Public Economics
5th Edition

Public Economics

5th Edition

EDITORS

Black • Calitz • Steenekamp

CONTRIBUTORS

Ajam
Siebrits
Van der Berg
Van der Merwe

OXFORD
UNIVERSITY PRESS
SOUTHERN AFRICA

Dedication

In memory of Daantjie Franzsen (1918-2008)

The leadership of Franzsen spanned more than half a century as teacher, researcher, policy adviser, and commissioner in the field of economics. He inspired many students of economics, influenced many decisions and decision-makers, and knowingly and unknowingly shaped the views of many ordinary people and officials in government and business in South Africa.

Born in 1918 and educated at the University of Stellenbosch, Daniel Gerhardus Franzsen was Professor of Economics at the Universities of Pretoria and Stellenbosch. He was Deputy Governor of the South African Reserve Bank, Chairperson of the Commission of Inquiry into Fiscal and Monetary Policy in South Africa (1967–1969), Chairperson and member of various other commissions and committees, Economic Advisor to the Minister of Finance, President of the Economic Society of South Africa, and author of many scientific books and articles.

OXFORD
UNIVERSITY PRESS

Oxford University Press is a department of the University of Oxford.
It furthers the University's objective of excellence in research, scholarship,
and education by publishing worldwide. Oxford is a registered trade mark of
Oxford University Press in the UK and in certain other countries.

Published in South Africa by
Oxford University Press Southern Africa (Pty) Limited

Vasco Boulevard, Goodwood, N1 City, Cape Town, South Africa, 7460
P O Box 12119, N1 City, Cape Town, South Africa, 7463

First published 1999
Second edition published in 2003
Third edition published in 2005
Fourth edition published in 2008
Fifth edition published in 2013

Public Economics

ISBN 978 0 19 599515 2

Fifth impression 2014

Typeset in Utopia Std 10 pt on 12 pt
Printed on 70gsm woodfree paper

Acknowledgements
Commissioning editor: Astrid Meyer
Development editor: Ilka Lane
Project manager: Nicola van Rhyn
Editor: Justine Creswell
Designer: Oswald Kurten
Typesetter: Orchard Publishing
Printed and bound by ABC Press, Cape Town
122604

The authors and publisher gratefully acknowledge permission to reproduce copyright material in this book.
Every effort has been made to trace copyright holders, but if any copyright infringements have been made,
the publisher would be grateful for information that would enable any omissions or errors to be corrected
in subsequent impressions.

Table of contents

Contributors

Philip Black is Extraordinary Professor of Economics at the University of Stellenbosch, a past President of the Economic Society of South Africa and the previous Managing Editor of the *South African Journal of Economics*. He teaches Microeconomics and Public Economics at post-graduate level.

Estian Calitz is Professor of Economics and a former Executive Director: Finance and Dean of Economic and Management Sciences at the University of Stellenbosch. During South Africa's period of political transition, he was the Director General of Finance of the national government (1993–1996). He is a former president of the Economic Society of South Africa.

Tjaart Steenekamp is Professor of Economics at the University of South Africa, where he teaches Public Economics and leads the Economics and Public Finance short-learning programme.

Tania Ajam serves as a Commissioner on the Financial and Fiscal Commission of South Africa, a constitutionally created independent body that gives independent, impartial advice on intergovernmental fiscal relations to Parliament and the legislatures.

Krige Siebrits is a Senior Lecturer in the Department of Economics at the University of Stellenbosch. His research interests include Public Economics and Institutional Economics.

Servaas van der Berg is Professor of Economics and National Research Chair in the Economics of Social Policy. His research interests focus on issues of poverty and inequality. He has undertaken a number of studies for National Treasury on fiscal incidence, documenting the shifts in the targeting of public spending. He has also done extensive research on social delivery, some of it for the World Bank. In recent years much of his research focuses on the Economics of Education.

Theo van der Merwe is Professor of Economics at the University of South Africa. He is the Chair of the Department of Economics. His research interests include Social Security issues.

Preface

Public Economics provides a comprehensive introduction to the study of public economics within a South African as well as an African context. In this book, theory is explained with reference to several important institutions, practices and examples. The aim is to equip the student with basic analytical skills and to demonstrate the application of these to practical issues.

Our emphasis is on developing the student's understanding of the theoretical issues pertaining to the role of government in a mixed economy, as it translates into expenditure on government functions. These functions are then financed by means of various taxes and loans. The conceptual framework for the book is that of a medium-sized, open developing economy, exposed to the forces of democratisation and globalisation. Many textbooks offer public economics as a study in applied microeconomics. Although this book follows the same approach to a large extent, fiscal policy is discussed in terms of both its macro- and microeconomic dimensions.

Fourth edition

In the fourth edition we maintain the approach followed in previous editions, which includes several cross-references to, and examples from countries making up the African region generally and Southern Africa in particular. The increased level of interaction and economic cooperation between the latter countries, and across the African continent as a whole, makes it almost impossible to look at the role of government and public policy in isolation. We cannot ignore the many economic spillover effects – both positive and negative – within our region; nor should we miss the opportunity to learn from one another by adopting a more integrated regional approach. In view of the interrelatedness of the economies of Southern African and other African countries as well as cultural and historical links between them, students from these countries should therefore also find the contents of the book accessible and relevant. We hope that the book will enable African students to have greater appreciation for the broader economic environment in which they operate.

As the book deals with constantly changing policy and analytical issues, we updated the material in this edition by using the latest relevant figures and information as provided in the March 2008 issue of the Quarterly Bulletin of the South African Reserve Bank and the 2008 Budget of the South African Government.

This edition of Public Economics is the product of a long process of discussions and deliberations amongst ourselves and colleagues, and students who have used the earlier editions. We are grateful to them, and also to our co-contributors, for the efforts they have put into the edition. A special word of thanks is due to our colleagues at Oxford University Press Southern Africa: Astrid Meyer (Development Editor), Meryl Abrahams (Editor) and Nicola van Rhyn (Project Manager), as well as to Mthunzi Nxawe (the former Education Publisher) for their strategic contributions, technical proficiency and, above all, patience.

Fifth edition

Much has happened since the time we started work on the previous edition of *Public Economics*. We have witnessed a major global recession in 2007–2009, several natural disasters and, more recently, widespread social unrest in the Middle East and certain North African countries. These developments have had significant implications for the conduct of fiscal policy, with banks and even governments being bailed out and international aid and additional defence spending putting strain on fiscal budgets generally. If anything, these crises have highlighted the importance of the subject matter covered in this book.

Throughout this new edition we have updated all the statistical information and also included the results of relevant research that has been undertaken over the past five years and earlier. In Part 1, for example, we have added a critique of the concept of market failure; reported on estimates of the size and composition of alcohol-related externalities; provided a critique of Pigouvian tax hikes on tobacco and alcohol products; expanded the sections on emission fees and cap-and-trade policies; added a new section on the regulation of natural monopolies; and expanded the section on rent-seeking by including a brief analysis of corruption. Similarly, an updated version of Chapter 14 has been brought forward and included as Chapter 8 in Part 2 dealing with *public expenditure*; while some recent applications of cost-benefit analysis have also been included in the final chapter of Part 2.

In Part 3 we applied the theory of tax incidence to the taxation of tobacco and alcohol consumption, revealing some important policy implications; extended the calculation of the excess burden by introducing the efficiency-loss ratio as a means of minimising tax inefficiencies; added a section on the neoclassical treatment of optimal tax evasion; analysed the effect of personal income tax on the supply of labour; extended the discussion of tax incentives aimed at promoting FDI by analysing tax holidays and taxable and non-taxable cash grants; added a new section on two important alternatives to the comprehensive income tax system, i.e. the flat rate and dual income tax systems; and included an extended discussion of tax reform in the last chapter of Part 3.

Part 4 on fiscal policy had to be substantially revised in light of the global financial crisis, with a new section entitled 'The great recession: new fiscal activism in practice' being added to Chapter 15. The section on 'fiscal rules versus discretion' was likewise updated and extended to include a discussion of the role played by fiscal councils. Finally, in Part 5 we have extended the sections dealing with fiscal federalism and also added new material to sections focusing on conditional grants and local government financing.

As before we would like to thank our colleagues at Oxford University Press for the important contributions they have made to the fifth edition. We are especially grateful to Astrid Meyer (Commissioning Editor), Ilka Lane (Development Editor) and Nicola van Rhyn (Project Manager).

Plan and outline of this book

We have three objectives with this book:
- To provide students with an opportunity to study public economics with reference to South African and African institutions and practices.
- To teach public economics as a field representing the dynamic interaction and tension between macro- and microeconomic considerations.
- To explain public economics with reference to the enormous challenges posed by recent constitutional changes in the region and the re-integration of individual countries into the global economy.

The book is divided into five main parts.

Part 1 contains a theoretical perspective on the **role of government** in the economy. We begin in Chapter 1 with an introduction to the study field of public economics, and we also discuss the nature of the public sector in South Africa. It includes a discussion of the political and institutional context within which the public sector conducts its business as well as a brief overview of the major views of the role of government in the economy. In Chapter 2 we explain the rationale for the role of government in the economy in terms of market failure, and distinguish between the allocative, distributive, and stabilisation roles of government. The next two chapters (3 and 4) examine the different dimensions of the government's allocative role, focusing on the nature of public goods, externalities, and imperfect competition. Chapter 3 includes a section on 'regional and global public goods', and also has a section on global warming as an example of a major negative 'global' externality. Chapter 4 contains an extended discussion of privatisation and regulation, and also provides an overview of several high profile cases of collusion being investigated and acted upon by the South African competition policy authorities. Inequality as a type of market failure is the focus of Chapter 5, which also examines the criteria for government intervention. We also briefly discuss results from 'experimental economics' which question the validity of the 'self-interest hypothesis'. Chapter 6 discusses the institutions and mechanisms of public (or social) choice and examines their efficiency and equity properties.

In **Part 2**, which deals with **public expenditure**, we first discuss the phenomenon of public expenditure growth in South Africa (Chapter 7) with reference to international experience. Theories of expenditure growth are studied with a view to determining their explanatory value for South Africa. We also study the positive impact of public expenditure on economic growth, with reference to both Keynesian economics and new growth theory. This chapter includes a discussion of the role of infrastructure investment in lowering production costs and 'crowding-in' private investment. Chapter 8 deals with fiscal and social policy issues pertaining to poverty, socio-economic development, and the distribution of income in Southern Africa. This is not such

an unusual theme for a textbook on public economics if one considers the importance of these issues to developing countries in Africa, as well as the amount of time spent by politicians and government officials in finding solutions to the challenges. These issues cannot be dealt with by public administrators, sociologists, political scientists, and engineers alone. An analysis of spending patterns in respect of various social services is also included in this chapter. Chapter 9 focuses on expenditure efficiency and the nature and use of cost-benefit analysis.

A major part of this book is devoted to **taxation (Part 3)**. In Chapter 10 we focus on the principles of taxation and equity. Tax efficiency and related aspects of tax reform form the main focus of Chapter 11; this chapter also includes a new and extended treatment of tax competition and harmonisation within a regional context. In the next three chapters we analyse different types of taxes, placing the emphasis on both theory and the South African and Southern African experience: taxes on income (in which a new section has been included which analyses the impact of a selective tax on interest income) (Chapter 12); taxation of wealth (including a more detailed treatment of property taxation) (Chapter 13); and taxes on goods and services (Chapter 14).

In South Africa the debate on fiscal policy and the role of government in the economy has been strongly influenced by two seemingly opposing forces. On the one hand, there are severe demands on the fiscus to deal with poverty, unemployment, and the high degree of inequality in the region. On the other hand, severe constraints are imposed on the fiscus by the need to maintain macroeconomic stability and at the same time to promote sustained economic growth within a very competitive global economy.

In **Part 4 (fiscal and social policy)** we capture this debate. We spell out the development of policies at the macroeconomic level, as well as sectoral policies (sometimes referred to as social policies in books on public policy, for example, with regard to welfare and housing). Chapter 15 (fiscal policy and the national budget) and Chapter 16 (public debt) are particularly pertinent to the second objective of this book, namely to highlight the dynamic interaction and tension between macro- and microeconomic considerations. Chapter 15 has been largely re-written and now includes a discussion of the evolution of views on the macroeconomic role of fiscal policy, focusing on the distinction between the Keynesian and structural approaches and the choice between discretionary and rules-based fiscal regimes. As in the fourth edition, this chapter closes with an overview of fiscal reforms in sub-Saharan Africa. Chapter 16 deals with theories of public debt and includes several sections on public debt management.

The last part (**Part 5**) deals with **intergovernmental fiscal relations**. In the sole chapter of this part (Chapter 17), we discuss the theoretical issues pertaining to fiscal federalism. We focus specifically on the structure of government as embodied in the constitution and the implications for intergovernmental fiscal relations in South Africa.

How to use this book

As lecturers at both residential and distance-learning universities, we share among us a great deal of research and practical experience in different aspects of public economics and fiscal policy. We have therefore designed this book with different kinds of students in mind: students at distance-learning universities who will have a fairly self-contained text that the lecturer can supplement with further explanations and tutorial exercises; residential students who will be able to study on their own, leaving lecturers time to analyse and debate topical issues, discuss the self-assessment exercises, and explain the more difficult material; postgraduate students who are completing a course in public economics for the first time and need to do self-study in

order to digest more advanced material; and postgraduate working students who did not complete an undergraduate course in public economics but who need to acquire this knowledge for non-degree purposes in order to advance their careers.

The material contained in this book may be more than can be digested in a semester course at undergraduate level. If public economics is presented as a theoretical course in applied microeconomics, the focus could be on Parts 1, 2, and 3 and Chapter 16. If the course designer requires a good mix of theory and practice, Parts 4 and 5 are a must, and one could then scale down by omitting Chapter 9. The material can therefore be adapted to suit specific courses.

Our educational approach is fairly straightforward. We explain public economics to students with a basic understanding of macroeconomics and microeconomics at the undergraduate level. We make extensive use of diagrams and some basic algebra. Each chapter begins with an aim and a number of study objectives or learning outcomes. The student should use these to maintain a focus on what is essential in the chapter. We highlight important concepts in bold in the text and list them (together with page references) at the end of each chapter. Each chapter also contains a list of self-assessment exercises at the end that the student can complete to test his or her understanding of the material. A comprehensive literature list is included at the end of the book, containing sources consulted and references that the serious reader may wish to consult.

Throughout the book we have tried to present factual information about public economics in Southern Africa and other African countries in relation to theory and international experience, rather than as separate and dull descriptions of statistical trends and superficial features. We trust that this will enhance the relevance of both empirical observation and theoretical understanding.

PART

1

Perspectives on the role of government in the economy

Chapter
ONE

Estian Calitz

The public sector in the economy

The aim of this chapter is to demarcate the study field of public economics with reference to key issues and fiscal challenges facing the South African economy and the Southern African region in general. The role of government is fairly similar across the region, and in the sections and chapters that follow we describe the nature of the South African public sector against the backdrop of the theory of public economics and contemporary views on the role of government in the economy. We also consider the interaction between the public, household, and private (business) sectors of the economy.

Once you have studied this chapter, you should be able to:
- give a brief overview of different views of the role of government in the economy
- list key issues confronting Southern African governments regarding their role in the economy
- distinguish between the main institutional categories of the public sector
- discuss the salient features of and trends in the size and composition of the South African public sector
- discuss various aspects of the relationship between the public sector and the rest of the economy.

1.1 **Introduction**

In economics we study the way in which society chooses to allocate its resources in order to satisfy a multitude of needs and wants. As these resources are both scarce and have alternative uses, it is necessary for society to prioritise its needs and ensure that they are met in a declining order of importance. The income or budget constraint necessitates these choices. In the process, needs are converted into effective demand and resources are allocated and used accordingly. We are therefore interested in the allocation of resources and in the distribution of the benefits derived from resource use. In public economics we study the impact of the public (government) sector on resource allocation and distribution.

In the mixed economy the balance between the supply of and demand for resources is pursued either through the market system or the political system. In the market system, prices are the equilibrating mechanism in the interplay between supply and demand which, in turn, are determined by such factors as the preferences and income of consumers, the costs of production factors and the prevailing technology. Needs which cannot be or are not satisfied via the market system are channelled through the political process. The equilibrating mechanism between supply and demand in a political system based on democratic principles is the ballot box, and the 'price' is the tax which people pay.

Most Southern African countries have a parliamentary democracy with an executive president elected by parliament. In South Africa a constitutional change requires a two-thirds parliamentary majority (or a 75 per cent majority in respect of articles pertaining to the supremacy of the constitution and the rule of law). Key features of the South African democratic state, as established on 27 April 1994 under its new constitution, are the Constitutional Court, the Bill of Human Rights and the Human Rights Commission. Other important features of the democracy and of good governance are an independent judiciary, an independent Auditor-General reporting to Parliament and an independent central bank (the South African Reserve Bank). The seat of Parliament is Cape Town (the provincial capital of the Western Cape), the Appeal Court is located in Bloemfontein (the capital of the Free State province) and the Constitutional Court is in Johannesburg (the mining and industrial 'capital' of the country and the capital of the Gauteng province). There are three tiers of government: the executive (the national public service) functions on the national level and is situated in Pretoria[1] (the nation's capital city); on provincial level there are nine provincial governments; on local government level there are 283 municipalities. We will discuss the financial interaction between the different tiers of government in Chapter 17.

A large portion of Southern Africa's total resource use is channelled through the political process. Resource use in the public sector differs from profit-driven resource use in the private sector, which is nonetheless indirectly influenced by the nature of the political environment, and the functioning of the political system, including a variety of economic policies and regulatory measures. The efficiency and equity with which resources are allocated in the public sector as well as the impact of political decisions on private economic behaviour are therefore of paramount importance to the economic performance of a country. This point is best illustrated by South Africa's recent economic history and the major rethink internationally of the appropriate role of government in market-based economies.

---

[1] Proposals to change the name of Pretoria to Tshwane have invoked a lot of controversy and at the time of publication the name change had not been instituted.

1.2 **Legacy of the past**

During the 10–15 years prior to the constitutional change and during the first few years of the new state, the South African economy performed poorly. Real economic growth did not keep up with population growth: in 1994 real per capita gross domestic product (GDP) was 16 per cent below its most recent peak (recorded in 1981). It was only in 2006 (25 years later) that the 1981-level was surpassed. Broadly defined, about one-third of the labour force is unemployed and South Africa has one of the most uneven distributions of income ever measured internationally.

At the time of the constitutional change, poverty was indeed – and still is today – the most discomforting feature of the South African economic landscape. The lack of job opportunities among millions of previously disenfranchised citizens of the new South Africa is partly the result of statutory and other regulatory measures that inhibited occupational and geographical labour mobility in the past. More recently the impact on job losses of the international financial crisis of 2007–2009 aggravated the unemployment problem in South Africa. Furthermore, the allocation of government resources on a per capita basis has historically been very skew, resulting in many of the poor having only limited access to basic social services. A large proportion of the population has had experience of undernourishment, inadequate housing, and poor education, and of only limited access to basic public services such as primary healthcare. Generally speaking, millions of people are ill-equipped to participate meaningfully in the modern (formal) sector of the economy. Under these circumstances the need for appropriate policies is evidently urgent. Faced with high expectations of the citizenry, fiscal measures that promote economic growth and improve people's ability to participate gainfully in the market economy constitute an important policy instrument in the hands of the government.

Government's share in the economy increased steadily in the period between 1960 and 1990 (see Table 1.1, which contains different financial indicators of the size of government). When the first full democratic elections took place in 1994, many experts felt that the total tax burden, the national budget deficit (or borrowing needs), and the public debt were too high to achieve sustainable economic growth and development. Concerns for government finances at the time included the increasing arrears and leakage in tax collection at the national level as well as the tendency for government expenditure to regularly exceed budgeted figures. The growth of the government's current expenditure was such that it crowded out public investment, that is, ever-decreasing funds were available for government investment in social and physical infrastructure such as schools, hospitals, and roads.

The growth in public employment, which constitutes the main component of current expenditure, was a source of alarm. Between 1990 and 1999 the number of employment opportunities in the general government sector (i.e. excluding public sector business enterprises and corporations) was on average 16 per cent higher than in the previous 10 years. Between 1989 and 1999 job opportunities in the formal private sector dropped by 19 per cent. These were hardly the characteristics of a thriving economy.

1.3 **Fiscal challenges**

During the 30–40 years before and up to the 2007–2009 international financial crisis a strong consensus emerged that the efficient management of developed and developing economies required smaller rather than bigger budget deficits as well as lower rather than higher levels of public debt. There was also general agreement that fiscal prudence required a thorough revision of the basic functions for which government should be responsible in order to contain the growth of government expenditure. Along with the international shift towards market-based economies that followed the demise of communism and the command economies of Eastern Europe during the late 1980s and early 1990s, key ingredients of economic restructuring included the privatisation of various activities hitherto undertaken by the state, a total revision of the role and functions of the state, and a concomitant reprioritisation of government expenditure. It is important to note that the emphasis was on how the public sector could be restructured to free more resources for the development function of government and to target the destitute effectively, without jeopardising macroeconomic stability or increasing the share of government in the economy – preferably even reducing it.

The case for smaller and more efficient government was the result of a growing dissatisfaction with the effectiveness of government. Contributing factors included the failure of the command economies of Eastern Europe; the increasing unaffordability of the welfare state in Western Europe; the poor economic performance of, especially, developing countries with increasingly ineffective and ballooning governments; the negative impact on economic freedom and initiative of excessive and poorly functioning government regulations; the alarmingly high prevalence of corruption and rent-seeking activities; the poor service delivery of government agencies in developing countries – which corresponded with an inability to attract and/or retain expertise; and – generally – the failure of governments to generate wealth in cases where they wanted to engage in or prescribe on production activities better left to the private sector.

Countries seldom have the opportunity to thoroughly revamp all their institutions and policies at once; yet this has been one of the main features of the South African experience since the 1990s, which occurred against the backdrop of the above-mentioned changing views on the role of government in the economy. Similar institutional changes are also taking place or have been effected in Angola, Namibia, Mozambique, Zambia and many other African countries. The restructuring of the public sector in South Africa after 1994 affected all groups in society. It affected the way in which business is conducted in the domestic private sector, as well as the nature of the trade and investment relations with the rest of the world. It affected the nature of public goods and services to be provided by the different tiers of government. It affected the individuals and groups of individuals who benefit from public goods and services as well as the way in which the tax or financing burden is distributed amongst individuals and firms. It changed the way in which consultation takes place between politicians and the electorate and between politicians and various sectional interest groups in society, be it interest groups in business, organised labour or civil society. Finally, it affected the basis on which employees are appointed and managed in the public sector as well as the nature of interaction between politicians and bureaucrats, and between bureaucrats and the clients of government. What was remarkable about the development of fiscal policy in South Africa since 1994 was the ability of the government to strike a good balance between the dictates of the market (requiring fiscal prudence) and the fiscal pressures for redistribution, poverty reduction and socio-economic development. Unfortunately, some of the good policy decisions were undermined by poor service delivery. These are themes to which we will return in later chapters of the book.

The international financial crisis of 2007–2009 was a serious wake-up call. Confidence in mainstream (consensus) views on the respective roles of government and the private sector in the mixed economy was shaken. The sub-prime financial crisis in the United States resulted in the bankruptcy of huge and prominent financial institutions, thus posing a systemic risk to their financial system. The subsequent financial contagion rapidly spread globally. The ensuing biggest economic recession since the Great Depression jeopardised the solvency of companies in the real and financial sectors of developed economies all over the industrial world and resulted in bailout and rescue plans by governments of unprecedented proportions. More than that, the fiscal sustainability of entire countries like Greece, Spain and Ireland was threatened and required multilateral rescues. The recession in developed countries had a major adverse effect on developing countries like South Africa although the impact was generally less severe than in the industrial world.

At the time of writing serious analysis and debate about the causes of the 'Great Recession' (as it became known) was still continuing. The events led to a major review of the appropriate role of government in the economy. The cost of bailouts of financial institutions and fiscal measures to counter the recessionary impact led to dramatic increases in the ratio to GDP of budget deficits and public debt in many industrial countries. Countries who had joined the European Union in terms of the Maastricht prescriptions of a budget deficit-to-GDP ratio of no more than 3 per cent and a debt-to-GDP ratio of no more than 60 per cent quickly found themselves in huge transgression of these fiscal criteria. For example, in 2009/10 the United Kingdom recorded a government budget deficit-to-GDP ratio of 11,1 per cent and a government debt-to-GDP ratio of 71,2 per cent.[2] Proponents of fiscal activism argue that their views had been vindicated: contra-cyclical fiscal policy is justified and financial markets need more regulation. But the huge deficits and debt levels clearly threatened fiscal sustainability and the appropriate way towards sustainability was and still is heavily debated.

Subsequent to the establishment of full democracy in 1994, the South African government carved out a particularly good fiscal track record, at least at the macro level. In tandem with monetary policy, macroeconomic stability and fiscal sustainability were achieved up to the time of the 2007–2009 international financial crisis. Although not spectacular by international standards, the economy had recorded 16 consecutive years of positive economic growth, averaging about 3,5 per cent per year. The economic upswing which started in September 1999 and ended after 99 months in November 2007 was the longest by far since World War II. After introducing inflation targeting in 2002, the monetary authorities succeeded in containing inflation within the target range of 3 to 6 per cent or bringing it back into the target range fairly quickly. The country's performance with regard to economic growth, job creation, and the combating of poverty improved on the performance during the 15 years before the constitutional change, but still fell far short of the country's economic needs. Moreover, the recession which followed the international financial crisis of 2007–09 was a major setback, causing about one million job losses. Many of the fiscal reforms that formed part of the economic policy package since 1994 are highlighted in this book, often with reference to theoretical issues. Attention is also given to new challenges to fiscal policy on account of the unemployment which accompanied the

---

[2] By comparison South Africa's debt-to-GDP ratio of 33,5 per cent in 2010 is relatively low (see Chapter 16, Section 16.2).

economic downswing since November 2007 and the continued high incidence of poverty.

1.4 The study field of public economics

Public economics is the study of the nature, principles, and economic consequences of expenditure, taxation, financing, and the regulatory actions undertaken by the non-profit making government sector of the economy.

In order to understand this definition, we first note that economic policy entails the application by government institutions of measures (instruments) that are designed to influence economic behaviour in order to achieve certain outcomes. Besides various macroeconomic goals, such as economic growth, balance-of-payments stability or income redistribution, many sectoral and microeconomic goals are also pursued; the ultimate objective being to improve the material well-being of people.

Turning now to the elements of our definition of public economics, note firstly that the main areas of decision-making are: expenditure, taxation, financing and regulation. These are also called the **instruments of fiscal policy**. In public economics we study the nature and impact of these instruments. The first three entail the procurement by the state of private funds and the spending of these funds. In economic terms the use of these instruments constitutes the direct mobilisation and allocation of scarce resources. Examples would be the spending of tax income on primary healthcare and borrowing funds to build an irrigation dam or a highway. **Regulation**, by contrast, entails enacting a law or administratively proclaiming an enforceable instruction that leads to a different allocation of private resources from that which would apply in the absence of such government intervention. The allocation of resources is now influenced indirectly. An example is a regulation by government that forces the manufacturers of motor vehicles to install platinum catalysts in the exhaust pipes of vehicles to reduce the emission of carbon monoxide.

Different types of expenditure, taxation, government borrowing, and government debt can be distinguished. In taxation, for example, we distinguish between taxes on income, wealth, and goods and services. The various categories of taxation or expenditure have different economic consequences. For instance, a tax on wealth (e.g. a property tax) will affect different people in society than a value added tax on red meat would. In other words, the distributional effects differ. The choice of a particular tax therefore depends on how the government wants to change the distribution of income or wealth in the economy, or on how an efficient allocation of resources can be pursued. Economists have developed several important fiscal criteria on which economic decisions in the public sector are or should be based and which may be applied when recommendations on taxes or expenditure allocations are formulated. These governing criteria are derived from the two concepts of efficiency and equity, which are paramount and distinguishing features of economics.

The study of the nature and economic consequences of decisions falls in the realm of positive economics, posing questions such as: if I take step a (e.g. raise income tax), what will happen to b (e.g. the supply of labour in the economy)? The development of criteria, on the other hand, has to do with normative economics, focusing on what ought to be. For example, if I want d (e.g. a more even distribution of income), what should step c be (e.g. what type and level of taxation should be introduced)? Public economics enters the realm of normative economics when we consider such diverse questions as the rationale for government involvement in the economy and how political decisions should be taken (i.e. what kind of voting system should be used) to ensure efficiency and equity in the allocation of resources.

Generally two broad views of the role of government in the economy are often encountered. The first, which recognises the supremacy of the individual and his or her freedom of choice, is known as the **individualistic view of government** (sometimes also called the mechanistic view). The main point of departure and test for whether or not government intervention is called for, is the maximisation of individual welfare. Government action is seen as a reflection of individual preferences and government institutions have no role independent of these preferences. The role of government is limited to correcting for market failure, a topic that we explore in various chapters of Part 1. This view is closely associated with the proponents of the free-market economy and gained widespread international support towards the end of the twentieth century, notably after the collapse of the command economies of Eastern Europe. The other view is called the **public interest or collectivist view** of the role of the state (sometimes also referred to as the organic view). Collective choice and preferences are thought to exist independently of individual preferences and the goals of society as a separate organism differ from the goals of the constituent individuals. Instead of individual welfare, it is social welfare or the national interest that should be maximised. The benefits to the individual, consequently, are derived from the benefits accorded to or achieved by the group.

From a policy perspective, the individualistic approach focuses relatively more on the efficiency of resource allocation and economic growth, whereas the collectivist approach is relatively more concerned with combating poverty and equity issues, notably the distribution of income as justification for government intervention. In practice, government policies often reflect a combination of the two approaches.

One is indeed likely to find a combination of policies emanating from both views in the model of the **developmental state**, a term coined in 1982 by Chalmers Johnson, an American political scientist. The ANC government propagates this model, although many features of South African society arguably do not fit this mould. Leftwich (1995: 401) describes developmental states as those states whose politics have concentrated sufficient power, autonomy and capacity at the centre to shape, pursue and encourage the achievement of explicit development objectives, whether by establishing and promoting conditions and the direction of economic growth, or by organising it directly, or a varying combination of both. The developmental state has been characterised as embodying inter alia a determined development elite, a powerful, competent and insulated economic bureaucracy, a weak and subordinate civil society and the effective management of non-state economic interests (Leftwich, 1995: 405–420). The focus appears to be more on the way in which political and economic control is obtained and exercised, and seems to allow for much variety as regards the nature and principles of the economy and economic policy. Selective government intervention that distorts relative prices, rather than a neoclassical minimisation of price distortions by government, has nonetheless been identified as a feature of the successful developmental state (Grabowski, 1994: 413). Countries regarded as examples of the developmental state,[3] as well as their economic policies, are too diverse to allow for the defining of a common economic policy of success. As always, many other

---

[3] For example Singapore, Botswana, Malaysia, South Korea, Indonesia and, more recently, China.

factors besides economic policies determine economic success.

Returning to the elements of our definition of public economics, the term **'non-profit making'** signifies the absence of profit maximisation as the leading motive, or one of the leading motives, in decision-making on the mobilisation and allocation of resources. The absence of the profit motive means that other criteria for decision-making have to be employed. We will see that the nature of public goods is such that their supply does not allow for decentralised price determination in a competitive market economy. Note that the government is not the only non-profit making sector in the economy. Many welfare, church, and service organisations exist as non-profit organisations. These institutions are often referred to as **non-governmental organisations (NGOs)**.

Does our definition of public economics include a study of **public corporations** (such as Eskom in South Africa)? If these entities were driven strictly by the profit motive, they would not fit our definition. However, as long as political appointees serve on or control the board of such entities, as long as these entities render certain socio-economic services on behalf of the government and rely on government financial support, and (or) as long as they behave in a monopolistic manner, they are not pure private institutions. These enterprises then operate in the hybrid area between the government and the private sector. In countries that have embarked on privatisation, such as South Africa, public enterprises often find themselves in transition between a public entity and a private company. Consequently, it is not easy to pinpoint their exact position on the spectrum between public and private entities, and the criteria in terms of which to study their behaviour are not that clear. In our study of public economics we do not include a separate section on these kinds of

activities. We do, however, analyse aspects of their functioning when we discuss topics such as externalities, imperfect competition, user charges, privatisation, public-private partnerships and macroeconomic stabilisation.

1.5 The public sector in South Africa

From our discussion in the previous section it is clear that public economics studies a wide range of diverse activities. In order to structure our thoughts, we will examine the composition and size of the public sector in South Africa, which is fairly typical of public sectors elsewhere in Africa, before we briefly review the relationship between the public and the private sectors.

1.5.1 Composition of the public sector

What are the constituent institutional components of the **public sector**? We present them in Figure 1.1 as a set of rectangles within rectangles. The South African constitution specifies three levels or spheres of government. The **central (or national) government** (see the inner rectangle in Figure 1.1) consists of all the national government departments. When the various **extra-budgetary institutions** are added (such as the National Research Foundation, the National Health Laboratory Service and the Urban Transport Fund, a number of government business enterprises that sell most of their output of goods and services to government institutions or departments at regulated prices, social security funds and universities), we refer to the combination as the **consolidated national government.** (Note that in the national accounts the universities are in fact classified as part of the public sector.) The aforementioned entities have access to funds additional to budgetary allocations, such as user charges, levies and other non-tax income.

As pointed out earlier, the second and third tiers of government in South Africa constitute nine **provincial governments** and 283 **local authorities**; these are shown in the second rectangle in Figure 1.1. Together with the central government, the general departments of provinces and local authorities (and certain business enterprises such as the trade departments (for electricity, water, transport, etc.) of local governments) are constituent components of the **general government**. For the most part, general government thus represents the non-profit activities of the public sector. The allocation of resources is determined by political considerations and is financed through the tax system and user charges (or loans which have to be repaid out of taxes at a later stage).

The next category of public entities (see the outermost rectangle in Figure 1.1) consists of financial and non-financial **public enterprises** such as Eskom, Mossgas, the South African Broadcasting Corporation (SABC), Telkom, Transnet, the Land Bank and the Public Investment Corporation. These activities are managed much more along business lines and, in the case of corporations like Eskom and Telkom, decisions are often taken on the same basis as in the private sector. Since, and for as long as these corporations are subject to government control, however, either in the form of shareholding or the appointment of directors, they are classified as part of the public sector. Conversely, should any public-sector activity or body (or a part of it) be privatised, it will thereafter be reclassified as part of the private sector.

To summarise: we refer to the three tiers of government (i.e. the general services and certain business enterprises of national, provincial and local government) as the general government, and to the combination of

general government and public corporations as the public sector.

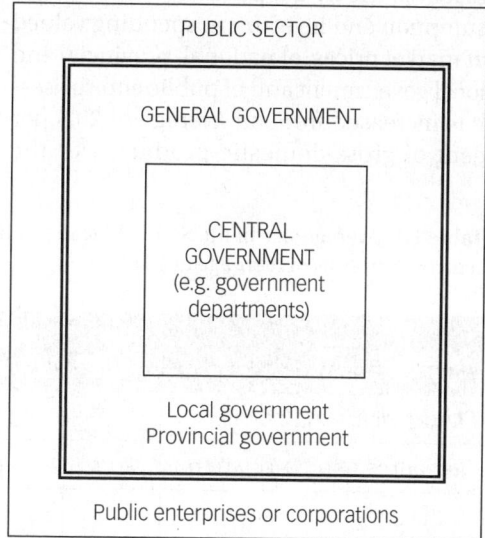

Figure 1.1 The composition of the public sector

1.5.2 Size of the public sector

The size of the public sector differs according to the indicator used. If we are interested in the size of the burden that the government imposes on current taxpayers, we may use the total tax income of the general government as indicator and express it as a percentage of the gross domestic product (or national income). By this criterion the government's average share in the South African economy during the period 2005–2009 was 28,1 per cent. We know, however, that government expenditure is not only financed through tax revenue, but by means of non-tax income (such as dividend and property income, mining leases and administrative fees) as well as borrowing (loans). We will thus obtain a more accurate picture by looking at government expenditure. We identify two aggregate indicators. The first is the total amount of **resource use** by government (i.e. the final demand by, or exhaustive expenditure of government) in any year. From Table 1.1 we note that the total resource use by the public sector (i.e. consumption and investment spending valued at market prices, of national, provincial and local government and of public enterprises) has increased from an average of 20,9 per cent of gross domestic product over the period 1960–1969 to an average of 27,0 per cent during the 1980s. It then decreased to 23,6 per cent in the first half of the 2000s, before rising to 26,2 per cent for the period 2004–2009.

Even this is not the complete picture. Not all of government expenditure is in the form of final demand for goods and services (i.e.

Table 1.1 Average size of the South African public sector by different measures, selected periods (current prices as percentage of GDP)

Measure	1960–1969	1970–1979	1980–1989	1990–1994	1994–1999	2000–2004	2005–2009
Taxes (direct and indirect)	15,8	19,1	22,9	24,1	25,1	25,4	28,1
Resource use (1), of which	20,9	28,1	27,0	25,2	23,6	22,8	26,2
General government consumption[a]	11,3	14,6	18,0	20,0	18,8	18,8	19,6
Investment[b], of which	9,6	13,5	9,0	5,2	4,8	4,0	6,6
General government	7,6	8,7	5,3	2,9	2,6	2,4	3,3
Public corporations	2,0	4,8	3,7	2,3	2,2	1,6	3,3
Transfer payments (2), of which	4,1	5,4	7,9	10,8	12,1	10,8	11,8
Interest on public debt[c]	1,0	1,9	3,8	4,6	6,2	4,6	3,2
Subsidies and current transfers[d]	3,1	3,5	4,1	6,2	5,9	6,2	8,6
Total public sector resource mobilisation (1) + (2), of which	25,0	33,5	34,9	36,0	35,7	33,6	38,0
General government	23,0	28,7	31,2	33,7	33,5	32,0	34,7
Public corporations	2,0	4,8	3,7	2,3	2,2	1,6	3,3

Notes: [a]   National accounting figures.
       [b]   Government finance statistics data.
       [c]   Data after 1994 exclude Financial Intermediation Services Indirectly Measured (FISIM). Data before 1994 adjusted by ratio between two sets of figures for 1994–1996, namely interest inclusive and exclusive of FISIM.
       [d]   Includes social benefits to households and production subsidies; also miscellaneous transfers, transfers to international organisations and capital transfers – for latter three, average ratio to GDP between 1994 and 2009 used as estimate for data before 1994.

Source: SA Reserve Bank *Quarterly Bulletins* (various issues) and electronic data. Available online at http://www.resbank.co.za/qbquery/timeseriesquery.aspx

exhaustive expenditure). The government also makes **transfer payments** (subsidies, current transfers, interest on public debt) to targeted beneficiaries or entities outside the public sector. These are called **non-exhaustive government expenditure**. The government mobilises the resources, but they are used by the recipients who exercise the final demand. (Note that the national government also makes transfer payments to provinces and local governments. These are regarded as internal flows within the public sector and not counted as payments from the government sector to other sectors of the economy.) If we add interest payments and transfers to the household, business, and foreign sector, we can obtain an accurate picture of the extent of **resource mobilisation** by the government. During 2005–2009 the South African public sector was instrumental in mobilising 38,0 per cent of the national resources. This figure is higher than the average figures for all of the previous periods in Table 1.1.

Due to the diverse nature of government activities and the corresponding differences in the factors that determine the allocation and distribution processes in the public sector, we are not only interested in the aggregate size of the public sector, but also in its constituent components. Note in particular the opposite trends of general government consumption expenditure and public investment, as well as the rising share of transfer payments (especially interest on public debt) until the second half of the 1990s as a percentage of GDP, and again during the period 2004–2009, especially on account of increased subsidies and current transfers. These are recurrent themes in this book (see for example Chapters 7 and 8).

1.5.3 The relationship between the public and the private sectors

What is the relationship between the public sector and the rest of the economy? A number of important aspects of this relationship may be identified with reference to the familiar circular flow of income, expenditure, and goods and services (see Figure 1.2).

▶ Government is a supplier of public goods and services. Households and businesses pay for these goods and services through taxes (and user charges). Government then uses this revenue to acquire factors of production and to purchase private goods and services (as intermediate inputs), all of which are used in order to produce public goods and services. Government departments, of course, use outputs of other departments as intermediate inputs as well. Government activities are relatively labour intensive and, as a result, salaries and wages constitute the largest input cost (averaging 38 per cent of total general government cash payments during 2000–2009).

▶ The size of government in the mixed economy is such that its purchases of goods and services exert important influences on the economy. At the sectoral level, for instance, government spending is often decisive for the construction and engineering sectors. **Privatisation** entails goods or services formerly supplied by government as part of the flow of public goods and services, redefined as goods and services supplied by private firms. In the case of **public-private partnerships**, one may actually find linked goods; some are part of the flow of public goods and services and some are private products. Often private

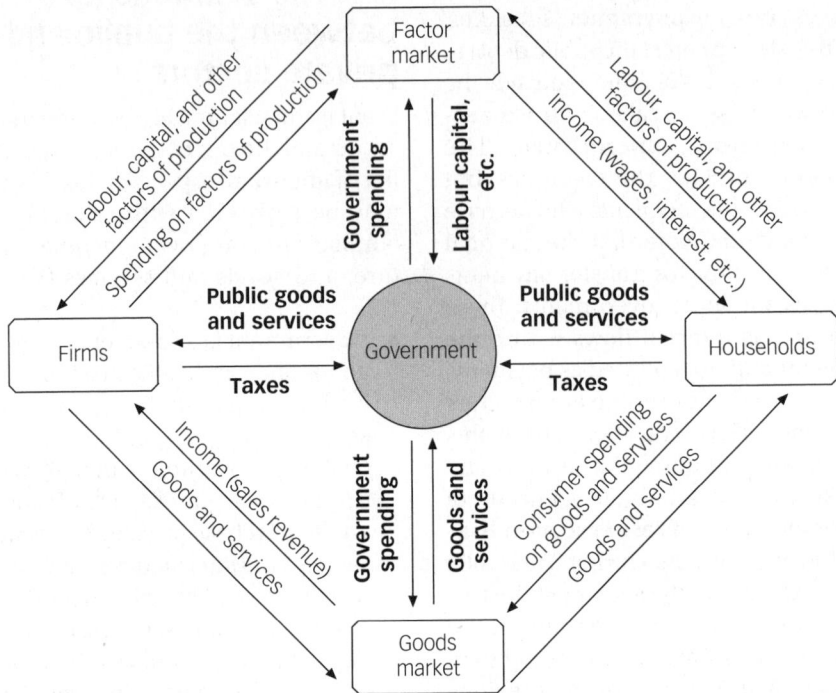

Figure 1.2 The government in the circular flow of income, expenditure, and goods and services

investment cannot be undertaken unless the necessary public infrastructure is in place (e.g. roads and electricity networks). At the macroeconomic level, changes in the aggregate level and composition of government expenditure are important factors in determining economic stability and growth. Excessive expenditure growth can, for example, be inflationary or crowd out private investment, thus retarding economic growth.

▶ The way in which government finances its expenditure also has important economic consequences. The kind of taxes used and the rates levied influence the after-tax distribution of income and thus the well-being (utility) of individuals, and also the decisions by private businesses regarding the allocation of resources in the private sector. The tax system can promote or obstruct efficiency and equity.

▶ If there is a budget imbalance (surplus or deficit), the government exercises an influence on the balance between saving (S) and investment (I), or on the balance of payments (i.e. the balance between exports (X) and imports (M)). This is shown in Figure 1.3. In national accounting terms, a budget imbalance (i.e. $G \neq T$) is reflected in either an imbalance between private investment (I) and saving (S), that is, $S \neq I$ (internal imbalance), or an imbalance between exports (X) and imports (M), that is, $M \neq X$ (external or balance of payments disequilibrium).

- If there is a budget deficit, for example, tax revenue (T) is less than government expenditure (G), or $T<G$, and the government has to borrow. The size of its deficit and the way in which it is financed is very important for macro-economic stability, depending on one's view of the impact of budget deficits on the economy. Government borrowing occurs via the financial markets and represents a use of either domestic (S_d) or foreign savings (S_f), as shown in Figure 1.3. (In Figure 1.3 T, S, and M represent leakages from the income-expenditure circular flow, while G, I, and X are additions to or injections into the circular flow.) Part of the savings may find their way into financing government investment, which is included in government expenditure (G). In the case of a budget surplus, the government supplements the supply of savings in the economy.

- While the government can influence the course of the economy, it is also extensively affected by what happens in the economy. In an economic recession, for instance, government revenue falls or grows at a slower rate. This may impair its ability to provide public services, especially if its debt or budget deficit is already relatively high. Government also bears the brunt of its own decisions via their adverse effect on the economy, such as when high budget deficits result in higher interest rates, thereby increasing the government's interest bill.

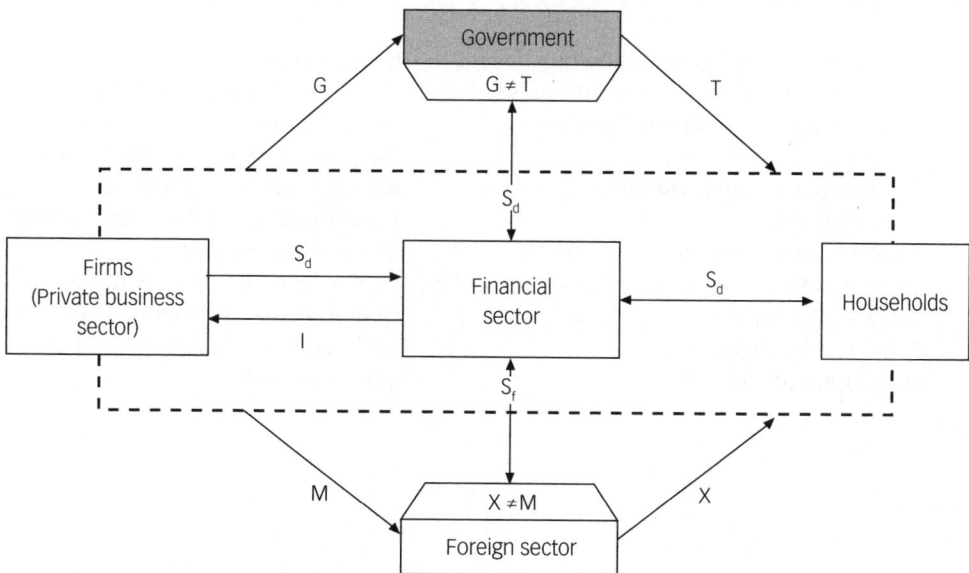

Figure 1.3 The impact of a budget imbalance on the financial sector in the context of the circular flow of income and expenditure

IMPORTANT CONCEPTS

central (or national) government (page 10)

consolidated national government (page 10)

developmental state (page 9)

exhaustive expenditure (page 13)

extra-budgetary institutions (page 10)

general government (page 11)

individualistic (or mechanistic) view of government (page 9)

instruments of fiscal policy (page 8)

local authorities (page 11)

non-exhaustive government expenditure (page 13)

non-governmental organisations (NGOs) (page 10)

non-profit making (page 10)

privatisation (page 13)

provincial government (page 11)

public corporations (page 10)

public economics (page 8)

public enterprises (page 11)

public interest or collectivist view of government (page 9)

public-private partnerships (page 13)

public sector (page 10)

regulation (page 8)

resource mobilisation (page 13)

resource use (by the public sector) (page 11)

transfer payments (page 13)

SELF-ASSESSMENT EXERCISES

1.1 Distinguish between the following:
  ▶ positive and normative economics
  ▶ general government and public sector
  ▶ resource use and resource mobilisation.

1.2 Explain the difference between the individualistic and public interest view of government.

1.3 What are the features of the developmental state?

1.4 Briefly review the salient changes in the size and composition of the South African public sector during the past few decades. Which of the changes, in your opinion, are incompatible with the requirements of a thriving economy?

1.5 Give an overview of the various dimensions of the relationship between the public sector and the rest of the economy.

Chapter
TWO

Philip Black

Benchmark model of the economy: positive and normative approaches

We begin this part of our book with a brief review of the neoclassical theory of general equilibrium which, over the years, has become something of a benchmark model. It is a benchmark model precisely because it does not presume to provide an accurate description of the real world. Rather, it should be seen as a frame of reference, or a starting point, that helps us to better understand and appreciate real-world problems. As we shall see in the chapters that follow, the model can in fact accommodate a large variety of alternative assumptions, and it is this built-in flexibility that enables it to yield alternative predictions that bring us closer to the real world.

Section 2.1 of this chapter provides a brief description of the basic assumptions of our benchmark model, while Sections 2.2 and 2.3 discuss the equilibrium properties of the model. These three sections thus provide a vision of how the world ought to work, and as such can be viewed as a good example of what some commentators refer to as 'normative' economics. In Section 2.4 we begin to compare our normative model with the real world and, in so doing, enter the domain of 'positive' economics. This is done by introducing the concept of '**market failure**' – a generic term describing broad categories of human behaviour that deviate from the ideal assumptions of the benchmark model. Sections 2.5 and 2.6 briefly deal with the role of the public sector in coming to grips with these market failures and related real-world problems. These issues will be dealt with in greater detail in Chapters 3–6. This chapter concludes with a note on government failure.

the indifference curve) equals the corresponding commodity price ratio, $\frac{P_x}{P_y}$ (or the slope of the budget line), that is

$$MRS^a{}_{xy} = \frac{P_x}{P_y} = MRS^b{}_{xy} \qquad [2.6]$$

where $MRS^a{}_{xy}$ is consumer a's marginal rate of substitution of commodity X for commodity Y, and P_x and P_y are the corresponding equilibrium prices.

Consider Figure 2.4 (which is similar to Figure 2.3) and assume that the economy is producing the Pareto-optimal combination given by point F on the PPC. Our second condition simply means that the two individuals will together consume 0_aX_2 of good X and 0_aY_2 of good Y, and in the process maximise their respective utilities subject to their respective budget constraints. This is shown by the box diagram for consumption indicated as the area $0_aY_2FX_2$ in Figure 2.4, and by the associated contract curve for consumption, $0_a F$, along which the indifference curves of the two consumers are tangent. As before, each point along the contract curve for consumption represents a Pareto-optimal allocation of the two goods, X and Y, between the two consumers, a and b.

How much each individual consumes eventually will depend on: (a) his or her tastes, or relative preferences for the two goods, and (b) his or her income which will, in turn, depend on how much of the initial resources (K and L) he or she owns. At point F' in Figure 2.4, for example, individual a maximises her utility ($U^a{}_2$) subject to the budget constraint given by the line vv', consuming 0_aX_a of good X and 0_aY_a of good Y. Individual b does likewise, maximising his utility ($U^b{}_3$) subject to the budget constraint, vv', and consuming 0_bX_b of good X and 0_bY_b of good Y. Each consumer's total income is given by the distance between vv' and their respective origins, 0_a and 0_b; though both consumers face the same market determined commodity prices, P_x and P_y, the ratio of which is, of course, equal to the slope of vv'.

Pareto optimality in consumption thus implies a situation in which it is impossible to increase the utility of either of the two consumers (for example by reallocating

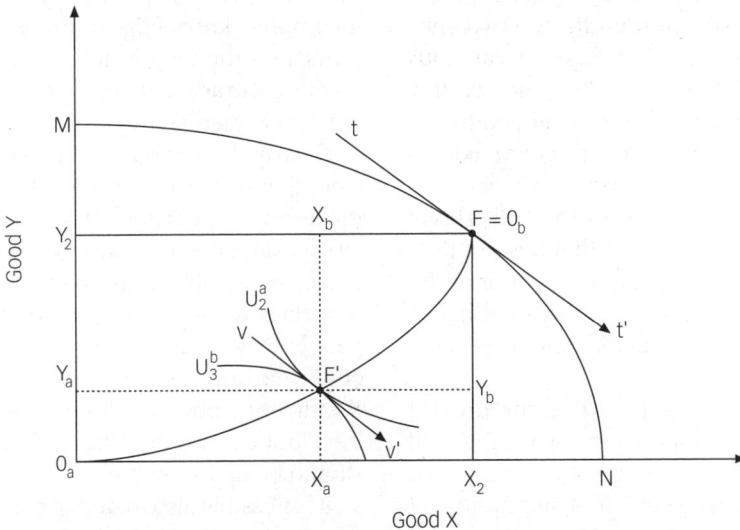

Figure 2.4 Consumption and overall equilibria

Once you have studied this chapter, you should be able to:
- identify the critical assumptions of the two-sector model
- define what is meant by a Pareto-optimal allocation of resources
- articulate the three conditions for a general equilibrium
- distinguish between allocative efficiency, X-efficiency, and 'dynamic' efficiency (or economic growth)
- discuss the broad categories of market failure
- explain the allocative, distributive, and stabilisation functions of government
- distinguish between direct and indirect forms of government intervention.

2.1 Basic assumptions of the benchmark model

Our benchmark model is based on a host of patently unrealistic assumptions that are set out in Box 2.1. The individual consumer or producer is assumed to be fully informed about the economy, unaffected by the actions of other consumers or producers, completely mobile in the occupational and spatial sense of the word, and always striving to maximise his or her own utility or profit within perfectly competitive markets. Any exogenous disturbance will merely set in motion a series of more or less instantaneous adjustments that will automatically return the system to a stable equilibrium. Indeed, in such a blissful state there would be few economic problems to speak of and little need to write this and many of the subsequent chapters.

One does not have to be an economist to realise that real-world economies do not behave in the way that the neoclassical model predicts. Perhaps the only real market that comes close to it is an auction, where suppliers and demanders all come together to reveal their preferences to an independent and knowledgeable auctioneer who establishes the equilibrium price before any trading takes place. In the neoclassical model we simply assume the existence of such a knowledgeable and omnipresent auctioneer – also called the 'Walrasian auctioneer' – and give him or her the task of establishing equilibrium prices in all markets, more or less simultaneously.

Before looking at the model itself – in Sections 2.2 and 2.3 below – it is perhaps worth noting that a theory does not necessarily stand or fall by its assumptions. To be sure, if one wanted to explain and predict some real-world phenomenon, assumptions are important, as are the functional relations used to make predictions and test the validity of the theory. But if one's aim is merely to develop a normative theory – such as our benchmark model of resource allocation – it is hardly appropriate to judge it only in terms of the realism of its assumptions.

BOX 2.1 Assumptions of the two-sector model

▶ There are two individuals, *A* and *B*, who are the suppliers of two factors of production, the producers of two commodities, and the consumers of both these commodities – all at the same time. Each individual is initially endowed with fixed quantities of the two factors, capital (*K*) and labour (*L*), that are both used in the production of the two commodities, *X* and *Y*, both of which are consumed by the two individuals.

▶ There are no external effects on consumption and both individuals have fixed tastes – this is reflected in the existence of smooth and well-behaved individual indifference curves. These curves are convex with respect to the origin, cannot intersect, and exhibit diminishing marginal rates of substitution.

▶ The two production processes are both characterised by unlimited factor substitutability, diminishing marginal productivities, and constant returns to scale. The latter assumption rules out internal (dis)economies of scale, while there are also no external costs or benefits in production. These assumptions together ensure the existence of smooth and well-behaved isoquants.

▶ As consumers, *A* and *B* maximise utility and, as producers, they maximise profit. Both are perfectly informed about their respective environments and are also perfectly mobile in the occupational and spatial sense of the word.

▶ The commodity and factor markets are all perfectly competitive, which implies that each market behaves 'as if' there were a large number of individual demanders and suppliers involved, none of whom can influence price.

▶ These assumptions together ensure the existence, uniqueness, and stability of a general equilibrium.

2.2 The benchmark model and allocative efficiency

Economic efficiency is conventionally defined in terms of both allocative efficiency and technical efficiency (or X-efficiency), and can also refer to a country's ability to achieve economic growth. In this section we confine ourselves to allocative efficiency only, leaving our discussion of X-efficiency and economic growth for the next section.

Allocative efficiency refers to a situation in which the limited resources of a country are allocated in accordance with the wishes of its consumers. An allocatively efficient economy produces an 'optimal mix' of commodities. Under conditions of perfect competition, the optimal output mix results from the fact that utility-maximising consumers respond to prices that reflect the true costs of production, or the marginal social costs. It is thus evident that allocative efficiency involves an interaction between the consumption activities of individual consumers and the production activities of producers.

In an economy with no public sector and in which there are no consumption or production externalities, allocative efficiency in the general equilibrium context requires the simultaneous concurrence of three familiar conditions. These are briefly discussed below.

Condition 1: Production activities must be Pareto optimal. **Pareto optimality** in production means that it should not be possible to increase the output of any one commodity without thereby bringing about a decrease in the output of at least one other commodity; or, put differently, in a non-optimal situation it is always possible to increase the output of one commodity without thereby decreasing the output of other commodities. In terms of the familiar two-sector model, this condition requires that each of our two sectors, X and Y, should maximise output subject to its own cost constraint. In Figures 2.1(a) and 2.1(b) each sector does exactly that. At points r and s each sector employs a combination of the two inputs, capital (K) and labour (L), for which the marginal rate of technical substitution (given by the slope of the isoquant), equals the corresponding factor price ratio, $\frac{w}{r}$ (given by the slope of the isocost). It can be formulated as follows:

$$MRTS^x_{lk} = \frac{MPL_x}{MPK_x} = \frac{w}{r} \qquad [2.1]$$

$$MRTS^y_{lk} = \frac{MPL_y}{MPK_y} = \frac{w}{r} \qquad [2.2]$$

$MRTS^x_{lk}$ is the marginal rate of technical substitution of labour for capital in sector X, MPL_x and MPK_x are the marginal productivities of labour and capital in sector X respectively, and w and r are the market-determined equilibrium factor prices. The same applies for sector Y (Equation [2.2]).

Under perfectly competitive conditions, each sector will face the same equilibrium factor prices, as set out in the next equation:

$$MRTS^x_{lk} = \frac{w}{r} = MRTS^y_{lk} \qquad [2.3]$$

Equation [2.3] implies, inter alia, that the economy is operating at some point on its contract curve for production. This is illustrated in Figure 2.2 in the form of the familiar Edgeworth-Bowley box diagram. The dimensions of the box are determined by the total (fixed) supplies of our two factors of production: total capital supply is given by either of the two vertical axes, $0_x V$ or $0_y W$, and total labour supply by either of the two horizontal axes, $0_x W$ or $0_y V$. Sector X's production function, or isoquant map, is shown with respect to the South-western corner, 0_x, and sector Y's with respect to the North-eastern corner, 0_y. Only three out of a large number of isoquants are indicated for each of the two sectors, that is X_1, X_2, and X_3 for sector X, and Y_1, Y_2, and Y_3 in the case of sector Y. The next step is to find all those points where the two sectors' respective isoquants are tangent, for example, points e, f, and g. If this exercise is repeated many

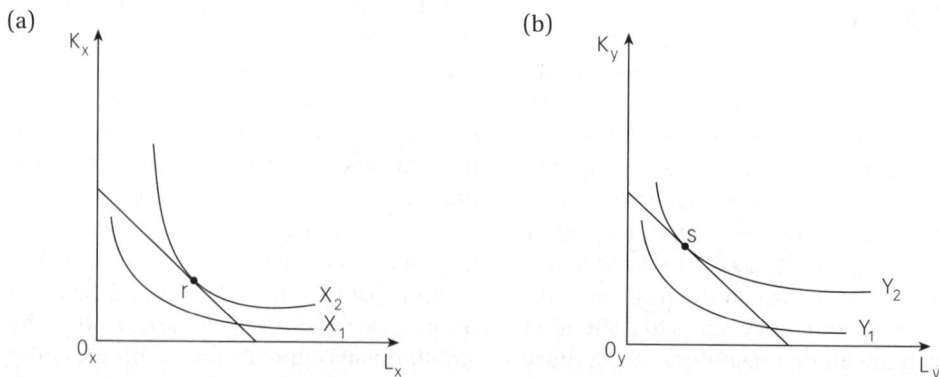

Figure 2.1 Individual sector equilibria

times, we can derive the contract curve for production – $0_x 0_y$ in Figure 2.2.

It is important to note that each point on the contract curve represents a Pareto-optimal allocation of the two resources, K and L, between the two sectors, X and Y: at point e (or f or g), it is not possible for either sector to increase its output without the other sector having to cut back its own output. This is clearly not true of a point such as q where either of the two sectors can increase its output without causing a reduction in the output of the other. Point q is not on the contract curve and, as discussed in the next section, represents an 'X-inefficient' outcome.

Not only does perfect competition ensure that our two sectors will operate at the same point on the contract curve – for example e, f, or g in Figure 2.2 – but it also implies that the economy will find itself at a point on the production possibility curve (PPC). The latter is simply the flip side of the above contract curve: it brings together all the output combinations along the contract curve within a more conventional diagram and is shown in Figure 2.3. There the PPC is depicted as the curve MN, on which the points E, F, and G represent the same output combinations as their equivalents on the contract curve in Figure 2.2.

The slope (or rate of change) of the PPC in Figure 2.3 is given by $\frac{\Delta Y}{\Delta X}$, and is known as the marginal rate of product transformation, or $MRPT_{xy}$. The latter, in turn, equals the corresponding marginal cost ratio – which is easily proved with the aid of Figure 2.3.

Consider a small movement from point F to point h such that the resources gained by sector X equal the resources lost by sector Y. With factor prices assumed unchanged, this means that the increase in the total cost of sector X will equal the decrease in the total cost of sector Y; or $\Delta TC_x = \Delta TC_y$. Now, since

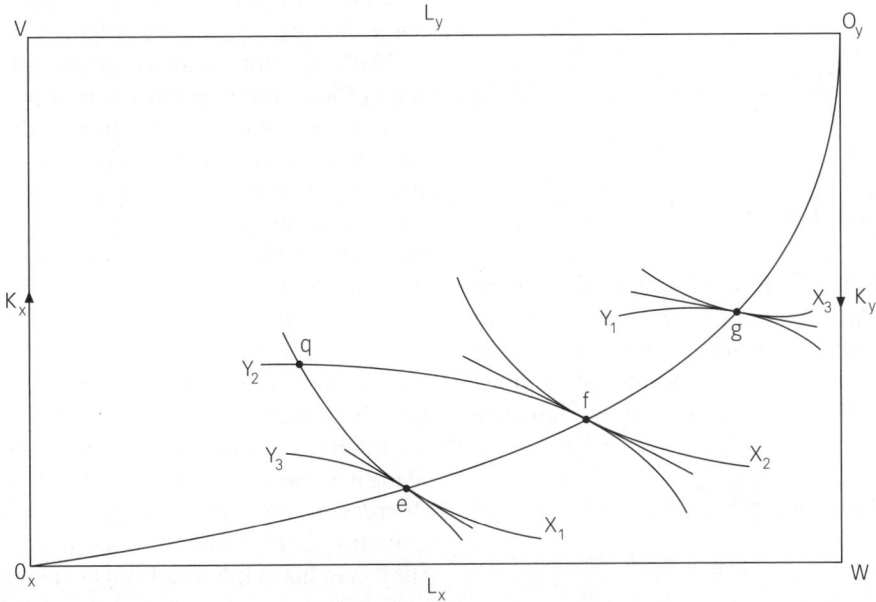

Figure 2.2 Edgeworth-Bowley box diagram

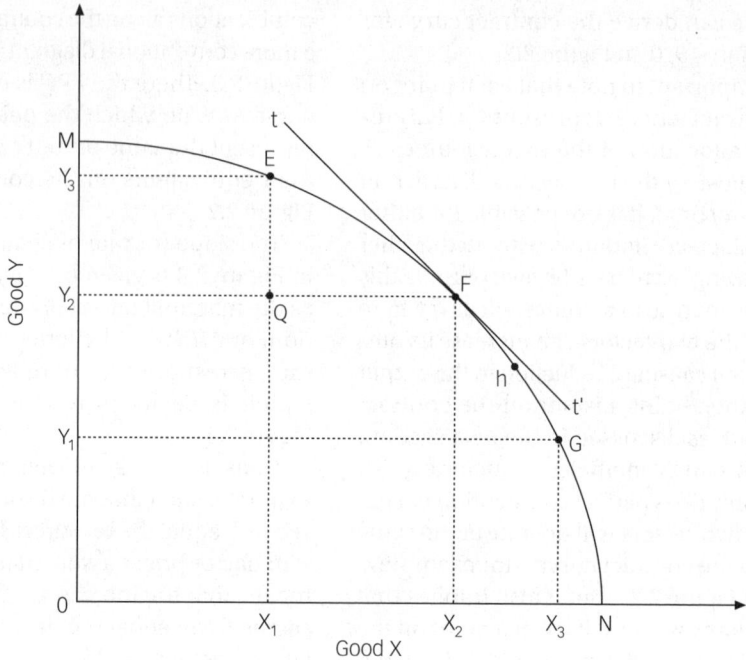

Figure 2.3 Production possibility curve

$$MC_x = \frac{\Delta TC_x}{\Delta X} \text{ and } MC_y = \frac{\Delta TC_y}{\Delta Y} \quad [2.4]$$

or

$$\Delta X = \frac{\Delta TC_x}{MC_x} \text{ and } \Delta Y = \frac{\Delta TC_y}{MC_y} \quad [2.4a]$$

therefore

$$\frac{\Delta Y}{\Delta X} = MRPT_{xy} = \frac{MC_x}{MC_y} \quad [2.4b]$$

MC_x is the marginal cost of production in sector X. Since under perfect competition each sector will ensure that its own marginal cost equals the corresponding market price, that is, $MC_x = P_x$ and $MC_y = P_y$, we have the following:

$$MRPT_{xy} = \frac{MC_x}{MC_y} = \frac{P_x}{P_y} \quad [2.5]$$

This is given by the slope of a tangent drawn to a point on the PPC – for example, the slope of line tt' at point F in Figure 2.3.

The first condition thus implies a point on the PPC according to which it is impossible to increase the output of either of the two sectors without thereby decreasing that of the other. Under perfect competition price will equal marginal cost in each sector, so that the MRPT, which equals the marginal cost ratio for the two sectors, also equals the corresponding price ratio.

Condition 2: Economic efficiency in consumption must occur in such a way that no interpersonal re-allocation of commodities can increase the utility of either of the two consumers, *a* or *b*, without thereby decreasing the utility of the other. Each consumer will therefore maximise utility subject to his or her own budget constraint; or choose that commodity mix for which the marginal rate of substitution (or the slope of

consumer goods between them) without thereby decreasing the utility of the other.

Condition 3: The third or top-level condition requires that producers and consumers achieve equilibrium simultaneously. Given that the slope of the PPC, or the $MRPT_{xy}$, equals the corresponding ratio of marginal costs, $\frac{MC_x}{MC_y}$ and hence also the corresponding equilibrium price ratio, our third condition can be written as follows:

$$MRPT_{xy} = \frac{MC_x}{MC_y} = \frac{P_x}{P_y} = MRS^a_{xy}$$

$$= MRS^b_{xy} \qquad [2.7]$$

This indicates equality between the (marginal) rate at which each consumer is willing to substitute one commodity for the other, and the rate at which it is technically possible to do so.

Simultaneous compliance with these three conditions will ensure production of the optimal output mix – shown by the parallel lines tt' at point F and vv' at point F' in Figure 2.4. The slope of the line tt' equals the $MRPT_{xy}$ and the corresponding marginal cost ratio, while the slope of vv' equals the marginal rates of substitution for the two consumers. Points F and F' in Figure 2.4 are thus consistent with Equation [2.7] above: they represent our third or top-level condition, and hence also our first and second conditions for a general equilibrium.

Point F is a **Pareto-optimal top-level equilibrium**, in the sense that it is not possible to increase the output of either of the two commodities, or the utility of either of the two consumers, without thereby reducing that of the other.

It is important to note that the precise location of the top-level point on the PPC will depend on the underlying assumptions of the model, particularly the initial distribution of resources between the two individuals, a and b. If one of the two individuals owns most of the initial capital and labour resources and has a particularly strong relative preference for commodity Y, it stands to reason that our model will generate a top-level equilibrium lying on the PPC and close to the Y-axis in Figure 2.4. We will revisit this important issue in Chapter 5.

2.3 Efficiency and economic growth

Technical efficiency or **X-efficiency** refers to a situation in which existing resources are utilised in the most efficient manner. Obtaining the maximum possible output from a given set of resources – or technically efficient production – necessarily implies a position on the PPC, such as points C_0 and S in Figure 2.5.

A point such as R indicates the presence of X-inefficiency. All economic inefficiencies other than allocative inefficiency fall under the term X-inefficiency. Leibenstein (1966) argued that although X-inefficiency (sometimes also termed organisational slack) derives primarily from a lack of motivation by production agents, factors such as a lack of information about market conditions, incomplete knowledge of production functions, and the incomplete specification of labour contracts can also explain the existence of X-inefficiency.

Clearly, X-efficiency alone is an insufficient measure of economic efficiency since the technically efficient production of goods by itself does not necessarily reflect the needs of consumers. In common sense terms, it is pointless to produce goods efficiently if people would rather consume some other combinations of goods. Put differently, X-efficiency ensures that society is on its PPC, but cannot determine where society should be on this curve.

It is possible also to define economic efficiency dynamically (i.e. **dynamic efficiency**) in terms of given increases in the quantity

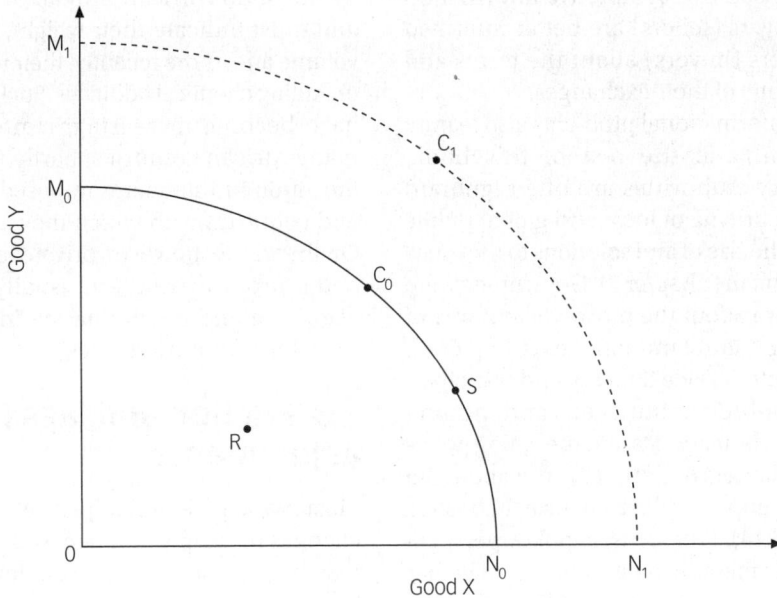

Figure 2.5 X-inefficiency and economic growth

and (or) productivity of the factors of production. The sources of growth are conventionally defined to include savings, investment in the form of both physical and human capital formation, technological inventions and innovations, and increases in the availability of labour of different skills. From a general equilibrium perspective, the net effect of sustained economic growth can be shown as an outward shift in the PPC, for example, from $M_0 N_0$ to $M_1 N_1$ in Figure 2.5, and by a concomitant change in the competitive equilibrium, for example, from point C_0 to C_1.

2.4 Market failure: an overview

The perfectly competitive model is nothing more than a theoretical nicety, a normative ideal against which real-world conditions can be judged, and in this section we briefly distinguish between several instances of market failure. The most important of these are discussed in more detail in the remaining chapters of Part 1.

2.4.1 Lack of information

Producers and consumers do not always have at their disposal the information necessary to make rational decisions. Producers may be unaware of the existence of certain resources or of the latest technologies available in their own lines of business. Similarly, consumers may be ignorant of potentially harmful properties inherent in some goods and services they consume, or of the fact that certain goods are available at lower prices than what they are currently paying for them (Bohm, 1978). Similar comments can be made in respect of the labour market where unemployed workers are often unaware of the existence of available job vacancies, or employers are unaware of available job seekers who can fill their vacancies. Many transactions are also characterised by asymmetric information where buyers (sellers) are better informed than sellers (buyers) about the terms and implications of their exchanges.

Such informational problems also feature prominently in the rest of this book. Regulatory authorities are often ignorant about the pricing of local and global public goods or the size of and solutions to the externality problem (Chapter 3). Governments are also unsure about the most efficient way of regulating natural monopolies (Chapter 4), dealing with service delivery and principal-agent problems between and among politicians, bureaucrats and the voting population (Chapters 6, 8 and 17), and about the economic impact of different taxes (Chapters 11, 12 and 14). From a fiscal policy perspective, governments can never be sure whether actual tax revenue one year down the line will equal the budgeted equivalent, due to unforeseen changes in GDP (Chapter 15); and neither do they know precisely what the cost of their debt will be in the future (Chapter 16).

Very few individuals and institutions have the information they need when having to make decisions that would maximise their own well-being. Even if consumers, producers and job hunters and seekers were prepared to pay for the required information, this too does not always help. It would be clearly impossible for them to calculate such costs without knowing precisely what the additional information is. But if they knew the latter there would be no need to acquire it, let alone calculate the cost. They thus have no choice but to accept their lack of information as a binding constraint.

This raises the question whether governments in free societies should bear the responsibility of providing individual citizens with information for private decision-making. In some cases governments do perform this function. In South Africa, for example, virtually all consumer goods must be cleared by the South African Bureau of Standards and must indicate their weight, mass, and volume and, more recently, their ingredients, including chemical additives. Such standards have become increasingly important for many African countries, partly because of the minimum standards imposed by regions and countries with which they are trading. On the whole, however, private institutions, being profit-driven, are usually better at acquiring and disseminating information than government agencies.

2.4.2 Friction and lags in adjustments

Most markets do not adjust very rapidly to changes in supply and demand. While this may be partly due to a lack of information, it is also true that resources are not very mobile at the best of times, that is, even when the necessary information is at hand. This has given rise to the development of search markets in which agents spend time and resources searching for information and, in the process, incur so-called friction costs (see work done by the 2010 Nobel laureates, Diamond, Mortensen and Pissarides, in http//nobelprize.org/nobel_prices/economics/laureates/2010/). Labour may take time to move from one job to another or from one place to another, while physical capital can only move from one location to another at very irregular intervals. It takes time for an entrepreneur to move out of textile production into computer software production, or for a civil engineer to become retrained as an electrical engineer – even when they are fully aware of the new opportunities available in the market place. Acquiring and adapting the latest technologies may also take both time and money, especially when the requisite skills are not readily available. We will revisit the issue of lags when we evaluate their impact on the effectiveness of fiscal policy in Chapter 15 (Section 15.3.2).

2.4.3 Incomplete markets

Markets are often incomplete in the sense that they cannot meet the demand for certain public goods such as street lighting, defence, or neighbourhood security on their own. Neither do they fully account for the external costs and benefits associated with individual actions. When a company pollutes the air or river water, damaging the health of consumers using that air or water, it is not usually held responsible for its action; and neither are the consumers compensated for the additional health expenses that they might incur. These issues are discussed more fully in Chapter 3.

2.4.4 Non-competitive markets

Non-competitive markets are the rule rather than the exception. Commodity markets are characterised by the presence of monopolies and oligopolies, while labour markets are in turn constrained by minimum wages imposed by trade unions, governments, and by large corporations themselves. Several of the new labour laws in South Africa, including the Basic Conditions of Employment and the Employment Equity Acts, may well raise the non-wage costs of employment, thus forcing firms either to reduce output or adopt labour-saving technologies.

While a lack of competition may well undermine allocative efficiency and X-efficiency as defined above, it may also be the net result of a competitive process in which one or more low-cost firms managed to dominate the market. In Chapter 4 we shall look at these issues in more detail and also consider the role of competition policy in a modern economy.

2.4.5 Macroeconomic instability

At the macroeconomic level, markets may be slow to react to sudden exogenous shocks to the system – witness the recent movements in Southern African currencies and the negative real effects they have had on the domestic economies. Left on their own, markets may take too long to adjust to changing external conditions and it is often necessary for domestic policymakers to take appropriate actions aimed at stabilising the currency (South Africa Foundation, 1998). The important role played by monetary and exchange rate policies today can be viewed as an attempt on the part of governments to deal with the problem of market failure at the macroeconomic level.

A more recent example of a serious exogenous shock is the 2008–2009 global financial crisis that has even been compared with the 1929 Great Depression. Swift and appropriate actions were required from policymakers the world over to mitigate its effects. It was prompted by a liquidity shortage in the American banking system and has led to the downfall of large financial institutions such as Lehman Brothers, the bail-out of banks by domestic governments, and downswings in stock markets throughout the world. The effects of the crisis were more severe in developed countries than in the developing world with the IMF and EU having to bail-out several countries – including Ireland, Greece and Portugal – whose public debt had become unmanageably large. This issue is taken up again in Chapters 15 and 16.

2.4.6 Distribution of income

Perhaps the most important shortcoming of the neoclassical model of general equilibrium is the fact that it is entirely neutral on the distributional issue. It basically operates like a 'black box': what you get out of it is what you put into it. The distributional outcome – as reflected by the precise top-level equilibrium on the PPC – is determined to a great extent by the initial distribution of capital and labour between the two individuals. If the initial distribution is highly unequal, then so too will be the final distribution. In Chapter 5 we take up this issue again and also spell out some of the relevant policy implication, while in Chapter 8 we discuss the distributional issue in South Africa.

2.4.7 Concluding note

These examples of market failure are but a small sample of the many things that can go wrong in a modern capitalist economy. It is clear that real-world economies are not very efficient in the conventional economic

sense of the word. They do not, and probably never will, achieve a Pareto-optimal allocation of resources. Neither will they on their own produce an equitable distribution of income – or a distribution that is acceptable to the broad community, or its representative government.

But this does not mean that any other form of economic organisation, such as a socialist or centrally planned economy, will be any better at allocating scarce resources in accordance with the true wishes of the community. There is now enough evidence to suggest that countries that have abided by the principles of the market have generally grown more rapidly and have spread the benefits of that growth more effectively, than those countries that have opted for an overly interventionist or centrally planned system. Indeed, not all economists have bought into

BOX 2.2 Market failure: alternative view

The Austrian school believes in the superiority of a free-market system in which government's role is limited to that of protecting the freedom of individuals and communities. To Austrian economists the notion of 'market failure', as conventionally defined, is something of a misnomer. Rather it should be viewed as being part of the dynamic process by which markets continually adjust to changing tastes and technologies, with individuals and enterprises constantly searching for and filtering information in an attempt to stay or get ahead of their rivals. Free and competitive markets operate in an evolutionary fashion, with only the fittest surviving, and with the only 'failure' being the 'creative destruction' of firms that are unable to produce at minimum cost or create or imitate new technologies (e.g. Schumpeter, 1987; Nelson and Winter, 1982).

Other economists would argue that market participants can and often do overcome the problem of imperfect information themselves. We have already referred to the creation of 'search markets' in which employers and work-seekers spend time and money to acquire information they need to secure their occupational well-being. Another example is the payment of efficiency wages by employers in order to save on monitoring costs and, in the process, avoid an otherwise serious principal-agent problem (Stiglitz, 1984). Yet another example is credit rationing on the part of banks when demand exceeds supply at the prevailing interest rate. There is also a view that too little is generally known about the nature and extent of market failures, and that governments have less of an incentive to fill such informational gaps than the private sector (Cowen and Crampton, 2011).

the notion of 'market failure' which, as Box 2.2 shows, can be viewed as part of the normal adjustments made by free agents in the face of changing circumstances. The key issue here is whether such adjustments are being made in response to negative or positive externalities imposed by others, and whether they can be made in good time with little or no cost to the broader society; or conversely, whether government intervention can speed up the process and close some of the gaps discussed above without undermining economic efficiency.

What cannot be denied is that in most market-based economies the public sector has played a significant role in creating wealth for their growing populations. In these economies the public sector has been charged with the task of providing certain public goods such as defence and law and order, dealing with the problem of externalities, protecting consumer interests through minimum health and other standards, regulating natural monopolies, and preventing abusive behaviour on the part of monopolies and oligopolies. We will deal with these issues in the sections and chapters that follow.

2.5 Enter the public sector: general approaches

We saw in the previous section that various kinds of market failure can render the benchmark model of perfect competition unworkable in the real world. These failures provide a prima facie case for government intervention and in this section we briefly focus on the broad approaches that governments can follow in coming to grips with such failures.

Economists conventionally distinguish between three broad functions of government: the allocative, distributive, and stabilisation functions.

2.5.1 Allocative function

The **allocative function of government** stems from the fact that market failures distort the allocation of resources in an economy. Market failures due to incomplete and non-competitive markets are particularly important sources of allocative distortions. The issues surrounding incomplete markets are discussed in greater detail in Chapter 3, but we will point out the main manifestations of incomplete markets briefly.

There are two manifestations of incomplete markets: the first one involves the fact that some goods and services have characteristics that prevent competitive markets from supplying them efficiently. Such market failures can take various forms. In the case of pure public goods (such as national defence and street lighting) potential consumers have a strong incentive not to reveal their demand. This makes it impossible to determine a price or to force users to pay for the benefits they derive from using the good or service. As a result, competitive markets cannot supply public goods at all, even though they are in great demand.

A second class of goods and services, known as mixed goods, has some public good characteristics. Consumers would either not reveal their demand for such goods and services, or producers would find it impossible to enforce payment of the price. Mixed goods can be supplied by competitive markets, but neither the quantity supplied nor the price resulting from market provision would be optimal. Examples of these goods are subscription television services and certain healthcare services.

A second manifestation of incomplete markets is the existence of externalities. In practice, the activities of individual consumers and producers often impact on other 'third parties', and failure to account for such external effects tends to create a divergence between actual market prices and quantities and their socially optimal equivalents. Externalities can be either negative, as in the case of air or river pollution, or positive. An example of a positive externality would be the 'additional' benefits that society derives from education, such as having a more literate voter population and a lower crime rate. Such benefits are additional to the private benefits accruing to individual recipients in the form of higher earnings.

As discussed in Chapter 4, non-competitive markets may take two forms. 'Artificial' monopolies operate in markets where perfect competition is technically feasible but is prevented by legal restrictions imposed by government or professional bodies. By contrast, 'natural' monopolies develop in industries characterised by large capital outlays that give rise to economies of scale over the entire range of their output. Only one firm can effectively operate in such a market. Examples include the markets for water and electricity. In both cases, firms operating in non-competitive markets maximise their profits by supplying less than the optimal quantity of the good or service at too high a price.

Governments have various instruments at their disposal for correcting the allocative distortions resulting from incomplete and non-competitive markets. We refer to some of these instruments in Section 2.6 and discuss them more fully in Chapters 3 and 4.

2.5.2 Distributive function

In Section 2.4 we pointed out that the general equilibrium model of the neoclassical school is decidedly agnostic when it comes to the *distribution* of wealth or income in a society. It yields a distributional outcome largely determined by the initial distribution of labour and capital between the market participants. The model can thus be used to determine the Pareto-optimal allocation of resources for a given distribution of income only. In fact, there exists a Pareto-optimal allocation for each income distribution. However, the model is silent on the *fairness* of that distribution.

Market outcomes tend to exhibit considerable inequality in the distribution of income. The fact that all governments use combinations of taxes, transfer payments, and subsidies to alter these outcomes, suggests that no society regards the market-determined distribution of income as being fair or just. Some commentators have even suggested that a redistribution of income could improve the general well-being of society, even if it carried a cost in terms of lower levels of productivity or slower economic growth. In practice, however, there is considerable disagreement about the appropriate criteria for evaluating the **distributive function of government** – this remains a key aspect of its role in a modern capitalist economy. These issues are investigated in greater detail in Chapter 5.

2.5.3 Stabilisation function

The **stabilisation function of government** refers to its macroeconomic objectives, which include an acceptable rate of economic growth, full employment, price stability, and a sound and manageable balance of payments (see Chapter 15). An inability on the part of competitive markets to realise these objectives would represent market failure on a grand scale, and often induces governments to correct for such failure by means of appropriate monetary, exchange rate, and fiscal policies. Being a macroeconomic issue, however, a detailed analysis of stabilisation policy falls beyond the scope of this book, though some of the fiscal aspects will be dealt with in Chapters

15 and 16. Our purpose here is mainly to provide a brief overview of the stabilisation role of government.

The notion that governments have an important stabilisation function to fulfill is associated primarily with the Keynesian school of macroeconomic thought. The Keynesian approach to stabilisation rests on three premises:

▶ the market economy is inherently unstable
▶ macroeconomic instability is a form of market failure that is highly costly to an economy
▶ governments are able to stabilise the economy by means of appropriate macroeconomic policies.

Keynesians therefore propose active counter-cyclical policies to stabilise economic activity. Their proposed policies mainly work on the demand side of the economy. In times of recession, governments should reduce taxes, increase their expenditure, and boost credit expansion in order to raise aggregate demand and stimulate economic activity. Conversely, inflationary overheating of the economy should be addressed by higher taxes and lower levels of state spending and credit expansion, thus moderating aggregate demand.

The stabilisation function of government – as described above – is not without its critics. Economists from the New Classical Macroeconomics school believe that the economy is self-adjusting and that government intervention would worsen rather than improve matters. They argue that Keynesian economics lack a proper microeconomics foundation, and fail to realise that individual agents could rationally anticipate the actions of government and act upon them even before they are executed, or at least before they have their intended effect. New Classical economists thus believe that there is no need to stabilise the market economy and that,

even if there was a need, governments would be unable to do so effectively.

In response to these criticisms, the so-called Neo-Keynesian school has tried to revive Keynesian theory by providing it with a credible microeconomics foundation. Neo-Keynesian economists argue that many rigidities characterising the modern economy are perfectly consistent with rational economic behaviour and that some of them, such as wage and price contracts, can prevent the economy from responding or adjusting rapidly to exogenous shocks. These theories provide some justification for demand-management policies, although Neo-Keynesians do acknowledge some of the practical difficulties facing policymakers, such as policy lags and shifting expectations.

2.6 Direct versus indirect government intervention

Another way of approaching the role of government in the economy is to look at the nature of government interventions. Viewed very broadly, it is useful to distinguish between direct and indirect forms of intervention.

Direct government intervention refers to the actual participation of government in the economy. It includes the government's constitutional right to tax individuals and companies, borrow on the financial markets, and execute its budgeted spending programmes. As far as the latter programmes are concerned, governments intervene directly when they respond to a market failure by producing or supplying a good or service, such as national defence, waste disposal, or electricity; or by financing production undertaken by the private sector on a contract basis, such as school textbooks and much of the state's infrastructure.

Indirect government intervention refers to the regulatory function of government. **Regulation** entails enacting a law or proclaiming a legally binding rule that gives rise to market outcomes that are different from those that would have been obtained in the absence of the intervention. Examples abound and in South Africa they include the following: the new labour laws that are aimed at improving the working conditions of labour; the new anti-tobacco law through which it is hoped to curb tobacco smoking; the new competition policy that is aimed at preventing abusive behaviour on the part of monopolies; and several new environmental control measures. Indirect taxes and subsidies, which also change market outcomes, constitute indirect fiscal measures as well.

The distinction between direct and indirect interventions can make an important difference to our estimates of the size of the public sector and its effects on the economy. Conventional indicators of the size of the public sector, that are based on the total tax burden, government expenditures, and the budget deficit or surplus, provide a reasonably accurate picture of the size and extent of direct government intervention in the economy (or of the 'resource use' by government, as explained in Chapter 1). The problem is that regulatory interventions, whose total effect on the private sector may well be as important as that of direct measures, do not show up in the national or government accounts. Conventional measures of the size of the public sector, such as those used in Chapter 1 and in Chapter 7, may well underestimate the overall effect of public sector activity on an economy. However, as yet there is no suitable quantitative indicator that fully accounts for the impact of government regulations on the economy.

2.7 Note on government failure

Irrespective of how we define the public sector or how we measure its size or impact on the economy, it is important to realise that governments, like markets, can also fail. Those involved in the business of government – politicians, bureaucrats, and public employees – are no different from the rest of us. They often pursue their own self-interest, rather than the public interest and, due to the protected nature of their business, they are not particularly X-efficient. They make mistakes, wittingly or unwittingly, and are even corrupt at times – just like many of the rest of us are.

In Chapter 6 we argue that 'government failure', like market failure, is nothing sinister or extraordinary. It is a perfectly natural outcome of the way in which politicians and government officials behave. Like their counterparts in the private sector, they are utility maximisers: politicians want to maximise votes, virtually at all costs, while bureaucrats often strive to maximise the size of their departmental budgets, or 'empires'. The net effect is usually an excess supply of public goods and services – or a government that is bigger than its optimal size.

It is therefore important – indeed imperative – for the tax-paying public, including students of public economics, to know how efficiently their government is performing its various functions. But to make this judgement it is not only necessary to know *why* governments intervene in the economy in the first place (which is the focus of the rest of Part 1) but also to know *what* it is that governments are supposed to do – the focus of the remaining parts of this book. Only then will we be able to make an informed judgement about the role of government in our economy.

IMPORTANT CONCEPTS

allocative efficiency (page 19)

allocative function of government (page 29)

direct government intervention (page 31)

distributive function of government (page 30)

dynamic efficiency (page 24)

indirect government intervention (page 32)

market failure (page 17)

Pareto optimality (in consumption) (page 23)

Pareto optimality (in production) (page 20)

Pareto-optimal top-level equilibrium (page 24)

regulation (page 32)

stabilisation function of government (page 30)

technical or X-efficiency (page 24)

SELF-ASSESSMENT EXERCISES

2.1 Distinguish between allocative efficiency, X-efficiency, and economic growth ('dynamic' efficiency) and briefly consider their relevance to South Africa.

2.2 Outline the conditions for a top-level general equilibrium and explain why they represent a Pareto-optimal allocation of resources.

2.3 Explain the meaning of market failure and provide a few pertinent examples.

2.4 Distinguish between the allocative and distributive functions of government.

2.5 Should governments have a stabilisation function?

2.6 Distinguish between direct and indirect government intervention.

Chapter
THREE

Philip Black and Krige Siebrits

Public goods and externalities

In Chapter 2 we introduced a benchmark model that explains the allocation of scarce resources within a perfectly competitive environment. We emphasised the point that the model itself provides a normative standard against which the performance of real-world markets can be judged. In Chapter 2, Section 2.4 we briefly introduced the notion of 'market failure', that is, the inability of real-world markets to achieve the efficient outcomes of our benchmark model.

In this chapter we provide a more detailed discussion of two important sources of market failure, namely public goods and externalities. Both sources of failure reflect the incompleteness of markets. On their own, free markets cannot meet the demand for public goods or fully account for the external costs and benefits associated with individual actions. These market failures therefore provide a rationale for complementary government actions aimed at improving the allocation of resources. In addition to the theory of public goods and externalities – discussed in Sections 3.1 to 3.6 – we also look at some of the relevant policy implications in Sections 3.7 and 3.8. Public goods may also have a regional or global dimension, while externalities may have spillover effects across international boundaries; and in Section 3.9 we discuss relevant examples of these dimensions.

Once you have studied this chapter, you should be able to:
- distinguish between private, public, mixed, and merit goods
- derive the conditions for the optimal allocation of private, public, and mixed goods with the aid of supply and demand analysis
- explain why competitive markets fail to provide public and mixed goods efficiently
- explain the distinction between the financing of public goods and services and their physical production
- explain the concept of an externality
- identify the main types of externalities
- explain the effects of positive and negative externalities with the aid of supply and demand analysis
- discuss the policy options to correct for externalities
- discuss the relative importance of property rights and transaction costs in market-based approaches to dealing with the problem of externalities
- discuss cap-and-trade programmes
- provide examples of global or regional public goods and consider some of the relevant policy implications.

3.1 Private goods and the benchmark model

We begin our discussion of public goods by reflecting on the nature of the goods produced and consumed in the benchmark model. In Chapter 2 we simply labelled these goods X and Y and gave no further information about them. We then proceeded to derive the conditions under which X and Y would be produced and consumed in a Pareto-efficient manner. The issue that we now have to consider is whether the nature of X and Y has any bearing on the outcome of the analysis. Can we substitute any actual commodity or service for X and Y and still achieve allocative efficiency? As suggested in Section 2.4 of Chapter 2, the answer to this question is 'no'. Not all goods and services can be supplied efficiently by competitive markets.

Efficient production under competitive conditions requires that consumers reveal their preferences (or demand) for goods and services. By doing so, they signal to producers what types and quantities of goods they prefer. On the basis of these signals, producers then decide on what and how much to produce. Competition among producers ensures that they do so at minimum cost. Provided that consumer preferences are fully revealed, the market performs like a huge auction that meets the third or top-level condition for allocative efficiency: simultaneous achievement of equilibrium by producers and consumers.

Conversely, competitive markets will fail if there are no satisfactory mechanisms through which consumers can reveal their preferences. Whether or not such mechanisms exist depends on the nature or characteristics of goods and services. They certainly exist in the case of **private goods**, which we can define in terms of the following two characteristics:

- Rivalry in consumption: private goods are wholly divisible amongst individuals; this means that one person's consumption of the good reduces its availability to other potential consumers. For example, if Thandi wears a particular dress, it is not possible for Christine to wear it simultaneously. Similarly, the consumption of an apple by Christine reduces the quantity of apples available for consumption to Thandi by one.

▶ Excludability: the consumption of a private good can be restricted to given individuals, typically those who pay the indicated or negotiated price. Once private goods have been paid for, ownership (or the assignment of property rights) is certain and uniquely determined. For example, if Thabo pays for a drink in a restaurant, he gains the sole right to consume that specific drink and has legally excluded Charles from enjoying it.

The benefits of consuming private goods are therefore restricted to those individuals who reveal their preferences for such goods. The rivalry and excludability of private goods force potential consumers to reveal their preferences, thereby setting in motion the competitive processes resulting in allocative efficiency.

We can illustrate this point by referring to the market for compact discs as illustrated in Figure 3.1. *DB* and *DJ* are the individual demand curves for two consumers, Bongani and Joan. Each demand curve depicts the quantities of compact discs that the respective consumer would demand at different prices. The market demand curve – given by *DB +J* – is simply the horizontal sum of the individual quantities demanded at each price. Market equilibrium occurs at point *E*, where market demand equals market supply, thus yielding a single equilibrium price at point *P*. Joan and Bongani cannot affect the equilibrium price they pay for compact discs

and are therefore price-takers. The equilibrium output of compact discs is *0Q*, with the quantities demanded by Joan and Bongani given by *0J* and *0B*, respectively. Note that although *0J* and *0B* sum to *0Q*, there is no reason why the two should be equal. The respective quantities demanded at the equilibrium price may differ according to the tastes, income levels, and other characteristics of our two consumers. They are therefore quantity-adjusters, in the sense that each one determines the quantity he or she demands in accordance with the equilibrium price.

Our compact disc example enables us to highlight two important characteristics of a private good:

▶ Marginal utility equals marginal cost for each consumer: you will recall that the area underneath the demand curve gives the total utility derived from consuming compact discs, or the sum of the marginal utilities derived from consuming each compact disc, while the area under the supply curve gives the sum of the marginal costs of producing each compact disc. Therefore, at equilibrium price *0P* the marginal utilities of Bongani and Joan (*BF* and *JG*, respectively) both equal the marginal cost *QE*. This is the condition for the efficient supply of a private good.

▶ The price of a private good equals its marginal cost: this is the efficient pricing rule for private goods, as is evident from Figure 3.1.

3.2 Pure public goods: definition

The fact that private goods have two defining characteristics implies that there are three classes of 'non-private' goods. Two of these classes each share one characteristic with private goods – these are known as

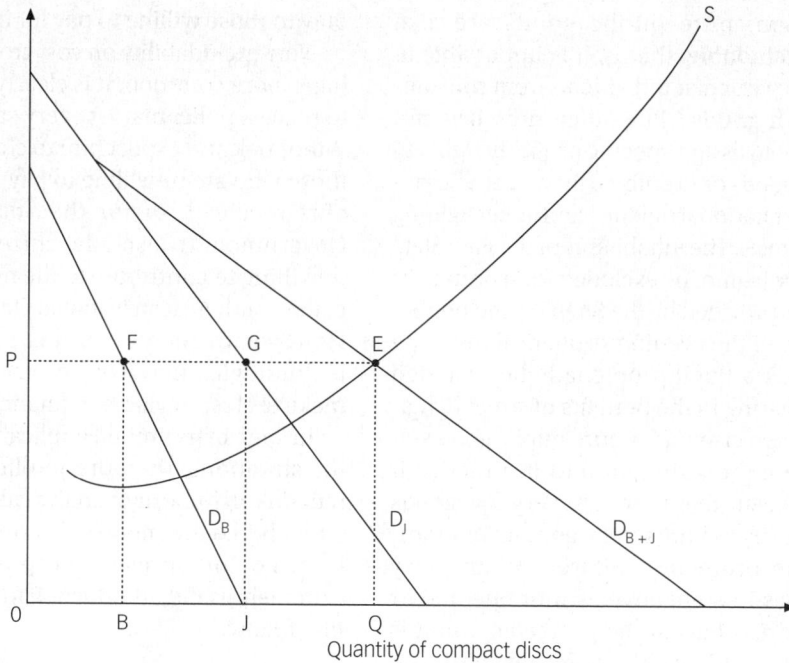

Figure 3.1 Equilibrium of a private good

mixed goods and are discussed in Sections 3.5 and 3.6. In this section we discuss goods to which neither of the characteristics of private goods applies. Such goods are called **pure public goods** or pure social goods.

Pure public goods such as street lighting and national defence are indivisible – that is, they cannot be divided into saleable units – and are therefore non-rival in consumption. For a given level of production of a public good, one person's consumption does not reduce the quantity available for consumption by another person.[1]

If Thandi uses a street light to guide her during her walk to a postbox, Roger can use that same street light to establish whether he has found the street in which a distant relative of his lives. Similarly, the protection provided by the South African National

Defence Force (SANDF) to the inhabitants of Tshwane does not reduce the 'quantity' of protection available to the inhabitants of Johannesburg or Polokwane.

Non-rivalry in consumption has two important implications:

Firstly, the fact that one person's consumption does not reduce the quantity available to other consumers implies that the marginal cost (i.e. the cost of admitting an additional user) is zero. The second implication follows from the first, namely that excluding anyone from consuming a non-rival good, even if it was feasible to do so, is Pareto-inefficient. The reason is straightforward: allowing Ibrahim to use the above street light at zero marginal cost will clearly make him better off than before; yet it will not detract from the enjoyment that Thandi and Roger derive from that same street light. We will return to these implications in the next section.

---

[1] The use of the word 'consumption' in the context of public goods could perhaps be misleading. Such goods are not really consumed; they generate a stream of benefits that can be enjoyed by all.

In addition to being non-rival in consumption, pure public goods are also **non-excludable**, that is, it is impossible to exclude particular individuals from consuming such goods.[2] Put differently, it is not possible to assign specific property rights to public goods or to enforce them. Let us again consider national defence and street lighting as examples. The inhabitants of the Free State Province cannot be excluded from protective services provided by the SANDF; and neither can any of the evening strollers along Cape Town's Sea Point promenade be excluded from sharing in the benefits of street lights.

The two criteria for pure public good status are quite stringent and in practice it would seem that there are very few goods that qualify as pure public goods. For example, the protection offered by an army becomes less effective as more people or larger areas have to be protected and it is therefore debatable whether national defence is fully non-rival at all levels of provision.

Similarly, very few goods are non-excludable in the true or 'technical' sense of the word. The development of new technologies continuously expands the scope for the application of the exclusion principle to more goods. Consider the standard case of the lighthouse. For many years the lighthouse was the favourite example of a non-excludable public good. However, the service offered by a lighthouse is not so much a beam of light as a navigational aid. Nowadays it is technologically feasible and cost-effective to provide this service in the form of an electronic signal made available only to those willing to pay for it.

Non-excludability on cost grounds is perhaps more common. It is clearly very costly to place a policeman at every street light in Windhoek and expect him to chase away all those who are unwilling to pay for the benefits received, or for the South African Government to 'exclude' citizens who are unwilling to contribute to the maintenance of the South African National Defence Force. However, in such cases it is possible that technologies may yet be developed that make exclusion viable in financial terms.

In spite of its limited applicability to real-life situations, the pure public good case remains an important analytical benchmark – much like the model of perfect competition. For our present purposes it is an extremely useful introduction to the sections that follow.

3.3 The market for public goods

Let us now consider the market for pure public goods from a partial equilibrium perspective. We are going to analyse the public good equivalent of the private good case that we analysed in Section 3.1. The implications of the divergent characteristics of public and private goods will therefore become apparent from a comparison of the results obtained in Figure 3.2 below with those derived from Figure 3.1.

The two music-lovers we met in Section 3.1, Bongani and Joan, live in neighbouring houses. They spend many enjoyable evenings at home listening to their latest purchases of compact discs, often developing a strong demand for snacks in the process. A convenience store is located nearby, but the sidewalks in their neighbourhood are so poorly maintained that street lights are

---

[2] In his path-breaking analysis of public goods, Samuelson (1954 and 1955) defined public goods in terms of non-rivalry in consumption only. As we have just shown, non-rivalry is indeed a sufficient condition for public good status since it makes exclusion inefficient even when it is feasible. Some textbooks follow Samuelson in defining public goods in terms of non-rivalry only, but we shall follow the more conventional approach of using non-rivalry and non-excludability as criteria for public good status.

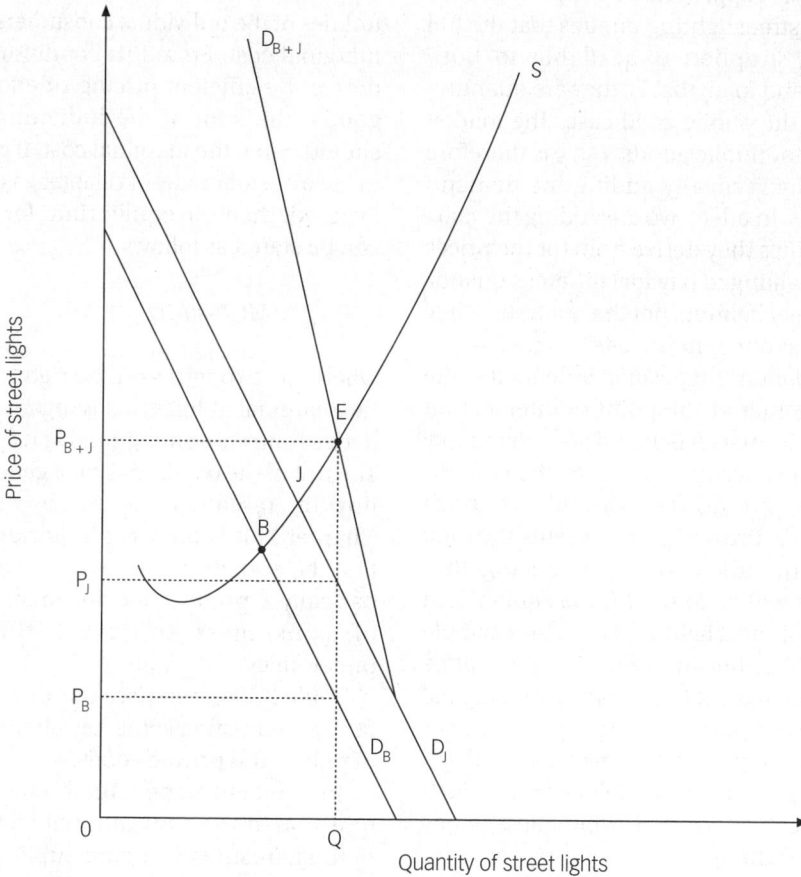

Figure 3.2 Equilibrium of a pure public good

essential to prevent slipping and tripping at night.

Figure 3.2 depicts the market for street lights in Joan and Bongani's street. We assume that they are the only 'consumers' of the light. Their respective demands for street lighting are given by curves D_J and D_B. Note that these are what Samuelson (1954) called 'pseudo demand curves', because they can be drawn only if consumers accurately reveal the quantities that they demand at different prices. As we have indicated in Section 3.1, however, such a revelation of preferences occurs only with private goods. We will return to this point and its implications

below, but for the moment we assume that Bongani and Joan do accurately reveal their preferences for street lighting. Given this assumption, the individual demand curves and the total supply curve S are drawn similar to those in Figure 3.1.

The fundamental difference between the public and private good cases is the manner of deriving the market demand curve. In Figure 3.1 we derived the market demand for compact discs by horizontally adding the demand curves of Joan and Bongani. But in the case of a public good which is indivisible, horizontal summation of the quantities demanded by each consumer at each price is clearly not appropriate. The non-exclud-ability of street lighting implies that the full quantity supplied is available to both Bongani and Joan, that is, they are quantity-takers in the public good case. The market demand for public goods, D_{B+J}, is therefore derived by vertically adding the demand schedules. In effect, we are adding the marginal utilities they derive from (or the prices they are willing to pay for) different quantities of street lighting, not the quantities they demand at different prices.

The equilibrium position is defined in the usual manner at the point of intersection between the market demand and total supply curves. This occurs at point E. The equilibrium output $0Q$ is available to both consumers. Price $0P_{B+J}$ represents the total amount that the two consumers together would be willing to pay for the equilibrium quantity of street lighting, $0Q$. In the example of Figure 3.2 Bongani is willing to pay a price or equivalent tax of $0P_B$ (equal to his marginal utility), while Joan is willing to pay a price or tax of $0P_J$ (equal to her marginal utility). Bongani and Joan are therefore price-adjusters who can adjust their willingness to pay for street lighting.

A similar model was developed by Lindahl (1958) in which each user paid a different price per unit of the public good based on his or her tax share (or Lindahl price). Through an auctioneer-driven competitive process equilibrium is achieved when all users agree to their respective tax shares and the associated quantity of the public good, e.g. $0P_B$, $0P_J$ and $0Q$ in Figure 3.2.

The rules for the efficient allocation and pricing of public goods are also different from those for private goods. Returning to Figure 3.2 above, keep in mind that the areas under the demand and supply curves show the sum of marginal utilities and the sum of the marginal costs, respectively. The equilibrium position implies that the condition for the efficient provision of a public good is

equality between the sum of the marginal utilities of the individual consumers and the marginal cost. From this condition we can derive the efficient pricing rule for public goods: the sum of the individual prices should equal the marginal cost. If good X in the two-sector model of Chapter 2 is the public good, then the equilibrium for sector X can be stated as follows:

$$P^x_{B+J} = MC^x = MU^x_B + MU^x_J \qquad [3.1]$$

where the two terms on the right represent the marginal utilities that Bongani and Joan derive from consuming good X, respectively. The rest of the conditions for a general equilibrium remain the same as shown in Chapter 2. It is however important to add that the equilibrium shown in Figure 3.2 is basically a 'pseudo' one due to the inability of consumers to reveal their true preferences.

Table 3.1 summarises our discussion so far by contrasting some key characteristics of public and private goods.

In a recent paper Agiobenebo (2006) questioned the conventional view on the optimal quantity of a pure public good. He argued that the optimal quantity is the largest quantity demanded by any single consumer (individually or as a collective). In Figure 3.2 this quantity would be determined at point J where Joan's demand equals the supply; and where the quantity is a bit lower than $0Q$ and the (combined) price is a little lower than P_{B+J}. Although the principles involved are the same as before – e.g. equality between the sum of the individual marginal utilities and marginal cost – Agiobenebo's definition does imply a smaller quantity of the public good, and a lower price, than the conventional approach; which may in turn imply a smaller tax burden (see Part 3 on taxation).

Table 3.1 A comparison of key characteristics of public and private goods

	Public goods	Private goods
Property rights	Non-excludable	Excludable
Consumption	Non-rival	Rival
Aggregate demand curve	Vertical addition of individual demand curves	Horizontal addition of individual demand curves
Partial equilibrium condition for optimum provision	The sum of marginal utilities equals marginal cost $[\Sigma MU_i = MC]$	Marginal utility of each consumer equals marginal cost $[MU_i = MC$ with i the individual consumer]
Efficient pricing rule	The sum of individual prices equals marginal cost $[\Sigma P = MC]$	Price equals marginal cost $[P = MC]$

Source: Adapted from Freeman (1983: 482).

3.4 Who should supply public goods?

Why do private markets fail to supply goods and services characterised by non-rivalry and non-excludability? We have already touched on the effects of non-rivalry when we stated that the marginal cost of admitting additional users of non-rival goods is zero. The condition for efficient pricing by competitive markets $(P = MC)$ therefore requires the price to be zero as well. Clearly, profit-maximising producers cannot apply the efficient pricing rule in this case, as charging a zero price would not enable them to cover the costs of providing the good or service.

The alternative of setting a cost-covering price (equal to the sum of the individual prices) would potentially enable a competitive market to supply the good; it would, however, not be efficient as exclusion cannot occur.

Any price other than zero exceeds the zero marginal cost of admitting additional users and consequently reduces consumption of a non-rival good. Such exclusion is

Pareto-inefficient, as its annulment would increase the welfare of previously excluded consumers without reducing the welfare of those already enjoying access to the good. In sum, it is impossible to determine an equilibrium price for the private provision of a non-rival good.

The non-excludability characteristic of public goods and services creates incentives for '**free riding**', that is, the phenomenon of misrepresenting preferences (or hiding them completely) on the expectation that a benefit may be enjoyed without having to pay for it. Let us return to our example of street lighting. Being rational individuals, Bongani and Joan know that they cannot be excluded from enjoying the benefits once street lighting is provided. Both of them therefore have an incentive to understate the intensity of their preferences for street lighting in the hope that the other will reveal his or her demand and pay for the service – they become free riders. If Bongani reveals his preference for street lights while Joan attempts to 'free ride', a competitive market will under-supply street lighting at the level where Bongani's marginal utility equals the marginal cost of provision;

this is represented by point *B* in Figure 3.2. In the extreme case where both Joan and Bongani attempt to 'free ride', no street lighting would be provided at all: their true preferences would then not be revealed. See Box 3.1 for some recent discoveries pertaining to free riding.

Government provision of public goods and services can improve on the inefficient outcomes of the market; yet it cannot ensure an optimal provision of public goods. Compared to the market, the government has the advantage that it can use its coercive powers to enforce payment for public goods. However, it is no more able than the market to get consumers to reveal their demand for such goods and therefore cannot determine efficient prices. These points may be

illustrated with the aid of Figure 3.2. Ideally, the government wishes to apply the efficient pricing rule for public goods, $\Sigma P = MC$. To do so, however, it would have to know the demand curves of the two consumers so that it can charge each consumer a price that is equivalent to his or her marginal valuation of the benefits of street lighting. In this case, the government would charge Bongani OP_B and Joan OP_J, thus recovering the full marginal cost (OP_{B+J}) of providing street lighting (OQ). Optimal provision of a public good thus requires the application of price discrimination, that is, the practice of charging different consumers different prices.

In practice, however, the government does not have the required knowledge about people's preferences to enable it to apply

BOX 3.1 Do people 'free ride'? Experimental results

The notion of free riding has recently been brought into question. In the comparatively new field of 'experimental economics', several experiments have been conducted among students to test one of the basic tenets of neoclassical economics, i.e. the 'selfishness axiom' or, in the present context, the temptation to free ride (see Kagel and Roth, 1995). In the so-called public goods game (PGG) the experimenter gives each participant or player an initial endowment – not known to others – either in the form of real money or a token which may or may not differ in value. Each player is then asked to make an unspecified and entirely voluntary contribution to a public fund – to be used to the benefit of all. The players also know that once all contributions have been made, the experimenter will augment the public fund – e.g. by 50 per cent – and then share it out *equally* among all the players.

Now, in terms of the selfishness hypothesis the dominant strategy in this game

would be free riding; and yet the vast majority of PGG players actually contribute, on average, between 40 per cent and 60 per cent of their endowments. Although there was great variation in the responses, including some evidence of no contributions being made, free riding definitely did not constitute a dominant strategy.

In a similar experiment conducted among secondary school kids in Cape Town (Hofmeyr, Burns and Visser, 2007), where the distribution of endowments reflected a high degree of inequality, it was found that low and high endowment players contributed roughly the same *fraction* of their endowments to the public fund. The latter result emerged after 10 rounds of the game during which time players could adjust their contributions to what they considered to be a 'fair share'. This and most other studies show that reciprocity and a sense of fairness do feature in the utility functions of individuals.

perfect price discrimination. This is the reason why governments typically cover the costs of supplying public goods by collecting a 'tax price' from consumers. The mandatory nature of tax payments eliminates the 'free rider' option and gives taxpayers a direct stake in revealing their preferences for public goods. Once Bongani and Joan have been forced to surrender a part of their hard-earned salaries to the government, they clearly have an incentive to participate in decisions on the use of their tax contributions, for example, by insisting on better maintenance of sidewalks or the provision of street lighting in their neighbourhood. Such participation could take the form of voting in a referendum on tax and expenditure measures, or voting for political parties in a democracy – as we will discuss in more detail in Chapter 6.

The actual production of public goods need not necessarily be undertaken by government as such – it could be done on a contract basis by the private sector. The critical difference between public and private goods therefore lies in the financing of these goods. When we refer to public goods, we essentially refer to the need for public (or collective) financing rather than private financing through the private financial sector. In an extreme sense one may say that all public goods could be produced privately as long as they are financed publicly. Many economists would argue that such a system is more efficient than one in which the government produces public goods, as governments are not subject to the profit and loss discipline of the market.

There are many examples of goods and services that are privately produced and publicly financed: school textbooks, free medicines, roads, dams, and the like. In addition, governments often use private goods and services as a means of meeting public demands, with the labour of public employees being the only significant value that is added in the 'production process'. Examples include the sophisticated equipment used by the military to produce a national defence system, the equipment and buildings used by diplomats in overseas embassies, and the electronic equipment used by administrators in the public sector. It is clear that a substantial part of government activity is in a sense already 'privatised'. The much-debated issue of further privatisation largely involves the service component and the important financing issue.

Of course, government financing presents its own problems, and we will highlight some of the efficiency implications of using tax increases or debt-financing as sources of government revenue in subsequent chapters.

3.5 Mixed and merit goods

As the name suggests, **mixed goods** possess both private and public good characteristics. Such goods and services are common in the real world and raise several vital questions about the economic role of government. Two classes of mixed goods and services can be distinguished:

- Non-rival, excludable mixed goods and services. Consider the part of the N14 highway between Vryburg and Kuruman. The exclusion principle can be applied by installing a toll gate, as has already been done on the N1 and N3 highways from Johannesburg to Bloemfontein and Durban. (This is indeed an old method of exclusion. At the entry to the old Montagu pass between George and Oudtshoorn in the Western Cape, a toll house survives to remind us that the government applied it as long ago as 1849.) Yet, on an average day, there is no rivalry in getting access to the N14 as road users have no need to compete for scarce space. The public good characteristic of non-rival access to the road prevents competitive markets from providing such roads efficiently. As discussed in the case of pure public goods, the problem is the impossibility of determining a competitive price. The competitive solution of setting the price equal to marginal cost is inappropriate since the marginal cost of access to the road is zero and, similarly, charging a cost-covering price will lead to Pareto-inefficient exclusion. The subscription television channels M-Net and DSTV are other examples of this class of mixed goods.

- Rival, non-excludable mixed goods and services. On weekdays, main thoroughfares in downtown Luanda are a good example of the class of mixed goods characterised by rivalry in consumption and non-excludability. Rivalry in the form of competition for the scarce road space is fierce, and the marginal cost of road usage increases as congestion increases. Efficient price determination at the level of the marginal cost becomes theoretically possible. The problem, however, lies in applying the exclusion principle. Imagine the congestion effects of levying toll charges at the entrances and exits to the central business district of a city like Luanda. In this case, market failure arises from the non-excludability characteristic of the mixed good.

Mixed goods as a group represents a 'grey area' and the question of whether they should be supplied by the public or the private sector remains open. The influence of technology on the application of the non-excludability characteristic is particularly important in this regard. We mentioned earlier that technological innovation changed the status of navigational aids from a pure public good (the lighthouse) to a non-rival but excludable mixed good (electronic information signals). In the same way, congested urban roads may in future become private goods through the use of road sensors to measure traffic volumes, detect licence plate numbers, and bill road users.

Political factors also come into play. In the case of some mixed and even private goods it is possible to apply the exclusion principle, but the goods in question are politically regarded as so meritorious that they are often provided via the national budget. Examples of such **merit goods** are education and health services. The reason for treating merit goods and services in a special way is that the individual who buys or receives them often confers certain 'external' benefits on other people and hence on the broader community – we will return to this issue in the next section.

In many other cases, such as enforcing the use of seatbelts in cars and making primary school education mandatory, the provision of merit goods simply reflects the belief that individuals are unable to act in their own best interest. The same belief guides the prohibition of certain harmful practices, for example comprehensive bans on smoking or on the use of certain drugs. There is an undeniable element of paternalism to the merit goods argument, which makes it quite controversial, particularly among those who fear that special interest groups would attempt to use the government to further their own views of how people should behave.

On the whole, mixed goods can be provided either by the government alone – such as in the case of healthcare services in some countries – or by the private sector – as with private toll roads or subscription television services. Most mixed goods, however, are provided by a combination of the private and public sectors. In addition to wholly owned government schools, for example, we also have a growing number of privately owned schools and training colleges in this country. Likewise, universities get their income partly from government and partly from students in the form of registration fees. The latter split can be viewed as an attempt to share the costs of university education in accordance with the public and private good components of the service.

3.6 Externalities

Externalities, or external effects, can either be positive or negative. They are **positive** when the actions of an individual producer or consumer confer a benefit on another party free of charge; and they are **negative** when those actions impose a cost on the other party for which he or she is not compensated. Such actions can be either of a 'technological' or of a 'pecuniary' nature. They are **technological** when they have a direct effect on the level of production or consumption of the 'other party'; and they are **pecuniary** when they change the demand and supply conditions, and hence the market prices, facing the other party. In either case, however, the beneficiary gets a windfall by not having to pay for the benefit, while the prejudiced party gets no compensation at all.

As far as pecuniary externalities are concerned, it can be argued that they do not have a net effect on society – resources are merely transferred from one owner to another, and markets adjust efficiently to changing demand and supply conditions (Browning and Browning, 1994: 49). Consider an area in which crime is rampant and house prices are falling rapidly: current owners and sellers will be disadvantaged but buyers will have the benefit of lower house prices. There is therefore no net loss to society and no real external effect – only a redistribution from one group to another. Nonetheless, it is still true to say that house buyers enjoy a windfall

while house sellers – the losers – get no compensation.

External effects drive a wedge between the private (or monetary) and the social costs and benefits associated with everyday market transactions. Social costs (benefits) are simply the sum of the private costs (benefits) and the external costs (benefits). In the following section we shall focus on the respective marginal equivalents.

Externalities can originate on either the supply side or the demand side of the market, and it is possible to distinguish between the following four broad categories:

As far as the supply side is concerned, the productive activities of a producer can have one of the following effects:

- a negative external effect on other producers or consumers, in which case the marginal external cost (MEC) > 0 and marginal social cost (MSC) > marginal private cost (MPC)
- a positive external effect, in which case $MEC < 0$ and $MPC > MSC$.

Likewise, on the demand side, the consumption activities of an individual consumer can have one of the following effects:

- a positive external effect on other consumers or producers, in which case the marginal external benefit (MEB) > 0 and marginal social benefit (MSB) > marginal private benefit (MPB)
- a negative external effect, in which case $MEB < 0$ and $MPB > MSB$.

This four-pronged taxonomy is ideal for analysing the effects of externalities and the scope for remedial government intervention with the aid of demand and supply curves. Each of the four types of externalities can be analysed separately, but we shall consider only two cases: a negative production externality and a positive consumption externality.

3.6.1 Negative production externality

Assume that a coal-fired power station on the Mpumalanga Highveld pollutes the air and the water used by nearby livestock and crop farmers. This example of a negative production externality can be analysed with the aid of Figure 3.3.

The diagram shows the normal private (= social) demand curve and the private supply or marginal cost curve ($S_p = MPC$) for the electricity generated by the power station. Recall that these curves represent the consumers' benefits from using electricity and the supplier's cost of providing it respectively. In a typical market situation equilibrium would occur at point E_0 with $0Q_0$ electricity supplied at a unit price of OP_0.

From the perspective of the community as a whole, however, the costs incurred by the supplier do not reflect the full cost of providing the electricity. The external costs of pollution to nearby farmers are ignored, yet are in fact part and parcel of the full or social cost of providing electricity. This is shown in Figure 3.3 by the 'social' supply curve labelled $S_s = MSC$. This curve indicates that the negative externality raises the social costs of providing electricity above the private costs of the supplier. By producing $0Q_0$ units of electricity, the supplier incurs a marginal private cost equal to Q_0E_0 and a marginal external cost of E_0F which together make up the marginal social cost of Q_0F. At the private equilibrium point E_0 total private costs equal $0Q_0 E_0K$ and total external costs are KE_0F.

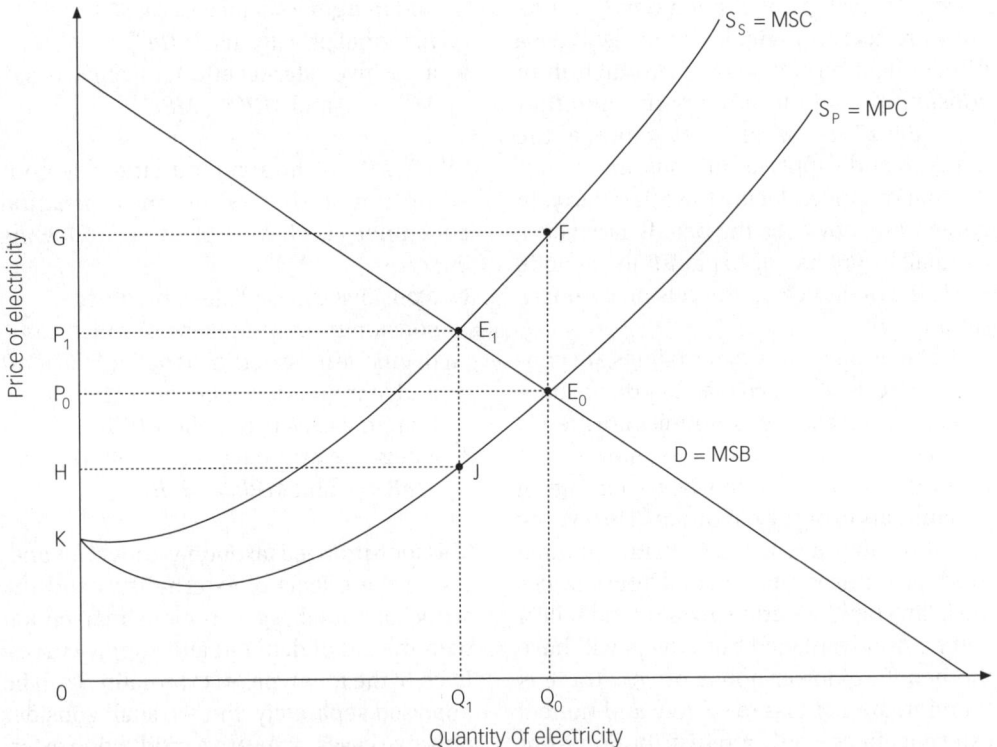

Figure 3.3 External cost and Pigouvian tax

If the externalities were taken into account, the 'social' equilibrium would be at point E_1, where social supply (or MSC) equals demand (assumed to equal MSB). At point E_1 only $0Q_1$ units of electricity are supplied at a unit price of $0P_1$. Two points are worth emphasising here. Firstly, $0Q_1$ represents a lower quantity of output than $0Q_0$ whereas P_1 is a higher price than P_0. Thus, from a social point of view, the presence of a negative production externality in a competitive market causes inefficiency in the form of over-provision and under-pricing of the good in question.

Secondly, in moving from point E_0 to point E_1 the externality has not been eliminated. It has merely been reduced – from KE_0F to its optimal level KJE_1. The latter is an optimal level because our farming community is basically prepared to accept this negative externality from electricity generation in exchange for the value that it adds to their personal comfort and farming activities.

The opposite case – of a positive production externality – implies the presence of negative external costs, that is, a situation where the social supply (MSC) curve lies below and to the right of the private supply (MPC) curve. A good example is the classic case of a bee farmer's bees pollinating the apple blossoms on an adjacent farm.

3.6.2 Positive consumption externality

The market for education provides an example of a positive consumption externality. In Figure 3.4 the curve S represents the (social)

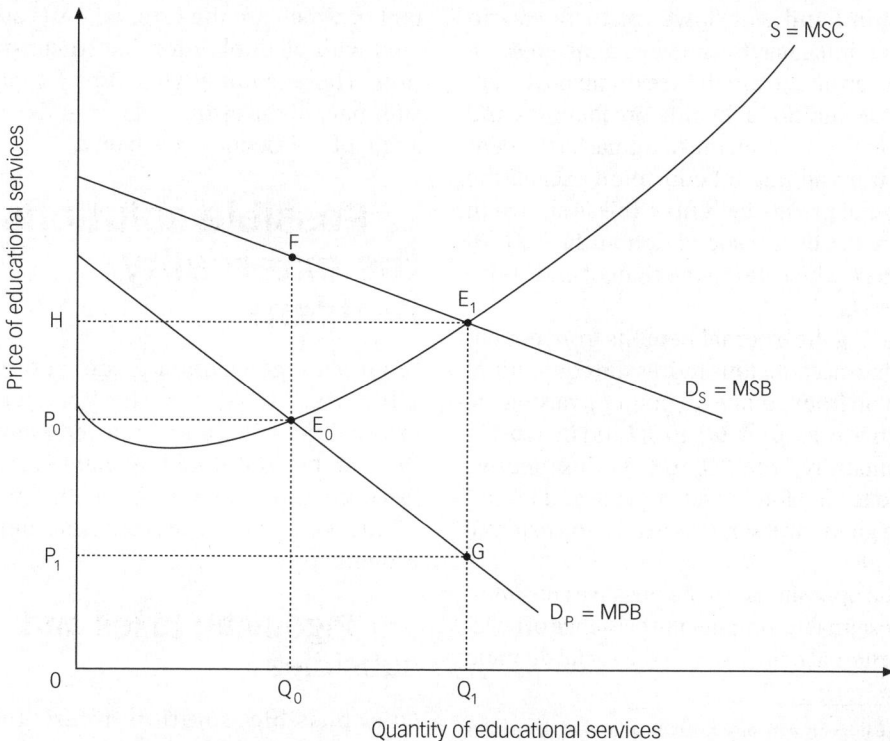

Figure 3.4 External benefit and Pigouvian subsidy

supply of educational services, that is, the marginal social cost of providing education. Curve D_p depicts the private demand for education, indicating marginal private benefits in the form of skills accumulation, expected higher earnings, and the sheer enjoyment to be had from being more knowledgeable. The market equilibrium therefore occurs at point E_0 with $0Q_0$ education being supplied at a 'unit price' of $0P_0$.

In this case the externality originates on the demand or consumption side of the market. The benefits of education are not restricted to the individual recipient. Society as a whole also derives considerable benefits from the effects of education. The educated individual may, for example, disseminate valuable information to other producers and consumers free of charge, thus enabling them to become more productive or happier citizens. Higher education levels also go hand in hand with lower birth rates and lower crime rates, thus relieving the pressure on government, and hence on taxpayers, to provide additional healthcare facilities and policing. As a result, the marginal social benefits from additional education exceed the marginal private benefits.[3] This is shown in Figure 3.4 by the social demand (or MSB) curve D_s which lies to the right of and above curve D_p.

Taking the external benefits from education into account thus moves the equilibrium position from point E_0 to point E_1, raising the effective price from $0P_0$ to $0H$ and increasing the quantity from $0Q_0$ to $0Q_1$. Competitive markets therefore under-provide and under-price goods and services exhibiting external benefits.

The opposite case – of a negative consumption externality – implies the existence of negative external benefits, with the social demand

(MSB) curve lying below and to the left of the private demand (MPB) curve. If Bongani had a particular liking for the music of Mandoza and played his compact discs into the early hours of the morning, he may impose a negative externality on his next door neighbour, Prudence, who prefers the music of Bach and Mozart.

3.6.3 Concluding note

External effects – whether negative or positive – are an everyday occurrence and affect not only individual consumers and producers but also the fauna and flora via their potentially harmful effects on biodiversity. Air and water pollution or the provision of education, as in the above examples, are the typical textbook cases because they are undoubtably important. But there are many other examples, perhaps the most important of which are the external costs associated with alcohol and tobacco consumption. The accompanying Box 3.2 gives a summary of the estimated size and composition of the alcohol externality.

3.7 Possible solutions to the externality problem

What can governments do about the allocative inefficiencies caused by externalities? There are four interventions that can be considered, namely Pigouvian taxes and subsidies, regulation, the creation of markets, and the establishment of property rights.

3.7.1 Pigouvian taxes and subsidies

One possible solution refers to the introduction of **Pigouvian taxes and subsidies** – named after the famous British economist A.C. Pigou. Such taxes and

[3] These benefits may be subject to a form of decreasing returns. Most empirical estimates of the returns to education indicate that the excess of the social benefit over the private benefit decreases as education becomes more advanced (Todaro, 1997: 390–93).

BOX 3.2 Size and composition of alcohol externality

Alcohol consumption by private individuals results in a number of external costs experienced by the society at large. These costs are usually divided into three broad categories. The first type of cost refers to 'direct' expenditures on policing, healthcare and repairs arising from fatal and non-fatal traffic accidents, person-to-person assault, property damage and 'avoidable' illnesses (e.g. liver and cardiovascular disease) – all caused by alcohol abuse. The second category refers to 'indirect' labour and productivity costs which result from a loss of output due to alcohol-related premature death, injury, illness and absenteeism in the workplace. These two cost categories, i.e. direct and indirect costs, are referred to as financial tangible costs as they can be measured in monetary terms if the requisite data is available. The third category is non-financial intangible welfare costs, and they include emotional pain, depression and feelings of regret which come about as a result of alcohol-related harm. Although these costs are non-financial because they do not have a monetary value, they can nevertheless be estimated. This can be done by finding out, through appropriate surveys, how much the affected individuals and institutions would be prepared to pay to *avoid* such costs – a point we return to briefly in Chapter 9.

There have been many attempts to estimate the first two cost categories mentioned above. In a recent overview of international studies the weighted average tangible external cost of alcohol consumption was found to be 1,58% of GDP per year, with individual estimates ranging between 1% and 2% of GDP (Mohapatra et al., 2010). Similarly, Parry (2009) estimated the tangible external cost of alcohol consumption in South Africa at 1,5% of GDP. There have been very few attempts to estimate the intangible costs of alcohol abuse, but in a recent study it was estimated that intangible costs in the EU came to more than double the tangible costs (Anderson and Baumberg, 2006). If this was true of other countries, including South Africa, the total size of the alcohol externality may be as high as 3% of GDP.

subsidies attempt to internalise externalities, that is, to force parties to include the external effects of their actions in their cost and benefit calculations.[4]

The effect of a Pigouvian tax can be illustrated by revisiting our case of a negative production externality – as illustrated in Figure 3.3. Recall that a negative production externality leads to an over-provision and under-pricing of the good in question. By levying a Pigouvian tax on the party whose actions cause

the externality, the government can increase the producer's marginal private cost to the level of the marginal social cost. In Figure 3.3 this would be achieved by levying an *ad valorem* tax on the price charged by the power station, that is, a percentage tax equal to the corresponding value of the externality. In unit terms the tax would equal E_0F at price $Q_0F(= 0G)$ and JE_1 at price $Q_1E_1(= 0P_1)$, thus shifting the private supply curve S_p to $S_s = MSC$. But, since supply exceeds demand at point F, the new equilibrium will settle at point E_1 where MSC equals MSB. Note that for this tax to be efficient it must equal the marginal external cost measured at the new

---

[4] Internalisation of externalities could also be viewed as a means of conferring property rights on the individuals involved in order to account for divergences between private and social costs and benefits. See Section 3.7.4.

social equilibrium. At Q_1 the marginal external cost is the vertical difference between MPC and MSC, i.e. JE_1.

At point E_1 the tax per unit of output is JE_1 and the (internalised) externality equals KJE_1 – its optimal size. The net effect of the policy is that a large portion of the original externality – given by the area JE_0FE_1 – has been eliminated.

Instead of levying a Pigouvian tax on each unit of output, it could be levied on each unit of the externality itself – commonly known as an **emission fee** or a **congestion tax**. If such a unit tax exceeded the unit cost of *reducing* the polluted emissions, the polluting firm could reduce output or it could use pollution-free inputs and new technologies in order to reduce its emissions level. It would do so until the marginal cost of such reductions equalled the unit tax. Congestion taxes can be imposed on vehicles entering highly congested urban areas, especially during rush hours, and cities like Singapore and London have recently done so to good effect (Kennedy, 2003).

The use of a Pigouvian subsidy to correct a positive consumption externality can likewise be illustrated by revisiting Figure 3.4. If the government subsidises education by E_0F (or GE_1) per unit, again on an *ad valorem* basis, it will bring the marginal private benefit in line with the marginal social benefit, that is, private demand D_p effectively shifts to D_s = MSB. At point F the price inclusive of the subsidy is high enough to induce a positive supply response. At the new equilibrium point E_1, where the marginal social benefit equals marginal social cost, the price paid by consumers will be Q_1G ($= OP_1$), the subsidy per unit will be GE_1 ($= P_1H$), and the supplier will receive Q_1E_1 ($= OH$). Again, note that for the subsidy to produce the optimal result, it must equal the marginal external benefit at the optimal output level Q_1. Clearly, the final equilibrium represents a more efficient

outcome with more educational services being provided at a lower unit demand price.

Although Pigouvian taxes and subsidies are widely used in the real world, they are subject to the same informational constraints as most of the other regulatory options discussed below. The Pigouvian option unrealistically assumes that the authorities are perfectly informed about the size of the externality and hence about the slopes and shapes of the respective demand and supply curves, all of which are supposedly costless to obtain.

In the case of tobacco and alcohol products (the so-called 'sin' goods) the Pigouvian tax becomes a crude measure in the sense that it may not in fact achieve its objective of reducing consumption and, with it, the attendant externalities; and it may even produce perverse results. This point is further explained in Box 3.3 and in Chapter 10.

3.7.2 Regulation

The option of regulation is particularly relevant to the case of negative production externalities such as pollution. This option – also known as **'command-and-control' regulation** – entails telling each polluter to reduce pollution to a certain level or else face legal sanction. In the example used in Figure 3.3, the power station would be ordered to reduce its output from $0Q_0$ to the socially-optimal level $0Q_1$. This approach has two shortcomings:

- It assumes that the government is sufficiently well-informed to determine the output level $0Q_1$ – in practice this is very difficult to do.
- The second objection to regulation would be valid even if the problem of determining the socially-optimal output level could be overcome. Regulation of this nature is simply not efficient in industries consisting of more than one firm, since it requires each firm to

BOX 3.3 Pigouvian taxes: perverse effects

It is generally accepted that consumption of both tobacco and alcohol products – the perennial 'sin' goods – inflicts huge externalities on the broader community. Tobacco smoking is a major cause of heart and lung-related illnesses that require expensive medical treatment mostly paid for by the tax-paying public. The South African government, in line with many other countries, has therefore introduced a range of control measures aimed at cutting down on tobacco smoking and reducing the attendant externality. The most important of these measures are (annual) excise tax hikes which are supplemented, through the Tobacco Products Control Amendment Act of 1999, by the prohibition of smoking at work and other public places, comprehensive bans on tobacco advertising, promotion and sponsorships, and restrictions placed on the tar and nicotine content of tobacco products.

One of the unintended effects of a tax hike on tobacco products is an increase in smuggling, or the substitution of illicit and cheaper products, often imported, for the legally taxed local equivalents, as has happened in Canada, the USA, England, Belgium and many other countries. Tobacco smuggling has a long history in South Africa due partly to the size and extent of informal trading networks within the country and also because of the availability of cheaper substitutes in neighbouring countries. It is estimated that the illicit (and unrecorded) market comprises between 40 and 50 per cent of the total tobacco market in South Africa (Lemboe, 2010).

The potentially perverse nature of the problem is straightforward. To the extent that tax hikes do boost smuggling activity, the government may in fact fail to achieve its objective of reducing tobacco consumption. International evidence also shows that smuggled cigarettes are typically of a lower quality than their legal counterparts, thus potentially causing a larger negative externality per cigarette than before the tax hike. The net effect of the tax hike may thus be an increase, rather than a reduction, in the overall size of the externality.

A similar substitution effect also applies to tax hikes on alcohol consumption. Official figures fail to capture a significant portion of the alcohol market, i.e. the unrecorded market, which is characterised by privately produced and imported alcoholic beverages, often at prices lower than those in the recorded market. The World Health Organisation estimates that world-wide unrecorded consumption makes up 27 % of the total alcohol market, while in South Africa it is estimated that unrecorded consumption constitutes 26,32 % of the total alcohol market (Econex, 2010). As is the case with tobacco consumption, evidence shows that homebrewed sorghum beer, which is highly toxic and unhealthy, is being substituted on a large scale for legal alcohol in response to excise tax increases. In such cases the excise tax is unlikely to fulfil its mission of reducing alcohol-related harms to an acceptable level, and may even have the perverse effect of adding to it.

Yet another unintended effect, applying to both tobacco and alcohol consumption, is the adverse impact that tax hikes may have on income distribution *within* especially poor households. This may happen when tax hikes raise the amount spent on tobacco and alcohol products relative to other goods making up the household budget, thus impacting negatively on non-drinking members of the household.

In patriarchal households the male head, who controls the household budget, is often egotistical and addictive and would maintain his consumption of tobacco and alcohol products in the face of excise tax increases – often at the expense of other important household goods and services, e.g. food, healthcare and education (Black and Mohamed, 2006). The rest of the household is thus made worse off than before as a direct consequence of the tax hikes.

Alternatively, and as mentioned before, household heads may respond to the tax hikes by diverting tobacco and alcohol spending to poor quality substitutes which may in turn compromise their health status. In either case the tax hikes may have the perverse effect of actually enlarging the negative externalities experienced *within* households, and in the community as a whole.

reduce its output by equal absolute amounts or proportions. But by doing so, individual firms may be forced into violating the efficiency criterion of producing at the point where marginal social cost equals marginal social benefit. The reason is that these costs and benefits may vary significantly between firms within the same industry, so that the application of a blanket rule would result in some of them producing too much and others producing too little.

The regulatory role of the state stretches far and wide. Most countries have Bureaux of Standards whose task it is to ensure that all goods and services adhere to certain minimum standards. Such standards are also aimed in part at addressing an externality problem: consuming sub-standard food may cause illnesses that require treatment paid for by the general public, whilst a defective automobile may cause accidents negatively affecting both the owner-driver and other innocent persons. Similar arguments also apply to a host of measures regulating industries such as telecommunications, tobacco products, alcoholic beverages, gambling and prostitution.

In many of these cases the externality can be better controlled by more direct or **regulatory measures** than Pigouvian taxes (or subsidies). In the case of tobacco and alcohol consumption, for example, we have already

referred to the problem of smuggling, or the substitution of lower quality and cheaper surrogates for their legally taxed counterparts. It may therefore be worth allocating public resources to combating smuggling *before* Pigouvian taxes are used in an attempt to reduce legal consumption. Similarly, the external costs of drunk driving seem to constitute a significant portion of the total external costs caused by excessive alcohol consumption. Here too, it would seem that road blocks would, given law enforcement capacity, be a better means of addressing the problem than excise tax hikes (Black, 2008).

3.7.3 Creation of markets

A third option is an incentive-based one generally referred to as the **'cap-and-trade' programme**. It was developed in the context of the pollution problem and consists of the creation of a market in which the government would issue or sell legal permits giving owners the right to pollute. The first step would be for government to establish the overall quantity of pollutants that it considers to be an efficient level – for example, the area KJE_1 in Figure 3.3 – and then to issue or sell a limited number of individual permits to the relevant polluters. Permit holders are free to sell their permits, or buy additional ones, and will do so by comparing the price of the permit with the marginal cost of *reducing* their own emissions, e.g.

by shifting to cleaner technologies. If the permit price exceeded the marginal cost of pollution reduction, permits will be sold and the proceeds can be used to help fund the costs involved in reducing pollution. Those who buy permits can, of course, increase their emission of pollutants and possibly contribute to a more concentrated distribution of a fixed total quantity of emissions. But if the cost of reducing pollution should fall, e.g. through new technologies, more permits will be offered for sale at lower prices until, eventually, there are few or no takers left. Given the fixed (and theoretically optimal) total supply of permits, a declining price is a sure sign that the quantity of emissions is also declining.

The market-creation approach also assumes that the government possesses perfect knowledge about the sources of pollution and the level of pollution commensurate with the efficient level of output. But some pollutants, such as the emission of sulphur dioxide from electricity power plants, can be measured and monitored, and the USA has, via amendments to its Clean Air Act, set a national cap (of 9 million tons per year) for sulphur dioxide emissions, together with issuing a limited number of permits. The success of this programme is reflected in the continuous decline in the permit price. Similar cap-and-trade programmes have been introduced to protect fisheries and wildlife in the USA and elsewhere (Rosen and Gayer, 2008:Chapter 5).

3.7.4 Property rights

Our fourth approach to solving the externality problem derives from the view that regulation and Pigouvian taxes and subsidies are both costly to administer and in any case not likely to achieve their purpose. The Nobel Laureate Ronald Coase argued that the divergence between marginal private cost and marginal social cost arises due to insufficiently defined property rights over the use of resources. **Property rights**, broadly defined, represent the legal specification of who owns what goods, including the rights and obligations attendant upon such ownership. The problem of externalities thus boils down to disputes over the ownership of resources.

Let us illustrate with an example: does Prudence have the right to paint her front door a garish pink when it not only offends Bongani every time he passes it to enter his own adjacent front door, but it may also reduce the value of his apartment? Or, returning to our earlier example, do the producers of electricity on the Mpumalanga Highveld possess the right to discharge pollutants into the atmosphere? Do farmers possess rights to unpolluted air and water? If property rights are well-defined, they can be exchanged on a voluntary basis by means of a straightforward market transaction. If Prudence had the right to paint the outside of her front door any colour she wished, then Bongani could offer to pay her a certain amount not to paint it pink. Likewise, if our Highveld farmers had a right to clean air and water, the electricity supplier could buy that right from them by offering to compensate them for the damage caused. The externality problem can thus be resolved without having recourse to potentially unsuccessful government intervention.

The **Coase theorem** holds that market incentives will generate a mutually beneficial exchange of property rights through which externalities can be fully internalised, provided that property rights are well-defined and enforceable and transaction costs are negligible. **Transaction costs** are the costs of the exchange process. They comprise the resources used when economic agents attempt to identify and contact one another (identification costs), negotiate contracts (negotiation costs), and verify and enforce the terms of contracts (enforcement costs).

These transaction costs, together with the costs of enforcing property rights, may well be lower that the costs of regulation and taxing or subsidising goods and services. In the Coasian approach, the government's role in respect of externalities mainly consists of the maintenance of a judicial system to define and enforce property rights and a market system to lower transaction costs.

The Coase theorem is crucially predicated on the twin assumptions of well-defined and enforceable property rights and zero or negligible transaction costs.

As suggested above, the definition and enforcement of property rights are largely determined by the quality of the judicial system. If transaction costs are non-trivial however, they may prevent parties from exchanging their property rights and in the process internalising the externality. In general, the higher the transaction costs, the lower will be the degree of internalisation of externalities and the greater will be the resultant divergence between marginal private cost and marginal social cost. Transaction costs are bound to be high when large numbers of people are involved, such as the many consumers experiencing respiratory illnesses from inhaling the polluted air of the Mpumalanga Highveld, Sasolburg and many other industrial areas. It may be too costly for them to take the necessary steps to have their right to clean air legally enforced.

3.8 Property rights, transaction costs, and the theory of market failure

We mentioned in the previous section that the Coasian solution to the externality problem rests on the assumptions of well-defined and enforceable property rights as well as negligible transaction costs among the bargaining parties. In emphasising the importance of property rights and transaction costs, Coase made a significant contribution to the theory of market failure. In fact, his contribution provides a way out of a fundamental weakness in the standard benchmark model.

In Chapter 2 we pointed out that the neoclassical theory of general equilibrium assumes rational utility-maximisation on the part of all economic agents. Such behaviour implies, among other things, that agents would exploit all mutually-beneficial opportunities for exchange. Yet the present chapter has shown that many such opportunities remain unexploited, especially those characterised by external effects. This divergence between actual behaviour and the fundamental behavioural assumption of our benchmark model suggests that the model is a poor yardstick for objectively judging the efficiency of real-world conduct.

Coase's analysis of property rights and transaction costs provides a lifeline for the benchmark model by suggesting that the model is not wrong in assuming rationality but is merely incompletely specified. If the model of perfect competition can be expanded to include transaction costs, in particular, it would conform much better in explaining actual behaviour. Thus agents are not necessarily irrational when they decline to undertake certain transactions – in fact, they are responding rationally to the fact that the costs of undertaking the transaction are higher than the corresponding benefits.

This view has quite dramatic implications for the theory of market failure as set out in the current and subsequent chapters of this book. Taken to its extreme, it implies that there is no such thing as market failure. Economists such as Harold Demsetz (1982), Dahlman (1979), and Toumanoff (1984) have argued that what we conventionally define as market failures, such as externalities and the formation of monopolies, can be explained in terms of the failure of the standard general equilibrium model to consider various forms of transaction costs. In their view, the problem is one of 'model failure', not market failure.

Literature on transaction costs is in many respects still in its infancy and as yet does not provide a fully-fledged challenge to the theory of market failure. From a policy point of view, it would become much more useful if it could provide a coherent framework for analysing the sources of transaction costs and their effects on market institutions. Toumanoff (1984: 538) rightly points out that to attribute all instances of unexploited exchange to the existence of transaction costs would amount to rationalising the economic status quo. If we accept that all agents behave rationally in the face of transaction costs, we are confronted with the so-called **Panglossian dilemma**: whatever is, is optimal. But if this problem can be overcome by further research on transaction costs, it may be possible to equip future policymakers with a variety of original, market-based policy instruments that could complement or replace some of the more traditional ones discussed in this chapter.

3.9 'Global' public and merit goods

Neighbouring countries often agree to take joint responsibility for, and share the burden of, providing certain cross-border public (including mixed) and merit goods – these are called **'global'** or **'regional' public and merit goods** (Kaul, Grunberg and Stern, 1999; Calitz, 2000). Such agreements can apply to global or regional defence systems and cross-border road and rail networks, or to measures aimed at addressing the 'externality problem' as well as other forms of market failure.

One country's national defence system may confer benefits on neighbouring countries free of charge – unless they enter into an agreement that forces each country to contribute *pro rata* to the cost of the service. There may in fact be an important 'economies of scale' argument here: providing an effective defence system or a subsidised electricity network at minimum unit cost may require high levels of production capable of serving several countries at the same time. There is also no point in constructing a road or railway line that stops at the border separating two countries trading with each other. Countries making up the European Union (EU) all derive huge benefits from being connected by single road and railway networks; likewise, the road linking Gauteng Province in South Africa with the Maputo harbour in Mozambique clearly benefits holiday makers, transport companies, and importers and exporters in both countries.

In all these cases it is important to know who the beneficiaries are, how they are spread across different countries, and how payment – in the form of taxes and user charges – should be divided among the beneficiaries. This point can be illustrated by referring back to Figure 3.2 and replacing the two individuals (Bongani and Joan) with two countries (e.g. South Africa and Mozambique). The optimal price-discriminating solution again occurs when each country pays a price equal to its marginal value of the service, that is, P_J and P_B, where the subscripts now refer to the two countries. We already know that such a pricing strategy is not a feasible solution, partly due to a lack of knowledge about (country) preferences and the attendant problem of free riding. The only alternative is a 'tax price' to which each country contributes, presumably based on some pre-determined formula – this clearly calls for a formal bilateral agreement, or a multilateral agreement if more than two countries are involved. An agreement of this kind would normally form part of a more broadly based regional trade agreement, such as those associated with the Southern African Customs Union (SACU), the Southern African Development Community (SADC), the Common Market for Eastern and Southern Africa (COMESA), and the Economic Community of West African States (ECOWAS).

Similar arguments also apply to externalities: air and water pollution may impose negative externalities on producers and consumers in neighbouring countries. These producers and consumers should ideally have a say in resolving the problem, including the task of defining property rights and determining compensation in terms of the Coase theorem. A truly global example is the emission of carbon dioxide into the atmosphere, which happens virtually everywhere in the world where automobiles are used and fossil fuels are burnt. Such emissions – as Box 3.4 shows – can give rise to dramatic climate changes in different parts of the world, adversely affecting producers and consumers alike and threatening the well-being of future generations (see Nahman and Antrobus, 2005). The solution here evidently calls for a binding international agreement, such as the Kyoto Protocol, which aims to reduce CO_2 emissions on a global scale, and the details of which are provided below.

Yet another example concerns the so-called 'brain drain'. When, for instance, a Namibian citizen, schooled and trained in that country, accepts a job offer in Germany, the latter country may benefit greatly in that it obtains human capital free of charge, but paid for by Namibian taxpayers. Such positive spillover effects do, of course, happen on a large scale in many parts of the world, and can be viewed as a manifestation

BOX 3.4 Global warming

Much of our natural energy comes from the sun in the form of shortwave radiation that warms the earth and its inhabitants; and when some of this energy is again released into the atmosphere, in the form of longwave radiation, the result is a delicate temperature range that is life-giving and makes the earth inhabitable. The 'incoming' short waves are capable of penetrating man-made greenhouse gases like carbon dioxide, ozone, methane and other industrial gases, but the 'outgoing' long waves are not, and are absorbed by the same greenhouse gases. If the emission of these gases reaches and surpasses a critical level, as many commentators are claiming, the result is an 'enhanced greenhouse effect' that raises average global temperatures, changes precipitation levels and may give rise to extreme weather patterns (Stowell, 2005; Lutzeyer, 2008). Now, the earth's atmosphere can be considered a free resource and a global public good in the sense that it is largely non-excludable, thus either benefiting all or most inhabitants on earth or, in the case of a greenhouse effect, harming many innocent individuals, countries and regions. Excessive carbon dioxide emissions in one region may have negative spillover effects in many other regions (without any compensation changing hands); or conversely, steps taken to reduce emissions in one country may benefit many others. These are examples of global externalities that call for appropriate forms of intervention on the part of a supranational or global institution – as discussed in the accompanying text.

of an individual's constitutional right to choose his or her place of work. Over time the net effect may be small for various reasons: Namibia may also benefit from human capital created in Germany; the brain drain may be reversed when our earlier Namibian citizen returns home as a more experienced and productive worker; or the brain drain can contribute to the development of global networks that encourage international trade and capital flows between the countries concerned.

A final comment refers to our earlier discussion of market failures other than 'missing markets'. Within a sovereign country, monopolistic abuse (as discussed in the next chapter) can be avoided or minimised by means of an appropriate competition policy authority. Similarly, the problem of ignorance about the harmful properties of certain goods and services can be addressed by means of a 'bureau of standards' through which minimum standards can be legally enforced. Likewise, a national government can apply tax and other measures to internalise positive or negative externalities within its geographical borders. In the case of regional and global public goods, however, there is no single government with jurisdiction over the entire set of activities. Addressing the 'problem' of public goods then becomes dependent on international cooperation in the form of agreements, treaties, and different forms of integration. One possibility is a mutual agreement whereby the public institutions of one country are allowed to exercise their authorities also in neighbouring countries. This will arguably ensure that they operate more efficiently (i.e. at lower unit cost), provided due cognisance is taken of relevant differences between the countries – one size does not necessarily fit all.

Alternatively, new regional or global institutions may be formed. For example, exogenous shocks at the macroeconomic level usually have a similar negative contagious effect on countries that are economically integrated, such as those of SADC, and may call for a regionally coordinated approach to the conduct of macroeconomic policy. In the case of the European Union, the extent of economic integration has actually reached the advanced state of using a single monetary system.

Going beyond the regional dimension, many countries stand to benefit from a world that is becoming more integrated by the day – economically, culturally, and geopolitically. At the same time, however, the same countries are also becoming more vulnerable to a range of negative spillover effects emanating from exogenous financial shocks, technology-driven climatic changes, ethnically driven regional conflicts, international terrorism, and a host of contagious diseases. In the absence of a world government, it is therefore imperative that global institutions like the International Monetary Fund (IMF), the World Bank (WB), the World Trade Organisation (WTO), the World Health Organisation (WHO), the Food and Agricultural Organisation (FAO), and the Kyoto Protocol should take the necessary steps to eliminate or at least minimise the incidence and extent of such negative spillovers.

One of the major obstacles has been the reluctance of industrialised and high polluting countries to accept the need for a Coasian-type redistribution of resources, i.e. of limiting their own levels of carbon emissions while compensating poor and low polluting countries at the same time. But at a recent UN conference in Cancun in 2010, involving 193 countries, industrialised countries accepted the proposal to reduce greenhouse gas emissions by between 25 per cent and 40 per cent of 1990 levels within the next ten years; while also agreeing to create a Green Climate Fund aimed at helping developing countries to cope with the effects of global warming.

The relevant greenhouses gases (GHG) are carbon dioxide, methane, nitrous oxide, sulphur hexafluoride and two groups of gases (hydrofluorocarbons and perfluorocarbons) produced by them, all of which are measurable by known techniques. Furthermore, both the UN conference and the (latest) Kyoto Protocol actively support the use of clean and green forms of

renewable energy that can be easily replaced and repeated. This specifically refers to the use of solar energy, wind energy, biomass energy and geothermal energy. Finally, it is also worth noting that although nuclear power has a waste disposal problem and is vulnerable to earthquakes, it does not pollute the air or water, while natural gas causes less pollution than coal-driven electricity plants.

IMPORTANT CONCEPTS

cap-and-trade programmes (page 52)
Coase theorem (page 53)
command and control regulation (page 50)
emission fee (page 50)
excludable (non-excludable) goods (page 38)
free riding (free rider) (page 41)
global and regional public goods (page 55)

merit goods (page 44)
mixed goods (page 43)
negative externality (page 45)
non-excludable (page 38)
Panglossian dilemma (page 55)
pecuniary externality (page 45)
Pigouvian subsidy (page 48)
Pigouvian tax (page 48)

positive externality (page 45)
private goods (page 35)
property rights (page 53)
pure public goods (page 37)
regulatory measures (page 52)
rivalry (non-rivalry) (page 37)
technological externality (page 45)
transaction costs (page 53)

SELF-ASSESSMENT EXERCISES

3.1 Explain the difference between a private and a pure public good. How do their respective equilibria differ?

3.2 Who should supply pure public goods?

3.3 Explain the meaning of mixed and merit goods. Who should supply them?

3.4 Explain the concept of 'externality' and distinguish between the different types of externality that one might encounter in the real world.

3.5 Should Pigouvian taxes be used to internalise the negative external effects of tobacco and alcohol consumption?

3.6 Critically discuss the 'cap-and-trade' approach to addressing the externality problem.

3.7 Discuss Coase's theorem and consider its usefulness as a means of solving the externality problem.

3.8 Do you agree with the view that 'market failure' is something of a misnomer, and that the problem to which it refers is rather one of 'model failure'?

3.9 Discuss the phenomenon of 'global' or 'regional public' goods.

Chapter
FOUR

Philip Black

Imperfect competition

The widespread existence of monopolies and oligopolies represents perhaps the best-known example of market or institutional failure in a modern economy. It is customary to distinguish between two types of monopoly: firstly, an 'artificial' or statutory monopoly operating in a market where perfect competition is technically feasible and, secondly, the case of a 'natural' monopoly. The former refers to a situation in which potential competitors are prevented from entering the market in question, either due to certain legal restrictions imposed by the government or a professional body, or due to efforts on the part of the incumbent firm itself to limit entry, for example by exerting control over critical suppliers or by temporarily setting price below its profit-maximising level (Harrod, 1952).

Since the latter practices are difficult to detect or control in practice, we shall confine ourselves in Section 4.1 to the case of an artificial barrier that limits productive activity within an otherwise competitive market. Section 4.2 deals with the decreasing cost case and considers the question of whether a natural monopoly should be regulated or owned and controlled by the state. Section 4.3 discusses other forms of imperfect competition, while Section 4.4 looks at the conduct of competition policy in South Africa. Finally, Section 4.5 considers some of the modern views on monopoly, including the so-called 'efficiency hypothesis' introduced to the literature by Harold Demsetz (1973).

Once you have studied this chapter, you should be able to:
- discuss the social costs of a monopoly and indicate its relevance for 'deregulation'
- outline the characteristic features of a natural monopoly
- discuss the case for and against regulating a natural monopoly

> ▶ explain the meaning of the 'structure-conduct-performance' (SCP) hypothesis and discuss its relevance for competition policy in South Africa
> ▶ explain Demsetz's 'efficiency hypothesis' and discuss its relevance for competition policy generally.

4.1 On the social costs of monopoly[1]

Our starting point is the familiar distinction between perfect competition and monopoly – as illustrated in Figure 4.1. Here we assume that both the demand function, D, and marginal cost, MC, are the same for the two market forms. The only difference is that under perfect competition MC represents the sum of the marginal cost curves of the individual firms making up the market, whereas under monopoly it represents the marginal cost of the monopolist only.

The perfectly competitive equilibrium occurs at point E in Figure 4.1 where supply equals demand and $0Q_c$ of the good is produced at a price of $0P_c$. Under monopoly, equilibrium occurs at point F where $MC = MR$ and the market produces a smaller quantity, $0Q_m$, at a higher price, $0P_m$, than it does under perfect competition.

The loss in consumer surplus is the area given by P_mGEP_c, part of which – P_mGHP_c – is a straight transfer from consumers to the producer with the remaining triangle, GEH, being the net welfare (or 'deadweight') loss. Although the value represented by the rectangle labelled HEQ_cQ_m is usually assumed to be transferred to other sectors in the economy, this is evidently easier said than done. In a neo-Keynesian economy with all its frictions and time lags, the resources contributing

to this value, e.g. labour and capital equipment, may remain unemployed for long periods, at least until they find alternative employment. The value thus lost represents yet another social cost of monopoly.

The difference highlighted in Figure 4.1 can also be shown in terms of the two-sector model discussed in Chapter 2. The implications of monopoly for this model are straightforward. Recall (from Equation [2.5] in Chapter 2) that the marginal rate of product transformation ($MRPT$) equals the marginal cost ratio for the two commodities, that is

$$MRPT_{xy} = \frac{MC_x}{MC_y} = \frac{P_x}{P_y} \qquad [4.1]$$

If Y is now assumed to be a monopolist and X a perfectly competitive industry, then $P_y > MC_y$ while $P_x = MC_x$. It follows that:

$$MRPT_{xy} > \frac{P_x}{P_y} \qquad [4.2]$$

indicating that the first, and by inference, the third or 'top-level' condition for a Pareto optimum has been violated. This is illustrated in Figure 4.2 by the difference between the slope of the production possibility curve, R_0T_0, and the commodity price line, P_MP_M, passing through point M_0. Specifically, in contrast to the competitive equilibrium at point C the effect of introducing a monopoly here is to lower the output of good Y and raise its relative price.

The difference between points M_0 and C in Figure 4.2 is often taken to reflect the degree of allocative inefficiency arising from the presence of a monopoly in one of the two

---

[1] This and the next section are partly based on Black and Dollery, 1992: 10–16.

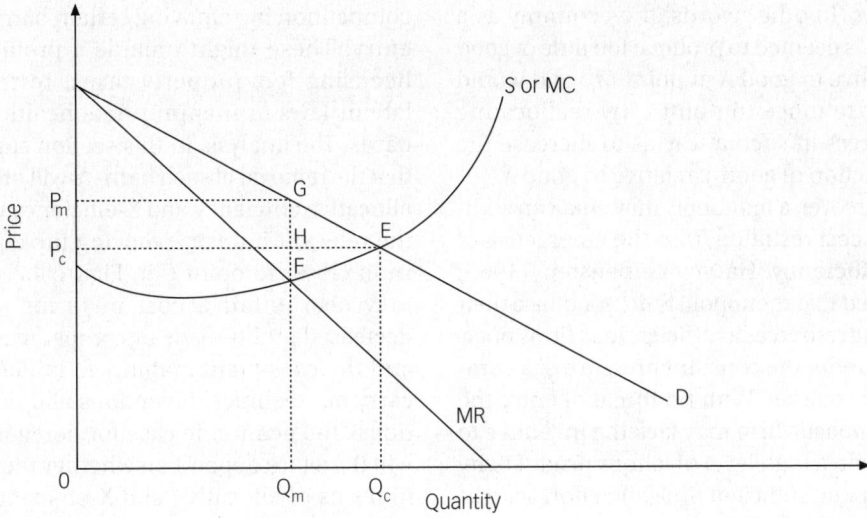

Figure 4.1 Monopoly versus perfect competition

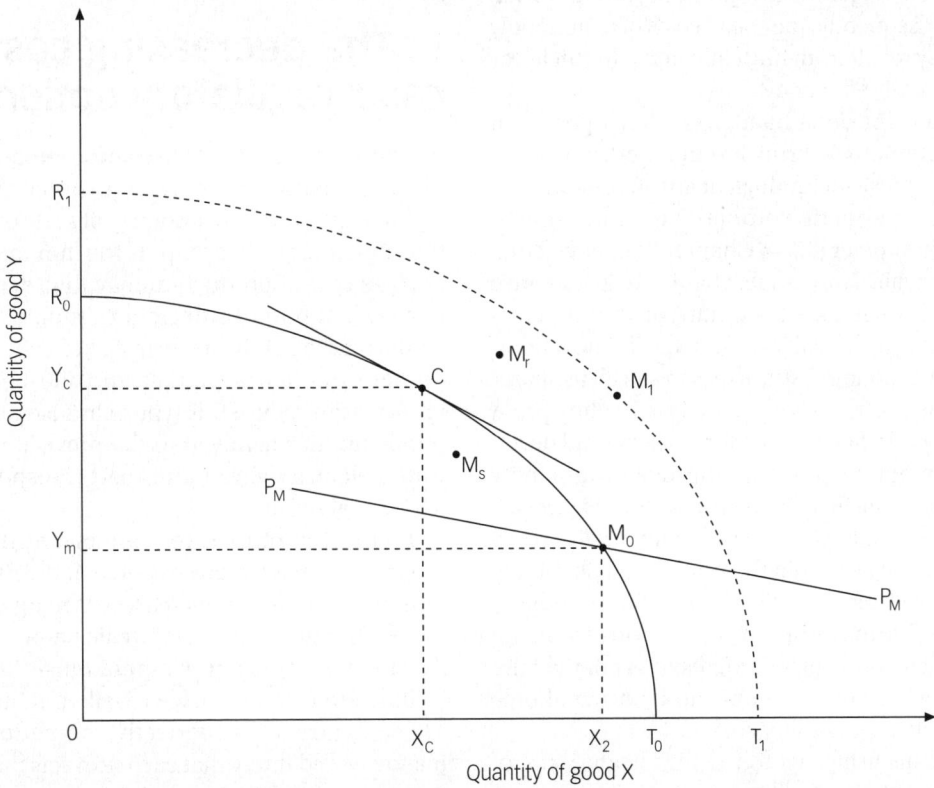

Figure 4.2 Efficiency implications of monopoly

sectors. In other words, the economy as a whole is deemed to produce too little of good Y relative to good X at point M_0, and would prefer to move to point C by reallocating resources in such a way as to increase the production of good Y relative to good X.

Moreover, a monopoly may entail an additional cost resulting from the emergence of **X-inefficiency**. Harvey Leibenstein (1966) believed that monopolists do not utilise their existing resources as efficiently as firms operating under the constant pressure of a competitive market. With no threat of entry the monopolistic firm may lack the incentive to maintain a high level of labour productivity or to spend sufficient time and effort searching for and acquiring the necessary information. Such a situation would imply an equilibrium lying inside the production possibility curve, just below point M_0 in Figure 4.2. Consequently, the social costs of a monopoly may result from both allocative inefficiency and X-inefficiency.

On the other hand, it is often argued that monopolistic firms are in a better position to achieve **technological advancement** than their perfectly competitive counterparts. Schumpeter (1954, Chapter 8) believed that the typical monopolist has both an incentive and the means to initiate or imitate cost-saving technical inventions and innovations. If the monopolistic firm is to satisfy its shareholders, it will have to make a healthy profit that can then be used for research and development purposes to improve productivity within the firm. Referring back to Figure 4.2, for example, the effect of technological progress will be to shift the production possibility curve from R_0T_0 to R_1T_1 and the monopoly equilibrium from M_0 to M_1, thus implying that technological progress has enabled the economy to move beyond its original production possibility curve.

This brings us to the important issue of **deregulation**. As it is commonly understood, deregulation represents an attempt on the part of the authorities to promote competition by removing certain barriers to entry. These might include a prohibitive licensing fee, property taxes, restrictive labour laws or inappropriate health standards. The analysis in this section suggests that the removal of such barriers will improve **allocative efficiency** and **X-efficiency** within the relevant industry, moving the equilibrium closer to point C in Figure 4.2. But it may also entail a cost in terms of the decreased profits made by competitive firms and their resultant inability to initiate and carry out technical inventions and innovations. The economic case for deregulation will therefore depend on whether the gains in terms of allocative and X-efficiency are sufficient to offset the slower pace of technological advancement amongst competitive firms.

4.2 The decreasing cost case: regulatory options

An industry is said to be a **natural monopoly** if it is characterised by large capital outlays that give rise to economies of scale over the entire range of its output. The minimum average cost of production may thus occur at a level of output sufficient to supply the whole market. Only one firm can effectively operate in such a market and the best-known examples of this type of industry are public utilities involved in the provision of water, electricity, rail and road transport, and postal services.

Increasing returns to scale means that the long-term average cost (AC) of the firm diminishes as output increases. Its marginal cost (MC) curve will therefore lie below the AC curve over the entire output range. This is illustrated by the curves labelled AC and MC in Figure 4.3. A perfectly competitive market would imply that each firm sets marginal cost equal to the market price, e.g. at point E in Figure 4.3 where $P_e = MC$. With increasing returns to scale, however, the

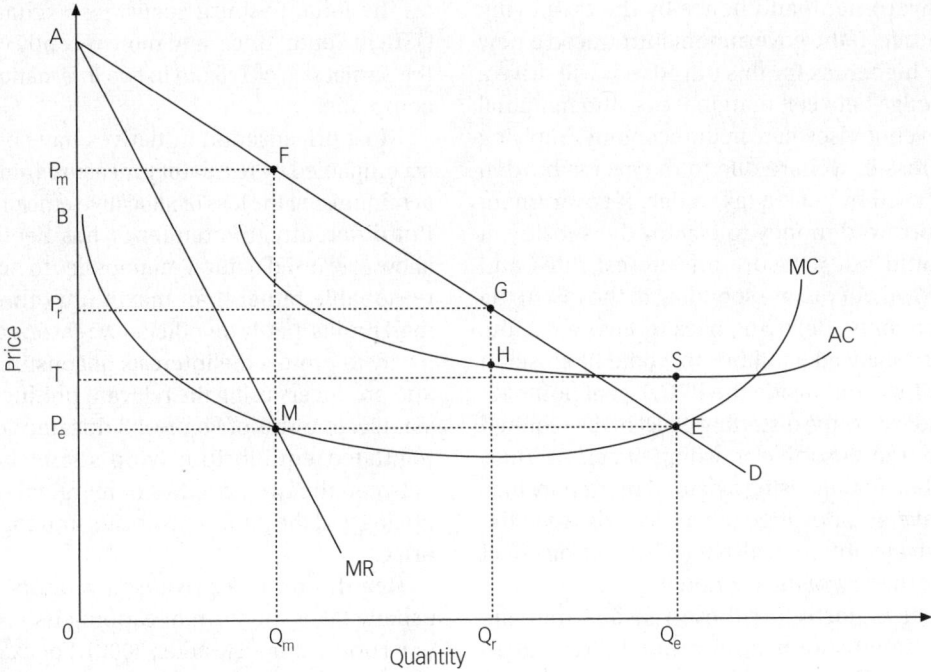

Figure 4.3 Decreasing cost cause

industry will make a unit loss equal to *ES* so that individual firms will eventually close down until a natural monopoly emerges.

If the natural monopoly is not controlled by the government, it will maximise profit at point *M* where its marginal cost equals marginal revenue. At point *M* the equilibrium price, OP_m, exceeds the socially efficient price, OP_e, while the corresponding level of output, OQ_m, is smaller than the Pareto-optimal level, OQ_e. The profit-maximising behaviour of the monopolist may therefore result in too little output being produced at too high a price, giving rise to a concomitant loss of welfare. The latter refers to the difference in consumer surplus between the two equilibria. Under monopoly, consumer surplus equals the area AFP_m, which is evidently much smaller than consumer surplus under the hypothetical competitive solution, given by the area AEP_e in Figure 4.3.

The question that arises is whether something should be done about this loss of welfare. As may be expected, there is no simple answer to this question, but the government does have several options at its disposal. These all depend on whether the good or service in question is used as an important input by many other sectors and industries in the economy – such as electricity and water supply. So if *D* and *MC* in Figure 4.3 represent marginal social benefits and marginal social costs, respectively, production at point *M* clearly implies that *MSB* > *MSC*. The only way to create and confer pecuniary externalities on other industries is then to expand production and lower the price, e.g. to OQ_e and OP_e.

One option is for government to start up and/or take ownership of the natural monopoly itself, as has happened in many countries during the previous century. It could then apply marginal cost pricing at point *E* in Figure 4.3 and cover the resultant loss by means of a unit subsidy equal to *ES*. But the required subsidy would have to be paid for by government, and hence by the tax-paying public. If the government introduced a new or higher tax for this purpose, it will drive a wedge between marginal cost and marginal revenue elsewhere in the economy, implying a loss in welfare due to the excess burden caused by such a tax wedge. If government borrowed money to pay for the subsidy, it could put pressure on interest rates and crowd out private spending in the rest of the economy. Referring back to Figure 4.2, the nationalised equilibrium would lie closer to point *C* but inside the PPC, e.g. at point M_s, indicating the distorting effect of the required tax and a possible crowding-out effect. Thus, while nationalising a natural monopoly may have an allocative advantage vis-à-vis the private option, it also has a distorting effect on the rest of the economy.

It is partly for these reasons that the nationalisation option has fallen out of favour. Government-owned monopolies are also less X-efficient than private monopolies (Leibenstein, 1978: 171–178) and certainly have less of an incentive to initiate and implement cost-saving innovations than their profit-driven private counterparts. After all, a privatised monopoly has little choice but to remain reasonably profitable and satisfy its shareholders if it is to avoid the threat of a possible takeover. The nationalised monopoly, by contrast, is under no such threat and can always rely on the seemingly endless resources of the state. Yet another advantage of **privatisation** is that the proceeds from the sale of state assets, albeit a windfall, can be used to redeem the public debt or boost investment in the physical infrastructure of the country.

It is therefore not surprising that the world has witnessed a strong shift towards privatising government monopolies (or 'public enterprises') during the past three decades. South Africa is no exception in this regard, and the privatisation drive there has gathered much momentum with the listing of Iscor

on the Johannesburg Securities Exchange (JSE) in South Africa, and more recently with the partial sale of Telkom to two international companies.

Most privatisation initiatives have been accompanied by **regulatory measures** aimed at minimising the loss of allocative efficiency. Put differently, the tendency has been to allow privatised natural monopolies to make reasonable rather than maximum (abnormal) profits, partly for efficiency reasons and partly to protect the interests of consumers and producers using the relevant product or service. In terms of Figure 4.3 this implies a regulated equilibrium lying somewhere between the two extremes of marginal cost pricing and the profit-maximising monopoly price.

Regulation of a privatised monopolist usually takes the form of capping its profit or its price, or both (Parker, 2002). For example, the government could cap profit at point *G* in Figure 4.3 where the maximum profit allowed would be *GH* per unit. The same result can be achieved by capping price at OP_r. Profit capping has become less popular because of the problem of 'cost padding' (Kahn, 1988) whilst price capping, first introduced in the UK, has gained ground as it can act as an incentive to cut costs and boost profit. But price capping regulation can also be administratively burdensome because regulators have to make forecasts of the future growth of demand and input costs. There is also a 'sliding scale' regulation that combines the two capping regulations. Thus if the monopolist's profit should rise to some pre-determined level, price is immediately adjusted downwards. The main advantage of this form of regulation is that both the producer and the consumers benefit from the **efficiency gains** secured by the monopolist (Parker, 2002: 502–503).

These efficiency gains imply an outward shift in the PPC similar to that shown in Figure 4.2, where the unregulated monopoly equilibrium occurs at point M_1. The fact that price capping regulation entails additional administrative costs means that the *regulated* equilibrium will occur closer to point C but *inside* the (new) PPC, e.g. point M_r. Regulation can thus strike a neat compromise between the need for economic growth (as reflected in the shift of the PPC) and the need for a higher level of allocative efficiency than under the unregulated scenario.

Although **regulated privatisation**, as described here, may well confer sustainable long-term benefits on the community, the transfer of ownership itself may be costly in the short run. It may involve heavy job losses which, in countries experiencing high levels of unemployment such as the SADC, may make it politically untenable. Even the proceeds of the sale of state assets may accrue to those who are already rich, thus worsening the distribution of wealth in the country. It is partly for these reasons that governments try to cushion job losses through the use of employment guarantee schemes and targeted safety-nets, at least in the short term, while ensuring that privatisation is carried out within an appropriate institutional and regulatory framework (see Heracleous, 1999; Gupta, Schiller and Ma, 1999).

On the whole, it would appear that the case for regulated privatisation is a pretty powerful one. The transfer of state monopolies and other public functions to the private sector is likely to boost efficiency and economic growth, lessen the burden of the public debt, reduce interest payments and government expenditure, broaden the tax base and, ultimately, enable the government to cut taxes and initiate a process of sustained economic growth. It is largely for these reasons that governments across the world have begun to dismantle their own empires in an attempt to restore the incentive-providing mechanisms of the market and thereby promote economic efficiency in their respective countries.

4.3 Market power and competition policy

Most real-world markets fall between the two extremes of perfect competition and monopoly, and are usually characterised by varying degrees of market power. In this section we briefly refer to the standard textbook cases of **monopolistic competition** (where many firms produce close substitutes and each firm has some control over price) and **oligopoly** (where only a few firms produce a homogeneous product and each one has considerable control over price). We will then focus on the reasons for the high degree of seller (and owner) concentration and the related policy implications.

Monopolistically competitive markets and oligopolies generally produce equilibria that fall between the two extreme cases. This means that they tend to produce higher equilibrium quantities at lower equilibrium prices than those achieved under an equivalent pure monopoly, but lower quantities at higher prices than those applicable to an equivalent perfectly competitive market. We can state this more formally as follows:

$$Q_{pc} > Q_{ic} > Q_m \qquad [4.3]$$

and $\quad P_{pc} > P_{ic} > P_m \qquad [4.4]$

where Q and P represent the equilibrium quantities and prices, and the subscripts pc, ic, and m, stand for perfect competition, imperfect competition, and monopoly respectively.

The general equilibrium equivalent of these inequalities is straightforward: if sector X is assumed to be perfectly competitive and we let sector Y vary between perfect competition, imperfect competition, and monopoly, then:

$$\left(\tfrac{P_x}{P_y}\right)_{pc} > \left(\tfrac{P_x}{P_y}\right)_{ic} > \left(\tfrac{P_x}{P_y}\right)_m \qquad [4.5]$$

which indicates the corresponding differences in the respective top-level equilibria. These are shown in Figure 4.4. As before, point C is the top-level equilibrium when both sectors are assumed to be perfectly competitive, while point M is the corresponding equilibrium when sector Y is assumed to be a monopoly. Inequality [4.5] implies that our intermediate cases, where sector Y is either monopolistically competitive or oligopolistic, will generate a top-level equilibrium lying somewhere between points C and M on the PPC in Figure 4.4 – for example, at point I where the slope of the price line falls between those of the price lines at points C and M.

It is clear from Figure 4.4 that imperfectly competitive markets have a smaller negative effect on allocative efficiency than a pure monopoly; however, compared to perfect competition, they do cause at least some degree of allocative inefficiency.

This analysis is, of course, a purely theoretical one. In practice, policymakers have been more concerned with the degree of concentration within particular markets both in terms of the number of firms and the ownership pattern. This concern stems partly from the so-called 'structure-conduct-performance' (SCP) hypothesis. According to this hypothesis, the structure of an industry determines the conduct of its constituent firms which, in turn, determines their performance. A highly concentrated industry, for example, may encourage collusive behaviour on the part of the few large firms comprising that industry, which will ultimately give rise to monopoly pricing. Empirically too, several observers (e.g. Leach, 1997) have found a strong and significant positive correlation between the degree of concentration and the profitability of industries within the manufacturing sector of South Africa. The latter finding can be ascribed either to the monopoly power of firms or the concentrated nature of ownership within the industry. It can also reflect the outcome of efficient behaviour on the part of low-cost firms – an issue to which we return in Section 4.5 below.

Adherents to the SCP paradigm believe that the power of highly concentrated industries should be broken down in order to eradicate or avoid monopoly pricing. The

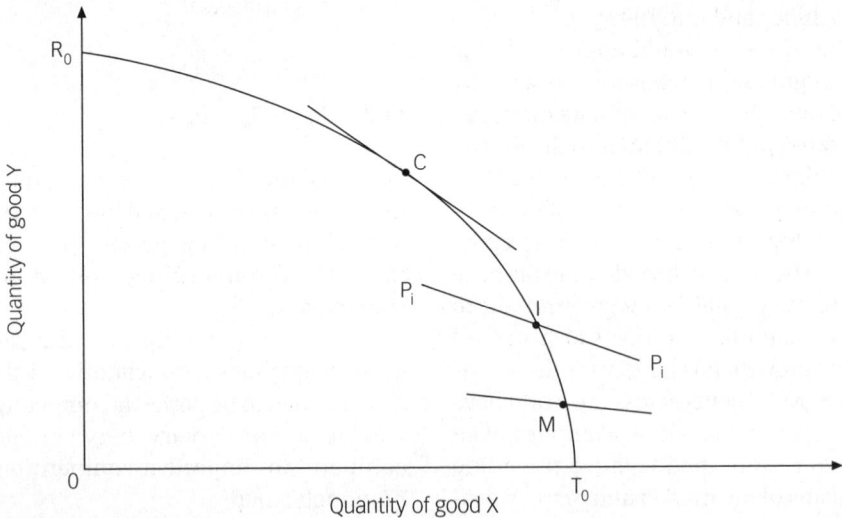

Figure 4.4 Imperfect competition

instrument through which this is to be achieved is **competition policy** – a prime example of regulatory or 'indirect' government intervention, as explained in Chapter 2. The need for a national policy on competition is widely accepted in the world today and many countries have recently begun to revise their own policies, often with a view to making them less country-specific and more consistent with prevailing international trends. South Africa is no exception and in Section 4.4 we highlight some of the main features of the country's Competition Act of 1998.

Competition policy should ideally be aimed at preventing or eradicating **restrictive practices** arising from the abuse of a dominant position. The issue here is not dominance as such, or the degree of market power, but rather the **abuse of a dominant position**. Likewise, a practice can only be deemed 'restrictive' if it prevents others from entering the market while at the same time exposing consumers to unnecessarily high prices or a limited choice.

Competition policy – correctly applied – can lead to lower prices, an expanded choice, technological progress, and higher levels of capital investment; and to the extent that it does, it will ultimately contribute to a process of *equitable* economic growth. Not only will the policy redistribute incomes through lower prices, but it will also see to it that restrictive entry barriers are dismantled, thus paving the way for new firms, including small and medium-sized ones, to enter lucrative markets.

4.4 **Competition policy in South Africa**

After many years of intense debate and negotiations between government, the business sector, and organised labour – under the auspices of the National Economic Development and Labour Council (Nedlac)

– a new Competition Act was promulgated in 1998. The act made provision for the establishment of a new Competition Commission, which consists of the following: a governing body called the Competition Management Board; a new Competition Inspectorate, responsible for investigating alleged contraventions of the Act; and a new Competition Tribunal whose functions include the assessment of alleged contraventions, the provisional authorisation or prohibition of existing or proposed **mergers**, and making recommendations to the Minister of Trade and Industry.

The main features of the new Competition Act can be summarised as follows:
- The main reason for the new policy stems from Government's view that South African markets are dominated by a few large firms and that ownership and control of the economy are unusually centralised.
- Abuse in the form of non-competitive conduct (for example monopoly pricing) could result from horizontal mergers, where a small number of firms or shareholders end up controlling the market and selling the same or similar products; vertical mergers, where one or a few firms own and control not only the same or a similar product, but also its suppliers and distributors, all within the same sector or industry; and conglomerate mergers, where one or a few firms have both horizontal and vertical control of production and distribution across several unrelated sectors and industries.
- The overriding objective of the new policy is to eradicate or avoid abusive behaviour and promote competition where feasible, in order to encourage efficiency and international competitiveness, provide easy access to small and medium-sized enterprises, diversify ownership in favour of historically

disadvantaged people, and create new job opportunities in the economy.

- The focus is not on dominance as such – said to exist where market share is at least 35 per cent – but rather on the abuse of a dominant position. The latter includes a number of potentially restrictive practices such as the fixing of purchase and selling prices, establishment of production quotas, exclusivity agreements, restriction of technical innovations not patented, and collusive tendering. New mergers and takeovers must be authorised by the competition authority, with the burden of proof resting with the companies involved.

Competition policy authorities in South Africa have been very busy during recent times with several high profile cases of collusion being investigated and acted upon (see Box 4.1).

4.5 Is competition policy necessary?

Before deciding on a competition policy it is surely appropriate to ask whether there is a need for such a policy in the first place. Is dominance of a market likely to result in abusive behaviour? Do high profit levels or 'non-competitive' conduct necessarily imply abusive behaviour?

The answer to these questions is 'no' according to the **efficiency hypothesis** proposed by Harold Demsetz (1973). He argued that the high degree of market power and ownership concentration in many markets across the world is merely the outcome of a competitive process in which superior low-cost firms have managed to outperform their less efficient counterparts. Prices in these markets are lower than they would have been otherwise, and any attempt to break down the power of dominant firms will undermine efficiency and put pressure

on prices, thus harming the interests of consumers. He turned the conventional SCP hypothesis on its head: efficient low-cost production ('performance') goes hand in hand with competition ('conduct') that inevitably gives rise to dominance of the industry ('structure'). He was able successfully to test for the direction of causation, and found that the profitability of dominant firms was positively related to their ability to produce at low cost. In a more recent study Leach (1997) found that Demsetz's efficiency hypothesis also applied to the manufacturing sector in South Africa.

It can be reasonably asked why dominant firms should use their profits to improve the quality of their products or to cut production costs and hence prices. One reason is that dominant (even monopolistic) **industries** are often '**contestable**', in the sense that the incumbent firms are subject to *potential* competition rather than actual competition. Provided that there are no barriers to entry and that exit from the market is not prohibitively costly, the mere threat of competition may be sufficient to keep incumbent firms on their proverbial toes. The Southern African beer market is a case in point. Even though the South African beer market is dominated by a large conglomerate – SAB Miller – nothing prevents overseas or other local brewers from entering the market. They might well consider doing so if local beer prices were too high, either because production costs were too high or because the profits of the incumbent brewer were deemed to be relatively attractive. It is therefore in the best interests of incumbent firms not to misuse their positions of power.

Contestable market theorists (e.g. Baumol, 1982) also argue that market structure depends on the relationship between the market demand and the nature of the product or service in question – as explained in Section 4.2 earlier. If economies of scale featured prominently in the

BOX 4.1 Competition policy in action

- In 2002 one of the big private hospitals in South Africa, Netcare, acquired a 44 per cent share in a smaller group, Community Health Care Group, without notifying and getting permission from the Competition Commission. This failure was discovered when evidence of price fixing by the two groups was reported by a medical fund. At the time of writing the Competition Tribunal was investigating the case and determining an appropriate penalty. The latter can be as high as 25 per cent of the preceding year's turnover which, in the case of Netcare, would amount to R600 million.

- In 2005 the Competition Commission found sufficient evidence of price fixing and market segmentation on the part of what was effectively a milk cartel. Several large milk suppliers were involved and the Commission proposed charges of 25 per cent of their (preceding year's) turnover. This case has been referred to the Competition Tribunal for confirmation.

- In 2006 the Commission laid charges against the four large commercial banks – Standard Bank, Absa, First National Bank and Nedbank. These charges relate to the Commission's assertion that bank charges were too high and that there was a paucity of transparency around them. In 2011 the banks agreed to the implementation of very significant reforms to reduce transaction fees, increase transparency and promote competition within the banking industry.

- In 2007 Tiger Brands, a major producer and distributor of bread, was found guilty of price fixing and market segmentation and had to pay a penalty of R98,8 million.

- In 2008 the Commission laid charges against Adcock Ingram Critical Care (an affiliate of Tiger Brands) and two other pharmaceutical companies, Dismed and Thusanong. These charges relate to collusive behaviour in respect of large tenders for the supply of medical equipment to state hospitals – a practice that has reportedly been in operation since the 1990s.

- In 2011 the Commission supported the United States retail giant Wal-Mart's proposed acquisition of 51 per cent of equity in the South African wholesale retailer, Massmart Holdings, without any conditions. The proposed acquisition has, however, drawn opposition from the Government and COSATU who fear that should the acquisition be approved without any conditions the result could be significant job losses, adoption of discount pricing strategies, the discontinuing of domestic supplier agreements and a surge of cheap imports. The Government and COSATU recommended that the Commission attach conditions that include a commitment from Wal-Mart to use mostly domestic suppliers and to utilise a pricing strategy that would not undermine the local industry.

production process, for example, then it can be expected that the market will be dominated by one or a few large firms. Furthermore, if the market was also globally contestable, these firms will avail themselves of the latest technologies in order to remain competitive vis-à-vis imported substitutes and to stay ahead of potential entrants. The optimal size of a firm depends largely on the nature of the product or service it produces and on the nature of the technology used in production.

Of course, the above arguments do not rule out the possibility that dominant firms may at times abuse their positions of power, for example by engaging in some of the 'restrictive practices' mentioned above. There are many factors that may give rise to such an abuse of power – 'structure' being one of them – but it is imperative that policy-makers consider all the relevant facts. We have shown here that 'big can be beautiful', especially if it allows one to utilise the latest technologies in order to improve quality and cut production costs. Populist intervention in the corporate structure of a country – merely on the grounds of size – could undermine efficiency, damage investor confidence and, above all, harm the interests of ordinary consumers.

It is also worth pointing out that growing global competition has already forced several dominant firms to restructure their operations with some unbundling into smaller entities and others – especially in the financial services sector – merging into bigger ones. These dramatic changes illustrate that inefficient corporate structures are simply not viable over time – they tend to disappear of their own accord.

IMPORTANT CONCEPTS

abuse of a dominant position (page 67)
allocative efficiency (in the context of monopoly) (page 62)
competition policy (page 67)
contestable market (industries) (page 68)
deregulation (page 62)
efficiency gains from privatisation (page 64)
efficiency hypothesis (page 68)

financial gains from privatisation (page 64)
increasing returns to scale (page 62)
mergers (page 67)
monopolistic competition (page 65)
natural monopoly (page 62)
oligopoly (page 65)
privatisation (page 64)
regulation of privatised natural monopolies (page 64)

regulatory measures (page 64)
regulated privatisation (page 65)
restrictive practices (page 67)
structure-conduct-performance (SCP) hypothesis (page 66)
technological advancement (with reference to monopoly) (page 62)
X-efficiency (in respect of monopoly) (page 62)
X-inefficiency (page 62)

SELF-ASSESSMENT EXERCISES

4.1 Illustrate the effect on general equilibrium of introducing a monopoly into the two-sector model. What are the efficiency implications?

4.2 Should natural monopolies be regulated?

4.3 Critically discuss the case for and against privatising natural monopolies.

4.4 Discuss the basic objectives and nature of competition policies with specific reference to the 'structure-conduct-performance' hypothesis.

4.5 Outline the new competition policy in South Africa.

4.6 Discuss Harold Demsetz's 'efficiency hypothesis' and consider its implications for the conduct of competition policy.

Chapter
FIVE

Philip Black

Equity and social welfare

Yet another potential market failure concerns the distribution of wealth or income within a community. In Chapter 2 we referred to the black box nature of our benchmark model of general equilibrium – or to the fact that its predictions are basically determined by the initial assumptions on which it is based. The same applies to the distributional issue: the model predicts a particular distributional outcome that is a mirror image of the distribution assumed initially. If the initial distribution is deemed unacceptable, then so too, will be the final distribution.

Once you have studied this chapter, you should be able to:
- distinguish between the Pareto and Bergson criteria for a welfare improvement
- discuss Nozick's entitlement theory and its relevance to the recent history of South Africa
- explain how a redistribution of income can be justified in terms of the theory of externalities
- distinguish between the cardinal and ordinal social welfare functions
- discuss the efficiency implications of policies aimed at redistributing income from rich to poor people.

5.1 Introduction

In terms of the two-sector model illustrated in Figure 5.1, all points along the PPC are Pareto-efficient as defined in earlier chapters. Each of these points also corresponds to a particular distribution of income between the individuals participating in the economy. This means that the distribution at point S is different from that at point C. In particular, one individual is in a better position relative to the other at point S than he or she is at point C.

Two important implications arising from our familiar two-sector model are relevant here:

▶ a competitive economy producing the output mix given by point C will not necessarily also yield the most preferred distribution of income; the latter may, for example, occur at point S;
▶ a policy-induced movement along the PPC, for example, from point C to point S, will necessarily change the distribution of income and thus place one individual in a worse position compared to the other.

Economists normally distinguish between two criteria when assessing the welfare effects of public policy: the **Pareto criterion** and the so-called Bergson criterion. The Pareto criterion implies that a policy-induced change is justified only if it improves the well-being of at least one person *without* harming any other. The **Bergson criterion** is much broader and allows for a welfare improvement even if one or more individuals are harmed in the process. In this chapter we shall consider both criteria: Section 5.2 focuses on Robert Nozick's (1974) well-known entitlement theory which provides a Pareto-based justification for a redistributive policy aimed at redressing past injustices; Section 5.3 examines several other Pareto criteria and does so in terms of the familiar theory of externalities; Section 5.4 considers the Bergson criterion and introduces what is conventionally referred to as 'welfare economics'; and finally, Section 5.5 looks at some of the efficiency implications of policies aimed at redistributing income from rich to poor people.

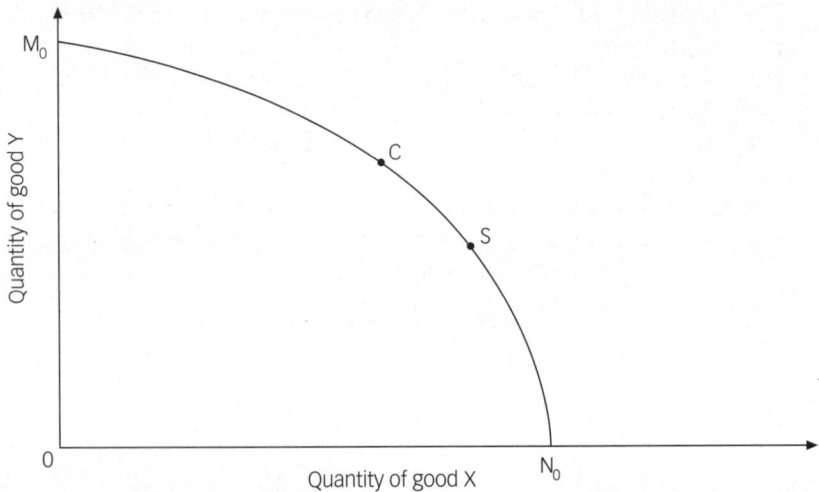

Figure 5.1 Potential top-level equilibria

5.2 **Nozick's entitlement theory**

The Pareto criterion is commonly associated with the libertarian approach to public policy, according to which individual freedom is viewed as the primary goal of the community. This is usually defined in terms of the maximisation of 'negative freedom', or protection of the right not to be coerced by others (Hayek, 1960; Nozick, 1974). The libertarian school thus advocates a *laissez faire* system in which the role of government is reduced to that of a caretaker charged with the responsibility of protecting individual freedom. Libertarians are in principle opposed to distributional policies that infringe upon the freedom of individuals.

There is, however, an important exception to the libertarian rule that derives from Robert Nozick's (1974) **entitlement theory**. Nozick distinguished between three 'principles of justice' in which he sets out the conditions for a just distribution. The first two principles can be defined as follows:

▶ Principle 1: **Justice in acquisition**, which states that individuals are entitled to acquire things that do not belong to others or do not place others in a worse position than before. Such 'things' refer to property and capital goods only – not to labour income, which Nozick regards as an inalienable individual right.

▶ Principle 2: **Justice in transfer**, according to which material things can be transferred from one individual to another on a voluntary basis, for example, in the form of gifts, grants, and bequests, or through voluntary exchange.

In terms of these principles '... a distribution is just if it arises from a prior just distribution by just means' (Nozick, 1974: 58).

Violating either of the first two principles gives rise to Nozick's third principle of justice:

▶ Principle 3: **Rectification of injustice** in holdings, in terms of which a redistribution of wealth is potentially justified only if one or both of the first two principles have been violated.

Nozick's third principle provides his only justification for a policy aimed at redistributing resources between individuals. But it is evidently easier said than done. Nozick (1974: 67) himself recognises the practical difficulties involved when he asks: '...how far back should one go in wiping clean the historical slate of injustice?' This question is clearly relevant to many peace initiatives and conflict resolutions undertaken in many parts of Africa and, in particular, to South Africa's recent past. Nozick's principles presumably formed one of the cornerstones of the investigations undertaken by the **Truth and Reconciliation Commission** (TRC) in South Africa. The TRC limited its focus to the apartheid era, in particular to the period between 1 March 1960 and 5 December 1993 during which the National Party was in power, though it did recognise the many historical precedents set by earlier regimes. Some of the functions of the TRC are outlined in Box 5.1.

According to Nozick, proper rectification requires a thorough analysis of the historical events that gave rise to the violation of his first two principles. It also calls for an accurate assessment of the distributional pattern that would have emerged in the absence of the violation. While both tasks are needed to determine the extent of rectification, neither can be said to be straightforward. Both require a wealth of historical data, much of which will be largely hypothetical and based on anecdotal evidence, and neither is likely to produce outcomes that are free of human prejudice.

On the other hand, Nozick's third principle is restricted to a redistribution of improper holdings of fixed property and capital only – not of labour income. The latter reflects a person's innate endowments and cannot therefore be taken from him or her, either for equity or efficiency reasons. While this restriction is perhaps highly contentious, it does at least simplify the practical application of Nozick's rectification principle.

The Pareto flavour of Nozick's rectification principle is straightforward: if Tom enriched

---

BOX 5.1 Rectification in South Africa

The overriding objective of the Truth and Reconciliation Commission was to develop a human rights culture in the country and to bring about national unity and reconciliation. The Commission was divided into three committees whose primary functions can be summarised as follows:

▶ The Committee on Human Rights Violations was responsible for identifying victims of 'gross human rights violations' committed during the period 1 March 1960 to 5 December 1993. The committee assessed the nature and magnitude of those violations, and referred legally prepared reports on the victims to the Committee on Reparations and Rehabilitation. During its deliberations the former committee also identified alleged perpetrators, as well as persons already being prosecuted or found guilty in a court of law, and submitted reports on them to the Committee on Amnesty.

▶ The Committee on Amnesty considered applications from persons who had committed human rights violations and based its decision on whether these were committed for political reasons, rather than for personal gain or any other reason. The Committee also looked at the nature and the degree of seriousness of violations before reaching a decision. Those who were granted amnesty could not be held liable for damages and could not be criminally charged in a court of law, while those who were unsuccessful were liable for prosecution.

▶ The Committee on Reparations and Rehabilitation had to submit proposals to the Cabinet for reparations in the form of monetary payments to individual victims, as well as 'community rehabilitation programmes' aimed at providing a range of basic services to communities that had suffered under apartheid. The TRC Act required Parliament to establish a President's fund from which payments were to be made.

After consulting across a broad spectrum of the community, and adopting a strict legalistic approach to its deliberations and findings, the TRC concluded that an amount of R2,8 billion was needed to pay reparations to apartheid-era victims. The Department of Land Affairs had been involved in a process of investigating and legally processing a number of land claims arising from past violations of individual and communal property rights (another legacy of the Group Areas Act and human resettlement programmes implemented during the apartheid era). In addition, several politicians, including former president Nelson Mandela, have appealed to the private sector to make voluntary contributions to the government's own job creation fund – aimed at 'achieving racial reconciliation in South Africa'.

himself at Thandi's expense and did so against her will, the principle demands that Tom should give back to Thandi what rightfully belonged to her so that both parties would be in the same position as they would have been in the absence of the injustice.

5.3 Other Pareto criteria

Policies aimed at redistributing income from rich to poor people can be justified on Pareto grounds in terms of the theory of externalities, i.e. the **externality argument for redistribution**, as discussed earlier in Chapter 3. In communities characterised by a high degree of inequality it is possible that the poor may impose certain negative externalities on the rich. High levels of crime and violence often go hand in hand with widespread poverty, and these may undermine the quality of life of the rich. Likewise, a lack of sanitation and other health-promoting services among the poor may give rise to a variety of contagious diseases that may ultimately threaten the health status of the rich.

Under these conditions, rich people may be prepared to transfer part of their income to the poor in an attempt to reduce poverty and minimise its negative external effects. However, no single rich person can do so alone and it is partly for this reason that the distribution of income is often viewed as a public good: all or most rich people stand to benefit from a reduction in poverty, and hence in the level of crime and violence or in the incidence of disease, but individuals acting on their own cannot bring about such changes. Poverty relief thus calls for appropriate government action aimed at bringing down the negative external effects of poverty to an optimal level. Government policy could take the form of direct transfer payments to the poor, or it could be used to provide basic services or strengthen the security system, in which case both poor and rich people

stand to benefit from a healthier and more secure environment.

A related justification for **redistribution** derives from the so-called **insurance motive**. Individuals may view their tax payments as a relatively inexpensive means of insuring themselves against a possible future loss of income or ill-health. On becoming unemployed, for example, they may qualify for support from a state-run unemployment insurance fund. If they should become ill, they could likewise avail themselves of health services provided by the state. These individuals may view tax payments as a superior or cheaper alternative to taking out private insurance.

In all these cases there is no charity involved, but rather a quid pro quo principle: rich people give up part of their income for distribution among the poor because they expect to derive commensurate material benefits from such actions.

By contrast, a redistribution of income can be justified on Pareto grounds if one or more individuals are assumed to be altruistic, that is, both concerned and generous (Hochman and Rodgers, 1969). Such individuals could experience a net increase in utility from a policy that taxes their own income and redistributes it in favour of another (non-altruistic) individual. In terms of our two-sector model, a movement along the PPC would then improve the welfare of both individuals.

It is important to note that the notion of **altruism** implies the existence of external effects in consumption. Reverting back to our earlier examples in Chapters 2 and 3, if individual a is an altruist but b is not, we can write a's utility function (U_a) as follows:

$$U_a = f[M_a, U_b(M_b)] \qquad [5.1]$$

where the first derivatives are all positive. Equation [5.1] simply states that a derives utility not only from her own income, M_a, but also from individual b's level of utility $[U_b(M_b)]$ – presumably up to some maximum level. Individual b derives utility only from his own income, M_b.

Simplifying Equation [5.1] by setting

$$U_a = g(M_a, M_b) \qquad [5.2]$$

we can state the condition for a 'Pareto-efficient' redistribution of income from our altruist, a, to the non-altruist, b. Mathematically it implies that:

$$0 > g'(M_a) > g'>M_b) > 0 \qquad [5.3]$$

Therefore, the increase in a's utility resulting from b's higher income $(g'(M_b) > 0)$ must exceed the decrease in a's utility resulting from the drop in her own income $(0 > g'(M_a))$. In other words, the fact that b is in a better position gives rise to a net increase in a's utility.

There are presumably many real-world examples of Pareto-efficient redistributions. When people contribute towards charitable organisations, or give money to beggars, they presumably do so because it makes them feel better – this is why we view altruism as a Pareto-based justification for redistribution. Such transactions are, of course, voluntary while redistribution via the fiscal process is not. Nonetheless, it can be suggested that some taxpayers do derive utility from that part of their taxes earmarked for the relief of poverty and the care of old and disabled people (See Box 5.2).

5.4 Bergson criterion

In terms of the **Bergson criterion**, a redistribution of income can be justified on welfare grounds even if it places one or more individuals in a worse position. The Bergson criterion is best explained in terms of the

---

BOX 5.2 Experimental games

In the field of behavioural economics we have witnessed the results of a large number of experimental games aimed at testing the 'self-interest hypothesis' that lies at the root of many of our standard economic models. These games include the so-called ultimatum game, the gift exchange game, the trust game and, as we saw in Chapter 3, the public goods game.

In the ultimatum game, for example, the experimenter gives an amount of money to a so-called proposer with the instruction of sharing it with a responder. If the proposer gives some portion to the responder who then rejects it, both players get nothing; but if the responder accepts it, the proposal stands. Now, in terms of the self-interest hypothesis, the smallest possible amount would be offered and accepted. And yet in many such games played across the world most proposers offer in excess of 20 per cent of the original amount, whilst the probability of rejection falls dramatically with the size of the offer. The conclusion here is that both players have a sense of 'fairness'. Other experimental games show that people are generally altruistic, or have social (as opposed to only individual) preferences, and also have an 'aversion' to inequality (e.g. Bowles, 2004).

From a public economics perspective, one implication of these experimental findings is that people would be willing to give part of their income to the fiscus if it will, directly or indirectly, benefit the poor.

familiar **social welfare function**, according to which a community's welfare is defined in terms of the utilities of all the individuals making up that community.

We can distinguish between two such welfare functions. The first is the so-called 'cardinal' or **additive welfare function**:

$$W = U_a + U_b + \ldots \qquad [5.4]$$

where W represents the level of community welfare, and U_a and U_b are individual utilities. According to Equation [5.4], community welfare equals the sum of individual utilities – these are assumed to be measurable on the same scale.

The additive welfare function does illustrate the Bergson criterion very neatly: it allows for the Pareto criterion insofar as W will increase if *either* U_a or U_b increases, or if both U_a and U_b increase at the same time. It also allows for a welfare improvement consequent upon a decrease in either U_a or U_b – W will increase so long as the increase in U_a (or U_b) exceeds the decrease in U_b (or U_a). In addition, if a poor person, say individual a, derives greater additional utility from an extra R10 than does his or her rich counterpart, individual b, then the stage is set for a welfare-improving redistributive policy: taking R10 away from b and giving it to a will raise U_a by more than it will reduce U_b. This conclusion assumes that an individual's marginal utility from income diminishes as his or her income increases.

Equation [5.4] represents a very restrictive welfare function. Apart from the measurability issue, it assumes that individual utility functions are identical and depend only on their incomes. It is also highly debatable whether increases in income engender smaller increases in utility at higher levels of income.

It is partly for these reasons that economists prefer the more generalised welfare function:

$$W = W(U_a, U_b) \qquad [5.5]$$

This **function is ordinal** in nature and does away with the assumption of measurability. By letting W take on different (constant) values, it is possible to derive a set of social or community indifference curves, such as those labelled W_1, W_2, and W_3 in Figure 5.2. These functions have the same properties as individual indifference curves: they are convex with respect to the origin, cannot intersect, and exhibit diminishing marginal rates of substitution.

Figure 5.2 also shows a utility possibility frontier (also known – rather grandly – as the 'grand utility possibility frontier') that is

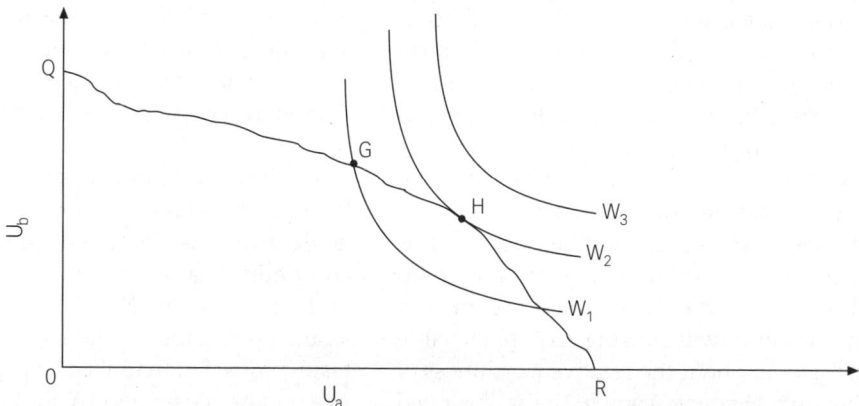

Figure 5.2 Utility possibility curve and welfare maximum

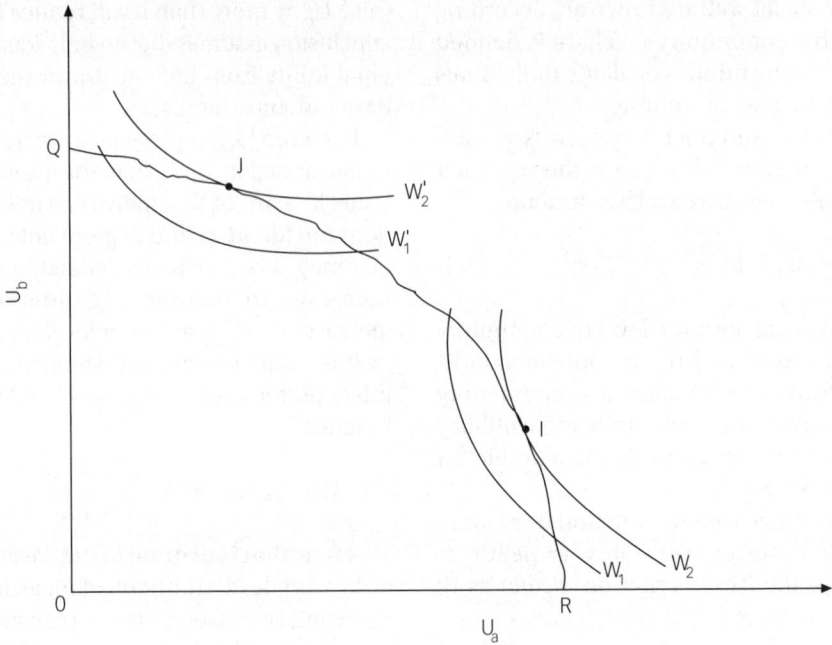

Figure 5.3 Alternative welfare functions

directly derived from the familiar PPC. The utility possibility frontier, QR, gives the utility combinations associated with all the top-level equilibrium points along a conventional PPC. In the example of Figure 5.2 the community prefers the combination at point H – the welfare maximum – to any other point along the frontier.

This analysis crucially depends on two closely related assumptions. Firstly, the community is assumed to be able to choose between different points along the utility possibility frontier, for example, point H as opposed to point G; the question of how a community makes such choices has given rise to a vast literature – referred to as public choice theory – and we shall return to this issue in the next chapter. Secondly, when choosing a particular point on the frontier, the community is making an explicit value judgement about the relative worthiness of the two individuals a and b. This is illustrated in Figure 5.3 where two alternative sets of

welfare functions are shown, one labelled W_1, W_2, ..., and the other W_1', W_2' ... . The similarly numbered subscripts indicate the same level of social welfare. It is clear that the former function embodies a relatively strong preference for individual a, generating a top-level equilibrium at point I; whereas the function W_1', W_2', ..., embodies a strong relative preference for individual b. Individual a is in a better position at point I than at point J, while the opposite is true of individual b, and yet the two **social indifference curves**, W_2 and W_2', represent the same level of welfare.

It is but a small step to show that the difference between the two welfare functions in Figure 5.3 also implies a difference in the community's assessment of the worthiness of the two sectors, X and Y. All we need to assume is that the individuals have different tastes. Thus if individual a has a strong relative preference for good X, and individual b has a strong relative preference for good Y,

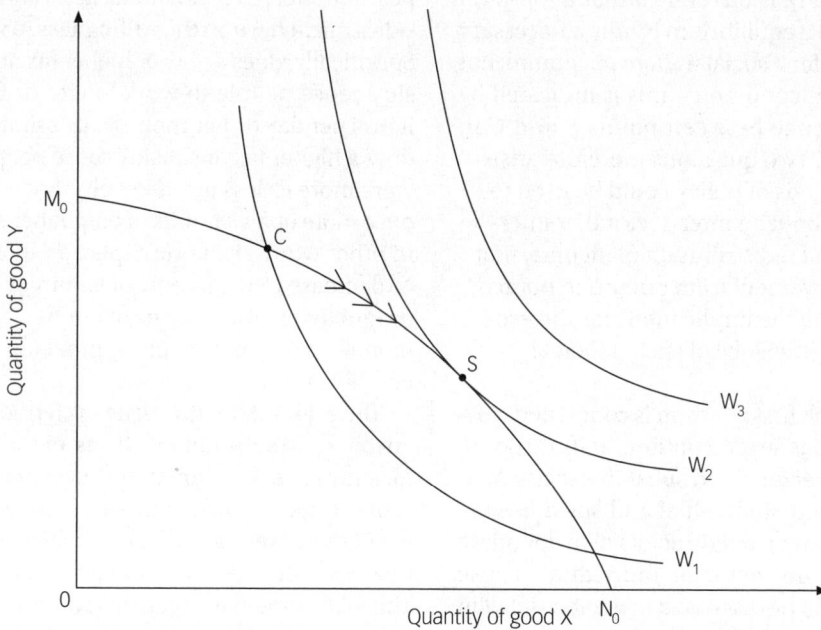

Figure 5.4 A competitive equilibrium versus welfare maximum

then it follows that the function labelled W_1, W_2, ... indicates, by implication, that the community has a strong relative preference for sector X. Similarly, the function W_1', W_2', ... would indicate a strong relative preference for sector Y.

Consider the following two individual utility functions:

$$U_a = U_a(X_a, Y_a) \qquad [5.6]$$

$$U_b = U_b(X_b, Y_b) \qquad [5.7]$$

Given that $X = X_a + X_b$ and $Y = Y_a + Y_b$, application of the 'function-of-a-function' rule to Equation [5.5] provides the following:

$$W = V[(X_a + X_b), (Y_a + Y_b)] \qquad [5.8]$$

$$W = V(X,Y) \qquad [5.8a]$$

where V indicates a different functional relationship from our earlier function. Equation [5.8a] simply states that the welfare of society depends on the production levels of the two commodities X and Y. Equation [5.8a] is a very general version of the welfare function (defined in terms of individual commodities) and it can be specified in many ways. However, most of these specifications will embody the above value judgement, that is, that the community has to make a judgement about the relative worthiness of the two sectors and, by implication, of the two individuals as well.

The commodity-based welfare function is shown in Figure 5.4 where we assume that the top-level competitive equilibrium occurs at point C. But this does not coincide with the welfare maximum at point S: the community prefers point S to point C, thus establishing a prima facie case for appropriate state intervention to move the economy to point S.

This analysis has shown that a top-level competitive equilibrium is only a necessary condition for a social welfare maximum, not a sufficient condition – this is indicated by the difference between points S and C in Figure 5.4. Two questions therefore arise:

▶ What kinds of policy could be used to bring about an inter-sectoral or inter-personal redistribution of income, that is, a movement from point C to point S?
▶ What are the implications for the economic efficiency of such policies?

As far as the first question is concerned, government has several options at its disposal: it can tax sector Y and subsidise sector X, or it can tax one individual and subsidise the other; it can also redirect its own spending towards one sector or individual. These options will be discussed in greater detail in subsequent sections of this book. Note, however, that a movement from C to S entails an improvement in social welfare even though U_b may be reduced on account of the reduced supply of good Y. This is the difference between the Bergson welfare function and the Pareto criterion discussed earlier.

In the meantime we turn our focus to the second question raised above.

5.5 Efficiency considerations

It would be surprising if a redistributive policy comprising a suitable tax-subsidy mix had no effect on efficiency levels in the economy. As we shall see in subsequent chapters, most taxes and subsidies do have distortional effects on markets, and the real question is whether the perceived benefits from such policies justify these distortions.

We shall briefly introduce two such distortions here, both of which are discussed in more detail in Chapter 11. The first is the

possible effect that individual taxes and subsidies might have on the **willingness to work**. Specifically, does a new or higher tax or subsidy cause people to work longer or fewer hours per day or per month? And similarly, does a higher tax or subsidy cause people to work more or less productively, that is, produce more or fewer units of output per hour? In other words, can one expect an increase or decrease in the supply of labour or in its productivity – or, in terms of our two-sector model, an optimal or sub-optimal top-level equilibrium?

The evidence on this issue – referred to as 'income and substitution effects' or the '(dis)incentive effect' – is anything but conclusive. What it does show is that, above a certain level, increased taxes tend to have a small negative effect on the willingness to work. This is illustrated in Figure 5.5 where the initial competitive equilibrium again occurs at point C_0 on the PPC labelled M_0N_0, representing an initial welfare level of W_1. Now, a policy aimed at redistributing resources from sector Y to sector X (for example by taxing sector Y and/or subsidising sector X) will move the economy in the direction of point S – the policy target. However, if the policy does have a small disincentive effect, labour productivity may fall below its potential and the economy may end up at a sub-optimal allocation lying inside the PPC – for example point F in Figure 5.5.

Although point F is inferior to point S, it nevertheless represents a higher level of welfare than the original allocation at point C_0 – W_2 as opposed to W_1. A stronger disincentive effect would have a bigger negative impact on labour productivity and hence on the level of social welfare. Thus the policy could move the economy to a point such as E on the social indifference curve W_0, which is clearly inferior to the original allocation at point C_0.

The second possibility referred to above concerns the dynamic consequences of a

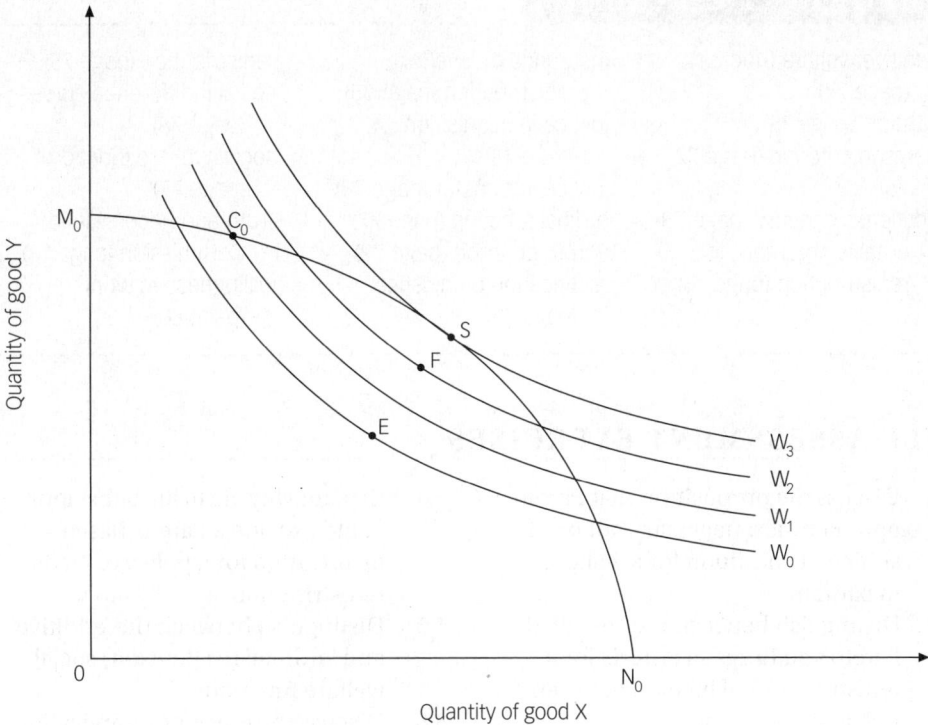

Figure 5.5 Disincentive and savings effects of redistribution

distribution policy aimed at taxing the rich and subsidising the poor. The imposition of a new or higher tax (on sector Y or on individual b) may limit savings and investment and hence economic growth and, in the limit, keep the economy on its existing PPC, for example, at point S in Figure 5.5, or at the inferior points F and E. In the absence of such a policy, however, the economy may experience positive economic growth over time, in which case the PPC will, as before, shift outwards thus enabling the economy to move beyond its original PPC.

On the whole, the above analysis indicates that there are many good reasons why societies might want to achieve a more equitable distribution of income. But whatever the justification might be, it is clearly important that the expected benefits of a policy of redistribution should be carefully weighed against the possible negative effects it might have on labour supply and on savings and investment, and hence on economic growth in the long term. We will return to this theme in subsequent chapters.

IMPORTANT CONCEPTS

additive welfare function
(page 77)
altruism (page 75)
Bergson criterion (page 72,
76)
entitlement theory (page 73)
externality argument for
redistribution (page 75)

insurance motive for
redistribution (page 75)
justice in acquisition
(page 73)
justice in transfer (page 73)
ordinal function (page 77)
Pareto criterion (page 72)
rectification of injustice
(page 73)

redistribution (page 75)
social indifference curves
(page 78)
social welfare function
(page 77)
Truth and Reconciliation
Commission (page 73)
willingness to work
(page 80)

SELF-ASSESSMENT EXERCISES

5.1 Discuss the proposition that Pareto optimality is a necessary but not a sufficient condition for a welfare maximum.

5.2 Distinguish between the so-called Pareto and Bergson criteria for a redistribution of income between rich and poor people.

5.3 Discuss Nozick's entitlement theory and briefly consider its relevance for South Africa.

5.4 Explain why altruistic behaviour could provide a Pareto-based justification for a policy of income redistribution.

5.5 Distinguish between the 'additive' and 'ordinal' (or Bergson) social welfare functions.

5.6 Discuss the efficiency implications of an inter-sectoral (or interpersonal) policy of income redistribution.

Chapter
SIX

Philip Black

Public choice theory

In the previous chapters we looked at a range of so-called market failures and highlighted the point that private markets cannot on their own supply public goods or make allowance for external costs and benefits. Similarly, although it is conceptually possible to regulate imperfectly competitive markets or to evaluate the desirability of various income distributions by means of the Pareto and Bergson normative criteria, we have not as yet addressed the question of how a community can practically express its collective preferences on these matters. In this chapter we focus on the way in which communities make public choices.

Once you have studied this chapter, you should be able to:
- ▶ discuss the Rawlsian theory of justice and comment on its relevance to recent political developments in South Africa
- ▶ explain the median voter theory and indicate its potential strengths and weaknesses
- ▶ discuss the meaning and importance of Kenneth Arrow's impossibility theorem
- ▶ consider whether logrolling (or vote trading) is an efficient means of improving the outcomes of a majority voting system
- ▶ explain the theory of 'optimal voting rules' and consider the question of whether it does indeed provide an 'optimal rule' for majority voting
- ▶ discuss the maximising behaviour of politicians and bureaucrats, and consider the implications of such behaviour for majority voting
- ▶ explain the origins and consequences of 'rent-seeking'.

6.1 **Introduction**

Many public issues are discussed and resolved in the political market place where the quantities of public goods and services and the levels of taxes and subsidies are decided. These decisions are usually made by elected politicians, on behalf of the voting population, and in this chapter we look at the way in which such public decisions are made from a strict economic perspective. We investigate the mechanisms – or 'social choice rules' – by which individual preferences are transformed into social or public preferences, and ask whether these will ensure that governments act in accordance with the wishes of the people they represent.

The most straightforward method of effecting such a transformation lies in simply imposing the ethical views of some dictator or central politburo on society and then adjusting economic policy accordingly. Viewed historically, however, dictatorial rule has often led to abusive behaviour and clearly does not represent a desirable social choice rule. Most countries today prefer some method of collective decision-making based on and legitimised by mass participation on the part of their citizenry. Indeed, the characteristic social choice rule employed in most democracies is majority rule whereby citizens elect representatives who must act within certain constitutional parameters.

Thus in the absence of dictatorial rule, the range of social choice rules varies between the **unanimity rule**, in terms of which a proposal requires 100 per cent support before being accepted, and ordinary majority rule, for which 50 per cent plus one vote are required. In this chapter we first look at the unanimity rule, and focus specifically on John Rawls's well-known theory of justice (1971), partly because of its relevance to the dramatic recent shift towards a full democracy in South Africa. This is followed in Section 6.3 by a discussion of the '**ordinary majority-voting rule**' as expressed in median voter theorem. Sections 6.4 and 6.5 look at some of the problems associated with majority voting, focusing specifically on its inability to allow for differences in the intensities of individual preferences. Section 6.6 deals with an important variation on the ordinary majority-voting rule, that is, Buchanan and Tullock's (1962) notion of 'optimal voting rules'. In Section 6.7 we shift our attention to 'positive public choice theory', and consider the behaviour of politicians, bureaucrats, and private interest groups within a typical representative democracy.

6.2 **The unanimity rule and the Rawlsian experiment**

The **unanimity-voting rule** means that each member or representative group within a community must support a proposal before it becomes the collective decision. The unanimity rule is the only voting rule that will lead to a Pareto-optimal outcome and, since it requires that collective decisions be in the interest of *all* parties, it can be viewed as a positive sum game.

A good, if somewhat unusual, example of the unanimity principle is provided by John Rawls or the **Rawlsian theory of justice**. The theory is essentially a normative one setting out the conditions under which 'free and rational' persons will choose certain principles of justice that govern the 'basic structure of society'. These principles determine the fundamental rights and duties of individuals and regulate the institutional framework within which allocative decisions are made on a collective – and unanimous – basis. The 'social contract' that ultimately emerges is described by Rawls as a case of 'justice in fairness'.

What sets the Rawlsian theory apart from others is its focus on the process by which individuals reach unanimity over the principles of justice. He thus asks his readers to *imagine* a situation in which the contracting parties, representing the whole community, all step through a 'veil of ignorance' and enter a hypothetical 'original position' – a position reached through intensive personal discourse during which all barriers are broken down and each party is able to rid itself of all prejudices and prior knowledge. In the original position, each party is wholly unaware of its 'place in society' and has no knowledge of the probability distribution of expected outcomes, let alone its current well-being. They all stand as equals on the same playing field.

What is important for our purpose is that each party in the original position is assumed to be equally risk-averse. All parties would thus support a risk-minimising social welfare function that effectively insures them against the worst possible outcome. Such a welfare function could take the following form:

$$W = Minimum\ (U_a,\ U_b) \qquad [6.1]$$

indicating that social welfare depends on the lower of the two individual utilities. Thus, if $U_a < U_b$, then welfare reduces to $W = U_a$. This implies that for W to increase, there must be an increase in U_a. The latter condition does not preclude an increase in U_b; it is perfectly in order for U_b to increase, as long as U_a increases as well. The **Rawlsian welfare function** is therefore perfectly consistent with a Pareto-based policy benefiting both parties.

From a Rawlsian perspective, Equation [6.1] implies that all parties in the original position will adopt a so-called maximin strategy, giving priority to the party potentially finding itself in the worst position. This will provide them with a measure of protection in case they end up being that party. All parties

will therefore choose, and unanimously approve, a political constitution embodying the Rawlsian welfare function and, by implication, also an institutional system and a set of policies aimed at allocating and distributing resources in accordance with that function.

It hardly seems prudent to suggest that recent negotiations for a new constitution and democratic dispensation in South Africa, Namibia, Mozambique, and several other African countries even approximated a Rawlsian original position – none of the negotiating parties can be said to have been 'completely impartial', while the underlying principle would appear to have been one of compromise rather than unanimity. Nonetheless, the growing concern for the poor and 'historically disadvantaged' in South Africa, as reflected in several empowerment 'charters' and the redistributive nature of recent budgets (see Chapters 15 and 17), does seem to come close to acceptance of a Rawlsian welfare function – that is, one that affords priority status to the disadvantaged members of the community.

The unanimity rule is not without its shortcomings. Reaching a unanimous decision may take a very long time, partly because of the divergent nature of individual preferences and the number of issues involved – consider, for instance, the drawn-out nature of the ('Kempton Park') negotiations that preceded the drafting of a new constitution in South Africa, as well as the extensive research and administrative tasks many African countries have to perform in order to meet the NEPAD (New Partnership for Africa's Development) requirements. The point here is that the costs of reaching consensus may be inordinately high, and it is important that cognisance be taken of the opportunity costs associated with the unanimity rule. The time spent lobbying and influencing individuals and groups of individuals can arguably be spent more productively elsewhere in the economy.

Viewed more practically, the unanimity rule could give rise to strategic actions on the part of certain individuals or groups who might want to enter into bargaining contracts with other parties in order to secure special benefits. Under such conditions parties may be persuaded to engage in '**logrolling**' (or **vote trading**) by forfeiting something they want in exchange for something about which they feel particularly strongly. We shall return to the issue of logrolling in Section 6.5, but suffice it to say here that the outcome of such a process is hardly likely to be Pareto-efficient.

A final objection to unanimity rule is that it gives minorities the right of veto; in the extreme case, the last unpersuaded voter has the decisive vote. Exercising such a veto right will clearly render the unanimity rule obsolete as it may lead to a situation in which a minority effectively rules.

6.3 Majority voting and the median voter

The most common social choice rule is the 'ordinary' **majority rule** (or **majority voting**). Every individual is given one vote and the issue or policy receiving the most votes wins the day. Under a **direct democratic dispensation** where each voter reveals his or her preferences directly via a referendum, the majority-voting rule requires that a proposal receives '50 per cent plus one vote' support before it can be imposed on the community. If South Africa had a direct democracy and the public were asked in a referendum to vote for or against an increase in the rate of value added tax (VAT), the rate would not be increased if 4 000 001 voters out of a total of eight million voted against such an increase.

In a **representative democracy** individual voters elect representatives who make decisions on their behalf. A representative democracy is generally less costly to administer than a direct democracy, and it is largely for this reason that the former is most widely used in the world today. Some countries like Switzerland, however, do combine the two systems, utilising the direct method when important national decisions have to be made.

Voters' interests in a representative democracy are represented by several influential actors including elected politicians, bureaucrats, and private and public interest groups. The role of politicians is paramount and one can reasonably ask: What are they in the 'market' for? What do they want to maximise? Following Anthony Downs (1957), politicians act like any other utility-maximising consumer or profit-maximising entrepreneur; the only difference is that they are in the business of maximising the number of votes they collect in an election. In an ideal world, the vote-maximising behaviour of politicians is an important means of transforming individual preferences into a logically consistent set of social preferences.

What is required to maximise votes in a representative democracy? To answer this question we must examine the **median voter theorem**. We begin our explanation of this theorem by defining the median voter as the voter whose set of preferences divides the voting community exactly into two. Let's assume we have a community of five people: Ndlovo, Mary, Thandi, Johan, and Ibrahim. We assume furthermore that we know their precise preferences concerning the size of the national health budget. Table 6.1 sets out the budgets for which each of them will vote.

Let us adopt a step-by-step approach towards discovering the majority decision on the size of the budget, beginning with a zero budget. Assuming that there are no extreme preferences (see below), all five voters will prefer a R50 million budget instead of a zero budget. It will, however, be the preferred option of Ndlovo only. A movement from

Table 6.1 Voter preference for size of health budget

Voter	Amount (R million)
Ndlovo	50
Mary	200
Thandi	400
Johan	600
Ibrahim	800

R50 million to R200 million will win the support of everyone except Ndlovo; that is, everyone except Ndlovo prefers a budget bigger than R50 million. A movement from R200 million to R400 million will be approved by Thandi, Johan, and Ibrahim, while only two voters will support an increase from R400 million to R600 million, and so on.

It is clear from Table 6.1 that three of the five options will enjoy majority support: all five voters (or 100 per cent) will support a budget of R50 million, four voters (80 per cent) a budget of R200 million, and three voters (60 per cent) a budget of R400 million. But which is the optimal one? Which one will make our voting population happiest, or cause the least harm?

The answer is provided by the median voter theorem: the best option is that of Thandi's – our median voter – whose preference divides the voters exactly into two. The reason is that both Johan and Ibrahim would prefer Thandi's option to that of Ndlovo and Mary; Ndlovo and Mary will likewise have a relative preference for Thandi's option vis-à-vis those of Johan and Ibrahim. It follows that our larger-budget supporters, Johan and Ibrahim, will rather give their support to a politician campaigning for the median voter's choice than to a politician promoting any other potential majority choice.

We can now formulate the median voter theorem: under a majority voting system in which preferences are not extreme, it is the median voter's preferred option that will win the day, since that is the option that will produce a minimum welfare loss for the whole group.

The median voter model provides a simplified explanation of the rational behaviour of politicians under ideal conditions. The model suggests that politicians interact with voters to determine their relative preferences. By doing so, they are able to identify the median voter, act upon his or her preferences, and in the process fulfil the wishes of the majority at minimum cost.

Of course, the real world of politics is a bit different from what the median voter theory would have us believe. Not all politicians are vote maximisers responding passively to individuals' demands. Some might pursue the 'public interest' rather than vote-maximising strategies, while others may appeal to voters because of their vision and personality, rather than any tangible benefits they might promise. The model also presumes that the median voter can be identified. This is not easy, especially since different political issues may have different median voters. The model furthermore assumes that voters are rational and that everyone will vote. Politicians and voters are often far from perfectly informed, which renders rational choice unlikely, if not impossible – an issue to which we return in Section 6.7.

On the whole, the majority-voting rule – although not Pareto-efficient – does have two important advantages vis-à-vis the unanimity rule:
- reaching majority approval takes much less time and is therefore less costly than achieving unanimous support
- under majority rule it is much less likely that a minority will be able to prevent the majority from getting their proposals accepted. On the other hand, majority rule can be criticised for its 'winner-takes-all' consequences and for its potential to ignore minority interests and even 'tyrannise' minorities.

6.4 The impossibility theorem

A potentially serious shortcoming of the majority-voting rule is the fact that it can lead to logically inconsistent results. This proposition was first proved by Nobel Laureate Kenneth Arrow (1951) in what is now referred to as his **impossibility theorem**. Arrow proved that it is not always possible to derive a logically consistent set of social preferences from a corresponding set of individual preferences on the basis of an 'ethically acceptable (or democratic) social choice rule'. He came to the conclusion that there is not a single voting rule – not even majority voting – that would meet all the minimum 'ethical' conditions he set for an 'acceptable' social choice rule.

Arrow's theory crucially depends on these ethical conditions, which can be summarised as follows:

▶ Rationality assumption, according to which individuals and the community must either prefer one option (X) to another (Y), or be indifferent between the two. This assumption is formulated as follows:

$$X > Y \text{ or } Y > X \text{ or } X = Y$$

where the symbols > and = stand for 'prefer to' and 'indifferent between'. The community must also adhere to the familiar transitivity condition:

$$\text{If } X > Y \text{ and } Y > Z, \text{ then } X > Z$$

which means that if X is preferred to Y and Y is preferred to Z, then X must be preferred to Z.

▶ Independence of irrelevant alternatives, which implies that if the choice is between two options, X and Y, then the effect of Z is irrelevant.

▶ Pareto principle, that is, if voter a prefers X to Y and voter b is indifferent between the two options, then the (two-person) community must prefer X to Y; or in algebraic terms:

$$\text{If } (X > Y)_a \text{ and } (X = Y)_b \text{ then } X > Y$$

▶ Unrestricted domain, that is, it should be possible for all eligible voters to vote.
▶ Non-dictatorship.

Although these conditions seem very reasonable indeed, it is important to note that Arrow's theorem is especially relevant to voters who have widely divergent preferences or who choose extreme alternatives. We can illustrate such a case by considering three voters, Brenda, Christelle, and Abdullah. Each of them has to choose between three alternative budgets, that is, a large budget (denoted by L), a moderate budget (M), and a small budget (S). Let the individual preferences be as follows:

Brenda: $L > M > S$
Christelle: $M > S > L$
Abdullah: $S > L > M$

It is clear from this example that if alternative budgets are voted for in pairs, a majority of the voters (i.e. Brenda and Abdullah) prefer L to M. A majority (i.e. Brenda and Christelle) also prefer M to S. Therefore, according to the transitivity condition, a majority should prefer L to S – yet that is not the case: a majority (i.e. Christelle and Abdullah) actually prefer S to L, and hence we have a logically inconsistent – or intransitive – outcome.

The reason for this outcome is straightforward. Abdullah has 'extreme' preferences: he prefers a small budget to a large one but also prefers the large one to a moderate one. Such a voter does not, when given the choice between any two budgets, consistently prefer a larger budget to a smaller budget, or vice versa. In a system of majority voting where voting often occurs in a pair-wise fashion,[1] the presence of extreme preferences[2] can have a number of consequences. The first is that there may be a new winner every time the sequence of voting is changed. Consequently it is impossible to get a consistent winner. While the preferences of individual voters may be consistent, their combined preferences or the community's preferences (as reflected in their voting) will not be consistent if the group of voters includes people with extreme preferences. This phenomenon is referred to as the voting paradox. Such voting can continue indefinitely, a phenomenon called cycling.

Furthermore, if the organisers of the election have prior knowledge of the existence of these extreme preferences, it is possible to organise the sequence of voting in such a way that a desired result is obtained. This is known as agenda manipulation. Any result that can be changed if the order of voting is changed, is not consistent and is not a true reflection of voters' preferences. Such a result therefore cannot claim to represent a choice for an optimal allocation of resources.

What is the practical relevance of all this? In a strict sense, Arrow's theory implies that the majority-voting rule does not necessarily produce outcomes that enjoy the support of the majority – which is something of a contradiction in terms. All is not lost, however. The theory only proves that logical

inconsistency is a possible outcome. In the above example of three voters choosing between three alternatives, for example, the probability of a logical inconsistency arising is only six per cent (Frey, 1978: Chapter 2). As one increases the number of voters and the number of alternatives, this probability rises only very gradually, reaching about 31 per cent when the number of voters becomes very large and the number of alternatives reaches six. It is thus tempting to conclude that perhaps too much is made of the impossibility theorem.

Nonetheless, the problem of inconsistency is compounded by the fact that majority voting does not allow for differences in the intensity of individual preferences and by the attendant problem of logrolling, as we shall see in the next section.

6.5 Majority voting and preference intensities

Another major shortcoming of the majority-voting rule is the fact that it cannot account for differences in the intensity of voters' preferences; or at least it cannot do so in a cost-effective way. Under these conditions it is quite possible that a small majority may have a relatively weak preference for a particular candidate, whom they nevertheless vote into power. If a large minority opposes the same candidate very strongly, it is possible that, in net welfare terms, the community as a whole will be in a worse position: given an additive welfare function (implying measurability of individual utilities), the cumulative decreases in individual utilities will exceed the corresponding increases.

Under majority voting there are two ways in which **preference intensities** can be accommodated. The first is to ask people to vote in the form of 'intensity units'. Instead of a straight yes-no vote, each voter can, for

---

[1] Suppose there are three candidates for a position. Pair-wise voting entails that the first vote is between the first two candidates. The one who wins is then paired with the other candidate in the second election. If the third candidate wins the second election, a third election will be required between the winner of the second election and the loser of the first to determine the ultimate winner.

[2] In the example of extreme preferences given above, the result is quite confusing if the voter is asked to vote in a pair-wise manner. If the first vote is between large and small, small wins. In small versus moderate, moderate wins. In the final vote between moderate and large, large now beats the candidate which conquered its own superior.

example, be given a total of 100 points that he or she can allocate between competing candidates. In this way the ordering of preferences will be weighted and the weights will be taken into account in the voting procedure. It is thus possible that a candidate, who would have come last under a straight yes-no system, may fare better under the weighted system. But weighting is a normative procedure: Thandi's '80 per cent' may mean something completely different from Johan's '80 per cent'. Weighting is also difficult to implement and administratively very costly, and it must be asked whether the additional benefits from introducing such a procedure are worth the additional costs.

Another – some would say better – way of accounting for preferences under a majority-voting rule is through logrolling or vote trading. Logrolling may occur between and among minority parties and the majority party. For example, an intense minority may trade its support for an issue enjoying strong support amongst the majority, in exchange for majority support of the minority issue; or the same exchange can be based on amendments being made to the issues involved. In practical terms, the latter exchange would only be feasible if the minority had a particularly strong preference for the 'minority issue' and the majority did not feel too strongly about it. It would also not help if the minority took a minority view on each and every issue: if the majority could never count on a minority's vote on any issue, there would be no point in trading votes. Nonetheless, to the extent that such logrolling enables a better expression of consumer preferences in respect of public goods, it may increase the social welfare of society.

Logrolling can also take the form of an exchange of votes between different minority groups. Such groups could gang up against the majority by supporting each other's causes. Suppose two minority parties in parliament each have a bill that will never get approved on its own. By voting for each other's bill they could get both bills passed if the majority party had less than 50 per cent of the votes in parliament. Such vote trading may be beneficial if it leads to the approval of economically viable projects, which may otherwise not have seen the light of day. It could, however, equally lead to the adoption of non-viable projects or to projects that do not meet with the approval of the majority. While vote trading on the part of minorities does reveal the intensity of individual preferences, it can either increase or decrease the ability of a majority voting system to truly reflect the wishes of the majority.

6.6 Optimal voting rules

Is there anything in-between an ordinary majority-voting rule and a 100 per cent unanimity rule? Is there anything more efficient than ordinary majority voting? The answer can be found in the theory of '**optimal voting rules**', as propounded by James Buchanan and Gordon Tullock (1962).

Their main hypothesis is that the 'optimal' voting majority varies in accordance with the particular public issue in question and that these optimal majorities depend on the costs involved in the act of voting. Voters are faced with two kinds of costs, namely external costs and decision-making costs.

External costs arise when a community takes a decision that goes against the interest of an individual voter or group. In other words, the greater the number of people not supporting a public decision, the higher the external costs will be or the higher the degree of unhappiness amongst the voting public will be. The expected external cost will be highest when public decisions are made by one person – a dictator – since such decisions will potentially ignore and undermine the interests of all other voters. By contrast, under a unanimity voting system, where public decisions require 100 per cent support, external cost can be expected to be zero. In other words, the closer one comes to unanimity, the smaller will be the risk of harming minorities. External costs are inherent in all decision-making rules except the unanimity rule. In Figure 6.1, which depicts majority size as a function of cost, the external cost curve falls from top left to bottom right.

Decision-making costs refer to the costs involved in persuading voters to support a particular public issue. The smaller the community of voters, the easier it will be to reach a majority or unanimous decision and the lower will be the decision-making costs. As unanimity is approached, however, it becomes increasingly difficult and costly to harness the support necessary to pass a new law or resolution. One also finds that the opportunities to act as a free rider increase as the size of the group whose consent is sought increases. Thus, as the size of the required support base increases, it becomes increasingly expensive to induce individuals to reveal their preferences accurately. In Figure 6.1 the decision-making cost curve rises from left to right as the number of individuals required for a collective decision increases.

We assume that voters take both types of costs into consideration when casting their votes. But since these costs will vary with the particular issue in question, the 'optimal' – that is, cost-minimising – voting rule will vary likewise. If the two kinds of costs are summed vertically, we obtain a total cost curve, as shown in Figure 6.1. The lowest point on the total cost curve, coinciding with the percentage given by M^*, determines the optimal majority for the particular public issue in question. There is likely to be a different set of cost curves for each issue on which a vote has to be cast. The characteristics of the optimal majority point are as follows: the higher the external cost (curve), *ceteris paribus,* the greater M^* becomes; and the higher the decision-making cost, *ceteris paribus,* the

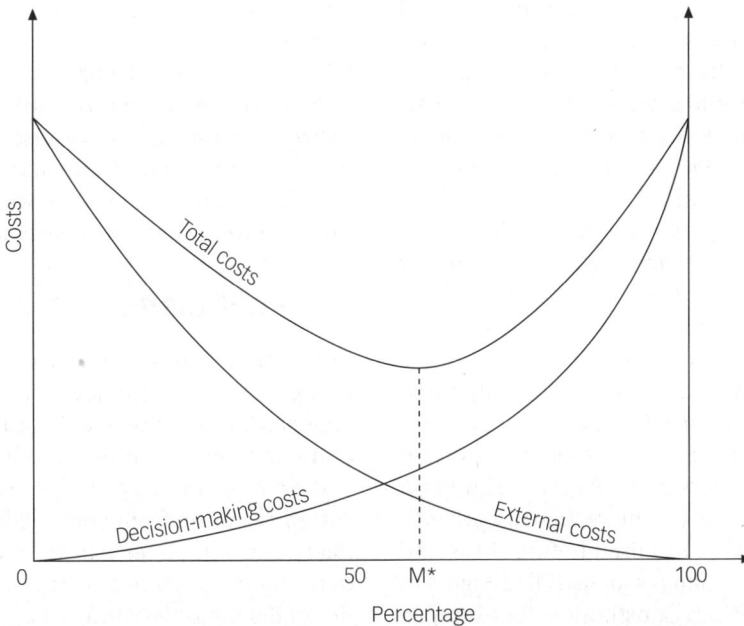

Figure 6.1 The cost of democratic decision-making

lower M^* will be. The shape of the curves will differ according to the type of activity that is to be decided on and the optimal majority need not be an ordinary majority (i.e. 50 per cent plus one vote).

A factor that influences both decision-making and external costs, is the degree of homogeneity among the voting community. In a homogeneous community it is probably easier to achieve a majority outcome or unanimity since individual tastes are relatively similar and, consequently, decision and external costs are relatively low. One implication is that a community characterised by sharp differences among individual citizens and groups may not be able to afford the high decision-making costs involved in near-unanimity rules for collective choice. However, the potentially adverse consequences – or high external costs – for minority individuals and groups may be the very factor that will prompt such individuals to press for costly near-unanimity rules.

The above analysis can be used to determine voting rules for different kinds of collective actions. All such actions need not be organised under the same voting rule. Voters, for example, will choose a voting rule with a high majority requirement for collective actions that incur high external costs (or a major loss of utility) for them. Conversely, there are collective actions that incur low external costs, which means that a lower majority-voting rule will probably suffice. However, one should bear in mind that individuals and groups will normally not deem it in their interests to support a voting rule that may promote the interests of other groups. The customary rule when important issues such as amendments to a constitution are concerned, is that more than just an ordinary majority is required before these can be executed. Changes to the Bill of Rights in the South African Constitution, for example, require a two-thirds majority in the National Assembly.

6.7 Government failure

A necessary condition for success of both direct and indirect (or regulatory) intervention by government is the presence of an adequate and efficient **institutional framework**. Important institutions include the legislative authority (e.g. parliament), law enforcement, the judiciary, tax collection or revenue services, and regulatory bodies. These institutions should ideally ensure that agents comply with the rule of law and honour their contractual and regulatory commitments. A sufficient condition for success refers to the value system of the community, including behavioural norms and customs, which should ideally entrench high levels of trust between and among consumers, producers and government institutions (North, 1991).

Both these conditions should ultimately ensure that government performs its functions in a transparent, accountable and consistent manner (Parker, 2002). But experience shows that such utopian outcomes are rare, especially in developing countries (Kahn, 2006), due to what economists refer to as '**government failure**'; and as we show below, governments fail because of the 'rational' behaviour of politicians and bureaucrats and also because of the influence that special interest groups has over government.

6.7.1 Politicians

As mentioned in Section 6.3, politicians can be viewed as entrepreneurs who engage in vote maximising strategies in order to secure and retain political office. It is important to consider the implications for resource allocation resulting from such behaviour. The likely consequences can be more readily determined given two further characteristics of the majority-voting rule:

▶ Voters are rationally ignorant of much of what politicians stand for, since they usually do not have a sufficient incentive to acquire all the information necessary to determine the desirability of all the relevant public issues.

▶ Politicians are elected on the basis of a package of policies and therefore do not have to please a majority of voters on each separate policy issue.

These characteristics can give rise to **implicit logrolling** favouring special interest legislation. We can illustrate this proposition by means of a hypothetical example, as shown in Table 6.2.

Imagine a politician standing for election for a political party with diverse interests. She explicitly supports three special interest programmes, namely the relocation of the South African Parliament to Pretoria, a rugby development programme, and a subsidised loan scheme for students. Each of these special interest programmes is likely to attract strong support from a particular group within the voting population – civil servants will strongly support the relocation of Parliament, rugby lovers will likewise support the proposed development programme, and students will lend strong support to the proposed subsidy scheme. But none of the programmes are likely to benefit a majority of the voters: the subsidy scheme will not benefit civil servants or rugby lovers directly, or at least not attract their strong support; when faced with a choice between the three programmes, they may have a relatively weak opposition to it. Civil servants and rugby lovers may therefore rationally decide to remain ignorant about the full cost of the subsidy scheme.

Meanwhile, the politician in question who supports all three programmes has an incentive to make the benefits of these policies clear to the three unrelated recipient interest groups, in order to form a coalition through implicit logrolling. She knows that the strong preference that civil servants have for

relocating Parliament to Pretoria probably outweighs their mild opposition to the student loan scheme and the rugby development programme: they would rather have all three programmes than none. And she can make sure of this by disguising or understating the cost of each of the programmes to the electorate as a whole – that is, by creating fiscal illusion. Table 6.2 illustrates the nature of this implicit logrolling.

Table 6.2 Coalition-forming and implicit logrolling

Policy	Strongly favoured by	Weakly opposed by
Relocation of Parliament	Civil servants (33,3%)	Rest of electorate (66,7%)
Rugby development	Rugby lovers (33,3%)	Rest of electorate (66,7%)
Student loan scheme	Students (33,3%)	Rest of electorate (66,7%)

It is evident that the politician supporting all three minority programmes will defeat an opponent who opposes them, or who supports only one or two of them, by mobilising the strong preferences of civil servants, rugby lovers, and students by means of implicit logrolling.

Two important consequences for resource allocation flow from this example:

▶ we can anticipate a preponderance of special interest legislation producing a variety of relatively unpopular public goods

▶ we can expect an aggregate oversupply of public goods in society.

It is clear that vote-maximising behaviour on the part of politicians can lead to outcomes inimitable to the wishes of the majority of voters. Some writers, most notably Buchanan and Tullock (1962), argue that this phenomenon is a consequence of constitutional failure and can only be dealt with by constitutional reform, for example, by limiting the proportion of scarce resources expended on public goods to some fixed percentage of national income and specifying the distribution of these resources between alternative kinds of public goods.

6.7.2 **Bureaucratic failure**

A second source of government failure stems from the maximising behaviour of government employees or so-called 'bureaucrats'. In essence, **bureaucratic failure** results from rational responses on the part of utility-maximising civil servants to the incentives presented to them by politicians and the institutional structures within which they operate.

Thomas Borcherding (1977: xi) notes that:

Individuals in the bureaucracy, like the rest of us, do react to different incentive schemes; they do have various preferences, and have the capacity, will and desire to fulfill these preferences. They prefer more rather than less income, power, prestige, pleasant surroundings, and congenial employees.

The rational behaviour of bureaucrats can be analysed in terms of the demand for and supply of public goods. The demand for public goods in a representative democracy is generated by the decisions of vote-maximising politicians, while the supply of public goods is usually the responsibility of the state bureaucracy. Unlike private firms, however, bureaucracies do not maximise profit. Instead, they receive annual lump sum payments from the legislature based on estimates – prepared by bureaucrats – of the costs of providing specified (and usually monopolised) public goods. Consequently, bureaucracies do not face any market test. William Niskanen (1971) argued persuasively that since higher salaries, more power, greater prestige, and other favourable attributes are positively related to bureau size and hence to bureau budgets, bureaucrats have an incentive to maximise their budgets.

The resultant bias towards the excess provision of public goods is illustrated in Figure 6.2. Part (a) of the diagram shows the total social cost (TSC) and total social benefit (TSB) curves for a public good. The usual marginal principles apply here: total cost rises at an increasing rate as output expands (due to the principle of diminishing marginal productivity), while total benefits increase at a decreasing rate as output expands. The rates of change of these curves, or their slopes, determine the shapes of the corresponding marginal curves shown in Figure 6.2 (b).

The socially optimal level of output of the public good is given by $0Q_0$, where marginal social benefit (MSB) equals marginal social cost (MSC) (in Figure 6.2 (b)), or where the difference between TSB and TSC is maximised (in Figure 6.2 (a)). But a budget-maximising bureaucrat would attempt to justify output $0Q_1 > 0Q_0$, where TSB equals TSC and where MSC exceeds MSB by the distance FG. The result is that the total value to consumers increases from $0AEQ_0$ to $0AFQ_1$ (in the (b) part) or by the area Q_0EFQ_1, while total cost increases from $0BEQ_0$ to $0BGQ_1$, or by the larger area Q_0EGQ_1. The increase in total cost thus exceeds the increase in total benefits by the area EGF – the net welfare loss to society.

Moreover, given the absence of a profit motive, bureaucrats may supply public goods inefficiently, for example, by using more than the required inputs to produce a given level of output. The resultant inefficiency (or welfare loss) thus stems from an excessive use

(a)

(b)

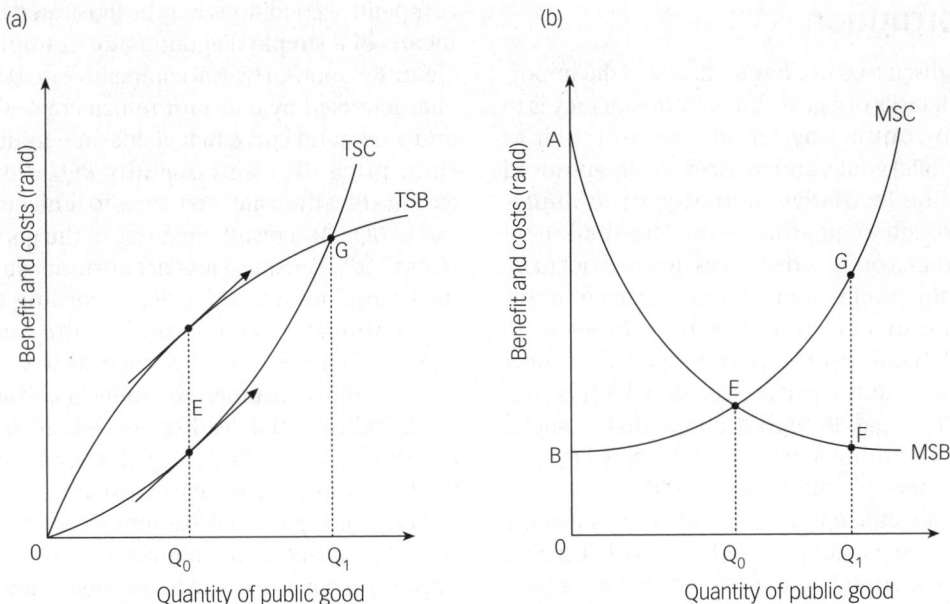

Figure 6.2 Bureaucratic failure

of inputs rather than from excessive production by the bureau.

In essence, the problem of bureaucratic failure is simply an example of a **principal-agent problem**. In the public sector bureaucrats act as agents for their principals, the taxpaying public, who are in turn represented by elected politicians. Since each individual bureaucrat benefits directly from a large budget, he or she has a strong preference for a high level of expenditure. Individual taxpayers, on the other hand, generally benefit only marginally from that expenditure and therefore remain rationally ignorant about it. Due to the size and divergent nature of the tax-paying public, there is little individual taxpayers can do to lobby against higher levels of state spending or in favour of lower taxes. Thus, there is a poor correlation between the objectives of agents and the objectives of principals. Put differently, bureaucrats have a greater incentive to increase spending than taxpayers have to

reduce taxes. It follows that one should expect spending levels on public goods to exceed their corresponding optimal levels.

Although Niskanen's model of bureaucratic failure provides a plausible explanation for excessive state intervention in the economy, it can be questioned on several grounds. Is it realistic to assume that politicians and the tax-paying public are entirely at the mercy of bureaucrats? Budgetary procedures have become more transparent everywhere, including South Africa and other African countries, while the salaries and perks of senior public servants are not usually linked to the size of their budgets. In a democratic environment, buttressed by strong institutions, it seems unlikely that bureaucrats will be allowed to get away with practices that run against the public interest, at least not for long. It is therefore difficult to confirm or deny the alleged empire-building motives and actions of bureaucrats.

6.7.3 **Rent-seeking and corruption**

As discussed in Chapter 2, one of the important tasks of a government bureaucracy is to sub-contract by tender the provision of (public) goods and services legally approved by the legislative authority; or to limit – through regulation – the production of certain goods and services deemed not to be in the public interest. Both forms of intervention can give rise to **rent-seeking** behaviour on the part of special interest groups in the private sector, which is perfectly legal, though it often adds to social waste attributable to the rent created by government (Buchanan et al., 1980).

The concept of economic rent is usually defined as that part of the reward accruing to resource owners over and above the payment that the resource would receive in any alternative employment. Rent is similar to monopoly profit: it cannot be competed away. In a perfectly competitive world market forces would ensure the dissipation of rent in a manner that produces socially desirable outcomes. The existence of positive rent in a competitive market will attract resources in the same way as the existence of potential profits, and consequently result in the erosion of such rent through an efficient re-allocation of resources. However, once we adjust the mechanisms through which this process occurs, the consequence of rent-seeking behaviour can be harmful to society at large.

The theory of rent-seeking deals with the origins of, and competition for, artificially created rent. The latter usually results from government protected monopoly power and in Southern Africa numerous examples abound, ranging from quantitative restrictions on licences for hawkers, liquor outlets and taxi drivers, to qualitative restrictions on purveyors of food and on people wishing to enter occupations like real estate sales, IT repairs, legal services and 'alternative' medicines.

The consequences of rent-seeking under competitive conditions may be illustrated by means of a simple diagrammatic example. Figure 6.3 shows a typical competitive market characterised by constant returns to scale and a demand curve that yields an equilibrium price OP_0, and quantity OQ_0. Now assume that the state intervenes to limit output to OQ_1. As a result, the price of the good rises to OP_1, causing a loss of consumer surplus equal to area $P_0E_0E_1P_1$. According to conventional economic theory, the area $P_0AE_1P_1$ denotes a socially costless wealth transfer from consumers to producers, while AE_0E_1 indicates the deadweight welfare loss to society. However, this may understate the net loss to society, as we will explain.

Under our present assumptions, the area $P_0AE_1P_1$ is available to potential suppliers to 'capture' in an attempt to boost their profits. They would thus be prepared to incur additional costs – by lobbying government, for example – in an effort to capture a share of this total rent. Two possibilities exist here.

If *participating suppliers* – taxi drivers, for instance – undertook the lobbying function themselves and the additional costs were internal to them, then marginal cost will increase to the critical level MC_1 in Figure 6.3. At this point the taxi drivers will have no further incentive to engage in rent-seeking activity since all rent consequent upon state intervention will have been dissipated; and with lobbying being largely a one-off expense, the suppliers could, like a cartel, share the future profits among themselves (when marginal cost would have fallen back to MC_0). But given the lobbying-induced exhaustion of $P_0AE_1P_1$, the social cost of state intervention will equal both areas $P_0AE_1P_1$ (or the social waste from rent-seeking) and AE_0E_1 (the deadweight loss). The point is that the taxi drivers will have transferred part of their own resources away from productive activities in favour of non-productive rent-seeking activities. Similar arguments may also apply to real estate agents, powerful

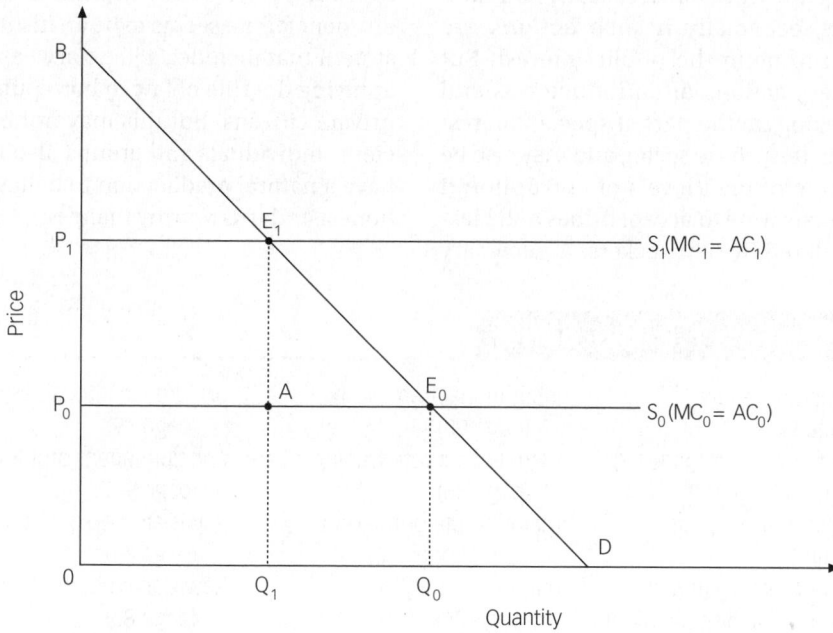

Figure 6.3 Rent-seeking

stakeholders in the fishing industry, and to many other profit-seeking special interest groups.

Alternatively, if a group of *concerned citizens* were to lobby government to reduce the number of taxis on the roads, then the additional costs will be external to the suppliers or taxi drivers, and the conventional theory will hold: the area $P_0AE_1P_1$ will indeed represent a wealth transfer from one group (the consumers) to another (the suppliers). The latter group will have received additional income (i.e. $P_0AE_1P_1$) that it can save or spend in the economy – much like a cartel.

Irrespective of who is doing the lobbying – taxi drivers or concerned citizens – the creation of rents by government, albeit *legal*, does establish a potential for **corrupt behaviour** on the part of bureaucrats. It is not beyond rent-seekers to offer bribes and kickbacks in an attempt to achieve their objectives more rapidly, and if such offers were accepted by bureaucrats they would be committing **corruption** which is, of course,

illegal. They would do so only if there were a net benefit in it for them, i.e. if the expected gain (of the bribe) exceeded the expected cost of being detected and punished. The fact that corruption is widely practised in many developing countries (Kahn, 2006; Merriman, 2003) would seem to point to an inadequate legal system which arguably constitutes the critical core of the institutional framework referred to above.

6.7.4 Concluding note

In broad terms then, the application of the microeconomic paradigm of rational maximisation provides further insight into the social costs attendant upon policy intervention by the state. The inefficiencies introduced into the market economy by vote-maximising politicians and budget-maximising bureaucrats generally take the form of an oversupply of public goods. Bureaucrats also have the responsibility of creating rents aimed at increasing or reducing the provision of certain goods and services, especially if such actions are deemed to be in the public interest. But these very actions often induce wasteful rent-seeking on the part of special interest groups in the private sector, and may also be the source of high levels of corruption if bureaucrats were to accept bribes and kickbacks offered by rent-seekers. A necessary condition for avoiding or minimising government failure seems to be an institutional system that includes a judiciary capable of applying the rule of law to both public and private citizens. But this may not be sufficient: individuals and groups also need to have a natural predilection to behave in an honest and trustworthy manner.

IMPORTANT CONCEPTS

bureaucratic failure
  (page 94)
corrupt behaviour (page 97)
corruption (page 97)
decision-making costs
  (page 91)
direct democracy (direct
  democratic dispensation)
  (page 86)
external costs (page 90)
government failure
  (page 92)
implicit logrolling (page 93)
impossibility theorem
  (page 88)

institutional framework
  (page 92)
logrolling or vote trading
  (page 86)
majority rule or majority
  voting (page 86)
majority-voting rule
  (page 86)
median voter theorem
  (page 86)
optimal voting rules
  (page 90)
ordinary majority-voting rule
  (page 84)

preference intensities
  (page 89)
principle-agent problem
  (page 95)
Rawlsian theory of justice
  (page 84)
Rawlsian welfare function
  (page 85)
rent-seeking (page 96)
representative democracy
  (page 86)
unanimity rule or unanimity
  voting rule (page 84)

SELF-ASSESSMENT EXERCISES

6.1 Discuss the Rawlsian theory of justice and briefly comment on its relevance to the political economy of South Africa.

6.2 Outline the median voter theorem and explain its importance to the successful application of a majority voting system.

6.3 Do you agree with the contention that majority rule does not necessarily produce outcomes representative of the majority view? Discuss with reference to the impossibility theorem and the phenomenon of vote trading.

6.4 Discuss the theory of optimal voting rules and briefly comment on its relevance to the future of majority rule.

6.5 Explain how the maximising behaviour of politicians could contribute to an oversupply of public goods.

6.6 In what way could the behaviour of bureaucrats cause 'government failure'?

6.7 Explain the meaning of 'rent-seeking' and show how it could undermine efficiency in the economy.

PART

2

Public expenditure

Chapter
SEVEN

Philip Black, Krige Siebrits, and Theo van der Merwe

Public expenditure and growth

Part 1 of this book explained in theoretical terms why governments should mobilise and spend scarce resources in a typical market-oriented economy. In this chapter we turn to 'real world' aspects of government expenditure in South Africa. We want to find answers to the following pertinent questions: What does the Constitution have to say about government expenditure? How much money is spent annually by government entities? What forms do such spending take and what services are provided? How has the composition of government expenditure changed over time, and how do these trends compare with those in other countries? Why has government expenditure grown so much over time? And, most importantly, how does government expenditure affect the economy over the medium to long term?

As indicated in Chapter 1, these questions are particularly topical in view of the economic challenges facing South Africa and the global context within which they have to be addressed. In this chapter we first look at the growth of government expenditure and at the change in its composition, both in this country and elsewhere in the world, before we discuss some of the theories explaining these changes. In the last section we turn our attention to the long-term effects of government activity on the economy.

Once you have studied this chapter, you should be able to:
▶ comment on the implications that the Constitution has on government expenditure in South Africa
▶ discuss salient trends in the size, growth, and composition of government expenditure in South Africa
▶ identify the main similarities and differences between government expenditure patterns in South Africa and other countries

> ▶ compare and contrast two or more of the theories that explain the growth of the government sector and indicate whether they have any relevance for South Africa
> ▶ consider the long-term effects of government spending in terms of 'new growth theory'
> ▶ discuss the role of infrastructure investment in the economy.

7.1 The constitutional framework

The Constitution is the supreme law of the Republic of South Africa. As such, its provisions for taxation and government expenditure are the basic contours within which the budgetary policies of the government are formulated.

7.1.1 The Constitution and public goods

The South African Constitution contains many provisions that directly or indirectly impact upon the extent and composition of government expenditure. At a very general level these provisions depend on how the government sector and its primary functions are defined in the Constitution. Government functions are derived from, and structured according to, the constitutional distinction between the legislative, executive, and judicial branches of government; the national, provincial, and local levels of government; the security services and certain constitutional entitlements (discussed below); and statutory bodies such as the Public Protector, the Human Rights Commission, the Auditor-General, and the Independent Electoral Commission. By granting powers and assigning functions to such institutions, the Constitution implicitly charges government with the task of

maintaining them and providing for the necessary public funding. Failing to do so would indeed be unconstitutional.

In addition, the government of the day is constitutionally obliged to provide or extend the provision of specified basic goods and services. The clearest examples of such provisions are found in the Bill of Rights, which entrenches the right of each citizen to adequate housing, healthcare, food, water, social security, and education. The Constitution (Section 26(2)) is explicit on this issue: '...the state should take reasonable legislative and other measures, within its available resources, to achieve the progressive realisation of this right'.

It is worth noting that these rights generally pertain to mixed and merit goods, rather than only to pure public goods (see Chapter 3), which partly confirms our earlier point that pure public goods are extremely rare in practice. But it is also indicative of modern thinking about the relative importance of the public sector in promoting sustained economic growth – a point to which we return in the last section of this chapter.

7.1.2 Constitutional entitlements

The rights to certain goods and services conferred by the Constitution could be regarded as constitutional entitlements. What are the practical implications of such entitlements for the way governments manage their own budgets? As we have pointed out, the wording of these entitlements in the Constitution does acknowledge that governments are subject to budgetary constraints, but many economists feel uneasy about the vagueness of phrases such as 'reasonable measures' and 'within its available resources.' They believe that such wording gives the government too much discretionary power that could threaten the macroeconomic sustainability of fiscal policy. Experts in human rights law also differ in their opinions on how enforceable these rights are in practice. To what extent can the government of a developing country like South Africa be held responsible for the provision of housing, social security, and other basic services to all its citizens? Which of these rights should be accorded priority when trade-offs arise?

From time to time the Constitutional Court has to respond to some of these very difficult questions. In an early case of this nature the Court ruled in November 1997 that a South African kidney patient was not entitled to receive expensive treatment at the state's expense. Two constitutional principles were involved in this case, namely the right to live and the right to have access to healthcare services. One of the grounds for the ruling was that the latter right is subject to the 'availability of resources.' In a number of subsequent cases, the Constitutional Court also refrained from granting individual claims and rather took the view that the government should adopt a comprehensive plan that provides in a reasonable manner for the progressive realisation of the rights in the constitution.

From a fiscal point of view, a strong case can be made for a ruling that the government's obligations to its citizens should be extended to include future generations. This means that any current attempt at fulfilling these obligations should take full account of the impact it is likely to have on the future growth of GDP, and hence on the growth of government revenue, since the latter is clearly a necessary condition for maintaining the supply of public services over time. At the same time, however, it can be argued that the future growth of GDP depends on the current provision of services such as education and healthcare. The matter is therefore far from simple. A steady and consistent supply of these services whereby backlogs and future demands are met within reasonable timeframes may help to resolve the conflict between constitutional entitlements and macroeconomic affordability. In this regard, medium-term expenditure frameworks may fulfil an important role, as we shall see in Chapter 15.

7.2 The size, growth and composition of public expenditure

In Chapter 1 we provided some indication of the size of the public sector in South Africa. Table 1.1 showed that the public sector had expanded considerably during the past few decades. In this section we take a closer look at trends in general government expenditure since 1960. As we explained in Section 1.2.1 of Chapter 1, general government spending includes the outlays of the national government, provincial governments, local authorities, and extra-budgetary institutions, but excludes the spending of public corporations such as Eskom, Telkom, and Transnet.

7.2.1 Size and growth of public expenditure

In this section we provide data for two measures of **general government expenditure**, namely the total amount of resources used and the total amount of resources mobilised (the concepts of resource use and resource mobilisation were explained in Chapter 1, Section 1.2.2).

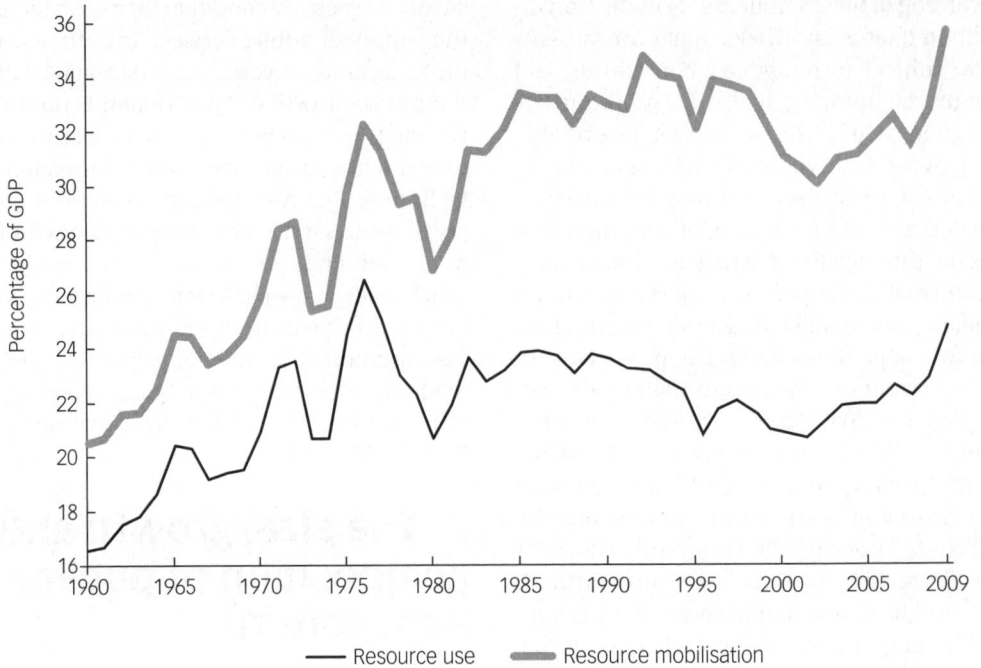

Figure 7.1 The size and growth of general government expenditure in South Africa[1]

We first look at the size and growth of **general government resource use** at constant 2005 prices.[2] This measure suggests that general government expenditure grew significantly in South Africa since 1960: real resource use increased from R66,3 billion in 1960 to R426,8 billion in 2009. On average, real resource use therefore grew at a brisk rate of 3,9 per cent per annum. This figure, however, masks a sharp decline in the average rates of growth in the decades from 1960 to 2000, followed by renewed growth in the early years of the new millennium. In the 1960s general government resource use increased at a rapid rate of 7,2 per cent per annum in real terms, but this slowed to 4,1 per cent in the 1970s, 2,4 per cent in the

1980s, and only 0,2 per cent in the 1990s. From 2000 to 2009, by contrast, real resource by the general government increased by 5,2 per cent per annum.

How did this pattern of growth affect the size of the general government sector relative to that of the South African economy as a whole? Figure 7.1 answers this question by showing **general government** resource use and **resource mobilisation** as percentages of the gross domestic product (GDP) at current market prices from 1960 to 2009. Over the period as a whole, general government expenditure clearly grew significantly in relative terms: resource use increased from 16,6 per cent of GDP to 24,8 per cent and resource mobilisation from 20,5 per cent to 35,8 per cent. However, the graph also emphasises that government spending did not grow uniformly or uninterruptedly. Resource use reached a peak of 26,5 per cent of GDP in 1976, while the broader measure, resource mobilisation, peaked at 34,7 per cent of GDP

---

[1] The data were obtained from the electronic database of the South African Reserve Bank (available online at http://www.resbank.co.za/Publications/QuarterlyBulletins/Pages/QBOnlinestatsquery.aspx).

[2] Data at constant 2005 prices are not available for the resource mobilisation measure.

Table 7.1 The economic composition of general government expenditure in South Africa, 1960–2009a

Item	% of total			% of GDP		
	1994	2001	2009	1994	2001	2009
Compensation of employees	32,3	37,8	33,2	11,9	12,6	12,1
Purchases of goods and services	22,2	24,5	26,4	8,2	8,1	9,6
Interest on public debt	13,9	15,3	7,0	5,2	5,1	2,5
Subsidies	4,8	1,4	2,8	1,8	0,5	1,0
Social benefits	10,8	8,2	10,7	4,0	2,7	3,9
Other expenses	8,5	6,5	9,3	3,1	2,1	3,4
Cash payments for operating activities (subtotal)	**92,6**	**93,6**	**89,6**	**34,2**	**31,2**	**32,5**
Purchases of non-financial assets (subtotal)	**7,4**	**6,4**	**10,4**	**2,7**	**2,1**	**3,8**
Total cash paymentsb	**100,0**	**100,0**	**100,0**	**37,0**	**33,3**	**36,3**

Notes: a Government finance statistics data, fiscal years ending 31 March.
         b Figures may not add up due to rounding.
Source: Calculated from South African Reserve Bank, *Quarterly Bulletin* (various issues).

in 1992. After reaching these peaks, both measures decreased, on balance, as percentages of GDP until 2001. Thereafter, both measures of the size of the general government sector regained their earlier upward momentum.

To summarise: general government expenditure grew significantly in South Africa from 1960 to 2009, both in real terms and as a percentage of GDP. Thus, in 2009 the general government sector was responsible for a markedly higher portion of aggregate expenditure in South Africa than was the case in 1960. In Sections 7.4 and 7.5 of this chapter we will outline various theories that try to explain why government spending grows in absolute terms and (or) relative to the rest of the economy. Chapter 15 explains why the growth rate of general government spending slowed so markedly in South Africa until 2001 before accelerating to growth rates last seen in the 1970s.

Significant changes in the composition of general government expenditure accompanied these trends in its size and growth. We now provide a synopsis of these changes.

7.2.2 The changing economic composition of public expenditure

Table 7.1 summarises trends in the **economic classification of government expenditure**, which distinguishes between the current and capital components of total outlays. The various expenditure categories are expressed as percentages of total general government expenditure and of GDP in the fiscal years 1994, 2001 and 2009.[3]

In 2009, cash payments for operating activities (formerly known as current

---

[3] In South Africa fiscal years run from 1 April to 31 March. The fiscal year 2009 therefore represents the period from 1 April 2008 to 31 March 2009.

expenditure) accounted for 89,6 per cent of general government spending in South Africa and purchases of non-financial assets (outlays for the acquisition of fixed capital assets, land, stock, and intangible assets – formerly known as investment) for the remaining 10,4 per cent. In descending order, the largest categories of cash payments for operating activities were compensation of employees (the government's wage bill), purchases of other goods and services (for example stationery, computers, vehicles, maintenance of capital assets), social benefits paid (mainly welfare payments such as old-age pensions or child support grants), other expenses and interest on public debt.

Table 7.1 shows that cash payments for operating activities (i.e. current outlays) increased from 92,6 per cent of total cash payments in 1994 to 93,6 per cent in 2001; over the same period, purchases of non-financial assets (i.e. capital spending) decreased from 7,4 per cent of total cash payments to 6,4 per cent. This represented a continuation of a long-term trend in general government expenditure highlighted in Chapter 1 of this book: Figure 1.1 indicated that current expenditure by the general government sector (the sum of consumption expenditure and transfer payments) increased from an average of 15,4 per cent of GDP in the period 1960–1969 to an average of 30,8 per cent in the period 1990–1994, while investment fell sharply from an average of 7,6 per cent of GDP in the period 1960–1969 to an average of 2,9 per cent in the period 1990–1994. It should be kept in mind that important components of infrastructure investment are not reflected in these numbers because such spending is undertaken by public corporations that do not form part of the general government sector (the outlays of Eskom and Transnet on electricity and rail infrastructure are prime examples). Moreover, the economic effects of government investment depend not on its extent but also on its nature: in the long run, the construction of power stations and roads, for example, is clearly more important for the promotion of economic growth than the construction of new buildings for government departments. Nonetheless, most economists believe that the decline in general government spending on economic and social infrastructure has hindered economic growth in South Africa. The fact that purchases of non-financial assets increased from 6,4 percent of total cash payments in 2001 to 10,4 per cent in 2009 (i.e. from 2,1 per cent of GDP to 3,8 per cent) is therefore significant, even though this recovery in investment spending is not yet sufficient in scope.

From 1994 to 2001, general government cash payments fell by 3,7 percentage points of GDP and the GDP shares of all the spending components, except compensation of employees, decreased. During this period of tight expenditure constraints the government gave high priority to outlays on interest on the public debt,[4] compensation of employees and purchases of goods and services: expenditure on these items increased as percentages of general government cash payments, while the spending shares of the other components decreased. By contrast, compensation of employees and interest on public debt were the only components that did not increase as percentages of total cash payments between 2001 and 2009 (the relative decrease in interest payments resulted from smaller budget deficits and lower interest rates, but efforts to restrain the growth of the wage bill at times led to conflict between the government and public sector labour unions). The reality that general government cash payments increased by 3 percentage points of GDP meant that the increases in the total spending shares of the other expenditure components (purchases of goods and

---

[4] Legislation decrees that the government should service the public debt before undertaking other expenditures.

services, subsidies, social benefits, purchases of non-financial assets and other expenses) also represented growth relative to the size of the economy as a whole.

7.2.3 Functional shifts in public expenditure

The **functional classification of government expenditure** refers to the amounts spent on the different goods and services provided by government. Table 7.2 contains data on the functional composition of general government spending in the fiscal years 1994, 2001 and 2009.[5]

In 2009 social services accounted for 49,3 per cent of general government spending in South Africa, making it by far the largest functional category. Social services expenditure includes spending on education, health, social protection, housing, community services, recreation, and culture. The second and third largest functional categories were general public services (interest payments and other public debt transactions, as well as the outlays of departments such as the Presidency, Foreign Affairs, Public Works, and Provincial and Local Government, including transfers from the central government to local authorities) and protection services (which consist of government spending on defence, policing, correctional services, and the justice system). The other expenditure category, namely economic services, encompasses the outlays of government departments that oversee and

[5] Data for the fiscal years before 2005 were compiled by Statistics South Africa on the basis of the 1986 version of the Government Finance Statistics (GFS) Manual, whereas data for later years reflect the conventions of the 2001 version. Hence, the two parts of the series are not strictly comparable and caution should be exercised when interpreting the information in Table 7.2. Note also that the total expenditure-to-GDP ratios in Tables 7.1 and 7.2 differ. According to the South African Reserve Bank, the main cause of the discrepancy is the exclusion from the functional classification of general government expenditure of data on the trading accounts of local governments.

assist various sectors of the economy (such as agriculture, mining, manufacturing, and transport), as well as those that are charged with cross-sectoral issues such as labour and technology.

As was indicated before, the period from 1994 to 2001 was one of fiscal restraint during which government spending fell markedly as a percentage of GDP. The GDP shares of all the functional categories except public order and safety decreased during this period. By comparing the total spending shares of the various categories in 1994 and 2001, one can get a sense of which items the authorities tried to 'protect' in terms of resources during this period of tight spending constraints. Apart from public debt transactions, these higher-priority items included outlays on public order and safety, education, health and transport and communication. The spending categories whose shares of total general government expenditure decreased most markedly were other general government services, defence, social protection, other social services and other economic services. Some of these changes had begun earlier: the period from 1983 to 1994, for example, already saw significant shifts in the composition of public spending away from economic services (mainly subsidies to farmers and businesses) and the defence component of protection services to social services and the public order and safety component of protection services (see Siebrits, 1998: 323–330). These shifts reflected efforts to increase the redistributive thrust of fiscal policy and the skill level of the labour force, the ending of South Africa's involvement in the Namibian and Angolan conflicts, rising crime, and a more market-oriented approach to economic development in which heavy subsidisation of particular economic activities was no longer seen as necessary.

From 2001 to 2009, more rapid growth in general government expenditure facilitated

Table 7.2 The functional composition of general government expenditure in South Africa, 1994–2009a

Item	% of total			% of GDP		
	1994	2001	2009	1994	2001	2009
Public debt transactions	13,5	16,0	6,9	5,0	4,9	2,3
Other general public services	14,2	10,1	16,0	5,2	3,1	5,4
General public services (subtotal)	**27,7**	**26,1**	**22,9**	**10,2**	**7,9**	**7,8**
Defence	6,5	5,2	4,1	2,4	1,6	1,4
Public order and safety	8,0	9,8	10,9	2,9	3,0	3,7
Protection services (subtotal)	**14,6**	**15,0**	**15,0**	**5,3**	**4,5**	**5,1**
Education	18,3	20,4	18,3	6,7	6,2	6,2
Health	8,9	10,3	10,4	3,3	3,1	3,5
Social protection	13,0	11,7	13,6	4,8	3,5	4,6
Other social services	5,1	4,3	7,1	1,9	1,3	2,4
Social services (subtotal)	**45,3**	**46,7**	**49,3**	**16,6**	**14,2**	**16,8**
Transport and communication	5,4	5,5	6,7	2,0	1,7	2,3
Other economic services	7,0	4,7	5,4	2,6	1,4	1,8
Economic services (subtotal)	**12,4**	**10,2**	**12,0**	**4,6**	**3,1**	**4,1**
Total expenditure[b]	**100,0**	**100,0**	**100,0**	**36,7**	**30,3**	**34,0**

Notes: [a] Government finance statistics data, fiscal years ending 31 March.
[b] Figures may not add up due to rounding.
Source: Calculated from South African Reserve Bank, *Quarterly Bulletin* (various issues).

growth in the GDP shares of almost all the functional categories. The only exceptions were education spending (which remained constant as a percentage of GDP), public debt transactions and defence outlays. Government spending on other general public services, social protection and other social services (especially housing and community amenities) increased significantly during this period as percentages of total general government expenditure and of GDP. The comparatively slower growth in outlays on public order and safety, education and health

did not imply that the government no longer regarded these items as spending priorities; instead, it reflected a growing emphasis on increasing the efficiency – that is, the ratio between inputs and outputs – of these large expenditure categories (see Chapter 8).

The net results of these developments have been that general government spending is now markedly more oriented towards the delivery of social services and the maintenance of public order and safety than was the case two decades ago. At the same time, the priority given to defence against external threats has clearly declined, while that of economic services has partially recovered after a sharp decline in the 1980s and 1990s. Authorities are also turning their attention increasingly to initiatives aimed at improving the efficiency and effectiveness of government programmes.

The links between trends in the economic and functional compositions of total outlays are now apparent. There is a close relationship between rates of growth in labour-intensive and supplies-intensive functions, such as public order and safety and education, and rates of growth in the government wage bill and of spending on other goods and services. Similarly, the extent of growth in transfers to households is closely associated with the importance assigned to social protection services. Changes in the government spending shares of subsidies and purchases of non-financial assets are major determinants of rates of growth in outlays on economic services.

7.3 **Comparisons with other countries**

For much of the twentieth century, increases in per capita incomes were accompanied by absolute and relative growth in government spending. One time-series study (Tanzi and Schuknecht, 1997) found that general government expenditure in the industrialised countries increased from levels of 10 per cent of GDP or less in 1870 to between 45 per cent and 50 per cent of GDP in 1994. Government spending also increased markedly in most developing countries in the 1960s, 1970s and 1980s (Lindauer and Velenchik, 1992). We discuss some of the theoretical explanations for such growth in government expenditure in the next two sections.

By contrast, the last quarter of the twentieth century was characterised by a fundamental reconsideration of the economic role of government. Various factors gave rise to this development, including the collapse of the controlled economies of the former Soviet Union, Central and Eastern Europe and parts of the developing world (notably Sub-Saharan Africa); mounting evidence that the expansion of the public sector beyond a certain point is more likely to contribute to macroeconomic problems and the erosion of economic incentives and personal freedoms than to meaningful improvement in the values of indicators of social and economic progress; and growing support for more market-based approaches to economic development. Halting or reversing the expansion of the public sector became a policy objective in many countries, and empirical studies (e.g. Fan and Rao, 2003; Tanzi, 2005) show that government spending did in fact decrease as a percentage of GDP in several of them. During the so-called Great Recession from the end of 2007 onwards, many governments launched fiscal stimulus packages to counteract the effects of severe economic downturns on production, demand and employment. Most of these packages included public spending programmes that raised government-expenditure-to-GDP ratios. It remains to be seen if these increases will be reversed as planned (the intention usually was that stimulus packages should be of a temporary nature), or provide more longer-lasting boosts to public spending levels via the ratchet effect outlined in Section 7.4.2 below.

International cross-section evidence on the composition of government expenditure at different levels of development (Van der Berg, 1991) have been summarised as follows:

▶ In low-income countries the bulk of government spending is typically directed at capital investment in the infrastructure, stimulation of industrial development through export subsidies and other incentives, and the establishment of primary education and healthcare systems.

▶ Middle-income countries give priority to education, healthcare, and research and development, and also usually begin to develop a social security system.

▶ High-income countries are characterised by huge increases in the share of transfer payments (especially social security-related ones) that are typically compensated for by reduced public investment.

Economic development is thus associated with a shift in the economic composition of government expenditure from capital expenditure to consumption spending, including transfer payments. The functional counterpart of this trend is a shift from protection and economic services to social services. In an authoritative study on the issue, Saunders and Klau (1985: 16) reached the following conclusion:

> *The structure of government expenditure has thus shifted away from the provision of more traditional collective goods (defence, public administration, and economic services) towards those associated with the growth of the welfare state (education, health, and income maintenance), which provide benefits on an individual rather than collective basis and where redistributive objectives are more dominant.*

The longer-run pattern of change in government outlays in South Africa broadly corresponds with these international trends. As indicated, South Africa has also experienced a shift from capital expenditure and economic services towards consumption spending and social services. These compositional trends have obvious distributional

effects, but recent advances in the theory of economic growth suggest that government spending on education and health also brings efficiency gains in the form of higher levels of human capital (see Section 7.6).

However, there are also interesting peculiarities to the evolution of government spending in South Africa. These include the following:[6]

▶ The shift in the economic composition of expenditure from capital to current outlays has left South Africa with a relatively high level of government consumption spending. In 2008, the ratio of general government consumption to GDP was higher in South Africa than in 111 of the 139 other countries for which data were available.

▶ As far as the functional composition of expenditure is concerned, public spending on education is also relatively high in South Africa. In 2008, public spending on education in South Africa amounted to 5,1 per cent of GDP. This ratio exceeded the averages for lower-middle-income countries (4,0 per cent of GDP) and upper-middle-income countries (4,6 per cent of GDP), and was only slightly lower than the average for high-income countries (5,4 per cent of GDP). South Africa's level of public spending on healthcare in 2008 (3,6 per cent of GDP) was significantly higher than the average for lower-middle-income countries (2,7 per cent of GDP) and marginally higher than that for upper-middle-income countries (3,5 per cent of GDP). In high-income countries, however, public spending on healthcare is significantly higher than in middle-income countries such as South Africa: in 2008, the average level for high-income countries was 6,9 per cent of GDP. It is also notable that South

---

[6] The data quoted are from World Bank (2010: 33–35; 120–122; 254–256; 316–318).

Africa is spending a relatively small portion of its national income on defence. In 2008, such spending amounted to 1,4 per cent of GDP, which was significantly lower than the averages for lower-middle-income countries (2 per cent of GDP), upper-middle-countries (2 per cent of GDP) and high-income countries (2,6 per cent of GDP).

Hence, international comparisons tentatively suggest that the scope for further reallocation of resources from capital to current spending and from protection and economic services to social services in South Africa is limited. Further increases in social spending would require that the burden of interest on the public debt be reduced and the crime situation be brought under control. However, it is questionable whether South Africa needs to invest even larger portions of its national income on publicly financed education and healthcare. Government spending on these items is

already relatively high by international standards, and the real challenge for the future is for government to utilise its existing education and health budgets more efficiently than before. Future increases in these budgets could perhaps more appropriately be achieved through additional revenues obtained from sustained real growth in per capita income – as illustrated in Box 7.1.

7.4 Reasons for the growth of government: macro models

In Chapter 1 we pointed out that there are different ways of measuring the size of the government; one is to express government expenditure as a percentage of gross domestic product. We saw that over the past five decades the South African government has steadily increased its share in the economy, in terms of both the use and the

---

BOX 7.1 Why economic growth is crucial for expanding service delivery

The relative effects on per-capita government expenditure of sustained economic growth can be illustrated with the aid of an example. Let us compare public spending on education in South Africa and Japan (the data are from World Bank, 2010). In 2008 the ratios of public expenditure on education to GNP were 5,1 per cent for South Africa and 3,6 per cent for Japan. South Africa's GDP per capita was US$5 820 and that of Japan US$38 130. In Japan the public sector therefore expended US$1 373 per person on education, compared to South Africa's US$297. To achieve the same level of public spending on education in per capita terms South Africa would have been required to

spend almost 24 per cent of its national income on education. Since the situation is much the same for healthcare, social security, and many other services, it is clear that South Africa (and other developing countries) cannot reach the same per-capita levels of government spending by simply increasing the portion of national income devoted to such spending.

That would require extremely high tax rates or unsustainable levels of borrowing. To achieve higher levels of government spending in per capita terms it is clearly more important to raise per capita income than to increase the share of national income devoted to government social spending.

mobilisation of national resources. From the information provided at the beginning of this chapter it appears as though the share of government has more or less stabilised at certain levels in the nineties of the previous century, but has resumed its increase over the first couple of years of the new millennium.

South Africa is not unique in this regard. Both industrial and developing countries have experienced an increase in the share of government in the economy and various theories have been developed in an attempt to explain this global phenomenon. Before we discuss these theories, two important qualifications should be made. Firstly, government expenditure growth is not necessarily the same as a growing share of government in the economy. Some of the theories (for example that of Brown and Jackson discussed in the next section) provide an explanation for the phenomenon of expenditure growth, irrespective of whether it is accompanied by an increasing share. Most of the theories under discussion, however, deal with the issue of an expanding government sector relative to the rest of the economy.

Secondly, it is important to distinguish between the empirical issue of expenditure growth and the reasons for it, on the one hand, and the normative question of what the appropriate size of government should be. The question of whether government is too big or too small is clearly a complex if not ambiguous one: the answer is bound to vary between different countries and cultures and, for any given country, is likely also to vary over time, as the sections below explain. Following Brown and Jackson (1990: 120), we distinguish between **macro models**, which tend to explain the broad patterns of government expenditure with regard to aggregate variables such as GDP, and (in the next section) **micro models**, which focus on the decision-making behaviour of public individuals and institutions.

7.4.1 Wagner and the stages-of-development approach

Both Adolph Wagner (1883) and the subsequent '**stages-of-development**' model developed by Musgrave (1969) and Rostow (1971) explain how government expenditure tends to increase when a country develops from a subsistence or traditional economy to an industrialised economy. During the first or early stages of development Wagner emphasised the need for government to create and maintain internal and external law and order and also set in place the critical legal and administrative institutions necessary to cut the costs of doing business. According to the stages-of-development approach, it is also important for government to get investment going in the first place. During the first stage, the formal sector of the economy is still relatively small and, as a result, government may have to participate actively by providing the basic infrastructure (e.g. roads, railways, and harbours) necessary to create an environment conducive to economic development. The implication of the first stage for government expenditure is that capital expenditures will feature prominently.

During the middle stages of development, government will continue to supply investment goods while private investment will also start to take off, partly due to the positive pecuniary external effects of government investment undertaken during the first stage (see Section 7.6). However, the development of the private sector may cause certain market failures, including externalities, monopoly pricing and high-density living conditions, that government would have to address, thereby giving rise to further increases in government expenditure.

In the last stage of development capital expenditure by government, expressed as a percentage of GDP, usually decreases because most of the necessary infrastructure is already in place. At this stage, however, expenditure on education, health, welfare programmes, and social security will tend to increase due to the high-income elasticity of demand for such expenditures. The result is a continuous increase in the share of government in the economy.

During the early stages of South Africa's industrialisation, the government (through state enterprises and public corporations) was heavily involved in major capital projects such as railways, harbours, roads, and public works, as well as in business activities such as the creation of Sasol and Iscor, which were subsequently privatised. The growth in public investment expenditure between the 1930s and 1960s, for example, corresponds with the first and middle stages discussed above. The subsequent decline in public investment is not, however, an indication that South Africa had entered the last stage of development: it is perhaps better understood in terms of Peacock and Wiseman's displacement effect or in terms of Meltzer and Richard's hypothesis (see the next two sections). Note in any case that many rural areas in the country can hardly be said to have entered the first stage of development, in the sense that public investment has hardly begun in these areas.

7.4.2 **Peacock and Wiseman's displacement effect**

Peacock and Wiseman (1967) used a political theory to explain the influence of political events on public expenditure. They did acknowledge a point made by Wagner, that is, that '...government expenditure depends broadly on revenues raised by taxation' (Peacock and Wiseman, 1967: 26). Governments would therefore be in a position to continue increasing their own expenditures and expanding their role in the economy – provided their economies continued to grow through industrialisation. On the other hand, individuals may not be prepared to continue paying higher taxes in order to finance such increased expenditure. In a democracy, government has to respect the wishes of the majority (50 per cent of voters plus one). Under normal circumstances government expenditure would therefore only increase when it is strictly necessary, and it can be expected that governments would take into account the possible resistance of voters against higher tax rates.

Social upheavals or disturbances may, however, change the established conceptions of the public. Examples of such upheavals are the two world wars, the Great Depression, the war on terrorism and the recent 'great recession'. National crises of such magnitude may cause a rapid increase in government expenditure, since they may convince taxpayers that higher taxes are necessary to prevent a national disaster. Peacock and Wiseman called this phenomenon the **displacement effect**, as certain government expenditures (e.g. war-related expenses) displace private expenditures as well as other government expenditures (such as non-war related expenses).

After a crisis had subsided, government expenditure could be expected to return to its pre-crisis level. According to Peacock and Wiseman (1967: 27), however, this was unlikely and government expenditure could even remain at the new post-crisis level, the reason being that taxpayers would become accustomed to the higher levels of taxation and accept them as a part of life.

The displacement effect of Peacock and Wiseman may help to explain the growth in government expenditure in South Africa. The previous political dispensation in South Africa resulted in a massive military build-up and excursions into neighbouring countries amidst widespread social unrest inside the country, especially since 1976. These crises triggered rapid increases in expenditures on protective services (defence and police), and also on social services. Expenditure on protective services at one stage (1983) reached almost 20 per cent of the national budget (see Table 7.2). Also, the share in total expenditure for education started to increase since the unrest at schools in 1976. It is, therefore, possible to argue that both social upheaval and the conflict situation on the borders contributed to the growth in government expenditure in South Africa during the period up to 1994. However, one may also argue that displacement pressures in South Africa were dampened by a redirecting of government expenditure (e.g. from economic services to social services). In a recent study, Lusinyan and Thornton (2007), came to the conclusion that there is some evidence that the displacement effect did in fact occur in South Africa since 1960.

7.4.3 The Meltzer-Richard hypothesis

Redistributive policies may have an important impact on the growth of government expenditure. Meltzer and Richard (1981) developed a general equilibrium model in which majority voting determines the magnitude of income distribution and, as a result, also the share of government expenditure in the economy. According to this model, the most important reason for the increase in government expenditure can be attributed to an extension of the franchise, which brings about a change in the **median** (or the decisive) **voter** (see discussion of median voter theorem in Chapter 6).

Meltzer and Richard (1981: 43) argued that the median voter plays an important role in determining the size of the government sector in a democracy. For example, if

all voters were ordered from left to right according to their income with the individual with the lowest income on the far left-hand side and the individual with the highest income on the far right-hand side, the median voter would be the one right in the middle. Therefore, if there were for example only five voters in a country, with incomes of R3 000, R4 000, R6 000, R15 000, and R25 000 per annum respectively, the median voter would be the individual with an income of R6 000. The median voter is important because in a two-party democracy he or she will determine which party will win the election. Both parties therefore try to gain the support of the median voter and will need the support of three individuals (including the median voter) for this purpose.

According to the model of Meltzer and Richard, there will be pressure for redistributing income if the income of the median voter lies below the average income. Redistribution would benefit the median voter and he or she will therefore vote for the party that proposes a programme of redistribution. In our example the income of the median voter (R6 000) lies below the average income (R10 600). To gain the support of the median voter, parties will emphasise redistributive policies that could result in higher taxes and higher expenditure on social services. The median voter effectively determines the tax level.

However, Meltzer and Richard's model (1981: 916) does not allow for unlimited redistribution, because they assume that voters are aware of the disincentive effects associated with high taxes and redistribution. The rational median voter will thus choose the tax rate that maximises his or her utility, while taking into account the possible impact on the economic behaviour of other individuals (i.e. their decisions to work and consume). If the median voter chooses a relatively high tax rate other individuals may decide to work less (consume more leisure)

to Baumol, technological changes do not have such an important effect on productivity in the non-progressive sector as they do in the progressive sector. It will, for example, be counterproductive to try and increase productivity in health services by halving the time individuals spend in an operating theatre or hospital. As a result there are only sporadic improvements in productivity in the non-progressive sector compared to relatively rapid increases in the progressive sector.

Baumol argues further that there cannot be too big a difference in the wages and salaries between the two sectors, otherwise employees would be leaving the non-progressive sector to join the progressive sector. This raises the relative costs of the non-progressive sector because salary increases are not accompanied by the same increases in productivity as in the progressive sector. Baumol (1967: 426) thus came to the conclusion that 'the costs of even a constant level of activity on the part of government can be expected to grow constantly higher.' Furthermore, if production in the non-progressive sector has to be maintained relative to that in the progressive sector, it will imply that a larger share of the labour market will have to be employed in the former sector, which could have negative effects on economic growth. One point of critique, however, is that Baumol may have underestimated the opportunities for technological advancement in the public sector, for example through the computerisation of certain services.

As we saw in Table 7.1, by far the largest share of government expenditure in South Africa goes towards the remuneration of employees. Education, health services, and policing, to mention but a few, all require labour inputs as an end in itself. The structure of government expenditure thus corresponds well with Baumol's notion of unbalanced productivity growth. However,

the Baumol hypothesis has not been tested empirically in South Africa or in other African countries; no firm conclusions can therefore be drawn about its relevance to government expenditure growth in the African continent.

7.5.2 Brown and Jackson's microeconomic model

The purpose of microeconomic models of growth in government expenditure is to study the factors influencing the demand and supply of public goods and services. Brown and Jackson (1990: 127) have developed a microeconomic model to derive the levels of publicly provided goods and services by, inter alia, taking the preferences, the income, and the tax rate of the median voter – all determinants of demand – into account, as well as the costs of the goods and services in question. Since the scope of this book does not permit a detailed description of this model, we will only briefly discuss some of the factors that may have an influence on the demand and supply of such goods, and hence on the level of government expenditure.

It often happens that government expenditure increases without there being a corresponding change in the level or perceived quality of service. Although such a state of affairs can be easily viewed as a sign of inefficiency, Brown and Jackson (1990: 137) argue that there may be other forces at work. It may in fact be the result of changes in the **service environment**. For example, an increase in the level of crime, as we have witnessed in South Africa, calls for increased policing and additional funding merely to arrest that increase and ensure that the same level of law and order as before is maintained. If a sufficient increase in expenditure did not occur, the service could be seen to have deteriorated as the service environment has become worse.

Changes in the size and density of the population and its age structure may also have an influence on the service environment. Population growth may lead to an increase in the demand for publicly provided goods and services. As far as pure public goods such as defence are concerned, we have seen that the marginal social cost of one additional consumer is zero by definition. However, governments do not only provide pure public goods but also mixed and merit goods such as education and health services. In such instances, increases in the population will lead either to higher levels of expenditure or to a drop in standards. On the other hand, population growth may also imply a decrease in the unit cost of such services because payment for those services will be shared by more individuals (i.e. economies of scale). If the relative price of services decreases, it may be an incentive to government to supply more of those services. However, population growth and human migration may also lead to changes in the density of the population, which may cause congestion and add to the costs of government. The fight against the HIV/Aids pandemic, malaria, and tuberculosis should also put pressure on government expenditure.

Another factor that may influence the level of government expenditure is the quality of goods demanded by the median voter. To define quality is not always easy. According to Brown and Jackson (1990: 139), however, a good or service is of superior quality if it requires more inputs in its production process than a good requiring fewer of those inputs, *ceteris paribus*. For example, a hospital which has 500 patients and 100 nurses should provide a service of superior quality to a hospital with 500 patients and 50 nurses. Increases in quality may therefore put further pressure on government expenditure if the additional costs cannot be recovered from the users.

On the whole, it would seem that the micro model of Brown and Jackson has identified and combined important and relevant factors that may influence the supply and demand of publicly provided goods and services. Their model provides a useful starting point for anyone interested in modelling government expenditure in African countries and identifying the explanatory variables that will determine future trends in government expenditure.

7.5.3 Role of politicians, bureaucrats, and interest groups

We have already discussed the role played by individual agents and interest groups in influencing government decisions and government expenditure. Politicians, bureaucrats, and other interest groups are often powerful enough to pressure government in a direction that is detrimental to the social welfare of the broader community. Their behaviour may result in a higher than optimal level of government expenditure, thereby contributing to the growth of government's share in the economy at the expense of the private sector.

Apart from engaging in various forms of vote-trading, as discussed in Chapter 6, there are many other ways in which the vote-maximising behaviour of **politicians** can bring about an increase in government expenditure. They may grant wage and salary increases to state employees just before an election, in order to gain the support of what is often a numerically significant and powerful constituency. From a macroeconomic point of view, the ruling party may be tempted to relax its fiscal and monetary policies in an attempt to stimulate the economy before an election. Such a relaxation may well please voters who stand to secure short-term gains in the form of lower interest rates, lower taxes, and better job prospects, and they may well respond by lending their support to the ruling party. But populist macroeconomic policies are not sustainable in the long term, giving rise to inflationary pressures and balance of payments problems, and ultimately calling for even tighter monetary and fiscal policies than had been the case prior to the election.

We also saw in Chapter 6 that **bureaucrats** tend to maximise the size of their departmental budgets, partly to help build their own personal 'empires', and that they are able to convince politicians of their actions as they are better informed about the activities of their own departments. The net result is a bureaucracy that is larger than the optimal size. In South Africa we have seen how the so-called homelands policy of the past and the increase in the number of provinces after the 1994 election have contributed to a duplication of government activities which has put additional pressure on government expenditure.

Individuals with shared interests are often able to organise themselves into powerful **interest groups** and put pressure on government to implement programmes and pass legislation that will meet their own parochial interests. South African farmers have formed an important lobbying group that has benefited greatly from agricultural subsidies and other forms of support over the years. The same is true of labour unions and organised business, and the government may well be tempted to grant them special favours such as tax allowances which will erode the revenue base of government. The persistent recurrence of such actions can also contribute to the growth of government expenditure in the economy.

7.6 Government and the economy: long-term effects

In the preceding sections we looked at the growth of the public sector in the economy and discussed the reasons for this growth. We saw that there are various theories explaining the secular growth of government in virtually all economies across the world. We now shift our focus to the economic effects – rather than the causes – of government activity, and deal mostly with the long-term effects that changes in government expenditure can have on the economy.

The short-term impact of government activity on the economy depends on the value of the familiar **spending multiplier** and on how government spending is financed on an annual basis (e.g. taxes or borrowing). These issues will be discussed in Chapter 15.

The long-term role of government can be usefully viewed within the context of the growing body of literature known as '**new growth theory (NGT)**' (Romer, 1986). Adherents to this school have all called attention to the contribution that government can make towards stimulating and reinforcing sustained economic growth. Several kinds of public investment and expenditure programmes are reputed to confer significant positive externalities (of both a pecuniary and technological kind) on private producers and consumers, and it is to these programmes that policymakers should turn in their quest to promote economic growth and development.

The origin of NGT can be traced to a general dissatisfaction with the classical and neoclassical theories of growth according to which private fixed investment, or additions to the physical capital stock, play a pivotal role in fostering economic growth. According to NGT, however, this is an oversimplification with the result that the economic 'pie' may become smaller and, as a result, the fiscal scope for redistribution as well.

This hypothesis would suggest that the extension of suffrage (which accompanied democratisation in South Africa) should have resulted in a major increase in the share of government expenditure in the South African economy. But this did not happen, despite the fact that the election of 1994 resulted in the appearance of a new median voter with an income well below the average income. It may be argued, of course, that the median voter model does not apply to South Africa, or that a substantial degree of redistribution had already occurred earlier in an attempt to counter social upheaval (as already explained). Expenditure on social services (as a percentage of both total government expenditure and GDP) increased between 1983 and 2004 (Table 7.2), while defence expenditure declined dramatically both prior to and after the 1994 elections. Also, the overall fiscal restraint imposed by the need for macroeconomic stability, forced the government to meet many of its distributional goals by means of a *reallocation* of social spending.

7.5 Micro models of expenditure growth

7.5.1 Baumol's unbalanced productivity growth

Government expenditure may also increase disproportionately due to an increase in the prices of inputs used by the public sector relative to those employed in the private sector. This phenomenon has drawn the interest of William Baumol (1967) who developed a microeconomic model of **unbalanced productivity growth** to explain the growth in government expenditure. He divides the economy into two broad sectors, a progressive sector and a non-progressive sector. The progressive sector is characterised by technologically progressive activities, such as innovation, capital formation, and economies of scale which all contribute towards a rise in the level of output. An important feature of this sector is a cumulative increase in the productivity of employees that justifies increases in wages and salaries. The inherent characteristics of the non-progressive sector, on the other hand, only permit sporadic changes in productivity.

The technological structure of a sector will therefore determine the increase in the productivity of labour inputs used. In the progressive sector labour is only one of the inputs in the production process, while in the non-progressive sector labour is often the end product. Baumol (1967: 416) illustrates this difference with the aid of several examples. Consumers are usually not interested in the labour used to produce an air conditioner; as they only care about the end product, that is, cold air. However, the labour input is of great concern when one has purchased a ticket to attend a one-hour concert by a Beethoven quartet. Any effort to increase the overall productivity of the concert to below four man hours, for example by doubling the tempo of the music, may upset listeners and detract from the end product, that is, the concert. In this case there is clearly a limit to productivity increases, which is greatly determined by the labour-intensive nature of the service.

The non-progressive sector usually consists of services that also constitute a large component of the public sector. In this sector labour plays an important role, for example in respect of functions such as education and law and order, where a certain teacher–learner ratio or a certain number of law-enforcement officers per thousand of the population is usually the aim. According

of what is really a very complex process. They adopt a much broader definition of 'capital' and focus attention on the role played by each of the components of capital in the growth process.

In addition to privately owned physical capital (e.g. factories, office buildings, and luxury homes), 'capital' also includes the following three components:

▶ the existing physical infrastructure (e.g. roads, street lighting, and sewage systems)
▶ accumulated human capital acquired through education, training, and healthcare
▶ the stock of technical expertise acquired through learning-by-doing and research and development (R&D).

The main thrust of NGT is that additions to any of the components of capital may yield increasing returns because they create externalities that benefit a range of sectors and industries in the economy. Investment in the physical infrastructure creates (pecuniary) externalities by lowering production costs and boosting returns in the private sector. Likewise, recipients of education may transfer their skills free of charge to third parties, healthier citizens will be more productive and limit the spread of disease, new users of electricity will boost the demand for electrical appliances, and so on.

Each of the components of capital can be influenced by government through appropriate policy intervention and, in the present instance, the case for such intervention is the standard one based on market failure. Since the marginal private benefits from investments in physical infrastructure, human capital, and R&D are lower than the corresponding marginal social benefits, the untrammeled operation of the market will lead to an under-provision of these services. NGT thus provides a strong justification for government intervention in these areas as it will create favourable conditions for private investment and economic growth.

Investment in a country's physical infrastructure usually boosts the productivities of a range of inputs used by existing private enterprises (see Aschauer, 1989). It may do so by lowering transport and communication costs, thus cutting down on travel time, reducing the time and costs involved in negotiations, and facilitating the discovery of new input and output markets. It may also 'crowd in' new private investment, including foreign direct investment (FDI), in the sense of new firms opening up or existing firms expanding their operations. The point here is that it is the new or improved infrastructure that triggers both the (mostly pecuniary) externalities and the new private investment, neither of which would have happened in the absence of infrastructure investment.

From a macroeconomic perspective, the role played by government capital investment can be briefly illustrated with the aid of a Solow-type aggregate production function. For example, let aggregate supply,

$$Y = f(K_p, K_g, eN) \qquad [7.1]$$

where K_p and K_g represent the levels of capital owned by the private and public sectors, respectively, e is a measure of labour productivity, and N is the quantity of labour (with eN being Solow's 'effective' labour). While an increase in K_g will directly boost Y in Equation [7.1], it may also either crowd in new private capital investment or, if the addition to K_g is financed by means of borrowing, putting upward pressure on interest rates, crowd out some private investment (see Chapter 15). In addition, an increase in K_g – for example, in the form of new school buildings or healthcare facilities – may boost labour productivity, e. We may therefore extend Equation [7.1] as follows:

$$Y = f[K_p(K_g), K_g, e(K_g)N] \qquad [7.1a]$$

where the relationship, K_p (K_g), is either positive or negative, depending on whether there is a net **crowding-in** or **crowding-out effect**, and where the first derivative of $e(K_g)$ is positive.

Infrastructure investment is usually financed by means of borrowing on the open market but it is generally accepted that such investments are more likely to have a net crowding-in effect than a crowding-out effect. The reason is that government borrowing usually constitutes a small portion of total borrowing, so that it is unlikely to have an effect on interest rates. But even if it did cause a rise in the interest rate, private investors would not necessarily be deterred by it – to them other things, including a country's infrastructure, are often more important when it comes to making important decisions about their own investments.

Empirically, too, several recent studies have produced evidence confirming this proposition. Although government spending as a whole tends to have a negative impact on economic growth – partly because it consists mostly of recurrent consumption expenditure – most studies show that public infrastructure investments do have a positive impact on factor productivities in the private sector. In its World Development Report 1994, for example, the World Bank (1994: 14)

summarised the results of these studies and concluded that '... the role of infrastructure in growth is substantial, significant and frequently greater than that of investment in other forms of capital.'

Much the same can be said of public investment in education, training, and healthcare. When these spending categories are suitably disaggregated, one finds significant differences between the constituent components of each category. Vocational training often produces higher returns than poor quality formal schooling, and so too does good quality primary and secondary education in relation to certain categories of tertiary education. Other categories of tertiary education in turn provide the specialised skills that are necessary for sustained economic growth (Bhorat, 2004).

These findings are clearly important in helping governments to prioritise their spending programmes, especially in view of the important redistributive role that such programmes play today – we will return to this theme in the next chapter. The prioritisation of state expenditures, based on efficiency criteria, can help governments to do two things – achieve a more equitable distribution of income and create the conditions for sustainable economic growth over the long term.

IMPORTANT CONCEPTS

crowding-in and crowding-out effects (page 120)
displacement effect (page 113)
economic classification of government expenditure (page 105)
functional classification of government expenditure (page 107)
general government expenditure (page 103)

general government resource mobilisation (page 104)
general government resource use (page 104)
macro models of government expenditure growth (page 112)
median voter (page 114)
micro models of government expenditure growth (page 112)

new growth theory (page 118)
politicians, bureaucrats, and interest groups (page 117, 118)
service environment (page 116)
spending multiplier (page 118)
stages of development (page 112)
unbalanced productivity growth (page 115)

SELF-ASSESSMENT EXERCISES

7.1 Discuss trends in the size, growth and composition of government spending in South Africa since 1994.

7.2 Distinguish between the various macro and micro models of public sector growth.

7.3 Explain the 'displacement effect' in Peacock and Wiseman's model of government expenditure growth.

7.4 Explain how unbalanced productivity growth may affect government expenditure, and briefly comment on its relevance to South Africa.

7.5 Discuss the influence of the different stages of development on government expenditure.

7.6 Explain the median voter hypothesis of Meltzer and Richard and indicate whether it can explain the growth of government expenditure in South Africa.

7.7 Consider the implications of new growth theory for the role of government in the economy.

7.8 Distinguish between the notions of 'crowding-in' and 'crowding-out' (of private investment).

Chapter
EIGHT

Servaas van der Berg

Poverty and inequality in South Africa: fiscal and social policy issues

The previous chapter focused on the growth and composition of government expenditure as a whole, and also looked at the mostly historical reasons for that growth, including the positive long-term impact that public investment in the physical and social infrastructure can have on economic growth. In this chapter we shift our focus to an important and critical component of government spending, one that is aimed at addressing what we considered (in Chapter 5) to be a serious and urgent form of market failure, particularly within a developing country context. We refer to the problem of inequality and the widespread incidence of abject poverty in Southern Africa and in many other countries of the world. Our particular focus is the category labelled 'social services' provided by the state, which comprises by far the largest part of the *functional* composition of general government expenditure in South Africa (see Table 7.2 and Chapter 1).

The theoretical underpinnings of the analyses in this chapter stem from the important conclusion we came to in Chapter 5, i.e. that an efficient (or Pareto optimal) allocation of resources does not necessarily coincide with what society considers to be an acceptable *distribution* of those same resources. The aim of this chapter is therefore to analyse in more practical terms the role of government in addressing problems of inequality, with special reference to the South African experience, although we also draw some examples from other Southern African countries. We first consider the distributional context in South Africa and include a brief overview of the nature of poverty and inequality in South and Southern Africa. Next we explain the role of public finance in redistribution, both in theory and with reference to international experience. This is followed by a discussion of changing patterns of fiscal incidence in South Africa. We conclude with an analysis of selected policy issues in which we concentrate on education, health, social security, welfare services, and the subsidisation of housing in South Africa.

Once you have studied this chapter, you should be able to:
▶ distinguish primary from secondary income distribution
▶ understand the redistributive impact of the budget on secondary income distribution
▶ explain the calculation of a Gini coefficient
▶ identify the excess burden of a subsidy
▶ show how a subsidy could be welfare-enhancing if there are positive externalities associated with consumption of certain goods (e.g. food for the poor)
▶ distinguish between the impact of a cash transfer and a subsidy in kind
▶ show how social transfers may create a disincentive to work
▶ identify major trends in fiscal incidence in South Africa, particularly with regard to social spending
▶ understand the redistributive impact of some major social policy interventions in South Africa.

8.1 The distributional context in South Africa and Southern Africa

Through its effect on resource allocation, the national budget is the most important redistributive mechanism available to any government to change the distribution of private earnings in the medium term. In the longer term, even earnings itself are strongly influenced by the current allocation of fiscal resources through its impact on human capital and economic growth in general. The budget therefore has a pivotal role in determining distributive outcomes. In South Africa, where poverty, socio-economic development, and income distribution are such important issues, the role of fiscal policy in this regard is particularly pertinent. At the same time one should guard against unrealistic expectations about the redistributive power of fiscal policy. In the words of De Wulf (1975: 95):

While an agnostic attitude may be extreme, at the very least a critical attitude with respect to any assertion concerning the extent of income redistribution through the budget seems warranted.

This chapter addresses the issue of the budget as redistributive device, focusing on the spending patterns that impact on distribution. Although there is a brief discussion of some social spending programmes and the problems encountered, these are important issues and warrant separate treatment. The approach here is rather to show how the budget affects redistribution, painting a picture with a broad brush and focusing on the analytical considerations underlying redistributive actions in general.

8.1.1 Poverty and inequality in South Africa and Southern Africa

South African society is characterised by extreme poverty and inequality in the distribution of income and earning opportunities. More or less a quarter of the total population lives below the international poverty line of $1 a day – an extremely high proportion for an upper middle-income developing country such as South Africa (Klasen, 1996: 10; Woolard and Leibbrant, 2001: 49). Indications are that poverty has improved only moderately since the turn of the century (Van der Berg, Louw and Yu, 2008). In Botswana, with a similar GDP per capita, the poverty rate is much the same, with 23 per cent of the population living on less than $1 a day. In Namibia, with a substantially lower per capita income, 35 per cent of the population live in poverty as defined by the $1 per day poverty line. Mauritius has a higher per capita income level and less income inequality than South Africa, and consequently has a lower poverty rate. Generally, in the remaining SADC countries the poverty rate is higher than in South Africa – in some cases considerably higher – and most countries fall in the low-income category. For instance, in Malawi 42 per cent of the population is poor (below $1 per day) and the average income per capita is roughly 5 per cent of income per capita in South Africa (World Bank, 2004a: 310).

The **Gini coefficient** developed by Corrado Gini (1884–1965) is often used to measure inequality and is usually linked to the Lorenz curve that was developed by Max O. Lorenz (1880–1962). The Lorenz curve is calculated after arranging the population from poorest to richest. It shows the cumulative percentage of the population (horizontal axis) against the cumulative percentage of income (vertical axis), as shown in Figure 8.1 for South Africa in 1995. If there were perfect

equality, the poorest 20 per cent of the population, for instance, would have earned 20 per cent of the income, as reflected in the diagonal line of absolute equality. The actual deviation from this line as a proportion of the maximum possible deviation, that is, the area between the line of absolute equality and the Lorenz curve as a proportion of the area under the diagonal, is then a measure of the inequality of income. Countries with extreme inequality of income, such as South Africa and Brazil, have Gini coefficients of around 0,60, while countries with relatively equal income distributions generally have ratios of between 0,20 and 0,35. The South African Gini coefficient has remained extremely high over a long time. Actual Gini coefficients vary due to the fact that different datasets as well as different measures (income or expenditure, per capita or per household, etc.) are used. Estimates of the Gini coefficient of per capita household income using comparable datasets indicate an increase in inequality between 1995 and 2000, and relative stability at a level that could be as high as 0,74 in 2007 (Yu, 2010). In Southern Africa, Namibia and Swaziland are other examples of countries that recorded Gini coefficients over 0,60 during the 1990s. In contrast, Tanzania, Mozambique, and Mauritius displayed much lower levels of income inequality over the same period (UNDP, 2004; World Bank, 2004a: 311).

The perseverance of poverty and inequality in South Africa despite substantial interracial redistribution during the past two decades may be attributed to widening inequalities within groups, especially amongst black South Africans. Since the mid-seventies the combination of rapid black wage increases and rising unemployment has had mixed outcomes for black households. While incomes among the top black income earners have increased greatly, some of the poor remained victims of unemployment. The racial divide in respect of poverty and affluence has been eroded ever since. Yet national household surveys have shown that poverty in post-apartheid South Africa remained concentrated among black, particularly rural, households (Woolard and Leibbrandt, 2001).

Table 8.1 presents recent estimates based on official surveys of per capita incomes and unemployment for each of the population groups. Access to employment has become a major dividing line between insiders sharing in the privileged situation formerly reserved for whites, and unemployed outsiders who through lack of skills, geographic location, and marginalisation in the wider society,

remain impoverished. Patterns of access to social services accentuate this cleavage, even in the post-apartheid period. The government thus faces a major challenge in effectively bringing services to the poor, both as a means of alleviating immediate acute poverty and of establishing a socio-economic environment conducive to economic growth that can incorporate the poor in the economic mainstream. In addition, the expansion of social grants (discussed in Section 8.4.2 below) assisted many of the poor to improve their position.

Table 8.1 South African per capita income and unemployment by population group

Population group	Per capita income 2005 (R)	Narrow rate of unemployment September 2005 (%)
Black	9 600	31,5
Coloured	18 400	22,4
Indian	35 600	15,8
White	102 500	5,0
Total	**19 600**	**26,7**

Source: Per capita income calculated from Statistics SA, Income and Expenditure Survey, (2005); Unemployment calculated from Statistics SA, Labour Force Survey September 2005.

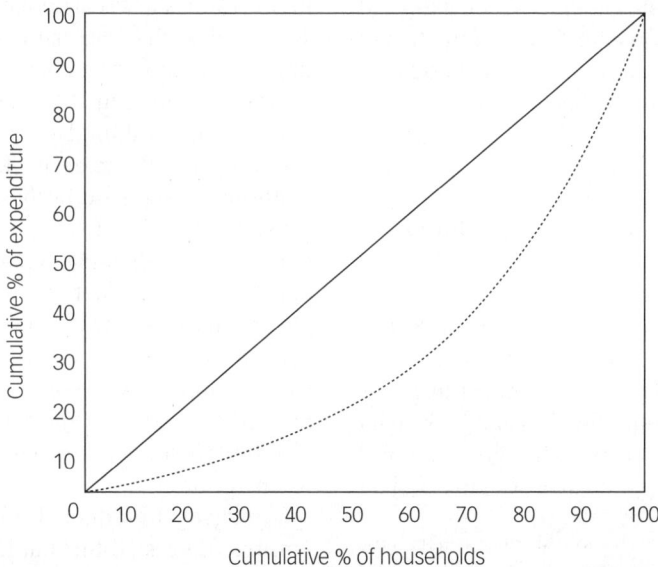

Figure 8.1 The Lorenz Curve for South Africa, 1995

8.1.2 **Primary income versus secondary income**

In order to determine the impact of the budget on distributive outcomes, note that a household's power of disposal over goods and services depends upon both the personal incomes of members and upon the taxation and spending of government. **Primary income** or personal income of any group is the actual value of income received in cash or in kind by individuals and households, including the value of subsistence production activities such as subsistence agriculture. **Secondary income** can then be regarded as primary income minus direct taxation (which leaves disposable income), to which is added the value of government services consumed (Bromberger, 1982). Therefore,

$$Y_s = Y_p - T_d + G \qquad [8.1]$$

where Y_s represents secondary income, Y_p represents primary income, T_d represents direct taxes, and G represents government spending.[1]

Social spending is the only category of government spending that can be assigned to beneficiary households with any degree of certainty. If other public expenditures are ignored, Equation [8.1] becomes

$$Y_s = Y_p - T_d + G_s \qquad [8.2]$$

where G_s represents social expenditure.

Considering the high degree of racial inequality of primary incomes in South Africa, it is indeed pertinent to ask what the role of the budget is in accentuating or reducing this inequality through its impact on secondary income. This goes beyond investigating only the fairness of the budget

itself, and also asks how much inequality remains once the budget has had its effect.

8.2 **The role of public finance in redistribution**

Conceptually the factor $(G_s - T_d)$ in Equation [8.2] combines the notions of tax and expenditure incidence (as discussed in previous chapters) into what is called fiscal incidence, that is, the net result of the incidence of tax burdens and expenditure benefits in society.

One approach to determining **fiscal incidence** is linked to the normative questions of fairness of the burdens and the benefits of public expenditure and taxation and focuses only on the budget, that is, the factor $(G_s - T_d)$. This type of fiscal incidence study often contrasts government expenditure benefits with all taxes paid by certain groups or households to determine whether, presuming no tax shifting takes place, they benefit in net terms and how the political process allocates fiscal benefits and burdens. The usual point of departure is the **balanced budget incidence**, a term encountered in Chapter 10 (Section 10.5.1): this entails calculating the combined effect of government spending and the taxes levied to finance it, assuming there is no budget deficit or surplus. In this context, the distributional impact of a tax depends not only on the incidence of the tax itself, but also on how the government spends the proceeds from the tax. An example is the very different redistributive impact when tax revenue is used to finance defence spending compared to when it is used to finance social old-age pensions for the poor.

However, balanced budget incidence ignores the distributional impact of fiscal policies on primary incomes and hence fails

[1] Strictly speaking, social transfers should for this purpose not be included in government spending, as they already form part of personal incomes.

to take into account the overall distributional context within which the budget is but one element. In other words, it ignores the fact that primary income has already been influenced by the impact of fiscal policies on market prices. For example, company tax has already influenced personal income by reducing the after-tax company income for distribution to shareholders, while value added and sales taxes enter into the price level and are reflected in the reduced purchasing power of consumers. At any point in time, therefore, the primary income distribution already incorporates an element of fiscal incidence. To avoid 'double counting', balanced budget incidence studies should adjust for this.

8.2.1 Government's distributive role

Fiscal redistribution addresses an enormously complex issue, as stated by Bromberger (1982: 167):

> *The distribution of income is determined by immensely complex processes in which government activity interacts with relatively autonomous initiatives and adjustments by 'the myriad forces of the market'. There does not exist a well-tested, widely endorsed body of theory to model all of these processes. But it is clear that governments cannot readily control all of them, and there are limits to what governments may be able to do to change distributions. We must avoid assuming that if there is a change, or no change, government policy is responsible. Nor should we assume that government policies are either coherent or necessarily successful.*

The government budget embodies the fiscal measures of redistribution. It influences income distribution by determining which services are provided to whom (government expenditure) and how these expenditures are to be financed (taxes and loans), including their impact on the long-term distribution of human capital that fundamentally determines the distribution of earnings (primary incomes). But the budget is only one part of the distributive role played by government.

From a broad economic perspective it is possible to identify a number of roles that the government can play in affecting distribution (see Bromberger, 1982: 168):

‣ as a rule-maker – in particular the rules of competition in markets, or phrased differently, rules of access to various levels of market opportunity

‣ as a controller of prices and wages in markets

‣ as a market operator – in particular as a major employer of labour and through the size and nature of its purchasing activities

‣ as an influence on the long-term pattern of activities, for example industrial decentralisation measures that affect location decisions of employers, or the impact of taxes on the capital intensity of production

‣ as taxer, supplier of public goods and welfare services, and payer of transfer incomes

‣ as (potential) redistributor of assets that carries claims to current and future income.

The first four roles mainly affect primary incomes in the market and are only indirectly related to public economics. The last two activities however influence secondary income through the budget. It is this role of government, as fiscal redistributor, that mainly concerns us in this chapter. Note that we will discuss the distributional impact of public debt (government loans) in Chapter 16.

8.2.2 Government taxation

The distinction between the statutory and the economic incidence of a tax is well known in the public finance literature and was discussed in Chapter 10 (Section 10.5). The extent to which taxes can be shifted of course differs, as does the progressivity of different forms of taxes. Just as the perceived equity of a tax system is very important for the legitimacy of taxes and for tax morality, so the perceived (statutory) incidence, in contrast to the economic incidence, is often quite crucial.

In terms of the statutory incidence, the most progressive taxes are usually income taxes. In its extreme form, an income tax may even be extended to include a negative income tax (i.e. a transfer) for low levels of income, thus strengthening its progressive distributional effect. This may be seen as an alternative to means-tested social transfers, which we will discuss in some detail in Section 8.5.1. Wealth taxes, where they apply, are also progressive, and appropriately selected excise duties too can have a progressive impact. By contrast, most other indirect taxes are usually relatively regressive. This regressivity can in some instances be reduced through certain exclusions, for example zero-rating certain food items from value added tax; however, this process has to be weighed against the increased complexity of administration and the erosion of the tax base that it entails.

8.2.3 Government spending, subsidies, externalities, and income transfers

The distributive stance of a government can furthermore be determined from its spending priorities and, in particular, its social spending. Social spending includes important income transfers as part of social security, as well as publicly provided or subsidised goods and services such as education, health, and housing.

In analysing social spending, one should take note that subsidisation or the public provision of goods or services gives rise to economic inefficiencies in the form of the excess burden of a subsidy. The concept of consumer surplus as developed by Marshall and Hicks may be used to show that the costs of a subsidy are larger than its benefits, thus leaving an excess burden (Rosenthal, 1983: 88). This is illustrated in Figure 8.2. Assuming constant production costs, if the full benefit of a subsidy were passed on to consumers, it would result in a lowering of the price charged from P_0 to P_1 and an increase in quantity demanded from Q_0 to Q_1. This would increase consumer surplus (the difference between what the consumer is willing to pay and the actual price) from the area aP_0E_0 to the area aP_1E_1. Thus, the subsidy results in a benefit for consumers measured as area $P_0E_0E_1P_1$, consisting of area $P_0E_0CP_1$ due to the lower price for the original quantity demanded, and area E_0E_1c, originating from the extra quantity purchased due to the lower price.

However, the cost of the subsidy to the state, that is, area $P_1P_0bE_1$ (the subsidy per unit multiplied by the Q_1 units consumed) still has to be accounted for. This cost exceeds the consumer benefit by area E_0bE_1. This is known as the excess burden, or deadweight or welfare loss, of the subsidy (Rosenthal, 1983: 88–9).

As subsidies interfere with consumer choice and therefore lead to a socially suboptimal outcome, it seems that public subsidies should in principle be avoided, perhaps by rather providing income transfers if the intention is to redistribute resources.

The case for subsidies, however, is stronger where there are externalities, that is, where the marginal private benefit a consumer derives from a public good or service deviates from the marginal social benefit due to an external benefit to a non-user. Consider the case where society attaches value to

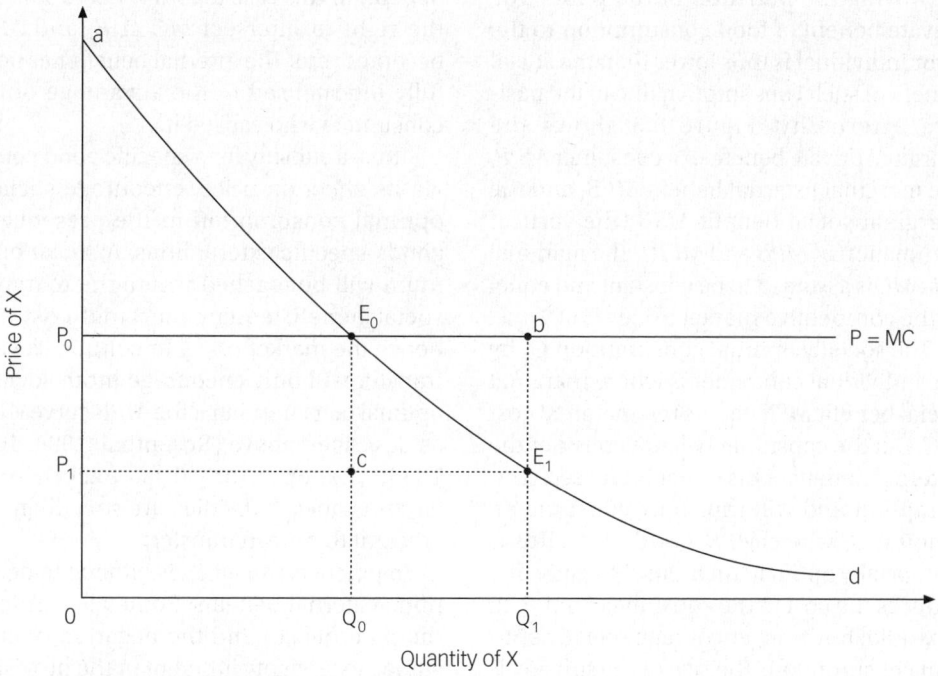

Figure 8.2 The excess burden of a subsidy

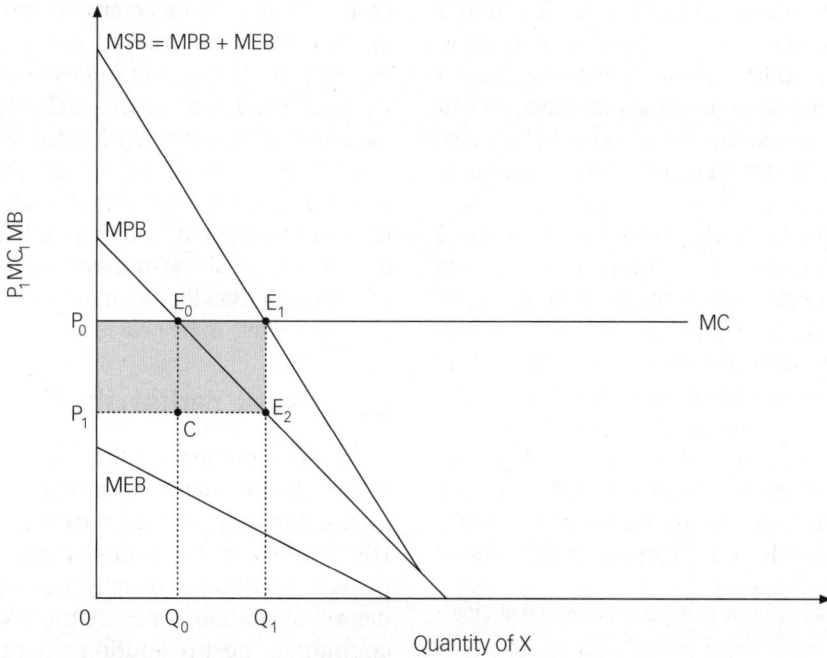

Figure 8.3 Externalities and subsidies for public goods or services

improving the nutrition of the poor.[2] The private benefit of food consumption to the poor individual is thus lower than the social benefit of such consumption due to the positive externality. Figure 8.3 shows the marginal private benefit to a consumer *MPB*, the marginal external benefit *MEB*, and the marginal social benefit *MSB* (the vertical summation of *MPB* and *MEB*). The marginal cost *MC* is assumed to be constant and equal to the competitive market price (P_0).

The socially optimal consumption Q_1 by the individual consumer is where marginal social benefit *MSB* equals the marginal cost *MC*. But the consumer will not consider the external benefit of his or her increased consumption and will thus only consume an amount Q_0 where $MPB = MC = P_0$. This is not socially optimal. An in-kind subsidy that reduces the cost to the consumer from P_0 to P_1 would, however, encourage socially optimal consumption. The size of the subsidy is indicated by the area $P_0E_1E_2P_1$.

Can a cash transfer achieve the same results as an in-kind subsidy? Note that a cash transfer is not targeted at increasing only the consumption of those goods to which society attaches value. Thus, a cash transfer to poor households could increase their consumption of food, but also of other goods such as alcohol and luxury items. A cash transfer is therefore less certain of improving the consumption of those goods to which a positive externality is attached. In Figure 8.3 a cash transfer could shift the *MPB* and the *MSB* curves to the right,[3] thus increasing the socially optimum level of consumption. Cash transfers will only lead to socially optimum consumption where the private benefit curve (*MPB*) is shifted enough to eliminate the marginal external benefit, consequently equating private with social benefit. In this case the *MPB* curve shifts to the right to intersect *MC* at E_1 and *MEB* becomes zero. The external benefit has been fully internalised to the advantage of the consumers who caused it.

Thus, a subsidy for a specific good could, via its effect on price, encourage socially optimal consumption in the presence of goods-specific externalities. A social optimum will be reached where the marginal social benefit equals marginal cost and hence the market price. In contrast, a cash transfer will only encourage more socially optimal consumption if the *MPB* curve shifts as described above (Rosenthal, 1983: 100–101). Except for this exceptional circumstance, subsidies are socially more efficient than cash transfers.

In practice, though, it is difficult to determine external benefits. Some also criticise the paternalism and the negation of consumer sovereignty inherent in the provision of public goods. Subsidies on specific goods furthermore entail high implementation costs, including enforcement costs to prevent the conversion of subsidised goods into cash equivalents. If in-kind subsidies can be readily converted into cash, such subsidies become very similar to cash subsidies. Costs and effects of subsidies are more complex to administer, understand, and analyse than income transfers. But since public support for specific subsidies or merit goods is usually stronger than for income transfers, these are more likely to be provided.

8.2.4 Asset redistribution

Asset redistribution usually takes place over a considerable period of time through the interaction of market and fiscal processes. Direct interventions to force rapid changes in asset distribution usually require a large degree of coercion and are therefore only common in post-revolution situations, for example nationalisation or land

---

[2] This explanation is derived from Rosenthal (1983: 100–101).

[3] It is assumed that *MEB* is not affected by the cash transfer.

redistribution without full compensation. The recent Zimbabwean experience can perhaps be placed in this category. Where full compensation does take place, such asset redistribution is usually much slower and has a high cost in terms of opportunities forgone for redistributive social spending. Thus, land reform in South Africa and Namibia has to compete with other services such as education for public funds. For that reason, asset redistribution through direct measures has limited application in market-based economies and will not receive more attention here. Our focus is on redistributive fiscal measures that operate directly on flow rather than stock variables. Of course, given positive saving propensities on the part of recipients, income redistribution could also result in wealth accumulation.

8.2.5 International experience and practice

The rise of the modern welfare state has been the major force behind the secular rise in public expenditure ratios in industrial countries. Since the nineteenth century, the state's role has gradually shifted from an earlier emphasis on the indirect satisfaction of needs (e.g. infrastructure, defence, and administration) to a greater emphasis on the more direct satisfaction of needs (e.g. education, health, and social security) (see Chapter 7, Section 7.2). There was a particularly strong rise in income transfers in the form of social security spending. Increased expenditures also necessitated increased taxation, which later caused growing tax resistance.

Social spending in developing countries is more constrained by limited fiscal resources. Nevertheless, the period after World War II saw social spending ratios rising to levels far above those that had prevailed in today's industrial countries at a similar stage in their economic development.

However, in trying to meet the demands of strong urban pressure groups, many governments embarked on social policies that were biased towards the urban population. Thus the major beneficiaries were often the non-poor. Moreover, spending often favoured higher-level services (e.g. tertiary rather than primary education, hospitals rather than primary healthcare facilities), which again benefited the relatively privileged.

The Republic of Congo (Congo Brazzaville) during the 1980s and 1990s is a case in point. Most public expenditure was devoted to the wages and salaries of an inflated public sector consisting largely of urban civil servants (e.g. the health budget was devoted to the university hospital rather than the urgent primary healthcare needs in rural areas) and cuts in education expenditure impacted severely on primary education while preserving tertiary scholarships that benefited mainly upper income groups (World Bank, 1997: ii). Swaziland followed a similar course with a 'strong urban bias' in the provision of healthcare and too little focus on primary or preventive care from which the poor benefit more (World Bank, 2000: iv). In most developing countries social security has been relatively neglected, with education usually dominating social spending, particularly in Southern Africa which has recorded many of the highest education spending ratios (expressed relative to GDP) in the world.

8.3 Changing patterns of fiscal incidence

8.3.1 Fiscal incidence in South Africa

We saw in Section 8.2.3 that, just as the burden of taxation is often shifted, so are public expenditure benefits. This may have all kinds of unintended consequences. The means test for social grants may, for example, affect labour force participation or saving for retirement. Most incidence studies reflect only the static effects of spending, without considering the dynamic effects or the effects of previous rounds of taxation or public spending on distributive outcomes. De Wulf (1975: 75), in an important overview of the incidence literature in developing countries, was highly skeptical of attempts at full net fiscal incidence estimates:

[I]t should be emphasized that the impression of preciseness left by the studies surveyed here is definitely questionable; the estimates obtained in these studies are at best approximations. In any study, the overall effective tax rate or the effective tax rates of those income classes that, from a political point of view, deserve more attention – the wealthy and the poor – can be changed considerably by altering the shifting assumptions or by using different consumption and income data.

Fiscal incidence studies in South Africa naturally focused on the racial incidence of taxation and particularly of public spending. Until recently, taxation was not often considered in these studies as the black population contributed only a small share of taxation. Such studies go back as far as the Native Economics Commission (1932: 170–178), which concluded that expenditures (both directly assignable to individuals such as social services, and an imputed value for non-assignable expenditures) of R8,3 million to the benefit of blacks in 1929/30 well exceeded the R6,6 million they paid in taxes.

Subsequent studies confirmed this finding that the black population gained far more from social spending than they contributed to taxes paid (e.g. Leistner 1968: 175), and pointed to significant shifts in social

spending towards blacks since the 1970s, leaving the net fiscal incidence considerably more favourable to blacks by the early 1980s. But throughout this period, disposable income and indeed secondary income (primary income plus the net effect of the budget on command over resources) remained highly skew. McGrath (1983) used data obtained from the tax and expenditure authorities for his estimates on racial fiscal incidence. 'Apartheid bookkeeping' assigned social expenditure on education, health, housing, and welfare by race. His conclusions for the period 1949 to 1975 were that blacks gained under all sets of assumptions, that redistribution from whites probably increased, but that a vast post-redistribution gap in racial (secondary) incomes remained. Later work (Lachmann and Bercuson, 1992) showed that even under conservative assumptions, it would have been fiscally impossible to extend white expenditure levels to the whole population, thus expenditure levels on whites had to decrease quite substantially. This further emphasised the need for accelerated economic growth to enhance fiscal resources, as available resources could not meet expectations in a simple static redistributive exercise.

Two competing norms can be identified that underlie views about socially just public expenditure. The first norm, based on the apartheid paradigm, saw groups as fiscally autonomous units, that is, it presupposed that the taxation paid by members of a particular group should also be used to fund public expenditures benefiting that group. Even under apartheid this norm was not fully applied as whites paid more taxes than the benefits they received from public expenditure. From an apartheid perspective, this was regarded as a form of 'development aid' to poorer groups.

The alternative norm for allocating public expenditure departs from the view that need, rather than the origin of taxes, should determine public expenditure. But need, approximated by population shares, clearly had not been the norm determining past public expenditure. The white population – only 17 per cent of the total – obtained a far larger share of the benefits of public expenditure. From the perspective of this unitary society paradigm, then, expenditure patterns in apartheid South Africa were grossly inequitable.

Fiscal incidence studies usually cannot distinguish between differences in the costs and the quality of providing a service to different households or in different areas. In apartheid South Africa, however, racial differentials in the costs of services provided were more readily determinable and, as this was a major source of discrimination, expenditure incidence analysis tried to incorporate these differences. For instance, Janisch (1996) determined the distribution of social services from the 1993 Living Standards and Development Survey, and then applied cost patterns by race and/or region from public expenditure data to these. Based on Janish's data, before the redistributive effect of the budget was considered, per capita income of blacks (excluding social pensions, which were part of social spending) was only 10,3 per cent of white levels in 1993. After incorporating the impact of the budget, black secondary income per capita was 15,6 per cent of white levels, due to a net gain from fiscal incidence of R895 per black person and a net loss of R3 421 per white person. But even though the budget did effect a considerable redistribution, the racial post-budget gap remained extremely large.

The scope for further redistribution through the budget is rather limited, however. The government's macroeconomic strategy on Growth, Employment And Redistribution (GEAR) (Department of Finance, 1996) acknowledged that taxation was already too high. Even parity in social spending per capita would have had a limited

effect: secondary incomes of blacks would then still have been only 17 per cent of white levels. The latter conclusion emphasises the limits to the budget as an instrument of redistribution and points to the importance of the distribution of pre-budgetary or primary income.

A recent study for the National Treasury by Van der Berg (2005) found that spending per capita on blacks exceeded that of whites. This is a result of the means test that ensures that social grants are targeted at the poor, the fact that poor people have more children who benefit from school education subsidies (and there is almost universal access to schools until about age 15), and because many of the more affluent have opted out of the public health system in favour of private health services, thus leaving spending to go to the less affluent. The South African government has succeeded in shifting fiscal resources on a massive scale, particularly away from whites, who were unfairly advantaged under apartheid, to blacks. The largest part of this shift occurred in school education through the equalisation of teacher-pupil ratios funded through the public budget between historically white and historically black schools. However, higher salaries or even more teachers in poor schools did not automatically translate into improved education for the poor. Also, it remains difficult to employ well-qualified teachers and medical personnel in townships or deep rural areas where poverty is most acute; shifts in social outcomes thus lag far behind shifts in social spending patterns.

The budget has for a long time redistributed across race groups. Due to much higher incomes, whites always paid by far the largest share of taxes and, as was already discussed, even under apartheid part of these taxes was used to finance certain services to blacks. The secondary distribution of income by race has therefore been more equitable than the primary distribution, even though public

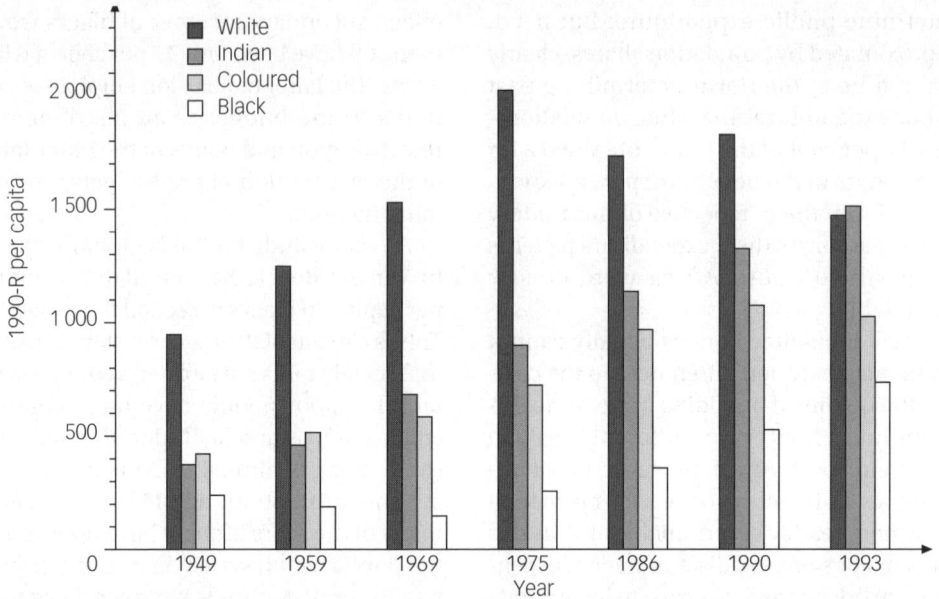

Figure 8.4 The estimated racial incidence of social spending for selected years

expenditure as such has been highly inequitable and clearly conflicted with the demands of social justice. It also appears from the available data that racial redistribution through the budget actually accelerated over time, even under apartheid. Fiscal redistribution across races before the 1930s may have been negligible, but rising social spending for blacks led to substantial redistribution through the budget. Figure 8.4 shows not only a narrowing gap between white and black, but also implies a real reduction in white benefit levels after 1975 that predates political democratisation. The combination of the strong rise in the general government expenditure ratio as a percentage of GDP, reprioritisation towards social spending, and the shift within social spending programmes towards blacks meant that real social spending for blacks grew at 6,5 per cent per annum from 1975 to 1991, despite the fact that economic growth was sluggish and apartheid had not yet been officially abandoned. The largest part of the remaining gap arose not from differentials in expenditure levels for specific services, but from differential service provision or utilisation.

The inherited racial spending inequalities from the apartheid era were translated into provincial spending gaps after the political transition. The new provinces were given the function of controlling most social spending and are funded predominantly from transfers from central government. The horizontal division of revenue between provinces was based on formulae that allowed only five years for fiscal equalisation between provinces (see Chapter 17, Section 17.7.2). Consequently, there was a sharp cutback in fiscal resources in the richer provinces which have historically had a relatively smaller black population. At the same time, racial expenditure gaps had to be eliminated in all provinces.

Expenditure cutbacks in some provinces may have resulted in a poorer utilisation of national fiscal resources. For example, the retrenchment of teachers in the Western Cape and Gauteng could not be matched by new appointments of skilled teachers in

Limpopo or Mpumalanga. The net result of such redistribution patterns across provinces may therefore well have been a reduction in the marginal efficiency of public resource use. That is, a million rand spent on additional teachers in Limpopo, for example, contributed less to educational output than the million rand saved in Gauteng.

Expenditure data provide little information on the efficiency of social spending or on how well it matches consumer preferences. The presumption in fiscal incidence studies that 'a rand is a rand is a rand' (the accounting approach), is palpably untrue. One billion rand spent on pensions, for instance, may make a greater difference to people's welfare than another billion rand spent on teachers. If teacher salaries were to double, would learners and parents experience a commensurate increase in welfare? These questions relate to who the presumed beneficiaries are (teachers or learners), how well the increase in spending translates into command over real goods and services, and how spending reflects the preferences of consumers – or matches the utility function of the consumers of public goods and services (see also Musgrave, 1987: 1057).

In the absence of data broken down by race, it is today impossible to even crudely estimate the fiscal incidence of the budget by race directly from the budget. The only source that offers some possibility for doing so, is socio-economic surveys, which show the distribution of access to various resources. This data shows continued disparities in access to some services, particularly tertiary education.

8.3.2 Social spending pressures in Southern Africa

Owing to obvious differences in history and demography, the racial dimension of fiscal incidence is not as important for analysis in the other SADC countries as it is in South Africa. Nevertheless, most of these societies have not been able to avoid protracted political instability and conflict that have left an indelible mark on fiscal processes in the region. This implies that an analysis of priorities in public spending and taxation remains a fruitful exercise.

For instance, it is remarkable that between 1990 and 2002 (a period that saw the cessation of several armed conflicts and increasing democratisation) military spending as a percentage of GDP dropped in every single SADC country with available data (UNDP, 2004). While it is fair to assume that this would free up resources for social spending benefiting the poor, as alluded to in earlier examples of the Congo and Swaziland, this type of fiscal prudence was certainly not automatic. For example, despite reductions in military spending, public expenditure on education as a percentage of GDP was lower in 2000 than in 1990 in Angola, Mauritius, Mozambique, the Seychelles, and Tanzania. In Swaziland, public expenditure on education dropped from 6,1 per cent of GDP in 1990 to 1,5 per cent in 2000 (World Bank, 2004a: 329).

That said there are governments that are responding to popular pressure for social investment in health and education. To do this, they need to increase tax revenues or run the risk of ballooning budget deficits. It is increasingly acknowledged that considerable scope exists for widening the tax base through strengthening collection systems, combating low compliance and evasion, and rolling back widespread exemptions. South Africa's recent success (in the form of billions of rands in surplus revenue collection) is ample evidence of the potential rewards to an efficient revenue service. A number of SADC governments have attempted to emulate that success by introducing autonomous revenue authorities as well as value added taxation (VAT) (African Development Bank, 2001: 86–87).

While certain SADC countries such as Botswana and Mozambique have made progress in achieving a balance between creating the fiscal climate conducive to economic growth and addressing issues of social urgency through the budget, some continued on a path of gross fiscal mismanagement. For instance, a lack of expenditure control and weak oil revenue monitoring systems saw the Angolan budget deficit for 2003 rise to 4,6 per cent of GDP despite a reasonable rate of economic growth. In Zambia a growing budget deficit resulted from the government bowing to public sector salary and wage pressure. A similar problem in Zimbabwe was compounded by a plethora of other policy abuses and errors including lax borrowing and price controls, causing a 2003 fiscal deficit of 8,8 per cent of GDP (African Development Bank, 2004: 83–85). Madagascar had fiscal deficits exceeding 13% of GDP in 2004 and 10% the following year (Bank of Namibia 2006: 9). Along with Zimbabwe, Madagascar was the only country not meeting the SADC regional deficit target of 5% or less (Bank of Namibia 2006: 18).

The overriding point is that all countries in the region are hard pressed to meet the enormous social challenges they face in a sustainable manner that protects and promotes the prospects of economic growth.

8.4 Selected policy issues in the South African context

With full democratisation in 1994, the trend towards reduced racial disparities in social expenditure was already well established. In education for instance, starting from a low base, spending benefiting blacks increased remarkably from the late 1960s as more blacks entered schools, those in school remained there longer, and expenditure per learner rose. As recently as 1982, total spending on black education was still less than half the amount spent on whites; five years later it had surpassed spending on whites for the first time. Yet even today, differential access to higher levels of education leave blacks worse off than their white counterparts, especially in rural areas.

We now turn to a brief discussion of some social programmes that illustrate the types of difficulties faced in social policy in the South African context. The areas are the following:

- School education, where there have been massive shifts in teacher resources to poorer schools after the abolition of apartheid, but where the major issue still remains the poor quality of education in the major part of the school system.
- Health, where the shift to primary healthcare was not always successful in providing quality healthcare for the poor, while the advent of Aids dominated public health debates and required major resource inputs.
- Social security, where the incentives that flow from the means test for social assistance and that inhibit the evolution of the system of occupational insurance remain a crucial issue.
- Social welfare services, where the restructuring of services is intended to ensure greater equity across both race groups and provinces, and greater responsiveness to the needs of the poor.
- Housing, where accelerated provision is sought to reduce the accumulated backlog by combining state and private funding and provision.

Other areas, such as tertiary education, public job creation programmes (public works), and water and infrastructure provision are not discussed here.

8.4.1 **School education**

As discussed in Chapter 3, school education is a good example of a merit good. A merit good is defined in the MIT dictionary of Economics (Pearce, 1986) as follows:

> *A good the consumption of which is deemed to be intrinsically desirable. In the case of such goods it is argued that consumer sovereignty does not hold and that if consumers are unwilling to purchase 'adequate' quantities of such goods they should be compelled to do so.*

In this respect, it is quite different from tertiary education, where most benefits accrue to the beneficiaries themselves through increased earning opportunities in the labour market, whereas it is less clear that there are major external benefits that flow from such tertiary education.

In South Africa spending on education formed a major part of discrimination in public spending under apartheid, and overcoming this legacy was a major challenge for the new government. They achieved this in a remarkably short space of time, in that the discriminatory teacher-learner ratios were eliminated by 2001, while racial barriers to school entry were eliminated. However, there are still differences in the average spending per child between rich and poor as a result of better qualified, and therefore also better remunerated, teachers being more common in richer schools. (Equity of school spending is well analysed in Gustafsson and Patel, 2006; Motala, 2006; and Van der Berg 2006). A large part of the challenge now is no longer a fiscal one, but one of ensuring that the resources available to all children are efficiently used. Education production functions seem to show large inefficiencies in many poor schools, where efficiency is measured as the ratio of outputs to inputs after taking into account differences in the socio-economic status of children, which also has an impact on learning outcomes (Crouch and Mabogoane, 1998; Van der Berg and Burger, 2003). The question is thus how to improve the functioning of schools and the quality of education.

8.4.2 **Health**

Attempts by government to improve health outcomes have largely entailed a shift in focus to poorer provinces and to primary healthcare within these provinces in an attempt to enhance access. This was also accompanied by a lowering of costs to certain users of primary health services, namely the provision of free healthcare to pregnant women and young children (i.e. the elimination of user charges). There are clear indications that quality of healthcare in the public sector is not perceived very positively and the demand for healthcare reflects a clear preference by users – even amongst the poorest – for private health facilities, despite their greater cost. Analysis of health demand shows public healthcare to be an inferior good for which the demand declines as incomes rise (Burger 2007; Burger and Swanepoel 2006; Grobler and Stuart 2007). As a result of the advent of Aids, pressure on the public healthcare system increased in terms of an increased workload for public health workers, greater pressure on health facilities, and fiscal pressures to deal with treatment and prevention programmes.

The ANC has recently adopted a plan for the introduction of a National Health Insurance scheme to be funded through a combination of member contributions for those earning above a threshold level of income, and general taxation. However, details of the scheme are not yet fully clear and serious reservations have been expressed about its fiscal and practical viability. As a consequence, government has not yet committed itself to any details, though it forms part of the Department of Health's Ten Point Plan. The 2011 Budget Overview (National Treasury 2011: 108) indicated that it will be phased in over a 14-year period due to its complexity and to ensure that the initial investment required in health service capacity is in place. National Treasury and the Department of Health are currently working on the fiscal and financial arrangements.

8.4.3 Social security

Unlike other types of social spending, social grants can directly influence the distribution of primary income. The embryonic welfare state erected for whites in apartheid South Africa was later expanded to other groups, leaving the country with a relatively advanced social security system for a semi-industrialised country. **Social security** protects people against various contingencies, such as income loss from unemployment, disability, injury sustained at work, illness or old age. The South African social security system has two major components:

▶ **Occupational insurance** is based on contributory insurance to protect those in formal employment and includes the following: retirement benefits for a large part of those in formal employment; a somewhat inadequate system of workers compensation; a system of unemployment insurance which cannot address the major unemployment risks associated with structural rather than cyclical unemployment; and health or medical insurance for some of the employed and their dependants.

▶ **Social assistance** (also called social grants or social transfers) has three main pillars, namely social old-age pensions, disability grants, and child

support grants. All are means-tested to ensure targeting at the poor and are funded from the national budget.

The interaction between occupational insurance and social assistance, particularly in the field of retirement provision, poses the greatest challenge to policy, for in this interaction – largely regulated by the means test – lies many incentive problems that perversely affect the behaviour of potential or actual recipients.

Occupational insurance

Occupational retirement insurance has expanded its coverage to most industries. Assets of pension funds amounted to R1 284 billion in 2003 (Registrar of Pension Funds, 2005: 11). In the same year, occupational retirement funds paid out retirement benefits of R85,9 billion, compared to just more than R50 billion paid by the state in the form of all social grants (National Treasury, 2008a: 95).

Insofar as convention and agreements between employers and employees have made occupational insurance for retirement the norm in the formal sector, occupational insurance can be regarded as social insurance, despite the absence of legal compulsion. It is mandatory for employees in most industries or firms to join their pension fund or provident fund. However, as the 'taxes' imposed on employers and employees do not flow through state coffers, fiscal comparisons understate social security provision in South Africa. Coverage is still low in agriculture, trade, catering, accommodation, and domestic service, and is probably much lower among women, who are disproportionately employed in some of these industries.

Insurance against certain types of risk is unlikely to be offered by the private sector due to the problem of adverse selection. This means that people most likely to face certain risks (e.g. of unemployment) and to collect

Chapter 8 *Poverty and inequality in South Africa: fiscal and social policy issues* 139

benefits from insurance, will have an especially high demand for, and are thus more
likely to buy, such insurance (Rosen and
Gayer, 2008: 187–188). However, the high
premiums needed to compensate for these
high-risk clients could lower the demand to
such an extent that it is unprofitable for a
private insurance firm to offer such coverage.
This problem is exacerbated by that of moral
hazard (explained further in Chapter 17)
which is said to exist when economic behaviour adjusts to incentives in such a manner
as to increase the likelihood that the event
insured against will actually take place. For
instance, the presence of lucrative unemployment insurance may make continued
employment less attractive and therefore
lead to greater unemployment than would
have been the case in the absence of such
insurance. This phenomenon ties in with the
question of asymmetric information: the
insurer's insufficient knowledge about the
insured persons' circumstances makes such
an insurer more susceptible to such moral
hazard. Thus, **adverse selection** and **moral
hazard** generally result in market failure and
an inefficient allocation of resources: there
is a lack of insurance against risks for which
a sufficient demand does exist (see Rosen
and Gayer, 2008: 220–231).

Occupational retirement insurance is vital
for many South Africans, but cannot reach
those outside paid employment, nor those
parts of the employed population presently
uncovered. It is estimated that, because of
large-scale unemployment and non-cover-
age of some sectors and low-income workers,
only 47 per cent of the economically active
labour force of 16,8 million are members of
a provident or pension fund (National Treasury 2008a: 100). Of particular concern is
that the interaction with the means test for
social old-age pensions may discourage private retirement provision for many
low-income workers, an issue to which we
will return.

Unemployment insurance applies only to
certain workers covered by the Unemployment Insurance Fund (UIF) against
short-term unemployment. Workers and
employers each contribute one per cent of
the wage (up to a ceiling income) to the UIF
which is publicly administered and to which
the government also commits funds from
time to time.

Workers' compensation requires employers to make risk-related contributions to the
accident funds and is paid to employed
workers who are temporarily or permanently
disabled as a result of injuries or industrial
diseases sustained at work.

Social assistance

Figure 8.5 explains the effect of a cash transfer or the free provision of public goods and
services on the work effort of an economically active individual who is therefore also
subject to income tax. We measure available
hours per time unit (e.g. a week or a month)
on the horizontal axis and the corresponding unit income on the vertical axis. $0A$
hours are available to the worker to allocate
between work and leisure. This distance is
referred to as the time endowment. The vertical line AX signifies that time endowment
is fixed at all income levels. The line AB
shows his or her combined budget and time
constraint, where sacrificing leisure would
allow him or her to earn a bigger wage
income and therefore to increase his or her
consumption of goods. Initially the worker
is in equilibrium at E_0 on the price line AB,
given his or her indifference curve (I_0)
between goods (income) and leisure, sacrificing CA hours of leisure (or alternatively,
working AC hours) in order to consume $0D$
of goods. $0D$ is the value of goods which can
be purchased with the revenue earned by
working AC hours and thus, assuming no
saving, is equal to total income earned.

If the government now provides an
income transfer irrespective of its effect on

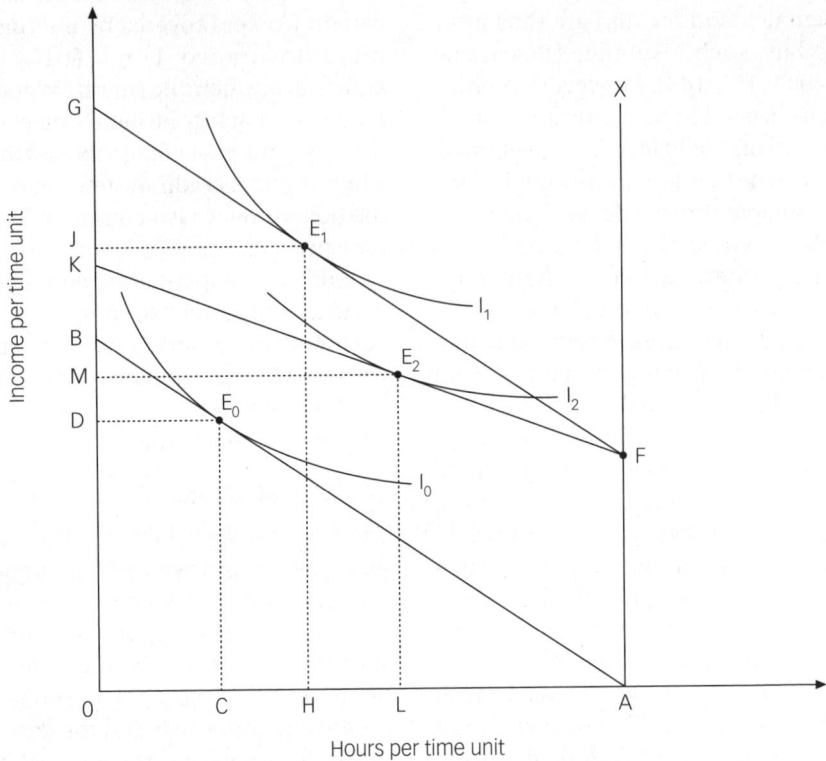

Figure 8.5 The effect of an income transfer on work effort

individual work effort, the budget constraint shifts parallel to the right to *FG*. Note that this parallel upward shift is similar though opposite to the downward movement of the budget constraint when a lump sum tax is levied (see Chapter 11, Section 11.4.1), that is, the relative prices of the items of choice remain unaffected. The worker is now at point E_1 on the new budget line and on the higher indifference curve I_1. Thus, consumption of both leisure and goods is increased (from *0C* to *0H* and from *0D* to *0J*, respectively). The individual now has a higher level of welfare but works fewer hours (*AH* as opposed to *AC*) due to the income effect arising from the cash transfer.

If an income tax is now imposed to finance the cash transfer, this would reduce the opportunity cost of leisure, thus

swivelling the budget line from *FG* to *FK*. The individual moves to E_2 (where *FK* is tangent to indifference curve I_2) and work effort is further reduced to *AL*. This is even lower than the work effort arising from the cash transfer alone (*AH*). The combined effect of the cash transfer and taxation to finance it is thus to reduce work incentives in two ways, namely the negative (income) effect *CH* of the cash transfer plus the negative net (income and substitution) effect *HL* of the income tax. Thus, the government needs to be as careful in the design of its cash transfer programmes as in its taxes to ensure that, in combination, they lead to as little reduction in work effort as possible. Social old-age pensions are an example where the cash transfer would not provide a disincentive to work as the beneficiaries are not part of the labour force.

In South Africa child support grants are the most important social assistance grants, covering more than half of the eight million recipients of social grants, followed by social old-age pensions and disability grants. Although grants and pensions to the old and the disabled effectively target many of the poor, not all the poor can be reached in this way. For 2011/12 R98 billion was budgeted for social assistance (National Treasury 2011: 103). This income largely ends up in the pockets of the poor, thus contributing substantially to their secondary income.

The absence of adequate occupational retirement insurance in the past has left most people of pensionable age with few other income sources than social old-age pensions to fall back on. Social old-age pensions were until 2007 paid to men from 65 years of age and to women from age 60, subject to a means test. In 2007 the government announced that the eligible age for men would also be reduced to 60 years. Applicants whose private incomes fall below the lower threshold (30 per cent of the value of the annual social benefit) qualify for the full pension. Above this level, every R2 increase in private income reduces the benefit by R1. This marginal 'tax' rate or claw-back of 50 per cent creates a typical poverty trap (see below) and has severe implications for the behaviour of low-income workers.

Disability grants were historically the second most important form of social assistance and are paid to the disabled (including the blind) from age 16 up to retirement age, subject to medical eligibility criteria and the same means test as for old-age pensions.

For many years child and family maintenance benefits consisted of child allowances and parent allowances, and were paid mainly to single mothers and their children without other means of support. Blacks were largely excluded. When the social assistance system was de-racialised, it became apparent that the cost of these grants could become astronomical, that there were potentially perverse incentive effects associated with them (e.g. the requirement that mothers had to be single to remain eligible for these grants), and that other equally poor children in intact families were not eligible for such support. Thus, following the Lund Committee's (1996) recommendations, the Cabinet approved the phasing out of the former child and parent allowances and the institution of a new flat rate child support grant of R100 per month to caregivers of the poorest children under seven years of age, identified through a simple means test. The benefit levels were increased gradually to R270 in 2011/12, and the age ceiling was raised in steps so that children up to the age of 14 were covered since 2004, and in 2008 it was announced that eligibility would be expanded in further steps to 18 years of age.

The large volume of social grant spending in South Africa (at about 3½ per cent of GDP more than twice as large as in any other developing country) has not only made it an important income source for many households, but also a major part of provincial expenditures. To reduce the pressure on provincial budgeting, this national programme has now been centralised in a national South African Social Security Agency (SASSA).

The means test for social pensions

A crucial area of concern is the interaction between social assistance and the tax system, especially with regard to retirement provision. This hinges particularly on the so-called poverty trap associated with most means tests. A **poverty trap** exists when certain regulations or tax systems make it unattractive for people to increase their private income beyond a certain earnings level, as this leads to a reduction in the resources obtained from the state. A poverty trap is then said to exist at that level of income. For instance, if a person receives a cash benefit of R100 from the state as long as his or her private earnings are below R500, it is not in his or her interest to expend any effort to increase private earnings marginally above R499. Someone with private earnings between R500 and R599 may actually be worse off than someone whose private earnings of R499 are supplemented by transfer payments from the state. For a low-income worker the means test may thus be a disincentive to work. Moreover, when income from pension or provident funds is also taken into account in the means-test, it could be a deterrent for making provision for retirement. The means test is also difficult to administer. This was not such a great problem when many low-income black workers were not covered by occupational insurance; however, now that most of them belong to pension or provident funds, the perverse incentives are coming into play to a greater extent.

For these reasons, removing the means test would remove the perverse incentives that favour premature withdrawal of retirement benefits, would encourage private retirement insurance for informal sector participants and domestic servants, and would affect the choice between lump sum retirement benefits and pensions as well as the form in which assets are held. Although the fiscal costs of a universal old-age grant could be reduced by removing the old-age tax rebate and raising income taxes payable by more affluent retired people, the ageing of the population may lead to the growth of the elderly population outstripping the growth of fiscal resources.

The limits to social security

The challenge for the state is to offer a safety net for the poor, who are often outside of remunerated employment, while insuring those in employment against major contingencies (loss of employment, old age, ill health, disability), in the process avoiding schemes that discourage the private provision of security. The poorly educated rural black population is worst affected by the major contingency against which no proper protection is given – unemployment. Occupational insurance can reach at best only half the labour force, leaving the most vulnerable dependent upon various forms of social assistance. But such social assistance is, in turn, almost exclusively tied to the presence of elderly or disabled members in households, thus leaving a major social security need uncovered. A proposal that received some support in the welfare community and amongst trade unions, the so-called Basic Income Grant (referred to often by its acronym, BIG), was strongly opposed by the South African Government and most economists. The proposal entailed providing a grant of R100 per month to all South Africans, rich and poor, and then recouping the costs through higher taxes on the rich, thus increasing their net tax burden and boosting the net benefits to the poor. Government's opposition to this plan was based on a number of considerations. These include the high cost of transferring grants, at about R20 per grant per month, which would have amounted to almost R11 billion per annum for 45 million South Africans, and the large tax increases required to fund the additional 5 per cent of GDP the grant would cost.

The government has announced plans to implement a broad-based wage subsidy that 'partially offsets social security contributions for employees earning less than the income tax threshold' (National Treasury 2008: 104), alongside the introduction of mandatory social security contributions. The government estimates that this policy will increase employment by 350 000 over five years and considerably reduce poverty. The exact details, and various alternative models, are still under consideration.

8.4.4 **Welfare services**

Publicly funded social welfare services are provided either directly by government or through subsidising private welfare organisations. Although there is a vibrant network of such private providers of welfare services, they are less active in rural areas (where the greatest unmet needs are) and many are currently experiencing financial pressures. Welfare spending takes place mainly at the provincial level. Almost four out of every five rand spent by the state in various fields of social welfare services – both for services provided by government and for financial support of private welfare institutions – goes to child and family care or care of the elderly. The only other major field of service is care of the disabled.

The White Paper for Social Welfare (Department of Welfare, 1997) advocated a major overhaul of welfare services in South Africa. In the past, welfare services were highly discriminatory, inequitably distributed across provinces, poorly directed at communities and families, mainly rehabilitative rather than preventive, and often based on a fiscally expensive model of institution-based care (e.g. old-age homes).

Discrimination in the provision of welfare services under apartheid was massive. In 1993, spending per member of the elderly population was seven times as much for whites as for blacks. When the new constitution was implemented, provinces with a large white and coloured population share (Western Cape, Northern Cape, and Gauteng) inherited far better welfare services than other provinces: in 1995 the Western Cape spent more than four times as much per capita as Mpumalanga, the worst served province. Inter-provincial redistribution of fiscal resources through the provincial funding formula (see Chapter 17) reduced welfare service spending in the historically better-served provinces and considerably narrowed the spending gaps. But lack of institutional capacity in welfare institutions and personnel remains an even more binding constraint in poorer provinces, than finance. In contrast, spending cuts in richer provinces placed severe strain on service provision and on the financial health and service provision of well-established welfare organisations in metropolitan areas. The government is attempting to move away from expensive models of institutional care to rehabilitation and preventive government intervention, with special attention to developmental needs. Preventive programmes are to focus on high-risk groups who are vulnerable to particular social problems, such as children and youth at risk.

8.4.5 **Subsidisation of housing**

The fact that poor consumers spend a large part of their income on housing, and that many others cannot afford or gain access to housing, provides a rationale for the emphasis placed by governments on subsidies in both private and public housing sectors (Rosenthal, 1983: 108–118). The case for government intervention in housing rests on the basic needs argument and the alleged existence of externalities (e.g. investment in housing enhances the return on non-residential physical and social investment (such as education), especially in a development context) (Calitz, 1986: 340–341). South Africa's huge housing backlog in urban areas has accumulated through the combined effects of influx control, which for a long time kept most of the poor out of the cities, and limited housing construction.

The impact of a housing subsidy depends on the price elasticity of housing supply and demand. This may be analysed on the basis of a shift in the supply curve of housing (which implies a producer subsidy), or in terms of a shift in the demand curve (a consumer subsidy). As in the case of an indirect tax (see Chapter 10, Section 10.5), the result in terms of the shifting of the subsidy benefit is the same. We can illustrate the impact of the subsidy by means of a shift in the market demand curve for housing, as shown in Figure 8.6. Assume firstly a perfectly price-elastic supply of housing S_0 (i.e. $P = MC$, which is constant). The initial equilibrium is at E_0, with P_0 and Q_0 the corresponding equilibrium price and quantity. A housing consumer subsidy will increase the purchasing power of prospective homeowners and thus shift the demand curve upwards and to the right, that is, from D_0 to D_1. (For simplicity we assume a fixed subsidy amount, which entails a parallel shift in Figure 8.6.) The new equilibrium is at E_1. Since the price of houses has not been affected, buyers enjoy the full benefit of the subsidy. No shifting of the benefit occurs.

At the other extreme, however, where there is a fixed housing supply (a perfectly price-inelastic supply curve such as S_1 in Figure 8.6), a housing subsidy will only result in an increase in house prices (from P_0 to P_1) to the benefit (increased capital gains) of existing homeowners, thus completely cancelling the benefit which the subsidy was supposed to have for potential buyers. In practice, neither of these extremes is likely, and the net impact is likely to be that some benefit will accrue to existing homeowners through an increased demand for housing and higher prices, and some benefit to the intended beneficiaries through an increase in their purchasing power (or a reduction in their costs) and an acceleration of housing supply. To the extent that the price of new houses is increased by the subsidy, some of the benefit is shifted to home-builders (the construction industry) as well or, in a general equilibrium context, to the owners of the factors of production (mainly labour and capital).

The major problem with housing provision in South Africa is that the incomes of a large part of the urban population are too low to allow them to afford even a relatively small house with rudimentary services. Early

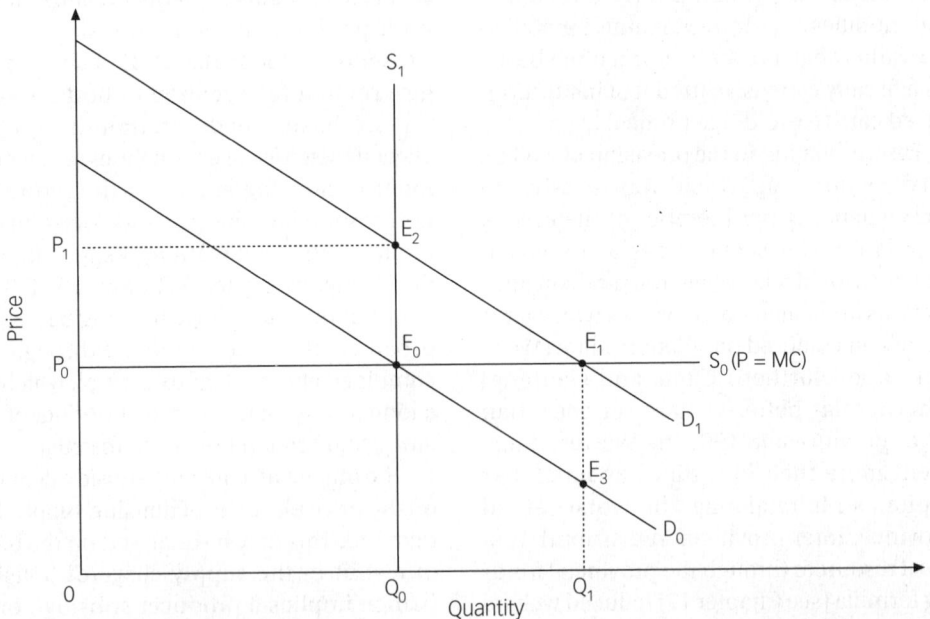

Figure 8.6 The impact of a housing subsidy

ambitions about providing a 'proper' house for every household have given way to an acceptance that this is simply not affordable. Now the policy is one of incremental housing provision, to try and reach as many households as possible within a reasonable time frame, and to supplement their own incomes where necessary to allow them to afford at least a minimal level of housing.

The housing subsidy scheme, considered a 'cornerstone of the government's approach to the housing challenge' (Department of Housing, 1995: 8), provided various forms of assistance to eligible households earning less than a certain threshold. Individual ownership subsidies assist recipients to own fixed residential properties (housing opportunities) for the first time, with higher subsidies for the lowest income-bracket (Department of Housing, 1996: 8; Department of Finance, 1999: 139). Subsidies can either be allocated to individual beneficiaries for housing units in projects approved by provincial housing boards, or enable an individual to acquire ownership of an existing property or a property not in an approved housing project. Part of these funds may even be paid directly to developers when certain conditions are met in order to smooth the payment procedure. The individual subsidy can also be linked to further credit provision, that is, a home loan to buy a property is obtained in addition to the subsidy amount. Institutions that give eligible people access to affordable subsidised residential properties based on secure tenure receive institutional subsidies from the state.

Initially, progress with housing provision was painfully slow. The problem often revolved around coordinating the financing, the provision of serviced land, and the selection and involvement of communities and households who qualify. Only by 1997 could a marked acceleration of housing output be seen and the annual target of 300 000 units a year was reached. By 2008, therefore, a full 2,3 million houses had been built since 1994

(National Treasury 2008a: 111), although recent years witnessed some deceleration of housing provision, because of capacity constraints rather than fiscal constraints at municipal and provincial government level and in the construction sector. In the Government's 2008/09 budget a total amount of R35,8 billion was indicatively allocated for the medium term (three years) for housing provision by provinces (National Treasury 2008a: 111).

8.5 Conclusion

The South African fiscal dilemma – a prime example of the economic problem of allocating scarce resources in a situation of unlimited wants – is the result of the conflict between the rising expectations of a mobilised urban workforce and the resource constraints of a middle-income developing country. This economic problem of scarcity requires a reprioritisation of needs via the political system (see the opening paragraph of Chapter 1). It is a problem that is becoming increasingly prevalent throughout Southern Africa as countries emerge from armed conflict, adopt democracy, and engage in economic reconstruction.

In Chapter 15 we provide an outline of the overall fiscal policy approach, emphasising the importance of fiscal sustainability. Considerable scope does however exist for addressing the expectations of the poor. Only in respect of education was the problem especially severe. Yet, even there financial resources could be freed and shifted to address the needs of the black school-going population.

In this chapter we saw that there was ample scope for a redistribution of resources via the expenditure side of the budget. This entails not only a reallocation of resources towards social expenditure but also a restructuring of the social budget towards services benefiting the really needy. Moreover, if the restructuring of social services could also ensure greater effectiveness in their delivery to the poor, these resources could be put to even better use without over-straining the capacity of the budget. Success in this regard would substantially lighten the burden of a government faced with the demands of a newly enfranchised and expectant constituency, and increase the likelihood of social stability and therefore economic growth. Economic growth is in turn a prerequisite for ensuring that the benefits of social expenditure can continue to keep up with a rapidly expanding need. If it does not, budgetary redistribution would have accomplished very little.

But there are limits to redistribution through the budget, and unless economic growth draws many more people into remunerative employment, the large inequalities in South African society and the widespread poverty will remain. The limits to budgetary redistribution again emphasise the need for job-creating economic growth. Thus, fiscal policy has to balance the short- to medium-term need for budgetary redistribution with the long-term need for growth to ensure a more substantial redistribution of both primary and secondary incomes. Similar pressures arise in other Southern African countries, most of which also face strong constituency pressures and severe fiscal resource constraints.

IMPORTANT CONCEPTS

adverse selection (page 139)
balanced budget incidence (page 126)
fiscal incidence (page 126)
Gini coefficient (page 124)

moral hazard (page 139)
occupational insurance (page 138)
poverty trap (page 141)
primary income (page 126)

secondary income (page 126)
social assistance (page 138)
social security (page 138)

SELF-ASESSMENT EXERCISES

8.1 Distinguish primary income from secondary income.
8.2 Explain the role of public finance in redistribution.
8.3 Is it possible for the budget to redistribute resources, and yet still to discriminate? Discuss with reference to racial fiscal incidence in South Africa.
8.4 Do you think racial fiscal incidence has become less discriminatory since the mid-1970s?
8.5 Under what conditions would a subsidy be welfare-enhancing? Do you think this is the case for social old-age

pensions in South Africa? Would it equally be the case for grants to single mothers?
8.6 Why is it so difficult for the private sector to provide insurance against unemployment?
8.7 Poverty traps can also exist for other social programmes and social security. Do the conditions for housing subsidies and South Africa also create a poverty trap?
8.8 Explain by means of a graph the incidence of a housing subsidy when both the demand and supply curves are moderately elastic.

Chapter
NINE

Philip Black

Cost-benefit analysis

In this chapter we will adopt a more microeconomic approach to our analysis of government expenditure. Government departments face the same basic economic problem as their counterparts in the private sector – how best to spend a limited budget. In the past governments used a variety of programming and financing methods aimed at providing public and merit goods in a cost-effective manner – much like an equivalent private enterprise would do. But unlike the private sector, government cannot base its decisions merely on the monetary or 'private' feasibility of projects. In the case of pure public goods, for example, this is simply not possible. In many other instances it is necessary also to consider the extent to which prevailing market prices deviate from their respective marginal *social* costs and benefits. In most countries, including South Africa, governments now use some form of cost-benefit analysis (CBA) according to which costs and revenues are defined in social rather than private terms. The South African government, for example, has produced CBA guidelines (CUTA, 2002) that attempt to use adjusted or 'shadow' prices representing the true social opportunity costs of inputs used and outputs produced by the public sector.

Standard evaluation techniques used in the private sector are thus insufficient and need to be modified and extended when applied to public sector projects. Some of these techniques are briefly discussed in Section 9.2, while the required modifications and adjustments – that is, cost-benefit analysis proper – are dealt with in the remaining sections of the chapter.

Once you have studied this chapter you should be able to:
- distinguish between the private and public sector approaches to project evaluation
- explain the net present value approach to project evaluation and compare it with the internal rate of return and the benefit-cost ratio
- show why, under ideal conditions, public sector projects should strive to maximise consumer (and producer) surplus
- explain the meaning of shadow prices and comment on some of the difficulties involved in quantifying benefits and costs
- discuss the importance of the social discount rate in determining the net present value of a public project
- indicate how risk factors can be taken into account in project evaluation.

9.1 Introduction

For a private business to be efficient it has to consider whether its shareholders will benefit from engaging in one particular undertaking instead of another. Likewise, the analyst in the public sector has to decide whether society as a whole will be in a better position given the choice between two or more mutually exclusive alternatives. Private shareholders, however, generally pursue a different set of objectives from that followed in the public sector, and it can therefore be expected that final choices will differ between the two sectors.

Cost-benefit analysis (CBA) is an analytical tool used to evaluate the relative merits of public projects financed by the state. It differs from evaluation techniques used in the private sector because it strives to maximise something other than monetary profits (or the difference between private benefits and private costs). Public projects generally aim to maximise the difference between total social benefits and total social costs, that is, achieve a level of output where marginal social benefit equals marginal social cost.

But this is easier said than done and, as we shall see, it is simply not possible in practice to identify – let alone quantify – all the relevant external costs and benefits associated with a particular public project.

Project evaluation in the private sector requires that a comparison be made between the expected private costs and benefits over the estimated time span of a new project. If the project is expected to yield a positive net benefit, then it can be said to be feasible and potentially acceptable. Final acceptance will depend on whether the positive net benefit exceeds the corresponding benefits associated with all other alternative projects. Standard techniques used in project evaluation include calculation of the net present value (NPV), the internal rate of return (IRR), and the benefit-cost (B-C) ratio, as discussed in the next section.

The same methodology can also be used to determine the relative merits of alternative projects in the public sector. But here it is necessary also to correct for prevailing price distortions arising from externalities, monopoly elements, and indirect taxes and subsidies. In Southern Africa the problem is compounded by the huge inequalities that exist between individuals and communities, and in the case of South Africa, by the fact that the government has taken it upon itself to correct the wrongs of the past by means of various affirmative action and other economic empowerment programmes. These include the public tender systems adopted by governments at all levels, according to which preference is given to tenders submitted by members from previously disadvantaged communities. In the private sector too, several large corporations have adopted affirmative procurement policies, many of which entail a loss in efficiency and profitability, at least in the short term (South Africa Foundation, 1998). In most cases, however, these institutions expect to derive additional benefits over the long term, including expanded markets and an enhanced reputation, which may ultimately outweigh the short-term losses (Black, 1993; Black, 1996).

The point to note is that project evaluation in the public sector is based on a different set of criteria than those used in the private sector. It is largely for this reason that conventional evaluation techniques are usually modified and extended in accordance with the particular objectives of the public sector.

Cost-benefit analysis has often been applied to determine the **economic efficiency** – broadly defined to include external costs and benefits – of a range of publicly funded infrastructure investments, e.g. new roads, railway lines and harbour developments. The same or a similar methodology is also used to determine the environmental impact of new capital investments as well as regulatory initiatives undertaken by the public sector. A good example of the latter is a recent attempt to determine the costs and benefits of wildlife conservation in Zimbabwe, which has to compete with other important forms of land use (Muchapondwa et al., 2008).

9.2 Evaluation techniques

9.2.1 Net present value (NPV)

Just as wages are the reward for labour services rendered, and rent is the payment received for the use of land, so interest is the return to capital. In the event that capital is employed for the development of a particular project, the **net present value** (NPV) approach is used to determine whether the return on such an investment will be greater than, or at least equal to, the interest that can be earned from simply putting the money into a banking account.

If you invested R1 000 in a bank at an interest rate of 10 per cent, then you would expect to receive R1 100 at the end of the first year, or

$$R1\ 000 + 0{,}10(R1\ 000) = R1\ 000(1 + 0{,}10)$$
$$= R1\ 100.$$

After two years you would receive

$$R1\ 100 + 0{,}10(R1\ 100) = R1\ 100(1 + 0{,}10)$$
$$= R1\ 210.$$

The latter can be written as

$$R1\ 000\ (1 + 0{,}10)(1 + 0{,}10)$$
$$= R1\ 000(1 + 0{,}10)^2.$$

After n years the future value, F, of your present investment, P, will be

$$F = P(1 + i)^n \qquad [9.1]$$

where i is the market rate of interest.

You could, of course, invest your money in some other financial asset, such as equity or government bonds, or in a physical asset. After allowing for inflation and different risk profiles, you will naturally choose the one yielding the highest future value.

Conversely, it follows from Equation [9.1] that the present value of your future income is simply

$$P = \frac{F}{(1 + i)^n} \qquad [9.2]$$

where i is now referred to as the **discount rate**. Thus if you knew the future value of your income, you could work out the present value. If a friend wanted to borrow money from you and promised to pay back R1 000 to you after two years, you would obviously not lend her R1 000 now – you could earn 10 per cent on it each year in the bank. But how much would you lend her? The answer is given by Equation [9.2]:

$$\frac{R1\,000}{(1 + 0{,}10)^2} = R826{,}45.$$

In other words, if you invested R826,45 in the bank you would receive R1 000 after two years. There is always an inverse relationship between the discount rate and the present value of an investment. The higher the interest rate, the higher your expected future stream of income will have to be to receive a given sum in the future.

The present value concept plays a critically important role in project evaluation. It is applied to both the expected costs and benefits of a project. In addition to the initial cost of a new project, one might typically expect to derive a stream of benefits in each subsequent year, which must then be compared with the corresponding expected costs. The difference between the discounted benefits and costs is the net present value (NPV).

The NPV after two years, for example, is as follows:

$$NPV = \frac{\{B(x)_1 - C(x)_1\}}{(1 + i)} + \frac{\{B(x)_2 - C(x)_2\}}{(1 + i)} - C(x)_0$$

$$NPV = \sum_{t=1}^{2} \frac{\{B(x)_t - C(x)_t\}}{(1 + i)^2} - C(x)_0$$

where $B(x)_t$ and $C(x)_t$ are the expected benefits and costs associated with project X in the first year of operation, and $C(x)_0$ is the initial capital costs. After n years the NPV is the following:

$$NPV = \sum_{t=1}^{n} \frac{\{B(x)_t - C(x)_t\}}{(1 + i)^n} - C(x)_0 \qquad [9.3]$$

This method can be used to determine the relative merits of two or more mutually exclusive projects. Given that the present values of two such projects are positive, the one yielding the higher net present value after a given date in the future will be the obvious choice. Higher discount rates will count against projects that yield returns further into the future, rendering the choice of an appropriate discount rate and cut-off date crucial to the NPV exercise.

9.2.2 Internal rate of return (IRR)

The **internal rate of return** (IRR) method is used to determine the actual rate of return earned by an organisation when undertaking a particular project. Simply stated: a R1 000 project that yields R1 100 in a year, has an IRR of 10 per cent. If the organisation could earn 7 per cent by investing the funds in the bank, the project will be viewed in a favourable light. The actual arithmetic solves for the IRR of the project such that, when discounted, the present value of future costs and benefits equals zero. In this example,

$$- R1\,000 + \frac{R1\,100}{(1 + r)} = 0$$

will yield an IRR (r) of 10 per cent. It follows that, in general, the IRR for any given project over any given time period can be solved by using this equation:

$$- C_0 = = \sum_{t=1}^{n} \frac{B_t - C_t}{(1+r)^n} - C(x)_0 \qquad [9.4]$$

Prima facie, this method appears to be a corollary of the present value method. However, the problem is that it does not allow for comparisons between two or more projects of different sizes. For example, consider project *A* involving an initial investment of R1 000 that yields R1 200 in a year giving an IRR of 20 per cent. If the opportunity cost of the investment is 15 per cent (using, say, a given bank interest rate), the firm is better off by R50. Compare this with a smaller project, *B,* for which the initial investment is R100 and which yields R130 in one year's time, thus giving an IRR equal to 30 per cent. Using the IRR method you will choose project *B,* and yet the firm is only better off by R15.

The IRR method clearly produces ambiguous outcomes. If the same projects are compared using the NPV method, we get a different outcome. Using the discount rate, $i = 15$ per cent, the NPV for project *A,*

$$- R1\ 000 + \frac{R1\ 200}{1,15} = R43,50$$

and for project *B* it is

$$- R100 + \frac{R130}{1,15} = R13,00$$

indicating that project *A* is now preferred.

9.2.3 Benefit-cost (B-C) ratio

As with the IRR method, the **benefit-cost (B-C) ratio** represents a simple and therefore attractive method at first glance. Hidden pitfalls, however, will lead us back to the NPV as the preferred method of evaluation. The B-C ratio also involves discounting the future streams of expected benefits and costs for a given project. Once this is determined, the ratio simply gives the (present value of) benefits divided by the corresponding costs. If the B-C ratio is greater than one (B-C ratio > 1), the project is admissible.

Problems arise when costs can also be classified as negative benefits, like air pollution caused by a factory; or when benefits are classified as negative costs. By reducing the numerator by the value of a negative benefit, for example, a completely different ratio will be derived than if the denominator was increased by the equivalent amount.

It follows that the only consistent and reliable method of project appraisal is the NPV.

9.3 Valuation of benefits and costs

In a perfectly competitive environment in which there are no distortions or external effects, we already know that market prices will equal the corresponding marginal social costs and benefits. Under these conditions it is sufficient to value the inputs used by a new project at their prevailing market prices, and value output in terms of its expected market price. From a policy perspective, however, it is necessary first to find and quantify the appropriate *private* costs and benefits before considering the possible existence of *technological* externalities.

Of course, real-world markets are characterised by a host of market failures, including monopoly pricing, unemployment, and the presence of positive or negative technological externalities. Where market prices do exist, they will not usually reflect the true opportunity costs of the production factors and final goods in question: in an imperfectly competitive world prices will generally exceed marginal cost, while **technological externalities** will tend to drive a wedge between private and social marginal costs and benefits. In the case of pure public goods, prices do not even exist and recourse will have to be taken to alternative ways of appraising the relevant benefits and costs. In all these cases the project analyst will attempt to value the costs and benefits in terms of so-called **shadow prices**, that is, Pareto-optimal prices based on the true opportunity costs.

Project evaluation in the public sector usually begins by utilising information based on prevailing input and output prices in the private sector. Irrespective of whether the project involves provision of a pure public good or a mixed good, it will employ a range of labour skills, capital goods, and material inputs for which markets do exist. These input prices must, however, first be adjusted and converted into their shadow-price equivalents.

9.3.1 Labour

As far as labour is concerned, it is important to note that the existence of involuntary unemployment, experienced by many developing countries, implies that the social opportunity cost of employing unemployed labour is zero. A new public project making use of unemployed workers will not lower employment or output elsewhere in the economy, and the prevailing market wage rate cannot be used to value the cost of employing such labour on the project. The practice has been to set the shadow wage equal to the average unemployment benefits received by the unemployed. An alternative would be to use per capita income levels earned and received in the informal sector, which can be easily obtained from available household surveys.

9.3.2 Non-labour inputs

In pricing non-labour inputs, the project analyst should ideally allow for the presence of monopoly elements among suppliers. Recall that the demand (or actual) price charged by a monopolist exceeds the supply (or marginal cost) price. A public project using monopolistically priced inputs can use either of the two prices, and the choice will depend on the impact that the transaction has on the relevant input market. If the increased demand for the input leads to a corresponding increase in production, then the input should be priced at marginal cost which, after all, represents the value of the additional resources used in the production of the input. Alternatively, if the required inputs were simply transferred from existing users to the new project without any increase in production, then the appropriate price would be the demand or market price, since it represents the value to current users. In the event of there being a combined response, the project analyst should devise a suitably weighted average of the two prices.

9.3.3 Indirect taxes and subsidies

The prices of non-labour inputs may also include indirect taxes and subsidies. Here too it is necessary to consider the artificial gap that exists between the demand and supply prices: under a typical sales tax, for example, consumers pay more than what producers receive, while the opposite is true of a subsidy. As before, the decision whether to use the demand or the supply price will depend on the impact that the increased demand has on the input market. If production of the input increases, then the project analyst should use the supply price and consider only the factor cost of the input; if a transfer occurs without any change in production, the demand price will suffice; and if a combined response occurs, a weighted average price should be used.

9.3.4 Price variation

Where a new public project does give rise to increased production (of the input), and the lower (supply) price is used for valuation purposes, the project analyst could use the lower price or, in a more dynamic setting, a weighted average of the initial and subsequent prices. But the problem may be a lack of information about the underlying demand and supply functions. In certain instances it may be possible to obtain the necessary information directly from suppliers themselves and, after allowing for monopoly influences and indirect taxes and subsidies, price the input accordingly.

9.3.5 Pecuniary external effects

Perhaps the most important adjustment that has to be made concerns the multiplier or indirect effects that many public projects tend to have. These are usually **pecuniary external effects** that nonetheless constitute real benefits or costs (Dasgupta and Pearce, 1974: 121). Provided the economy is operating at a less-than-full-employment level of real income, a new public project could give rise to multiplied increases in output and employment in many other sectors, and it is imperative that these effects be taken into account in determining the relative attractiveness of the project. Apart from the direct impact on supplying and purchasing industries, the multiplier (and accelerator) process works its way through the spending activities of new workers on the project itself, and of workers in the supplying and purchasing industries, which ultimately add further value in the rest of the economy. Given the relevant information, including

up-to-date input-output tables, it is not too difficult to estimate the overall economic impact of a new public project. Multiplier coefficients ranging between 1,4 and 1,6 are fairly common, and can make an important difference to the relative values afforded to different public projects (Black, 2004; Black and Saxby, 1996).

Of course, under conditions of full employment and maximum capacity utilisation, these multiplier effects will be offset by cut-backs in output and employment elsewhere in the economy. Thus it may be that shop and restaurant owners located along or near a new rapid railway system may become more profitable as a direct result of increased traffic. If these benefits are offset by losses experienced by shop and restaurant owners along the old routes, however, it can be viewed as an income transfer from one group to another in which case total welfare will remain the same as before. In this instance we are dealing with pecuniary externalities that do not constitute net benefits or costs and that should not therefore be included in the calculation of the discounted net benefit of a project.

If all the above adjustments could indeed be made, it should at least be possible to quantify the **adjusted marginal private cost** of the project which is bound to be much lower than the unadjusted equivalent (as discussed in Chapter 3). In equilibrium the adjusted marginal private cost will equal the corresponding marginal private benefit. This equilibrium is shown as point M in Figure 9.1, where supply or MPC – *adjusted* for unemployment, monopoly elements, indirect taxes and subsidies and pecuniary externalities – equals the correspondingly adjusted MPB.

9.3.6 Questionnaire studies

There still remains the problem of having to quantify the technological external costs and benefits, which, as we have seen, should be added to the (adjusted) private costs and benefits in order to derive the true social value of the project. The problem here is that the analyst cannot use market prices to begin with, because there are none. Nonetheless, the basic aim remains that of estimating the net willingness to pay, or consumer surplus. Two possibilities suggest themselves, one entailing survey work and the other intelligent guesswork.

Technological externalities can be gauged by means of questionnaire studies. The creation of a park in a CBD will benefit some and harm others, each of whom can presumably put a monetary value on the benefit or cost. Likewise, the installation of an express train directly from Khayelitsha to the CBD of Cape Town will save commuters the time spent waiting for taxis and the time wasted in rush-hour traffic. The challenge here is to quantify the value of time or the value of leisure to the commuter, that is, the amount

she would be willing to pay in order to substitute the time spent in rush-hour traffic for more leisure time. Thus the benefits from the new rapid railway system can be gauged through questionnaire surveys that ask commuters how much they would be willing to pay to reduce their current commuting time. Similarly, in addition to the (adjusted) direct or monetary costs of the project, external costs could be proxied by asking those negatively affected by the new railway line how much compensation they would need in order to put up with it.

It is important to add that we are referring here to technological externalities only as discussed in Chapter 3 and Section 9.3.5 earlier – not pecuniary ones, which feature in the calculation of adjusted costs and benefits, as discussed in the previous section. Technological externalities affect the utility functions of consumers and the production functions of producers and do not, as a rule, alter market prices.

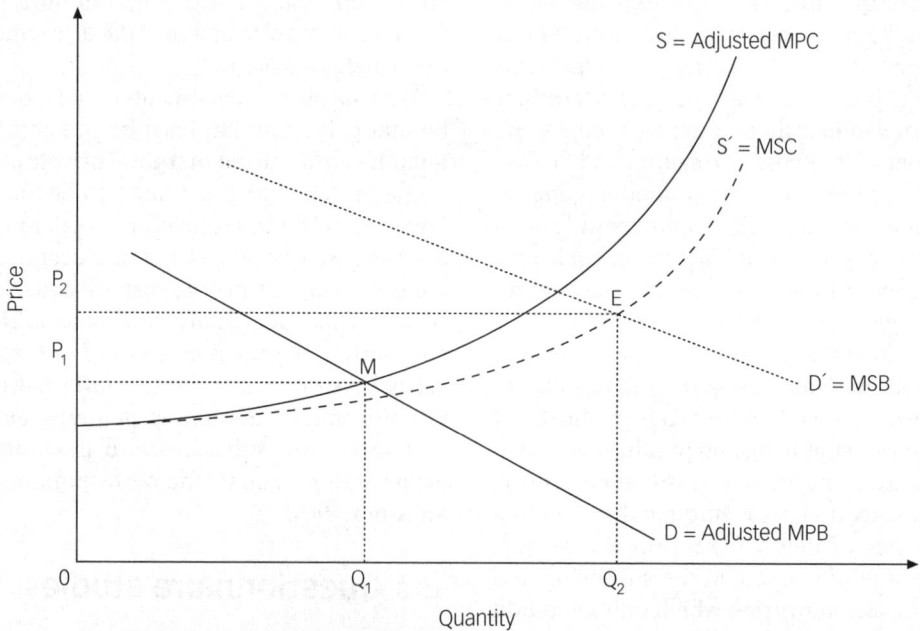

Figure 9.1 Adjusted private values versus social values

9.3.7 Contingencies

If the survey method should prove to be too costly, the analyst could consider using the results of similar studies undertaken elsewhere in the world. However, care should be taken to adjust such findings in accordance with the particular characteristics of both the project itself and the environment in which it will be operating.

The alternative would be to treat the expected external effects as 'contingencies' in the budget, rather than simply ignoring them altogether. For many public projects, such as a new school or healthcare facility, it seems reasonable to assume that they will confer a net external benefit on the community; in such a case the project analyst would be justified in budgeting for a larger output at a higher price than would otherwise apply using only the adjusted private costs and benefits of the project. Such a procedure clearly involves a judgement call on the part of the decision-maker, who should ideally base his or her judgement on the social preferences of the broader community as expressed through the ballot box (see Chapter 6).

This discussion can be illustrated with the aid of Figure 9.1. S and S' are the adjusted marginal private and social cost curves, respectively, while D and D' represent the adjusted private and social marginal benefit curves. If technological externalities were entirely ignored, and the project analyst used appropriate shadow prices for all the inputs, the adjusted private equilibrium would occur at point M, indicating production of $0Q_1$ units at price $0P_1$. But technological externalities evidently do exist with the marginal social benefit exceeding the marginal social cost of the project at point M. Clearly the social equilibrium occurs at point E, requiring a larger output at a higher price than before.

9.4 The social discount rate

Our discussion thus far, has focused on the valuation of benefits and costs. Recall that Equation [9.3] had three variables: benefits, costs, and the discount rate. In the private sector the profit derived from undertaking an investment (as measured by the return on capital or ROC) must exceed the rate at which capital for the project can be obtained, as there would otherwise be no incentive to begin the project in the first place. The discount rate is thus simply the appropriate market rate of interest charged by the lending institution. But as argued before, when private firms undertake new investment projects they generally pursue their own individual interests. It is often claimed that in doing so, they choose a discount rate – i.e. the interest rate – that does not necessarily serve the broader interests of society. We briefly discuss some of the reasons for this claim.

9.4.1 Insufficient investment

Private investments do not benefit investors only, but may also confer external benefits on 'third' parties not involved in the initial investment activity. Investments in new technologies generally tend to benefit many more firms than only those who have taken on the initial risk of such investments. Similarly, a firm investing in the training of its own workforce would indirectly benefit other firms when its trained workers change jobs (Arrow, 1962). Individual South African firms will likewise have little or no incentive to train employees belonging to historically disadvantaged groups if they expect them to be poached by other firms once they are trained. The conventional argument is that such training should become the responsibility of the public sector, which is at least potentially capable of achieving the requisite optimal level of training.

If private investments do create positive externalities, it can be expected that private markets on their own will invest too little, at least when viewed from a social welfare perspective, establishing the usual case for appropriate policy intervention. One option would be to lower the discount rate used in public projects below the prevailing market rate of interest. Such a downward adjustment would immediately increase the discounted net present value of all public projects, making more of them feasible and potentially acceptable. The difficulty here is that of measuring the size of the externality. Even if this could be done, the most efficient means of intervention does not necessarily involve adjusting the discount rate. The government could instead grant private firms an investment subsidy equal to the marginal external benefit, leaving it to the private sector to make up the investment shortfall (see Chapter 3).

9.4.2 Current and future generations

A second consideration concerns the relative importance of future generations vis-à-vis the current generation. It is sometimes argued that the community as a whole, and hence its representative public sector, places a higher relative value on the well-being of future generations than do self-interested private individuals and institutions. The private sector thus saves too little and applies too high a discount rate to the future returns of their investments. This preference for the current generation may well explain why private individuals do not, as a rule, invest large amounts in the provision of social services such as education and healthcare – these tend to have long gestation periods before they render positive returns. Likewise, the planting of trees in a

residential suburb may only produce benefits in, say, 20 years. Such benefits are clearly unlikely to exceed the return on capital (ROC) demanded by private investors. But if society as a whole placed a high value on the benefits that fully grown trees could have on the next generation, it can choose a lower **social discount rate** now to increase the discounted net present value of the project.

If CBA can be used to discriminate between different generations, then it can also be used to discriminate between different groups within the current generation. Governments pursuing a more equitable distribution of income can do so by applying different discount rates to public projects in different regions and neighbourhoods. It is often true that the cost of investing in an established urban area is lower than the cost of the same investment in a poor and remote rural area. Given that the benefits are roughly the same, the government can avoid this distributional bias by either applying a lower discount rate to the rural area, or by simply applying a higher quantitative weight to NPV in that area. In either case, however, the distributional gain may entail a loss in efficiency, the size of which will ultimately depend on the value judgments of the project analyst.

9.4.3 Risk

A final issue concerns the riskiness of different investment projects. Public projects are generally considered to be less risky than equivalent projects in the private sector. The reason is that project risks in the public sector are spread more widely across the tax-paying public than equivalent risks taken on by private entrepreneurs. Public project analysts could therefore use a lower risk premium than that which applies to the private sector. The lower risk premium usually implies an adjustment to the relevant market rate of interest, and hence to the private discount rate, thus implying that the public project analyst could use a discount rate that is lower than the prevailing market rate of interest. It goes without saying that risk premiums will vary among different public projects, and it is therefore important that such differences be duly taken into account.

9.5 Concluding note

All in all, it would seem that CBA does enable governments to evaluate and compare public and merit goods in terms of their *social* rather than private (or monetary) values and to deliver those with the highest net present values at socially optimal quantities and prices. It is partly for this reason that CBA has been successfully applied in many parts of the world (see Box 9.1). But the strict application of CBA in practice does tend to give a great deal of discretionary power to project analysts and decision makers in the public sector. It is therefore imperative that the decisions they take should truly reflect the wishes of the community they serve. While this is clearly a tall order – perhaps a wishful one – we know from Chapter 6 that successful delivery will ultimately depend on both the political system – or 'social choice rule' – that is in place as well as the ability of politicians and bureaucrats to control 'government failure'.

BOX 9.1 CBA Examples

Cost-benefit analysis (CBA) has been applied to many public projects across the world, including those involving land-use, irrigation, hydro-electric power, rail and road transport, health services and education (Prest and Turvey, 1978). In a recent study in Namibia, Pienaar (2008) conducted a CBA on a major new road coupled with the upgrading of an existing road linked to the former. He used the net present value (NPV) technique and estimated income multipliers for the construction phase as well as the 'recurring accelerator effect' resulting from the increased usage and shorter distances and time travelled between two industrial towns. Similarly, Meier et al. (2008) used the World Bank's 'road economic decision' (RED) model to conduct CBAs of two adjacent roads in South Africa, one being a single-lane road and the other a more recently constructed and tolled double-carriageway national road. They found that the diversion of traffic to the latter road generally conferred a net economic benefit to the region as a whole.

In another recent study in Zimbabwe, focusing on wildlife preservation, Muchapondwa et al. (2008) used a technique similar to CBA, i.e. the contingent valuation method (CVM). They used this method to estimate inhabitants' valuation of wildlife (in particular the African elephant) residing in an adjacent game reserve. While a majority viewed the elephants as a 'public bad', damaging crops on occasions, and preferred them to be relocated elsewhere, the authors recommended that the inhabitants be compensated for their discomfort in order to preserve the tourist value of the national park.

IMPORTANT CONCEPTS

adjusted marginal private
    costs (page 153)
benefit-cost ratio (page 151)
discount rate (page 150)
economic efficiency
    (page 149)

internal rate of return
    (page 150)
net present value (page 149)
pecuniary external effects
    (page 153)
shadow prices (page 152)

social discount rate
    (page 156)
technological externalities
    (page 151)

SELF-ASSESSMENT EXERCISES

9.1 Outline the net present value (NPV) method of project evaluation and briefly compare it to the internal rate of return.

9.2 Compare the different approaches to project evaluation followed by the private and public sectors.

9.3 Explain the process by which market prices can be adjusted to reflect the true opportunity cost of inputs used in a public project.

9.4 Under what conditions should the multiplier effects of a new public project be taken into consideration?

9.5 Distinguish between pecuniary and technological externalities and show how they might feature in the evaluation of public projects.

9.6 Illustrate with the aid of a diagram what you consider to be the optimal value of a public project.

9.7 How would you justify the use of a social discount rate that differs from the prevailing market rate of interest?

PART

3

Taxation

Chapter
TEN

Tjaart Steenekamp

Introduction to taxation and tax equity

In Parts 1 and 2 we explained the role and functions of government as well as the nature and patterns of government expenditure. The need and demand for public goods and services would appear to be varied and extensive. However, like all other demands (wants) and needs, the demand for public goods and services is also constrained by limited resources on the supply side. Furthermore, like all other goods and services, the supply and distribution of public goods and services must be financed. John Coleman aptly remarked: 'The point to remember is that what the government gives it must first take away' (quoted in Mohr et al., 2008: 339).

This chapter will focus on taxation as a source of finance for public expenditures. Different sources of finance are identified in Section 10.1. In the following section tax bases are identified and a distinction is made between different types of taxes such as general taxes, *ad valorem* taxes, and direct taxes. Criteria for analysing taxes are proposed in Section 10.3 after which the equity criterion is described and discussed in depth in Section 10.4 as well as the rest of the chapter. When the fairness of a tax is considered the effects of tax shifting are paramount. In Sections 10.5, 10.6, and 10.7 the incidence of taxes is discussed using both a partial equilibrium and a general equilibrium analysis.

Once you have studied this chapter, you should be able to:
- ▶ list alternative sources of government revenue
- ▶ define a tax and describe the structure of tax rates
- ▶ distinguish between general and selective taxes, specific and *ad valorem* taxes, as well as direct and indirect taxes

> ▶ list the properties of a good tax
> ▶ explain what is meant by an equitable tax
> ▶ distinguish between the statutory and economic burden of a tax
> ▶ analyse the shifting of a tax and its impact on tax incidence using both a partial and a general equilibrium framework.

10.1 Sources of finance

The dominant source of finance for public expenditure is taxation. In 2009/10 tax revenue constituted approximately 81,1 per cent of total cash receipts from operating activities of the consolidated general government (South African Reserve Bank 2010: S-70). Government expenditure may also be financed from alternative sources. In addition to taxation there are four other important sources of finance: user charges, administrative fees, borrowing, and 'inflation taxation'.

User charges (also referred to as benefit taxes) are prices charged for the delivery of certain public goods and services. The role these charges play in the allocation and distribution of resources is analogous to the role of prices in the market mechanism. The important difference is that user charges are set in the 'political market'. User charges can only be levied if exclusion is possible (see Chapter 3, Section 3.9). In other words, it should be possible to exclude those who do not pay for the consumption of the public good or service in question. Examples of user charges include toll roads, public swimming pools, ambulance services, and university education (see Section 10.4.1 for a further discussion of benefit taxes).

Administrative fees are similar to user charges but differ in the sense that the service (or benefit) received in return for the fee is defined rather broadly and imprecisely.

Such fees include business licences, television licences, diamond export rights, fishing licences, and motor vehicle licences. The dreaded parking ticket and speeding fine can also be added to the list. Administrative fees and fines are insignificant sources of revenue.

Government can borrow from its own citizens and from abroad. Borrowing is often used to finance capital expenditure. Borrowed funds must be repaid at some point and can therefore amount to deferred taxes. Because lenders have to be adequately compensated for current consumption forgone, it is imperative that borrowed money should be spent on productive activities. Sometimes government uses borrowed funds to finance current consumption, a practice that cannot always be defended on economic grounds (see Chapter 16, Section 16.2).

Government-induced inflation can also be regarded as a source of revenue. If public expenditure is financed in such a way that increases in the money supply occur, such financing may eventually raise the price level. Inflation changes the real value of public debt. If government borrows R2 000 from a taxpayer (e.g. if government imposes a loan levy on all taxpayers with incomes in excess of R100 000) and inflation is 10 per cent, then in a year's time the real value of the loan is only R1 800 (R2 000 − $[\frac{10}{100} \times 2\ 000]$). If the value of the loan is not linked to a price index, the real value of government debt decreases. In this case it may also be said that government finances its expenditure with an '**inflation tax**'.

10.2 Definition and classification of taxes

In 1789, Benjamin Franklin wrote: 'In this world nothing can be said to be certain, except death and taxes' (Cohen and Cohen, 1960). What, then, is so abhorrent about taxes? **Taxes** are transfers of resources from persons or economic units to government and are compulsory (or legally enforceable). There is not necessarily a direct connection between the resources transferred to government and the goods and services it supplies. In fact, government can compel one group of individuals to make payments that are used to finance activities to the benefit of another group. Taxes are compulsory due to the free rider problem. As no one will pay taxes voluntarily, people have to be compelled to do so. The fact that government has legally been granted the power to tax distinguishes government's confiscation of resources through taxation from other involuntary transfers of resources (e.g. theft).

Government, however, does not have unlimited powers as far as taxation is concerned. The Constitution of the Republic of South Africa (1996) provides for money Bills, that is, Bills that provide government with the legal right to appropriate amounts of money or impose taxes, levies, or duties. All money Bills must be considered in accordance with the procedure established by Section 75 of the Constitution, and an act of parliament must provide for a procedure to amend money Bills before parliament. Since the National Assembly must pass such a Bill, it implies that, in addition to procedural limits, the imposition of taxes and changes to taxes are subject to the checks and balances of parliament. In a representative democracy, parliamentarians must take cognisance of the preferences of voters as well as of other parties (e.g. vested interests) that may influence fiscal decisions. The influence of interest groups in this process is considered to be particularly important (see Chapter 6) and may even explain why the fear that 'the numerous poor will out-vote the rich and middle classes, and tax away much of their wealth' is more apparent than real (Becker, 1985).

Taxes can be classified in many ways. The classification used in South Africa is the one that conforms to the International Monetary Fund's Government Finance Statistics Manual, published in 2001. Tax revenue is grouped into six categories, each of which is then sub-divided further. The main tax categories in respect of central government (with the approximate percentage contribution to total tax revenue net of South African Customs Union payments for 2010/11 in brackets) are as follows (National Treasury, 2011a: 156):

▶ Taxes on income and profits (59,1 per cent)
▶ Taxes on payroll and workforce (1,3 per cent)
▶ Taxes on property (1,4 per cent)
▶ Domestic taxes on goods and services (37,8 per cent)
▶ Taxes on international trade and transactions (4,1 per cent)
▶ Stamp duties and fees (0,001 per cent).

Income taxes clearly constituted the most important category of taxes in 2010/11. Taxes on the income of individuals contributed 60,0 per cent towards the total taxes on income and profits while tax on the income of non-mining corporations (excluding secondary tax on companies) contributed 44,9 per cent.

In order to do a proper analysis, we will classify taxes according to tax base in the next section. We will then distinguish between general and selective taxes, specific and *ad valorem* taxes, and direct and indirect taxes in the subsequent sections.

10.2.1 **Tax base and rates of taxation**

Taxes can generally be imposed on three **tax bases**: income, wealth, and consumption. A tax on people can be added to these three bases. A poll tax (or **lump sum tax** per head) is an example of a tax on people. Tax bases can also be viewed in terms of their flow and stock characteristics. Flows are associated with a time dimension and are measured over a period. Income and consumption are flow concepts since both are measured over a period of time (normally a tax year). Stocks have no time dimension and are measured at a particular point in time, for example wealth. Which of the three potential tax bases is the best is a much-debated issue. Most countries have hybrid systems, exploiting three (or four) bases simultaneously. Tax systems differ according to historical and political circumstances as well as the stage of development. This aspect is discussed in Chapter 14, Section 14.5.

Once the tax base has been identified, the **tax rate structure** can be set. The **tax rate** refers to the amount of tax levied per unit of the tax base. Three variants can be distinguished: proportional, progressive, and regressive taxes. The rate structure can be described in at least two ways. One way is to compare the average tax rate (the total rand amount of taxes collected divided by the rand value of the taxable base) to the size or value of the tax base. Therefore, when the average tax rate remains constant with respect to variations in the tax base, the tax is **proportional** – see Box 10.1. When the average tax rate increases as the tax base increases, the tax is **progressive**. If the average tax rate decreases as the tax base increases, the tax is **regressive**.

The rate structure can also be described by focusing on the ratio of taxes paid to income. All taxes are then evaluated in terms of the income base as a common denominator for comparison purposes, even though the tax may in practice be imposed on a different base. In this way the distributional consequences of taxes can be determined. Taxes that generate the same proportion of income as income rises are proportional (e.g. corporate income tax). A tax with a proportional rate structure is also called a flat-rate tax. Taxes that take an increasing proportion of income as income increases are progressive taxes (e.g. personal income tax). If a tax generates a decreasing proportion of income as income increases, it is a regressive tax (e.g. a value added tax without any zero-ratings) – see Box 10.1.

10.2.2 **General and selective taxes**

Taxes can be classified as general or selective taxes. A **general tax** (also called broad-based tax) is one that taxes the entire tax base and allows for no exemptions. A value added tax (VAT) without any exemptions or zero-ratings is a general tax on consumption. Similarly, an income tax that taxes all sources of income (including capital income) without any tax deductions would be a general tax.

Selective taxes (also called narrow-based taxes) are imposed on one or a few products or only income, that is, excluding leisure. The whole tax base is therefore not taxed. An excise tax on cigarettes is an example of a selective tax. The importance of the distinction between general and selective taxes lies in the fact that under certain assumptions[1] general taxes are similar to head or lump sum taxes that leave relative prices unchanged.

---

[1] The most important assumptions are that the supplies of work effort and of savings remain unchanged (i.e. are unaffected by the tax).

BOX 10.1 Proportional, progressive, and regressive taxes

Consider a tax on the consumption base. Suppose a tax of 10 per cent is imposed on the consumption of all food and non-alcoholic beverages (in short food products). Suppose furthermore that there are two households: the Peterson household with a monthly income of R2 000 and the Chetty household with a monthly income of R100 000. Is this tax progressive, proportional, or regressive? According to the 2005/06 Income and Expenditure Survey conducted by Statistics South Africa (SSA), the low-income group (lower expenditure quintile) spends approximately 37 per cent of its income on food products, whereas the high-income group (the fifth expenditure quintile) spends only 10 per cent of its income (Statistics South Africa, 2008). The Petersons thus spend approximately R740 on food products per month and the Chettys R10 000 (more than ten times the amount of the Petersons). A 10 per cent tax on food products will therefore 'cost' the Petersons R74 per month in taxes while the Chettys will pay R1 000. In absolute terms the Chettys thus contribute more in tax on food products to the South African Revenue Service (SARS) than the Petersons. When we divide the tax collected (R74 or R1 000) by the rand value of the taxable consumption base (R740 or R10 000), the average tax rate is the same ($\frac{74}{740} \times 100 = 10\%$ or $\frac{1\,000}{10\,000} \times 100 = 10\%$). Our first conclusion would therefore be that the tax is proportional since the average tax rate does not vary with the size of the tax base. However, if we evaluate the tax in terms of the income base, as is commonly done, the picture looks rather different. The Petersons have to transfer 3,7 per cent of their income ($\frac{74}{2\,000} \times 100$) to SARS, but in the case of the Chettys it is only 1,0 per cent of their income ($\frac{1\,000}{100\,000} \times 100$). Thus the tax structure is regressive with respect to the income base but proportional with respect to the consumption base.

In other words, the behaviour of economic role players is assumed to be unaffected by these taxes. In contrast, selective taxes distort relative prices by driving a wedge between the before-tax price and after-tax price of a commodity. This violates the Pareto efficiency condition. This aspect will again receive attention when we consider the efficiency of different taxes in Chapter 11, Section 11.1.

10.2.3 Specific and *ad valorem* taxes

Taxes can also be specified according to the size or the value of the tax base. The size of the tax base can be measured in terms of weight, quantities, or units. When a fixed amount is imposed per unit of the product, the tax is called a **unit tax** or **specific tax**. Examples of specific taxes in South Africa in 2011/12 are excise duties on sparkling wine (R6,97 per litre), beer made from malt (R0,92 per average 340 ml can), and cigarettes (R9,74 per 20 cigarettes).

Taxes imposed on the value of products are called *ad valorem* taxes. Such a tax is usually levied as a rate (i.e. a percentage) of the excisable value (or price) of a commodity. VAT and excise duties are examples of *ad valorem* taxes. *Ad valorem* taxes (sometimes called *ad valorem* duties) are often imposed on 'luxuries'. *Ad valorem* excise duties were introduced in 1969 for revenue purposes and were levied on certain locally manufactured goods with a corresponding *ad valorem* customs duty (at the same rate) levied on imported goods of the same kind. For example, in South Africa commodities such as sun protection products with a sun protection factor of less than 15, perfumes and toilet waters, golf balls, video cameras for non-commercial application and cellphones are taxed at rates varying between 5 per cent and 7 per cent of the price. Motor vehicles are taxed using a graduated formula that distinguishes between vehicle type and weight and translates into a higher excise duty on high ('luxury') priced cars.

10.2.4 Direct and indirect taxes

Yet another possible distinction can be made between direct and indirect taxes. Direct taxes are imposed directly on individuals and companies (e.g. personal income tax and company tax). Indirect taxes are imposed on commodities (e.g. excise taxes and VAT). This distinction fundamentally revolves around the issue of tax incidence (i.e. the question of who really pays the tax). Tax incidence is a complex issue and is analysed in Section 10.4. It would suffice to say that we simply cannot tell with certainty in advance what the outcome is going to be.

From the perspective of tax shifting, **direct taxes** are defined as taxes that cannot be shifted readily. They are collected from individuals, households, or firms and allow for the possibility of adjusting the tax according to the personal circumstances of the taxpayer (e.g. the marital status, gender, size of household, wealth status). These taxpayers are the intended bearers of the tax burden and it is assumed that they pay the tax over to SARS. Personal income tax is nowadays mostly deducted from employees' salaries and paid over by employers. Nonetheless, the employer does not have complete information on non-salary income (e.g. donations, interest, rent, capital gains) and the individual is therefore still responsible for the completeness and correctness of the tax assessment.

Indirect taxes are taxes that are imposed on commodities or market transactions and are likely to be shifted. Examples are excise duties and fuel levies. It is also more difficult to adjust the tax rate to the personal circumstances of the consumer. In the case of indirect taxes it is often possible to shift the burden of the tax to someone else. VAT is collected from merchants who, in turn, can pass on the tax to consumers by way of a price increase. The consumer then indirectly bears the burden.

Although there are differences of opinion on the exact distinction between direct and indirect taxes, this classification is widely used. The relative importance of direct versus indirect taxes is much debated, also in South Africa. In 1975/76 the ratio of direct to indirect taxes was 2,7, that is, for each rand in indirect taxes collected, R2,70 was collected in direct taxes. In 2010/11 this ratio was 1,4 which shows a clear shift in the direction of indirect taxes. These trends will be discussed in Chapter 14, Section 14.5 when the topic of tax reform is considered. The merits and demerits of indirect taxes will receive attention in Chapter 14.

10.3 Properties of a 'good tax'

Tax systems evolve from time to time as new taxes are introduced and others are amended. The question is whether such changes are good or bad. To evaluate these changes we can use a list of criteria, some of which date back to the 'maxims of taxation' proposed by Adam Smith in 1776. A good tax system must first of all generate sufficient revenue to finance budgeted government expenditure. The other more important criteria or properties of a 'good' tax system can be classified under four headings:

▶ Equity: Taxes should promote an equitable (or 'fair') distribution of income. Cognisance has to be taken of the fact that the burden of taxes can be shifted. To determine fairness, the incidence of taxes, therefore, has to be examined. These topics are covered in Section 10.4.

▶ Economic efficiency: All taxes impose a burden and most taxes affect the behaviour of taxpayers (i.e. they cause an 'excess burden'). Taxes should be designed in such a way that their distorting effects on the choices made by taxpayers are minimised. This aspect is discussed in Chapter 11 (Section 11.1).

▶ Administrative efficiency: Taxes are levied to yield sufficient revenue but in order to be efficient, administration and compliance costs have to be kept low. This calls for tax simplicity and certainty. This topic is discussed in Chapter 11 (Section 11.3).

▶ Flexibility: As economic circumstances change, taxes and tax rates need to adjust. Taxes should therefore be flexible enough to facilitate macroeconomic stability and economic development. This aspect is discussed in Chapter 11 (Section 11.4).

10.4 Taxation and equity: concepts of fairness

One of the most important judgements in tax analysis is whether or not the distributional impact of a tax is equitable or fair. Fairness, however, is a subjective concept and, like beauty, it lies in the eye of the beholder. Although fairness is a value-laden concept, economists can help to make informed value judgements. In his first maxim of taxation, Adam Smith (1776), as quoted in Musgrave and Musgrave (1989: 219), stated:

> *The subjects of every state ought to contribute towards the support of the government, as nearly as possible, in proportion to their respective abilities; that is, in proportion to the revenue which they respectively enjoy under the protection of the state.*

This statement contains a **tax equity** principle that is still used in theory and practice to evaluate the fairness of the impact (or incidence) of taxes, that is, the **ability-to-pay principle**. Another principle is based on benefits received. We will first consider the benefit principle.

10.4.1 Benefit principle

The **benefit principle** stipulates that the tax burden of government expenditure should be apportioned to taxpayers in accordance with the benefits each receives. Consider the example of a bridge: the more an individual uses the bridge, the more he or she will have to pay for this benefit. If the bridge is financed out of general revenues instead of through a benefit tax (e.g. a toll) levied on those using the bridge, those who do not use the bridge will be in a worse position. It seems unfair to expect non-users also to pay for the construction and maintenance of the bridge. Here we have an example of **forced carrying**: while free riding refers to someone failing to carry a 'proper' tax burden, forced carrying refers to someone being made to carry a heavier than 'proper' burden. It can also be argued that tax morality will be undermined if taxpayers do not benefit from a tax system and that a democratic society will become intolerant of such a system in the long run.

A major advantage of the benefit principle is that it links the expenditure side of the budget to the revenue side. In this way it serves to discipline or regulate government expenditure. A further benefit is that the allocative procedures of market behaviour are approximated. Individuals can adjust their consumption of services until price is equal to the marginal cost. In a voluntary exchange model, if the price is higher than the marginal cost, society places a higher value on an additional unit of the service than the resources required to provide the additional unit. In terms of Pareto optimality conditions, society's welfare can then be improved by allocating more resources to the provision of the service, that is, at least one person's position can be improved without causing anyone else to be in a worse position. Benefit taxes assume the role of prices and can therefore ensure that resources are efficiently allocated.

Unfortunately the scope for applying the benefit principle to government funding is rather restricted. Governments generally provide goods and services that are public in nature. In other words, the benefits are generally non-excludable (see Chapter 3). For example, how would one apportion the benefits of protection (e.g. policing) to different beneficiaries? There is no straightforward answer. Some would argue that the rich benefit most because they have so much to lose and that they therefore have to contribute more. Others would argue that the poor are the most vulnerable (i.e. most in need of protection) and that they thus have to pay more.

Another shortcoming of benefit taxes is that it takes the existing distribution of income and wealth for granted. The effective demand for public goods and services is often determined by this distribution. If the distribution is skewed towards the rich, the provision of public services might therefore be tailored largely to their needs. The benefit approach can ideally only handle a tax-expenditure process that has no redistributive objectives (i.e. where redistribution is not a significant justification for the service being provided). It cannot handle a tax-expenditure programme designed for redistributive purposes (e.g. taxes levied to finance transfer payments or expenditure programmes designed to benefit the poor rather than the rich) or where it is administratively not feasible to exempt poor people from paying for the benefits of a particular service (e.g. a toll road). It would, for example, be somewhat ridiculous if pensioners have to bear the current taxes required to finance the transfers to themselves. The benefit principle can therefore undermine redistributive objectives of government and result in conflicting outcomes.

Benefit taxes (often referred to as user charges) are nevertheless levied in some cases, for example, tolls for roads and bridges, admission charges to museums and parks, license fees, and (to a certain extent) university tuition fees and school fees. Note that in the case of user charges the link between the financing of the use of the service and the benefit is reasonably direct.

The benefit approach may therefore be rationalised on the grounds of equity. However, a frequent criticism against user charges is that they may contradict the equity objective by preventing the poor from using government-supplied services. For example, it is argued that education and publicly supplied cultural and recreational facilities such as art galleries, museums, and parks, often referred to as merit goods, should be made available free of charge to all people. This will enable those who are unable to pay for the use of these facilities to enjoy them. A problem with this approach is that the implicit subsidy that is involved when general financing is applied accrues to both the rich and the poor. If the services are heavily used by the rich, the subsidy to the rich may be substantial. To the extent that the poor contribute to general revenue, a part of the cost of the subsidy is borne by the poor. In certain circumstances, general-fund financing could even redistribute income from the poor to the rich. This dilemma may be resolved by imposing a charge for the use of facilities but offering special reductions to targeted groups such as children, the elderly, and so on.

Sometimes services are financed in such a way that the link is more indirect. This occurs when charges are assigned (or dedicated) to special funds or accounts for financing services that are indirectly related to the source of the funds. In such cases the taxes are called **earmarked taxes**. Examples of earmarked taxes are levies on the sale of fuel, social security taxes (e.g. unemployment insurance contributions), and skills development levies. Fuel levies at provincial level have been proposed in some provinces, for example the Western Cape, and are intended for transport infrastructure maintenance. At the time of writing, fuel levies consisted of a general levy of 177,5 cents per litre (in respect of 93 octane petrol), the Road Accident Fund (RAF) levy of 80,0 cents per litre and a customs and excise levy of 4,0 cents per litre. Only the RAF has the character of an earmarked tax since the general fuel levy finances general government expenditure and accrues to the National Revenue Fund. On the recommendation of the Katz Commission (1995), government decided that a portion of the general fuel levy would be allocated to a National Road Agency for road construction and maintenance. The Skills Development Act (No. 97 of 1998) as amended (2003) provides for a levy of 1 per cent of payrolls aimed at, for example, developing skills of the South African workforce, improving productivity in the workplace, promoting self-employment, and increasing the levels of investment in education and training in the labour market.

The shortcomings of the benefit principle generally apply to earmarked taxes as well. In addition, earmarked taxes affect the procedural fairness of the budgetary process. Since earmarked funds have assured sources of revenue, these funds need not compete with other departments for finance. In the case of earmarked funds, accountability and the responsibility for efficient resource allocation are also shifted to the managers of these funds. Earmarked taxes also complicate fiscal policy aimed at achieving macroeconomic objectives. The Katz Commission (1995: 24) therefore recommended against a proliferation of earmarked taxes (especially in respect of general tax revenue such as VAT where the link between benefits and costs is extremely vague).

10.4.2 Ability-to-pay principle

As already mentioned, the benefit principle cannot be applied to the financing of public goods and services that are non-excludable. Public expenditures are predominantly of this type. Total cost of such public expenditure therefore has to be apportioned according to the ability of people to pay. In contrast with the benefit principle, the application of the ability-to-pay principle implies that the tax problem is viewed independently from the expenditure aspect.

The ability-to-pay principle calls for people with equal capacity to pay the same amount of tax (**horizontal equity**), and for people with greater capacity to pay more (**vertical equity**). Horizontal equity requires similar treatment for tax purposes of people in similar economic circumstances, while vertical equity requires that individuals in different economic circumstances be treated differently.

The implementation of a tax system based on ability to pay requires public consensus on an appropriate definition (i.e. measure, indicator, criterion, or basis) of ability to pay.

It also calls for consensus on the rate structure. Income is generally regarded as one such measure or criterion. Other possible measures include consumption, wealth, and utility. Much of the discussion concerning the appropriate measure or base is theoretical, but, in practice, income is commonly used.

Income, however, is by no means a perfect measure of a person's ability to pay. Income measures outcomes and does not necessarily reflect ability or capacity. Consider, for example, two persons, Ms Moleketi and Ms Pienaar, with similar economic circumstances and the same capacity to earn income. The economic circumstances referred to here include gender, race, religion, marital status, level of education, disability, number of dependants, and so on. Ms Moleketi, however, is much more hard-working and works ten hours a day at a rate of R50 per hour compared to the five hours that Ms Pienaar works for the same hourly pay. Ms Moleketi therefore earns R500 per day compared to Ms Pienaar's R250. Using income as the yardstick of ability to pay implies that Ms Moleketi has a greater ability to pay and that she should therefore make a greater tax sacrifice. Is this fair? In this case, is the wage rate, instead of total wage income, not a more appropriate measure of ability? Not surprisingly, the inclusion or exclusion of the various possible determinants of economic circumstances in the search for an appropriate base for ability to pay has been hotly debated.[2]

The appropriate measurement of horizontal and vertical equity is not only a complicated issue but also requires subjective evaluations. Economics alone cannot provide unambiguous answers to the measurement of 'ability' and the final decision therefore has to be taken via the political process.

Once the appropriate measure of ability to pay has been established, fairness suggests that people with the same ability should pay the same amount of tax and people with different abilities should pay different amounts. Suppose income is used to measure ability to pay. This still leaves the question of how to determine the taxes payable by people with different incomes. For example, if person A's income is double that of person B, should person A pay exactly twice as much tax as person B? This relates to vertical equity and is a rate structure issue. Various concepts involving sacrifice have been developed in an attempt to deal with the problem of vertical equity.[3]

Suffice it to say that most countries try to deal with vertical equity by applying the progressive tax rule to income (i.e. by taxing an increasing proportion of income as income increases). But this does not solve the dilemma. To determine whether a tax is truly progressive, proportional, or regressive, one needs to know who really pays the tax. In other words, the impact of a tax on the distribution of income has to be investigated. This is what tax incidence is all about.

10.5 Tax incidence: partial equilibrium analysis

10.5.1 Concepts of incidence

All taxes reduce the real disposable income of taxpayers. All taxes therefore involve a burden. At the outset it should be noted that only people bear the burden. Companies, for example, cannot bear the tax burden.

Only people (e.g. shareholders, workers, landlords, consumers) bear the burden of taxation. Exactly who ultimately bears the burden is a matter for theoretical discourse and empirical evidence. To deal with this question, we first have to distinguish between the statutory (or legal) incidence of a tax and the economic (or effective) incidence.

The **statutory incidence** refers to the legal liability to pay the tax over to the revenue authorities. Economists are not really interested in who is legally obliged to make the tax payment to SARS. Since taxes affect economic behaviour, economists are more concerned with who ultimately bears the tax burden, that is, the **economic incidence** of the tax. For example, customs and excise taxes are levied on cigarettes. At the time of writing, an importer of cigarettes had to pay a customs duty of R9,74 per 20 cigarettes to SARS. However, the importer can shift the actual burden forward to retailers who, in turn, can pass on the tax to the consumers (the smokers) in the form of higher prices. The tax burden can also be shifted backward if, for example, the importer cuts back on staff or lowers real wages. In addition to tax shifting, the tax can be avoided by cutting back on the taxed activity, that is, by reducing imports of cigarettes. What we notice here is that the economic incidence issue is fundamentally about how taxes affect prices (including wages).

Tax incidence studies may apply either a balanced-budget incidence methodology or a differential-incidence methodology. According to the **balanced-budget** incidence approach, the overall distributional effect of a tax and the spending financed by the tax is considered. Income taxes lower real disposable income but, at the same time, the income tax revenue is spent on education and other public services that raise real disposable income (at least for those with school-going children). The advantage of the balanced-budget incidence approach is that it relates the cost of spending programmes to those who pay for it. The disadvantage is that, in reality, government uses a number of different taxes to finance expenditure – tax revenue is pooled in the national revenue account. Linking a particular expenditure item to a tax source is almost impossible.

Since not all taxes are earmarked for a particular expenditure programme, the differential tax incidence approach comes in handy. The **differential tax incidence** methodology considers the distributional impact as one tax is substituted for another, holding total revenue and expenditure constant. The benchmark tax often used for purposes of comparison is a lump sum tax (e.g. head tax) that does not affect relative prices and hence economic behaviour. For example, suppose government replaces a lump sum tax on all redheads with an excise tax on beer drinkers that yields the same tax revenue. Assuming that redheads are not beer drinkers, they would gain and beer drinkers would lose. Furthermore, the owners of breweries and their employees will be affected by the tax. By comparing the total impact of the tax change on the incomes of beer drinkers to those of redheads, we are engaging in differential tax incidence analysis.

Ultimately the economic incidence of a tax depends on how the economy reacts to a tax change. The response of the economy can be determined by tracing the effect of the tax on prices. Taxes change the relative prices of goods and services. For example, if a R2,00 dairy levy on butter increases the price of butter from R20,50 to R22,50 per 500 g while other prices remain unchanged, the relative price of butter also increases. If it is assumed that the initial change in the price of butter does not have significant repercussions on prices in other markets, tax incidence can be analysed in terms of a **partial equilibrium framework**. In other words, we can then study the effect of the tax in a single market in isolation. In partial equilibrium analysis price and quantity in each market are determined by demand and supply with the assumption that other prices remain unchanged (i.e. the *ceteris paribus* assumption is used).

However, when a tax is imposed on one good it usually means that the prices of other goods change as well. For example, a levy on butter will affect the price of margarine, a substitute. After the imposition of the levy, butter will be relatively more expensive and margarine relatively cheaper than before. Consumers will therefore tend to substitute margarine for butter and the increased demand for margarine will probably lead to a rise in the (absolute) price of margarine. This will leave margarine consumers with less real disposable income than before. Once the secondary effects of a tax are taken into account, tax incidence is studied in a **general equilibrium framework**.

Both partial and general equilibrium analyses can be used in incidence studies. Partial equilibrium studies are less complex since all the ramifications of a tax change are not considered. It is ideally suited to studying taxes levied on goods and services that are characterised by low degrees of substitutability or complementarity. Where the secondary effects are considered to be small, uncertain, or spread thinly over a number of other markets, economists would argue that these can be ignored and that the conclusions based on partial equilibrium analysis will not differ significantly from those based on general equilibrium analysis. The general equilibrium framework, however, is more suitable for studying the incidence of a general sales tax that is levied on a broad base, or a levy on an important product such as fuel that has important ramifications for the economy. Since general equilibrium analysis considers relative price changes in more than one market, it is conceptually superior to partial equilibrium analysis.

10.5.2 Partial equilibrium analysis of tax incidence

In this section we analyse the incidence effect of taxes within a partial equilibrium framework. The ability to shift the tax burden under partial equilibrium conditions depends on a number of factors, but we will consider only two: market structure and price elasticity.

Two types of taxes are considered: a unit tax (i.e. a fixed amount per unit of a good or service sold (see Section 10.2.3)) and an *ad valorem* tax. We start by assuming that there is perfect competition and that the tax is levied on an increasing-cost industry (i.e. the supply curve slopes upward).

Incidence of a unit tax

In Figure 10.1 D_0 is the demand curve and S_0 the supply curve for sparkling wine. The before-tax equilibrium price is P_0 and the equilibrium quantity is Q_0. Suppose that an excise tax (a unit tax) of t per unit is imposed on sparkling wine. The excise tax is a fixed amount per unit of the product. If the tax is collected from the seller (i.e. the statutory burden is on the seller), it means that the minimum price at which firms will supply the equilibrium quantity Q_0, is $P_0 + t$. Since the sellers are interested in the after-tax price, they will try to recover the full tax amount at any given quantity – they will charge a higher price (the original price + the tax) at each output level. The supply curve therefore shifts up vertically by the tax amount to $S_1 (= S_0 + t)$. Note that because it is a unit tax, S_1 is parallel to S_0. The new market equilibrium is at point A with price P_m and quantity Q_1. The market price, which is the price paid by buyers of sparkling wine, increases from P_0 to P_m. Sellers receive the after-tax price, P_s (i.e. $P_m - t$).

What is the total tax revenue that accrues to government? The formula for total revenue is price multiplied by quantity. Total tax revenue is the tax per unit t ($= P_m P_s = AC$)

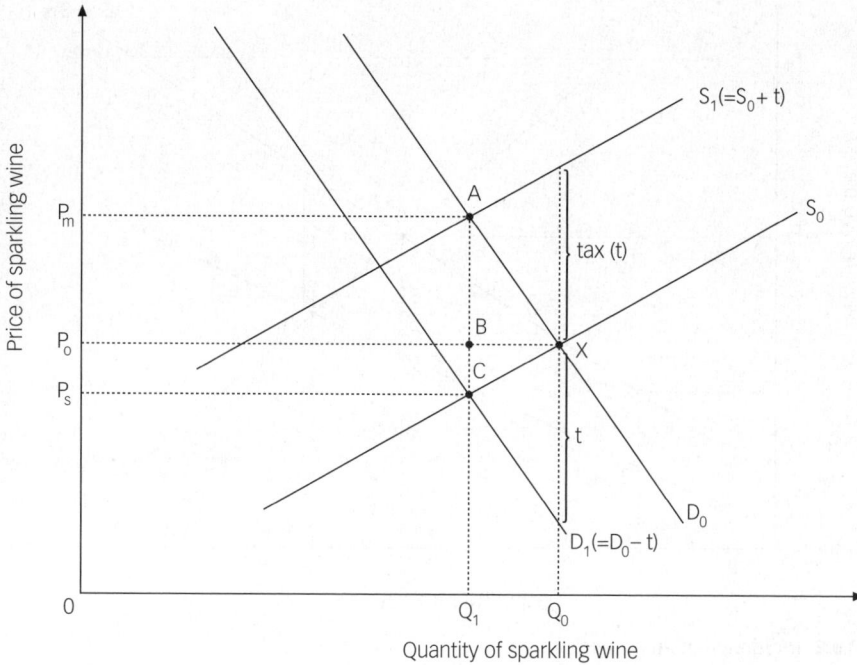

Figure 10.1 Incidence of a unit tax on consumption imposed on the supply side or the demand side

multiplied by the number of units sold, $0Q_1$ ($= P_sC$). Geometrically the total revenue is represented by the rectangle P_mACP_s. The important question now is: Who pays what part of the total tax amount? The answer to this question will tell us what the economic incidence of a unit tax on consumption is.

Before the imposition of the tax, consumers paid a price P_0 for the product. After the tax they pay P_m. Note that the price that buyers have to pay did not increase by the full amount of the tax (P_m minus P_0 is less than t or AB is less than AC). The total tax amount paid by consumers is equal to the rectangle P_mABP_0. What about the sellers? The before-tax price received was P_0. The after-tax price received by sellers is P_s which is less than P_0. Producers therefore also pay part of the tax. The total tax amount paid by sellers is equal to the rectangle P_0BCP_s. From this analysis it is clear that the total tax burden is split between buyers and sellers, that is, the tax

incidence falls on both. Uninformed observers generally assume that sellers simply pass on the total tax burden to consumers. Partial equilibrium analysis shows that this need not be the case.

Would the result be any different had the statutory burden been on buyers (i.e. the consumers)? The answer is no. To show this, one must remember that the demand curve in our example indicates the maximum price consumers are willing to pay for each different quantity of sparkling wine. In Figure 10.1 the before-tax equilibrium price is P_0 and the equilibrium quantity is Q_0. At the equilibrium quantity Q_0 the consumer is willing to pay only P_0. If a tax of t is now collected from the buyer for this quantity, the buyer will still be willing to pay only P_0. The price paid to the seller, however, will be reduced by the tax amount ($P_0 - t$) that is paid over to SARS by the buyer. This will hold for each point on the demand curve. In this case, therefore,

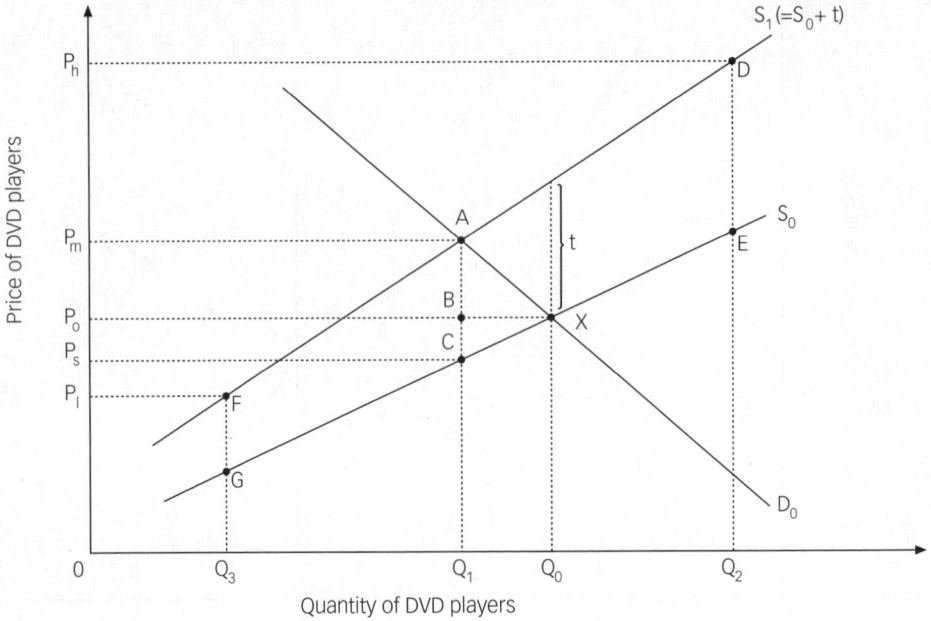

Figure 10.2 Incidence of an *ad valorem* tax

the effective demand curve (i.e. as perceived by the seller) shifts downward by the tax amount. The new demand curve is $D_1 (D_0 - t)$. Since a unit tax of t is imposed, D_1 is parallel to D_0. The after-tax equilibrium is at point C with price P_s and quantity Q_1. While the original demand curve D_0 shows what price buyers are willing to pay for each quantity, the demand curve D_1 shows the price received by sellers (i.e. the after-tax price) for each quantity. Thus for quantity Q_1 buyers are willing to pay P_m and sellers receive $P_s (= P_m - t)$. The result is exactly the same as the result obtained when the tax was levied on sellers – the tax incidence is on both buyers and sellers.

Incidence of an *ad valorem* tax

An *ad valorem* tax is levied as a percentage of the price of a good or service (see Section 10.2.3). We now examine the imposition of an *ad valorem* tax, collected from the producers of DVD players, for example, with the aid of Figure 10.2.

The most important difference between the analysis of an *ad valorem* tax and a unit tax is that the after-tax supply curve swivels in the case of an *ad valorem* tax (compared to the parallel shift in the case of a unit tax). Because the tax is proportional, the higher the price, the greater the amount of tax to be paid over by producers (or the higher the after-tax price paid by consumers) will be. For example, at a price of R1 000 per DVD player and an *ad valorem* rate of 20 per cent, the absolute amount of tax is R200 ($= \frac{20}{100} \times$ 1 000). If the price is R2 000, the absolute amount of tax is R400.[4]

Thus, when an after-tax supply curve such as S_1 in Figure 10.2 is constructed, the vertical distance between S_1 and S_0 (the before-tax supply curve) at a relatively high price such

---

[4] The *ad valorem tax* can be levied as a percentage of the gross price (i.e. the price received by sellers). A 20 per cent tax on the gross price is equivalent to a 25 per cent tax on the net price. If the buyer pays 20 per cent on R1, the seller receives R0,80 (the net price). The tax is R0,20. Twenty cents as a percentage of the net price is equivalent to 25 per cent of the gross price ($\frac{20}{80} \times 100 = \frac{25}{100} \times 100$).

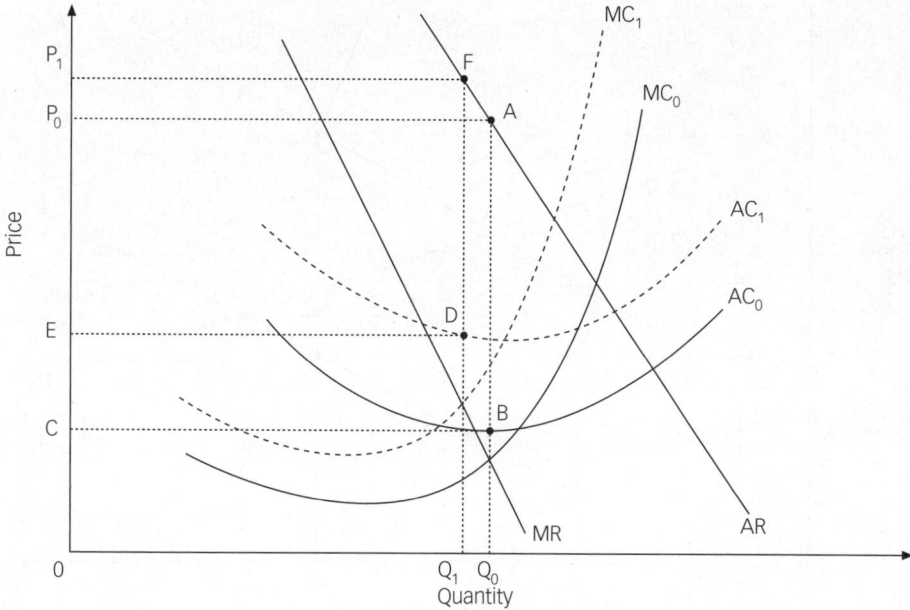

Figure 10.3 Incidence of a tax on a pure monopoly

as P_h ($= DE$) should be greater than at a low price such as P_l ($= FG$). The rest of the incidence analysis of an *ad valorem* tax is similar to that of a unit tax. In Figure 10.2 the total tax burden of buyers is the rectangle P_mABP_0 and that of sellers is P_0BCP_s. The *ad valorem* tax rate, expressed as the ratio of tax to the gross price paid by the buyer, equals $\frac{AC}{AQ_i}$.

Incidence and pure monopoly

Until now we have investigated tax incidence under conditions of perfect competition. Pure monopoly is another extreme form of market structure. It is often taken for granted that a monopolist, being a price maker, can always shift taxes forward in full. Under certain circumstances (e.g. where a monopolist is not maximising profit) this may indeed be the case; however, the conclusion does not necessarily apply. Let's consider the tax shifting capacity of a monopolist-maximising profit.

A monopolist maximises profits where marginal cost (*MC*) equals marginal revenue (*MR*). In Figure 10.3 the before-tax equilibrium of the pure monopolist is at quantity Q_0 and price P_0. The before-tax profit is the area P_0ABC. Assume that a unit tax on output is now imposed on the monopolist.

A unit tax on the output of the monopolist will raise the average cost (*AC*) and the marginal cost of the firm. The reason why both *AC* and *MC* increase is that the tax is levied on each unit produced and is therefore viewed by the firm as a variable cost. In Figure 10.3 the average cost curve shifts from AC_0 to AC_1 and the marginal cost curve from MC_0 to MC_1. Profits are now maximised at an output of Q_1 and at price P_1. When you compare the before-tax equilibrium to the after-tax equilibrium, you will notice the following:

▶ The after-tax price is higher and the quantity is lower than before the imposition of the tax. The increase in the

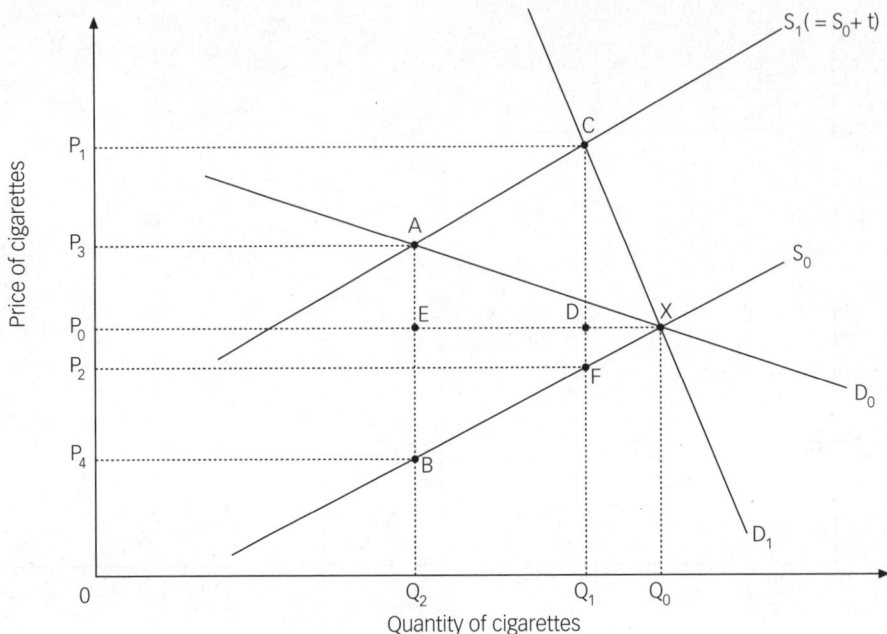

Figure 10.4 Tax incidence and price elasticity of demand

price from P_0 to P_1 indicates the extent of forward shifting.

▶ The after-tax profit (the rectangle P_1FDE) is less than the before-tax profit (the rectangle P_0ABC). The pure monopolist therefore does not shift the tax burden fully.

Monopolists can also be taxed (at least in theory) on their economic profits. Economic profit (or excess profit) is the difference between total revenue and total costs (i.e. both explicit and implicit costs). Implicit costs include the opportunity costs of self-owned resources (i.e. normal profit). The cost curves in Figure 10.3 represent economic costs. In other words, if average revenue exceeds average cost, economic (or excess) profits are earned. In Figure 10.3 the pure monopolist's before-tax profit (area P_0ABC) is considered to be economic profit. A tax at a rate of t per cent on the monopolist's profit of P_0ABC will simply reduce its

economic profit by the tax amount. Neither the average nor marginal cost curves will be affected. The monopolist will maximise after-tax profit at the same before-tax level of output and price. The tax is therefore borne fully by the owners of the firm and in such circumstances the profits tax cannot be shifted.[5]

Incidence and price elasticities of demand and supply

As mentioned at the beginning of Section 10.5.2, tax incidence is affected by market structure (e.g. perfect competition or pure monopoly) and price elasticities. When a tax is imposed, both the quantity demanded and the quantity supplied at equilibrium decreases. The magnitude of the decrease depends on the elasticity of demand and

---

[5] This conclusion holds only if the firm is maximising profit prior to the introduction of the tax on economic profits. In the case of unrealised profits or non-profit maximising behaviour, tax shifting is possible.

supply. Likewise, the impact on the tax burden and the relative tax shares of buyers and sellers also depend on the price elasticities.

The importance of price elasticities in tax incidence analysis can be illustrated with the aid of diagrams. We will first consider the effect of demand elasticities and then the effect of supply elasticities.

Figure 10.4 shows two demand curves D_0 and D_1 and a supply curve S_0, all intersecting at X. The before-tax equilibrium price (P_0) is the same, irrespective of the demand curve used. The intersection of the demand curves enables us to compare elasticity at this point. The demand curve D_1 is more inelastic at any price than demand curve D_0, that is, quantity demanded is less responsive (or sensitive) to price changes in the case of D_1. Suppose the taxed good is cigarettes. If a unit tax (t) is now imposed on the importer or seller, the effective supply curve shifts upwards and to the left from S_0 to S_1 (where $S_1 = S_0 + t$). Let us consider the relatively inelastic demand curve D_1 first.

If the demand for cigarettes is represented by D_1, the price charged to buyers increases from P_0 to P_1. The price received by the seller (or importer) decreases from P_0 to P_2. The proportional price change for the buyers therefore exceeds that of the sellers. The tax burden (P_1CFP_2) is divided between the portion borne by buyers (the area P_1CDP_0) and the portion borne by the sellers (the area P_0DFP_2). In the case of the more elastic demand curve D_0, the proportional price changes for buyers and sellers are approximately the same in this example. The total tax burden of P_3ABP_4 is then divided between the buyers (the area P_3AEP_0) and the sellers (the area P_0EBP_4). Thus, the more price-inelastic the demand for a product is, the greater the relative portion of the tax borne by buyers, *ceteris paribus* (sometimes referred to as the **inverse elasticity rule**). Conversely, the more price-elastic the

demand for the product, the greater the relative portion of the tax borne by the sellers.

Remember that the flip-side of the tax burden for consumers and producers is government's tax revenue. Comparing demand curve D_1 to D_0 it is evident that the more price-inelastic the demand curve, the greater the total tax revenue government collects (P_1CFP_2 compared to P_3ABP_4).

We can also show that, *ceteris paribus*, the more price-inelastic the supply of a product, the greater the relative portion of the tax borne by sellers. In Figure 10.5 we have two supply curves S_0 and S_1 intersecting a demand curve D_0 at point X. The supply curve S_1 is relatively more inelastic than supply curve S_0. To simplify the analysis, suppose that the unit tax (t) on cigarettes is now imposed on buyers (i.e. the statutory burden is on smokers). This means that the effective (after-tax) demand curve shifts downwards to the left from D_0 to D_1 (where $D_1 = D_0 - t$). Let us first analyse the shifting of the tax burden in the case of price inelastic supply S_1. The new equilibrium quantity is Q_1. The after-tax price paid by smokers increases from P_0 to P_2 whereas the after-tax price received by sellers decreases from P_0 to P_1. The proportional price change for sellers is greater than for buyers. Put differently, the share of sellers in the total tax burden P_2ACP_1 is P_0BCP_1 which is greater than the share of buyers (i.e. P_2ABP_0). By contrast, in the case of the elastic supply curve S_0 we notice that the proportional change in the after-tax price of sellers is less than that of buyers. The new equilibrium quantity is Q_2. The buyers pay a price (P_4) per unit and the sellers receive a price (P_3) per unit. The portion of the total tax burden P_4DFP_3 borne by the sellers (i.e. P_0EFP_3) in the case of the elastic supply curve is less than the burden of the buyers (i.e. P_4DEP_0).

From our discussion of price elasticity so far we can generalise by stating that the more inelastic the demand and the more elastic the supply, the easier it is to shift the burden

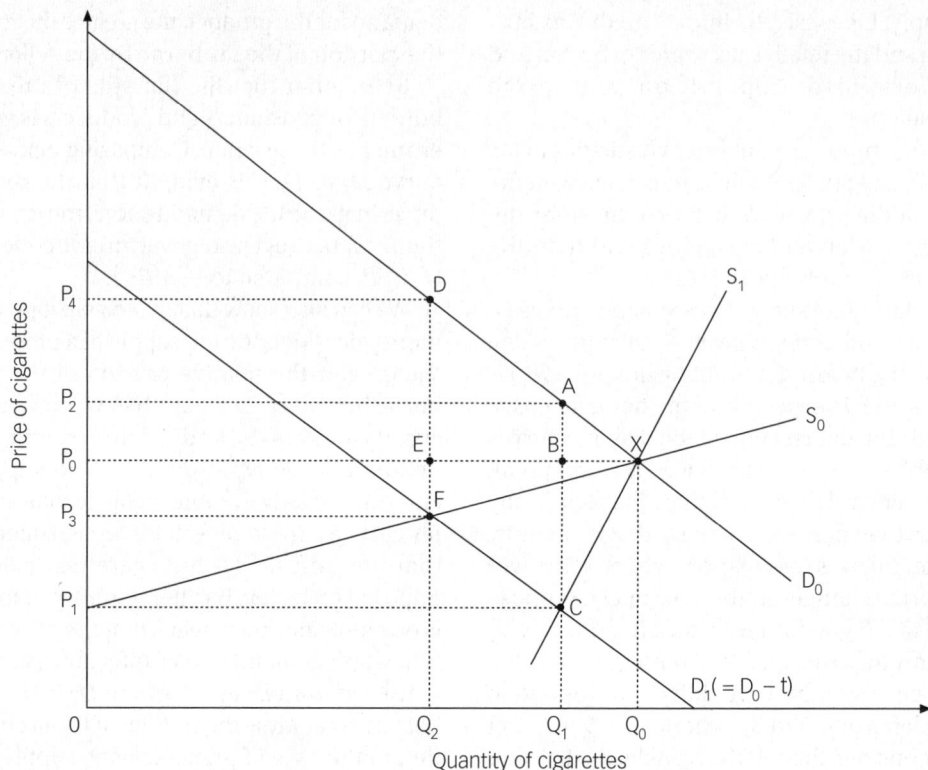

Figure 10.5 Tax incidence and price elasticity of supply

of a tax forward through a higher selling price. This conclusion is illustrated in both Figures 10.4 and 10.5. By rotating the demand curve D_0 and supply curve S_0 around X in each case, we note that the buyer's portion of the burden increases as the demand curve becomes steeper (i.e. more inelastic) and the supply curve becomes flatter (i.e. more elastic). In addition to the examples provided here, the extreme possibilities of perfectly (in)elastic demand and perfectly (in)elastic supply also exist; however, we will not consider these possibilities here.

Applying the theoretical discussion of tax incidence to, for example, taxing tobacco and alcohol consumption ('sin' products) reveals some interesting policy perspectives and dilemmas. There is some empirical evidence that in South Africa the price elasticity of

cigarette demand ranges between -0,5 and -0,7 (see Boshoff 2008: 128–129). Consumption is thus relatively price inelastic (it is less than 1 in absolute value) and the quantity demanded is not that responsive to price (tax) changes (see demand curve D_1 in Figure 10.4). A 10 per cent increase in the price of cigarettes will lead to a reduction in quantity demanded of only 5 per cent. Expectations regarding how high(-er) excises on sin products will reduce consumption should not be too optimistic. There are also other factors that impact on cigarette consumption such as income (higher disposable income leads to higher consumption) and smoker health awareness. Policy interventions improve greater awareness of health risks and reduce consumption. Higher cigarette prices also impact on the number of smokers who substitute legal for illicit cigarettes. Thus lower official consumption figures may not reflect the full picture. The price elasticity coefficients noted above may thus be over-estimating the reduction in the number of smokers caused by higher excises on cigarettes.

Another interesting consideration when analysing excise taxes ('sin' taxes) imposed on cigarette and alcohol products, is how these taxes may affect the welfare of, in particular, those earning low incomes. We have noticed that the incidence of an excise on cigarette consumption is mainly on consumers (the area P_1CDP_0 in Figure 10.4). This tax burden is distributed unevenly across households and categories of users (e.g. moderate drinkers versus abusers). Studies for the USA and UK have found that these taxes tend to be regressive – tobacco and alcohol spending of the poor as a percentage of total income is much higher than that of the rich. According to the Income and Expenditure Survey for 2005/06 poor households in South Africa (the 20% of households with the lowest income) spent 1,5 per cent of total expenditure on alcoholic beverages and tobacco compared to 1,0 per cent by the richest households (Statistics South Africa 2008: 18). Indirect taxes (excises) on these products will therefore be shared approximately in this proportion – implying that taxes on sin products are regressive. Black (2008: 607–611) and Econex (2010: 7–38) also eloquently argue that an excise tax on alcohol is a blunt instrument in addressing the negative external effects of abusive (heavy) drinking. The Econex study (2010: 19) shows that the vast majority of (moderate) drinkers pays 87 per cent of the tax yet contributes perhaps 20 per cent to the externality. A better option would be to target heavy drinkers directly by enforcing stiff penalties for drunken driving, abusive and intrusive behavior (see Chapter 3, Section 3.7).

There is evidence that low and middle-income groups are more sensitive to price increases in tobacco and alcohol goods than the high-income group. And if – as argued in Chapter 3 – many low-income household budgets are controlled by males who are also addicted to nicotine and alcohol, an increase in excise taxes may have perverse effects (see Black and Mohamed 2006: 131–136 and Econex 2010: 36–38). Money may be diverted from the household budget to maintain the user's level of addiction who may also substitute lower quality sin goods (e.g. cigarette butts and low quality wine in foil bags or home-brewed beer concoctions which may be damaging to health) for high quality ones – the negative externality is actually aggravated. The potential for policy conflict is apparent; applying the inverse elasticity rule to tobacco and alcohol consumption implies that tax revenue objectives must be traded-off against reducing negative externalities and ensuring that the burden is shared fairly between the rich and poor and abusers and non-abusers alike.

10.6 General equilibrium analysis of tax incidence

In Section 10.5 we distinguished between partial equilibrium analysis and general equilibrium analysis. Partial equilibrium analysis examines a single market in isolation (i.e. on the basis of the *ceteris paribus* assumption) and ignores the secondary effects of a price change. When the secondary effects of a tax are taken into account, we are studying tax incidence within a general equilibrium framework.

Because general equilibrium analysis considers what happens in all markets simultaneously, modelling tax incidence becomes rather complex. To make it manageable, certain assumptions have to be made.[6]

We assume that only two products are produced in the economy: shoes and reed baskets. There are two factors of production, labour and capital, that are perfectly mobile between sectors. Both factors of production are fixed in supply (i.e. the supply curves are vertical). Shoes are produced using a capital-intensive technique (i.e. the capital–labour ratio is high) whereas reed baskets are produced using a labour-intensive method (i.e. the capital–labour ratio is low). We will analyse the incidence of a tax on one product (i.e. a selective tax) and the incidence of a tax on both products (i.e. a general tax). In Chapter 13 we will discuss a selective tax on one factor of production (e.g. land).

10.6.1 A selective tax on commodities

Suppose that a tax is imposed on shoes. The price of shoes increases relative to that of reed baskets. Remember that the after-tax price does not necessarily increase by the full amount of the tax (in Figure 10.1 the tax was equal to *AC* but the price increase was only *AB*). The price increase has two effects – one is on the consumption (uses) side, the other is on the factors of production (sources) side.

On the uses side, the price increase of shoes (which is, of course, also a relative price increase) causes consumers to demand fewer shoes (illustrated by a movement along the demand curve for shoes) and demand more reed baskets. When the demand for reed baskets increases (illustrated by a shift of the demand curve to the right), the price of reed baskets increases, *ceteris paribus*. The

tax thus causes an increase in the price of both products, that is, the tax burden (and incidence) is spread to the consumers (and producers) of the non-taxed product as well.

On the sources side, the fact that the tax on shoes results in fewer shoes being demanded implies that fewer shoes will need to be produced. When fewer shoes are produced, some of the capital and labour used in the production process become redundant. But since shoes are produced using capital-intensive technology, relatively more capital than labour is released into the market. The redundant labour and capital must now find employment in the sector manufacturing reed baskets. Since the reed basket sector is a labour-intensive sector (and technology is assumed to remain unchanged), all the redundant capital cannot be absorbed into the sector. The additional capital can only be absorbed if the capital–labour ratio increases. But with capital in excess supply, its relative price will decrease, so that both sectors will end up using more capital-intensive production techniques. Thus, in addition to the rise in the relative price of the non-taxed commodity (reed baskets), a tax on shoes also causes the relative price of capital (i.e. the return on capital) to decrease. The burden of the tax is therefore also spread to the owners of the factor of production used most intensively in the production of the taxed commodity.

10.6.2 A general tax on commodities

If a tax is imposed on shoes and reed baskets simultaneously at the same rate, the tax is a general one as opposed to a selective tax. The general tax is equivalent to a tax on income (e.g. a tax on capital and labour at the same rate). The tax will be borne in proportion to the consumption (or income) of each member of the economy. A general tax on commodities leaves relative prices

[6] This approach to tax incidence theory was pioneered by Harberger (1962). For a discussion of the extensions to and limitations of the simplified model we are considering, consult Boadway and Wildasin (1984: 368–374).

unchanged (including the relative price of leisure).[7]

10.7 Tax incidence and tax equity revisited

When we introduced the topic of tax shifting and tax incidence, we stated that most taxes alter the distribution of income. To make inferences about the equity of a tax, it must be ascertained whether the tax alters the distribution in a progressive, proportional, or regressive way.

In the preceding sections we examined the question of who contributes what part of the tax burden in the case of consumption taxes in particular. If the economic burden of the tax is on buyers and the expenditure on this good or service increases as individuals move up the income scale (i.e. if the demand is relatively income elastic), the tax is progressive. Luxuries tend to fall in this category of goods and services – as income increases, individuals tend to spend more on luxuries. In contrast, expenditure on necessities tends to fall as total income rises (i.e. low-income earners spend proportionally more on these goods and services than high-income earners). A tax on necessities that is shifted to buyers is therefore regressive. A value added tax or a general sales tax levied on a broad base will be regressive. The reason is that consumption as a percentage of income decreases as individuals move up the income ladder – high-income earners tend to save proportionally more, leaving them with a proportionally lower tax burden than low-income earners (since saving is exempt from the tax).

When the tax is shifted to the seller it also has distributional implications. If the seller has to bear the tax, his or her real factor income (wage, rent, interest, profit) is reduced. Whether the tax is progressive or regressive now depends on the factor income shares of the 'sellers' and their relative positions on the income ladder. If the tax is shifted to unskilled workers who find themselves at the bottom end of the income scale, the tax could be said to be regressive. On the other hand, if the tax is shifted to highly skilled workers earning high incomes, the tax will be progressive.

To determine the final impact of a consumption tax on distribution, the effect on buyers and sellers should be considered simultaneously. According to Musgrave and Musgrave (1989: 254), there is no systematic relation between the distribution in consumption of a good and the distribution of the factor income that the production of a good generates. They conclude that in the absence of evidence to the contrary, the distribution of the tax burden is dominated by what happens to consumption (i.e. the extent of tax shifting to buyers) since the initial impact is on the uses side.

The incidence of alternative taxes will be addressed when they are examined in later chapters. In addition to the impact of individual taxes on distribution, we would also like to know the overall impact of taxes on income distribution. This is a daunting task since we need to know the incidence of each tax beforehand. Based on plausible assumptions about the shifting of different taxes, empirical studies have found the tax structure of countries to be progressive for the low-income and high-income groups and regressive for the intermediate income groups.[8] Similar results have been obtained for South Africa.[9]

---

[7] This assumes that leisure can be taxed. The tax therefore cannot be shifted and consumers have to bear the entire burden.

[8] For references see Boadway and Wildasin (1984: 384–385).

[9] See McGrath, Janisch and Horner (1997). In the same study the authors calculated the tax share of the high-income group to be 75,7 per cent of the total tax burden, compared to the tax share of the low-income group of 2,8 per cent.

It seems that not much redistribution is taking place through the fiscal system from the tax side. This conclusion has persuaded many economists to argue that if the objective is to improve the position of poor people, it is best to pursue the objective through the expenditure side of the national budget rather than through the tax system (see Chapter 14, Section 14.5 as well as Chapters 8 and 16).

IMPORTANT CONCEPTS

ability-to-pay principle (page 167)

administrative fees (page 162)

ad valorem tax (page 165)

balanced-budget (page 171)

benefit principle (page 167)

differential tax incidence (page 171)

direct tax (page 166)

earmarked tax (page 169)

economic incidence (page 171)

forced carrying (page 167)

general equilibrium framework (page 172)

general tax (page 164)

horizontal equity (page 169)

indirect tax (page 166)

inflation tax (page 163)

inverse elasticity rule (page 177)

lump sum tax (page 164)

partial equilibrium framework (page 171)

progressive tax (page 164)

proportional tax (page 164)

regressive tax (page 164)

selective tax (page 164)

specific tax (page 165)

statutory incidence (page 171)

tax base (page 164)

tax equity (page 167)

taxes (page 163)

tax rate (page 164)

tax rate structure (page 164)

unit tax (page 165)

user charges (page 162)

vertical equity (page 169)

SELF-ASSESSMENT EXERCISES

10.1 Distinguish between taxes and other sources of government revenue.

10.2 A R1 000 tax payable by all adults could be viewed as both a proportional tax and a regressive tax. Do you agree? Explain.

10.3 Indicate whether the following taxes or levies are general or selective, specific or *ad valorem*, direct or indirect, and explain your answer in each case:
- personal income tax
- a 10 per cent tax on DVD players
- value added tax
- R1,02 per litre on fuel
- a R200 levy on all economics students.

10.4 'When taxes are evaluated we need look at fairness only.' Do you agree? Discuss.

10.5 Explain what is meant by tax equity.

10.6 By using the partial equilibrium framework, explain who bears the burden of an *ad valorem* tax levied on buyers (i.e. consumers) if there is perfect competition and demand is relatively inelastic.

10.7 'It is a misconception that a monopolist can simply pass on the burden of a tax on its product to consumers.' Discuss this statement.

10.8 Explain what is meant by the general equilibrium analysis. Then discuss the incidence of a selective sales tax using the general equilibrium framework.

Chapter
ELEVEN

Tjaart Steenekamp

Tax efficiency, administrative efficiency and flexibility

In Chapter 10 we identified a number of properties of a good tax and considered the equity criterion in some detail. Most taxes affect relative prices and consequently also the economic choices of participants in economic activity. This chapter focuses on the impact of taxes on efficiency in the allocation of resources. Because tax efficiency is handicapped by the fact that people do not like paying taxes, the issue of tax compliance will be discussed. Since tax systems are continuously being adjusted in response to changing economic and political influences, issues surrounding tax reform will be highlighted.

We begin this chapter with an explanation in Section 11.1 of what the excess burden of a tax is, using budget lines and indifference curves. The measurement of excess burden is discussed in Section 11.2 by applying the consumer surplus approach. Once the impact of taxes on economic efficiency has been analysed, we focus on the two remaining criteria for analysing taxes: administrative efficiency (Section 11.3) and tax flexibility (Section 11.4).

Once you have studied this chapter, you should be able to:
- explain what is meant by tax efficiency
- compare the excess burden of different taxes using indifference curves
- determine the magnitude of excess burden using the consumer surplus concept
- explain the meaning of administrative efficiency and how it can be achieved
- show what is meant by tax evasion and how to reduce it
- define tax flexibility.

11.1 Excess burden of taxation: indifference curve analysis

All taxes place a burden on consumers, workers, or producers. In addition to this direct burden, most taxes cause a burden that is greater than what is necessary to generate a certain amount of tax revenue. This additional burden is called the **excess burden**, welfare cost, or deadweight loss of a tax. It measures the loss in benefits (well-being) to consumers and producers that results when prices are distorted by a tax and then inhibits the markets for the taxed goods to achieve efficient levels. An example will help to illustrate this concept.

We know from Chapter 2 that for a given set of relative prices perfectly competitive markets will allocate resources in a Pareto-efficient way. This means that the marginal rate of substitution (MRS) of, say, (x) for (y) will be equal to the marginal rate of transformation (MRT) of x for y ($MRS_{xy} = MRT_{xy} = \frac{P_x}{P_y}$). Furthermore, given this set of relative prices we know that the consumption of x and y yields a certain amount of consumer satisfaction (or a certain level of welfare). Suppose that a tax (t) is now levied on x. The price of x becomes $(1 + t)P_x$. Suppose also that the tax is such that the consumption of x becomes zero. This is an extreme example of excess burden. If this is the case, no tax revenue will be forthcoming and there will thus be no direct tax burden. However, there must be some burden since consumers can now enjoy only y. Because the relative price ratio changed from $\frac{P_x}{P_y}$ to $\frac{(1+t)P_x}{P_y}$, consumers reallocated their resources (i.e. their after-tax income) towards y. The expenditure pattern moved away from what was previously regarded as optimal and desired and consumers therefore experience a welfare loss (or loss in utility), even though there is no direct tax burden. On the production side

production of good x must be discontinued and the resources used to produce it, must be reallocated to producing more of y. In practice workers will probably have to be reskilled and some may even lose their jobs if the technology used in the production of y is less labour-intensive. Also machinery used in the production of x may have to be moved to a different location and reprogrammed to produce more of y. These additional costs are (deadweight) losses that result from the tax-induced price distortion.

Another example, which is often cited to illustrate the effect of taxes on the behaviour of taxpayers, is the 'window tax' levied in England between 1695 and 1851. The tax was levied in proportion to the number of windows in a house. The tax was levied obviously for revenue but because the wealthy, having had the largest houses, paid the most it can be viewed as a form of wealth tax. But people do not like to pay taxes and some owners simply avoided the tax by bricking up some of their windows. This loss in daylight they had to endure (i.e. the excess burden of the tax) led some to believe that the phrase 'daylight robbery' came from the window tax!

The theory of excess burden of different taxes can be explained using two approaches: the **indifference curve** approach and the **consumer surplus** approach. The consumer surplus approach is useful in measuring the excess burden and is discussed in Section 11.2. Here we focus on the indifference curve approach, which is useful for comparing the price distorting effects of different taxes. We will first look at the impact of tax-induced changes in relative prices on the welfare of a particular consumer. We then distinguish between the impact of a general tax and that of a selective tax. For comparison purposes we use a lump sum tax as our general or benchmark tax. We will therefore evaluate the excess burden of a selective tax by comparing its impact on welfare with that of a lump sum tax.

11.1.1 **Lump sum taxes and general taxes**

A **lump sum tax** is a fixed amount of tax an individual would pay in, for instance, a year and is independent of his or her income, wealth, or consumption. These taxes do not distort relative prices and therefore do not affect people's choices. For example, a person will not be able to avoid a lump sum tax by working shorter hours or by reducing consumption of a particular commodity. Put differently, a lump sum tax does not cause a substitution effect. It reduces the taxpayer's disposable income and thus has an effect on income only. Because relative prices are not distorted, lump sum taxes have no excess burden. A head tax, levied on each member of society or on all breadwinners, is an example of a lump sum tax.

Lump sum taxes have one major disadvantage. Since the tax as a percentage of income (i.e. the average tax rate) decreases

as income increases, lump sum taxes are regressive. They therefore leave the after-tax distribution of income more unequal than the before-tax distribution. For most policymakers the price tag of such a trade-off between equity and efficiency is simply too high. The perceived unfairness of the poll tax (a prime example of a lump sum tax) introduced in 1990 by the Thatcher government in Britain is widely regarded as one of the factors that led to her downfall later that year.

A head tax is not an unfamiliar tax in Africa, and in South Africa in particular. An early version of a head tax can be found in the Glen Gray Act (Act 25 of 1894). This tax generated insignificant tax revenue (R9 million or approximately 0,1 per cent of total tax revenue in 1978/79) and was abolished in 1978/79, the year in which general sales tax (GST) was introduced.

The effects of a lump sum tax are illustrated in Figure 11.1. *X* is measured horizontally and *Y* vertically. The before-tax

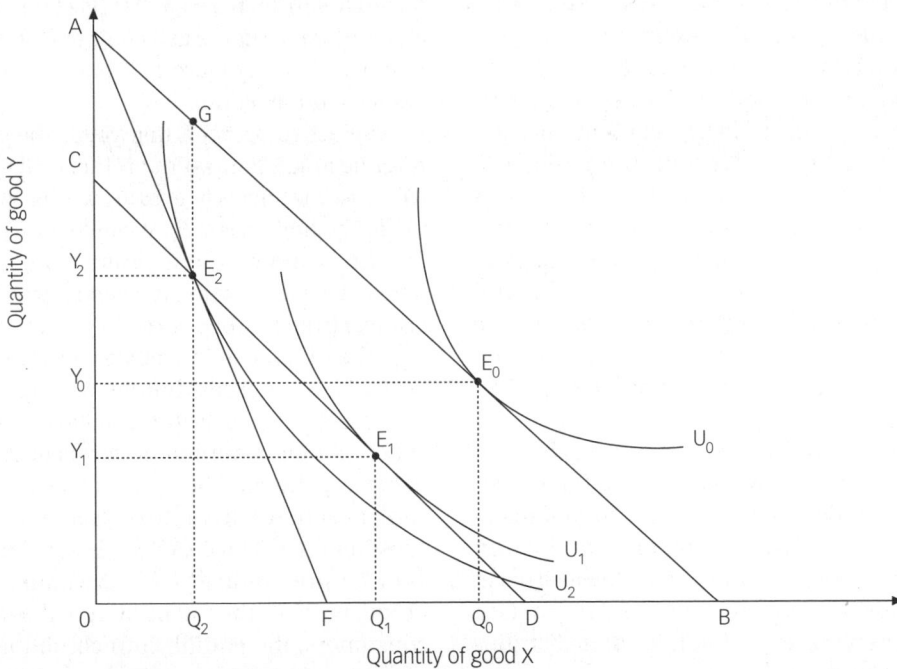

Figure 11.1 The excess burden of a tax using indifference curves

budget line is AB. The consumer is initially in equilibrium at point E_0 where the indifference curve U_0 is tangent to (i.e. touches) the budget line. A lump sum tax is introduced that lowers the income of the consumer and causes the budget line to shift from AB to CD. The lump sum tax yields revenue equal to AC if measured in terms of Y, or DB in terms of X. Note that the after-tax budget line, CD, is parallel to AB since relative prices are unchanged. The consumer is now in equilibrium at E_1 where fewer of X and fewer of Y are consumed than before.

Note that the consumer is in a worse position after the tax, since consumption is on a lower indifference curve, U_1. This is due to the normal burden of the tax. The condition for Pareto optimality has not been disturbed ($MRS_{xy} = \frac{P_x}{P_y}$) and resources are allocated efficiently at the new after-tax income level. A lump sum tax thus causes a normal burden but it has no excess burden.

In Chapter 10, Section 10.2.2 a general tax was defined as one that taxes the entire tax base and allows for no exemptions. If a general tax is imposed at the same rate on Y and X and it is assumed that these are the only products produced in the economy, the budget line in Figure 11.1 shifts from AB to CD. Equilibrium is again at E_1. Tax revenue equals AC. A general tax does not distort relative prices. This means that the after-tax price ratio $[\frac{(1+t)P_x}{(1+t)P_y}]$ is the same as the before-tax price ratio $(\frac{P_x}{P_y})$. The condition for a Pareto efficient allocation of resources in the economy is therefore not distorted $[MRS_{xy} = MRT_{xy} = \frac{(1+t)P_x}{(1+t)P_y}]$.

General taxes resemble lump sum taxes and do not have excess burdens. These taxes have the added advantage that, from a practical point of view, general taxes at uniform rates are easy to administer. However, as in the case of lump sum taxes, the disadvantage of general taxes is that it ignores distributional implications.

11.1.2 Selective taxes

Suppose a selective tax is now imposed on X. To analyse its welfare implications, we compare the impact of the selective tax to that of a lump sum tax that generates the same tax revenue (i.e. AC) in Figure 11.1. We know that a selective tax on X will increase the price of X and leave the price of Y unchanged. If the consumer spends his or her entire budget on X, fewer of X can be obtained after the tax than before the tax. If the consumer spends his or her entire budget on Y, the same amount of Y can still be purchased (because the price of Y has remained unchanged). The budget line showing combinations of Y and X will, therefore, swivel inward (or pivot around point A). To obtain the after-tax budget line, which yields the same tax revenue as the lump sum tax, we must find an equilibrium point which is also on budget line CD. A budget line therefore has to be drawn through A in such a way that it is tangent to an indifference curve at its point of intersection with CD. In Figure 11.1 budget line AF is such a budget line.

A selective tax on X that yields the same revenue as the lump sum tax (i.e. $E_2G = AC$) will cause the budget line AB to pivot (or swivel) to AF. Equilibrium is at E_2 on indifference curve U_2. This is an important observation. Compared to the lump sum tax, consumer welfare is lower (indifference curve U_2 is lower than U_1). The difference in welfare indicates the welfare cost or excess burden of a selective tax. **Selective taxes** distort relative prices and cause an excess burden. In terms of Pareto optimality, the equilibrium condition for consumers is now where the marginal rate of substitution of X for Y (MRS_{xy}) is equal to the after-tax price ratio $[\frac{(1+t)P_x}{P_y}]$. Assuming that producers shift the full burden of the tax to consumers, the equilibrium condition for producers is where marginal rate of transformation of X for Y (MRT_{xy}) is equal to the before-tax price ratio $\left(\frac{P_x}{P_y}\right)$. The price ratios for consumers and producers thus differ and, as relative prices are distorted by the selective tax, resources are allocated inefficiently in the economy ($MRS_{xy} \neq MRT_{xy}$).

11.1.3 Tax neutrality

Economic efficiency is considered as one of the properties of a 'good tax'. Efficient taxes are taxes that minimise the distorting effect on the choices of decision makers. In other words, taxes are considered efficient when the excess burden is as small as possible. This brings us to the concept of tax neutrality.

The **tax neutrality** concept must be understood in its traditional, narrow context and also in its wider, modern context. The traditional, narrow neutrality concept is mainly concerned with allocation, the idea being that taxes should not prevent consumers from maximising utility or producers from maximising profit – in other words, taxes should be neutral. The tax should have little or no impact on economic decisions about what to buy, how much to invest or save, and how many hours to work. This view of neutrality rests on the assumption that resources in the economy are allocated optimally and that non-neutral taxes would result in a reallocation and therefore a non-optimal allocation. A broader view of tax efficiency, however, also takes account of market imperfections.[1]

In reality the market economy is imperfect (meaning it is inefficient and inequitable), and optimality is the exception rather than the rule. Hence non-neutral taxes may be beneficial or harmful, depending on whether they steer the economy in the direction of optimality or away from optimality.

These two possibilities are called positive non-neutral and negative non-neutral effects respectively.

A selective tax is clearly non-neutral as it disturbs relative prices. Economic choices are affected and, according to the traditional view, selective taxes are therefore inefficient. According to the modern approach, however, a selective tax can move the economy in the direction of optimality, which amounts to positive non-neutral action. In contrast, a general tax such as a head tax, is a neutral tax and does not influence allocation decisions. From the modern perspective, a general tax may well perpetuate existing distortions in the economy or perpetuate a socially unacceptable income distribution, which implies that tax non-neutralities can sometimes improve allocative efficiency. Examples include levying taxes to correct for negative externalities and taxing sumptuary consumption (e.g. excises on cigarettes and liquor).

The term **optimal taxation** is derived from efforts to design tax systems to improve efficiency (minimise excess burden) and to achieve a socially more equitable distribution of income (maximise social welfare). In the following sections we will touch upon some of the 'tax optimisation rules' to minimise excess burden (e.g. the inverse elasticity rule – see Section 11.2.2). Related to the theory of optimal taxation is the theory of second best. We saw in Chapter 2 and subsequent chapters that the market sometimes fails due to certain inefficiencies (or distortions). The theory of second best is concerned with designing government policy (and therefore tax systems) in situations where some inefficiencies cannot be removed. More accurately, the theory of second best states that whenever there are distortions in several markets, removing one may not necessarily improve matters. In fact, it may introduce other distortions and, in general, may result in a lower level of welfare

---

[1] In addition, the modern approach to neutrality applies a balanced budget framework. According to this approach, the concept of fiscal neutrality relates to both the revenue side and the expenditure side of the budget.

for consumers (see Lipsey and Chrystal, 1995: 414–415).

11.2 Excess burden: consumer surplus approach

11.2.1 The magnitude of excess burden

Until now we have made some progress in comparing different taxes in terms of their excess burdens. Selective taxes cause an excess burden, whereas general taxes do not. Using the indifference curve approach,

we have shown that the same tax revenue can be obtained by levying a general tax or lump sum tax and at the same time leave the consumer better off. In this section we follow the consumer surplus approach in order to measure the excess burden of a tax. To enable measurement, we employ a partial equilibrium framework and focus on the burden of a unit tax on a particular commodity or output of an industry. Suppose the commodity is grams of butter. We can simplify the example by assuming that supply is produced under constant-cost conditions (i.e. the supply curve is horizontal). Furthermore we use standard demand curves. Although it is theoretically more correct to use compensated demand curves to calculate the excess burden, we

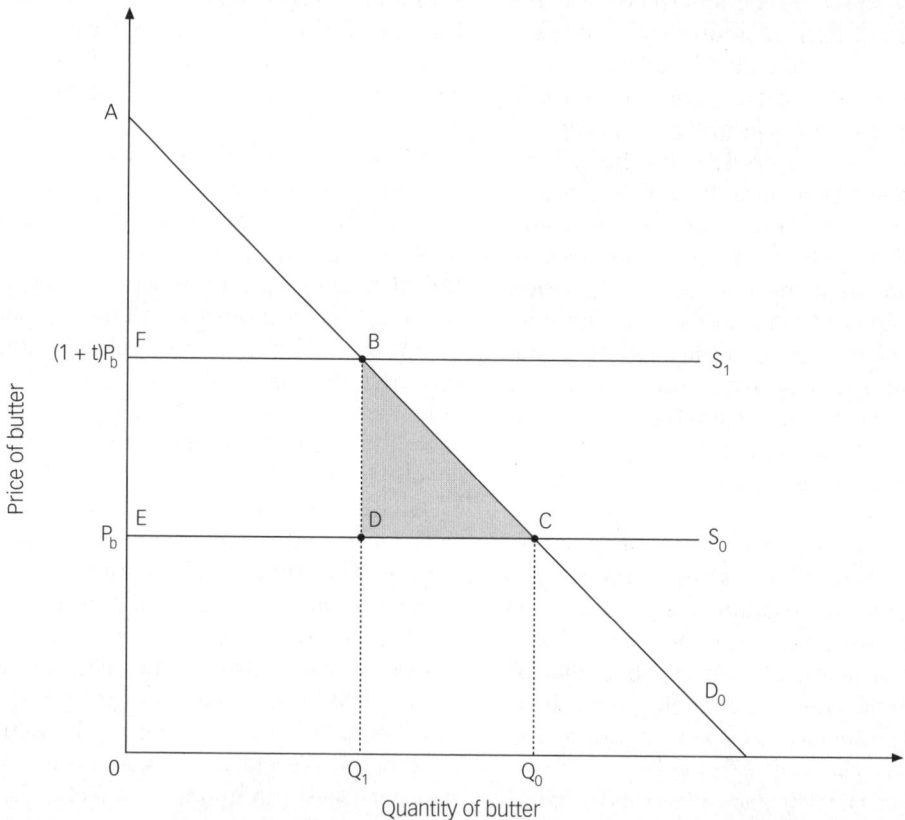

Figure 11.2 The magnitude of the excess burden of a tax on a constant-cost industry

use standard demand curves. Ignoring this subtlety will not significantly affect our analysis.

In Figure 11.2 the demand curve for butter is shown as D_0 and the supply curve is S_0. The equilibrium price is P_b and equilibrium quantity is Q_0. We now have to introduce the consumer surplus. Recall that the demand curve indicates what consumers are willing to pay for different quantities. However, once the market price is determined, it applies to all consumers. The difference between what consumers are willing to pay for a good and what they actually pay is the consumer surplus. This is represented by the area under the demand curve and above the price line. The consumer surplus measures the rand value of consumer welfare at different quantities.[2] In Figure 11.2 the consumer surplus is *ACE*.

Suppose a selective tax (t) is levied on the producers of butter that increases the price of butter to $(1+t)P_b$. The supply curve S_0 shifts parallel upwards to S_1. The equilibrium quantity of butter decreases from Q_0 to Q_1, and the consumer surplus is reduced from *ACE* to *ABF*. The loss in consumer surplus is the trapezoid *FBCE*. But this is not the total welfare cost (or loss) to the consumer. The tax revenue is the tax per unit (tP_b) multiplied by the quantity of butter purchased (Q_1) (i.e. $FE \times 0Q_1 = FBDE$). The tax on butter therefore yields revenue equal to the area *FBDE*. If government, which after all spends the tax revenue, were to return this amount of tax to consumers as a lump sum, the consumers are worse off by the triangle *BCD* (i.e. *FBCE – FBDE*). The triangle is the welfare loss or excess burden of the selective tax on butter. In other words, the tax causes a reallocation

of resources (less butter and more other goods are produced than without the tax). The triangle measures the welfare loss caused by this misallocation of resources.[3]

The size of the triangle (i.e. the excess burden) is determined by the price elasticities of demand and supply and the tax rate. These determinants are discussed below.

The magnitude of the excess burden can be measured using simple algebra. We know that the formula for the area of a triangle is one half the base multiplied by the height. In Figure 11.2 the excess burden can therefore be expressed as

$$E_b = \tfrac{1}{2}tP\,\Delta Q \qquad [11.1]$$

where E_b is the excess burden (area *BCD*), tP is the *ad valorem* tax ($= BD$), and ΔQ is the decrease in quantity demanded ($= DC$). This formula can be refined by also considering two other determinants of the excess burden, namely price elasticities and the tax rate.

11.2.2 **Price elasticities**

Price elasticity of demand indicates how sensitive the demanded quantity is to a price change, while price elasticity of supply indicates the same sensitivity in respect of the supplied quantity. If demand is inelastic, buyers will tend not to adjust their quantities demanded by much if the price changes. In other words, they are insensitive to price changes. If demand is elastic, buyers will tend to adjust their quantities demanded significantly if the price changes. In other words, they are sensitive to price changes.

What is the impact of price elasticity of demand on excess burden? Figure 11.3 is

[2] Assuming that the marginal utility of income is constant, the demand curve can be interpreted as measuring marginal utility. The area under the demand curve (i.e. the sum of the marginal utilities) represents the total utility (welfare) of consumers. The difference between the total utility and the actual cost of the benefits (the market price) is the consumer surplus (Mohr and Fourie, 2008: 129).

[3] In the case of an increasing-cost industry (i.e. where the supply curve is positively sloped), the excess burden is the area between the original demand curve and the supply curve and restricted by the after-tax equilibrium quantity. The excess burden triangle therefore contains some consumer and producer surplus.

almost the same as Figure 11.2. The only difference is that in Figure 11.3 we compare the impact of a selective tax on butter for two cases of demand. In the one case, the demand curve (D_1) is relatively inelastic and in the other case the demand curve (D_0) is relatively elastic. The before-tax quantity (Q_0) and price (P_b) are the same for both. The selective tax (t) causes the supply curve to shift upwards from S_0 to S_1. In the case of demand curve D_0, the equilibrium quantity decreases to Q_1. With demand curve D_1 the equilibrium quantity decreases to Q_2, indicating that the quantity demanded is less sensitive to the imposition of the tax than in the case of D_0. Comparing excess burdens we notice that for demand curve D_0 the excess burden is BCD (the same as in Figure 11.2) and for demand curve D_1 the excess

burden is GCH. This illustrates that the welfare cost of a given tax is less where the demand for a good is relatively inelastic. In other words, the more elastic the demand, the greater the excess burden (or welfare cost).

Figure 11.3 also illustrates how price elasticities impact on the amount of tax revenue that can be collected from a tax. Consider first the relatively elastic demand curve D_0. The tax revenue is the tax per unit (tP_b) multiplied by the quantity of butter purchased (Q_1) (i.e. $FE \times 0Q_1 = FBDE$). With the more inelastic demand curve D_1 the tax revenue is clearly much greater (i.e. $FE \times 0Q_2 = FGHE$). From a revenue perspective it would make perfect sense for tax authorities to levy taxes on commodities for which demand is relatively inelastic.

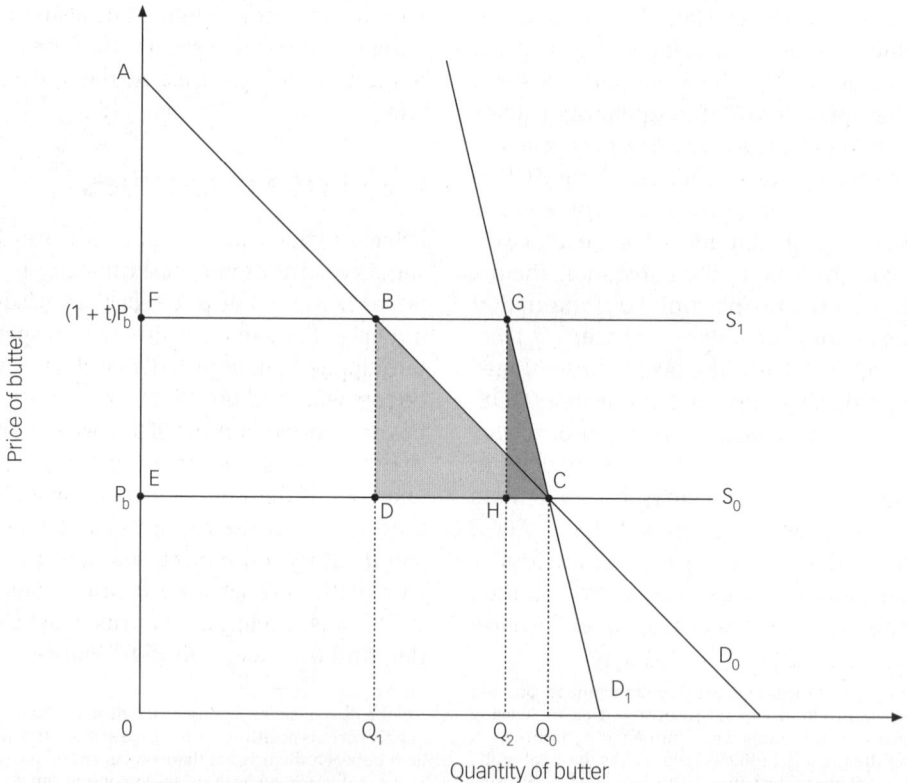

Figure 11.3 The effect of demand elasticity on excess burden

The implications are that it is more efficient from an economic efficiency point of view (i.e. low excess burden) and tax revenue perspective (i.e. high tax revenue) to levy taxes on price inelastic commodities than on price elastic commodities. Commodity taxes should thus be high on inelastic goods and services and low on goods and services with high demand elasticities. This tax rule, commonly referred to as the **inverse elasticity rule**, is attributed to Frank Ramsey (1927). A further implication of this tax rule is that uniform tax rates are not necessarily efficient, since the higher the elasticity of demand of good X relative to that of good Y, the lower the tax rate on X should be relative to that on Y.

Applying the Ramsey rule to the design of taxes leads to interesting results. Luxury goods and services typically have high price elasticities – the possibilities for product substitution are greater. Consumer products with high elasticity coefficients would include marijuana (-1,50), transatlantic travel (-1,30), restaurant meals (-2,27), lamb and mutton (-2,65) and motor vehicles (-1,20). Necessities have lower elasticity coefficients such as food (-0,21), bread (0,15), petrol (0,60) and medical services (-0,18) (see Nicholson and Snyder 2010: 131 and McConnell and Brue 2005: 363 for a list of price and income elasticities for the USA). The price elasticity of demand for necessities tends to be low compared to luxury goods. In Chapter 10, Section 10.5.2 we noticed that in South Africa the price elasticity of cigarette demand ranges between -0,5 and -0,7. A non-smoker would hardly consider cigarettes necessities but it would not surprise a smoker. The low coefficients are inter alia indicative of the addictive nature of nicotine. The elasticity tax rule implies that a high tax rate on, for example, bread or insulin would be efficient (the excess burden is small and the tax revenue would be high). However, distributional implications are ignored in arriving at these

conclusions. Expenditure on bread constitutes a major proportion of the income of poor people. The tax is therefore regressive and inequitable. Diabetics depend on insulin to keep them alive and would probably pay anything to obtain it. Few would disagree that it would be very unfair to apply optimal taxation rules to this product. Tax design often calls for a trade-off between equity and efficiency.

The effect of elasticity on the magnitude of the excess burden can be expressed in mathematical terms. In Equation [11.1] the term ΔQ depends on the elasticity of demand. The price elasticity of demand (ε) is defined as

$$\varepsilon = \frac{\Delta Q}{Q} \div \frac{\Delta P}{P} \qquad [11.2]$$

which can be expressed as

$$\Delta Q = \varepsilon(\Delta P)\frac{Q}{P} \qquad [11.3]$$

The change in price caused by the tax (ΔP) is equal to the selective tax (tP). The right side of Equation [11.3] can therefore be rewritten as $\varepsilon(tP)\frac{Q}{P}$. By substituting this expression for ΔQ in Equation [11.1], we obtain

$$E_b = \frac{1}{2}\varepsilon t^2 PQ \qquad [11.4]$$

Equation [11.4] tells us three things. Firstly, the value of ε indicates the importance of price elasticities of demand. If the value is low (demand is price inelastic), it means that the excess burden will be small, and vice versa. Secondly, PQ is the amount spent on butter before the tax. In our equation it means that the higher this original amount spent, the greater the excess burden. Finally, we notice that the excess burden is a function of the tax rate. We focus on this finding in the next section.

11.2.3 **The tax rate**

The magnitude of the excess burden also depends on the tax rate. As the tax rate increases, the excess burden increases by a multiple of the tax rate.

In Figure 11.4 the initial equilibrium is at price P_b and quantity Q_0. The commodity, butter, is produced under constant-cost conditions. If a selective tax of t_2 is levied on butter, the after-tax price is $(1 + t_2)P_b$ and the equilibrium quantity decreases to Q_2. The excess burden is the triangle ACH. The tax revenue is the area GAHE. Suppose that the tax rate is halved to t_1. The new equilibrium price is $(1 + t_1)P_b$ and the equilibrium quantity is Q_1. Tax revenue is now equal to the area FBDE. The excess burden is now the triangle BCD. We notice that although the tax rate was halved, tax revenue did not halve. More

importantly, the excess burden fell by about three-quarters. This can easily be confirmed geometrically by decomposing the triangle ACH into four smaller triangles of equal size: ABK, KBH, BDH, and BCD.

We can conclude that low tax rates on a large number of commodities will produce smaller excess burdens (and more tax revenue) than high tax rates on a few commodities that yield the same total revenue. This analysis therefore suggests that broad-based taxes such as VAT and income taxes are more efficient than narrow-based selective taxes.

Excess burdens are real and, according to some estimates, quite significant (see below). Knowing the excess burdens of different taxes are useful in designing taxes. If, for example, an *ad valorem* tax of 30 per cent is levied on a good of which the price elasticity

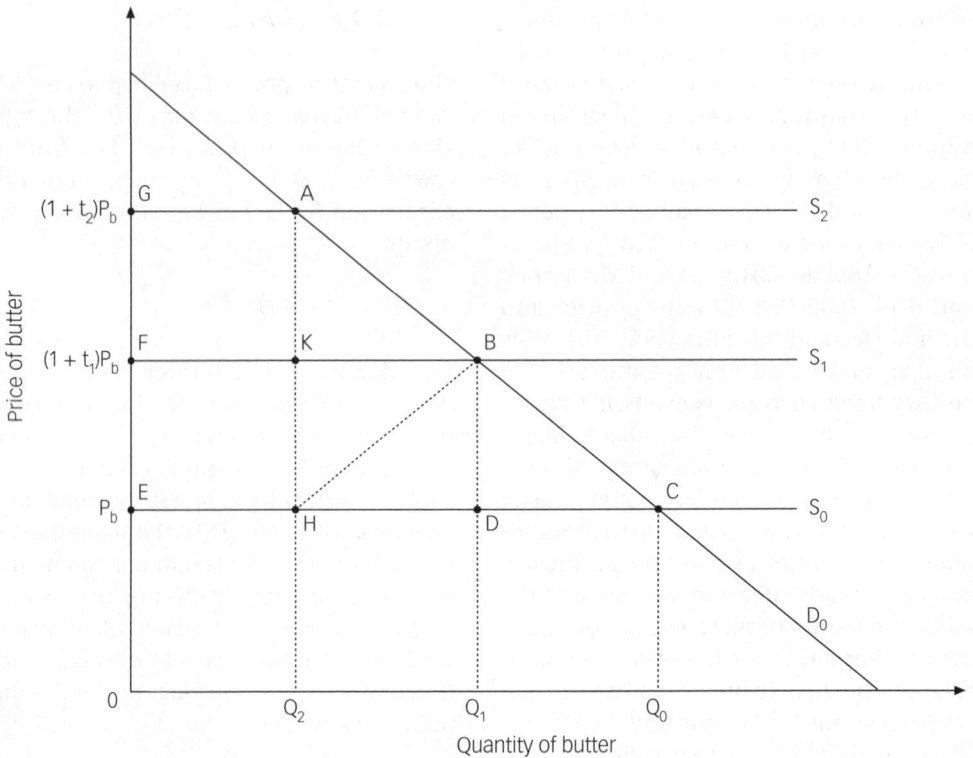

Figure 11.4 The effect of tax rates on excess burden

of demand is equal to one and total expenditure on the good is R200 million, it can be shown (using Equation [11.4]) that the excess burden will be R9 million (i.e. 15 per cent of the tax revenue). Put differently, if the excess burden is expressed per rand of tax revenue the **efficiency-loss ratio** of the tax can be calculated (i.e. excess burden ÷ tax revenue). Given tax revenue of R60 million from the *ad valorem* tax, the efficiency-loss ratio is 0,15. This means that for each rand raised in taxes, the deadweight loss (excess burden) is 15 cents. By comparing the efficiency-loss ratios of different taxes, tax designers can attempt to minimise the total excess burden of the tax system. Overall economic efficiency can be improved by reducing taxes on goods and services with high efficiency-loss ratios and increasing taxes on goods and services with low efficiency-loss ratios.

Excess burden calculations are subject to theoretical and empirical limitations. When excess burdens are estimated, compensated demand and supply curves should be used. Using standard demand and supply curves overestimates the excess burden. The problems associated with attempts to make the concept operational are illustrated by its absence in public budgets. The excess burden costs of taxes are not recorded as expenditure items in public budgets. Given an uncompensated demand elasticity of -0,75 for alcohol, and assuming constant costs, Econex (2010: 11) estimate the total current value for the excess burden to be R881,0 million (figures for 2009). Of this amount 87,26 per cent, or R769,0 million, is carried by moderate drinkers. The estimated excess burden for alcohol may be lower or higher depending on the size of the income effect and the possible loss in producer surplus if increasing costs are assumed (the supply curve is upward sloping). For the USA it was estimated that for each $1,00 of tax revenue raised in the personal income tax system in 1994, the additional loss in net

benefits (excess burden or deadweight loss) was $1,65 (Feldstein 1997). The loss is attributed to the impact of the tax-induced distortion on labour participation rates and hours as well as the effect on investment in education, occupational choice, effort, location, more attractive fringe benefits, nicer working conditions and all of the other aspects of behavior that affect the short-run and long-run productivity and income of the individual.

11.3 Administrative efficiency

The excess burden is not the only cost of a tax. Taxes have to be administered and this generates costs. In 2010/11 the estimated expenditure by the South African Revenue Service (SARS) amounted to R8 142,2 million which was approximately 1,2 per cent of total tax revenue collected. In addition to administration costs borne by government, and ultimately taxpayers, individual taxpayers incur costs in order to meet their tax obligations, called **compliance costs**. These include the cost of time spent filling in tax returns, as well as the cost of employing tax specialists (accountants and lawyers). When taxes are designed, these costs must also be considered. There is some evidence that the compliance costs are significantly greater than the administrative costs incurred by government. For example, Slemrod and Sorum (1984) estimated compliance cost in the USA at between 5 and 7 per cent of revenue collected from income taxes. In New Zealand, Sandford and Hasseldine (1992) estimated compliance costs at approximately 2,5 per cent of GDP.

Administrative efficiency entails minimising both administration costs and compliance costs. Two phenomena are related to these costs: tax avoidance and tax evasion. **Tax avoidance** is perfectly legal and includes the actions by taxpayers to take advantage of special provisions (tax loop-holes) in the tax code so that their tax liability is reduced. Although tax avoidance is legal, it is wasteful in the sense that taxpayers make choices on the basis of tax considerations rather than economic considerations, that is, it entails high opportunity costs. Avoid-ance practices often arise from errors or loosely drafted tax legislation. Exploiting these loopholes through careful tax planning is therefore not in the 'spirit of the law'. An example would be where a business is split up into smaller units to take advantage of the graduated company tax rate for small businesses.

Tax evasion is illegal and consists of actions that contravene tax laws. The most common forms of evasion are not registering as a taxpayer, under-reporting of income and claiming more deductions than warranted. Tax evasion is quite prevalent in the informal sector (also called the unrecorded sector) and is characterised by cash transactions that are difficult to trace.

To get a clearer understanding of the actions that can be taken to reduce tax cheat-ing we need to know the extent of tax evasion, the reasons why taxpayers engage in evasion practices, and what the optimal level of tax evasion is from the perspective of the cheat-ing taxpayer.

In some countries tax evasion is said to have become a national pastime. South Africa is not untouched by taxpayers' attempts to reduce their tax burden. The extent of tax evasion can be measured by considering the **tax gap** which is the differ-ence between the tax liability declared to tax authorities (the actual revenue collected) and the tax base calculated from other sources (the expected tax revenue). Knowing the size of the tax gap is important as a per-formance measure for the revenue authorities and identifies problems with tax legislation, national statistics and what the

impact of the informal sector is on tax rev-enue. Various attempts have been made by countries to estimate the gap for different taxes and the total tax gap but it remains a difficult task to accurately quantify the gap (see McManus and Warren 2006: 77–79 for examples of tax gap studies). The Margo Commission (1986: 406) and the Katz Com-mission (1994: 62) refer to tax gap studies which indicate that the gap is in the order of 10 per cent for developed countries and an average of 33 per cent for developing coun-tries. The Katz Commission (1994: 66) guesstimated the tax gap in South Africa to be around 20 per cent. This would amount to approximately R120 billion in lost tax rev-enue in 2009/10. Another indicator of tax evasion and avoidance is the difference between persons who have chosen to register for personal income tax purposes and the number of persons employed (that is the potential tax base). In 2007 there were approximately 13,6 million employed work-ers but only 5,2 million were registered as individual taxpayers. We return to this aspect in Chapter 12 when we look at the personal income tax base.

Various factors or reasons contributing to the tax gap can be listed and include tax illit-eracy, cultural attitudes, the level of **tax morality** and deficient tax legislation. Ober-holzer (2008) studied the differing perceptions of taxation which result from people's cultural, political and social back-grounds. All the respondents were of the opinion that waste and corruption in govern-ment were high and almost 80 per cent felt that taxes were used by government for meaningless purposes. This of course affects taxpayers' willingness to pay taxes. At local government level similar problems apply. Fjeldstad (2004) argues that the prevailing view explaining non-payment is that non-compliance is caused by poverty (i.e. an inability to pay) and the existence of an 'entitlement culture'. In addition the paper argues that non-payment is related to whether citizens trust the local government to act in their interest. Trust has three dimensions: the local authority will use tax revenues to provide the expected services; the authorities will apply fair procedures in collecting tax; and other citizens will pay their share. In other words, taxpayers want value for their money and taxes must be fair from a horizontal and vertical equity point of view. Suffice to say there are psychological reasons and economic reasons for tax evasion (see Gcabo and Robinson 2007). We are more interested in the economic reasoning behind tax evasion and what the optimal level of tax evasion is.

Neoclassical economic theory considers decision makers as rational beings who attempt to maximise their expected income and utility. Note that in deciding how much to evade implies that the taxpayer has already made up his or her mind about the morality of tax evasion (that is the taxpayer acts illegally). We can then employ an ordinary demand and supply framework to answer the 'how much' question. Tax evasion generates benefits and costs. If we assume a progressive income tax structure, the

marginal benefits from evading an extra rand's income decline as evasion increases. The individual faces lower tax brackets and thus lower taxes. For example if the marginal tax rate is 35 per cent, the tax liability for the extra rand not reported is reduced by R0,35. This is the marginal benefit received by the taxpayer. If more tax is evaded the marginal tax rate may be reduced to, say, 18 per cent translating into a tax liability of only R0,18 for the extra rand evaded. We can plot this relationship in Figure 11.5(a) as a downward-sloping marginal benefit (MB) curve. A marginal benefit curve can also be interpreted as a demand curve for underreported income (D_0).

When evading taxes the taxpayer runs the risk of being caught and penalised. Marginal costs of evasion, therefore, increases as evasion increases and this can be plotted as a marginal cost (MC) curve or supply curve for underreported income that increases from left to right (S_0). To complete the picture we consider both the marginal benefits and marginal costs of evasion in Figure 11.5(a). Equilibrium (E_0) is where $MC = MB$. At this point the optimal level of underreported income is Q_0.

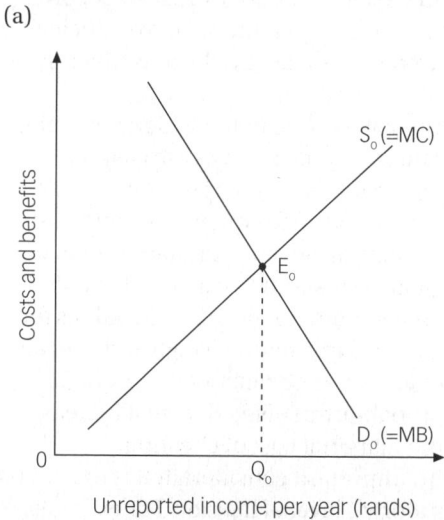

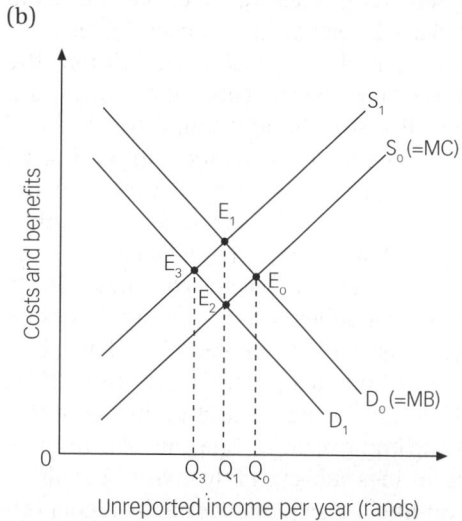

(a)

(b)

Figure 11.5 Optimal tax evasion and policy options

To reduce the level of underreporting taxes the revenue authorities have two clear policy options: increase the marginal cost for underreporting and/or decrease the marginal benefits taxpayers derive from tax cheating. The marginal cost can be increased by higher penalties if caught and by increasing the probability of getting caught. Both would have the effect of shifting the supply curve in Figure 11.5(b) from S_0 to S_1. The new equilibrium is at E_1 thereby reducing underreported income from Q_0 to Q_1. The revenue authorities, however, cannot monitor all taxpayers at all times. In their enforcement programme they encourage compliance by randomly auditing taxpayers. The audit coverage ratio of the South African Revenue Service (SARS) has been increasing over time and in 2009/10 amounted to about 1,88 per cent of taxpayers (SARS 2009: 29), which compares favourably with that of other countries. Although economic theory predicts that increased sanctions against underreporting of income or non-payment of service charges should lead to better compliance, this may not necessarily always result. Experience from local authorities in South Africa shows that the more severe the sanctions observed, the greater the resistance to pay. Fjeldstad (2004: 552) ascribes this 'perverse' relationship to reciprocity considerations: 'the proposition that the authorities' unresponsive, disrespectful and unfair treatment of ratepayers fosters disrespect for and resistance against local authorities and the service providing agencies...'. A softer approach was followed by SARS at one stage by encouraging taxpayers who have failed to meet their obligations to voluntary disclose their sins in return for a waiving of penalties or additional tax (National Treasury 2005: 97). But to ensure fairness in the tax system and to improve budget revenue, the revenue authorities subsequently revised penalties, requiring higher penalties on the higher taxable evaders (National Treasury 2009: 39).

Penalties for income tax evasion can be up to double the amount evaded (that is 200%).

The alternative to combating tax evasion through penalties is to decrease marginal tax rates in an effort to lower the benefits from underreporting tax. Lower marginal tax rates would cause the demand curve in Figure 11.5(b) to shift from D_0 to D_1. Equilibrium is at E_2 and the amount of income underreported also decreases from Q_0 to Q_1. There is some evidence that lower marginal tax rates may positively affect underreporting. In a study measuring the effect of tax rates on tax evasion on Chinese imports, Fisman and Wei (2004) found that the evasion gap is highly correlated with tax rates and that much more tax revenue is lost in respect of products with higher tax rates.

Of course, by applying both compliance options (higher penalties and lower marginal tax rates) simultaneously, equilibrium E_3 can be reached in Figure 11.5(b) resulting in underreporting decreasing from Q_0 to Q_3.

Thus, in addition to taxes having to be designed to minimise the excess burden, administration costs, and compliance costs, good tax administration requires that tax evasion and avoidance be kept to a minimum. When taxes are evaluated according to the criterion of administrative efficiency, a number of issues should consequently be considered:

▶ The golden rule in tax design is simplification. Simple tax laws are easy to understand and comply with. Incentives for 'tax delinquency' should also be minimised. For example, high marginal rates should be avoided and the poor should not be taxed. Penalties for tax evasion should be high and actively enforced. High penalties and a high probability of being detected increase the marginal cost of cheating.

▶ An important consideration is the community's level of literacy. For example, income taxes require high levels of skill, whereas a head tax is fairly easy to understand.

▶ A further consideration is the efficiency and expertise of the tax administration. The importance of this was recognised in the first Interim Report of the Katz Commission (1994). Considerable attention was devoted in this Report to tax administration and it was made clear that the South African system required major structural changes. At that time the Commission estimated that at least R5 billion in additional revenue could be netted through administrative reform, a figure that turned out to be much higher.

▶ To improve tax collection, taxes should be withheld at source. Most taxpayers are subject to the pay-as-you-earn (PAYE) system, according to which tax is withheld at the source (e.g. by the employer) and paid over directly to the tax authorities. (Note that PAYE is a tax collection system and not a particular kind of tax.) Under the PAYE system government receives its revenue before the employee can lay his or her hands on it. Moreover, there is a regular flow of revenue that, in turn, reduces the lag in the operation of the tax multiplier and makes stabilisation policy more effective. On the other hand, the PAYE system significantly increases the compliance costs borne by companies and other institutions in the private sector on behalf of taxpayers. Clearly, a trade-off between administrative and compliance costs is required.

▶ A further consideration is the tax morality of the community. Taxpayers' willingness to part with their hard-earned money is linked to perceptions about the vertical and horizontal equity of taxes as well as the way in which the tax revenue is spent. If taxpayers feel that the tax system is inequitable and that government is spending their tax

money wastefully (or not in their interest), the willingness to pay tax will be undermined. Government's proposal to publish the names and particulars of persons who have been convicted of tax law offences in the Government Gazette ranks as a measure to improve tax compliance and tax morality.

▶ Tax efficiency is also affected by the political will to enforce tax laws.

▶ For taxes to be administratively efficient they should be certain and transparent. The tax to be paid should be certain (predictable) to ensure rational decision-making on the part of both taxpayers and the government. Both the tax collector and the taxpayer should thus be given as little discretion as possible. There should also be no uncertainty about who bears the tax burden. Personal income tax satisfies this requirement, but in respect of company tax there is still too much uncertainty as to who actually bears the burden. Indirect taxes are also characterised by obscurity as to who carries the tax burden, as we saw (Chapter 10, Section 10.5.2) when tax shifting and tax incidence of tobacco and alcohol products were explained.

▶ Transparency means that the government should not take advantage of people's ignorance. Transparency also means that the government has a responsibility to subject tax decisions to the political decision-making process – tax decisions should be embodied in legislation and be actively debated. Taxation through inflation is an example of a tax on income that is not legislated for explicitly (see Chapter 12).

11.4 Flexibility

Economic activity is characterised by recurrent recessions and booms, that is, cyclical changes. Moreover, structural changes occur in the economy as well. Taxes should be flexible enough to provide for changing economic conditions. Taxes can influence economic activity from both the supply and the demand side.

On the supply side, economic growth can be influenced by changing the incentive to work and spend (or save). For example, if the price elasticity of the supply of female labour is greater (i.e. labour supply is more sensitive) than that of males, female labour should be taxed at a lower marginal rate (according to the inverse elasticity rule). This should, theoretically, induce more females to enter the labour market or increase their work effort. Hence the supply of labour can be influenced. This topic is discussed in more detail in Chapter 12.

In macroeconomics the use of demand-side measures to smooth out business cycles is a standard topic of discussion. This is known as stabilisation policy and a distinction is made between automatic and discretionary stabilisers. The timing of discretionary fiscal action is decisive. The problem of timing, however, is not too serious in the case of automatic stabilisers. Automatic stabilisers are characterised by built-in flexibility. An example of an automatic stabiliser is a progressive income tax system. When the economy is entering a recession, for example, the average income tax rate will automatically begin to decrease. As individuals' incomes decline, they are automatically assessed at lower rates, and in this way they are left with relatively more disposable income than they would have had otherwise. By the same token, tax revenue for the government declines more rapidly than the national income. In Chapters 12 and 15 we will note that inflation has largely rendered tax policy's role in automatic stabilisation ineffective.

IMPORTANT CONCEPTS

administrative efficiency (page 193)

compliance costs (page 193)

consumer surplus (page 184)

efficiency-loss ratio (page 193)

excess burden (page 184)

indifference curve (page 184)

inverse elasticity rule (page 191)

lump sum tax (page 185)

optimal taxation (page 187)

selective tax (page 186)

tax avoidance (page 193)

tax gap (page 194)

tax evasion (page 194)

tax morality (page 194)

tax neutrality (page 187)

SELF-ASSESSMENT EXERCISES

11.1 Explain why a lump sum tax is used for comparing the excess burden of different taxes.

11.2 'A tax on cigarettes is inefficient since it is non-neutral.' Do you agree? Explain your answer by using indifference curves.

11.3 Assuming that government needs to raise a certain amount of tax revenue from two goods with different price elasticities of demand, what would your advice be to government if the excess burden had to be minimised? How would your answer differ if other tax criteria had to be considered as well?

11.4 Briefly discuss administrative efficiency as a property of a good tax.

11.5 'Marginal tax rates should be reduced for high-income taxpayers to increase tax compliance.' Discuss this statement by making use of a diagram.

11.6 Use examples to explain what tax flexibility means.

Chapter
TWELVE

Tjaart Steenekamp

Income taxation

Once you have studied this chapter, you should be able to
- define the comprehensive income tax base
- discuss the international principles of taxing income
- discuss the reasons why the personal income tax base differs from the comprehensive income tax base
- explain what a progressive personal income tax is and how progressiveness is achieved
- discuss the economic effects of personal income tax
- explain why companies are taxed separately
- define the company tax base
- describe the classical and fully integrated company tax systems
- describe company tax in South Africa
- explain the efficiency of company tax
- discuss the importance of company tax in the investment decision
- discuss the merits of tax incentives for investment
- explain the equity implications of company tax
- discuss the arguments for and against capital gains taxation
- explain a flat rate income tax
- explain the dual income tax.

12.1 **The comprehensive income tax base**

When we introduced the tax base in Chapter 10, we distinguished between three bases: income, wealth, and consumption. In this chapter we will focus on income. We first need to know what income is.

We are all familiar with a budget (e.g. our own personal budget) which has an expenditure (or uses) side and a revenue (or sources) side. Income can be defined from both the sources side and the uses side of the budget. From the uses side, income is the monetary value of consumption plus any change in the net worth over a year. Net worth (or the net value of assets) is obtained by subtracting liabilities from assets (see Chapter 13). Put differently, income is the net increase in the power to consume in a particular period (e.g. a year). It can be expressed as

$$Y = C + S$$

where Y is income, C is consumption, and S is saving (or the change in net worth).

From the sources side of the budget, anything that makes consumption possible (i.e. anything that is available to finance consumption) is considered as income. Income thus includes salaries, wages, interest, capital gains, rent, profits, royalties, dividends, gifts, employer contributions to pension funds, unemployment benefits, and income in kind. This definition of the **comprehensive income tax base** is referred to as the Haig-Simons definition, named after two early twentieth-century economists who advocated its use. Haig and Simons believed that such a definition of income most accurately reflects the ability to pay (one of the criteria of fairness) or purchasing power.

For administrative and other reasons, governments tax some of the sources of

income separately. In South Africa and most other countries, income received by individuals is subject to personal income tax. The income of incorporated businesses (i.e. profits) is subject to company tax and in some countries net capital gains from increases in the value of assets are subject to capital gains tax. These three income tax bases are discussed separately in this chapter. Gifts, which can also be treated as additions to wealth, are discussed in Chapter 13.

Another dimension of the comprehensive definition of income is that income is recorded as it accrues and not only when it is realised. For example, if an asset increases in value during the course of the year, the capital gain is an addition to net worth. The asset need not be sold (i.e. realised) for the increased value to be regarded as income. The reason is that an increase in the value of an asset represents an increase in the owner's purchasing power (i.e. ability to pay). In practice, the accrual principle causes considerable administrative complications (e.g. valuation problems) and it may also result in cash flow problems for those who have to pay tax on accrued amounts not actually received in cash.

12.1.1 **International taxation of income: the residence principle versus source principle**

Income is generated within countries but also across national borders. In recent years the economies of countries have become increasingly internationalised and this has impacted on a tax jurisdiction's ability to tax individuals and companies. In an integrated and open economy the returns of factors of production (e.g. salaries, dividends, profits, royalties, interest) flow much more freely within a country and across national borders. When rates of return differ between countries due to taxation, these tax-induced differentials can be exploited by capital and highly skilled individuals causing distortions within countries and across countries. Over the years tax authorities have dealt with the international taxation of income using two general principles: the residence of taxpayer principle and the source of income principle.

The **residence principle** (or worldwide basis) is based on the view that the country of residence of the person or business that receives the income determines the tax liability and collects the tax. Thus, a person residing in South Africa would be liable for taxes on his or her total (worldwide) income in South Africa if a residence system was applied. For example, if the person earns R300 000 from a source in South Africa and R120 000 from a source in Zimbabwe, the combined income of R420 000 is taxable in South Africa. For a legal person (e.g. a company), residence is determined where the business is registered or has a permanent presence. Only income that can be allocated to the activities (at home and abroad) of the business would be taxable.

According to the **source of income principle**, income is taxed by the country where the income is generated. Using the example above, only the R300 000 which originated in South Africa would be taxable in South Africa if the source principle was applied.

In practice most countries apply a combination of both systems. This hybrid form of taxing cross-border flows of income could result in double taxation of such income. If South Africa applies the residence principle and Zimbabwe the source principle, then, in our example above, a person residing in South Africa would be taxed on his or her worldwide income of R420 000 in South Africa. In addition, the Zimbabwean tax authorities would tax the person on the R120 000 generated in

Zimbabwe. To eliminate or reduce the extent of double taxation, countries using the worldwide basis unilaterally grant tax relief in the form of an income deduction for the income earned in the source country or a tax credit for the tax paid in the source country. Alternatively, countries enter into bilateral tax treaties or attempt to harmonise the tax treatment of cross-border income.

On a multilateral basis, however, it is difficult to harmonise tax systems as countries perceive the net benefits of each system differently. The debate on the merits of each system is extensive and not clear-cut at all (see Faria, 1995: 216–221; Tanzi, 1995: 65–89; and Katz Commission, 1997b). The issues that developing countries have to consider include the following:

▶ The source basis resembles the benefit principle of taxation. The entity generating the income benefits from public expenditures, for example, uses public roads and schools, and should therefore be taxable. This is not a very convincing argument since a resident who earns foreign-sourced income also benefits to some extent from public roads and schools. The residence basis, on the other hand, approximates the ability-to-pay principle and enables countries to tax the worldwide income of residents on a progressive scale. Countries with low levels of foreign income (e.g. dividends, interest, and royalties) would have to consider using the source basis on grounds of administrative expediency. On the other hand, where income from investments abroad is considerable, the residence basis has to be considered on revenue grounds.

▶ From a tax neutrality point of view, a tax system (e.g. tax rates) should not influence locational decisions of businesses. From the perspective of a capital-importing country, a source-based system would have the advantage of being neutral with regard to capital imports, since it does not discriminate between domestic investment and foreign investment, regardless of where the capital originates. Developing countries tend to be capital importers. On the other hand, from a capital-exporting perspective, a residence-based system would be neutral with regard to capital exports. The only concern to an investor would be the tax rate in his or her country of residence.

In South Africa the taxation of income was based on the source principle of international taxation in the past. Due to the increasing globalisation of the economy and the relaxation of exchange controls, a residence-based income tax system was introduced as of 1 January 2001. It was argued that by doing this, the South African income tax base would be broadened, opportunities for tax arbitrage would be limited, and the tax system would be brought in line with accepted norms for taxing international transactions (Department of Finance, 2000: 84).

This move was contrary to the recommendations of the Katz Commission (1997b). In its *Fifth Interim Report*, the Katz Commission (1997b) distinguished between active income (income derived from operational activities, such as manufacturing and rendering services) and passive income (income derived from investment, such as interest and royalties). The Commission recommended that active income should be taxed on the source basis and passive income on the worldwide basis. It argued that taxing active income on a worldwide basis and at the relatively high domestic effective tax rates, would encourage South African multinational companies to relocate to low tax jurisdictions. Changing the tax system to a worldwide basis would also be administratively complex. The Commission argued that

taxing passive income on a worldwide basis would be necessary to protect the tax base. Passive capital is very mobile when exchange controls are limited.

There remain differences of opinion on the relative merits of the change to a worldwide (or residence) basis in South Africa. The application of the residence principle may enhance equity by taxing the off-shore income of South African residents. After all, these amounts increase taxpayers' ability to pay and allow for progressive rates of taxation. On revenue grounds it is also sound to protect the system from undue losses as exchange controls are relaxed. However, converting to the worldwide basis involves many administrative problems, including problems of definition (e.g. when is an establishment resident) and requires the (re-)negotiation of various double taxation agreements. The

---

BOX 12.1 Calculating personal income tax liability

TOTAL (COMPREHENSIVE) INCOME
minus Exclusions
(e.g. imputed rent and unrealised capital gains)

GROSS (CASH) INCOME
minus Exemptions
(e.g. tax-free portion of interest)

NET INCOME
minus Deductions
(e.g. contributions to medical scheme)

TAXABLE INCOME
Tax according to tables

GROSS TAX LIABILITY
minus Rebates
(e.g. primary rebate and rebate for age 65 and over)

NET TAX LIABILITY

possible impact on net foreign investment is unpredictable at this early stage.

12.2 The personal income tax base

Gross income is the starting point in calculating personal income tax. In South Africa, **gross income** consists of all receipts and accruals (e.g. wages and salaries, rents, royalties, dividends, capital gains, and interest) of South African residents irrespective of where in the world it was earned. Exempt income (e.g. interest) is deducted from gross income and the resulting amount constitutes net income. Taxable income is obtained by deducting all the amounts allowed as deductions (e.g. medical expenses) from net income. Normal tax is calculated at the applicable rate on taxable income.

The comprehensive definition of income is much broader than the definition of taxable income in South African tax law. The reason is that government provides **tax expenditures**, sometimes referred to as tax loopholes. Tax expenditures include exclusions, exemptions, deductions, and tax rebates (or credits) which all affect the size of the tax base. It was estimated that in 2008/09 tax expenditures to the amount of R29,3 billion were provided to personal income taxpayers (National Treasury 2011: 181). This revenue forgone represents about 15 per cent of the income tax revenue collected from persons in 2008/09. The calculation of personal income tax liability in South Africa is shown in Box 12.1.

12.2.1 Exclusions

Income tax is generally levied on cash income. Some forms of non-cash income, such as in-kind receipts, are excluded from the tax base. Here are some examples of **tax exclusions**. If a person were employed as a cook or child minder, the salary of such a person would be taxable; but if a housewife or mother performs the same functions, the value (or opportunity cost) of her services is not taxed. If a homeowner lets his or her house, the rent received is taxable. If, on the other hand, the owner lives in the house, the rent forgone is an opportunity cost (i.e. imputed rent) that ought to be taxable in terms of the comprehensive definition of income but it is excluded from tax.

In the past, companies could also offer generous fringe benefits (e.g. motor vehicle allowances, subsidised meals, low-interest loans, and housing subsidies) to employees that were not taxed. Nowadays most fringe benefits are taxable, but the real value of such benefits is not always taxed in full. For example, in the case of bursaries for relatives of employees, R10 000 per year is tax free for employees earning up to R100 000 per year. The taxation of fringe benefits is sometimes also difficult to administer. For example, it is often difficult to distinguish between personal use and business use (e.g. the use of a company cellular phone or company stationery for private use). Finally, non-cash transactions such as barter arrangements are also difficult to detect and frequently go untaxed (e.g. a dentist filling a plumber's tooth in exchange for the plumber clearing a drain at the dentist's residence).

12.2.2 Exemptions

A second category of tax expenditures is exempt income (or exemptions). As a method of providing tax relief to the poor and the aged, an amount of income is **tax exempt**. In 2011/12 the exempt amount for persons below the age of 65 was R59 750 and for those over the age of 65 the exempt amount was R93 150. A further threshold was added for those aged 75 years and older (R104 261). In practice, the exempt amount is determined by tax rebates allowed on the amount of tax that is due (see the discussion on rebates in Section 12.2.4). The first R22 800 of interest income received by a natural person under the age of 65 from a South African source is also exempt from income tax in South Africa.

12.2.3 Deductions

In addition to the exempt categories of income, certain expenditures may be deducted from income for tax purposes. There are a variety of deductions (or allowances) that serve different purposes. Some deductions, such as those in respect of pension fund contributions and contributions to retirement annuity funds, are intended to serve as incentives for taxpayers to provide for their old age. This is particularly important in a country like South Africa, which does not have a comprehensive social security network. Deductions are also allowed (within limits) for contributions to medical aid funds and medical expenditures. These are expenses over which the individual sometimes has no discretion and that can significantly affect his or her ability to pay (e.g. in the case of major heart surgery). The tax-deductible medical contributions and expenses are capped at a monthly monetary threshold of R720 for the first two beneficiaries. It is important to note that a tax deduction of a given amount is worth more to a person with a high marginal tax rate than a low marginal tax rate. It is for this reason that it was announced that the monthly deduction for medical contributions and expenses will be converted into tax credits from 1 March 2012 (see rebates below). Another category of deductions is in respect of expenditures incurred with the purpose of producing income (e.g. travelling and motoring expenses or allowances).

12.2.4 Rebates

A further tax expenditure, which affects revenue from income tax, is **tax rebates (or credits)**. Tax rebates involve the subtraction of a specified amount from the amount of tax to be paid (i.e. taxable liability). In contrast to a tax deduction of a specified amount, a tax rebate is independent of the taxpayer's marginal tax rate and therefore more equitable. These rebates are primarily aimed at providing tax relief to the poor and middle-income groups and to provide for differences in taxpayers' personal circumstances. In 2011/12 our personal income tax system provided for a primary rebate of R10 755 while persons aged 65 and over (the secondary rebate) are allowed an additional R6 012 and persons aged 75 and over (the third rebate) a further R2 000 to be deducted from their tax liability. What does this mean? The primary rebate determines the de facto tax-exempt income (see exemptions in Section 12.2.2). When the primary rebate of R10 755 is deducted from the gross tax liability of a person earning a taxable income of R59 750, the net liability is zero. The income level at which the effective tax rate is zero is referred to as the minimum **tax threshold**. Any taxable income above this amount would incur a tax liability. It should be obvious that rebates benefit the poor more than the rich. For example, a rebate of R10 755 is worth more to a person with taxable income of R100 000 than to a person with taxable income of R200 000. Without the rebate, a person earning R100 000 would have had to pay R18 000. With the rebate, the tax liability falls to R7 245. The benefit is 59,8 per cent of the unadjusted tax liability. For the person earning a taxable income of R500 000, the benefit (calculated in the same way) is only 7,8 per cent.

12.3 The personal income tax rate structure: progressiveness in personal income taxation

In the case of personal income tax, most observers agree that the ability-to-pay principle should apply. This principle generally takes taxpayers' income as a yardstick. However, it is not so simple to determine taxable income and to combine it with the tax rate in such a way that fairness is achieved. For example, one of the most prominent features of personal income tax is that the structure can be adapted to the personal circumstances of the taxpayer, but such adaptations complicate the rate structure.

Ability to pay (and thus the rate structure) is affected by the filing status (or **unit of taxation**) of the taxpayer, that is, whether he or she is single, married, or has children. If two people live together, their living costs (per person) should be lower than when they live apart (e.g. because they share certain things). Their combined ability to pay should therefore be greater than it would have been if they had lived apart and they could, therefore, be taxed at a higher rate (on their combined income). But the issue is not quite so simple. For example, a married couple, with both partners working, can be at a disadvantage compared to a couple where there is only one breadwinner. In the case where both spouses work, families have to purchase a number of services that would normally be rendered at no additional cost by a non-working spouse (e.g. cleaning services and child-caring). If imputed income is not taxed, the two-breadwinner couple should be taxed at a lower rate.

There is a further complication when children are included in the relationship. Having children involves costs and affects the disposable income of the parents. Some would argue that these costs are non-discretionary (e.g. where contraception is ruled out due to religious beliefs) and that tax deductions or rebates for children should be allowed. Others argue that children are a matter of choice and that there is no reason why special provision should be made for expenses involving children and not for other expenses that are incurred by choice such as private overseas trips. The particular view taken on these issues also depends on the values of society in respect of the family. Should mothers be encouraged to return to work, or should the income tax system discriminate against women to promote a stable family life? Whether or not the personal income tax structure should be used for social engineering purposes is a much-debated issue. It should be obvious that all kinds of cultural, religious, and moral factors can enter the picture. This brief discussion shows that an individual's tax rate and tax liability do not necessarily depend solely on his or her income.

Until the mid-1990s the tax unit in South Africa was the married couple. Married and single people were taxed using different schedules. The choice of unit was scrutinised carefully by the Margo Commission. It was argued that joint taxation of spouses amounted to a marriage penalty for income earning wives. Such taxation discouraged people from marrying, discouraged married women from entering the labour market, and affected the status of married women as individuals. The Margo Commission (1987: 151) recommended that the individual replace the couple as the unit. The Katz Commission also considered the issues of discrimination on the basis of marital status, gender, age, ethnic or social origin, religion, and so on. Their perspective was mainly a constitutional one. The Katz Commission (1994: 73) recommended that all provisions in the Income Tax Act, based on gender and marital discrimination, violated the Constitution and should therefore be eliminated. The Katz Commission (1994: 73) also recommended that child rebates no longer be granted, but that discrimination on the basis of age remains for the time being. These recommendations were introduced in 1995 and in the current personal income tax system in South Africa the individual is indeed the unit of taxation.

Whether the unit of taxation is the family, a married couple, or the individual, the principle that people should pay according to their ability to pay still holds. In Chapter 10 it was said that a tax system based on ability to pay requires consensus on how ability is to be measured as well as on the rate structure. In the case of vertical equity, the question is what the respective tax liabilities of rich and poor taxpayers should be. For this purpose, each taxpayer's sacrifice of utility due to taxation has to be evaluated. Most countries apply the equal marginal sacrifice principle. According to this principle, the income tax rate should increase progressively as taxable income increases (i.e. the richer the person, the higher his or her tax rate should be). The aim is to achieve a more equitable distribution of after-tax income.

What is meant by progressivity and how can it be achieved? In Chapter 10 it was explained that the progressivity of the rate structure could be determined by looking at the average tax rate. When the average tax rate (i.e. the total amount of taxes payable divided by the value of the taxable base) increases as taxable income increases, the tax is progressive. Progressivity can be obtained by using a combination of income exemptions (or tax rebates) and by taxing blocks or brackets of income at different rates. A higher tax rate is specified for each higher income bracket, but the higher rate is applicable to only that part of the taxable amount that falls into the relevant bracket. These graduated rates are called **marginal tax rates** since they represent the change in taxes (i.e. the marginal or extra tax amount) paid with respect to a change in income (i.e. the marginal or extra income).

Table 12.1 shows the tax rates for individuals for 2011/12. The first column shows the taxable income brackets. The second column shows the basic amount of tax paid for each bracket. The basic amount in the schedule is simply the sum of the marginal tax amounts of the preceding brackets and is specified to simplify tax calculations. Thus, a person with taxable income of R200 000 pays R27 000 on the 'marginal' income in the first bracket (R150 000 × 18%) plus R13 500 on the 'marginal' income in the second bracket [(R200 000 – R150 001) = R44 999 × 25%] which is equal to R40 500. Note that this amount is not the effective tax liability. The

Table 12.1 Personal income tax rates in South Africa, 2011/12

Taxable income bracket (R)	Basic amount (R)	Marginal rate (%)	Lowest average rate in each bracket (%)
0–150 000		18	–
150 001–235 000	27 000	25	10,8
235 001–325 000	48 250	30	16,0
325 001–455 000	75 250	35	19,8
455 001–580 000	120 750	38	24,2
580 001 and above	168 250	40	27,1

Source: Calculated from National Treasury, *Budget Review 2011*, (2011: 182).

primary rebate of R10 755 has to be subtracted from this amount, which leaves a tax liability of R29 745. This converts to an average tax rate (or effective tax rate) of 14,9 per cent ($\frac{29\,745}{200\,000} \times 100$) on taxable income. If we repeat this exercise for an income of R580 001, an average tax rate of approximately 27,1 per cent of taxable income is obtained. Since the average tax rate increases as income increases, the tax structure is progressive. The importance of the distinction between marginal and average rates will again be emphasised when the economic impact of personal income taxes is discussed in the next section.

A much more simplified personal income tax rate structure applies in Lesotho. On the first M30 000 (one rand equals one Lesotho maloti) a rate of 25 per cent is applied (a personal credit of M2 640 may be deducted). Income in excess of M30 000 is taxed at 35 per cent. This structure almost resembles a flat rate tax (see below). In Botswana individuals with an income of more than P30 000 are liable for personal income tax. Five brackets are used. At the threshold income level of P30 000 (one rand equalled 0,93 Botswana pula in February 2011) a rate of 5 per cent applies and graduates to a maximum of 25 per cent for incomes over P120 000.

12.4 Economic effects of personal income tax

In Chapters 10 and 11 we laid the foundations for analysing different taxes. Recall that we identified four properties of a 'good tax': economic efficiency, equity, administrative efficiency, and flexibility. These properties or criteria will now be applied to the personal income tax.

12.4.1 Economic efficiency

From Chapter 11 we know that, when the economic efficiency of any tax is considered, economists try to establish whether or not the tax has an excess burden. Recall that the excess burden is a burden in addition to the normal burden of a tax that reduces the taxpayer's welfare (i.e. leaves the taxpayer on a lower indifference curve). To determine whether an income tax has an excess burden, we will first consider a general tax on income and then a selective tax on labour income. Since personal income tax is levied on interest income as well, we will also consider the economic efficiency of this practice separately.

General tax on income

The impact of a general tax (a tax which is levied on the entire tax base) was analysed in Chapter 11. We concluded that such a tax has no excess burden since relative prices are not distorted. An example of such a tax is a head tax. If the entire income base (personal income and company income) is taxed and leisure is ignored (or it is assumed that leisure can be taxed at the same rate as income), an income tax is also a general tax. The effect of such a tax was illustrated using Figure 11.1. The tax on income will simply shift the after-tax budget line (CD) parallel and downwards to the origin. Relative prices remain unchanged and there is no excess burden. The tax has a normal burden only, which is illustrated by consumption occurring on a lower indifference curve (U_1) than before. An income tax that taxes the entire tax base (excluding leisure) is therefore an efficient tax. Unfortunately, leisure cannot be ignored and neither can leisure be taxed that easily.

Selective tax on labour income

Once we include leisure in our analysis, it can be shown that a personal income tax does have an excess burden. Workers have a choice between income and leisure. Since leisure cannot be taxed easily, a tax on income only is in fact a selective tax. If income (or the goods that can be purchased with that income) and leisure are viewed as two commodities, we can argue that an income tax distorts the relative prices of income and leisure. People may decide to work more or less as a result of the tax (i.e. the supply of labour is affected). The net result will depend on the relative strengths of the income and substitution effects of the price change. We focus on these two effects below and show that it is the substitution effect that has an adverse impact on the incentive to work. We also show that the substitution effect is determined by the marginal income tax rate. We start by examining how the supply of labour is determined using budget lines and indifference curves.

Assume that a person, say, Peter, has 18 hours a day (his time endowment), which can be used for two activities: work and leisure. In Figure 12.1 the daily time endowment is measured on the horizontal axis as the distance $0L$. Carefully observe that on this axis we measure two things. From left to right (i.e. from point 0 to point L) we measure the number of hours spent on leisure activities. From right to left (i.e. from point L to point 0) we measure the number of hours worked. For example, if LQ_1 hours are spent working, it means that $0Q_1$ hours are available for leisure.

Suppose Peter earns a wage of R10 per hour. If he uses his entire daily time endowment (18 hours) to work, he can earn an income of R180 per day. Peter's income (or the goods that can be purchased with that income) is plotted on the vertical axis. If the full-time endowment is used to earn income, one combination of income and leisure or

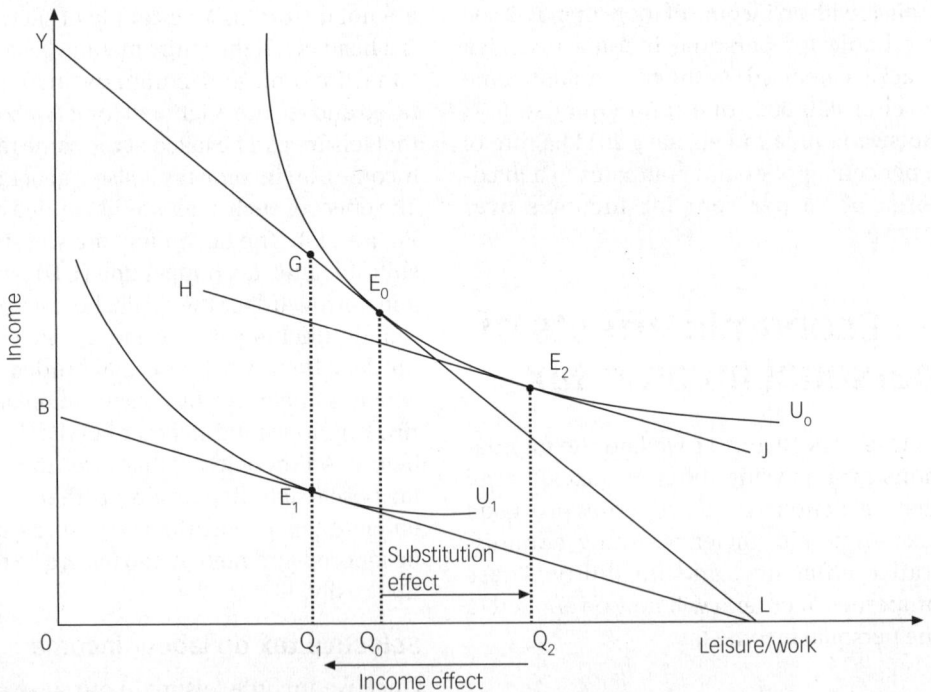

Figure 12.1 The supply of labour and an income tax on personal income

Chapter 12 Income taxation   **209**

work is obtained (i.e. point *Y*). If, instead, he wastes all his time doing nothing, zero income is earned and we have another combination of income and leisure/work which we can plot (i.e. point *L*). We can continue in this way and trace out the different combinations of income and leisure or work for each number of hours worked. This is shown as line *YL*, that is, Peter's budget line. The two 'goods' in this case are income and leisure. By adding indifference curves (which indicate Peter's preferences or tastes), we can determine the combination of income and leisure or work most preferred by Peter. Suppose that the highest indifference curve that Peter can attain is U_0. He is then in equilibrium at E_0 where $0Q_0$ hours are spent on leisure and LQ_0 hours are used or supplied for work.

Suppose a proportional tax or flat rate tax (e.g. 14 per cent) is now levied on income only. A proportional tax lowers the after-tax wage. This means that Peter's income (his after-tax wage multiplied by the number of hours worked) is now less at each number of hours worked. The after-tax budget line pivots (or swivels) from *YL* to *BL*. The after-tax equilibrium is at E_1 where indifference curve U_1 is tangent to the new budget line *BL*. Peter's welfare has declined as indicated by the fact that he finds himself on a lower indifference curve. At the new equilibrium Peter has a tax liability of E_1G (i.e. the difference between his before-tax and after-tax income earned by working LQ_1 hours). The quantity of labour supplied has increased from LQ_0 to LQ_1 hours per day. This, however, need not always be the case. The movement from E_0 to E_1 is due to the combined effect of the income and substitution effects of the tax change. Whether the number of labour hours supplied increases or decreases, will depend on which effect is the stronger.[1] The budget line *DF* and indifference curve U_2 are discussed later in this section.

What is the **income effect**? The tax reduces Peter's after-tax income. Peter is worse off as a result of the tax and will tend to work more to partly offset this loss in income. Put differently, Peter has a lower after-tax income and can therefore not afford the same amount of leisure than before – less leisure means more hours of work. The income effect will therefore cause the quantity of labour supplied to increase. What about the **substitution effect**? To understand the substitution effect it is important to note that leisure has a price. The price of one hour of leisure is the hourly wage sacrificed by not working. Thus, the opportunity cost of leisure is the wage. Since the introduction of an income tax reduces the after-tax wage, the opportunity cost of leisure therefore decreases – leisure becomes cheaper. In other words, consuming leisure involves a smaller sacrifice in income than before the introduction of the tax. Because leisure is now relatively cheaper, it is substituted for work. The substitution effect increases leisure, which means that it reduces the quantity of labour supplied.

The income and substitution effects can also be explained using Figure 12.1. After the introduction of the proportional tax, equilibrium changes from E_0 to the new equilibrium at E_1. The movement from E_0 to E_1 can be decomposed into the income and substitution effects. By hypothetically compensating the individual with an amount just enough to make him as well off as before the tax, the budget line *BL* shifts parallel outwards to *HJ* which is tangent to indifference curve U_0 at E_2. The movement from E_2 to E_1

[1] The decision to work less or more is also affected by non-economic factors (e.g. the status of work in a society and the need to avoid boredom and to get out of the home environment). We concentrate only on the economic effects.

is, therefore, the income effect of the tax. The income effect shows that the individual increases work effort in response to the imposition of the proportional tax. The movement from E_0 to E_2 depicts the substitution effect, which is a consequence of the change in the relative price of labour alone. The movement shows how the individual substitutes more leisure for less work if a proportional tax on labour is imposed or increased.

As stated earlier, the income and substitution effects combine to determine whether a person will work more or less. If the income effect dominates, the after-tax quantity of labour supplied will increase. In contrast, if the substitution effect dominates, the number of hours worked will decrease and the quantity of leisure will increase. On the basis of this analysis alone it is impossible to say what the outcome will be. Empirical evidence, however, suggests that the labour supply elasticities for prime-age men (from about 20 to 60 years of age) are generally

close to zero (see Brown and Jackson 1990: 456). This means that the supply curve is almost vertical or, put differently, that the quantity of labour supplied is very insensitive to changes in the net (after-tax) wage. On the other hand, the estimated elasticities are generally positive and high for married women. In their case, the quantity of labour supplied is thus quite sensitive to changes in the net (after-tax) wage. For example, there is evidence in the UK that the hours men work are not very responsive to changes in work incentives; however, participation by those with low levels of income is responsive. In contrast the hours of work and participation of women with young children are quite sensitive. For men with high levels of education, their income is responsive to tax but in the sense that they shift their income to nontaxable forms (see Meghir and Phillips 2010: 204 and 252).

The analysis used for a proportional tax can be repeated for a progressive tax on income. One difference would be the shape

BOX 12.2 Marginal tax rates and the substitution effect

In the case of the proportional tax, every taxpayer faces the same marginal tax rate, but in the case of the progressive tax the marginal tax rate varies with income (for example in Table 12.1 – for each income tax bracket the marginal tax rate exceeds the average rate). What does this mean?

The size of the income effect is determined by the average tax rate, whereas the size of the substitution effect is determined by the marginal tax rate.

The average tax rate indicates how much of his or her income the taxpayer sacrifices to the revenue authorities for his or her total work effort. To recover some of the income lost due to the tax, the taxpayer will work more. Recall that this is the income effect of

the tax change. The income effect is therefore related to how much tax is paid and, for a given income, this is determined by the average tax rate. The marginal tax rate, on the other hand, indicates the additional income an individual sacrifices to the revenue authorities for additional work effort (i.e. changes in work effort) and is therefore related to the substitution effect. The higher the marginal tax rate, the more of the additional income a taxpayer must sacrifice. As the marginal tax rate increases, the incentive to substitute leisure for income becomes greater. It is therefore the size of the marginal tax rate that determines the incentive to work (the substitution effect).

of the after-tax budget line. In the case of a progressive tax, the budget lines will be kinked or curved (see Rosen and Gayer 2010: 418). This does not fundamentally change the conclusion with regard to the impact of the tax on the supply of labour, but there is one important difference between progressive and proportional taxes. For a proportional tax the average tax rate is equal to the marginal tax rate, but for a progressive income tax the marginal tax rate is greater than the average tax rate. This means that the adverse incentive effects due to the substitution effect are likely to be more important for a progressive tax than for a proportional tax (see Box 12.2).

We know at this stage that a tax which selectively taxes income (and not leisure as well) has income and substitution effects which together may cause the quantity of labour supplied to increase or decrease. We also know that the taxpayer's welfare is reduced by the tax (as illustrated by the movement to a lower indifference curve). However, we still have to determine the economic efficiency of the tax, that is, whether or not it has an excess burden. To arrive at an answer, we have to compare the results of the proportional tax to a lump sum tax of equal revenue. Remember that a lump sum tax does not distort the relative prices of leisure/work and income and therefore has no excess burden. The impact of the personal income tax on economic efficiency (the excess burden) is explained in Figure 12.2. This figure is similar to Figure 12.1 except that the income and substitution effects are not illustrated.

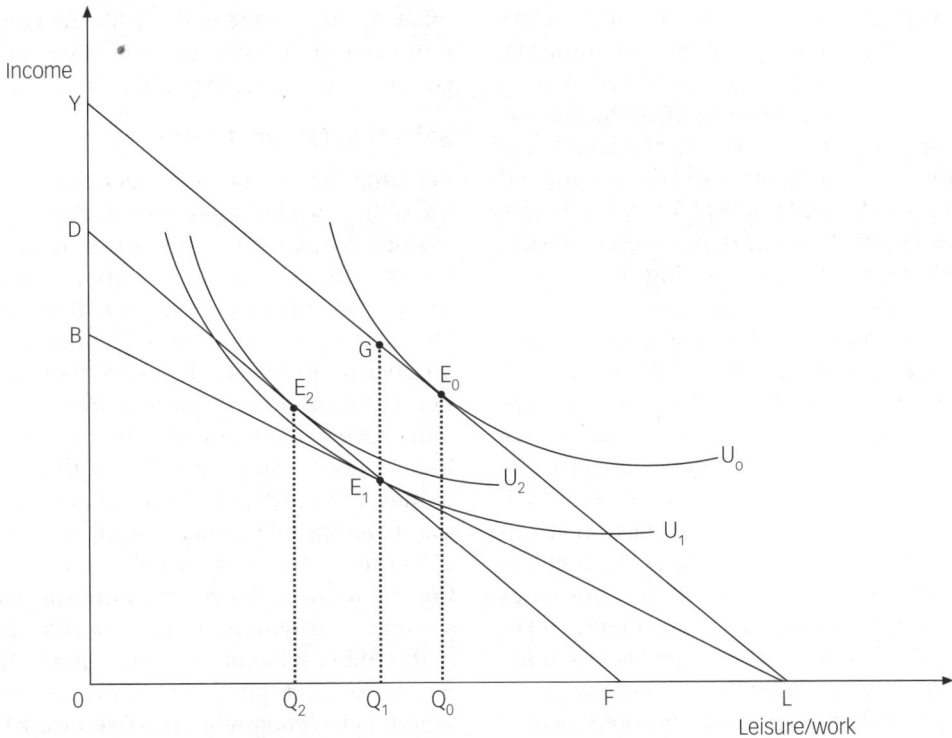

Figure 12.2 The excess burden of a proportional tax on personal income

If a lump sum tax (e.g. head tax) is introduced to raise the same tax revenue as the proportional tax in Figure 12.1 and Figure 12.2 (i.e. E_1G at Q_1 hours), the after-tax budget line shifts parallel to the original budget line (YL) to DF, which intersects BL at point E_1. Peter will now be in equilibrium at E_2 where the highest indifference curve U_2 is tangent to the (new) budget line. Peter is working LQ_2 hours a day which is more than the LQ_1 hours worked under the proportional tax. Peter's welfare is also higher under the lump sum tax than under the equal-yield proportional income tax as illustrated by the attainment of a higher indifference curve (U_2) than before (U_1). The difference between U_2 and U_1 can be ascribed to the excess burden of a proportional income tax that selectively taxes income. Note that, compared to lump sum taxes, selective income taxes lower the incentive to work even though they may lead to increased work effort (labour supply increases from LQ_0 without any tax to LQ_1 with the tax). A lump sum tax of equal revenue yield thus results in an even greater quantity of labour being supplied (the quantity of labour supplied increases from LQ_0 to LQ_2). We can therefore conclude that income taxes are economically inefficient, the reason being that relative prices are distorted by the tax.

Our conclusion that income taxes are distortional rests on the premise that it is difficult or impossible to tax leisure. If it were possible to tax both labour and leisure hours, we would have had a tax that generates no excess burden. One option put forward and which became known as the Corlett-Hague rule, was to tax goods and services complementary to leisure (Corlett and Hague, 1953). Consumers use certain goods such as golf clubs, DVDs, television sets, and romance novels along with leisure time. On their own, these goods have little value – they only become useful if used in combination with leisure time. Therefore, if you cannot tax leisure explicitly, the policy solution would be to tax goods complementary to leisure at a rate that would reduce demand for leisure indirectly. In this way the excess burden of the income tax system could possibly be reduced.

From this analysis it follows that taxing women who are not the main breadwinners at lower marginal tax rates than men may, for example, increase the supply of labour. This would induce more women to enter the labour market. This option is not available, however, since the South African Constitution does not permit discrimination on the basis of gender or marriage.

Based in part on the theoretical arguments that lower marginal tax rates will increase work effort and improve tax compliance (the incentive to cheat is lower if tax rates are lower), there has been a worldwide trend towards lower marginal tax rates (see Chapter 14, Section 14.5.2). South Africa has followed suit. In the early 1970s the maximum marginal tax rate was 72 per cent compared to the present rate of 40 per cent.

Selective tax on interest income

Personal income tax impacts not only on the supply of labour but also affects private savings if interest income is taxed. South African households have a poor savings record. Savings as a percentage of disposable income of households declined from 4,1 per cent in 1993 to -1,0 per cent in 2008. Because taxation may affect savings behaviour, governments attempt to encourage individuals to save more. In South Africa domestic interest income is exempted up to a certain threshold depending on the age of the individual (above or below 65 years). Contributions to retirement annuities, pension and provident funds are also tax deductible up to certain levels to provide incentives for individuals to save for their retirement. A comprehensive framework for social security and retirement reform has been proposed in 2007. This framework provides consistent tax incentives for mandatory contributions and supplementary voluntary contributions. To analyse the impact of taxation on savings we will show that the supply of savings is a function of **lifetime income**, the interest rate and the preferences (tastes) of individuals. We then introduce a tax on interest income and show that because the tax changes the opportunity cost (or 'price') of present consumption it has income and substitution effects. The supply of individual savings may increase or decrease.

We know that income (Y) is equal to the sum of consumption (C) and saving (S). Less saving implies more consumption. We can understand the impact of a tax on a person's savings choices by analysing consumption in two periods: the present and the future. In deciding how much to save the individual will have to consider his or her lifetime income, that is, the income which is now received and what is expected to be earned in the future. Because individuals prefer present consumption to future consumption, our individual (let's call her Grace) would require some form of compensation for postponing consumption to the future. The compensation for giving up one rand of present consumption (i.e. saving) can be seen as the interest that can be earned on her savings. Put differently the opportunity cost of one rand of present consumption is $(1 + r)$ rand in the future, where r is the interest rate. If Grace has R2 000 available now and the interest rate is 10 per cent, she would be able to postpone her consumption of this amount (the principal) in return for future consumption of R2 200, that is, [R2 000 + (0,10)2 000]. This can also be analysed graphically.

In Figure 12.3 present consumption is measured on the horizontal axis and future

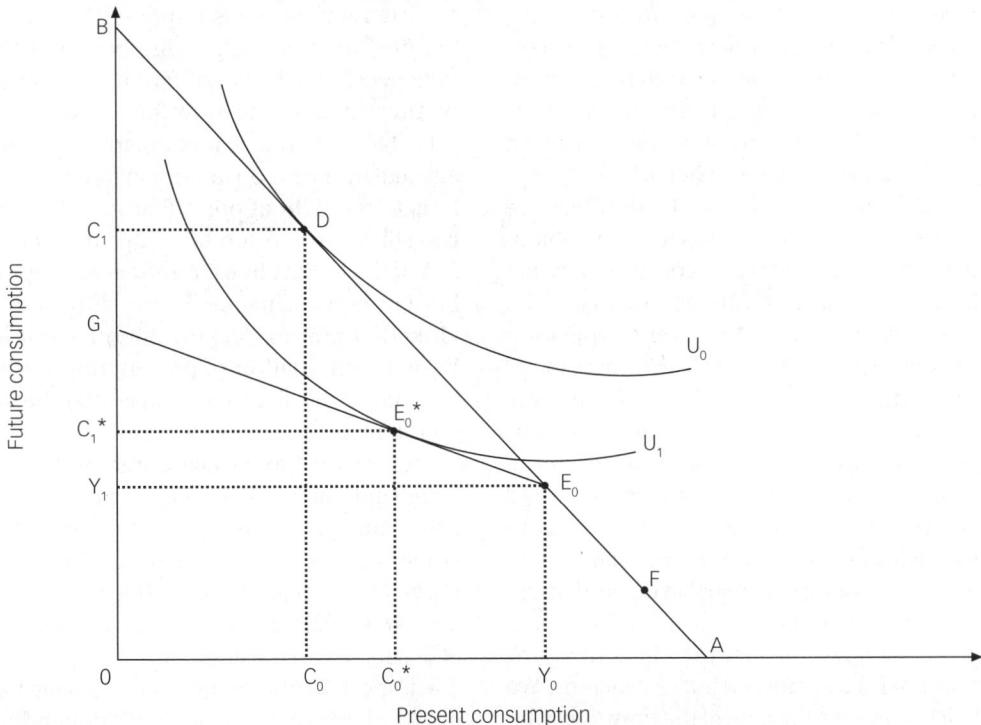

Figure 12.3 Effect of an income tax on savings

consumption on the vertical axis. Suppose Grace has an initial endowment of present income (Y_0) and future income (Y_1). If she neither saves nor borrows this income and consumption bundle would correspond to point E_0 (the endowment point). She now decides to save S. This can be shown as a movement to the left of E_0 and a reduction in present consumption equal to the distance Y_0C_0. In the next period Grace will be able to enjoy increased consumption equal to $(1 + r)S$. This represents a movement to a point above and to the left of E_0 such as D, entailing an increase in future consumption equal to the distance Y_1C_1. But Grace can also decide to borrow, that is, her present consumption exceeds her present income leaving her with less future consumption. In Figure 12.3 the net effect is represented as point F, a movement to the right and below the initial endowment point E_0. By linking points D and F through E_0 and by considering all the other possible values of savings and borrowing, the **lifetime budget constraint** AB is derived. This budget line shows the different combinations of consumption over the two time periods and has a slope of $-(1 + r)$. But which combination will Grace choose?

Each person has a set of indifference curves and each curve gives those combinations of present and future consumption that leaves the person indifferent, that is, at the same level of utility. Whatever the person's preference, each person will attempt to maximise utility subject to his or her lifetime budget constraint. If Grace prefers to consume less today in return for more in the future, a point such as D can be attained where her indifference curve U_0 is tangent to the lifetime budget line AB. She prefers present consumption equal to $0C_0$ and future consumption of $0C_1$.

Let us now consider the effect of a proportional tax, at rate t on interest income. We will not analyse the case of the borrower who has to pay interest and who may in some cases deduct interest payments from income tax. Deductible interest payments are permissible in countries such as the USA. Some taxpayers in South Africa may also claim part of their interest payments on their housing bonds as a personal income tax deduction. The tax reduction on interest payments on housing bonds is the exception and we will focus on the more important practice where interest income (i.e. the return on savings) is taxed.

A tax at a rate of t reduces the rate of interest received to $(1 - t)r$. The opportunity cost of present consumption changes to $[1 + (1 - t)r]$ compared to the before tax opportunity cost of $(1 + r)$. How does this affect the budget line? First of all, the after-tax budget line must include the initial endowment (Y_0, Y_1) since the individual may still opt to neither save not borrow at that income. If Grace decides to save (i.e. move above and to the left of point E_0 in Figure 12.3) she will be able to increase future consumption by less than before. The new budget line becomes the flatter section GE_0. Put differently, the slope of the budget line now has a slope of $-[1 + (1 - t)r]$. The cost of borrowing is not affected by the tax on interest income. Therefore, to the right of point E_0, the individual can still consume combinations on section E_0A of the budget line. The after-tax lifetime budget constraint becomes AE_0G and is kinked at point E_0. Again the question is: Which combination of present and future consumption will Grace choose after the tax on interest?

Before the tax Grace consumed at D where indifference curve U_0 touches the lifetime budget line AB. After the tax consumption is at E_0^* where indifference curve U_1 is tangent to the after-tax budget line AE_0G. Present consumption is now at $0C_0^*$ and future consumption is equal to $0C_1^*$. The important observation is that saving has declined from Y_0C_0 to $Y_0C_0^*$. But depending on her taste for future and present consumption (the shape of the indifference curves) the outcome could have been different – saving could have increased. The net result is ambiguous. Why?

The tax has changed the relative 'price' of present consumption and a price change has a substitution effect and an income effect. Let us consider the substitution effect first. Since the opportunity cost of present consumption has decreased (the product has become 'cheaper'), Grace would increase present consumption. This implies that savings must be reduced resulting in less future consumption. The income effect can be explained by noting that the reduction in the interest rate received caused after-tax income in the future to become less. The only way in which Grace could maintain her consumption level in the future is to reduce present consumption. The income effect implies more saving. One could also understand the income effect by considering that many persons aim at reaching a certain retirement goal or that they are target savers. If the return on their savings declines, they have to compensate by saving more (reducing present consumption). To summarise: the substitution effect causes saving to decrease; the income effect causes saving to increase. If the substitution effect dominates the net result would be lower saving. If the income effect dominates the net result would be increased saving. The end result is therefore theoretically ambiguous and remains a matter for empirical research.

We have established that an income tax levied on interest income causes the relative price of present consumption in terms of future consumption to change. The impact on the supply of savings remains uncertain. How is economic efficiency affected? To determine whether the tax on interest income has an excess burden we could repeat the procedure we employed when we analysed a selective tax on labour income. We simply contrast the effect of the interest income tax with a lump sum tax of equal revenue. A lump sum tax does not have an effect on the consumption choices of the individual in the two periods (i.e. the relative price ratio between present and future consumption remains unchanged). We can conclude that an income tax on interest income is economically inefficient since it causes the individual to substitute between present and future consumption (an excess burden is created). The magnitude of the burden may also be compounded when different forms of savings are taxed differently, thereby changing the rates of return on savings vehicles. This would imply a further distortion of relative prices.

Empirical results of the effect of taxation on saving are inconclusive. Some economists estimated a low interest elasticity of supply of savings whereas others came to different conclusions. The consensus opinion is that the rate of return effects on saving is at best small (Jappelli and Pistaferri 2002). The evidence on whether saving may have an impact on pension savings is also not clear. People do not necessarily increase their net savings – they shift their savings in response to tax incentives (Gale and Scholz 1994). The Katz Commission (1994) came to similar conclusions noting that the impact of non-tax factors are much more important and that it is only the composition of savings that is affected by personal income tax. In this regard by stimulating personal saving, the loss in revenue for government could result in an increased budget deficit (i.e. greater government dissaving). Promoting savings through mandatory contributions to pension funds also crowd out voluntary savings. But there may be other reasons for introducing compulsory savings programmes. These include equity reasons. Low-income earners below the income tax threshold have no tax incentive to save while the high-income earners have resources and financial information to exploit tax incentives. To leave saving for retirement entirely in the hands of individuals could lead to free-riding behaviour which could cause a burden for future generations. The reform of the social security system was given attention in Chapter 8.

12.4.2 Equity

As mentioned, personal income taxation lends itself to the application of the ability-to-pay principle. Through a system of exemptions, deductions, tax rebates, and marginal tax rates, the rate structure can be made to conform to society's notion of fairness. However, before we can make final conclusions in respect of tax equity, we need to know who ultimately bears the burden of the tax. If the tax can be shifted quite easily, the achievement of equity objectives could be compromised.

Even though the statutory burden of the tax is on the individual, it may be possible for individuals to shift the burden. The critical issue is how sensitive the supply of labour is to price and tax changes. As already noted, the net effect on work effort will be determined by the relative strengths of the income and substitution effects. Empirical evidence points to an insensitive or inelastic supply of labour for men (i.e. the supply curve is almost vertical). If the supply curve is relatively inelastic, the burden is on the supplier, that is, the employee in this case (see Chapter 10, Figure 10.5). If the supply curve is less inelastic, the employer and the employee will share the burden. This scenario is possible in the case of married women and high-income professionals who are internationally mobile. Thus, governments should take due cognisance of tax shifting possibilities when personal income taxes are levied with the purpose of affecting income distribution. Intentions and actual policy outcomes do not necessarily point in the same direction.

12.4.3 Administrative efficiency and tax revenue

In the discussion of administrative efficiency in Chapter 11 a number of references were made to income tax (Section 11.3). We will highlight some of the issues here. Income taxes are complex and administrative efficiency requires relatively sophisticated taxpayers and administrators. In countries where these requirements are generally lacking, the income tax code should be as simple as possible. To simplify tax administration and ease the compliance burden for some taxpayers, SARS introduced an electronic filing facility for individuals.

Personal income tax is a major source of government revenue. In 2010/11 taxes on persons and individuals raised R228 000 million which contributed about 33,9 per cent to total tax revenue (gross). It must be recognised that the tax base is rather small – approximately 5,9 million registered taxpayers in 2009 compared to about 8,1 million employed people in the non-agricultural sectors in September 2009. Many of the total number of potential taxpayers are not liable for income tax due to tax rebates. The tax base can be increased by lowering tax rebates (i.e. raising the minimum tax threshold). This would cause hardship for the poorer taxpayers and increase tax administration. Alternatively, efforts could be made to capture those outside the tax net such as those in the informal sector and other groups that are difficult to tax. These groups can be taxed using presumptive taxes. **Presumptive taxation** involves the use of certain indicators (e.g. ownership of certain assets, personal servants, average profit margins, or average gross turnover) to determine tax liability.

Another method that has been proposed to increase tax revenue (or maintain the same level of tax revenue) is to reduce tax rates. This recommendation is based on the alleged tax rate–tax revenue relationship that has become known as the **Laffer curve**, named after the economist Arthur B. Laffer (1941) who popularised the idea. The logic of his argument is that higher tax rates will not necessarily produce more tax revenue, since the tax base will shrink as taxpayers reduce their work effort in response to the higher rates. Fundamentally, the debate is again about how sensitive labour supply is to tax changes. Without discussing this issue again it should be recognised that the higher the tax rate, the more likely it is that the substitution effect will dominate. For example, if income is taxed at increasingly higher marginal rates and ultimately at 100 per cent, work effort will not only decline, but a person will eventually not be prepared to do any additional work whatsoever. Tax revenue is the product of the tax rate and the tax base, where the tax base depends on work effort (the number of hours worked). At low tax rates, an increase in the tax rate will tend to increase tax revenues (at low rates people will still work more, i.e. the income effect dominates). However, this will only continue up to a point beyond which further tax rate increases will reduce tax revenues (people will eventually reduce their work effort, i.e. the substitution effect will dominate).

The Laffer curve is illustrated in Figure 12.4. Total tax revenue is plotted on the vertical axis and the tax rate on the horizontal axis. If the tax rate is at A, government can still increase tax revenue by raising the rate. Once the tax rate is at B, however, a further

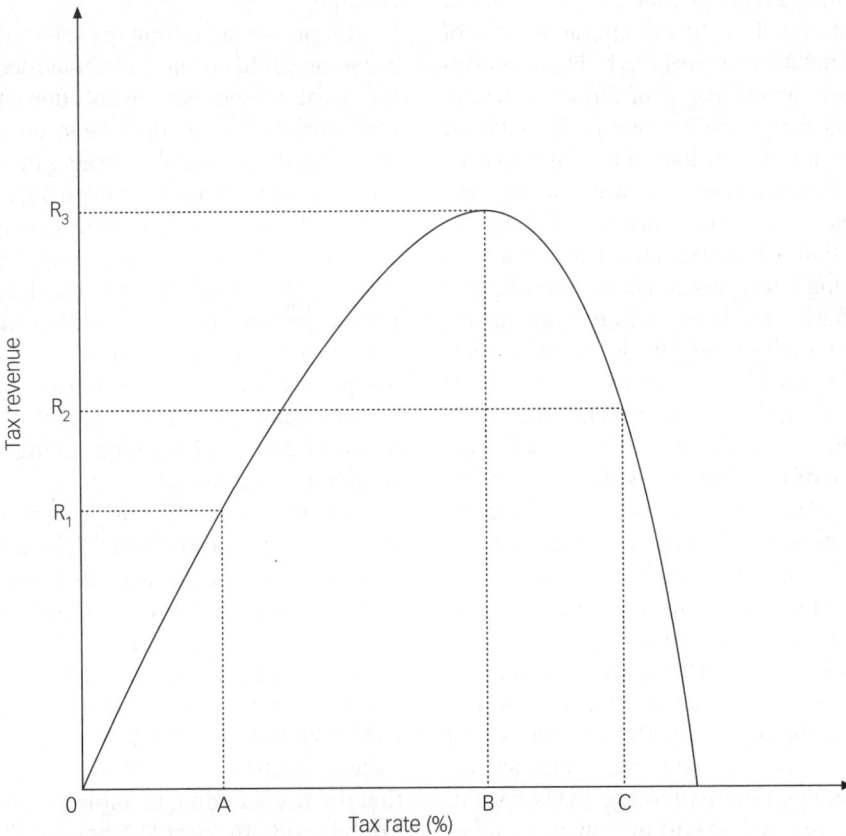

Figure 12.4 The Laffer curve

increase in the rate will cause tax revenue to decline (e.g. from R_3 to R_2). The supporters of the Laffer hypothesis use the mechanism to show that if the tax rate is at C, the authorities should lower the rate since this will result in higher tax revenue as illustrated by a movement from R_2 to R_3. The critical question, of course, is to determine where countries are on the curve. The proponents argue that some countries may well be beyond point B. The debate can only be settled empirically but it does appear that labour supply elasticities are such that it is unlikely that rate reductions would be fully counteracted by increased work effort.

12.4.4 Flexibility

In Section 11.4 of Chapter 11 it was pointed out that one of the 'good' characteristics of a personal income tax is its built-in flexibility to counter cyclical economic behaviour. Personal income tax is thus considered to be an automatic stabiliser. On the negative side, inflation has serious implications for a progressive personal income tax to the extent that it has rendered the automatic stabilising effect meaningless (see Chapter 15). Inflation erodes the value of tax thresholds and deductions and leads to **bracket creep**; this is a process whereby a person is pushed into a higher income tax bracket as his or her nominal income increases (irrespective of what happens to the person's real income). This could be beneficial to government (it raises more and more revenue without the legislative process to increase tax rates), but if tax brackets and the value of tax preferences are left uncorrected, all taxpayers could end up paying the maximum marginal tax rate. Such a disguised way of increasing the tax burden is of course not conducive to transparency, an important requirement of a good tax system. Sometimes the phenomenon of bracket creep is erroneously referred to as 'fiscal

drag'. This concept really refers to the dampening effect on the economy of the higher tax revenues (caused by bracket creep), that is, rising tax revenues automatically push the government's budget into a surplus creating a restrictive fiscal policy. This could have very adverse implications if substantial inflation occurs in recessionary times (when a deficit on the budget would be more appropriate in Keynesian terms) unless tax brackets are adjusted for inflation.

To understand the bracket creep phenomenon it is essential to distinguish between nominal income and real income. **Real income** refers to the purchasing power of income (i.e. income after adjustment for inflation) whereas **nominal income** is the actual monetary value or rand value of income.

The personal income tax schedule taxes a person on his or her nominal income. In inflationary times employers often compensate workers for the decline in purchasing power by increasing their wages or salaries. If the rate of increase is equal to the inflation rate, workers' nominal income increases, but their real income stays the same. However, if the personal income tax schedule is not corrected for inflation, individuals are pushed into higher tax brackets with higher marginal tax rates because their nominal incomes have increased. Consider the following numerical example using the tax schedule in Table 12.1.

Suppose that Ms Shope received an income of R140 000 in 2011/12. Now assume that the general price level increases by 10 per cent in 2012/13 and that Ms Shope's employer raises her salary by 10 per cent. In real terms her income stays the same, but in nominal terms her income increased to R154 000. We can calculate Ms Shope's tax liability in 2011/12 and 2012/13, assuming that the tax schedule in Table 12.1 remains unchanged. In 2011/12 her tax liability (based on her income of R140 000) was

R14 445 (remember to take the primary rebate of R10 755 into account). In 2012/13 her nominal income of R154 000 pushed her into the higher (R150 001 and more) tax bracket and the last R4 000 of her income is taxed at a marginal tax rate of 25 per cent. In 2012/13 her tax liability increases by 19,4% to R17 245, much more than the inflation rate of 10% with which her salary increases. Ms Shope therefore pays R2 800 more tax, even though her real income has not increased. Her average tax rate increased from 10,3 per cent ($= \frac{14\,445}{140\,000} \times 100$) to 11,2 per cent ($= \frac{17\,245}{154\,000} \times 100$). This increase in her average tax rate (while her real pre-tax income remains unchanged) is what bracket creep is all about. If left unchecked, bracket creep undermines vertical equity. Even poor taxpayers will be drawn into the tax net and will eventually be taxed at high marginal tax rates.

The tax authorities can temper or eliminate the effects of bracket creep by linking the rate structure to a price index (i.e. raise the income brackets each year in line with the increase in the general price level). Alternatively, government can adjust the brackets and rebates on an ad hoc basis. This has been the preferred method of the South African tax authorities. Following the recommendation of the Margo Commission (1987: 81), government also reduced the number of tax brackets to slow down the inflationary creep to increasingly higher marginal rates. For example, in 1991/92 the income tax schedule for married couples provided for 15 brackets compared to the six brackets in 2011/12.

12.5 Company taxation

Due to certain unique properties of company income, most countries tax this source of income separately. These are the main reasons for taxing companies:

▶ From a legal point of view, companies are separate entities (legal persons). They function as institutions with their own identity and are independent from their shareholders who are taxed in their own right.
▶ Companies receive benefits from government and should be taxed for these privileges according to the benefit principle. The benefits include companies' limited legal liability to shareholders, the creation of an orderly environment by government which is necessary for conducting business, the use of infrastructure, etc.
▶ If companies are not taxed, it is possible for shareholders to limit their personal income tax liability by retaining profits in the company. This increases the capital value of the shareholders' investment in the company. If capital gains are also not taxed, the integrity of the whole system of income taxation is jeopardised. Tax avoidance by individuals is therefore limited by taxing company profits. Since it is generally the higher-income group who are shareholders in companies, taxing this income is fair from an ability-to-pay perspective.
▶ By taxing the excess profits of imperfectly competitive firms (e.g. monopolies and oligopolies) market failures are addressed. The government can also achieve other economic policy objectives such as promoting foreign and local investment and achieving regional development aims by manipulating company tax rates and providing tax incentives (e.g. liberal depreciation allowances, training allowances, and tax credits).
▶ Company taxation is administratively simple and generates significant revenue as a separate tax, particularly in developing countries (see the

discussion of tax reform in Chapter 14, Section 14.5).

> By taxing companies, revenue is derived that would otherwise accrue to foreign investors and their home governments. Foreign investors are usually taxed on their investment income at company tax rates in their home countries. For example, when South Africa (the host country) levies company tax, the profits repatriated to the home country (e.g. the USA) will also be taxed at prevailing USA company tax rates. To avoid double taxation, countries usually enter into double taxation agreements whereby the home country credits taxpayers with taxes paid in the host country. In other words, only the difference between the home country tax liability and host country liability is payable in the home country.

Company tax is a significant but declining source of tax revenue. In 1975/76 income tax on companies amounted to R1 969 million, or about 41 per cent of total tax revenue (net collections) in South Africa. In 2010/11 company tax came to R132 500 million, or about 20,3 per cent of total tax revenue (excluding SACU payments). There are various reasons for this decline, one of which concerns the nature of economic development. As a country develops economically, the consumption tax base broadens and the personal income tax base also becomes more important. Another set of possible reasons are factors that reduce company profit margins, such as rising wage costs, import costs, and debt finance charges. Tax exemptions, tax evasion, and tax avoidance are further possible causes, since they lead to effective tax rates that turn out to be much lower than the nominal or statutory rates. Changing domestic and global economic conditions also cause volatility in the contribution of company income tax to total tax

revenue as profits track upswings and contractions in economic activity.

One of the most important explanations for the declining contribution of company tax to total tax revenue in South Africa is the decline in tax revenue from income tax on mines, particularly gold mines. Tax revenue from gold mining declined from approximately 10 per cent of total tax revenue in 1975/76 to less than 0,2 per cent in 1998/99 (the last year in which revenue from gold mining companies was reported separately from other companies). This is indicative of the decline in the gold mining industry as well as of structural change as South Africa moved from a mining economy to an industrial economy. The decline in the gold mining industry can also be attributed to the relatively low international gold price at times, rising wage costs, and lower ore grades. Although the contribution of company tax revenue shows a declining trend, South Africa uses company taxation very intensively compared to other low- and middle-income economies. When countries are ranked according to their company income tax efforts, South Africa ranks second out of 27 countries studied (Steenekamp 2007).

12.6 The company tax structure

12.6.1 The company tax base

Businesses can be classified as incorporated or unincorporated. Incorporated businesses or companies include private and public companies and close corporations. Unincorporated businesses include sole proprietorships and partnerships. In South Africa, mining companies are also distinguished from non-mining companies. The nature of business differs so much between these two categories that they are taxed differently. The taxing of mining enterprises is still receiving the attention of government. The South African government has indicated that it is committed to a differentiated *ad valorem* royalty on gross sales and is preparing legislation in this regard. In the rest of this chapter we focus on the taxation of non-mining companies only.

Taxable income is defined as total receipts (or revenue) of the company minus certain allowable expenses (or costs). Expenses comprise costs incurred to run the business. The definition seems simple enough, but a number of issues in respect of expenses complicate company taxation. These are the two most important complications:

▶ Interest payments can sometimes be deducted from taxable income but dividends cannot. This has implications for company finance. Companies have three basic sources of finance: share capital, borrowing (debt financing), and retained earnings. In the case of borrowing, the company can write off the cost of the loans (interest) against income for tax purposes. When share capital is used in South Africa, the cost of shares (dividends) cannot be written off against income. Therefore, there is a built-in bias against the use of share capital as a source of financing. In other words, the tax system encourages the use of loan finance but excessive use of loans increases indebtedness and may lead to bankruptcy.

▶ Companies are allowed to deduct depreciation on assets when taxable income is calculated. The rationale for a depreciation allowance is that assets (e.g. machinery) lose some of their value each year and wear out over their lifetime; this constitutes a cost of production. But it is difficult to precisely determine the true rate of depreciation (i.e. economic depreciation). Sometimes the allowance exceeds economic depreciation. From time to time governments also allow companies to depreciate assets at an accelerated rate. This is sometimes used, for example, as an incentive to attract foreign investors. Such practices have the effect of reducing the effective company tax rate below the statutory tax rate. Assets are also classified into different categories and depreciation allowances differ accordingly. For example, 5 per cent per annum is allowed on commercial buildings (i.e. a write-off period of 20 years) but 40 per cent of the cost of manufacturing machinery will be deducted in the first year and 20 per cent of the cost for the subsequent 3 years.

In 2004 a special depreciation allowance for investment undertaken for construction or refurbishment of buildings in under-utilised designated urban areas was introduced. Taxpayers refurbishing a building within such a zone will receive a 20 per cent straight-line depreciation allowance over a five-year period. If a new commercial or residential building is constructed within such a zone, taxpayers will receive a 17-year write-off period with a 20 per cent write-off in the first year and 5 per cent thereafter. The incentive is aimed at encouraging investment in areas with high population-carrying capacity and central business districts. This depreciation allowance applies to 15 municipalities including areas such as Johannesburg, Cape Town, Polokwane, Sol Plaatjie Metropolitan (Kimberley), and Nelson Mandela Metropolitan (Port Elizabeth).

The problem with differentiated depreciation rates is that this practice tends to open up tax arbitrage opportunities. Investors, for example, will invest in assets that they can write off quickly or immediately for tax purposes, but which actually depreciate much slower or even appreciate over time. The tax authorities usually become aware of such shelters only after a while and it then takes some time to eliminate the loopholes. In South Africa investments in forests, ships, motion pictures, and aircraft were, and are still, examples of such tax shelters. Needless to say, such tax-driven schemes are not models of efficient resource allocation.

12.6.2 Type of company tax

There are two extreme types of company tax. At the one extreme, companies are regarded as entities separate from their shareholders, and both are taxed on the same income source (referred to as the **classical system** or partnership approach). Company income is thus taxed twice, first as company tax and then also as personal income when distributed as dividends. This is commonly known as double taxation of dividends. At the other extreme, the company is simply seen as a conduit for all company income to the shareholders. All company income (retained as well as distributed) is taxed in full in the hands of the shareholders at their marginal income tax rates. The company tax then only serves as a withholding tax, which is credited in full at shareholder level. This type of company taxation is referred to as the **full integration** system.

Prior to 1990, South Africa had a modified classical company tax system incorporating a tax on company income and a tax on dividends, with a certain portion of dividends being excluded from taxation in the hands of the shareholders. On recommendation of the Margo Commission (1987: 204) the double taxation of dividends was discontinued in 1990 when dividends became tax-exempt in the hands of resident individuals and close corporations.

The company tax system was modified again in 1993 in an effort to (a) reduce the company tax rate without undue revenue loss, and (b) encourage companies to finance

themselves. A dual tax rate was introduced, that is, a basic and secondary rate. Non-mining companies are taxed at a fixed percentage on their taxable income. This is the **basic tax on companies**. Company tax is therefore a proportional tax. The basic company tax rate was lowered from 48 per cent to 40 per cent in 1993 and to 30 per cent in 1999. In 2005 the rate was further reduced to 29 per cent and again in 2008 to 28 per cent. The basic rate applies to all retained profits, that is, profits that are used to finance company investment or build company reserves and that are therefore not paid out as dividends to shareholders. In addition to the basic rate, a **secondary tax on companies (STC)** was introduced in 1993. STC was levied on all profits distributed to the company's shareholders (i.e. dividends). STC was levied at company level and paid by companies. The rate was originally set at 15 per cent in 1993 but it was raised to 25 per cent in 1994, reduced to 12,5 per cent in 1996 and reduced again to 10 per cent in 2007. To determine the company tax rate, both rates had to be considered.

The Katz Commission (1994: 175–177 and 226–227) thoroughly investigated the advantages and shortcomings of STC. The Commission concluded that STC has served its purpose and that 'it has become desirable to consider better ways to achieve its objectives'. Starting in 2007, STC is being phased out and replaced with a dividend tax at 10 per cent. The dividend tax becomes effective on 1 April 2012. It applies to all distributions and is administratively enforced as a withholding tax at company level – legally it is not a tax on companies. The withholding tax will only apply to dividends paid to individuals and non-resident shareholders (dividends to all South African tax resident companies are exempted). No deductions may be claimed against the dividends received and such dividends will not be included in the shareholder's taxable income. The phasing out of STC was introduced to bring dividend taxation in line with international practice. Since STC impacts on the cost of financing businesses using equity its removal would lower the cost of doing business.

Company tax rates differ somewhat between the BLSN countries. In Botswana resident companies pay company tax at 25 per cent. Where a business falls within the definition of 'manufacturing', it is entitled to a reduced corporate tax of 15 per cent. This relief is conditional on the approval of the Minister of Finance on consideration of, for example, the number of citizens employed, training, replacement of non-resident employees with skilled citizens, and citizen management participation. The Kingdom of Lesotho taxes companies at a rate of 25 per cent. Income derived from manufacturing activity is taxed at a rate of 15 per cent. In Namibia corporate income is taxed at 34 per cent. Special rebates may be granted to approved manufacturing companies. Taxable income (after the special deductions) derived from manufacturing is taxed at 18 per cent for a total period of ten years. A tax-free regime applies in Namibian export-processing zones (EPZs).

12.6.3 Taxation of small and medium-sized enterprises

It is generally recognised that small and medium-sized enterprises are important for economic growth and creating job opportunities in the economy. It is also recognised, however, that the tax system severely affects these types of businesses in so far as tax compliance is concerned. In addition, small businesses are highly dependent on working capital provided by the owners. When their profits are taxed, owners often have to use short-term debt that increases their risk exposure. To assist small enterprises through the tax system, various options can be pursued including taxing these businesses on

their cash flow, taxing enterprises at differentiated rates (e.g. a progressive corporate rate structure) and using tax incentives (e.g. tax holidays, accelerated depreciation allowances) (see Steenekamp, 1996).

The real and financial cash-flow tax base equals [(sales + borrowing + interest received)-(real purchases + interest payments + debt repayment)]. The main advantages of a cash-flow tax (Mintz and Seade, 1991: 177–190; Shome and Shutte, 1993; and Sunley, 1989) are:

▶ The definition of the tax base is simple as the tax does away with problems of defining depreciation, measuring capital gains, costing inventories, and accounting for inflation.
▶ The tax is neutral with respect to the use of capital. Immediate expensing implies that the tax does not discriminate between debt and equity.

The cash-flow tax has a number of shortcomings:

▶ During the transition from an accrual to a cash-flow system, the tax creates windfall tax revenue gains or losses, depending on whether government allows or denies companies depreciation on earlier investment.
▶ Full and immediate expensing seems to reduce the tax base compared to the accrual income tax base. However, this conclusion is disputed by some, who argue that it has to be considered that the corporate income tax base is also eroded through all kinds of tax expenditures.
▶ The incentive for base shifting is high (the tax base can be shifted from a high-tax entity to a low-tax entity). This could be done by purchasing inputs from the low-tax entity at inflated prices, by low-rate leasing and expensing by a high-tax party to a low-tax party, and by the sale of expensed assets at understated prices

to the low-tax entity. Monitoring these practices is difficult and increases the administrative burden.

▶ The cash flow tax raises serious problems in international taxation, as it may not be creditable in home countries.

▶ Since no country has implemented the tax as yet, administrative problems are difficult to predict.

The Katz Commission (1994: 157–158) considered cash flow accounting and recommended that it be introduced as an option for small enterprises. The South African government accepted this recommendation in principle and considered implementing cash-flow taxation in a particular sub-sector of the economy, namely the micro and small business sector. Limiting cash-flow taxation to a sub-sector has the advantage of improving its cash flow and capital requirements. Although the theoretical case for a cash-flow tax system is quite strong, one serious problem concerns the international consequences. On the negative side, cash-flow taxation increases the incentive for tax evasion and avoidance. The application of this form of taxation to a sub-sector of the economy will probably add to opportunities for tax arbitrage.

In 2000 the South African government opted for a graduated tax rate structure and generous depreciation allowances for small business corporations. The tax rate structure is set out in Table 12.2.

Small businesses may write off investment in manufacturing assets in full in the tax year in which the assets are brought into use. An accelerated allowance for machinery, plant, implements, utensils, articles, aircraft or ships (other than plant or machinery used in a manufacturing or similar process) acquired by small business corporations can be depreciated at 50 per cent of the cost of the asset in the tax year during which it was first brought into use, 30 per cent in the

Table 12.2 Graduated tax rate structure for small business corporations

Taxable income	Tax rate
R0 – R59 750	0%
R59 751 – R300 000	10% of amount above R59 750
R300 001 +	R24 025 plus 28% of amount above R300 000

Source: South African Revenue Service (SARS), *Pocket Tax Guide, Budget 2011* (2011).

second year and 20 per cent in the third year (a 50:30:20 per cent rate over a three-year period). At the time of writing, these benefits were limited to businesses with an annual turnover of less than R14,0 million. Businesses in which more than 20 per cent of gross income consists collectively of investment income are excluded. Small businesses with a payroll of less than R500 000 are also not required to pay the skills development levy as a measure to reduce compliance costs. These tax reliefs are thus mainly intended for manufacturing businesses and are aimed at promoting job creation and improving the cash flow of small businesses. Small businesses engaged in the provision of personal services qualify for relief as long as they maintain at least four full-time employees for core activities.

To further reduce compliance costs (income tax and VAT paperwork) for very small businesses, the government proposed a simplified tax regime in 2008. The regime is a turnover-based presumptive tax system. Businesses with a turnover of less than R1 million per year will have the option to elect this form of tax. Tax liability is calculated using a graduated tax rate structure based not on taxable income but on turnover (sales) (see Table 12.3).

Globally the use of presumptive taxes is widespread and is an approach where tax

Table 12.3 Presumptive turnover tax for micro businesses

Turnover	Tax liability
R0 – R150 000	0%
R150 001 – R300 000	1% of each R1 above R150 000
R300 001 – R500 000	R1 500 + 3% of the amount above R300 000
R500 001 – R750 000	R7 500 + 5% of the amount above R500 000
R750 001 and above	R20 000 + 7% of the amount above R750 000

Source: South African Revenue Service (SARS), *Pocket Tax Guide, Budget 2011* (2011).

liability is administratively determined using criteria such as turnover, sales, employment, assets or size of the firm. It is intended to capture a minimum tax amount from hard-to-tax groups of taxpayers such as those operating in the informal (or unrecorded) sector. The aim is to eventually draw these taxpayers into the regular tax net once they have reached a certain maximum threshold (e.g. R1 000 000 of turnover in Table 12.3). Above this limit firms do not qualify for presumptive tax status and must migrate to the regular company tax options.

Presumptive taxation has some advantages of which simplification is important. It not only reduces compliance cost for the business but makes it easy for the revenue authorities to administer. They can use readily available data to benchmark and verify tax liability and it also releases them from spending too much time on large numbers of small tax entities – they can concentrate on the 'big fish'. On the negative side, presumptive taxes may cause inefficiencies in the tax system as firms try to take advantage of the regime by restructuring their activities to qualify for presumptive tax status. Alternatively, if the maximum threshold is set too high (resulting in a tax liability that is low compared to the regular tax liability), firms will attempt to remain in the presumptive tax net. This may compromise horizontal fairness in the company tax system.

12.7 The economic effects of company tax

12.7.1 Economic efficiency

In analysing the economic efficiency of company tax we again have to consider the excess burden of the tax. Does company tax cause an excess burden, that is, are relative prices (or returns) distorted, resulting in resources not being optimally allocated? The answer depends on whether company tax is seen as a tax on excess profits (or economic profits) or as a selective tax on capital.

If company tax is regarded as a tax on economic profits only, then company tax has no excess burden. The economic profits of firms are simply reduced by the tax and firms still maximise profits. The tax does not cause any other changes in behaviour (i.e. marginal costs are unchanged) and prices are not affected. But companies are taxed on their accounting profits (i.e. economic profit plus normal profit).[2] In the short term, normal profits are a fixed cost. Therefore, marginal costs, which change only when variable costs change, are not altered by the tax. However, in the long term there are no fixed inputs (all become variable) and taxing normal profits as part of accounting profits may then affect

[2] See Mohr et al. (2008: 202–203) for an explanation of the profit concept.

marginal cost. Thus, in the long term a tax on accounting profits may cause a change in the behaviour of owners and prices, which could result in an excess burden.

The return on capital of shareholders invested in companies (i.e. dividends) is a non-deductible expense. Company tax can therefore be regarded as a tax on capital. However, all forms of capital are not taxed at the same effective rate. In South Africa incorporated businesses (e.g. public companies) are taxed at a rate of 28 per cent. Non-incorporated businesses (e.g. sole proprietorships) are taxed at marginal personal income tax rates which vary between 18 and 40 per cent. Small business corporations are taxed at graduated rates which vary between 0 and 28 per cent.

The important point about differential taxes on capital is that if companies are taxed at different rates, the net (after-tax) returns differ from sector to sector. Capital will then move from the sectors with lower net (after-tax) returns to sectors where a higher net (after-tax) return can be obtained. This process will continue until net returns are equal in all the sectors. This migration of capital is purely in response to tax-induced differences in returns, and not because capital can be used more productively elsewhere. Resources are therefore misallocated and an excess burden results. In the United States this loss in welfare has been estimated at between 12 and 24 per cent of total tax revenue (see Shoven 1976: 1261–1283; and Jorgenson and Yun 2001: 302).

12.7.2 Company taxation and investment

The decision to invest

Another issue concerning the economic efficiency of company taxation is its impact on local and foreign fixed investment. The company tax structure can lower or raise the user cost of capital. The **user cost of capital** includes, firstly, the opportunity cost of holding an asset in a company. By investing capital in a company instead of, for example, saving it, an opportunity cost is incurred (i.e. the interest forgone). Secondly, the user cost of capital includes depreciation costs. Capital invested in, for example, machines decreases in value. Finally, the user cost of capital is affected by company tax. The returns on share capital (realised profits and dividends) are taxed and constitute a cost to the investor. By lowering nominal company tax rates, providing depreciation allowances, or giving tax incentives (e.g. tax holidays and tax rebates), the user cost of capital can thus be lowered, and vice versa.

The question in developing countries is whether taxes impact on foreign direct investment (FDI), that is, can developing countries attract new capital to meet various economic, social and political objectives (see below). Empirical studies on the impact of taxes on FDI in developed countries generally conclude that taxes have a strong effect. Limited evidence for developing countries also show some impact of tax rates on location decisions of investors (see Zee, Stotsky and Ley 2002: 1509–1510; Keen and Mansour 2009: 22; and Norregaard and Kahn 2007:18–19;). Using dynamic panel data econometrics Klemm and Van Parys (2010) find evidence that lower company income tax (CIT) rates and longer tax holidays (see below) are effective in promoting foreign direct investment in Latin America and the Caribbean but not in Africa. This is a surprising result. It means that investment incentives are ineffective in Africa and simply lead to a loss of revenues. This ineffectiveness of tax incentives is presumably attributed to a generally poor investment climate in Africa, thus indicating that non-tax factors are important considerations when investors make locational decisions.

Based on the evidence brought before the Katz Commission (1994: 213), the Commission observed that 'while tax is an important investment consideration, it ranks well down the list of priorities unless it poses a specific and actual inhibition'. However, corporate taxation might be a major policy issue for the following reasons:

▶ A punitive corporate tax regime constrains investment while a liberal regime could result in an unnecessary loss of revenue to the treasury, thus allowing foreign treasuries to capture bonus revenue.

▶ An unfavourable corporate tax regime might lead to other forms of profit-taking (e.g. repatriation of profits through transfer pricing and setting up branches instead of subsidiaries). The willingness of multinational corporations and others to lower their effective tax rates through transfer pricing indicates their sensitivity to tax rates.

▶ When non-tax factors are approximately the same in countries competing for investment, taxation becomes all-important, as is evident from the intense tax competition in the East Asian region.

Non-tax factors

One should guard against overemphasising the impact of the company tax structure and rates on the decision to invest. Overall it appears that there is much more empirical evidence indicating that the effect of taxes is minor compared to the impact of other factors that affect investment decisions (see Norregaard and Kahn 2007: 18 and Zee, Stotsky and Ley 2002: 1509–1510). The following non-tax factors are important to investors:

▶ Business opportunities. Investors look for market opportunities to maximise profits, for example, by increasing market size or vertically integrating their production processes across national borders. Portfolio investors look for speculative profits (such as those offered by exchange rate differentials) or are interested in spreading risk.

▶ Political stability and good governance. Political instability disrupts investors' calculations of the expected rate of return on their investment. Badly governed countries impact negatively on the business environment.

▶ Economic stability. This includes price and exchange rate stability as well as fiscal stability (i.e. a sustainable fiscal deficit).

▶ Labour stability. Rigidities in the labour market can result in labour costs becoming internationally uncompetitive. Work ethic is important for certain types of investors. For a businessperson interested in manufacturing goods that use labour-intensive technology (e.g. clothing) a reliable workforce is essential.

▶ Security and respect for property rights. Investors are sensitive to policy in respect of nationalisation and privatisation, and to the honouring of international commitments, such as double taxation agreements and debt repayment obligations.

▶ Transportation costs and communication infrastructure. In principle it is always desirable to manufacture goods as close as possible to the market(s) they serve. Poor communication infrastructure can raise the cost of doing business.

Tax incentives

Tax incentives (e.g. tax holidays, capital allowances, incentives for research and development, deductions for training expenses) are used in many developing countries in an effort to attract investment to particular regions, sectors, and industries. They are used for specific purposes such as export promotion, employment creation, local participation, local sourcing of materials, improved infrastructure, the promotion of technological transfers, skills development, and the development of geographical regions.

The reasons for and arguments in favour of the use of tax incentives (see Zee, Stotsky and Ley 2002: 1499–1501; Boadway and Shah, 1995; and Chia and Whalley, 1995) are as follows:

- In the case of market failures (e.g. positive externalities) incentives may correct these. To reduce congestion and pollution in urban areas economic activity could be promoted in rural areas using tax incentives. Similarly projects that use new technology or require much research and development (R&D) input can be targeted.
- Incentives are regarded as a means of offsetting the effects of regulations and controls in developing countries, such as exchange control and licensing restrictions. Incentives compensate for these distortions.
- Likewise, labour market distortions may be corrected by using investment incentives as a second-best policy and in this way employment can be created.
- Capital markets are often imperfect in respect of small firms. By targeting these firms selectively, incentives can be used to overcome these constraints.
- Temporary investment incentives may be effective devices for assisting infant industries.
- To the extent that they are effective in encouraging investment, incentives generate external benefits for the economy over and above those accruing to the investor, for example, innovation and training.
- Tax incentives can be used to signal to investors that a country is open for business. They announce to investors that

government has certain priorities and that investors will be compensated for their commitment. Niche markets can also be promoted through income tax incentives.

Various analysts have questioned the use of incentives to promote investment and other objectives. The arguments raised against incentives (Zee, Stotsky and Ley 2002: 1501–1502; Easson, 1992: 387–439; Shah, 1995; and World Bank, 1991) include:

- Incentives complicate tax administration and increase administration costs.
- Tax concessions erode the revenue base and necessitate higher tax rates. In some cases profitable investments would have taken place without the tax incentive. The incentives then become a free gift from the government to the investor or even treasury of the investor's home country if the latter uses the residence principle.
- Incentive schemes are often the result of pressure group action rather than an analysis of the economy as a whole, thus favouring certain sectors over others (socially unproductive rent-seeking). If the incentive is not aimed at correcting a market failure, it may actually create distortions and economic costs (inefficiencies).
- Tax incentives result in an uneven tax burden among taxpayers.
- Tax incentives are less likely to succeed in attracting foreign investment than a general reduction in corporate income tax.
- Investment incentives often lead to windfall gains in respect of investments that would have taken place anyway – they have little impact on new investment.
- If there are obstacles to investment (e.g. untrained labour) it is better to address these problems directly instead of using

tax incentives, since such incentives simply add further distortions to the economy.

In developing countries tax incentives for investment are now much more widely used than in the 1980s. Low-income countries use incentives more extensively than do middle-income countries. It appears that tax holidays are very popular. At the same time the use of free zones (e.g. export processing zones, free trade zones and economic development zones) has increased to attract footloose industries (see Keen and Mansour 2009: 20). Research by Klemm and Van Parys (2010) confirms that countries in Africa, Latin America and the Caribbean compete for FDI by lowering company income tax rates and offering tax holidays. There is no evidence of spatial interaction (competition) using investment allowances and tax credits.

The popularity of tax holidays runs counter to best practice tax advice. **Tax holidays** exempt (for a period) investment projects from company income tax (CIT) or offers a rate lower than the regular rate. The advantage of tax holidays and preferential CIT rates is ease of administration. The disadvantages are many: these incentives favour investors expecting high profits and who would have undertaken the investment without the incentive; it encourages shifting of profits from non-exempt to exempt firms; it attracts short-run projects, rather than sustainable ones; and the revenue losses are not transparent. Some forms of incentives, for example, investment allowances or tax credits and accelerated depreciation are preferred to tax holidays (see Zee, Stotsky and Ley, 2002: 1504–1505). These incentives (e.g. shorter write-off periods for investment costs) provide for investment in plant and equipment thereby raising capital intensity. They are more targeted and transparent in addressing, for example, human resource training needs and cash-flow problems

associated with new investments and are also less prone to abuse than tax holidays. To ensure that incentives achieve their beneficial outcomes well-designed incentives must follow three basic rules (Bird 2008: 9): keep it simple; keep records on who receives and what the costs are in revenue sacrificed; and evaluate the numbers at regular intervals to check the results.

The Katz Commission (1994: 204) thoroughly reviewed tax incentives in South Africa and concluded that '... the range of incentives should be narrowed as far as possible and that those which exist should all be justified in terms of the objectives in the Reconstruction and Development Programme.' This, however, is a very vague guideline. The Commission also endorsed the principle that tax incentives be subject to thorough cost-benefit analysis. Incentives can be economically justified mainly where markets fail (e.g. when investments generate positive externalities). When granted such incentives should be transparent and discretion should be minimised.

South Africa has for some years been encouraging foreign and domestic investment using a range of incentives. Investment support is provided by the Department of Trade and Industry and consists of an extensive grant system. Tax incentives (see Box 12.3) are also provided to promote investment and consists of accelerated depreciation allowances, graduated tax rates for small businesses (see Section 12.6.3) and incentives for capital expenditure on research and development (R&D). In the late 1990s South Africa also experimented with a tax holiday scheme for certain companies but it applied only until September 1999. Much emphasis is now placed on grants and depreciation allowances. This augers well for transparency and better targeting of projects. In the 2011 Budget Review, a statement concerning tax expenditures was provided in an effort to quantify revenues forgone due to tax incentives. It was estimated that incentives amounting to approximately R1,2 billion were provided to the corporate sector in 2008/09 (National Treasury 2011: 181). Compared to the approximate R185 billion tax revenue collected from companies in the same year, the revenue forgone due to tax incentives is insignificant. Nevertheless, with expenditures now quantified, analysts will be able to attempt a proper cost-benefit analysis of tax incentives.

12.7.3 Fairness

When we considered tax incidence in Chapter 10 we explicitly stated that only people could bear the burden of a tax. In the case of companies, the people in question are shareholders, workers, and consumers. We will now analyse the incidence of company tax on each of these groups.

In Section 12.7.1 we noted that when companies are taxed at different rates, capital

---

BOX 12.3 Grants and tax incentives for investment

A generous system of taxable and non-taxable cash grants are provided by the Department of Trade and Industry to promote new investment in South Africa. Programmes benefitting from this grant system include:
▶ The Clothing and Textile Competitiveness Improvement Programme
▶ The Automotive Investment Scheme
▶ The Enterprise Investment Programme for manufacturing investment and tourism support
▶ Black Business Supplier Development Programme
▶ Critical Infrastructure Programme
▶ Sector-Specific Assistance Scheme
▶ Film Production Incentive
▶ Industrial Development Zones

Tax incentives to support investment are provided in terms of the Income Tax Act 58 of 1962 and are limited to accelerated depreciation allowances, graduated tax rates for small businesses and incentives for research and development (R&D) capital expenditure. Accelerated depreciation allowances permit investors to use a 40:20:20:20 regime for manufacturing assets (plant and machinery). Investments in renewable energy and biofuels production and capital expenditure on R&D can be depreciated over a three-year period on a 50:30:20 basis. Furthermore an

accelerated depreciation regime applies to buildings within Urban Development Zones (see Section 12.6.1). Other tax incentives are:
▶ A tonnage tax regime for South African shipping companies according to which companies are taxed not on their business income but on the size of the ship, thus lowering the effective tax rate.
▶ Investments in energy efficient equipment get an additional tax allowance of up to 15 per cent.
▶ The government's industrial policy strategy provides for investment and training allowances for large manufacturing projects. It is designed to support Greenfield investments (i.e. new industrial projects that utilise only new and unused manufacturing assets), as well as Brownfield investments (i.e. expansions or upgrades of existing industrial projects). A points system is used to determine qualifying status (i.e. energy efficiency, skills development and size). Between 35 and 55 per cent of the cost of fixed capital investment and employee training is deductible from taxable income.
▶ Expenditure in respect of scientific and technological research and development can be deducted at a rate of 150 per cent of expenditure.

will move from high-taxed sectors to low-taxed sectors so that a higher net return can be obtained. Theoretically this process will continue until net (after-tax) returns are equal in all the sectors. All owners of capital therefore bear the burden of the tax, not only the capital owners in the taxed sector. The real controversy regarding the incidence of company tax is whether capital owners bear the full tax burden. Empirical studies indicate that capital bears almost the entire burden, but it is still worth examining how the tax can theoretically be shifted to other groups.

When the net (after-tax) return of taxed businesses declines, firms will attempt to recover the tax by increasing their prices to consumers. The extent to which the taxed businesses can shift the tax will, of course, depend on the price elasticities of demand and supply of goods and services produced by these businesses (see Chapter 10).

How can the company tax be shifted to workers? Just like firms may attempt to pass on the tax burden to consumers in the form of higher prices, so they may try to shift the burden to workers in the form of lower wages or lower levels of employment. Some observers argue, for example, that company tax affects savings and investment over time. Since capital is internationally mobile, a tax on capital will cause capital to move to lower tax jurisdictions. This lowers the amount of capital available per worker in the country where capital is taxed and causes the marginal physical product of labour (MPP or labour productivity) to fall. A decline in labour productivity may lead to a decrease in wages or lower employment. Thus labour may bear a part of the company tax burden. Details about how company tax can be shifted to labour fall beyond the scope of this chapter. However, the incidence of company tax on consumers and labour remains controversial.

Ultimately, equity (or fairness) depends on who the owners of capital are. Capital is usually owned by the higher-income group. If the burden of company tax falls mainly on capital owners, vertical equity is thus achieved.[3] Horizontal equity depends on the type of company tax system in operation and will not be discussed here. The fully integrated income tax system (Section 12.6.2) appears to serve both horizontal and vertical equity objectives best, but this type of tax system is unfortunately administratively complex.

12.8 Capital gains tax

Capital gains can be defined as increases in the net value of assets over a period (e.g. an accounting period or fiscal year). According to the Haig-Simons definition of comprehensive income, anything that makes consumption possible without diminishing wealth at the beginning of a fiscal year is considered to be income. Capital gains are, accordingly, often classified as a form of income and are taxed as such. Capital gains can be taxed as they accrue (an unrealised gain) or when they are realised. An unrealised capital gain occurs when an asset increases in value in a given fiscal year and the asset is not sold, for example, an increase in the rand value of a Krugerrand when the rand depreciates against the dollar. A capital gain is realised when an asset has increased in value and is sold for cash.

Capital gains tax is currently levied in a number of developed countries, such as Canada, the USA, the UK, Australia, and Japan, as well as in some developing countries, including Argentina, Brazil, India, Nigeria, and Zimbabwe. In South Africa capital gains were generally not taxable in the past. Where assets were kept as an investment

---

[3] It should, however, be recognised that there are people with low incomes (e.g. pensioners) who derive their income mainly from capital. This could affect our equity conclusion with regard to company taxation.

and then sold, the yield on realisation of the asset was regarded as a receipt of a capital nature: one asset (capital) was simply converted into another (cash) and the yield was therefore not taxable. But where assets were sold in the course of normal business, that is, to make a profit, such profit was regarded as income and taxed as such. In many cases the courts had to rule on the application of this principle, which caused a great deal of uncertainty about the taxability or otherwise of capital gains. On 1 October 2001 South Africa implemented a capital gains tax (CGT).

Capital gains tax comes into play when there is a change in the ownership of an asset, that is, when it is sold, given away, scrapped, swapped, lost, or destroyed. It is thus a 'realisation' or transaction-based tax and, when capital gains are realised or deemed to be realised, such gains form part of the income tax base. The capital gain (or loss) is determined as the difference between the realised proceeds from the sale of the asset and the total base cost of the asset. The base cost of an affected capital asset includes the original acquisition costs and related transaction costs (e.g. legal fees and brokerage), the costs of any improvements, and VAT.

Capital losses may only be deducted against capital gains – there is no such thing as a negative CGT. Capital losses incurred on assets not used for business purposes cannot be subtracted from realised gains for tax purposes. These include assets used for personal consumption such as sailboats, second vehicles, and aircraft.

The first R20 000 of net capital gains of a natural person during a tax year is excluded from CGT. Although capital gains in excess of R20 000 are included in taxable income, some relief is granted to individuals and other legal persons. In the case of an individual, only 25 per cent of the net capital gain is included in taxable income. A company has to include 50 per cent of its net capital

gain. This means that the effective capital gains tax rate in respect of individuals varies between 0 per cent and 10 per cent, depending on the marginal tax rate, and for companies it is 14 per cent. The effective capital gains tax rate for small businesses ranges from 0 per cent to 14 per cent.

Any individual or legal person (e.g. a company, close corporation, or trust) resident in South Africa is liable for CGT in respect of the disposal or deemed disposal of capital assets held both inside and outside the country. Where an individual or legal person is not resident, a liability will only arise in the event of the disposal of immovable property inside South Africa or the sale of the assets of a local branch, permanent establishment, fixed base, or agency through which a trade, profession, or vocation is being carried out.

Capital assets liable for CGT are property of any kind, whether movable or immovable or tangible or intangible, and include land, mineral rights, office blocks, plant and machinery, motor vehicles, boats, caravans, trademarks, goodwill, shares, bonds, and Krugerrands. Some assets are exempted from CGT, such as trading stock and mining assets qualifying for income tax deductions as capital expenditure; and in the case of individuals, principal owner-occupied residences (gain/loss of less than R2,0 million), private motor vehicles, and personal belongings (e.g. clothing, stamps, works of art, antiques, medallions, foreign exchange, and coins not minted in gold or silver). Small business assets (businesses with a market value of assets of less than R5,0 million) realised by individuals over 55 who use the proceeds for retirement purposes are also exempted from CGT, provided the assets had been held for at least five years. This provision is limited to a once-off exemption of R900 000 per taxpayer.

In order to safeguard the reinvestment of profits, a capital gains tax liability may in certain cases be deferred until a subsequent

CGT event. Deferral (rollover) relief applies to asset disposals such as certain transfers of property to establish or reorganise a business, transfers of property from a deceased estate, donations of property, and transfers between spouses.

The Franzsen Commission (1968) recommended the introduction of a separate capital gains tax. This Commission regarded profits arising from the sale of shares and fixed property (with the exception of property that the person liable for tax uses for residential purposes) as the principal components of the capital gains tax base. The Margo Commission (1987) opposed a capital gains tax primarily because of the administrative problems involved. The Katz Commission (1995: 49), in its Third Interim Report, also recommended that '... by reason of the lack of capacity on the part of the tax administration, there should not be capital gains tax in South Africa at this stage'. The low revenue potential of such a tax reinforced the Katz Commission's conclusion.

Capital gains are not really taxed for the sake of the revenue they yield, but rather for other reasons. At the time of introduction it was estimated that CGT could raise about 1 per cent of total tax revenue a year directly (i.e. around R5 to R6 billion). The most important reasons for capital gains taxation are:

▶ To protect the integrity of the personal income tax base. If capital gains are not taxed, taxpayers have an incentive to convert income into capital gains in order to avoid taxation. Consider the example of a sole proprietor who reinvests his or her profit instead of taking it as a salary (which is taxed at marginal income tax rates). The reinvested income increases the value of the business. When the business is sold eventually, the benefits are reaped in the form of long-term capital gains (regarded as non-taxable capital

income in the absence of capital gains taxation).
▶ To ensure horizontal equity. A capital gain represents an increase in economic power and increases the individual's ability to earn income and to be taxed. Consider two persons with the same net additions to wealth (income plus net assets): person A's net additions consist of salary income and capital gains; person B's net additions consist of salary income only. Both have the same horizontal ability to pay in terms of the comprehensive definition of income (i.e. the Haig-Simons definition). If capital gains are not taxed, person B is unfairly taxed on his or her income.
▶ To ensure vertical equity. Capital gains accrue mostly to higher-income taxpayers. If they are not taxed on these gains, the vertical ability-to-pay principle is jeopardised.
▶ To improve economic efficiency. If investments are chosen on the basis of tax considerations, the allocation of investment funds is distorted and an excess burden results.

There are also a number of arguments against capital gains tax of which the the most important are:
▶ Capital gains taxation is subject to numerous administrative problems. Assets have to be valued and there is a need for accurate and up-to-date deeds registers in the case of, for example, works of art and real property. The valuation problem is more acute in the situation where an accrual base is used (i.e. where unrealised capital gains are also taxed). The problem of valuation is less severe when a realisation base is used – in other words, when the selling price is compared to the purchase price when the asset is sold and tax payment is only due when the asset is sold.

- If nominal profits (instead of real profits) are taxed, equity is at risk. Inflation causes imaginary capital gains (i.e. increases in the nominal value of assets) and it may be unfair to tax someone just because inflation has increased the nominal value of an asset. Nominal capital gains should therefore be deflated by an appropriate price index. The choice of a suitable index is a further complication.
- Capital gains are usually once-off events and to avoid the tax, taxpayers tend to lock in rather than realise investments. This lock-in effect can affect investment negatively. Concessions are therefore usually made either in the form of lower personal income tax rates on capital gains, or by not taxing capital gains once a certain period has elapsed. To compensate for the effects of inflation and the lock-in effect, the South African tax authorities opted for low effective capital gains rates.

12.9 Income tax reform

In the preceding sections attention was devoted to personal income taxation and company taxation within the broad framework of a comprehensive income tax system (the Haig-Simons definition of income). This tax base includes labour and capital income and ideally applies the same rate structure to all forms of income. In practice tax systems are far removed from the intended comprehensive income tax. Capital income and labour income are taxed at different rates and some forms of income are not taxed. Certain activities are encouraged using tax incentives, deductions and credits, all leading to a smaller tax base. Because of the international mobility of capital, and to some extent labour, countries try to outcompete their rivals using the tax

system. But distortions are created which impact on the work effort as well as saving choices (that is, tax efficiency). The comprehensive income tax does not adequately deal with irregular income earned over the lifetime of the taxpayer and results in excessive progressivity in this case. Tax systems also include other taxes than income such as consumption taxes (e.g. VAT and excises) and wealth taxes (e.g. inheritance tax). This mix of taxes has different distributional effects and spoils both horizontal and vertical equity. The problem becomes even bigger considering the administrative complexity and compliance issues resulting from the comprehensive income tax system. In addition to the tax preferences and expenditures the integration of the personal income tax and company income tax adds to the administrative difficulties. What are the alternatives? In this section we consider two reform options which have received attention in recent times, namely the flat rate income tax and the dual income tax.

12.9.1 The flat rate income tax

The flat rate income tax option is a response to mainly the administrative complexity of the comprehensive income tax and the inefficiencies created by taxing labour income and capital income at different rates (see Barreix and Roca 2007: 127). Two broad variants of the flat rate income tax can be considered. One received particular interest in the USA and was proposed by Hall and Rabushka (1983 and 1995). Their proposal provides for a combination of a cash-flow tax on business income (with full allowance for capital expenditure but not labour expenditure) and a tax on labour income (with a non-taxable personal exemption) at a single (low) flat rate. In principle it is none other than an origin-based VAT collected by the subtraction method and supplemented by a (non-refundable) tax credit against labour income (see Chapter 14 for a description and discussion of the destination-based VAT system). This design, therefore, taxes consumption but has some progressivity build in (the personal income tax exemption). This system has not been implemented in this form anywhere.

The second variant has been adopted in a number of Eastern European countries (including Russia) and has attracted much attention. It deviates from the Hall-Rabushka form in that only labour income is taxed at a single positive rate (with some income allowance based on the taxpayer's circumstances). Sometimes company income is also taxed at the same rate but not necessarily. Therefore, when we refer to a **flat rate income tax** we mean a single low rate on personal income (see Keen, Kim and Varsano 2008: 714 for a comprehensive discussion and analysis of the flat rate income tax).

Supporters of the flat rate tax base their arguments on various advantages (see Keen et al. 2008: 712–751, Browning and Browning, 1994: 378–379 and Boskin, 1996):

▶ A flat rate tax is simple to administer and complexity is reduced by the elimination of all kinds of exemptions and exceptions. Tax liability can be determined on a single page tax return where all forms of income are entered and then multiplied by the tax rate. Tax compliance should improve because of the lower marginal tax rate. Improved compliance may also lead to higher tax revenue (see the Laffer-curve analysis in Section 12.4.3).

▶ To get some perspective on the size of the tax rate required to maintain tax revenues, it should be considered that in 2009 current taxes on income and wealth of households in South Africa were R216 123 million. This amount was raised with average tax rates ranging from zero per cent to in excess of 27,3 per cent (taxpayers with taxable income

of R525 001 in 2009/10). If the gross balance of primary income of households as defined in the national accounts is used as the tax base (R1 578 607 million), the same amount of tax could have been obtained by levying a tax of approximately 14 per cent on all income (with zero personal income exemptions).

▶ Lower marginal tax rates increase productivity and the incentive to work.

▶ Horizontal equity is promoted since different special provisions are not available to people with the same taxable income.

▶ Bracket creep (explained in Section 12.4.4) during inflation is eliminated.

▶ A political economy argument favours the adoption of a flat rate. The public choice school would reason that a single low tax rate will limit the amount of tax revenue government can extract from voters. The size of a government pursuing its own interest and wasting resources is consequently restricted. It should be noted that there are other ways of constraining government, such as fiscal rules (see Chapter 15, Section 15.4).

One disadvantage of the flat rate tax regime is that the built-in flexibility of income taxation is reduced if the aggregate marginal tax rate falls, although this will be less the higher the basic allowance accompanying the flat tax. Another problem is that capital income and labour income are in most cases still taxed at different rates resulting in tax arbitrage and competition between different countries. The most important shortcoming of the flat rate tax proposal, and probably its nemesis, lies in its redistributive impact. The tax burden will be redistributed – the burden of the high-income group will be reduced while the burden of the low-income group will increase (although some adjustments may be possible to counteract these effects). Its impact on the tax burden of the low-income and even the middle-income group can, therefore, be curtailed by applying the tax rate to all income above a minimum income. It would thus introduce a degree of progressivity in the tax structure.

Another serious equity problem with the flat rate tax is the treatment of taxpayers with income around the threshold. For example, if a flat rate of, say, 14 per cent were levied on incomes equal to or in excess of R30 000, a taxpayer with an income of R30 001 would be taxed at an inordinately high rate – of 14 per cent – whereas a person with an income of R29 999 would have no tax liability.

The distributional and work incentive effects of the flat rate tax are not obvious and Keen et al. (2008: 722–732 and 741) show they are somewhat complex. The reason is that progressivity (or lack of equity) of the flat rate tax must be compared to that of the system it replaces. In addition the tax revenue yield and implications for compliance must be considered. Empirical evidence and the practice in flat rate income tax countries to allow for a personal income tax allowance, show that the equity impact is not unambiguously adverse for the low-income group. The impact on work incentives is also not clear-cut and there is no evidence that the high-income taxpayers improve their work effort significantly. Complexity is somewhat reduced and the potential for arbitrage lessened but this is not necessarily due to the rate structure itself; it is due to fewer exemptions and special treatments. Finally the sustainability of the flat rate tax movement is unclear: the low(er) rate imposes constraints on revenue and the framework does not adequately provide for internationally mobile capital income (see Keen et al. 2008: 742).

12.9.2 The dual income tax

An alternative to the progressive comprehensive income tax system and the flat rate income tax system is the dual income tax (DIT). Variants of the DIT were introduced in the 1990s in the Nordic countries and this system is now also being suggested as an option for developing countries.[4] The potential for introducing the dual income tax in developing countries is discussed in great detail in Bird and Zolt 2010.

In contrast to the comprehensive income tax system which includes in the tax base all income minus the costs to acquire and maintain that income, the **dual income tax** is a 'schedular' tax system. This means that different types of income are taxed separately and at different rates. The DIT has the following characteristics:

▶ Personal capital income is taxed separately from labour income and is levied at a flat or single rate. Under a pure dual tax system the single proportional rate is set equal to the lowest income tax rate (the first income tax bracket) on personal (wage) income. **Personal capital income** includes interest, dividends, capital gains, rental income, royalties, imputed rent on owner-occupied housing, accrued returns on pension savings, and profits from personal businesses (small enterprises). Profits from small enterprises is the aggregate return on capital invested and labour provided by the owners of sole proprietorships, closely held companies and partnerships. An important element of the DIT is the taxation of capital income on a broad basis and at a low flat rate to ensure uniformity and neutrality in capital income taxation.

---

[4] For a comprehensive analysis of the dual income tax system see Boadway (2005: 910–927), Sørensen (2005: 777–801), Sørensen (2007: 557–602) and Sørensen and Johnson (2010: 179–235).

- **Labour income** (wages, salaries and transfers from government) or non-capital income is subject to a progressive rate structure and it provides for tax deductions and exemptions to achieve equity objectives. Overall the taxation of labour income is therefore higher than the taxation on capital income.
- Company income (incorporated businesses) is taxed at the same rate that applies to personal capital income. In a pure system the company income tax is fully integrated with the personal income tax to eliminate double taxation. This can, for example, be achieved using the imputation method whereby shareholders receive credit for company tax paid. The company tax thus becomes a simple withholding tax at source (see Section 12.6.2).

The DIT system was implemented in Sweden, Norway, Denmark and Finland in the early nineties and a number of other industrialised countries have adopted forms of the dual income tax system. Uruguay is one of the few developing countries that have moved to a dual income tax system. The reasons in favour of the DIT were specific to Nordic countries at that time but still have relevance. These are listed below. In addition there are convincing economic and administrative considerations to consider.

Firstly, the Nordic countries were feeling the impact of globalisation and the international mobility of some forms of capital (e.g. portfolio investment). Because of their comparatively high tax rates investors were moving their capital to lower-tax jurisdictions. High inflation also meant effective tax rates on capital were high which led to arbitrage actions. High-income taxpayers could exploit tax preferences for capital investment using, for example, interest rate deductions to lower their earned income. This eroded the labour income tax base. Because of high

unemployment political support could be mobilised in favour of a dual tax by arguing that lower tax burdens on capital will increase economic activity and thus reduce unemployment. A dual tax left marginal tax rates on labour income untouched, which would not have been possible to change from an equity point of view. The combination of a lower flat tax rate on capital income and a progressive tax on labour income was therefore considered to be a rather pragmatic way to deal with problems of capital flight, tax arbitrage activities and inflation.

Secondly, the economic argument for lower tax rates on capital income and progressive rates on labour income needs to be considered (see Boadway 2005: 913–922). The basic efficiency argument is that the more elastic the source of income, the more appropriate a lower tax rate would be. Capital income has the characteristics of being more elastic than labour income, is mobile and it is used for riskier investments. High capital income tax rates, therefore, will lead to evasion and discourage investment. Other efficiency arguments include that investment generates externalities which should be encouraged by having lower tax rates on savings. The broadening of the capital income tax base and the imposition of a low flat rate reduce the distortions associated with the differential treatment of different sources of income: e.g. avoidance through tax planning, shifting of assets or selecting a business form on tax grounds.

Levying a single (proportional) tax on those who choose to save, reduces discrimination against savings. When taxing capital income (e.g. interest) at progressive rates (as under a comprehensive income tax system) can cause horizontal inequities because some individuals use savings to smooth their income over their life-cycle. Someone who saves for a rainy day or retirement, will end up paying a higher lifetime tax bill compared to a person with similar earnings who does not save.

Taxing labour income at a progressive rate can be justified easier than a corresponding tax on capital income. Taxing labour income causes some distortions as it affects the choice between labour supply/effort and leisure. The variability of labour income is however more predictable (e.g. seasonable work) and the impact can be determined based on knowledge of the worker profile and the income distribution. The responsiveness to progressive taxation of individuals to work and how much to work is reasonably known (see Section 12.4.1). The personal income tax system can be designed to compensate for individuals who experience income variability that is beyond their control. In addition a social security network can play a supporting role (see Boadway 2005: 917).[5] In short, progressiveness of the tax system as a whole is important, but not all taxes need to be progressive. It can be argued that the most efficient way to achieve progressiveness is to tax labour income using a progressive rate schedule, a provision which continues to characterise a dual tax system. The DIT thus provides the flexibility developing countries need in order to meet the international competition for capital on the one hand and to maintain the progressiveness generated by the personal income tax system. However, globally personal income tax rate schedules have become more flat which means that the advantage of flexibility of the DIT is somewhat dissipated (see Bird and Zolt 2010: 201).

Thirdly, from an administrative perspective the dual income tax system has the advantage that capital taxes are rationalised by treating all income from capital uniformly. The base is broadened and the accompanying removal of tax preferences and exclusions simplifies the personal and company tax system and reduces tax compliance costs.

Although much can be said in favour of the dual income tax system, it also has a number of disadvantages. One of the most important is that the DIT requires the splitting of income of active owners of small firms into a capital and labour component. This administrative challenge is the Achilles heel of the system (see Sørensen 2007: 566 and Sørensen 2005: 780–781). As noted above, profits from small enterprises is the aggregate return on capital invested and labour provided by the owners of sole proprietorships, closely held companies and partnerships. If capital income is to be taxed at a different rate to labour income, profits must be split into the two components. If it is left to the owners to decide, arbitrage opportunities arise or are sought, that is, attempts are made to reduce the tax liability. For example, if the tax rate on capital income is lower than the marginal tax rate of the taxpayer, the owner will attempt to have profits declared as capital income (e.g. dividends) or capital gains on shares. The problem becomes even more acute if the small enterprise makes losses – is the loss to be treated as labour income or capital income? In the Nordic countries **income splitting** rules are applied. This is done by imputing a rate of return to business assets (classified as capital income) and treating the residual profits as labour income. The imputed rate of return provides for a 'normal' return on capital (for example, the interest rate on government bonds) as well as a risk premium to compensate investors for their exposure to risk and a pure (excess) profit part (referred to as rent). One problem, for example, related to income splitting, is the practice by entrepreneurs to include low-yielding assets such as motor cars and real estate (used for private consumption) in the asset base. In effect this increases the part of the business profit imputed as capital

[5] Also see Boadway, Chamberlain and Emmerson 2010: 760–770 for a brief outline of the welfarist, equality-of-opportunity and paternalism criteria for evaluating a tax system.

income (the asset base to which the imputed return is applied increases) and is thus taxed at the lower capital income tax rate. The income splitting mechanism for self-employed and other small entrepreneurs, closely held companies and small companies remains imperfect and requires all kinds of special tax rules and anti-avoidance measures (see Sørensen 2005: 777–801), thus increasing the cost of tax administration.

A second disadvantage of the dual income tax system is the unresponsiveness of the company tax rate to international competition. Remember that the company tax rate is set equal to the capital income tax rate which is pitched at the lowest personal income tax bracket. If this rate is higher than global rates, investments and profits may be shifted between jurisdictions. The international mobility of capital requires a large degree of cooperation between financial institutions and governments to police these movements. In developing countries the alternatives for a company rate equal to the lowest income tax bracket would be to set the company tax rate either higher or lower than the personal income tax rate for income from capital. The choice would depend on whether the business is, for example, in resource extraction which generates location-specific excess profits. In this case the company tax can be higher. On the other hand, if small firms are to be encouraged to incorporate or formalise their activities (often developing countries have a large informal sector), the rate must be set lower. In the latter case incentives are unfortunately again created for small entrepreneurs to reduce their tax liability (see Bird and Zolt 2010: 203–204).

Thirdly, from a vertical equity perspective lower tax rates on capital may be viewed as unfair since capital income is earned mainly by the rich. Boadway (2005: 915–916 and 924) argues that this is a flawed argument since capital income must eventually be consumed and will then be taxed using the consumption tax system. Furthermore, the negative vertical equity effect can be mitigated by higher personal income tax rates on labour income of the well to do and by taxing inheritances of the rich.

Measuring capital income remains a problem. Included are accrued returns on human capital investment, imputed returns on consumer durables (e.g. owner-occupied housing), the return on investment in small businesses, and accrued capital gains. If capital income is taxed at a low uniform rate but excludes these hard-to-measure incomes there are still opportunities for avoidance and evasion since returns between assets are distorted.

In designing tax systems, it is almost inevitable that governments will be faced with policy conflicts and goal choices. Tax fairness, efficiency, neutrality and administrative simplicity cannot always be achieved simultaneously and must sometimes be traded-off. The dual income tax system appears to sacrifice neutrality; income from capital is taxed differently to income from labour. Vertical equity is sacrificed for horizontal equity. Efficiency gains can be achieved by taxing all capital at the same low rate. Countries face different policy objectives depending on economic and political considerations.

IMPORTANT CONCEPTS

basic tax on companies
(page 222)
bracket creep (page 218)
capital gains (page 231)
classical system (page 222)
comprehensive income tax
base (page 200)
dual income tax (page 236)
flat rate income tax
(page 235)
full integration (page 222)
gross income (page 203)
income effect (page 209)
income splitting (page 238)

labour income (page 237)
Laffer curve (page 217)
lifetime budget constraint
(page 214)
lifetime income (page 213)
marginal tax rate (page 206)
nominal income (page 218)
personal capital income
(page 236)
presumptive taxes
(page 216)
real income (page 218)
residence principle
(page 201)

secondary tax on compa-
nies (STC) (page 222)
source of income principle
(page 201)
substitution effect (page 209)
tax exclusions (page 203)
tax exemptions (page 203)
tax expenditures (page 203)
tax holidays (page 229)
tax rebates (page 204)
tax threshold (page 204)
unit of taxation (page 205)
user cost of capital
(page 226)

SELF-ASSESSMENT EXERCISES

12.1   Define and explain the 'comprehensive income tax base'.

12.2   Critically evaluate the introduction
of a worldwide basis of taxation in
South Africa.

12.3   Differentiate between the following
concepts:
 ▶ gross, net, and taxable income;
 ▶ nominal and real income;
 ▶ accrued and realised income;
 ▶ average tax rate and marginal tax
rate;
 ▶ tax exclusions, tax deductions,
and tax credits.

12.4   Explain the rationale behind the
progressive nature of individual
income tax structures.

12.5   With the aid of a graph, explain the
likely effects of an increase in individual income tax on the supply of
labour.

12.6   'Personal savings in developing
countries are at low levels. By
exempting interest income, governments can stimulate higher levels of
savings.' Do you agree? Make use of

a diagram and empirical findings in
your discussion.

12.7   Discuss the economic effects of personal income tax by referring to
economic efficiency, equity, administrative efficiency, and flexibility.

12.8   Why are policymakers so concerned about the impact of inflation
on personal income tax?

12.9   Discuss the relevance of the so-
called Laffer effect.

12.10   Why is company income taxed separately from other forms of income?
Explain.

12.11   Why are the economic consequences of company tax regarded
as controversial?

12.12   The combined effect of income tax
on companies and individuals
implies the double taxation of dividends. Explain the efficiency and
equity aspects of this interaction.

12.13   Explain the arguments for the integration of the individual and the
company income taxes.

12.14 If special provision is made in income tax law for small business or the agricultural sector, it means that the tax is not neutral. What is your opinion on this issue?

12.15 How will income tax on companies affect the decision of an entrepreneur to invest?

12.16 'Tax incentives are not effective instruments for attracting investment.' Do you agree? Discuss.

12.17 Analyse the following statement: 'Capital gains tax is an inappropriate form of taxation for South Africa.'

12.18 What is a flat rate tax, and what are the reasons for the interest in this type of tax?

12.19 Compare a progressive comprehensive income tax to a dual income tax.

Chapter
THIRTEEN

Tjaart Steenekamp

Taxation of wealth

In Chapter 10 we noted that taxes could be imposed on three bases: income, wealth, and consumption. In this chapter we consider the wealth base. Wealth is the product of accumulated savings, assets that gained in value, and the free gifts of nature. Richard Bird (1992: 134) argues that the existing distribution of wealth in a country is '... largely the outcome of historical accident, as condoned by the state and frozen in law. The result of this pattern of distribution of initial wealth is that many of those successful in life stand not on their own feet but on the shoulders of their fathers.' Wealth holdings therefore contain an element of personal effort (self-accumulated wealth) and an element of luck (inherited wealth). These characteristics make wealth taxation a much-debated topic and also an emotive one, especially in countries with vast inequalities of wealth. The aim of this chapter is to analyse the economic impact of the personal net wealth tax, property taxes, and capital transfer taxes.

We begin this chapter by distinguishing between different types of wealth (Section 13.1). In Section 13.2 we investigate the reasons why wealth is taxed. The taxation of real property, which is an important type of wealth, is studied in Section 13.3. The chapter concludes with a discussion of capital transfer taxes such as estate duty and gift taxes.

Once you have studied this chapter, you should be able to:
▶ define the wealth tax base
▶ explain the merits and shortcomings of taxing personal net wealth
▶ define the property tax base
▶ describe property tax rating and assessment
▶ explain the effect of property tax on equity using the benefit principle

- analyse property tax incidence using partial and general equilibrium analysis
- discuss the efficiency effects of a property tax
- define a capital transfer tax
- discuss the economic effects of capital transfer taxes.

13.1 Wealth and types of wealth taxes

Income and consumption are flow concepts since both are measured over a period of time. Income consists of wages, rental income from property, interest on savings, dividends on shares, and so on. In contrast to income, wealth is a stock concept that is measured at a particular point in time.

Wealth is the value of accumulated savings, investment, gifts, and inheritances. If a person does not save or receive inheritances or gifts, he or she will never accumulate wealth. A person's wealth consists of the net monetary value of assets owned. Another and technically more correct definition is that personal wealth is the present value of a person's expected real income. Personal wealth includes tangible things such as houses, durable goods (e.g. motorcars, jewellery, valuable paintings), and land. In addition, individuals hold financial assets such as cash, deposits in bank accounts, shares in businesses, and government bonds. These are all assets that can be traded in the market. We can also identify other items such as insurance policies and pension rights, although these types of assets are difficult to trade in the market and to value. Human capital acquired through investment in education and training should also be included as (intangible) forms of personal wealth, although valuing human capital is obviously difficult. A person's wealth must also take account of any liabilities since assets are often acquired through incurring debt. By subtracting liabilities from assets we obtain the net value of assets (i.e. personal wealth), which is also called net personal worth.

The wealth tax base is not restricted to personal wealth – company wealth should also be considered. Company wealth includes different forms of capital such as fixed capital (premises, plant, and machinery), floating capital (raw materials and inventories), and financial capital (stocks and shares, cash, and bank deposits). It is not difficult to see why the term capital is often used synonymously with company wealth. To these assets we should, in principle at least, add intangibles such as goodwill, brand name, and market power. As in the case of human capital, it is difficult to value these assets. To arrive at net company wealth we must subtract liabilities from the gross value of assets.

The taxation of the wealth base has a long history dating back to a form of property tax introduced in ancient Rome. The most important types of wealth taxes today include:

- annual wealth taxes (e.g. on persons and (or) companies)
- property tax (e.g. tax on land and improvements)
- capital transfer tax (e.g. tax on estates and gifts).

13.2 Why tax wealth?

The case for a wealth tax is best presented by considering the arguments in favour of an annual wealth tax on individuals (also called a personal **net wealth tax** or net worth tax).[1] The arguments for a net or gross assets tax on businesses are somewhat different and will not be addressed here.[2]

13.2.1 Equity considerations

When we discussed fairness as a criterion of a 'good' tax in Chapter 11, two principles emerged: the benefit principle and the ability-to-pay principle. A wealth tax is often justified in terms of the benefit principle. Governments provide public services that increase the value of real assets (e.g. property). Governments also provide protection for property (e.g. law enforcement and legislation). Consequently, owners of assets should pay for the benefits (expenditures) of the protection they receive. It may, however, be difficult to determine the extent of the benefits received – some properties, for example, need more protection than others.

As far as the ability-to-pay principle is concerned, monetary income, which may include income arising from realised or unrealised capital gains, is normally subject to income tax (see Chapter 12). From the horizontal equity perspective, however, wealth confers an additional ability to pay to the owners of wealth (over and above the monetary income derived from wealth itself and from work). Consider the example of a poor person with almost no income and a wealthy person who keeps his or her wealth in the

form of Krugerrands and Persian carpets. Surely, even if the wealthy person has no income, he or she is bound to have greater taxable capacity on account of the potential income-generating capacity of the assets than the poor person. Besides, because wealth owners have the ability to realise assets, they have economic security that enables them to exercise purchasing power (e.g. by obtaining loans). Wealth also provides them with the power to exploit economic opportunities.

From a vertical equity point of view, people with different taxable capacities should be taxed differently. Wealth is generally distributed very unevenly and it is argued that wealth taxes could reduce this skewness. The distribution of personal wealth in South Africa is also very uneven. See the Gini coefficient (Chapter 8, Section 8.1.1) in respect of the distribution of wealth in the former Transvaal.[3] This distribution, however, was not more skew than in other countries (e.g. 0,81 for the USA in 1983, 0,68 for the UK in 1968, and 0,52 for Australia in 1968). What makes South Africa's distribution different, is its racial dimension. In 1985 whites comprised approximately 36 per cent of the population of the Transvaal, but owned approximately 91 per cent of the wealth.

According to these equity principles it seems fair to tax wealth; however, we need to consider the incidence of a wealth tax as well. Remember that wealth is mostly accumulated savings. A tax on wealth is therefore largely a tax on savings. The incidence of a wealth tax therefore depends on the price elasticity of the supply and demand for savings. If the supply is perfectly inelastic, the tax is borne by the owners of capital (wealth) and, since wealth is concentrated in the hands of the middle- and upper-income

---

[1] The personal net wealth tax as implemented in a number of developed countries is discussed in detail in Organisation for Economic Co-operation and Development (OECD) (1988: 30–75).

[2] For a discussion of a gross assets tax on businesses, see Sadka and Tanzi (1993: 66–73).

[3] The land area largely corresponds to the present-day South African provinces of Gauteng, Mpumalanga, Limpopo, and North West Province province in 1985 was estimated at 0,67 (Van Heerden, 1996).

groups, the tax is progressive. If, however, the supply of savings is not perfectly inelastic, the incidence becomes complex but it is probable that wealth owners would then be able to pass on some of the tax to consumers and workers.

13.2.2 Efficiency considerations

Wealth taxes may affect economic efficiency positively or negatively. On the positive side, a net wealth tax has a smaller disincentive effect on work effort than an income tax. A tax on wealth is levied on past effort whereas income tax is levied on current effort. Furthermore, in the absence of a wealth tax, a person may invest in assets that do not yield income to avoid paying income tax. A wealth tax would counteract such tax avoidance to some extent. A wealth tax might therefore serve as an incentive to wealth holders to put their assets to productive use. We will address this issue when land taxation is considered in Section 13.3.5.

On the negative side, wealth taxes may affect saving because the tax base (wealth) is mainly accumulated savings. A tax on saving will also translate into a tax on labour, that is, insofar as the purpose of work is to save (for future consumption). When the tax becomes a disincentive to work, efficiency is lost. In addition, although wealth taxes may encourage a more productive use of assets, it may also have the opposite effect. High yield and efficiency are not necessarily the same. Assets are sometimes invested in ventures that yield little or no profit over the short term (e.g. investments in plantations). A wealth tax on these assets would cause an undue liability on its owners and ultimately on the community or economy, especially if taxes have to be paid when wealth increases even though there is no cash flow.

A discussion of the efficiency of wealth taxes will be incomplete without reference to the excess burden of such taxes. Wealth taxes reduce the net return on saving (i.e. the after-tax interest rate). Since wealth taxes distort the relative prices of goods that can be consumed presently and goods that can be consumed in the future, an excess burden results. The size of the excess burden will depend on how sensitive saving is to changes in interest rates.

13.2.3 Revenue and administrative considerations

Similar to all taxes, wealth taxes can be introduced to generate revenue although this is not a particularly important consideration. In fact, in most countries where such a tax is in force, the net wealth tax revenue rarely exceeds one per cent of total tax revenue.

Wealth taxes do have administrative advantages. The database for these taxes can be used to crosscheck income tax returns. Since the income tax base is often eroded by tax avoidance and evasion schemes, wealth taxes may complement income tax systems by curtailing these schemes. On the other hand, wealth taxes also have administrative shortcomings. In the past, wealth was relatively easy to tax since it was held in very visible forms (e.g. immovable property). Nowadays wealth holdings and their valuation have become very complex (e.g. derivatives such as options and swaps) and are often held in foreign countries. This calls for a sophisticated and costly tax administration, which deters many countries from introducing such taxes.

It appears as if the trend is to move away from taxes on wealth. In France a wealth tax was introduced in 1982 and scrapped in 1986. Other developed countries such as Japan and Ireland also abandoned the net wealth tax for reasons of equity, complex administration, and impeding economic growth. Colombia introduced a net wealth tax in 1935 but repealed it recently. In South Africa the Margo Commission (1987: 310–322) and the Katz Commission (1995: 50–55) both considered an annual wealth tax but concluded that such a tax (including an inheritance tax) should be avoided due to the administrative and compliance burdens involved. The Katz Commission (1995: 50) argued that redistribution is better achieved by other means, particularly through the expenditure side of the budget.

13.3 **Property taxation**

The property tax base can be defined very broadly to include **real property** (realty) and **personal property** (e.g. furniture, motor vehicles, shares, bonds, and bank deposits). We will focus exclusively on real property partly because it is the most common one. Such a tax is an **impersonal (*in rem*) tax**.

Property tax can be levied at the national level and provincial government level or local authority level. In South Africa it is collected mainly by (urban) local authorities. National government taxes on property are primarily in the form of transfer duties (payable by the person who acquires a property) and tax on donations and estates. In such cases, the tax is levied when immovable property is alienated or acquired in terms of a donation or an inheritance. However, the property taxes levied by local authorities are by far the most important form of property tax in South Africa.

Property tax is a major source of revenue for local authorities. Property tax revenue to the tune of R27,0 billion was generated in 2009/10. Property tax represented approximately 15,6 per cent of the cash receipts from operating activities of municipalities. Important as this source may be for local governments, its relative insignificance as a national revenue source is illustrated by the fact that it would contribute only about 4,2 per cent to the total tax receipts of the consolidated general government.

13.3.1 **The tax base**

The **real property tax** base includes land (farm, residential, commercial, and forest land) and capital invested in improvements (farm buildings, homes, business buildings, fences, and so on). The importance of the distinction between the two tax bases will become clear once we analyse the incidence effects of a property tax.

In South Africa all land and improvements in urban areas (from metropolitan local councils to small local councils) are rateable. In the past property tax (collected by local authorities) was not levied on rural land. The Katz Commission (1995 and 1998) considered the possibility of a national tax on agricultural land, but found that such a tax was not a viable option at the national level of government – neither as a means of raising revenue nor as an instrument of a land reform programme. It did, however, support a rural land tax at local authority level. It also acknowledged that a rural land tax may have certain social advantages such as encouraging the economic use of land.

A land tax on farmland was implemented in Namibia in 2004. The purposes of this tax are to fund the government's acquisition of agricultural land for resettlement of previously disadvantaged Namibians as well as to compel absentee landlords to sell unused land to the government.

As far as the urban property tax is concerned, municipalities in South Africa had the option of choosing between a **site value rating** (i.e. rating the value of the land only), a **flat rating** (i.e. rating the value of improvements), or a **composite** (differential) **rating** (i.e. rating both land and improvements, but at different tax rates). In four provinces the majority of municipalities used the site value rating system. Of the remaining five, Kwa-Zulu-Natal opted for composite rating while many councils in the other four provinces used flat rating (Franzsen, 1997).

In 2004 the Local Government: Municipal Property Rates Act, 2004 (hereafter the Property Rates Act 2004) was enacted, to be implemented over a four-year period. It empowers the six metropolitan municipalities (e.g. Tshwane, Johannesburg, and Cape Town), 231 local municipalities, and 47 district municipalities (or district management areas) to levy a rate on all rateable property. Property generally means immovable property and includes immovable improvements (excluding underground mining structures). Different categories of rateable properties may be determined and include residential properties, industrial properties, business and commercial properties, farm properties, smallholdings, and formal and informal settlements.

13.3.2 Tax rates

Property tax is usually levied as a percentage of the taxable assessed value of the property. The assessed value for tax purposes is often less than the market value of the property. Due to this difference between the assessed value and the market value, the nominal tax rate differs from the effective rate (the effective rate being the tax liability expressed as a percentage of the estimated market value). Tax rates generally differ between jurisdictions due to the selectivity of the property tax. Since the property tax is considered burdensome to certain categories of taxpayers (e.g. elderly homeowners), these taxpayers usually receive some kind of tax relief.

In the case of the Namibian land tax, a rate of 0,75 per cent is levied on the unimproved site value per hectare owned by commercial farmers. It increases by 0,25 per cent for each additional Namibian-owned

farm. If the land is owned by foreigners, the rate starts at 1,75 per cent of the site value for the first farm and increases by 0,25 per cent for each additional property.

In the past, flat (uniform) rates were levied in South Africa but differed between provinces and between municipalities within provinces. The taxes were levied annually but were generally collected in monthly installments. A maximum rate was prescribed in some provinces. Before 1994 a number of categories of properties were exempted from paying property tax (e.g. properties used for religious and educational purposes, hospitals, and national theatres). Since 1994, however, almost all exemptions were repealed and replaced by a system of grants-in-aid that could not exceed the equivalent rateable amount. Rebates were granted for certain classes of properties (e.g. residential properties) and categories of ratepayers (e.g. the handicapped, pensioners, and other ratepayers with annual incomes below a specified minimum).

In terms of the new Property Rates Act (2004), a rate levied by a municipality must be an amount in rand based on the market value of the property. The original four-year transitional period given to municipalities to implement the Municipal Property Rates Act (up to 1 July 2009) was extended by two years (up to 1 July 2011). Differential rates for different categories of rateable property may be set. The categories may be determined according to the use of the property or geographical area in which the property is situated. Certain categories of owners such as pensioners, owners temporarily without income, and indigent owners, may be exempted or may be granted a rebate. The ratio for residential property to public benefit organisation property (e.g. churches and schools), public service infrastructure property and agricultural property should not exceed 1:0,25. The rate for non-residential property is the same as that for residential property. The right to levying rates is limited by a number of provisions. One such provision stipulates that the Minister of Finance may set upper limits on the percentage by which rates may be increased annually. Furthermore, the rate may not:

▶ materially prejudice national economic interest and economic activities across its boundaries
▶ be levied on the first R15 000 of the market value of a residential property
▶ be levied on places of worship (including an official residence occupied by an office-bearer of the religious community) or
▶ be levied on property belonging to a land reform beneficiary or his or her heirs for a period of 10 years.

13.3.3 Assessment

Probably the most controversial part of property taxation is the valuation of property. There are a number of different approaches to assessing the value of property, such as the capital value of land and improvements, the site value system, the rental value of premises, and the comparable sales method (see Bahl, 1998). The **capital value system** attempts to determine the full market value of land and improvements (as a bundle) on a willing buyer and willing seller basis (i.e. the value they would agree to in an open market). In practice the capital value is determined by assessing land independent of improvements. Land is valued using data based on a judgemental approach and the expert opinions of professional appraisers and real estate agents are enlisted. Improvements are valued with the aid of schedules of value per square metre (based on building costs).

The **site value system** assesses the value of land only. The value of land can be based on sales of vacant land or estimated by means

of a residual method (e.g. by determining the bundled value of the property and then deducting the value of improvements).

The British tradition is to assess the value of property on the basis of some estimate of the rental value of the property or the rental income derived from the asset. The sales value of a property tax and the rental value are supposed to yield equal results.[4] However, in developing countries property is often under-utilised and an assessment based on the rental value would thus understate the value of the property. Idle land also generates no net income and rental value will therefore have to be imputed in such a case.

In South Africa the general basis of valuation will be the **market value** of a property, that is, the amount the property would have realised if sold on the date of valuation in the open market by a willing seller to a willing buyer (Property Rates Act, 2004). The market value would be inclusive of the land value and the value of improvements to the property. In the case of agricultural land, the value of any annual crops or growing timber that have not yet been harvested are disregarded for valuation purposes.

All rateable property must be valued during a general valuation. Physical inspection of the property to be valued is optional and comparative, analytical, and other systems or techniques may be used to determine the value, including aerial photography and computer-assisted mass appraisal systems. The valuation roll must remain valid in total for not more than four financial years.

The taxing of farm properties could be considered a new category of property that is now rateable by municipalities. The Property Rates Act (2004) provides that newly rateable property had to be phased in over a period of three financial years. Rating properties used for agricultural purposes must

---

[4] In theory the discounted stream of net rent payments is equivalent to the capital value of the property.

consider the extent of services provided by the municipality in respect of such properties, the contribution of agriculture to the local economy, as well as the impact of agriculture on the social and economic welfare of farm workers. These factors confirm that the property tax is not a national land tax on agriculture.

Using market values instead of **use value** for property, especially in respect of farm land, is a much debated issue. The Katz Commission (1998) was in favour of use value as a valuation base. Use value can be determined using the income capitalisation method, land resource quality index method, and lease value or rental value method (see Katz Commission (1995: 1–36) for a description of use value methods and their merits). According to the income capitalisation method, use value is determined by dividing net farm income by an appropriate capitalisation rate. A major shortcoming of this method is that income is volatile. The land resource quality index method compiles an index using information on the quality of the land obtained from farmers, population censuses, and the Weather Bureau. Farm land is then assessed on the quality of the land only. In terms of the rental value method, the value of land is assessed with reference to the potential market rent that could be obtained for a unit of land. The usefulness of this method depends on the size of the rental market. If properties in a geographical area are mainly owner-occupied, it would be difficult to determine rental value.

There is a tendency for use values to be lower than market values since market values are influenced by non-farm factors such as location and investment value. This discrepancy is most noticeable where farm land is close to urban concentrations. The market value of farm land is determined under conditions of supply and demand. If the farm is not actually going to be sold, it is difficult to accurately determine market value. The comparative sales method then has to be employed. According to this method the market value of the property is obtained by comparing it to similar properties that have recently been sold. Another shortcoming of the market value method is that rates based on the market value could put severe strain on the cash flow of property owners during periods of property price booms. The proponents of use value methods argue that these methods are more equitable from an ability-to-pay point of view compared to the market value method that would tax wealth. When the capacity of municipalities to appraise farm land was considered, the Katz Commission (1998: 51) noted that municipal property valuers have more experience in market valuation methods. In addition, not all rural land is used for agriculture. In the end we have to consider that, from an efficiency perspective, market values should reflect the value of the property when used in its most productive use (or best forgone opportunity). In other words, when valuing a property, the assessor should consider the best use of the property. If farm land close to an urban area could best be used for residential purposes, the market value should reflect this condition. It should also be clear that determining the highest or best use has a subjective element. For this reason valuation rolls are normally open for inspection and objections, and there is a right of appeal.

13.3.4 Equity effects

Benefit principle of taxation

According to the benefit principle of taxation, people should pay tax in relation to the benefits (or cost of expenditure) of public services received. At the level of local authorities, this rule suggests that owners should pay for services that raise the value of their properties such as pavements, tarred roads, and street lighting. A property tax on site value can then be viewed as a comprehensive benefit tax and may be regarded as a fair tax from this perspective.

Although the link between benefits received and the tax paid is not always clear, empirical studies indicate that property taxes and the value of local public services are capitalised into housing prices (see Box 13.1 for the meaning of capitalisation).

The implication is that we can expect property taxes to depress property values but that this effect could be countered by the positive effect of public services financed by these taxes (Rosen and Gayer 2008: 525–526).

Property taxes based on land values have until now not been considered as benefit taxes (or user charges) because benefit taxes are usually linked to specific services (e.g. access to a public park or bus fees for public transport). However, there are taxpayers who are eligible for, but do not use, these services. Consider the example of a childless couple: although an activity centre in a public park may affect the value of their property, they derive no further benefit from it. Taxing them

at the same (uniform) rate as other property owners would be unfair. Therefore, only if the revenue from property tax is spent on infrastructure and activities that genuinely benefit property owners as a group (individually and collectively), can it be said that the property tax is a benefit tax.

Incidence of a property tax

By now we know that information on the statutory (or direct) burden of a tax is insufficient to arrive at conclusions about the fairness and distributional implications of that tax. We also need to identify the economic incidence of the tax. The incidence of property tax can be studied using partial equilibrium analysis and general equilibrium analysis.

Partial equilibrium analysis

When property tax is analysed within a partial equilibrium framework, it is regarded as an excise tax that falls on land and on the capital invested in improvements.

Property tax on land. Since the quantity of land in a country is fixed, the supply of

---

BOX 13.1 The capitalisation of a property tax

The capitalisation principle can be illustrated by means of a simple example. Suppose a piece of land in Cape Town has an expected yield of R10 000 per annum and that the current interest rate (the opportunity cost of capital) is 20 per cent per annum. The capitalisation value is determined by answering the following question: What amount needs to be invested to earn this return? This amount can be determined by using the formula for capitalised value. The **capitalised value** (CV) is income from the property (R), divided by the interest rate (i): $CV = \frac{R}{i}$. Thus, the capitalised value of the land will be R50 000 (= $\frac{R10\,000}{0,20}$). Let a property tax of

R1 000 now be levied. This would be equivalent to a tax on the income from the land at a rate of 10 per cent (R1 000 as a percentage of R10 000 = 10 per cent). The capitalised value of the land changes to $CV = \frac{(1-t)R}{i}$ where t is the tax rate (equal to 10 per cent) or $CV = \frac{(1-0,10)10\,000}{0,20} = $ R45 000.

The value of the Cape Town property has been reduced by R5 000. When the owner wants to sell the property, he or she will have to absorb the loss since the new buyer will want to obtain a net return (after the R1 000 property tax) of 20 per cent on the investment (= R9 000).

land is in effect perfectly inelastic. This means that landowners cannot increase the quantity of land if prices increase. All they can do is to change the use of land and, to a very limited extent, to reclaim parcels of land (e.g. swamp land). In Figure 13.1 the supply curve (S_0) is vertical and the demand curve is D_0. The equilibrium rental before tax is P_0 and the equilibrium quantity is Q_0. Suppose that an *ad valorem* property tax (t) is now introduced. The before-tax demand curve D_0 swivels downwards to D_1 which is the new effective (after-tax) demand curve (the demand curve as perceived by landowners). The rent paid by the users of land remains unchanged at P_0. However, the rent received by the owners of land is reduced by the tax to P_1. The total tax revenue is equal to the area $ABCD$ and is borne entirely by the owners of land. Thus, the incidence of a tax on land is on the landowner. Since income from land ownership increases as income

increases, the tax falls relatively more on taxpayers with higher incomes. This makes a land tax progressive and, from the ability-to-pay point of view, the tax is therefore fair.

The lower rent on the land will cause the price of land to fall in order to account for the future tax burden – taxes are capitalised into the value of land (see Box 13.1). When subsequent buyers make property tax payments, these payments should not be seen as a burden in the true sense of the word since the payments have already been capitalised into a lower purchase price. In other words, the incidence of the property tax is only on the initial owner of the land (i.e. the owner at the time when the tax was imposed). Should property taxes be increased, the increase would again be capitalised. The extra tax burden would fall on whoever owns the property at that time. The determination of the incidence thus becomes quite complicated since the identities of the

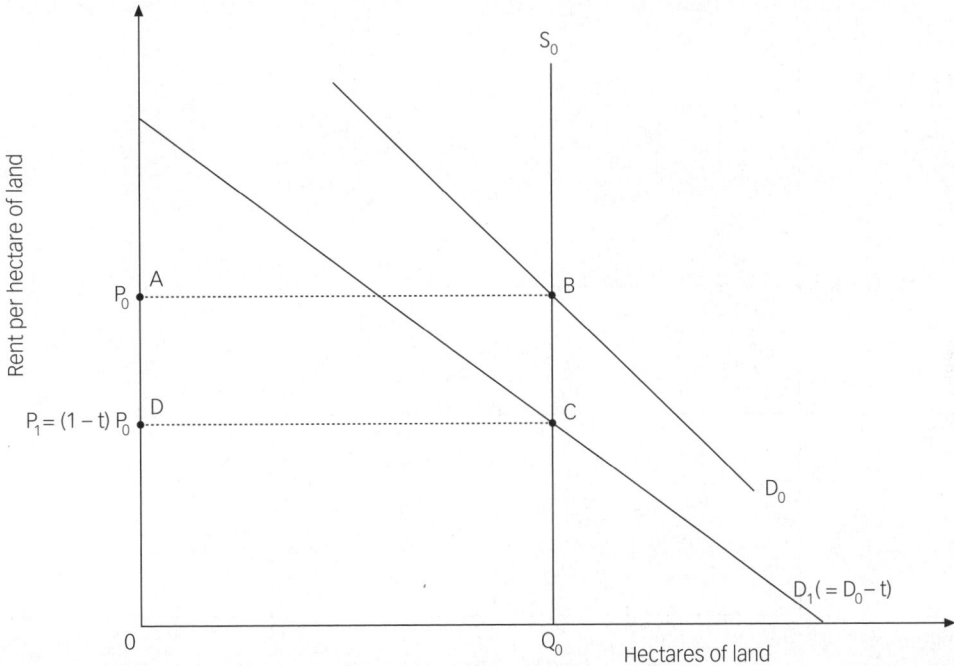

Figure 13.1 Incidence of an *ad valorem* property tax on land

owners at the time when the tax was imposed or increased must be known.

Property tax on improvements. In contrast to land that is fixed in supply, the capital invested in improvements is elastic in the long run. The argument is that, in the long term, investors can find all the capital they require at the market price. When market rents are taxed it is possible for property owners to shift the burden to the users of property (tenants and, indirectly, consumers and workers). This is illustrated in Figure 13.2. The supply of capital for improvements is the perfectly elastic curve S_0. The before-tax equilibrium is at Q_0 and P_0. If an *ad valorem* property tax is now levied on property, the effective (after-tax) demand curve becomes D_1. This is the demand curve as perceived by property owners. At the after-tax equilibrium property owners still receive P_0 but the users (e.g. tenants) have to pay P_1, which includes the property tax. Note that the after-tax equilibrium quantity of property

supplied is lower. Property owners are therefore able to shift the full tax burden (= $ABCD$) of a tax on improvements to users. The distributional implications depend on who the users are. If the users are lower- to middle-income tenants or owner-occupiers of residential property, the distribution tends to be regressive. The reason is that housing expenditures decrease with increases in income, that is, low-income taxpayers spend relatively more on housing than high-income taxpayers. If the users are tenants of commercial property, the higher after-tax rents will be reflected in higher prices for goods and services. Since consumption as a whole decreases as income increases, the regressive effect of a tax on the improvements part of property is again emphasised. However, since these effects disregard dynamic general equilibrium effects, the question of who bears the burden of the property tax is not fully resolved.

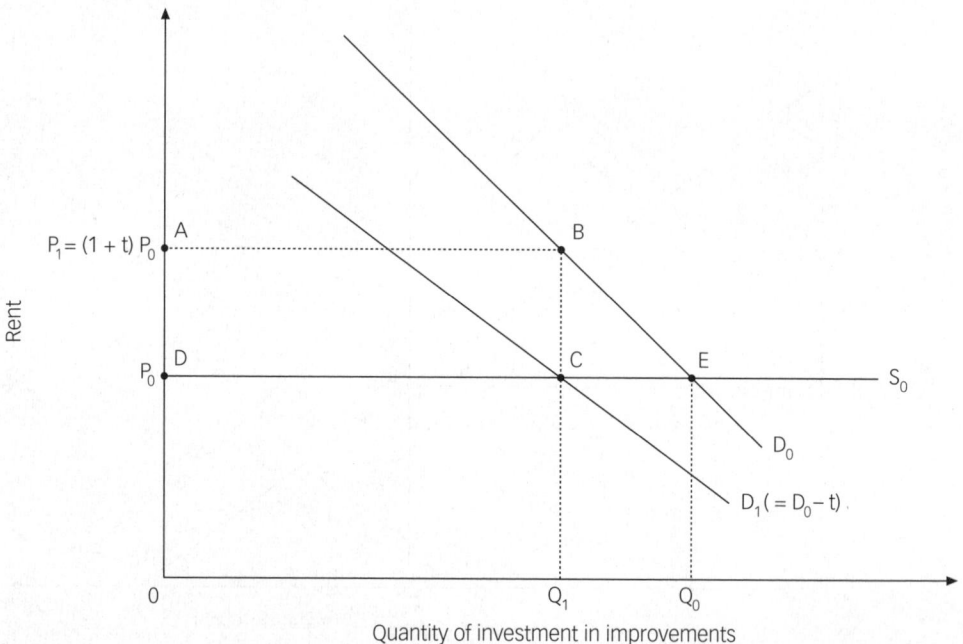

Figure 13.2 Incidence of an *ad valorem* property tax on improvements

General equilibrium analysis

In a general equilibrium framework the full effect of the tax is traced throughout the economy. Viewed from this perspective, a property tax levied at different rates is equivalent to a selective tax on capital. In the short term the tax will be capitalised and the value of property lowered. Since land and the capital invested in improvements are immobile in the short term, the incidence of the tax is on the initial owners of the assets. The burden is distributed progressively because property is not only heavily concentrated in the hands of the wealthy (particularly in developing countries), but income from ownership of property tends to be an increasing proportion of income.

In the long term the capital invested in improvements is more mobile. Capital then migrates from high tax rate areas to low tax rate areas. The stock of capital is reduced in the high tax rate area (increasing the net return on capital in this area) while the stock of capital in the low tax rate area increases (thereby reducing the net return of capital in this area). This process continues until net (i.e. after-tax) rates of return are equal throughout the economy or region. Therefore, even though the tax was imposed on capital in one area, the burden is shared by capital owners in other tax jurisdictions. The process does not stop here. When capital moves out of an area in which labour is immobile (often the case of unskilled labour), the labour in that area must now be combined with the reduced stock of capital in production. The capital–labour ratio decreases and this adversely affects the productivity of labour with the result that real wages decrease. Thus labour also bears part of the burden of the property tax and this adds a regressive element to the equity equation.

13.3.5 Efficiency effects

Note that the property tax is a selective tax on wealth. Elements of selectivity include:
- Only immovable property is taxed.
- The tax base can include land or improvements.
- Tax bases and rates can differ between tax jurisdictions (e.g. between urban and rural areas and between different urban areas).

Selective taxes have non-neutral allocation effects. As discussed in Chapter 11, tax non-neutralities can have positive or negative influences on resource allocation. These are some of the effects of selective property taxation:
- The industrial and residential locational decisions of entrepreneurs and individuals are influenced by tax differentials. These differentials cause a reallocation of resources away from jurisdictions with high property tax rates to those with low property tax rates. This kind of regional competition based on tax differentials can promote efficiency if, for example, agglomeration benefits[5] are created. However, it can also be very disruptive in areas where labour is not very mobile. A lower capital–labour ratio could depress already low wages even further or could result in unemployment.
- High property tax rates on improvements may discourage investment in the taxed property and lead to speculative purchases of low-taxed unimproved land. Large pockets of unimproved land in developed urban areas are inefficient since infrastructure such as roads and telephone lines have to be provided for the greater area.

---

[5] As firms concentrate (or agglomerate) in an area, benefits such as better access to a larger market and larger pools of managerial talent result.

High property tax rates on land may encourage more efficient use of land. A tax on land, for example, could serve as an incentive to develop the land to its most profitable use. Badly managed land or idle land that is taxed may generate no net (after-tax) income. The owner will have to improve the productivity of the land or sell the land to someone able to do so, or else the owner may go bankrupt.

Property taxes on improvements may have perverse effects. In 1695 a window tax was introduced in England, based on the number of windows in a house. Off course, larger houses tend to have more windows. The tax proved to be very unpopular and many households simply bricked up their windows to avoid payment; the tax was finally abolished in 1851 (Richardson, 1986).

13.3.6 The unpopularity of property taxation

Property taxation is known to be particularly unpopular (Rosen and Gayer, 2008: 527–528; and Skinner, 1991). Why?

Property taxation is a tax on unrealised capital income, which may cause solvency and liquidity problems for some taxpayers.

The burden of the land part of a property tax is on the owner of the property at the time of taxation. Since land ownership is mostly concentrated in the hands of a few property owners and ownership is often coupled with political power, the tax is fiercely resisted.

A land tax increases the riskiness of farming which is already subject to external risks and seasonal fluctuations in income.

The administration of property taxes has shortcomings. Properties and the liable taxpayers must be accurately identified.

The taxation of, for example, communal land is problematic. Each parcel of land must be valued and this process is difficult and sometimes judgemental. Since valuation is not done regularly, there is often outrage when values are updated. Property taxes are generally viewed as regressive and unfair. In addition, property taxes are highly visible forms of taxation and relatively easy targets for political action.

13.4 Capital transfer taxes

Capital transfer taxes are taxes on inheritances, estates, and gifts. Inheritance tax and estate duties are called death duties. The estate duty is donor-based, in other words, it is imposed on the estate out of which the legacy has been made. The liability is determined on the basis of the size of the total estate. Inheritance tax is donee-based (i.e. it is levied on the receiver of the legacy). The tax liability is determined by the size of the wealth transfer. Donations (gift) tax is levied on gifts. The reason for this tax is that estate duties can be avoided if such a tax does not exist – individuals would simply transfer wealth before their deaths. The donations tax is levied on the donor and certain exemptions are usually allowed.

13.4.1 Economic effects of capital transfer taxes

Equity issues

Capital transfer taxes are viewed as important tax instruments to reduce wealth inequalities, particularly vertical inequalities. Inheritances tend to perpetuate wealth inequalities and in this respect the inheritance tax has an advantage over estate duties – it targets the source of inequality.

Inheritance tax is also fair to the extent that it is levied according to the donee's ability to pay. Taxing the donee may also serve as an incentive to the donor to spread his or her wealth in order to minimise the tax burden of donees.

To fully comprehend the impact of death duties on wealth distribution, it must be realised that the act of leaving inheritances in itself can reduce wealth inequalities. Consider the example of a father leaving his worldly possessions to four low-income earning children with no accumulated wealth. Inter-generational inequality is reduced in this manner. Therefore, by taxing each child on his or her inheritance, the promotion of inter-generational equality of wealth is thwarted.

Efficiency issues

Capital transfer taxes affect an individual's choice between current consumption and saving. If bequests (accumulated savings) are taxed, the individual must give up more current consumption (i.e. save more) to maintain a given estate size. This is the familiar income effect of a price change. However, in addition to the income effect there is also a substitution effect. Capital transfer taxes increase the opportunity cost of accumulated wealth (i.e. savings) causing an increase in current consumption (i.e. lower saving). The final impact of capital transfer taxes therefore depends on the relative strengths of the two effects causing the outcome to be uncertain.

Administrative issues

Capital transfer taxes are probably easier to administer than an annual wealth tax as the estate is valued once only. By the same token, estate duties are easier to administer than an inheritance tax. In the case of estate duties there is only one tax identity, whereas under an inheritance tax there could be a number. Possibly the most serious problem

associated with death taxes is the ability of taxpayers to minimise tax liability through various forms of generation-skipping devices, such as trusts and interest-free loans. These devices not only erode the tax base, but are also utilised mainly by wealthy individuals, thereby perpetuating wealth inequalities. Tax avoidance activities are also unproductive (no new wealth is created). Other problems with death taxes relate to the hardships they may cause surviving spouses and children. Special provision has to be made for these categories of donees, which often complicates tax administration. Many forms of wealth (e.g. jewellery) are easy to hide and lend themselves to evasion under death duties. Transfers made in kind are also difficult to tax under a donations tax. It is no coincidence, therefore, that capital transfer taxes in the form of death and gift taxes are an insignificant source of revenue in developing countries (comprising less than 1 per cent of total tax revenue).

13.4.2 Capital transfer taxation in South Africa

Capital transfer taxation in South Africa includes taxes on estates and gifts. A flat rate of 20 per cent is applied in both cases. There is relief on a sliding scale where the same asset is taxable by reason of a second death occurring within ten years of a preceding death. A rebate of R100 000 is applicable to donations and a R3 500 000 rebate in respect of an estate. The assets bequeathed to the surviving spouse of the deceased are not subject to estate duty.

Estate duty is not only decreasing in importance but is also an insignificant source of total tax revenue. From 1984/85 to 2010/11 estate duty as a percentage of total tax revenue (net of SACU payments) declined from 0,42 per cent to 0,12 per cent. In 2010/11 approximately R800 million was raised in donations tax and estate duty.

Both the Margo Commission (1987) and the Katz Commission investigated transfer taxes. In its Fourth Interim Report, the Katz Commission (1997a) confirmed the viewpoint that a donations tax and a system of estate duty should be retained rather than be replaced by an inheritance tax. It was argued that:

▶ an inheritance tax is more complicated;
▶ the estate duty has been in place over many years and is well documented;

▶ estate duty has been the subject matter of numerous judicial decisions; and
▶ the administrative systems are geared to an estate duty.

The Katz Commission (1997a) recognised that the transfer tax system had deficiencies. It recommended that there should be provisions to deal with generation-skipping trusts that would tax capital transfers in a trust. It was suggested that net assets of a trust be valued at intervals of 25 to 30 years (more or less reflecting a single generation).

IMPORTANT CONCEPTS

capitalised value (page 250)
capital transfer tax
   (page 254)
capital value system
   (page 248)
composite rating (page 246)
donations (gift) tax
   (page 254)

estate duty (page 254)
flat rating (page 246)
impersonal (*in rem*) tax
   (page 246)
inheritance tax (page 254)
market value (page 248)
net wealth tax (page 244)

personal property
   (page 246)
real property tax base
   (page 246)
site value rating (page 246)
site value system (page 248)
use value (page 249)
wealth (page 243)

SELF-ASSESSMENT EXERCISES

13.1 Distinguish between annual wealth tax, property tax, and capital transfer tax.

13.2 'Wealth taxes tend to generate limited revenues for government and should therefore be eliminated.' Discuss this statement.

13.3 'Municipal rates boycotts in South Africa would confirm the notion that a property tax is a benefit tax.' Discuss.

13.4 'Property taxes on land are not only efficient but are also equitable.' Do you agree? Discuss.

13.5 Who really pays the property tax on improvements? Explain by using partial and general equilibrium analysis.

13.6 Discuss the possibility that high property rates in Sandton in Johannesburg can be shifted to other forms of capital and even to low-income earners in Soweto.

13.7 A factory located in Epping, an industrial area near Cape Town, is valued at R1,2 million. The opportunity cost of capital (or current interest rate) is 14 per cent. Due to the high incidence of crime, the Cape Town Metropolitan Council introduces a once-off 'protection levy' of R1 200 payable by all local property owners. Assuming full capitalisation, what will the impact be on the value of the property in Epping?

13.8 Discuss the economic effects of capital transfer taxes in South Africa.

Chapter
FOURTEEN

Tjaart Steenekamp

Taxes on goods and services and tax reform

In Chapter 10 we identified three major tax bases: income, wealth, and consumption. Until now we have studied taxes on income (Chapter 12) and wealth (Chapter 13). In this chapter we examine taxes on goods and services (i.e. the consumption base). When we introduced tax equity and efficiency in Chapters 10 and 11, we explained most of these concepts using excise taxes as examples.

In this chapter we identify first the types of indirect taxes in Section 14.1. The debate on the relative importance of indirect taxes versus direct taxes is an ongoing one and in Section 14.2 the advantages and disadvantages of indirect taxes are discussed. Value added taxes have increased in importance worldwide. This type of indirect tax is described and its economic effects are analysed in Section 14.3. In Section 14.4 we consider the personal consumption tax, which has until now only received theoretical attention by tax analysts. In Section 14.5 international tax reform is discussed and the chapter is concluded with a brief reference to tax reform in South Africa.

Once you have studied this chapter, you should be able to:
- distinguish between different indirect taxes and indicate their relative importance as sources of revenue
- discuss the merits of indirect taxation
- describe the consumption type VAT
- explain the economic effects of VAT
- describe the personal consumption tax base
- discuss the rationale for a personal consumption tax

> ◗ discuss the shortcomings of a personal consumption tax
> ◗ distinguish between patterns of taxation in industrialised countries and developing countries
> ◗ identify the direction of international tax reform
> ◗ compare tax competition with tax harmonisation
> ◗ contrast international tax reforms with the major tax reforms in South Africa since the late 1960s.

14.1 Types of indirect taxes

Indirect taxes are taxes that are imposed on commodities or market transactions (see Chapter 10, Section 10.2.4). The burden of an indirect tax is likely to be shifted. Consider, for example, an excise tax on locally produced washing machines. Although the statutory burden is on the supplier, the consumer usually indirectly bears the burden. Indirect taxes can be imposed at different stages of the production process: the resource (mining or farming) stage, the manufacturing stage, the wholesale stage, or the retail stage. If the tax is collected at one stage only, it is called a **single-stage commodity tax.** If it is collected at more than one stage, it is called a **multi-stage commodity tax**. VAT is an example of such a multi-stage tax.

We can distinguish between selective (narrow-based) taxes (e.g. specific excise duties) and general (broad-based) indirect taxes (e.g. turnover tax, general sales tax, value added tax) (see Chapter 10, Section 10.2.2). **Excise duties** are selective taxes levied on certain goods or transactions.

Excise duties can be specific (unit) taxes or *ad valorem* (percentage of value) taxes (see Section 10.2.3 of Chapter 10). Excise taxes are collected on both domestically produced and imported goods. When levied on imported goods, they are generally known as **customs duties** or tariffs. The personal consumption tax (see Section 14.5) is also included under indirect taxes.

From Table 14.1 it is clear that VAT is by far the most important indirect tax source in South Africa (contributing more than 70,0 per cent of the revenue from domestic taxes on goods and services), followed by the fuel levy (13,9 per cent) which is an excise tax. Specific excise duties are levied mainly on alcoholic beverages and cigarettes (the so-called sin taxes), whereas *ad valorem* excise duties are levied on a number of luxury goods. Excises imposed to reduce consumption of certain goods are known as **sumptuary taxes**. Specific excise duties (9,2 per cent) generate much more revenue than *ad valorem* duties (0,8 per cent). Included under 'Other' in Table 14.1 are various environmental levies such as the plastic shopping bag levy (4 cents per bag), a levy on incandescent light bulbs (between 1 cent and 3 cents per watt), a carbon dioxide (CO_2) emissions tax on new motor vehicles, a levy applied to electricity generated from non-renewable and nuclear energy sources of 2,5c/kWh and the international air passenger departure tax (R190 per passenger). These levies serve as incentives to reduce greenhouse gas emissions and to improve the environment.

Table 14.1 Main domestic taxes on goods and services

Source of revenue	Rate of duty (20011/12)	Tax revenue R m (% of total domestic tax on goods and services) (revised estimates for 2010/11)
1 Value added tax (VAT)	14%	181 335 (73,5%)
2 Excise duties		24 800 (10,0%)
2.1 Specific excises Beer Cigarettes and cigarette tobacco	R53,97 per litre of absolute alcohol or 15% of VAT inclusive price of R6,12 per 340 ml can R9,74 per 20 cigarettes or 38% of VAT inclusive price of R26,00 per packet of 20	22 900 (9,2%) 6 555 (2,7%) 9 685 (3,9%)
2.2 *Ad valorem* duties Beauty or make-up preparations Water scooters Cellular phones Golf balls Perfumes Fireworks	5% 7% 7% 7% 7% 7%	1 900 (0,8%)
3 Fuel levy	261,5c per litre or 29,6% of retail price of R8,84 per litre (93 octane petrol as in February 2011)	34 300 (13,9%)
4 Other		7 105 (2,9%)
4.1 Electricity levy	2,5c per kWh generated	5 200 (2,1%)
4.2 CO_2 tax –motor vehicle emissions	300 g/km x R75 per g/km CO_2 emissions or R22 500 (maximum levy)	505 (0,2%)
Domestic taxes on goods and services		247 540 (100%)

Source: Calculated from National Treasury, Budget Review 2011, (2011a) and South African Revenue Service (SARS), *Reference guide – Environmental levy on carbon dioxide emissions of new motor vehicles manufactured in the Republic* (SARS 2010: 8).

14.2 Indirect taxes: a general critical assessment

Indirect taxes have a number of advantages.

▶ Indirect taxation is a practical way of raising revenue from those who have small incomes and those who are not captured by the income tax net. This advantage hinges on the proposition that all citizens should contribute to some extent to the upkeep of government (i.e. it is based on the benefit principle).

▶ Taxes on goods and services are often invisible. Consumers hardly know that they are paying excise taxes, while the inclusion of VAT in prices is mostly noted only after the goods and services have been paid for. The advantage of fiscal illusion makes these taxes less susceptible to tax resistance.

▶ The tax liability is largely determined by how much is purchased of the taxed good. In the case of consumption goods (excluding certain necessities), consumers sometimes have a choice between different goods and services (i.e. substitution possibilities exist). For example, if an excise tax is imposed on golf equipment (e.g. golf balls), individuals may decide to rather take up jogging (an untaxed leisure activity). Within certain limits taxpayers themselves can thus determine their tax liability. In respect of direct taxes (income and company tax), the liability cannot be avoided that easily and the substitution possibilities are also fewer (e.g. in the case of income tax, bread-winners have to earn an income). Government enforces the tax liability much more strongly in the case of income tax.

▶ Consumption taxes can be used to achieve multiple objectives. Excise taxes can be used to correct market failures such as externalities. By levying a lower tax on unleaded petrol, environmental objectives are promoted. High sumptuary taxes on liquor and cigarettes are in part aimed at reducing alcohol abuse and smoking and, in so doing, help to improve general health levels. More broadly, it could be argued that in developing countries it may be worth levying the highest excises on luxury goods produced by means of capital-intensive technology, and the lowest on necessities produced by labour-intensive means.

▶ Taxes on goods and services are often levied on the value of the commodity, that is, on an *ad valorem* basis (e.g. *ad valorem* excises and VAT). Tax revenue from this source automatically increases, as the price of the commodity increases, and is therefore effectively indexed for inflation.

▶ Indirect taxes are relatively simple to administer. Consumers also have limited scope for evading taxes on goods and services and compliance is accordingly easier to enforce.

Analysts have also pointed to a number of disadvantages of indirect taxes.

▶ According to the ability-to-pay principle, broad-based taxes on goods and services tend to be regressive. The reason is that consumption declines as a percentage of income as income increases. This conclusion has led to the exemption or zero-rating of certain basic consumption goods and services from indirect taxation, in particular where a broad-based VAT applies (see Section 14.4). Even excise taxes, which are generally levied on sumptuary goods, can be regressive. According to

Statistics South Africa (2008: 18), the poor in South Africa spent approximately 1,5 per cent of their income on tobacco products in comparison to the 1,0 per cent spent by the wealthy in 2005. Even if it is assumed that cigarette prices are the same for both income groups (the poor often pay higher prices since they buy cigarettes at inflated prices in rural areas or townships and in units, e.g. a single cigarette), the tax is regressive. The same conclusion applies to excise taxes on beer and 'luxuries' such as skin care, hair, and shaving preparations (Steenekamp, 1994, and Katz Commission, 1994: 124).

▶ Indirect excise taxes are selective and lead to inefficiencies. For example, in developing countries the opportunity to purchase luxury goods may act as an incentive to work harder and save more. However, if high rates of indirect taxation are levied, this may result in a substitution effect in favour of leisure, thereby adversely affecting work effort (see Cnossen, 1990). In addition, high indirect tax rates may lead to smuggling and black market activities. To counter smuggling, the Swedish government lowered taxes on cigarettes and tobacco in 1998.

▶ Since indirect taxes can be levied for various purposes there is often a policy conflict (too many goals and only one instrument). When we considered economic efficiency as one of the properties of a 'good tax' in Chapter 11, we concluded that, to minimise the excess burden, commodity taxes should be high on goods and services with an inelastic demand and low on goods and services with high demand and supply elasticities. This tax rule is referred to as the inverse elasticity rule. In practice, excise taxes are imposed on luxuries for equity reasons. The demand for luxury

goods, however, tends to be both price and income elastic. Taxes on these commodities will significantly decrease the quantity demanded. Application of the inverse elasticity rule means that, from an efficiency point of view, such goods should bear low tax rates, which is contradictory to the equity requirement. Thus there is a policy conflict that requires a trade-off between equity and efficiency objectives.

▶ Indirect taxes may have an inflationary effect if wages are raised in response to tax increases. Some multi-stage commodity taxes also have a cascading effect on prices. If the tax at each stage of production is based on the gross price up to that stage, including tax levied at earlier stages, tax is in effect levied on tax. This may encourage vertical integration of production processes and thereby reduce the degree of competition in the markets concerned.

14.3 Value added tax

Value added tax is a multi-stage sales tax levied on the value added at the different stages of production. Roughly speaking, value added is the difference between sales and purchases of intermediate goods and services over a certain period (normally a month). If a retailer purchased goods to the value of R150 000 from suppliers in a month and had sales worth R300 000 in that month, the value added by the retailer would be R150 000 – the tax will then be applied to this value. The value added consists of wages, rent, interest, depreciation, and profit. The calculation of value added tax is illustrated in Box 14.1. South Africa's neighbouring countries, Namibia, Botswana, and Lesotho have all recently introduced VAT, while Swaziland will be introducing VAT within one to two years after the establishment of a

Revenue Authority in 2011. Their systems are broadly similar to that of South Africa but differ in some respects with regard to rates, exemptions, and goods and services that are zero-rated.

VAT comes in many forms. A tax authority wishing to introduce VAT therefore faces a number of choices. We now discuss these choices and the South African practice in respect of each.[1]

There are three broad types of VAT: a consumption type VAT, an income type VAT, and a VAT on gross product. When South Africa introduced VAT in 1991, the universal practice of a consumption type VAT was chosen. In a closed economy,

$$GNP = C + I = W + P + D$$

where GNP is gross national product, C is consumption, I is gross investment, W is wages, P is net profit after depreciation, and D is depreciation. The consumption VAT base is then,

$$C = W + P + D - I$$

The regime for international trade can be based on the origin principle (exports taxable, imports zero-rated) or the destination principle (exports zero-rated, imports taxable). Again, South Africa decided to follow the popular route of applying the destination principle. This is perceived to be a fair practice (domestic and imported goods are treated the same) and one that does not affect the competitiveness of exports.

Since destination-based VAT taxes imports but not exports, tax rate differentials between countries are normally offset at the border. This implies that production takes place in the least-cost location, or put differently, global allocative efficiency is achieved. The

destination principle, therefore, promotes neutrality in the taxation of internationally traded commodities. Within a customs union or union such as the EU where border controls on trades among members do not exist or are not effective, the destination principle breaks down. Cross-border shopping is, for example, encouraged if rate differentials between countries are significant. This has relevance for SACU (Southern African Custom Union – see Section 14.5.4) should there be a liberalisation of border controls in this union. Alternatives to the destination-based VAT include applying the **restricted-origin principle** to intra-union trades. This option provides for a clearing house allowing for exports of union members to be taxed at origin. Importers would be entitled to a tax credit for the VAT paid on imports. Tax-rate harmonisation could also lessen the impact somewhat. The incentive for cross-border shopping diminishes with the distance consumers have to travel to buy goods. The overall impact may not be that significant and reduces the need for rate approximation.[2]

Tax liability can be computed using three methods: subtraction, tax credit (or 'invoice'), or addition. The tax credit (invoice) method is generally used, also in South Africa. This is the type of VAT illustrated in Box 14.1.

Two techniques can be used to free goods and sectors from VAT (see Section 14.3.1): outright exemption (the firm need not file a VAT return and does not, therefore, levy VAT, but it also cannot claim refunds for any VAT included in the price of purchased goods and services) and zero-rating (the firm files a return but pays zero tax on sales and receives a refund in respect of VAT payments made at earlier stages in the production and distribution chain). South Africa uses both techniques. Education and health services as well as the services of various non-governmental

---

[1] For a comprehensive discussion of VAT see Gillis, Shoup, and Sicat (eds) (1990: 3–16; 219–233), and Katz Commission (1994: 101–147).

[2] See Cnossen (2003) in this regard and also for alternatives to the restricted-origin principle.

BOX 14.1 Value added tax: an illustrative example

Consider the transactions of three firms for the month of September. Agent A is an importer of bicycle components who, for argument's sake, is assumed to add no further value to the value of imports. Firm B is an assembler of bicycles and Firm C is a bicycle shop. Agent A imports bicycle components to the amount of R100 000, sells them for R100 000 to Firm B who, after assembling the bicycles, sells them for R150 000 to Firm C. Firm C sells the bicycles for R300 000 to the cycling public (consumers). The tax trail would be as follows:

Production stage	Goods, wages, profit etc.	VAT (14%)	Total on invoice
Agent A: Imports (value added is found in wages, rents, interest, profit, etc. in country of origin) VAT payable	100 000	14 000 14 000	114 000
Firm B: Purchases of inputs from Agent A Value added (wages, rents, interest, profit, etc.) Selling price VAT payable	100 000 50 000 150 000	(14 000) 21 000 7 000	114 000 171 000
Firm C: Purchases of inputs from Firm B Value added (wages, rents, interest, profit, etc.) Selling price VAT payable	150 000 150 000 300 000	(21 000) 42 000 21 000	171 000 342 000

VAT is collected at different stages of the production process and, at the end of the distribution channel, the tax is passed on to the consumer. The incidence (the burden) of the tax is therefore on consumers, but the sellers make the tax payments to SARS. VAT is collected by the seller at the point of sale (this is referred to as the output tax). The seller may then deduct taxes paid on intermediate products (this is referred to as the **input tax**). For example, Firm B purchases components from Agent A. Included in the price is input tax of R14 000 (this amount is collected by Agent A and paid over to SARS). Firm B may deduct the input tax from the VAT of R21 000 (the **output tax**) payable on his or her selling price. At the end of the month the total tax liability of Firm B is R7 000 (or R21 000 minus R14 000 on inputs). Firm C's tax liability is R21 000 (R42 000 on the selling price less input tax of R21 000). The total VAT collected is R42 000 (R14 000 from Agent A; R7 000 from Firm B; R21 000 from Firm C). Note that the same result can be obtained by levying 14 per cent VAT on the value added at each stage of the production process (remember to include the value added included in imports).

organisations are exempt. In addition to goods and services destined for export, a list of basic foodstuffs is zero-rated. This list includes brown bread, maize meal, samp, mealie rice, dried beans, lentils, pilchards, milk powder, dairy powder blend, rice, vegetables, fruit, vegetable oil, milk, cultured milk, brown wheat, eggs, and edible legumes.

VAT can be levied at a single rate or **multiple rates** (rates in addition to the zero rate). Namibia taxes most goods and services at a standard rate of 15 per cent. Lesotho levies VAT on most goods and services at a standard rate of 14 per cent. Alcohol and tobacco products are taxed at a rate of 15 per cent and 5 per cent on electricity and telephone services (including start-up SIM cards for cellphones). South Africa and Botswana have a single-rate VAT. In contrast to the 14 per cent VAT levied in South Africa, Botswana levies VAT at only 12 per cent.

14.3.1 The economic effects of VAT

Revenue

Value added tax (VAT) has a worldwide reputation of being a 'money machine' and in developing countries this has indeed proven to be the case. In South Africa VAT was introduced in October 1991 at a rate of 10 per cent, but the rate was increased to 14 per cent in April 1993. The revenue importance of VAT cannot be contested. In 1992/93 collections amounted to R17,5 billion, or approximately 21,7 per cent of total net tax revenue. In 2010/11 the revised budgetary estimate amounted to R181,3 billion or 27,7 per cent of total tax revenue (net of SACU payments). Likewise, Namibia netted 25,0 per cent of estimated 2010/11 tax revenue in the form of VAT. When countries are ranked according to their efforts at raising VAT revenue, South Africa ranks 21 out of 27

countries studied (Steenekamp 2007). While this weak performance can be attributed to South Africa's relatively low VAT rate, it would be an oversimplification to suggest that the VAT rate simply be raised. An important consideration would be the equity implications. To lessen the impact on low-income households, VAT rates can, for example, be restructured using different tax rates for commodities important to poor consumers (Go et al. 2005). This would again affect the economic efficiency and the administrative complexity of the system. To find a balance between revenue, equity and efficiency in taxation, for example, pursuing equity would imply trading off political and economic efficiency objectives.

Efficiency and the tax rate

In our discussion of the efficiency effects of general taxes in Chapter 10, we concluded that taxes imposed on a broad base and at a **uniform rate** resemble lump sum taxes and are efficient. In arriving at this conclusion we ignored equity considerations. Whether efficiency requires uniform rates is a much-debated issue. The theory of optimal taxation (see Chapter 11, Section 11.1.3) provides convincing arguments on efficiency and equity grounds, which refute the notion of uniformity (Newbery and Stern, 1987). The inverse elasticity rule is one example of this line of thinking (see Chapter 11, Section 11.2.2).

You will recall that the inverse elasticity rule states that the excess burden of selective taxes can be minimised by taxing price inelastic goods and services at higher rates. Put more eloquently, the rule states that the excess burden will be minimised if the proportional reduction in compensated demand that results when a set of selective taxes is imposed, is the same for all goods. When we move away from the one-person assumption of the model and also include equity considerations, the rule calls for higher taxes on goods with low distributional character- istics and lower taxes on goods with high distributional characteristics (goods where the share of the poor in its total consumption is high). The important conclusion from opti- mal tax theory is that, from an equity perspective, uniform taxation is not desir- able. In other words, to minimise inefficiency different tax rates should be applied to dif- ferent commodities. A case for uniform rates can only be made under certain strict condi- tions. One condition is that governments should make optimal lump sum transfers to households. In other words, when taxes are designed, one has to consider what govern- ment does with the tax revenue.

Using optimal tax theory in formulating policy is, however, severely restricted by data limitations. For example, to design separate rates for each commodity requires informa- tion on elasticities and patterns of complements and substitutes that are diffi- cult to come by. It is also doubtful whether the efficiency gain from designing a great variety of tax rates would outstrip the costs involved in administering such a system. One solution could be to lump together large cat- egories of commodities and to subject them to uniform *ad valorem* taxes. Another option is to achieve the desired equity objectives with a combination of differentiated or uni- form excises on luxuries and a uniform VAT rate. The lumping-together process is, how- ever, still analytically and empirically problematic. In the end there appears to be some agreement that the loss of economic efficiency due to VAT is likely to be mini- mised when uniform rates or a few rates (three or four) are applied to the broadest possible base. Moreover, if a system of income and expenditure supports for the poor is in place (see Chapter 8), the case for uniformity in rates is strengthened.

Equity

There is no question that a broad-based (comprehensive) VAT with no exemptions or zero-rating is regressive. To reduce the regressive impact of VAT, tax relief could be given to the poor, or transfer payments could be directed at them. As mentioned, tax relief includes exemption from VAT and zero-rating. **Exemption** of a good or service from VAT means that the firm or supplier need not levy VAT on sales, but at the same time such a firm may not claim refunds of the VAT already collected at earlier stages of the production process. The buyer of the service therefore pays VAT levied on all but the final stage in the production chain. **Zero-rating** of a good or service means that the firm charges a zero rate of tax on sales of the commodity and is also allowed to deduct VAT collected at earlier stages. The buyer of a zero-rated product does not pay any VAT. None of the stages of production is thus subject to VAT.

A major shortcoming of zero-rating is that the tax base is eroded, perhaps necessitating a higher VAT rate, given the total revenue that the government requires. For example, the estimated revenue loss due to zero-rating in South Africa in 1994/95 was R2 600 mil- lion. It was calculated that by abolishing zero-rating on foodstuffs the standard rate could have been reduced by about 1,25 per- centage points without affecting the yield from VAT. Furthermore, since zero-rated goods and services are consumed by the rich as well, they also benefit from the zero rate. Affluent households spend substantially more in absolute terms on zero-rated goods than less affluent households. It was esti- mated that of the above-mentioned R2 600 million loss in VAT revenue, more than two- thirds of the benefit accrued to households in the top half of the income distribution (Katz Commission, 1994: 113). Zero-rating may also lead to over-taxation of suppliers who cannot credit VAT collected at earlier stages. In South Africa this is of particular concern to unregistered vendors who operate in the informal sector.

Another method of reducing the regressivity of VAT is to levy multiple rates (e.g. higher rates on luxuries). This is similar to the option mentioned earlier of combining uniform VAT rates with differentiated excises on luxuries (as for example in Namibia). This option, however, is subject to various administrative and efficiency complications.

In its First Interim Report the Katz Commission (1994: 133) recommended that the further erosion of the VAT base through zero-rating or exemptions should not be considered and that targeted poverty relief and development programmes should receive priority. In addition, the Katz Commission (1994: 133) recommended against higher VAT rates on luxury goods or a multiple VAT rate system. The Commission argued that: such a system would make an insignificant contribution to reducing regressivity; would have high administration and compliance costs; and would not have much additional revenue potential. The South African government accepted these recommendations.

Administration

The credit-type VAT system has the reputation that it is effective against tax evasion. The anti-evasion features are its self-policing attributes, the possibilities for the cross-checking of invoices, and the fact that a large portion of tax revenue is collected before the retail stage. The self-policing feature reveals itself in the lack of incentives for sellers and buyers to collude to make under-payments of VAT. Sellers would prefer to understate the output tax whereas all buyers who are not final consumers would like to overstate the input tax since they can reclaim it. Therefore, if the seller does not

pay the full VAT, it increases the VAT liability of the buyer who will certainly complain about it. Since VAT requires the maintenance of records of both purchases and sales, the revenue authorities have a basis for cross-checking returns. The benefit from collecting VAT at the different stages of the production process can be seen from our example in Box 14.1. If the retailer (Firm C) is not a registered VAT vendor and therefore does not charge VAT on sales or claim an input tax credit, SARS will still collect R21 000 from Firms A and B.

Opportunities for fake claims increase when goods are zero-rated, exempt or taxed at different rates. A retailer can, for example, understate output tax by under-stating sales of higher-rated goods. Multiple rates not only open up avenues for tax evasion but also complicate administration for the tax authorities and taxpayers alike.

14.4 Personal consumption tax

In Section 14.3.1 we saw that one of the disadvantages of a VAT is its regressivity. An alternative tax on consumption that can address this shortcoming is the **personal consumption tax** (also known as the expenditure tax). The base of the personal consumption tax is income less net saving (saving minus dissaving). This tax is collected directly from the consumer, similar to the personal income tax, and can be made progressive by applying a rate schedule and allowing for exemptions on certain consumption items (e.g. medical expenditures). Although it looks simple enough, it is more complicated to design and implement than income tax or VAT. Nonetheless, there is a large body of support among economists for such a tax.

14.4.1 The rationale for a personal consumption tax

The proponents of a consumption tax argue that it is more equitable to tax what an individual takes out of the economic system (as reflected in consumption) than what an individual contributes to society (as measured by income). From this perspective it would be considered fair that a millionaire who lives like a miser ends up with a low current tax liability. This conflicts with the ability-to-pay principle which views potential consumption (the power to consume) as the yardstick. The counter-argument is that the millionaire is simply postponing the tax until he or she consumes the funds accumulated. The tax liability of the individual must therefore be viewed over a longer period, that is, a lifetime equity perspective is required.

It is further argued that a personal consumption tax is more efficient than an income tax. This conclusion rests on two assumptions: (1) that income tax affects saving; and (2) that the supply of labour is fixed. A tax on saving (e.g. an income tax) distorts the choice between present and future consumption. An income tax therefore causes an excess burden. In contrast, a tax on consumption does not create an excess burden since saving is not taxed. If the supply of labour (or work effort) is not affected by a tax on personal consumption, it has no excess burden. If, however, a tax on consumption induces a consumer to work less (i.e. enjoy more leisure time), it entails an excess burden. Nevertheless, there is some empirical evidence that a consumption tax is on balance more efficient than an income tax.

If consumption is taxed (as leisure is too difficult to tax), the price of consumption goods increases relative to leisure. It means that one hour of leisure (or labour sacrificed) is now equivalent to less consumption than before, that is, the opportunity cost (or relative price) of leisure has decreased. Put differently, a tax on consumption decreases the return to work effort. Leisure hours will increase and work effort decreases. Therefore, a tax on consumption does cause an excess burden. Since the consumption tax base is smaller than the income tax base, to yield the same tax revenue, the tax rate on consumption would have to be higher. Because the excess burden of a tax increases with the square of the tax rate, the excess burden of the consumption tax is higher than the equal-yield income tax. This efficiency loss must be subtracted from the efficiency gain derived from not taxing savings. The net effect must then be compared to the excess burden caused by an income tax. Whether the excess burden of a personal consumption tax is less than that of an income tax ultimately depends on empirical evidence. Some studies show that a consumption tax creates a smaller excess burden than an income tax and this has advanced the case of the proponents of the personal consumption tax (Rosen and Gayer, 2008: 479).

It is also argued that a consumption tax would be beneficial to developing countries. These countries have a critical shortage of saving. Since the personal consumption tax is neutral in respect of the choice between present and future consumption (saving), consumption would be a good tax base. Furthermore, consumption (like income) tends to be distributed highly unequally in these countries. A progressive expenditure tax could tap this base effectively and equitably.

The personal consumption tax is usually considered too complex to administer. It is argued, for example, that to arrive at the taxpayer's annual consumption, a list of expenditures would have to be made and then added up. This, together with the required record-keeping would be a mammoth task. Proponents argue, however, that these problems can be overcome by observing the individual's cash flow in qualified bank accounts. In addition, certain problems normally associated with income tax, such as valuing unrealised capital gains and depreciation, are also avoided when consumption is taxed. Under a consumption tax, capital gains are taxed when they are realised. Capital purchases are immediately expensed (written off when purchased), making allowances for depreciation unnecessary.

14.4.2 The disadvantages of a consumption tax

The personal consumption tax has not been successfully implemented anywhere in the world. India and Sri Lanka, for example, experimented with such a tax but abandoned it. The problem areas in designing a personal consumption tax are administration, treatment of bequests and gifts, and the problems of transition.

Critics are concerned about the risks of implementing such a tax because we know too little about the practical administrative problems to be encountered. In contrast the problems with the current income tax system are known and can be addressed. Furthermore, proponents of a consumption tax tend to compare an ideal consumption tax to the current income tax with all its impurities introduced over years. This is not really a fair comparison since there is no guarantee that a personal consumption tax will not follow the same route and become progressively more impure and complicated.

A personal consumption tax creates a host of specific administration problems. For example, under an income tax system taxes are withheld at source for administrative and compliance purposes (e.g. the PAYE system mentioned in Chapter 12). This would be difficult under a consumption tax. How would an employer estimate the consumption and saving of each employee?

A presumptive consumption-to-income ratio may have to be applied. As mentioned earlier, extensive record-keeping would also be required in respect of bank balances, expenditures, and assets.

It will be necessary (and difficult) to distinguish between consumption and investment. Consider expenditures such as housing and education. The purchase of a house, for example, should be regarded as investment and subtracted from consumption to determine the tax base. Owner-occupied housing, however, generates a service that should be classified as consumption. An imputed rent value would have to be determined for this purpose. An alternative would be to exclude housing altogether from the tax base, but this would erode the tax base. Education also has both an investment and a consumption component. Another source of base erosion is the consumption of goods and services in kind. The consumption tax system is not necessarily superior to the income tax system in detecting such consumption. Under the cash flow system, consumption is calculated as a residual (income minus saving). The definitional problems related to income all still apply and are compounded by problems relating to the definition of saving. Would it not be simpler to use an income tax system where only income needs to be determined?

Another major problem is the treatment of bequests and gifts. Should bequests and gifts be considered as consumption by the donor or as income of the donee (i.e. the recipient of the donation)? According to one view, a gift (e.g. cash) by a parent to a child is no different to any other form of expenditure and should be treated as consumption. From another point of view it is argued that consumption only occurs when the child spends the cash. Exempting bequests and gifts would solve the administrative problems but could lead to large concentrations of wealth. Some form of wealth taxation, however, could address this problem.

Finally, introducing a personal consumption tax will cause transition problems. One dilemma is the treatment of savings once the new system comes into effect. Under the income tax system saving comes from after-tax income. If an existing asset is now realised or previous saving is spent on consumption goods, the same base will be taxed again under a consumption tax, which appears to be unfair.

14.5 Tax reform: international experience

The existing tax systems of countries evolved over time. Changes to tax systems are implemented through ad hoc reforms or comprehensive tax reform programmes. The goals of such reforms are varied and differ from country to country. The driving force is often a desire for more revenue. In addition, non-revenue goals, such as redistribution or equity, promotion of growth, tax simplification, and a more efficient allocation of resources, are also pursued.

Tax reform can be triggered by various factors, one of which is political change. A change in government often implies different voter preferences. For example, if the new constituency is, on average, composed of relatively more low-income voters such as in Southern Africa, tax reforms that redistribute income to them may be forthcoming (see Chapter 7, Section 7.4.3). Political change may also be accompanied by ideological shifts (e.g. a shift away from centralised planning to a more devolved or federal-type structure). Developments in tax theory often provide new analytical insights, and attempts are then made to operationalise these through tax reforms. Some reforms are undertaken in response to

international trends. For example, there is a global trend towards VAT and lower marginal income tax rates and in the current integrated world economy it is difficult for a small open economy to ignore this trend. Tax reforms have also often resulted from a fiscal crisis (e.g. short-term budget deficits) or a concerted effort to prevent future fiscal crises (e.g. chronic deficits and inflation). Several African countries have recently introduced VAT, partly for these reasons.

14.5.1 Patterns of taxation in industrialised and developing countries

A cross-country comparison of tax systems indicates that there are vast differences in the composition of taxes between countries. As each country's tax system has been established over time by many – often unique – forces, one should be careful of overgeneralising best tax practices and reforms on the basis of international comparisons alone. Nevertheless, interesting patterns do emerge when countries are grouped together, for example, according to the level of economic development – as shown in Table 14.2.

Table 14.2 contains a comparison of central government taxes in a group of developing countries, a group of industrialised countries and South Africa. When total tax revenue as a percentage of GDP is considered we notice that the tax burden is slightly higher in the industrialised countries (21,6 per cent of GDP) than in developing countries (21,3 per cent of GDP). A number of observations can be made in respect of the composition of taxes (the percentages are unweighted average shares of tax types to total tax revenue):

▶ Taxes on income, profits, and capital gains constitute the predominant sources of revenue in industrialised

countries (58,9 per cent) whereas taxes on goods and services (mostly import tariffs) are the major sources of revenue in developing countries (44,0 per cent).
▶ In industrialised countries income tax on individuals (39,7 per cent) is much more important than income tax on companies (18,9 per cent). In developing countries the tax contribution of companies is almost double that of individuals.
▶ Taxes on payroll and workforce and property taxes are insignificant tax sources in both industrialised countries and developing countries.
▶ Developing countries rely on general sales taxes (29,7 per cent) and in

particular VAT for much of their tax revenue.
▶ Trade taxes are insignificant sources of tax revenue in industrialised countries (0,8 per cent) compared to developing countries (21,1 per cent).

Explaining differences in levels of taxation (the tax burden) and the composition of tax revenue is rather tricky. A few generalisations will suffice. The high tax burden and reliance on income taxes in industrialised countries can probably be attributed to their level of development. Not only does the level of development determine the size of the tax base, but it also has an effect on a country's capacity to administer taxes. In

Table 14.2 Tax revenue of central government by type, 2007

Tax type	Percentage contribution to total tax revenue		
	Developing countries[a]	Industrialised countries[b]	South Africa
1 Taxes on income, profits, and capital gains	28,0	58,9	57,3
1.1 Payable by individuals	9,6	39,7	29,2
1.2 Payable by corporations and other enterprises	18,0	18,9	28,1
2 Taxes on payroll and workforce	1,9	0,7	1,1
3 Taxes on property	4,7	2,0	2,1
4 Taxes on goods and services	44,0	36,8	34,9
4.1 General taxes (e.g. value added taxes)	29,7	26,3	26,0
4.2 Excises	10,6	8,9	8,7
5 Taxes on international trade and transactions	21,1	0,8	4,6
Total tax revenue as % of GDP Social contributions as % of GDP	21,3 3,7	21,6 10,1	28,8 0,6

Notes: [a] Sample of 7 African countries, 4 Latin American countries, 3 Asian countries
[b] Sample of 13 Industrialised countries
Source: Compiled from IMF, *Government Finance Statistics Yearbook*, 2008.

addition, taxpayers are more sophisticated in industrialised countries, enabling tax authorities to levy relatively complex taxes and thereby broadening the tax base even further. The greater reliance on taxes on international trade in developing countries can be explained by the administrative ease with which points of import and export can be targeted.

When South Africa's tax composition is compared to those of the industrialised countries and developing countries, it is evident that in most respects the South African pattern is almost identical to that of industrialised countries. An obvious deviation from most developing countries and some of the industrialised countries included in the sample, is the relatively high total tax burden South Africans face (28,8 per cent of GDP). It has to be considered that the percentage contributions are averages and the values for different countries in each group show considerable variation. Another difference between the two groups of countries is the importance of social security contributions to government revenue. In the past these contributions (compulsory social security payments by employees and employers) were included in the tax revenues of government but are now treated separately. The social security contributions add up to approximately 10,1 per cent of GDP for the industrialised countries but 3,7 per cent in developing countries. In South Africa social security contributions constitute only 0,6 per cent of GDP.

14.5.2 **International tax reform**

A number of countries have reformed their tax systems in recent years. Given South Africa's status as a developing country, we are particularly (although not exclusively) interested in reforms undertaken in developing countries. A detailed discussion of tax

reform in developing countries falls beyond the scope of this chapter, however. We will therefore focus on a selection of prominent tax issues in tax reform debates. The lessons for reform of specific taxes were discussed in the chapters on specific taxes (see for example Chapter 13, Section 13.9 on income tax reform). In the discussion below the emphasis is on the direction of tax reform.[3]

There has been a reappraisal of the redistributive role of taxes. The importance of using the tax system for redistributive purposes has been reduced, partly because both vertical and horizontal equity have proved to be elusive goals. Nonetheless, the contention is that the tax burden on the poor should at least be reduced or removed altogether. In this way a levelling-up process can take place. Bird and De Wulf (quoted in Brown and Jackson, 1990: 175) summarised the position as follows:

Taxes cannot, of course, make poor people rich ... If the principal aim of redistributive policy is to level up – make poor people better off – the main role the tax system has to play is thus the limited and essentially negative one of not making them poorer.

Consequently, more emphasis has been placed on public expenditure policies as instruments of redistribution (see Chapter 8). More attention is also given to efficiency considerations when raising revenues. This resulted in a larger role for consumption taxes and less reliance on the principle of comprehensive income taxation (see Norregaard and Khan 2007:5).

Concerted efforts have been made to broaden the base of the tax system. Tax

---

[3] For a more comprehensive discussion of international tax reform see Bernardi, Barreix, Marenzi and Profeta (2008), Norregaard and Khan (2007), Tanzi and Zee (2000), Stotsky and WoldeMariam (2002), Boskin (1996), World Bank (1991), and Khalilzadeh-Shirazi and Shah (1991).

systems in developing countries are known to be allocatively non-neutral, that is, they cause distortions in the goods and factor markets. To reduce the excess burden of taxation in these countries, various reforms have been introduced. The general direction has been towards a broadening of the tax base accompanied by reductions in tax rates. The concern with **base broadening** stems from the following: the narrower the base, the higher the rate required to generate a given income; the higher the rate, the greater the incentive for avoiding or evading the tax; resources used for evading taxes are socially unproductive; and high tax rates cause changes in relative prices that may lead to a reallocation of resources away from taxed activity. The objective, therefore, should be lower rates on a broader base. The base broadening policy debate focuses on the merits of a broad-based value added tax, a flat tax on consumption, and the reduction or removal of tax expenditures (e.g. tax incentives to promote economic activity).

Major efforts are being made to improve tax administration. Tax simplification is one of the mainstays of better administration. Tax simplification requires a rationalisation of the number of taxes. Taxes that provide little revenue and have high administrative costs should be done away with. Tax rates should also be streamlined (e.g. fewer personal income tax brackets). There is growing recognition that less complex taxes are easier to administer and will improve tax compliance. In addition, steps are taken to improve information systems and to limit political interference in tax administration.

Lower tax rates and a movement to more uniform tax rates (e.g. less differentiation in VAT rates) have been a worldwide phenomenon in the last decade. Lower tax rates are aimed at reducing the disincentive effects of taxation. Examples include lower import tax rates, lower marginal rates of personal income tax, and lower effective company tax rates. Lower tax rates and the transnational convergence of tax bases and rates are also the result of the increased tax competition that accompanies economic globalisation and the regional integration of countries in geographic proximity.

A popular development in tax reforms is the levying of 'green' and 'carbon' taxes to address environmental externalities. These taxes are aimed at reducing pollution and greenhouse gas emissions and to moderate climate change.

Recently the financial and economic crisis caused industrialised and developing countries to review their tax systems. For most of the last decade the countries of the EU and others experienced high economic growth and a cyclical fiscal dividend. This led to tax rate reductions and a weakening of automatic stabilisers. An aging population and the increasing burden of financing social pensions and healthcare systems further exposed structural fiscal balances. The crisis in the financial sector added an additional burden to the fiscus and the extent of bonuses received by executives raised the ire of taxpayers. Tax reforms, which are considered to meet these challenges, include a tax on financial transactions, shifting the tax structure towards taxes on property, consumption and environmental taxes and tax bonuses. Some of these reforms are short term but it is clear that public finances must be put on a sustainable path – governments need to finance the cost of the crisis and the increasing future cost of an aging population.

14.5.3 Globalisation and tax reform

Economic globalisation may be defined as the integration of economies throughout the world through trade, financial flows, the exchange of technology and information, and the movement of people (Ouattara,

1997: 107). It is a process whereby economic interdependence among nations has increased since World War II, and which gained particular momentum since the fall of the command economies in Eastern Europe towards the end of the 1980s.[4] This increasing interdependence has led to increasing competition and is reflected in cross-border economic integration between politically sovereign countries. In a globalised economy the policy measures of one country spill over into other countries. When the tax systems of the world came into being it was at a time when economies were by and large closed economies. Much of the economic activity was highly regulated and controlled and the tax policies of other countries could be disregarded.

Globalisation has altered the behaviour of economic actors in ways that required tax redesign. Firstly, cross-border shopping has increased in many regions in the world, including Southern Africa and Europe. This enables some countries to lower their excise taxes on high-value and easily transportable commodities to attract foreign consumers. In this way the tax base is extended to other countries and tax revenue is generated. Secondly, transfer pricing has resulted from the expansion of the multinational firm. Through transfer pricing, profits can be repatriated from high-tax jurisdictions to low-tax jurisdictions by over-invoicing imports and under-invoicing exports. Multinational enterprises are in the advantageous position of being able to minimise their global tax liability by shifting profits (through transfer pricing) from high-tax jurisdictions to low-tax jurisdictions. To entice multinational and other firms to locate in their countries, tax authorities compete by offering lower tax rates and other tax incentives. Thirdly, tax evasion and tax avoidance by individuals

became possible on a global scale as personal savings became more mobile. The proliferation of tax-haven areas or even countries and new financial market instruments have made it extremely difficult for tax authorities to monitor the non-reporting of personal income from savings invested.

How would globalisation impact on the future of tax systems? In his analysis of the globalisation phenomenon Tanzi (1996 and 2004) identified a number of possible trends. Globalisation tends to put pressure on developing countries to lower the level of taxation. As far as taxes on consumption are concerned, it is expected that as borders are effectively removed, countries that have high initial tax rates would be under pressure to reduce their rates in the face of competition. Such reductions would in particular affect excises on luxury products. The opening-up of economies requires that taxes on international trade be reduced or eliminated. International tax competition leads to reductions in marginal tax rates for personal income. In as much as taxation is a locational factor, tax competition will tend to drive down effective company tax rates. In an environment where multinational enterprises dominate it is even conceivable that income tax on profits may be replaced by another tax base such as a tax on net assets or gross assets. Due to the mobility of incomes from capital sources (e.g. interest and dividends), these sources could become taxed separately from wage income. This would enable tax authorities to either exempt these forms of income entirely or tax it using a separate schedule. Lastly, taxes on property will probably increase as the tax base is reasonably immobile.

The downward pressure on levels of taxation implies that developing countries have to increasingly rely on reforming personal income taxation and VAT. Personal income tax serves the purpose of raising revenue and ensuring that equity objectives are reached.

[4] The remarks made in this section are attributed to Tanzi (1996). For a more comprehensive discussion of the effects of globalisation on tax policy see Tanzi (1995).

Since it is mostly the high-income earners that benefit most from globalisation the personal income tax system is ideally suited to capture revenue from these income groups for redistributive purposes. At the same time, if the tax base is broad enough, tax rates need not be set that high. Value added tax should become the most productive source of revenue. Tanzi (2004) notes that it would be much better to have a low single rate on a broad base to generate sufficient revenue to deal with poverty and equity issues and the pressures of globalisation on spending. According to Keen and Mansour (2009: 38) most Sub-Saharan African countries have been successful in recovering much of the revenue losses due to trade liberalisation by implementing VAT systems in the 1990s.

14.5.4 International tax competition and tax harmonisation

Economic integration within some regions and between countries bordering each other has become more important in recent times. The economies of the European Union (EU) member states now form an integrated market. The same applies to the economies of bordering countries such as Canada and the United States of America (USA), and Mexico and the USA. In Southern Africa the economies of South Africa, Botswana, Lesotho, Swaziland, and Namibia (the BLSN countries) have been interlinked historically for many decades. The Southern African Customs Union (SACU) agreement between the BLSN countries aims to have goods interchanged freely between these countries. The Union provides for a common external tariff and excise tariff. All customs and excise collected in the common customs area are pooled and the revenue is shared among members according to a revenue-sharing formula. In the

BNLS countries, revenue from the common revenue pool (customs, excise and additional duties) is by far the most important source of revenue. In 2008/09 revenue from this source ranged from approximately 36 per cent (Namibia) to 63 per cent (Swaziland). The economies of South Africa and other Southern African countries such as Zimbabwe, Malawi, and Mozambique, as well as other African countries, are similarly interlinked through their membership of the Southern African Development Community (SADC). The aim of the SADC is to create a community providing for regional peace and security and an integrated regional economy. A number of Protocols have been signed promoting economic cooperation, planning, and assistance in areas such as trade, mining, tourism, and education. The SADC also provides the building blocks for the African Union (AU), which has the promotion of accelerated socio-economic integration of the continent as its vision.

Although each country remains an independent nation state with political autonomy, their economies have become much more integrated historically and by agreement. In such an integrated regional setting the monetary and exchange rate policies as well as the tax policies of these countries directly impact on each other. Added to the policy issues are the increased international mobility of consumers and factors of production such as capital and labour (e.g. professionals). The increased economic integration, coupled with mobility of factors of productions and consumers, have led governments to compete for investment capital and the purchasing power of neighbouring consumers by lowering tax rates. This may be welfare-reducing in that public services are under-provided. Others argue that tax competition is welfare-enhancing.

In this section we will approach the theory of **tax competition** and the need for **tax harmonisation** from the international tax perspective (i.e. we will consider competition between independent countries). The theoretical discourse also applies broadly to competition between independent governmental jurisdictions (or sub-national governments) such as local governments or federal states. The federal states perspective is provided in Chapter 17. In fact, the theory on tax competition has its roots in the local public finance (or fiscal federalism) literature.[5]

One of the earlier contributors to the debate was Oates (1972: 143) who noted that 'in an attempt to keep taxes low to attract business investment, local officials may hold spending below those levels for which marginal benefits equal marginal costs'. Put differently, there is a perception that high taxes on capital will drive mobile capital out of the country and even cause a lowering of wages, employment, and land rents. Governments then lower their public expenditure below efficient levels to reduce their dependence on tax. In addition, tax competition leads to 'fiscal externalities' or 'fiscal spillovers'. Some public services generate positive benefits for neighbouring countries, for example malaria control efforts. Countries engaging in tax competition would ignore these positive externalities when setting levels of public expenditure. These externalities also come in the form of negative costs, for example 'tax base externalities', which can be described as the result of a country lowering the tax rate on mobile capital to increase its welfare. The country gains the capital inflow but it is at the expense of another country in that their tax base is reduced and tax revenues decline. The same negative fiscal externality can be caused by a reduction in a commodity tax to attract cross-border shoppers. Other adverse effects of tax

competition include weaker environmental standards to attract investment and reductions in welfare payments by countries trying to make it unattractive for poor households to migrate or immigrate to their home countries. Another interesting negative outcome of tax competition between countries is that it may lead to 'market failure' in the provision of public goods and services. The argument is that government provides some goods and services when competitive private markets fail to do so, but when countries compete for the provision of such goods, governments might fail to provide the necessary public goods and services.

From an efficiency point of view, the potential adverse effects of tax competition suggest a role for tax rate harmonisation and also tax base harmonisation. That is, if all countries were to agree to raise their capital taxes or value added taxes simultaneously, to set minimum rates, or to unify tax bases, they would all benefit from increased levels of public expenditure. The welfare-enhancing effects of tax rate harmonisation can, in simple terms, be illustrated with the aid of Figure 14.1 (see Anderson 2003: 461). Assume two countries with identical demand curves and a world price given by P_w. The high-tax country sets its tax rate at (t_h) and the low-tax country at (t_l). The taxes create an excess burden in each country measured by ABC in the high-tax country and ADE in the low-tax country. By harmonising at a common rate equal to the average of the two rates, $0.5(t_l + t_h)$, the excess burden in the high-tax country is reduced by $BCFG$ and increased in the low-tax country by $GFED$. The net effect is a reduction of the global welfare loss (excess burden) equal to $BCFG$ minus $GFED$, implying a potential Pareto improvement under general conditions (e.g. assuming that tax revenues can be returned to consumers without additional distortions being created).

---

[5] For an excellent survey of theories of tax competition and formal models of tax competition, see Haufler (2001), as well as Zodrow (2003) and Wilson (1999). The discussion here is a summary of these surveys.

Tax harmonisation may however be unde-sirable, since tax competition may generate benefits that could offset the efficiency costs of the underprovision of public services.

In Chapter 17 the Tiebout model is dis-cussed. Modern formulations of this model argue that tax competition between local governments or states within a single nation will tend to limit overexpansion of the gov-ernment at the local level. A market-like solution to the efficient provision of public goods is reached due to the fact that local governments are closer to the people and therefore more accountable, and that indi-viduals tend to vote with their feet. This conclusion can be extended to the between-country situation. It is believed that tax competition is an important argument against tax harmonisation in unions such as the EU where labour is fairly mobile over national borders. Furthermore, when labour mobility and population economies of scale are considered together, the underprovision of public goods associated with tax competi-tion becomes even less of a problem. From a public choice perspective, we know that politicians and bureaucrats often attempt to maximise their self-interests and budgets, and it may thus follow that tax harmonisation benefits government officials. Tax competi-tion may curtail undesirable attempts at raising budgets.

The net effect of the positive and negative factors is very difficult to determine. Zodrow (2003) concludes that the argument for cor-porate tax rate harmonisation in the EU is not yet compelling. Economic models of the welfare costs of tax competition also suggest

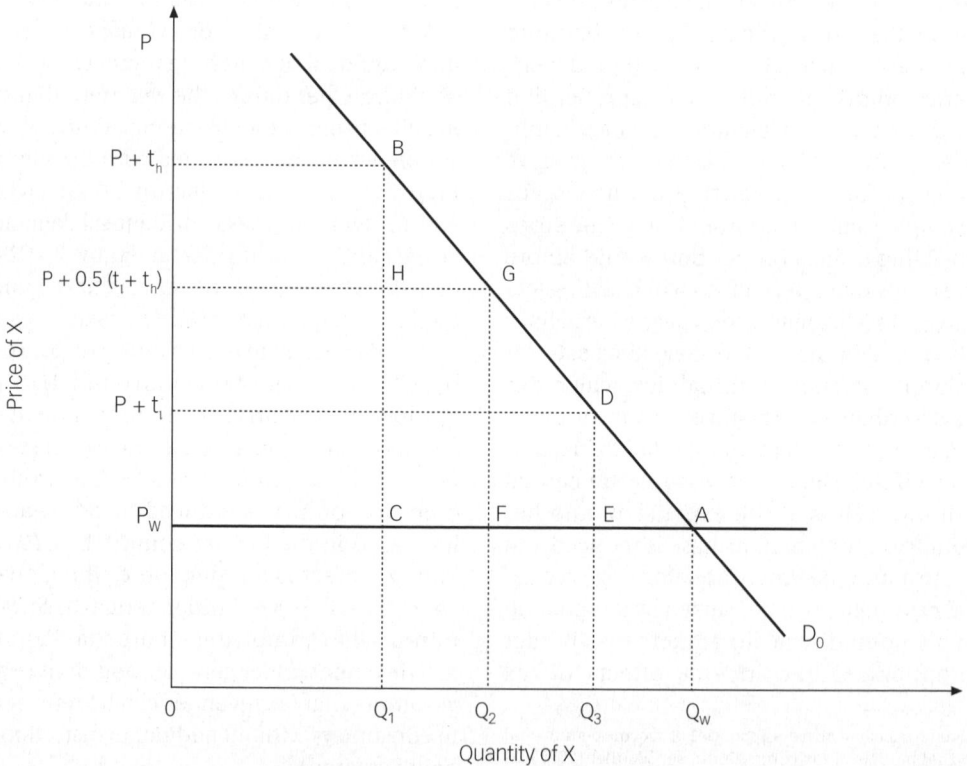

Figure 14.1 Efficiency gain from harmonising tax rates

that its costs may not be excessive. Zodrow suggests that a cautious approach to tax coordination (harmonisation) is appropriate. In designing or analysing tax regimes, tax autonomy must be traded off against tax efficiency and minimising tax administration. In this regard, Cnossen (2003) emphasises the importance of subsidiarity (or jurisdiction). Subsidiarity implies that the power to tax (or tax autonomy) rests with countries. With reference to the EU experience, Cnossen (2003) is of the opinion that all the proposals for VAT coordination require greater involvement of a central authority and thus a reduction in country autonomy and sovereignty.

We will gain a better understanding of the rationale for tax competition and tax harmonisation when we study certain basic principles of international taxation in later sections. These principles are the residence versus source principle (see income taxation in Chapter 12) and the destination versus origin principle (see value added tax in Section 14.3).

14.6 Tax reform in South Africa

Since the late 1960s South Africa has witnessed three government-appointed commissions of inquiry reporting on aspects of the tax structure: the Franzsen Commission (1968), the Margo Commission (1987), and the Katz Commission (1994 to 1999). The work of these commissions resulted in comprehensive reforms of the South African tax system. In addition to these comprehensive tax reforms, several major ad hoc tax reforms have also been introduced. Instrumental in these initiatives were the Standing Commission of Inquiry with regard to Taxation Policy of the Republic (Standing Tax Commission) and its successor, the Tax Advisory Committee (TAC), which was an advisory body to the Minister of Finance.

Presently the National Treasury organisational structure provides for a Tax Policy Unit which is responsible for advising the Minister of Finance on tax policy issues that arise at all three levels of government. In designing tax policy, the Unit cooperates with the South African Revenue Service (SARS) and interacts with the corporate sector and the general tax-paying public.

In the paragraphs below we highlight some of the main recommendations and reforms proposed by the different tax commissions.

The Franzsen Commission (1968) concluded in 1968 that the tax structure at that time was increasingly inhibiting economic growth. The focus of taxation was shifting from indirect to direct taxes and from direct taxes on companies to direct taxes on individuals. The Commission therefore believed that structural changes were required in the form of:

▶ reduced progression in direct taxes;
▶ a shift towards indirect taxes by broadening the base; and
▶ a broadening of the fiscal concept of income by including capital gains.

In its first report, the Commission consequently recommended that the maximum marginal income tax rate on individuals be reduced from 66 per cent to 60 per cent; that selective sales duties on a number of items (to be collected from manufacturers and importers) be introduced; and that capital gains tax of 20 per cent on net realised gains be introduced. With the exception of the recommendation in respect of capital gains tax, all the other proposals were accepted by government and duly implemented.

The next major tax reform occurred in 1978 when sales duties was replaced by a general sales tax (GST) at a rate of 4 per cent. The sales duties had inherent disadvantages (e.g. narrow base and high rates) and the major aim was to broaden the tax base and eliminate tax non-neutralities by introducing GST. GST was followed by the introduction of regional services councils levies in 1985. Of these levies that commenced in 1987, one on remuneration was paid to employees (0,25 per cent) and the other was paid on the turnover of enterprises (0,1 per cent).

The report of the Margo Commission (1987) was released in 1987. The Commission reported at a time when inflation was rampant, the business cycle was in an upswing, and foreign disinvestment was a threatening factor. The Commission took the view that tax reform should not be driven by short-term economic problems but rather by aspects of the existing tax structure that could hinder economic development. The Commission's general approach (1987: par 1.28) was founded in a base-broadening philosophy:

The ideal, both for direct and indirect imposts, is a broad-base, widely distributed, low-rate, high-yield tax, conforming to these other requirements (equity, neutrality, simplicity, certainty etc.) as far as possible.

Such a tax system would reduce the 'brain drain', encourage immigration, improve standards of tax morality and compliance, promote entrepreneurship and capital formation, and create job opportunities. The following are some of the major recommendations of the Commission that was accepted by government:

▶ the taxation of fringe benefits
▶ lower personal income tax rates with fewer brackets
▶ accepting the individual as the unit of taxation and phasing in marriage neutrality and the equal treatment of men and women
▶ the rejection of capital gains tax
▶ the scrapping of certain tax expenditures and allowances

▶ the modification of GST and the reduction of the rate; if the recommendation was not accepted, GST would be replaced by an invoice VAT system
▶ the imposition of a capital transfer tax to replace estate duty and donations tax.

Between 1987 and 1994 two of the most important tax reforms were the introduction of value added tax (VAT) and the lowering of the company tax rate (along with the introduction of the secondary tax on companies (STC)). Value added tax (VAT) was introduced in 1991 to eliminate the distorting effects of tax cascading inherent in GST and to reduce tax evasion. Initially the VAT rate was to be 12 per cent with very few exemptions and zero-rates. After much political lobbying by the trade union movement in particular, VAT was eventually introduced at 10 per cent with allowance for a number of zero-rated items. Secondary tax on companies (STC) was introduced in 1993. This was a tax on distributed profits, levied on firms. The aim was to encourage firms to reinvest their profits and thereby promote economic development. In a sense STC was also an astute way of reintroducing tax on dividends, since, in 1990, government had exempted the taxation of dividends.[6]

In 1994 the first interim report of the Katz Commission (1994) was released. It was supplemented by another nine reports between 1994 and 1999. The Commission conducted its investigations at a time when South Africa had just entered a new political and constitutional era. The major thrust of the first and third interim reports was to improve tax administration and collection and to reappraise the equity aspects of certain taxes.

---

[6] Some argued that, since dividends are paid out of after-tax income, it was previously double-taxed.

We have studied a number of taxes in the previous chapters. Tax reforms that were specific to these taxes were touched on and analysed. The following are some of the more important tax reforms introduced and proposed between 1994 and 2011:

▶ The status and independence of the revenue authorities were enhanced by the establishment of SARS as a separate department. Various changes and modernisation measures were introduced by SARS to improve tax collection and simplify tax administration and compliance. An electronic filing facility was introduced improving the quality of returns and timeliness.

▶ A general tax amnesty was introduced with a view to attract people into the tax system, such as the previously disenfranchised who challenged the equity of the tax system. A similar amnesty for small businesses was implemented in 2007 to broaden the tax base and increase tax compliance. This practice to improve compliance and to regularise the tax affairs of individuals and companies was again offered in 2010 under a Voluntary Disclosure Programme. Successful applicants are granted relief in terms of reduced interest and penalties. A foreign exchange control amnesty and accompanying tax treatment was introduced to encourage repatriation of illegally held assets abroad and to broaden the tax base.

▶ A single rate structure with six brackets for personal income tax was introduced.

▶ All gambling and fee-based financial services were subjected to VAT. Government proposed that gambling winnings above a threshold be subject to a final withholding tax.

▶ Interest, rental, and other trading income of the retirement fund industry became taxable but were abolished in 2007. Mandatory (tax) contributions to a national social security fund and incentives for additional savings to promote retirement savings were proposed.

▶ Capital gains became taxable.

▶ The source of income base was replaced by a residence-based income tax.

▶ The company tax rate was lowered for small businesses with turnover below a certain threshold. Furthermore, a turnover-based presumptive tax system was introduced as an elective system.

▶ Tax incentives to promote direct investment were introduced. Included is an accelerated depreciation allowance for investment in underdeveloped designated urban areas.

▶ Secondary tax on companies (STC) was phased out and replaced with a dividend tax on shareholders. The dividend tax will be enforced through a withholding tax at company level.

▶ Regional Services Council (RSC) levies and Joint Services Board levies were abolished.

▶ Various environmental charges and incentives were introduced in response to climate change. A carbon tax was proposed as an appropriate mechanism to reduce greenhouse gas emissions in South Africa.

▶ A national health insurance (NHI) scheme is to be phased in over the next few years (see Chapter 8). This will have a major funding impact and suggested options under consideration include a payroll tax payable by employers, an increase in the VAT rate and a surcharge on individuals' taxable income.

IMPORTANT CONCEPTS

base broadening (page 272)
customs duties (page 258)
economic globalisation
  (page 272)
excise duties (page 258)
exemption (page 265)
input tax (page 263)
multiple rates (page 264)

multi-stage commodity tax
  (page 258)
output tax (page 263)
personal consumption tax
  (page 266)
restricted-origin principle
  (page 262)
single-stage commodity tax
  (page 258)

sumptuary taxes (page 258)
tax competition (page 274)
tax harmonisation
  (page 274)
uniform rate (page 264)
value added tax (page 261)
zero-rating (page 265)

SELF-ASSESSMENT EXERCISES

14.1 Distinguish between the following indirect taxes:
  ▶ single-stage and multi-stage sales taxes
  ▶ excise tax and customs duty
  ▶ VAT and personal consumption tax.

14.2 Explain why the government should levy indirect taxes.

14.3 'Indirect taxes are not transparent enough and inhibit informed choices by taxpayers. The direct tax base should therefore be the major basis of government tax revenue.' Discuss this statement.

14.4 What are the characteristics of value added tax in South Africa? Why is it said that VAT is inequitable and what can be done to correct the inequity?

14.5 In designing VAT and other indirect taxes there is always a conflict between equity and efficiency. Do you agree? Explain your answer.

14.6 A uniform VAT rate is preferable to multiple rates. Discuss.

14.7 Personal consumption is a better tax base than income. Discuss

14.8 'Tax competition is preferred to tax harmonisation.' Discuss critically.

14.9 Evaluate tax reform in South Africa since the late 1960s in light of the patterns and directions of international tax reform.

PART

4

Fiscal and social policy

Chapter
FIFTEEN

Estian Calitz and Krige Siebrits

Fiscal policy

Fiscal policymaking and national budgeting are very complex tasks. Gerald Browne, Secretary of Finance in South Africa from 1960 to 1977, aptly describes the experience of the fiscal policymaker as follows:

> *Those who have not personally taken part in such an exercise [of budgeting] may find it difficult to appreciate the tremendous pressures for higher expenditure to which the Treasury is exposed – pressures applied, for the most part, with the best of motives and for expenditure on services of unquestioned merit. The Minister of Finance and his aides are condemned to fight a lonely and thankless battle for a cause that is seldom adequately understood.*
>
> Browne, 1983: 64

The aim of this chapter is to outline the nature of fiscal policy with reference to some of the theories and empirical observations discussed in earlier chapters. The chapter also discusses various aspects of fiscal policy in South Africa, and comments on aspects of the ongoing process of fiscal reform in sub-Saharan Africa.

Once you have studied this chapter, you should be able to:
▸ define fiscal policy and describe fiscal goals and instruments at the macroeconomic, sectoral and microeconomic levels
▸ discuss the evolution of views on the macroeconomic role of fiscal policy, focusing on the distinction between the Keynesian and structural approaches and the choice between discretionary and rules-based fiscal regimes

▶ distinguish between the various definitions of budget balance and explain the economic significance of each
▶ explain the importance of distinguishing between a cyclical and a structural budget deficit and between active and passive fiscal policy
▶ explain the fiscal consequences of the 2007–2009 international financial crisis and the ensuing Great Recession
▶ describe salient features of fiscal policy in South Africa with reference to theory, and against the backdrop of international experience and aspects of the performance of the South African economy
▶ describe some of the features of fiscal reform in sub-Saharan Africa in recent years.

15.1 Introduction

The decisions of government concerning the allocation and distribution of resources are embodied in its fiscal policies and reflected in its budgets. The term fiscal policy is normally used in relation to macroeconomic policy, and the contents of this chapter reflect that practice. Our discussion of the nature of fiscal policy (Section 15.2) nonetheless recognises microeconomic goals and instruments of fiscal policy as well. The reason why we do so is that fiscal policies aimed at achieving macroeconomic objectives seldom are sustainable unless they consider or map out the implications for resource allocation at the sectoral and micro levels as well. For example, if aggregate government expenditure has to be reduced to combat inflation and all spending programmes are simply cut in equal measure, the efficiency and equity consequences at the programme and project level of government can be profound. On the other hand, if the government yields to pressures for more government expenditure at the programme and project level without taking the consequences for the macroeconomy and the allocation of resources into account, it could have serious implications for inflation, balance of payments stability, and even long-term economic growth (which might jeopardise the perceived sustainability of fiscal policy). Fiscal policymaking and budgeting therefore constitute a juggling act of balancing 'unlimited' demands with limited resources. That, after all, is what economics is all about.

In this chapter we first explore the nature of fiscal policy, emphasising the South African experience and institutions that are in various respects similar to those in the rest of Africa. We will then discuss the evolution of views on the macroeconomic role of fiscal policy, with special attention to the worldwide shift during the last quarter of the previous century from active Keynesian anticyclical fiscal policies to what may be described as the structural approach to fiscal policymaking, as well as the apparent revival of Keynesian economics following the international financial crisis of 2007–2009 and the ensuing Great Recession. This is followed by a discussion of the choice between rules-based and discretionary fiscal regimes. Thereafter, salient aspects of fiscal policy in South Africa are outlined: the structure of the main budget, medium-term fiscal planning, the macroeconomic role of fiscal policy and the potential of fiscal rules in the South African context. The chapter ends with comments on the ongoing process of fiscal reform in sub-Saharan Africa.

15.2 The nature of fiscal policy

15.2.1 Definition

Fiscal policy may be defined as decisions by national government regarding the nature, level, and composition of government expenditure, taxation and borrowing, aimed at pursuing particular goals. Like all forms of economic policy, fiscal policy has both an active element (when a deliberate step is implemented to do something, e.g. to increase the budget deficit) and a passive element (when there is a deliberate decision to do nothing or to refrain from doing something, e.g. when no tax increases are announced in a particular budget).

15.2.2 Goals of fiscal policy

We distinguish the following **macroeconomic goals of fiscal policy**:
▶ economic growth
▶ job creation
▶ price stability
▶ balance of payments stability
▶ price stability
▶ a socially acceptable distribution of income
▶ poverty alleviation.

Note that this list contains none of the elements of the annual budget of the government, such as government functions, programmes and taxes. The reason for this is that these elements are not goals – they are the instruments that the government uses to pursue the above goals. Note also that price stability, balance of payments stability and cyclical economic growth are short-term goals; the others (including long-term economic growth) are of a longer-term or structural nature.

The **sectoral goals of fiscal policy** include the following:

▶ the development of particular economic sectors, such as agriculture, tourism, mining, manufacturing or the financial markets
▶ the pursuance of social goals pertaining to sectors such as housing, education, health and welfare (policies of this nature are often referred to as social policies – see Chapter 8).

It is also possible to specify **microeconomic goals of fiscal policy**. Such goals relate to fiscal action aimed at a single economic participant or group of participants. Normally they can be seen as sub-divisions of sectoral goals. The following are examples of microeconomic goals:
▶ Improving efficiency by addressing negative externalities in respect of a particular product (e.g. tobacco) or activity (e.g. toxic waste disposal by a chemical plant).
▶ Combating poverty (the equity consideration) by intervening in the market for a particular product (e.g. a bread subsidy).
▶ Pursuing goals with regard to a particular geographical area (suburban or rural), for example where government-financed infrastructure and housing subsidies for low-income earners are incorporated in a residential development project.

Fiscal policy is not the only tool for pursuing each of these sets of goals. Monetary policy, trade and industrial policy, competition policy and labour policy are important allies to achieve these goals. Quite often it is necessary to prioritise the goals and also to recognise that they are in conflict. For example, it may not always be advisable to stimulate economic growth further as doing so may fuel inflation. The government must then decide whether economic growth or price stability should receive the highest priority. In such circumstances we say that there is a trade-off between economic growth and inflation (a related example is the well-known Philips curve trade-off between inflation and unemployment). Fiscal policy differs, depending on whether the growth objective or price stability receives the highest priority.

Certain policies or policy instruments are more effective in pursuing some goals than others. An increase in interest rates (a monetary policy measure) may, for example, achieve quicker results than a tax increase (a fiscal policy measure) if private spending is to be reduced to combat inflation. The policy authorities must therefore not only decide on the priority of policy goals, but also choose the most effective policy instruments for the job at hand.

What happened to efficiency and equity, you might ask? Are they not the ultimate goals of economic policy? Have we not on numerous occasions emphasised these as the two pre-eminent considerations when assessing any fiscal action? In earlier chapters we have extensively studied various theories regarding public goods, government expenditure and taxation. Efficiency and equity were recurrent themes in all of these theories. We paid particular attention to the following:

▶ The conditions for Pareto efficiency in the allocation of resources between the supply of public and private goods and the equity implications (Chapters 2, 3 and 5).
▶ The extent to which different voting rules produce efficient outcomes (Chapter 6).
▶ Identifying those taxes that maximise efficiency (or minimise inefficiency) in the allocation of resources in the private sector and assessing the equity implications of different taxes (Chapters 10 and 11).
▶ The trade-offs between efficiency and equity that have to be considered when dealing with the issues of poverty and the distribution of income (Chapter 8).

In Chapter 16 we will pay attention to the choice between taxes and debt on the basis of efficiency criteria, while considering the inter- and intra-generational distributional consequences of debt financing.

The reason why we did not mention efficiency and equity before in this section is that they do not readily lend themselves to the specification of quantifiable targets at the macroeconomic level. Instead of equity, we therefore use more specific goals for which we can specify quantitative criteria, such as poverty alleviation or a socially acceptable distribution of income. The government may decide, for instance, on a programme to reduce the Gini coefficient (see Chapter 8, Section 8.1.1). Under certain conditions the promotion of economic growth and job creation will also serve the equity goal. Efficiency goals can be developed at the level of government programmes and the tax system can be designed with efficiency in mind, but it is not that easy at the macro level. In general terms, higher economic growth may be seen as a reflection of greater efficiency, but this is by no means obvious. Low inflation may also be a barometer of efficiency, just as high inflation might be indicative of a lack of it. The 'ultimate' goals of efficiency and equity are thus included (or subsumed) in the list of macroeconomic goals of fiscal policy.

15.2.3 Instruments of fiscal policy

As in the case of goals, we also distinguish between macro and micro instruments of fiscal policy. The macro instruments include total government expenditure, the economic categories of consumption and capital expenditure (i.e. the composition of government expenditure), the total tax amount, the budget deficit, as well as the way in which the deficit is financed. The sectoral or micro instruments include the various expenditure votes and programmes (e.g. education, health, and defence) and the concomitant criteria for the mobilisation and allocation of public and private resources; the different types of taxes and their rates; and the different dimensions of the public debt (such as maturity, ownership structure, etc.).

To form an idea of the many government activities that affect the allocation of resources in the economy, note that in 2010/11 no fewer than 201 government programmes were specified in the 37 **budgetary votes** in terms of which budgetary allocations were made in South Africa. These programmes cover a wide and divergent set of activities, ranging from food security and bio-security to disaster management; from state legal services to environmental quality and protection; from higher education to the promotion of mine safety and health; and from comprehensive social security to air defence. A total of 24 taxes or groups of taxes were identified. The economic impact of some of them is largely limited to a particular sector or a limited number of sectors of the economy (e.g. the excise tax on tobacco or the levy on plastic bags or the mining tax). Others, such as value added tax, the fuel tax, and income tax on individuals and companies, exert their influence throughout the economy, and changes in these taxes may therefore affect the macroeconomic performance of the country.

15.2.4 **The fiscal authorities in South Africa**

The key figure in fiscal policymaking is the Minister of Finance who is given certain statutory powers by acts of Parliament. He or she has the authority to levy taxes, allocate state income (tax and non-tax revenue), and borrow funds domestically and internationally. No state guarantees can be given to borrow money without the approval of the Minister of Finance. He or she is also responsible for the protection of the country's gold and foreign exchange reserves. On some matters the Minister has the authority to take and immediately implement decisions; these include changing the rates of value added tax,[1] excise duties or the fuel levy during the course of the government's financial year, or providing guarantees (at a cost) for foreign borrowing by parastatals such as Eskom and Transnet. On other matters, such as changing income tax rates or implementing the appropriation of state monies in the annual budget, parliamentary approval in the form of specific acts of parliament is required before any changes can be made. The Minister of Finance does not take important decisions without consulting and (or) obtaining the approval of Cabinet. He or she is accountable to Parliament for all decisions made.

The Minister is responsible for the coordination of macroeconomic policy and his or her statutory powers cover all the fiscal policy instruments of government expenditure, taxation, and borrowing. The South African Constitution furthermore requires consultation between the Minister of Finance and the South African Reserve Bank[2] regarding the implementation of monetary policy, the Bank's generic policy function. In practice, therefore, the Finance Minister is responsible for macroeconomic policy formulation and coordination, lays down the basic framework for monetary and exchange rate policy and manages fiscal policy.

The two key institutions that bear the responsibility for macroeconomic policymaking are the **National Treasury**[3] (macroeconomic and fiscal policy, expenditure allocation and control) and the South

---

[1] Section 77 of the Value Added Tax Act (Act 89 of 1991) authorises the Minister to make such adjustments, with the proviso that Parliament has to legislate this within six months after notification.

[2] For more information, visit the following website: http://www.resbank.co.za

[3] For more information, visit the following website: http://www.treasury.gov.za

African Reserve Bank (monetary and exchange rate policy). Another very important fiscal institution is the South African Revenue Service (SARS). The responsibilities of SARS not only include tax collection and the enforcement of tax law, as SARS also plays an important supportive and advisory role in the determination of tax policy. Close coordination between all these institutions is essential for effective economic policymaking.

There is an old saying that monetary policy begins in the Treasury. This signifies much more than the fact that public debt is financed by issuing government bonds, which constitute the main instrument of open-market policies by the central bank. It is a statement about the close links between fiscal and monetary policy in the pursuit of macroeconomic goals. The economic impact of fiscal and monetary policies is such that the fiscal and monetary authorities have to systematically study and regularly monitor the combined impact of these measures on economic behaviour. The fiscal policy menu that a particular country selects has to be framed in the context of a coherent macroeconomic policy strategy that includes monetary policy and a number of other policies (e.g. trade and competition policy). The implementation of such a strategy requires regular consultation and active coordination between the Minister of Finance and the Governor of the Reserve Bank and their respective staff. The issue of the coordination between the fiscal and monetary authorities will again feature in our discussion of public debt management (Chapter 16).

Another important form of coordination pertains to the formulation of tax policy, where close cooperation between the National Treasury and SARS is essential.

The final approval of the annual budget occurs by way of a law of Parliament, the watchdog of the public purse, thus giving effect to an important statement of fiscal policy at macro, sectoral and micro level.

Traditionally the South African Parliament only had the power to approve or reject the national budget in its entirety. One of the recent reforms in its role was in the form of the Money Bills Amendment Procedure and Related Matters Act (Republic of South Africa, 2009), which creates a procedure through which changes to appropriations may be considered in Parliament.

15.3 The macroeconomic role of fiscal policy

Mainstream views on the macroeconomic role of fiscal policy have changed significantly over time, reflecting the interaction between continuously evolving theoretical ideas and new policy challenges. This section first outlines the nature and shortcomings of the Keynesian approach to fiscal policy, which is known also as **fiscal activism** or **anti-cyclical fiscal policy**. We then discuss the structural view that largely superseded the Keynesian approach. The final part of the section points out that the cyclical effects of fiscal policy have recently come under renewed scrutiny, in that elements of the Keynesian or activist approach are complementing a revised structural approach to the macroeconomic role of fiscal policy.

15.3.1 The Keynesian approach

The **Keynesian approach** (also known as anti-cyclical fiscal policymaking) came to dominate fiscal policymaking after World War II. In the following three decades most governments saw it as part of their task to actively manage aggregate demand so that it equalled aggregate supply at the full employment level of income. Such manipulation of aggregate demand constitutes the active policy dimension of Keynesian fiscal policy. Keynesian economists and policymakers also believed that income taxes and unemployment benefits strengthen the demand-stabilising impact of active fiscal policy. The argument was that the income tax and unemployment benefits act as **automatic or built-in stabilisers**, because changes in income would automatically (or passively) trigger changes in tax revenue and transfer payments that would stabilise aggregate demand, income and output.[4] Given any set of statutory taxes and social security commitments, automatic stabilisers function much like rules in the sense of being nondiscretionary. In this section we explain the active and passive elements of Keynesian fiscal policy and then outline the shortcomings that caused it to fall out of favour from the 1970s onwards. In Section 15.4 we will say more about automatic stabilisers.

Figure 15.1 introduces an analytical apparatus that will feature at various points in this chapter.[5] The figure depicts government revenue and government expenditure as functions of national income (Y). The horizontal line G_0 represents government (or public) spending. We assume that the government sets its outlays annually; hence, public expenditure is not systematically related to the level of economic activity. (This assumption is realistic in the context of most developing countries, including South Africa, where unemployment benefit schemes are rudimentary or even non-existent. The governments of most industrial countries, however, maintain extensive unemployment benefit schemes. In such countries, the government expenditure line would slope downwards, because lower levels of income are associated with higher unemployment and, consequently, higher levels of government spending on unemployment benefits.) The government also sets tax rates, but the

---

[4] Section 10.4 in Chapter 10 introduced the notion of automatic stabilisers.

[5] This framework was adapted from El-Khouri (2002: 213–215).

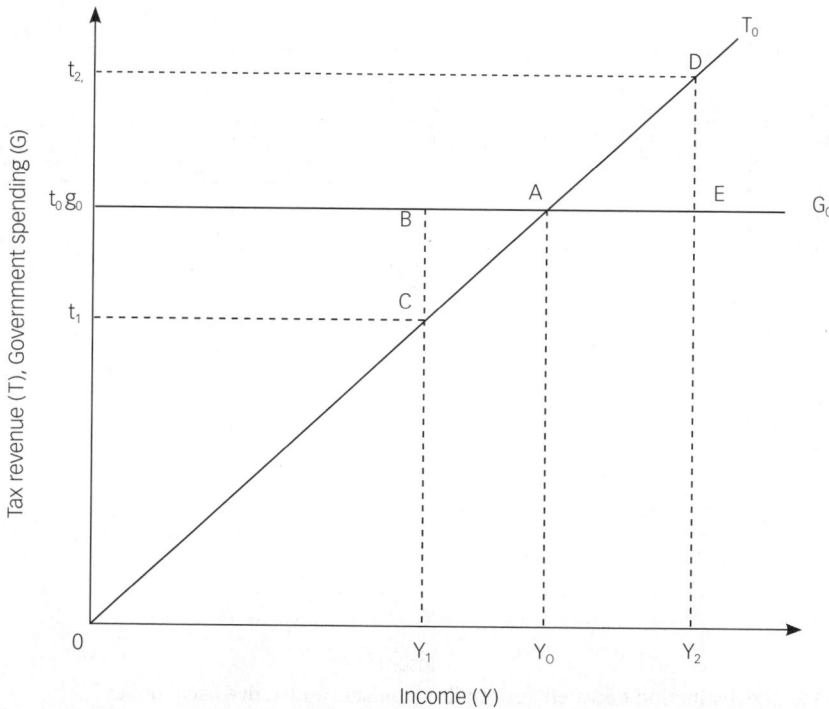

Figure 15.1 A framework for analysing Keynesian anti-cyclical fiscal policy

yields on the different taxes vary with the level of economic activity. Hence, the tax revenue curve (T_0) slopes upwards, because individuals pay more tax when income increases and vice versa. The positive relationship between income and tax revenues would be strengthened if some taxes have progressive rate structures (a common example is the personal income tax system – see Section 12.3.1 in Chapter 12). Figure 15.1 also shows examples of the three possible budget outcomes. At income level Y_0, the budget is in balance at point A, where tax revenue (t_0) equals government expenditure (g_0). Income level Y_1 yields a budget deficit equal to the distance BC; here, government spending (g_0) exceeds tax revenue (t_1). A budget surplus equal to distance DE occurs at income level Y_2, where tax revenue (t_2) exceeds government spending (g_0).

Figure 15.2 employs this framework to illustrate the distinction between active and passive fiscal policies. Our point of departure is point A at income level Y_0. The budget is in balance with tax revenue t_0 and government spending g_0. Suppose the economy in question experiences an exogenous shock (say, a decrease in export earnings) that reduces income to Y_1. This fall in income reduces total tax revenue to t_1 (point C on curve T_0). The drop in tax revenue cushions the impact of the adverse shock, because it represents a reduction in the extent of leakage from the circular flow of income and expenditure in the economy (see Section 1.2.3 in Chapter 1). The budget now exhibits a deficit (equal to g_0-t_1 or the vertical distance BC), which Keynesian economists traditionally regard as a stimulus to economic activity. Note that the government took no active steps. The stabilising influence and (or) countercyclical stimulus to economic activity are the entirely spontaneous results of structural aspects of the tax system – hence the

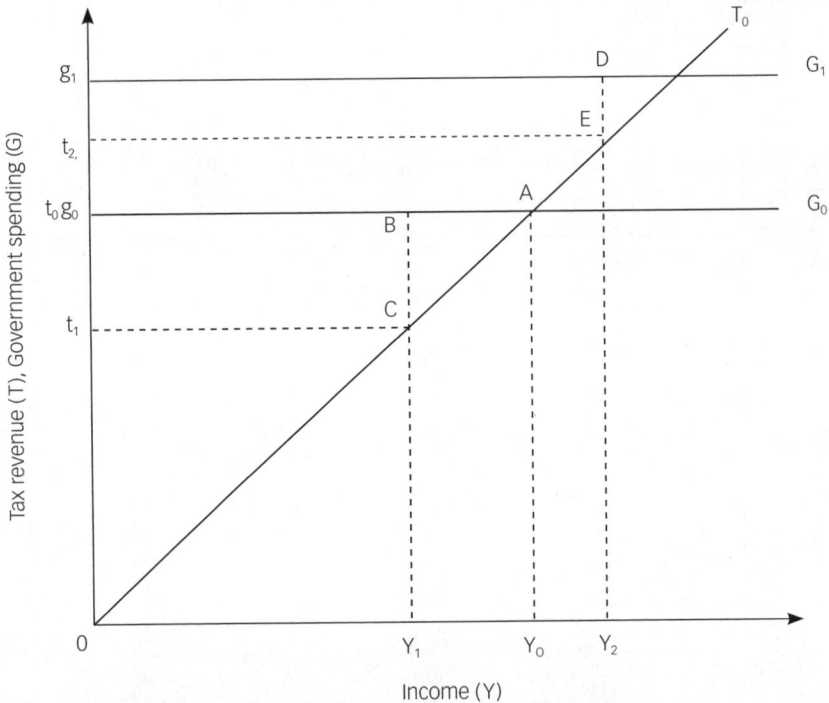

Figure 15.2 The distinction between automatic stabilisers and active fiscal policy

name 'automatic fiscal stabilisers'. The working of automatic fiscal stabilisers, or **passive fiscal policies**, is depicted as movements along the tax revenue and government spending curves. To illustrate **active fiscal policy** we return to point *A*. The government now increases its outlays, shifting the government spending line upward to G_1. Equilibrium income increases to Y_2, where tax revenue equals t_2 and government expenditure g_1. A budget deficit equal to g_1-t_2 (the vertical distance *DE*) has arisen. In contrast to the deficit depicted by the distance *BC*, however, deficit *DE* resulted from active manipulation of a fiscal policy instrument. Active fiscal policies are shown as shifts or rotations of the tax revenue and government spending curves.

As indicated, most Keynesian economists were optimistic about the ability of the automatic fiscal stabilisers to moderate cyclical fluctuations in economic activity. They agreed, however, that the stabilisers can only reduce such instability; they are not able to counteract it fully. Therefore active measures were the mainstay of the Keynesian approach to fiscal policy. In recessionary conditions,

policymakers tried to increase the budget deficit or change a budget surplus into a balanced budget or a budget deficit by increasing government expenditure (shifting the *G* line upwards) or by reducing taxes (shifting the *T* curve to the left or rotating the *T* curve in a northwesterly direction). They tried to do the opposite in situations where economies became overheated during an economic boom and experienced (rising) inflation, namely reduce government expenditure (shift the *G* line downwards) or increase taxes (shift the *T* curve to the right).

The most widely used barometer of the extent of anti-cyclical fiscal policy is the budget deficit. Box 15.1 contains an overview of different budget balances.

Practical efforts to expand or contract an economy by means of fiscal policy are subject to various limitations. These limitations can render fiscal policy largely ineffectual, and even cause it to produce perverse results by making fiscal policy pro-cyclical rather than counter-cyclical. In the next section we discuss the implications of these and other influences on the effectiveness of fiscal policy.

BOX 15.1 Different budget balances

Three concepts of the budget balance can be defined, each of which has a different use. In all three cases a negative balance signifies a deficit and a positive balance a surplus. Firstly, the **conventional balance** is equal to the difference between total revenue and total expenditure. **Total revenue** consists of tax and non-tax current revenue (the latter includes entrepreneurial and property income and administrative fees and charges), capital revenue (such as the sale of fixed capital assets), and other receipts (such as recoveries of loans and advances). All ad hoc income (such as privatisation income) is

treated as financing sources when the conventional balance is indicated. This balance is a measure of the total loan finance and other financing that the fiscal authorities require in a particular year. Calculations of budget balances normally rely on nominal amounts, which cannot be compared readily across countries or years. For this reason it is customary to express the budget balance as a ratio or percentage of nominal GDP (e.g. 2% of GDP). One should keep in mind when interpreting budget balances that:

▶ In most countries (including South Africa) the budget balance is not a comprehensive reflection of the borrowing requirement of the public sector as a whole, because public corporations and other extra-budgetary institutions are responsible for a significant portion of public sector loan financing. Many countries therefore also calculate and publish the **public sector borrowing requirement** (PSBR) as a more complete measure. The PSBR consists of the **net borrowing requirement** (i.e. after allowance for the refinancing of maturing debt) of the general government, extra-budgetary institutions, social security funds, and non-financial public enterprises. The non-financial public enterprises exclude institutions such as the Development Bank of Southern Africa (DBSA). As the DBSA lends to public institutions, we would be counting some borrowing requirements twice if the DBSA's requirements were also included.

▶ The state of the business cycle can significantly affect the extent of budget balances. During an economic downswing, government revenue (notably individual and company income tax) tends to be lower than the longer-term trend, while government expenditure tends to rise above the trend (especially if the country has a well-developed social security system). At the same time, nominal GDP (the denominator) is below the trend line. Hence, the budget deficit (in money terms and as a percentage of GDP) tends to be higher than its trend value. The opposite happens during an economic upswing. Analysts sometimes take the impact of the business cycle into account by calculating **cyclically adjusted budget balances**. We return to cyclically adjusted budget balances in Section 15.3.3 below.

Secondly, the **current balance** is the difference between total current revenue (tax and non-tax revenue) and total current expenditure (including interest payments). Calculations of the current balance therefore ignore capital revenue (e.g. income from the sale of non-financial assets) and capital expenditure (e.g. public outlays on the construction of dams, roads, schools, hospitals, etc.). The current balance is a measure of the extent of saving by government. A current surplus (a situation when the government's current revenue exceeds its current expenditure) implies that the government saves some of its current revenue by using it to finance capital expenditure. Conversely, a current deficit implies that the government dissaves: it has insufficient revenue to finance all of its current spending and has to borrow or sell assets to pay salaries and wages, interest on the public debt, etc. This is an example of what is sometimes described as 'selling the family silver to buy groceries'. As a rule, borrowing can be justified if it is used to finance capital expenditure, which should yield a return over a number of years. Borrowing to finance current expenditure cannot be justified on economic grounds, as it means that future generations will have to pay for the consumption enjoyed by the current generation. Moreover, government **dissaving** reduces the pool of savings that is available to finance capital formation in the economy. In the national accounts, gross saving consists of the consumption of fixed capital (formerly known as provision for depreciation) as well as saving by households, corporations and government. If the government dissaves, its contribution to gross saving is negative. The government sector then draws on the savings of the household and corporate sectors to finance current outlays that usually do not contribute to economic growth.

Lastly, the **primary balance** is calculated as the difference between total revenue and total non-interest expenditure. The primary balance should immediately be recognised as the conventional balance plus interest expenditure. This is a measure of the government's ability to service its debt (pay interest) through **ordinary revenue**. It measures the impact of the budget on the government's **net indebtedness**, that is, its liabilities net of assets. If the primary balance is positive (i.e. there is a **primary surplus**) and larger than the interest bill, government's ordinary revenue (which is predominantly tax income) is sufficient to pay all the interest on public debt and redeem at least part of its debt or finance some of the public investment. Net indebtedness (see Chapter 16, Section 16.2) is reduced. If the primary balance is positive (but smaller than the interest bill), a portion

of the interest bill is tax-financed. The rest is loan-financed (capitalised) and added to the public debt, thus increasing net indebtedness. If the primary balance is negative (i.e. there is a **primary deficit**), all of the interest and some of the current expenditure are loan-financed, thus adding to the public debt. In such a situation, government is borrowing to finance all its interest payments and some non-interest current expenditure. This would also increase the net indebtedness of the government. A negative primary balance is normally regarded as an unsound fiscal practice, particularly when it increases the risk of runaway public debt. A general rule of thumb is that a negative primary balance can be maintained for some time without an increase in the government's debt–GDP ratio, provided the real rate of economic growth is higher than the real rate of interest in the economy.

15.3.2 Shortcomings of anti-cyclical fiscal policy

As mentioned, the Keynesian approach to fiscal policy rose to prominence after World War II. Its heyday was comparatively short, however: its support waned steadily from the mid-1970s onwards and Martin Eichenbaum (1997: 236) summarised the opinions of mainstream macroeconomists at the end of the twentieth century as follows:

In sharp contrast to the views that prevailed in the early 1960s, there is now widespread agreement that countercyclical discretionary fiscal policy is neither desirable nor politically feasible. Practical debates about stabilisation policy revolve almost exclusively around monetary policy.

Why did fiscal activism fall from favour so dramatically? The answer to this question lies in several practical and theoretical developments in macroeconomics during the last third of the twentieth century and the first few years of the current century.

At least three sets of considerations made experts doubt whether it is possible to conduct anti-cyclical fiscal policy effectively. The first of these is that fiscal policymaking entails various stages, each with its own delays or time lags. There are four lags:

◗ The **recognition lag** is the delay between changes in economic activity and the recognition that the changes have occurred. It takes time to prepare and release economic data such as the national accounts (which provide information on economic growth and the state of the economy in general). In South Africa this data is published every three months in the Quarterly Bulletin of the South African Reserve Bank. When the annual budget of the South African government is presented in February every year, the latest available GDP figures are estimates based on figures from the end of the third quarter of the previous year. If, for example, the Minister of Finance wants to present a budget to stimulate economic growth, a significant margin of error is possible, since official information about the performance of the economy is lagging by six months.

- The **decision lag** refers to the time that elapses between the recognition of the problem and the decision on how to react. Various factors play a role in this regard, such as the analysis of various options, the time required for discussion between officials and ministers and, eventually, the speed with which Cabinet takes a decision. The South African constitution places a high premium on consultation and various consultative forums exist for this purpose, such as the National Economic Development and Labour Council (Nedlac) and the statutory Budget Council and Budget Forum (bodies of consultation with provinces and local government, respectively). These forums and various consultative processes, such as the public hearings of the parliamentary committees, may all contribute to the decision lag. These lags are particularly evident when legislation is required. The national budget, for example, is presented in February, but cannot be implemented before Parliament has enacted it. In South Africa this normally happens more or less during June of each year, that is, about three months after the start of the fiscal year. The government therefore has a standing legislative authority to spend funds

provisionally until the budget is approved by parliament. This includes provisions that enable the government to make limited changes during the course of the year when urgent matters arise. Such matters would otherwise have to stand over until the next year.

- The **implementation lag** refers to the period after the decision has been taken but before it is implemented. This lag arises mostly from procedures of orderly and accountable government. An example is the time it takes for government departments to implement approved capital expenditure programmes. The time lag between the approval of a capital project such as a national road and its opening for traffic is quite long. Administrative procedures in the private sector also influence the implementation lag. Changing the VAT rate, for example, requires adjustments to financial documentation, cash registers, and other automated business machines in the private sector. The fiscal authorities have to allow time for such adjustments before they can implement rate changes. Internet trade, on the other hand, reduces the implementation lag in the sense that transaction conditions and documentation can be adjusted and communicated much quicker.

- The **impact lag** refers to the period before an implemented policy measure begins to affect economic behaviour. An increase in income tax, for instance, can take quite some time to realise its full impact on private expenditure. Taxpayers may not immediately behave as though their after-tax spending power has dropped. They may reduce personal savings, for instance, in an attempt to maintain their living standard for some time. Another example of an impact lag arises when businesses delay price increases because of higher taxes to reap some temporary competitive benefits. On the expenditure side of the budget, certain programmes (e.g. welfare payments) have a much shorter impact lag than others (e.g. infrastructural projects). In the latter case the time lag may be quite long, for example when transport or defence equipment are ordered with long delivery lags.

These lags make it particularly difficult for fiscal policymakers to react to fluctuations in economic activity in time. If the economy is overheating, for example, it could take so long to implement a tax increase that a recession has already superseded the upswing by the time that the intended dampening of demand takes effect, by which time a stimulus would be more appropriate. Intended counter-cyclical fiscal policy then becomes pro-cyclical in the sense that it deepens and prolongs (rather than smoothes out) cyclical fluctuations in economic activity. Pro-cyclical fiscal outcomes were common in industrial and developing countries during the era of fiscal activism. And in South Africa Strydom (1987), for example, found that the structure of the public finances had a destabilising rather than a stabilising effect on the economy from 1960 to 1986. More recently, Du Plessis, Smit and Sturzenegger (2007) also found evidence of fiscal pro-cyclicality for the period 1994–2006, as did Thornton (2008) with regard to government consumption expenditure in 37 low-income countries between 1960 and 2004. In general, the decision and implementation lags are normally shorter in the case of monetary policy. This served to increase monetary policy's 'comparative advantage' over fiscal policy as far as macroeconomic stabilisation policy is concerned.

Monetarists emphasise a second constraint to the effectiveness of anti-cyclical fiscal policy: the possibility that an expansionary fiscal policy will push up interest rates and in this way crowd out private expenditure. Such **crowding-out** neutralises anti-cyclical fiscal policy measures by dampening the **multiplier** effect of a fiscal policy stimulus (see Chapter 16, Section 16.3.5). Monetarist analysis of fiscal policy also emphasises the effects of different ways of financing budget deficits. They are particularly concerned about the extent to which the government finances its spending by means of money creation, which fuels inflation (see Chapter 10, Section 10.1).

Macroeconomists from the new classical school raise a third objection to Keynesian fiscal policies. They argue that private agents would anticipate systematic counter-cyclical policies and respond to them in ways that neutralise their intended effects. The Ricardian equivalence theorem, which states that it is immaterial whether governments use tax or debt finance, is a well-known example of such thinking (see also Chapter 16, Section 16.3.4). In brief, the argument goes as follows. Government borrowing to finance budget deficits must be repaid in future from tax revenue. Rational economic actors realise that government borrowing now means a higher tax burden for them (or for their children) in future. They therefore would respond to any increase in loan-financed government spending by reducing their consumption spending and increasing their saving by equivalent amounts, thus ensuring that they can meet their future tax obligations. Such behaviour would mean that tax financing has exactly the same impact on the level of aggregate demand as deficit financing, which implies that the fiscal authorities cannot manipulate demand by varying the level of the budget deficit. The empirical validity of the Ricardian equivalence theorem is still being debated, but the possibility that countervailing behaviour by private agents has at times contributed to the disappointing outcomes of attempted anti-cyclical fiscal policies cannot be dismissed summarily.

Political constraints on anti-cyclical fiscal policy

In addition to the above sets of considerations that limit the practical effectiveness of anti-cyclical fiscal policy, a second reason why fiscal activism fell from favour was growing evidence that governments tend to be unwilling to implement such policies consistently (quite apart from their ability to do so). Considerations of political popularity make most governments far more inclined to adopt **expansionary policies** (increases in public spending and, at times, tax cuts) during recessions than to impose the short-term hardships associated with **contractionary policies** (tax increases and spending cuts) in economies facing the danger of overheating. Economists from the public choice school emphasise that this asymmetric approach to fiscal stabilisation contributed to the sharp growth in government spending in the second half of the twentieth century. One time-series study (Tanzi and Schuknecht, 1997) found that general government expenditure in the industrial countries increased from levels of 10 per cent of GDP or less in 1870 to between 45 and 50 per cent in 1994. More recently, South Africa showed a similar though less dramatic trend, with the ratio increasing from an average of 18,9 per cent (1960–1969) to 22,9 per cent (2005–2009) (see Table 1.1, Chapter 1).

Anti-cyclical fiscal policy and structural economic problems

The joint appearance of unemployment and inflation (i.e. **stagflation**) after the oil price shocks of 1973 also sharply dented the popularity of Keynesian anti-cyclical fiscal policy. Economists soon realised that the economic problems of the time were structural rather than cyclical in nature, and that short-term demand management measures are ineffective for solving structural problems such as supply shocks, structural unemployment and cost-push inflation.

15.3.3 The structural approach to fiscal policy

Taken together, these considerations gave rise to a strong perception that active anti-cyclical fiscal policy is ineffective at stabilising the economy, perhaps to the point of causing more instead of less volatility. **Supply-side economists**, however, advocated a particular brand of fiscal policy as a cure for stagflation. Members of this school of thought believe that the public sectors of most countries are too large and that the concomitant increases in tax burdens and tax rates are major disincentives to work effort, saving, investment and economic growth. They therefore recommend a reduction in marginal tax rates (to increase the incentive to work, save and invest)[6] and a concomitant reduction in government spending (to create more scope for private sector activity). 'Supply-side' has now become a catch-all word for all and any policy measure proffering to move the economy closer to its production possibility frontier or expanding the frontier.

In a sense, the supply-siders were part of the mind shift that took place from the mid-1970s onwards. The attention of fiscal policymakers shifted away from stabilisation policy – in the traditional Keynesian sense of attempts to 'fine-tune' the level of economic activity – to structural measures aimed at increasing the growth and job

---

[6] Recall our discussion of the impact which a selective tax on labour income may have on work effort (see Chapter 12, Section 12.4.1), and the Laffer hypothesis that there may be cases whereby a tax rate reduction could increase government revenue (see Chapter 12, Section 12.4.3).

creation capacity of the economy and the redistributive impact of the budget. This shift received further impetus from the development of unsustainable fiscal imbalances (excessive budget deficits and public debt burdens) in many industrial and developing countries during the 1980s and early 1990s, and generally dominated fiscal policy thinking until the international financial crisis of 2007–2009. For many policymakers, reducing these imbalances became a more pressing objective than using fiscal policy for cyclical stabilisation purposes, although – as some scholars have pointed out – signs of active fiscal policy could already be observed early on in the first decade of the twenty-first century.[7]

Key aspects of what could be described as the **structural approach to fiscal policy** include the following:

▶ Keeping the public debt (and the burden of servicing it) at a sustainable level by avoiding high budget deficits or reducing it to acceptable levels (such as was required after the dramatic surge in deficits and public debt levels as a result of the 2007–2009 international financial crisis)

▶ Keeping the overall tax burden at a level that does not seriously prejudice incentives to work, save and invest

▶ Keeping government spending in check to avoid crowding-out of private activity, inflationary financing, and the cost-push and disincentive effects of an excessive tax burden.

One of the major outcomes of the widespread acceptance of the structural approach to fiscal policy has been that more and more countries are adopting rules-based fiscal regimes in place of the discretionary regimes that characterised the Keynesian era. We discuss this trend in more detail in Section 15.4. Another outcome was that references to fiscal policy virtually disappeared from macroeconomic policy debates worldwide for almost two decades (recall the statement of Martin Eichenbaum quoted earlier).

A good example of how the focus in fiscal policy analysis has changed is the contrasting reasons why adherents of the Keynesian approach and the structural approach regard the extent of the budget balance as important. During the heyday of Keynesian anti-cyclical fiscal policy economists watched the budget balance closely as an indication of whether the short-run impact of fiscal policy on aggregate demand is expansionary or contractionary. The structural approach puts more emphasis on what the budget balance suggests about the current and future sustainability of fiscal policy and how the financing of budget deficits is likely to influence the economy. This leaves room for passive anti-cyclical fiscal policy to the extent that automatic stabilisers are effective.

There are several ways to finance a budget deficit. One option is to borrow from the central bank, which amounts to the government using its overdraft facilities. This type of financing increases the money supply and is potentially inflationary. Governments should therefore avoid it as far as possible. Another undesirable option is to run down the country's foreign reserves. Unless a country has an exceptionally large stock of reserves, financing the budget deficit in this manner would soon deplete them and cause a foreign exchange crisis. Most governments finance their deficits by borrowing from the domestic and international capital markets. In countries with well-developed financial systems (such as South Africa), governments borrow from the capital markets by issuing bonds (government stock) on which it has to pay interest. Such borrowing therefore

---

[7] Auerbach (2010) demonstrates this for the United States.

increases the public debt,[8] the sustainability of which also has become an important criterion for judging the soundness of fiscal policy and macroeconomic management in general. In practice, it is very difficult to determine the sustainability of the public debt: doing so requires an assessment of whether or not it is and will remain at levels that the particular country can repay and service. Economists often use a non-increasing (i.e. a decreasing or constant) public debt-to-GDP ratio as a benchmark to distinguish between sustainable and unsustainable fiscal policy (Chalk and Hemming, 2000: 3).

Apart from the possibility that it can become unsustainable (i.e. that the government would have to default on its debt obligations), a large public debt also has other undesirable effects. For one thing, government borrowing places a burden on future generations who have to pay the interest and repay the debt. Such intergenerational redistribution is especially problematic when the government uses the borrowed funds to finance current expenditure that only benefits the current generation. Another disadvantage of a large public debt is the associated interest burden that, for a given level of public expenditure, leaves the government with less money to use for productive purposes.

15.3.4 Renewed interest in active fiscal policy

Even before the international financial crisis of 2007–2009 and the ensuing Great Recession, there were clear signs that policymakers were showing greater interest in the cyclical effects of fiscal policy than had been the case only a few years previously. This development should not be interpreted as a fully-fledged return to fiscal activism of the traditional Keynesian variety. At the time of writing,

leading economists were still grappling with a full understanding of the causes and consequences of the global financial crisis and the appropriate macroeconomic and regulatory response. Nonetheless, a strong body of economists still maintain that, except maybe in most extreme situations, monetary policy is a better tool for stabilisation purposes than fiscal policy and that activist fiscal policies generally should be avoided. One is reminded of the view of a well-known Keynesian economist Alan Blinder (2006: 54):

Under normal circumstances, monetary policy is a far better candidate for the stabilisation job than fiscal policy. It should therefore take first chair. That said, however, there will be occasional abnormal circumstances in which monetary policy can use a little help, or maybe a lot, in stimulating the economy – such as when recessions are extremely long and (or) extremely deep, when nominal interest rates approach zero, or when significant weakness in aggregate demand arises abruptly. To be prepared for such contingencies, it makes sense to keep one or more fiscal policy vehicles tuned up and parked in the garage, and perhaps even to adopt institutional structures that make it easier to pull them out and take them for a spin when needed.

There are two reasons for the tentative comeback of fiscal policy in discussions of macroeconomic stabilisation. First, automatic fiscal stabilisers often become destabilising when inflation is high. In many countries lower inflation rates have now rejuvenated the working of the automatic fiscal stabilisers, thus restoring to fiscal policymakers a tool for influencing economic activity that is not subject to some of the shortcomings of activist policies. Second, the decisions to bail out certain financial institutions when financial markets in

---

[8] Chapter 16 provides a more detailed discussion of various aspects of the public debt and its management.

various countries were at perceived risk of systemic failure in 2007 and 2008, together with the ineffectiveness of monetary policy to counter the severe recessionary effects when interest rates approached the zero bound, seemingly left many governments with little choice but to fall back on fiscal measures. Depending on the condition of countries' public finances prior to the crisis, the scope for active fiscal policies varied. On the whole, however, the approach to the macroeconomic role of fiscal policy clearly shifted – at least temporarily – towards Keynesian anti-cyclical fiscal policy.

Appropriate indicators are needed to determine whether the fiscal policy stance complements or undermines the actions of the monetary authorities. We introduced the cyclically adjusted budget deficit in Box 15.1, and now discuss it in more detail with the aid of Figure 15.3 to show how countries have begun to use cyclically adjusted (or

structural) budget balances in assessing and designing fiscal policy.

The set-up of Figure 15.3 is similar to that of Figures 15.1 and 15.2: it also depicts government tax revenue and government spending as functions of income (Y). As before, the total tax revenue curve (T) slopes upwards and the government spending curve (G) has been drawn as a horizontal line. The economy experiences full employment when income is Y_F. At this level of income tax revenue and government spending are t_0 and g_0 respectively. The associated budget deficit (distance AB) is not distorted by the effects that any particular state of the business cycle may have on the levels of government revenue or expenditure. As such, it represents the 'underlying' budget balance that results from the tax structure and level of government spending at the full-employment, potential or trend-line level of income. This benchmark level of the budget balance is

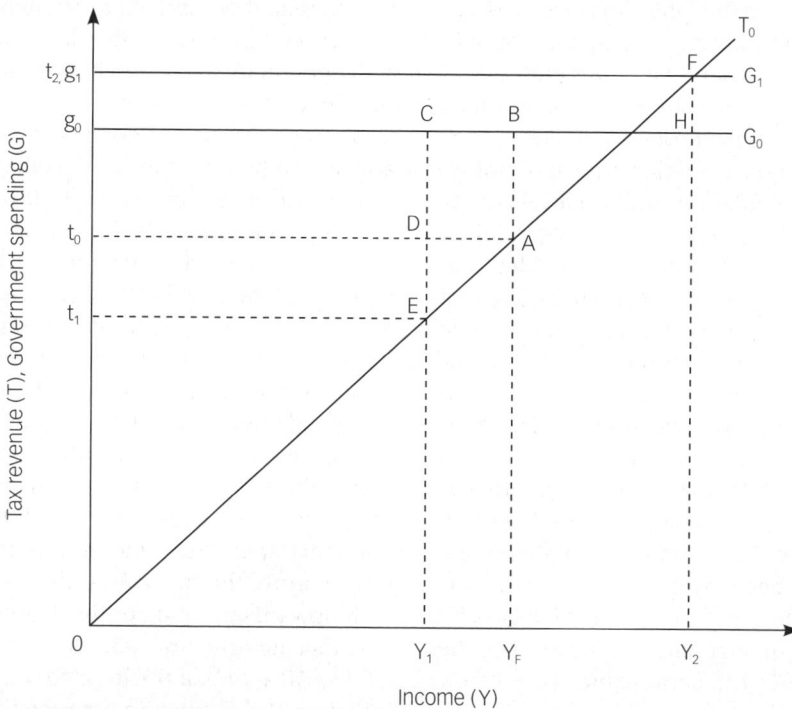

Figure 15.3 Structural and cyclical budget balances

known as the **structural budget balance**, the **full-employment income budget balance**, the **potential-income budget balance**, the **trend-line budget balance** or the **cyclically-adjusted budget balance**.

The calculation of structural budget balances is easier said than done. Whereas the conventional budget balance is usually expressed as a percentage of the estimated or actual gross domestic product, the structural budget balance is expressed as a percentage of the potential output of the economy or the full-employment level of income. Potential output and the full-employment level of income cannot be measured accurately. They can only be estimated using techniques that remain controversial. This explains why Vito Tanzi (2005: 9) once referred to cyclically-adjusted budget balances as 'counterfactual variables' and 'virtual variables'. Structural budget balances nonetheless are very useful indicators, because they enable policymakers to assess the extent and impact of observed budget balances in a dynamic manner and, therefore, more accurately. Consider, for example, the situation at income level Y_1 in Figure 15.3. The economy is well below the full-employment level of income, and the levels of tax revenue t_1 and g_0 result in a budget deficit depicted by the distance *CE*. Provided that they have a reasonably accurate estimate of potential output, policymakers would be able to distinguish between the structural component of this deficit (distance *CD*, which equals distance *AB*) and its cyclical component (distance *DE*). Given the assumption in our example that government spending is not sensitive to the state of the business cycle, the cyclical component of the deficit can be ascribed fully to a revenue effect. Tax revenue is lower than what it is likely to be at the full-employment income level by the distance $DE (=t_1 t_0)$ because income is below the full-employment level.

Hence, structural budget balances enable policymakers to distinguish between the permanent and transitory components of observed budget balances. This distinction can help policymakers to avoid errors, a typical example of which is taking long-lasting decisions on taxes and expenditures based on transitory movements in revenues. The situation at income level Y_2 illustrates this possibility. Here tax revenue is t_2 and government spending g_0, yielding a budget surplus equal to the distance *FH*. Many governments (supported by interest groups) would interpret the emergence of a budget surplus as an indication that they can and should increase public spending, for example to help the poor or to expand the country's physical infrastructure. Increases in public spending, however, are seldom easily reversible: once appointed, public servants cannot be retrenched at will, and newly created assets (such as schools and hospitals) have running expenses and require maintenance. Policymakers therefore should ensure that sufficient financing would be available on a sustained basis before expanding public outlays. Here the observed budget surplus appears to be a temporary (cyclical) phenomenon: income is well above the full-employment level (by the distance $Y_2 Y_F$) and this raised tax revenue from t_0 to t_2. What Figure 15.3 tells us is that income should eventually revert to the full-employment level Y_F, with a concomitant fall in tax revenue to t_0 and the re-emergence of the structural budget deficit. In fact, the budget surplus may be the very deflating factor that moves the economy back to Y_F. If, however, the government uses the windfall revenue to finance spending programmes of a long-term nature, the horizontal line G_0 would shift upwards to G_1 to cut the T-function at F, so that the structural deficit increases from *AB* to $(AB + FH)$, a position that may fuel inflation. The distinction between the cyclical and structural budget balances therefore could help policymakers to avoid the ratchet effects that many economists blame for persistent budget deficits and secular increases in government spending levels.

15.4 The fiscal consequences of the Great Recession – new fiscal activism in practice

The 2007–2009 international financial crisis caused the biggest economic slump since the Great Depression of 1929–1933. Due to the interconnectedness of financial markets and innovative financial instruments a crisis in the US subprime housing market was rapidly transmitted internationally and caused deep recessions in advanced and developing economies. The fallibility of financial markets and governments was exposed and invoked a serious debate about the rationale for and appropriateness of fiscal rescue plans and a thorough rethinking on and redesign of financial regulation followed.

We now demonstrate the fiscal consequences of the international financial crisis, using the same graphs as in Figures 15.1–15.3, but with a few different symbols. In Figure 15.4 G_0 is the initial government expenditure line (with the spending level indicated as g_0 on the vertical axis), determined through the political process and independent of income (Y). The upward sloping tax line T_0 reflects tax revenue as a positive function of income. We start by supposing a country with a structural budget deficit AB at its trend or cyclically adjusted level of output, Y_{sd}, which we measure as AB or the distance between g_0 and t_{sd} on the vertical axis, ignoring for the moment whether or not there also is a cyclical imbalance. (Y_{sd} corresponds to Y_F in Figure 15.3, but we use

the subscript *sd* instead to emphasise the initial **s**tructural budget **d**eficit.) This was the typical position of a number of OECD and developing countries prior to the international financial crisis.[9] The financial crisis is an exogenous shock which causes a deep economic recession that reduces the income level to Y_1, associated with a bigger budget deficit CE (or the distance between g_0 and t_1 on the vertical axis). A Keynesian liquidity trap develops and monetary policy becomes ineffective due to the lower interest-rate bound (interest rates fall to zero or near zero). The government, in fulfilling a 'rescuer of last resort' function, with all the associated moral hazards, decides to bail out financial institutions to avoid a total collapse of the financial sector, as well as certain manufacturing companies. Assistance is varied and includes loans, shareholding, guarantees and outright nationalisation. Some, but not necessarily all, of these measures stimulate or arrest the fall in aggregate demand. These rescue actions obviously occur at the cost of a higher budget deficit, which is further increased by active fiscal policies to further stimulate aggregate demand. These higher deficits are partly, if not entirely, financed through money creation.

What made the choice of fiscal measures so problematic was the uncertainty about the nature and depth of the crisis (every now and again news surfaced of firms and governments in trouble, dragging out the sense of crisis and the recessionary experience), the likely duration of the economic downswing, the reaction time to and strength of different stimulatory measures and the difficult trade-off between short-term fiscal stimulation (with the associated higher deficit and debt levels) and longer-term fiscal sustainability (associated with lower deficits and debt levels). Very quickly the importance of effective

[9] In 2001 the combined structural fiscal balance of the major advanced economies, relative to their combined GDP, was -2,1% (International Monetary Fund, 2010: 191).

international coordination of measures became evident, not only within the European Union where fiscal coordination was an imperative for supranational economic stability and the perpetuation of the economic union, but also further afield. In their consideration of the requirements of an optimal fiscal policy package, Spilimbergo et al. (2008: 2) concluded that the measures should be: timely, because the need for action was immediate; large, because the current and expected decrease in private demand was exceptionally large; lasting because the downturn would last for some time; diversified because of the unusual degree of uncertainty associated with any single measure; contingent, because the need to reduce the perceived probability of another 'Great Depression' required a commitment to do more, if needed; collective, since each country that had fiscal space should contribute; and sustainable, so as not to lead to a debt explosion and adverse reactions of financial markets. They then argued that spending increases, and targeted tax cuts and transfers, were likely to have the highest multipliers. General tax cuts or subsidies, either for consumers or for firms, were likely to have lower multipliers. In reality, different countries applied different measures. Countries like India, Indonesia and Mexico applied mostly tax reductions. The US, Australia, Korea, France and Russia made use of a mix of tax and expenditure measures. The UK, Canada, Germany and Turkey mostly resorted to expenditure measures. Countries like Greece, Portugal and Ireland had no room for stimulatory measures and had to rely on bailout support from other countries and the International Monetary Fund, in addition to harsh measures of fiscal restraint.

In Figure 15.4 we show the impact of these active fiscal policies with an upward shift in the government expenditure line, from G_0 to

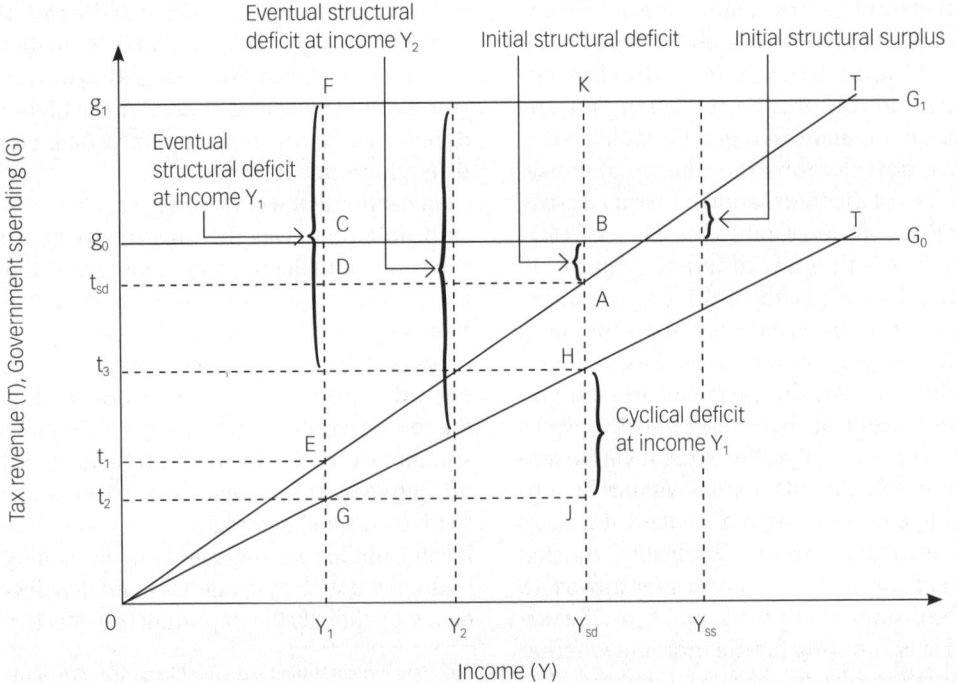

Figure 15.4 The fiscal implications of the 2007–2009 international financial crisis

the after-crisis line G_1 (measured on the vertical axis by g_1) and a downward rotation of T_0 to T_1, signifying a reduction in the average tax propensity (or the average tax burden).[10] The combined result is a new budget deficit FG at Y_1 (measured as the distance between g_1 and t_2 on the vertical axis). An important fiscal policy question is what the structural and cyclical components of the deficit are. We find the answer by asking what would happen to the deficit if the level of income were to return to the cyclically adjusted (trend or potential) level of output, Y_{sd}. The key to the answer lies in what the impact of the automatic stabilisers in the economy would be. Recent empirical evidence indicates that this effect is stronger in the low-inflation world of the past ten to twenty years than was thought to be the case earlier (see for example Debrun and Kapoor, 2010: 5). Because we have assumed that government expenditure is exogenous to the economy and independent of income, we only have to ask what would happen to tax revenue if income were to increase from Y_1 towards Y_{sd}. Note that the impact of the automatic stabilisers is now represented by a movement *along* the *new* (after crisis) tax curve T_1. If the output level were to return to Y_{sd}, the budget deficit will be reduced by the automatic stabilisers (passive fiscal policy) to the tune of HJ (i.e. the distance between t_3 and t_2 on the vertical axis). Note that the fiscal expansion on the expenditure and tax sides of the budget results in a higher structural deficit at Y_{sd} than before the crisis, namely $HK (>AB)$. It is precisely these higher structural budget deficits that were so controversial and caused major policy debates in most of the industrial countries of the world. Figure 15.4 shows that the structural deficit (which we always measure at the

cyclically-adjusted or trend level of output) is significantly bigger than the cyclical deficit, i.e. $HK>HJ$. This is a true reflection of the actual situation as shown in Figure 15.5 for a number of OECD countries in respect of 2010 and South Africa (2009/10). South Africa's position, by comparison, was much less disconcerting than that of some of the major economies.

One aspect of this debate was about the speed with which economic recovery should be pursued with fiscal activism. A huge fiscal stimulus (as witnessed in countries such as the USA[11] and the UK) would result in high public debt, imposing a huge debt service burden on future generations. A conservative fiscal approach might not generate as speedy a recovery, but would put fiscal sustainability less at risk. We will return to this point when we consider the impact of these developments on the regimes of fiscal rules which were in operation in most of the OECD countries. What added to misgivings about the effectiveness of active fiscal policies, is that consumers appeared to respond to some of the measures (for instance in the USA) by replenishing lost savings, rather than increasing consumption – in other words, behaviour resembling Ricardian equivalence (see Chapter 16, Section 16.3.4), rather than generating Keynesian increases in aggregate demand. Another complication was that a number of smaller countries (e.g. Greece and Ireland) exhibited fiscal unsustainability and had to be bailed out by the International Monetary Fund and the European Central Bank. The accompanying conditions entailed major fiscal austerity measures, cutting short the period of active fiscal policies and dampening the strength of the economic recovery. One of the major steps to reduce the structural deficit, was the raising of the retirement age in European

---

[10] Although the average tax burden was reduced in various countries, the distributional effect was to give more tax relief in the lower- and middle-income range, such as in the US.

[11] Blinder and Zandi (2010) reported that in the US close to $1 trillion, roughly 7 per cent of GDP, would be spent on fiscal stimulus.

countries. Although the retirement benefits of the welfare states of Europe varied, they had for a long time in general been regarded as increasingly unaffordable and unsustainable, although very hard to change. The grim realities of the Great Recession and the cost to taxpayers of the bailout and the active fiscal measures seemed to have made it politically feasible to increase the retirement age, that is, the age at which people become entitled to the benefits of the welfare state. This had the effect of reducing future fiscal commitments and social security costs, which were socio-politically easier to digest than a future cut in benefits or an increase in taxes.

Figure 15.4 enables us to demonstrate two further developments in the aftermath of the Great Recession. The first is the British experience, where the rising debt-to-GDP and deficit-to-GDP ratios resulted from a sharp decline in potential GDP during the crisis,

in addition to the fiscal response to the crisis. The financial and business services sector is very large in the United Kingdom compared with most other developed countries, therefore the impact of the financial crisis on potential output was more severe. This can be demonstrated by a leftward shift of the British trend (or cyclically adjusted) level of output. Let us assume the new level of British potential or trend output is Y_2 instead of Y_{sd}. As indicated by the curled brackets in Figure 15.4 this results in a bigger structural deficit than for countries whose trend output remains at Y_{sd}.

The other example is the position of countries that had budget surpluses before the crisis, like Germany, Chile and South Africa. Their position may be illustrated by assuming a country with an initial structural fiscal surplus at income level Y_{ss}, as shown by the curled brackets near the top of the dotted Y_{ss} line. What should be clear from

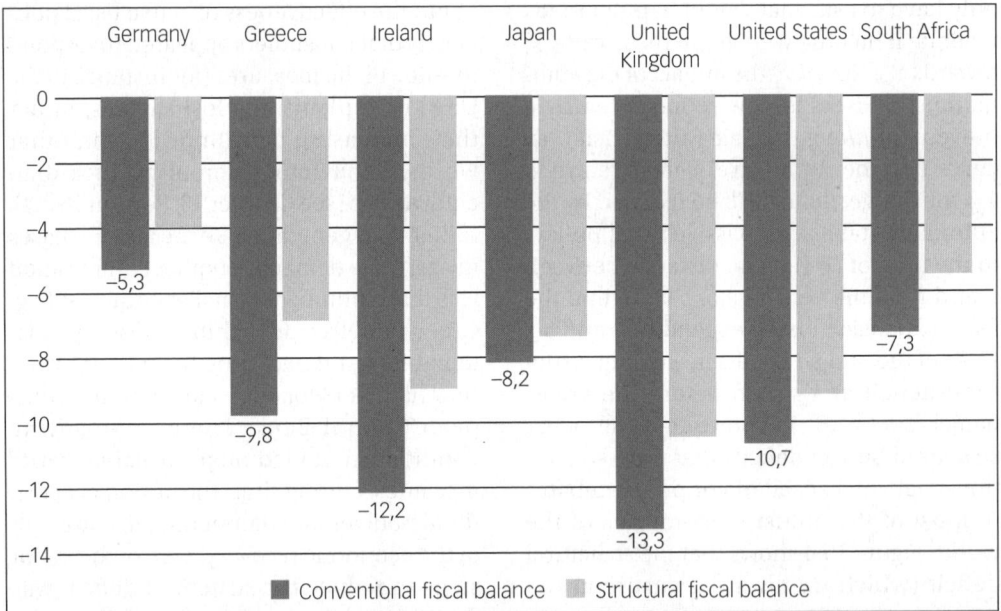

Figure 15.5 Conventional and structural fiscal deficits as a percentage of GDP, selected OECD countries and South Africa 2009/10
Source: International Monetary Fund (2010: 191) and National Treasury (2010: 64).

the picture is that such countries enjoyed much more scope for active fiscal stimulation than those countries who already had (high) structural deficits. The surplus countries (and also low-deficit countries) not only encountered a less severe recession but were also able to generate quicker economic recoveries. This was also experienced by many developing countries that had been applying prudent fiscal policies. Time will tell whether the resort to fiscal activism was an exceptional clutch at a rescue straw. If so, we are bound to see the structural approach to fiscal policy return to main stage. Traditional Keynesianism then becomes a tool that is put to use only when a major shock leaves policymakers with no real alternative.

15.5 Discretion versus rules in fiscal policy[12]

Kopits and Symansky (1998: 2) define a **fiscal rule** as '... a permanent restraint on fiscal policy, typically defined in terms of an indicator of overall fiscal performance'. We mentioned in Section 15.3.3 that a growing number of countries have been adopting such rules of late. The majority of industrial countries now use fiscal rules, and rules are growing in popularity in Latin America and elsewhere in the developing world. The most popular numerical rules are as follows:

▶ **Expenditure-limiting rules** cap the level of or growth in total government expenditure or specific categories of government spending. Such rules are in force in Argentina, Brazil, Canada, Peru, Sweden and the United States, among others.
▶ **Current-balance rules** stipulate that current government spending should

not exceed current government revenue or, what amounts to the same thing, that governments may not borrow to finance current expenditure. This so-called 'golden rule' of fiscal policy applies in Brazil and the United Kingdom.
▶ **Overall-balance rules** limit the extent of the budget deficit or prescribe budget surpluses. Rules of this nature apply in countries such as Argentina, Chile, India and Peru, as well as in the European Union.
▶ **Public debt rules** prohibit borrowing from certain sources (typically the central bank) or limit the extent of the public debt. The countries of the CFA franc zone in West Africa as well as the European Union, India, Indonesia and the United Kingdom use such rules.

The remainder of this section discusses the choice between discretionary and rules-based fiscal regimes in general terms. Section 15.6.4 explores the question of whether or not South Africa should adopt numerical fiscal rules.

15.5.1 Rules as binding constraints

Keynesian macroeconomics emphasised the sluggishness of market adjustment to shocks and the stabilising properties of active anti-cyclical fiscal policies (see Section 15.3.1). The dominant view during the heyday of Keynesian macroeconomics was that rules-constrained policymakers cannot pursue activist policies effectively. Discretion therefore was the norm in fiscal policymaking from the end of World War II until the mid-1970s. The failure of activist fiscal policies was interpreted widely as clear proof of the deficiency of **discretionary policy** regimes. Hence, one of the reasons for the growing popularity of fiscal rules is the belief that rules can prevent the

---
[12] This section draws on Siebrits and Calitz (2004).

problems associated with activist policies and improve the effectiveness of fiscal policymaking by making it very difficult (if not impossible) for the authorities to stray from sound policies. In this view, fiscal rules essentially have a negative purpose, namely to prevent policymakers (who allegedly cannot be trusted to do the right thing) from lapsing into fiscal profligacy.

The strongest argument against this view is that fiscal rules cannot bind policymakers to maintain fiscal discipline. There are two main reasons why governments find it relatively easy to circumvent, ignore, suspend or abandon fiscal rules: all rules are subject to sovereign political authority, and policymakers have only limited control over fiscal outcomes. As indicated above, numerical fiscal rules typically establish upper limits for the ratios of key fiscal aggregates to GDP (e.g. budget balances and the level of public debt). The values of such ratios are strongly affected by factors beyond the immediate control of governments, including GDP shocks (which impact upon the denominator and the tax revenue component of the numerator) and restrictions on the scope for changing the level of government spending in the short run.

15.5.2 **Rules as credibility-enhancing commitment devices**

Theoretical developments in macroeconomics have suggested a second reason why countries should adopt policy rules. The argument follows from the widespread adoption in modern macroeconomics of the **rational expectations hypothesis** for which Robert Lucas received the Nobel prize for economic sciences in 1995. This hypothesis states that all agents make optimal use of the information at their disposal by taking into consideration past, current and the expected future states of their environment – including anticipated economic policies – when they take decisions. If agents really are forward looking decision makers as the hypothesis states, announced policies affect their behaviour in the manner desired by policymakers only if such policies are deemed credible, that is, if the agents believe that policymakers will implement them fully.

Such thinking raises the following question: how can policymakers credibly commit themselves to policies in order to make them effective (that is, to ensure that they influence the behaviour of rational private agents in the desired manner)? Proponents of fiscal rules argue that the adoption of such rules represent a credible commitment to sound policies that should lessen or solve the credibility problem. Consider an example: to encourage investment, governments would like to reassure prospective investors that they would not resort to unsound fiscal practices that lead to high inflation and financial crises (e.g. running excessive budget deficits and financing them by borrowing from the central bank). The argument is that the adoption of a current-balance rule or an overall-balance rule would be an ideal mechanism to signal commitment to fiscal discipline, thus fostering investment and economic growth. This argument for fiscal rules differs from the one outlined in Section 15.5.1. The premise in Section 15.5.1 is that governments are inclined to stray from prudent fiscal policies and therefore should be constrained by rules. In what we have been discussing now, the government is fully committed to maintaining fiscal discipline, but requires a mechanism to convince rational private actors of its resolve.

In practice, whether or not the adoption of rules will make announced fiscal policies credible is likely to depend on the agents' view of the extent to which such rules can effectively 'bind' policymakers. Section

15.5.1 pointed out that rules generally are not very effective constraining mechanisms.[13] Hence, one could argue that the rational economic agents postulated by modern macroeconomic theory would recognise the fragility of rules and not regard rules-based commitments as credible. Critics have raised two other arguments against the adoption of fiscal rules as credibility-enhancing commitment devices as well.

▶ Rules may force governments to adopt ultra-conservative forecasting and budgeting techniques that result in excessively contractionary fiscal outcomes, or to undertake undesirable forms of tax increases and expenditure cuts. Unlike governments operating in discretionary fiscal regimes, rules-bound governments have little choice but to respond actively to small or transitory increases in budget deficits or public indebtedness caused by negative GDP shocks, for example. If they do not react to such shocks, their own credibility and that of the rules-based regime could come under threat. Yet the same policy lags that caused problems for active fiscal policies aimed at stabilising the business cycle will also cause problems for active fiscal policies aimed at complying with fiscal rules (see Section 15.2.3). Moreover, it tends to be very difficult to change the fiscal stance between budgets or reduce government spending significantly in the short term. The scope for doing so depends on factors such as legislative restrictions on the scope for changing tax rates and the contractual nature of major outlays such as compensation of employees, interest on public debt, procurement programmes and certain subsidies and transfer payments. Experience has shown that governments typically respond to shocks that threaten compliance with rules by using measures that are likely to provoke little political resistance, instead of those that are most appropriate from an economic point of view. For example, they often reduce growth-promoting capital spending programmes while maintaining subsidies to loss-making public enterprises.

▶ Numerical fiscal rules prescribe upper limits for the levels of aggregates such as the budget deficit, tax burden, government expenditure and public indebtedness, usually as percentages of GDP. While it may make sense to set such limits as short- or medium-term policy targets to redress fiscal imbalances, neither economic theory nor experience provides a basis for adopting them for long periods that transcend business cycles and structural economic changes. The optimal levels of fiscal aggregates – especially indicators of the size of the public sector – differ from country to country and from period to period during any specific country's development. It is both impossible and inappropriate to try to fix them by means of numerical fiscal rules.

Governments that are serious about using numerical rules as a device to signal their commitment to fiscal discipline are therefore likely to find that rules complicate the management of the economy in the short and long term.

15.5.3 Accountability-enhancing transparency

Fiscal transparency means being open to the public about the structure and functions of government, fiscal-policy intentions, the

---

[13] It could be argued that, in the context of a regional bloc (such as the European Union) fiscal rules could also be credibility-enhancing and 'incentive-driven' devices, reflections of the commitment to economic integration.

public-sector accounts, and fiscal projections (Kopits and Craig, 1988). Advocates of transparency argue that it improves fiscal policymaking by making the fiscal authorities more accountable. Some fiscal policy experts believe that **transparency-enhancing reforms** are more effective mechanisms to make fiscal policies credible than adopting fiscal rules.

Australia, New Zealand and the United Kingdom pioneered the adoption of transparency-enhancing measures aimed at making fiscal policymakers more accountable. The fiscal frameworks of these countries do not prescribe specified numerical targets, but require the fiscal authorities to disclose their fiscal objectives regularly. These objectives may or may not take the form of quantitative targets.

Transparency-based frameworks are more flexible than rules, but less flexible than discretionary ones. The extent to which transparency-based frameworks constrain policymakers depends on their specification and interpretation (for example, whether or not they are complemented by numerical targets). As far as the short-term and long-term management of economies is concerned, the greater flexibility of transparency-based regimes gives them a major advantage over rules-based regimes (especially to policymakers who are strongly committed to prudent fiscal policies and who therefore do not need binding by rules).

Another advantage of transparency-based regimes over rules-based ones is their superior ability to strengthen the effectiveness of market discipline over fiscal policymakers. 'Market discipline' refers to the phenomenon that the financial markets restrain the de facto independence of fiscal policymakers: the markets quickly 'punish' fiscal laxness by suspending lending, withdrawing capital and increasing risk premiums on borrowed funds. On the whole, the influence of market discipline on fiscal policymaking is benign but there is the danger that governments could become excessively concerned with gaining or maintaining the confidence of markets, and allow the short-term oriented preferences of market participants to bias their macroeconomic policy decisions. The problem with rules-based regimes is that they emphasise a small number of summary indicators of fiscal policy, and in this way foster the tendency of market participants to judge fiscal policy on a too narrow basis. Transparency-based regimes, on the other hand, can strengthen the effectiveness of market discipline by ensuring that the bigger picture receives due emphasis.

15.5.4 An overall assessment of fiscal rules versus discretion

The argument that the adoption of fiscal rules would enhance the credibility of policies cannot be dismissed out of hand. Adopting rules may well be useful, for example, when a new government without a record of accomplishment wishes to signal its commitment to sound fiscal policies. The potential benefits of adopting fiscal rules, however, should always be weighed against the potential drawbacks. Moreover, it should always be remembered that the ultimate determinant of fiscal outcomes is not the existence of rules (or, for that matter, any other institutional framework), but the strength of a government's commitment to fiscal discipline. Fiscal rules cannot substitute for government commitment in the sense that the mere existence of rules cannot prevent irresponsible policies.

The fiscal response to the international financial crisis of 2007–2009 did not entail a strict application of fiscal rules. In 2009, for example, none of the major member countries of the European Union recorded a fiscal deficit for general government within the

Maastricht fiscal rule of three per cent of GDP.[14] This transgression is clearly seen in Figure 15.4. Even if fiscal rules did not allow for an escape clause, the crisis was de facto managed as if there were an escape clause. Apparently, fiscal rules work better in periods of moderate instability, however defined. Fiscal rules, however, at least seemed to retain their value as points of fiscal responsibility to which countries should return by implementing medium-term fiscal consolidation measures, albeit within time frames varying greatly across countries.

There is a sense in which rules and discretion meet each other. Discretion with increased transparency and accountability (and the underlying institutional reforms to correct for destabilising incentives on the side of policymakers) amounts to constrained flexibility. Rules with escape clauses or rules specifying medium-term boundaries, or constraints to be met over the course of the business cycle, amount to flexible constraints.

A fairly recent institutional development complementing rules and adding to transparency has been the establishment of **fiscal councils**. A fiscal council typically consists of a group of independent experts with designated responsibilities to analyse and comment publicly on fiscal policy. Three types have been identified:[15]

▶ The first type is to provide an objective analysis of current fiscal developments, their macroeconomic context (such as the cyclical position of the economy), long-term sustainability considerations and the costing of budgetary initiatives. Examples are the US Congressional Budget Office (CBO), Japan's Fiscal System Council, Korea's National Assembly Budget Office and Mexico's Center for the Study of Public Finances.

▶ A second group is expected to produce independent projections and forecasts regarding both the budgetary variables as well as the relevant macroeconomic variables, such as is undertaken by the panels of independent experts in Canada and Chile.

▶ The third type is entrusted with the additional mandate to provide normative assessments (for example Belgium's High Council of Finance, Denmark's Economic Council and Sweden's Fiscal Policy Council). These estimates include, for example, an independent view on the appropriateness of fiscal policy in a given macroeconomic environment, or a recommendation of a particular fiscal stance for a given year within a medium-term framework previously defined through the political process. While theory and practice seem to suggest that fiscal councils can enhance the quality of fiscal policy, their effectiveness, just like with fiscal rules, ultimately rests on a societal consensus and on government's commitment to the mandate assigned to them.

15.6 Fiscal policy in South Africa

This section highlights and briefly discusses key features of fiscal policy in South Africa. The first two parts outline institutional aspects of fiscal policymaking in South Africa, namely the structure of the national budget and medium-term expenditure planning.

---

[14] For example, the following fiscal balances for general government were recorded in 2009: Germany (-3,0%), France (-7,6%), and the UK (-11,0%). Other EU countries with huge deficits (fiscal balances in brackets) were Greece (-13,7%), Ireland (-14,2%) and Spain (-11,1%). The US deficit was 11,3%. See International Monetary Fund (2010: 191.)

[15] The rest of this paragraph uses the classification and information by Debrun and Kapoor (2009: 61–62 and 66–70).

Section 15.6.3 discusses the evolution of the macroeconomic (stabilisation) role of fiscal policy in South Africa. We focus mainly on the period since 1990, but refer to longer-term trends and developments where appropriate. Section 15.6.4 explores the potential of fiscal rules in the South African context.

15.6.1 **The national budget**

The presentation of the annual budget of the national government is the major event on the fiscal calendar. It enables the Minister of Finance to present a systematic and comprehensive overview of the state of the public finances in a macroeconomic context and to motivate the expenditure, revenue (tax), and loan financing proposals of the government for the next fiscal year to the electorate and their political representatives in parliament. Although the budget always includes announcements of new decisions, it is largely a collection of fiscal decisions taken over a long period. The management of the finances of government is a continuous process of decision-making. Its annual culmination in the presentation of the budget merely provides an opportunity to present all the decisions coherently in a single set of documents.

In South Africa the presentation of the national budget normally takes place during the second half of February. The Minister of Finance then reads the **Budget Speech** in Parliament and tables a number of documents along with the speech. These include the **Budget Review** (which extensively covers macroeconomic and fiscal issues relevant to the budget and contains a wealth of fiscal information), as well as the proposed expenditure allocations and the revenue estimates for the next fiscal year, which runs from 1 April to 31 March.

Table 15.1, which contains a summary of the 2011/12 Budget together with the revised figures for 2010/11, shows the major components of the main budget. Note that this table consists of four parts: expenditure, revenue, borrowing requirement, and financing.

▶ The first part contains the expenditure estimates (heading 1). Item 1.1 represents the printed estimate of main budget expenditure. The provision for the **contingency reserve** is also stated separately (item 1.2). This amount is not allocated at the time of the budget, but acts as a cushion to finance unavoidable and unforeseen expenditures that may arise in the course of the year. If such additional allocations can be limited to the amount of the contingency reserve, the government will be able to meet them without exceeding the budget. Item 1.3 shows the total expenditure amount that has to be financed.

▶ The next section deals with revenue (heading 2). The first entry (item 2.1) is an estimate of the revenue that the South African Revenue Service would be likely to collect in the next fiscal year if all tax rates were to remain the same as in the previous year. This revenue estimate results from applying the previous year's tax rates to the projected value of the tax base of the current year. Item 2.2 indicates the net revenue increase or loss due to new tax proposals. In other words, this item represents the expected revenue increases from increases in tax rates, minus the expected revenue losses due to rate reductions. Item 2.3 provides the total budgeted revenue for the financial year.

▶ The third section deals with borrowing (heading 3). The difference between expenditure and revenue is the main budget deficit (item 3.1), which is expressed in item 3.2 as a percentage of GDP. From the different definitions of the budget balance or deficit explained

Table 15.1 Summary of the 2011/12 National Budget

Budget item	2010/11 Budget Revised Estimate (Rbn)	2010/11 Budget (Rbn)	Change 2010/11– 2011/12 (%)
1 EXPENDITURE			
1.1 Printed estimate		884,8	
1.2 **Plus** contingency reserve		4,1	
1.3 Total expenditure	**809.9**	**888,9**	**9,8**
2 REVENUE			
2.1 Estimate of revenue (existing rates)		734,0	
2.2 **Plus** proposals		-4,1	
2.3 Total revenue	**666,6**	**729,9**	**9,2**
3 BORROWING REQUIREMENT			
3.1 Main budget balance	-143,3	159,1	
3.2 Budget deficit as % of GDP ·	-5,4	-5,5	
3.3 **Plus** extraordinary payments	-0,8	-0.2	
3.4 Less extraordinary receipts	3,1	1,4	
3.5 Net borrowing requirement	**141,0**	**157,9**	
4 FINANCING			
4.1 Domestic short-term loans (net)	35,1	22,0	
4.2 Domestic long-term loans (net)	139,2	135,4	
4.3 Foreign loans (net)	-2,3	5,0	
4.4 Change in cash and other balancesa	-31,0	-4,5	
4.5 Total financing (net)	**141,0**	**157,9**	

Note: A negative sign signifies an increase in cash balances.
Source: National Treasury, *Budget Review 2011* (2011: 198–199).

in Box 15.1 it should be obvious that the deficit in Table 15.1 is the conventional budget deficit. By adding extraordinary transfers that occur from time to time (item 3.3) and subtracting proceeds from the sale of state assets (item 3.4) we calculate the net borrowing requirement, which indicates the amount of new loan finance that the government will require during the fiscal year (item 3.5).

▶ The last section contains the financing plan (heading 4). This indicates how much of the total net financing (i.e. financing after subtraction of loan redemptions) (item 4.5) will be contributed by short-term loans (treasury bills) (item 4.1), long-term domestic loans (government stock) (item 4.2), foreign loans (item 4.3) and changes in the Government's cash balances (item 4.4). In Chapter 16 we discuss the considerations behind these financing decisions of government.

15.6.2 Medium-term fiscal planning

In November 1997 South Africa entered a new phase of fiscal planning with the publication of the first **Medium Term Budget Policy Statement** (MTBPS) (Department of Finance, 1997). This enabled the presentation of the annual budget in the context of a medium-term policy framework.

Various countries have practiced **multi-year fiscal or expenditure planning** over the past 40 years. Various concepts are used, ranging from multi-year budgets to medium-term fiscal plans, strategies or frameworks, expenditure plans, and so on. An essential distinction is made between a **multi-year budget** (which signifies a formal, statutory, multi-year appropriation of funds) and a **multi-year plan** (a statement of intent, which serves as a reference framework or road map for the annual budget). South Africa's MTBPS is a multi-year plan; the budget is a legislated one-year appropriation of funds.

Over the years, governments in countries covering the whole range of economic systems have experienced the need for multi-year fiscal practices, albeit for different reasons. Multi-year economic plans were key policy instruments in centrally planned economies, but they have all but disappeared during the transformation of the Eastern European economies. In market-oriented economies the need for multi-year fiscal practices arose from macroeconomic, sectoral or microeconomic considerations.

From a macroeconomic point of view, the need for multi-year fiscal practices derived from the realisation that the problems of low economic growth and high and persistent unemployment and inflation that were experienced by developed and developing countries required structural economic reform. A multi-year fiscal plan was seen as an essential component of a medium-term economic or financial restructuring and development strategy. Inflationary environments, increasing international mobility of capital and strong expenditure demands in newly democratised countries all added to the risk of fiscal instability. The increasing complexity of the economic and fiscal scene and the multi-year nature of objectives strengthened the case for longer-term fiscal planning. Ironically this complexity tended to limit the usefulness of such planning. Some countries (e.g. Canada and the UK) have therefore reverted to less ambitious planning exercises over the years. Public investment expenditure, though, still requires proper long-term planning.

At the sectoral level there is also a strong argument for a longer-term approach with regard to various government functions (such as education or health) and government's role in certain economic sectors (such as construction or transport). In countries undergoing rapid change, such as South Africa, it is impossible to systematically and consistently achieve important social development goals and the concomitant expenditure reprioritisation without proper longer-term planning. The costing of policies and trade-offs between key choices often require a multi-year framework. Furthermore, government demand dominates certain economic sectors (e.g. construction) to such an extent that proper planning and phasing of expenditure are important requirements for private sector efficiency.

Several actions can be particularly harmful to sound financial management in both government and private business. These include stop-go policies (which may be the result of political indecision, even in a rules-based fiscal dispensation), across-the-board-cuts by Treasury in response to looming excess expenditure, or abortive attempts at deliberate anti-cyclical capital expenditure. Economic actors increasingly prefer smoothing of government expenditure to attempt to moderate expenditure peaks or troughs in the economy. For this, a long-term approach is required.

Finally, at the microeconomic (i.e. programme or project) level, efficiency also warrants multi-year financial planning. Proper cash flow planning, cost projection, and a measure of certainty about future resource commitments are important requirements for efficient delivery. (Naturally, a zero-based approach to budgeting also requires sufficient flexibility, constant re-appraisal, and cost-awareness to avoid complacency and the concomitant inefficiencies.)

In South Africa the medium-term budgetary policy statement consists of three-year rolling expenditure and revenue projections for the national and provincial governments, presented against the backdrop of economic and fiscal goals and prospects for the economy. This policy document and the planning processes that generate the information are cornerstones of the government's broader budget reform process. The three-year **medium-term expenditure framework** (MTEF) is regarded as being particularly important for bringing greater certainty and transparency to budget processes within and outside government, strengthening the link between policy priorities and the government's longer-term spending plans, and improving expenditure control (as reflected in reduced levels of overspending in recent years). In this sense, it has been an important aspect of the ongoing reforms aimed at making policymakers more accountable by increasing the transparency of fiscal policymaking in South Africa (see Section 15.5.4).

15.6.3 Macroeconomic aspects of fiscal policy in South Africa[16]

As was the case in most other countries, the South African fiscal authorities adopted Keynesian policies after the Second World War. Fiscal policy in South Africa continued to reflect aspects of Keynesian thinking well into the 1980s, and even continued to achieve anti-cyclical effects from time to time thereafter. Towards the end of the 1970s, however, there were indications that the authorities were beginning to abandon active anti-cyclical stabilisation policy in favour of longer-term fiscal planning. Thereafter, taxation and government expenditure were no longer used actively or deliberately to stimulate economic growth in times of recession, nor to dampen demand during boom times. South Africa's progressive income tax was no longer capable of exerting strong automatic stabilising effects due to bracket creep, which was not compensated for by indexing income tax brackets to inflation; moreover, the Treasury was under so much pressure to reduce government expenditure that it had lost the option of stimulating or cooling the economy by changing the level of government expenditure.

The longer-term focus that replaced the Keynesian approach emphasised fiscal discipline, which the authorities regarded as a prerequisite for improving the longer-term growth and job creation potential of the South African economy. The strong emphasis on the pursuit of price stability, based on the view that lower inflation is a necessary condition for sustained economic growth, further confirmed the longer-term and structural focus of fiscal policy. Statements in the annual budget speeches of successive Ministers of Finance suggest that price stability was the most important macroeconomic objective of fiscal policy from 1994 until 1997, and the second most important in 1990, 1993, and 1998. During the 1990s government budgets contained almost no measures aimed at deliberately stimulating economic growth in the short term. When growth regained pride of place as an objective of fiscal policy in 1999, the fiscal authorities emphasised its intention to promote growth

---

[16] This section draws on Calitz and Siebrits (2003) and Siebrits and Calitz (2004).

by microeconomic reforms to boost the supply side of the economy, instead of demand stimulation.[17] The government's decision to adopt medium-term expenditure planning in 1998 further cemented the movement away from expenditure fine-tuning.

During the 1990s, the focus on fiscal discipline and other structural aspects of fiscal policy was associated closely with the stabilisation or even the reduction of the public sector's claim on resources, including the total pool of savings. This development should be interpreted against the backdrop of longer-term trends in the major fiscal aggregates. Sections 1.2.2 (Chapter 1) and 7.2.1 (Chapter 7) showed that, on balance, the total tax burden and government expenditure increased as percentages of GDP during the 1960s, 1970s and 1980s. The budget of the national government was in deficit throughout the 1960s and the 1970s, and the loan debt of the national government increased more than sevenfold in nominal terms from 1961 to 1981. For most of this period the economy grew even more rapidly, however, and the debt ratio (national government debt expressed as a percentage of GDP) therefore decreased significantly. On average, national budget deficits were no higher during the 1980s than during the preceding two decades. Yet because of sluggish economic growth, these deficits tended to make the public debt grow faster than the gross domestic product. Hence the government debt ratio increased by about 6 percentage points of GDP during the 1980s.

---

[17] The shift to supply-side factors is in line with the thrust of new growth theory, which argues that growth-promoting capital formation is not limited to investments in privately-owned physical capital (e.g. factories and machinery). New growth theory indicates that additions to any of the following components of the capital stock may yield increasing returns by creating externalities that benefit a range of sectors and industries: the existing physical infrastructure (e.g. roads and electricity networks); accumulated human capital acquired through education, training, and healthcare; and technical expertise acquired through learning-by-doing and research and development. See Chapter 7, Section 7.6.

This experience confirms that the rate of economic growth can exert a powerful influence on the extent to which a budget deficit affects the government-debt ratio. The higher the rate of economic growth, the higher the deficit can be without increasing the debt ratio, *ceteris paribus*.

The period from 1989 to 1995 saw a marked deterioration in the overall fiscal situation: the long recession from March 1989 to May 1993 depressed tax revenues, while several extraordinary transfer payments and the expansion of social services sharply increased government expenditure. The budget deficit ballooned from 1,4 per cent of GDP in 1989/90 to 7,3 per cent in 1992/93. The resulting sharp increase in central government debt (from 36,4% on 31 March 1989 to 49,5% on 31 March 1996) caused widespread concern about the sustainability of fiscal policy. Some South African economists even predicted that the government was heading for a debt trap in which it would not be able to service its debt and might find it increasingly difficult to raise loans in the capital market. Such fears confirmed that the private sector had lost faith in the potential of Keynesian anti-cyclical fiscal policy. The government did not deliberately increase the budget deficit to stimulate the economy, but the rising deficit during a deep recession represented a strong anti-cyclical policy stance. In the heyday of Keynesian anti-cyclical fiscal policy, the private sector would have welcomed this as an appropriate attempt to soften the cyclical downturn. In the early 1990s, however, the relatively high deficits and rising public debt caused alarm in financial circles.

It is important to keep in mind that the debt ratio never reached a particularly high level in international terms – it remained, for example, well below the 60-per cent-of-GDP threshold that countries had to achieve to qualify for membership of the European Economic and Monetary Union (EMU). Analysts of fiscal policy were worried more about the growth of the public debt than about its level. The situation also was the first test of the democratic government's commitment to fiscal discipline. The first two Ministers of Finance after the political transition in South Africa, Derek Keys and Chris Liebenberg, were businesspersons whose perceived political neutrality gave them much credibility in local and international financial circles. The appointment of ANC politician Trevor Manuel as Minister of Finance in 1996 raised a crucial question: would the democratic government maintain fiscal discipline, or would it pursue unsustainable populist fiscal policies to achieve its well-publicised goals of fighting poverty and redistributing income?

It was against this background that the South African government adopted the Growth, Employment And Redistribution (GEAR) strategy in June 1996. From a fiscal policy point of view, the two most important goals of GEAR were to turn the deteriorating fiscal situation around and to quell fears about the democratic government's perceived lack of commitment to fiscal prudence. Hence, the fiscal goals of the GEAR strategy for the period 1996 to 2000 included a step-wise reduction in the budget deficit to 3 per cent of GDP, maintenance of the total tax burden at 25 per cent of GDP, the reduction of general government consumption expenditure as a percentage of GDP and the gradual elimination of general government dissaving. While also making major progress towards effecting a socially more acceptable distribution of income (see Chapter 8), the application of the strategy succeeded on both counts. From 1996 to 2001 a combination of buoyant revenue growth, strict control over public spending and wise use of privatisation receipts reduced the conventional budget deficit from 5,1 per cent of GDP to 1,9 per cent. Concern about a possible debt trap also evaporated

as the debt ratio dropped from a peak of 49,9 per cent of GDP in 1999 to 43,9 per cent in 2001. The achievements of the first ten years[18] after the political transition brought the authorities an enviable reputation for sound fiscal policymaking, as is evident from the consistent improvement in South Africa's international credit ratings since the first official ratings were issued in 1994. It has also drawn warm praise from experts on fiscal policy. Tanzi (2004: 539), for example, recognised this in an article about episodes of successful fiscal reforms:

> *Outside of the Americas South Africa merits a mention because... it has followed, in recent years, a steady path towards fiscal adjustment trying to use its public resources sparingly and efficiently and creating an efficient tax system while resisting the temptation of magic solutions. The country has managed to reduce its fiscal deficit by about five to six percent of GDP over the past decade through a careful reallocation of spending and tax reform...*

As indicated, the stated fiscal policy stance became more expansionary after 2001. A major aim of this stance has been to raise the growth rate of the South African economy through investment in social services and the country's physical infrastructure. The data does not reflect the more expansionary fiscal stance fully, however, because government revenue regularly exceeded budget forecasts and kept the budget deficit below 2,5 per cent of GDP. Assisted by relatively brisk economic growth, these modest budget deficits reduced the public-debt ratio further to 29,0 per cent of GDP as on 31 March 2007. The fiscal authorities also succeeded in eliminating government dissaving: whereas

---

[18] For an assessment of fiscal policies post South Africa's political transition, see Ajam and Aron (2007).

general government current expenditure exceeded general government current income by 7,3 per cent of GDP in 1992, general government saving amounted to 1,2 per cent and 2,4 per cent of GDP in 2006 and 2007 respectively. The longer-term perspective provided by Table 1.1 (Chapter 1) further amplifies the significance of the fiscal consolidation between the middle of the 1990s and the first half of the 2000s, during which time the share of public sector resource use and public sector resource mobilisation in the economy decreased significantly from the average levels recorded for the period 1990-1994. This curtailment of the longer-term growth of government is remarkable in that it occurred after the country's constitutional change and its adoption of constitutional social rights in recognition of all human rights. This expenditure pattern actually contradicts theories of public-sector growth, which predict that the share of public spending in national income is likely to increase in countries with unequal income distributions if lower-income groups receive voting rights.[19]

Section 15.3.4 discussed the recent worldwide revival of interest in the cyclical effects of fiscal policy and Section 15.4 the momentum gained by fiscal activism in response to the international financial crisis of 2007-2009. South Africa has been no exception in this regard: of late, several researchers have attempted to estimate the size of the automatic fiscal stabilisers and to establish how fiscal policy has affected the stability of the macroeconomy since 1994. The automatic stabilisers in South Africa appear to be of the order of 0,5 per cent of GDP (Du Plessis and Boshoff, 2007: 10; Swanepoel and Schoeman, 2003: 813), which suggests that they exert a modest, but by no means negligible, influence on fluctuations in economic activity. The

findings of efforts to determine whether fiscal policy has been pro-cyclical or anti-cyclical since 1994 have been sensitive to the empirical methods employed, but a careful analysis of the evidence (Du Plessis, Smit and Sturzenegger, 2007) concluded that fiscal policy had not significantly affected the stability of economic activity in South Africa since 1994.

Up to the time of the international financial crisis of 2007-2009, the approach followed by the fiscal authorities in South Africa was largely reminiscent of the view that regards monetary policy as a more potent instrument for stabilisation policy than fiscal policy. Attempts to 'fine-tune' the level of economic activity by means of fiscal policy (i.e. active fiscal policy) was therefore generally avoided. This did not mean, however, that the fiscal authorities were ignoring the cyclical state of the economy when formulating the Budget and the need for mutually supportive fiscal and monetary policy stances was increasingly recognised. A clear example of this approach was the inclusion of estimates of the structural budget balance in the 2007 Medium-Term Budget Policy Statement (National Treasury, 2007c) and the 2008 Budget Review (National Treasury, 2008a). The 2007 Medium-Term Budget Policy Statement (National Treasury, 2007c: 3) commented as follows on these matters:

Fiscal policy over the past few years has increasingly taken account of the economic cycle. Government revenue performance fluctuates in response to economic fortunes, influenced in turn by the economic performance of our major trading partners, commodity prices, interest rate cycles, inflation trends and business profitability. These are complex factors that affect the economy and tax revenue in ways that cannot be fully modelled or predicted. In the face of potentially destabilising cyclical factors, it is important to adopt a policy

---

[19] This is the main line of argument developed by Meltzer and Richard (1981) – see Chapter 7, Section 7.4.4.

stance oriented towards stable long-term growth.

In this MTBPS the National Treasury introduces the concept of a structural budget balance as a contribution to more systematic and consistent adaptation of the fiscal stance to cyclical factors. Simply put, when economic conditions are good, as they are now, we must invest and save in a manner that allows us to maintain public spending and societal welfare when economic conditions turn less favourable, as they inevitably will.

The 2008 Budget Review (National Treasury, 2008a: 42) contains a clear example of how the fiscal authorities use estimates of the structural (or cyclically adjusted) budget balance to inform policy decisions:

The 2008 Budget takes account of a more unsettled global economic environment. While total revenue growth is expected to moderate in line with economic activity, strong commodity prices are generating robust tax revenues from the mining sector. As a result, the cyclical element of tax revenue remains significant. Taking these factors into account, government is budgeting for a fiscal surplus, which keeps the cyclically adjusted budget balance from deteriorating. By saving a share of the cyclical revenue, the fiscus is protected from cyclical and external volatility, and ensures that the state does not contribute to pressure on inflation and the current account deficit.

Some commentators criticised the authorities for budgeting for a surplus in the 2008/09 financial year, arguing that it would have been better to further increase government spending to address various social needs. The quoted statement, however, confirms that contemporary views on the macroeconomic role of fiscal policy in South

Africa and elsewhere attempt to balance short-term considerations and the ever-present longer-term issue of the sustainability of the public finances.

The fiscal surplus turned out to be a blessing in disguise. As Figure 15.4 demonstrates, South Africa was one of the developing countries that was able to utilise its fiscal space to counter the recession that followed the international financial crises with active fiscal policy measures – without running the same fiscal sustainability risk experienced by some industrial countries. In 2010/11 the fiscal surplus did turn into a deficit equivalent to 5,3 per cent of GDP. This was the outcome of reduced revenue and the maintenance of medium-term expenditure patterns on economic and social services. At the same time the Government committed itself to a process of fiscal consolidation. The 2011/12 budget envisaged a reduction of the deficit-to-GDP ratio to 3,8 per cent in 2013/14.

15.6.4 Fiscal rules in South Africa

South Africa has recently adopted two institutional innovations in monetary policy, namely inflation targeting and constitutional protection of the independence of the central bank. The South African fiscal authorities have implemented multi-year expenditure planning, but have not committed themselves to numerical fiscal rules (yet). As indicated in Section 15.4, however, rules are growing in popularity in other countries and it is likely therefore that they will eventually come under consideration in South Africa.

South Africa has not used formal numerical fiscal rules since 1976, when the local version of the current-balance rule was abolished. We pointed out earlier that the South African authorities from time to time in recent years have adopted annual or medium-term fiscal targets to give effect to the more structural approach to fiscal policy. These targets, however, never achieved the status of formal numerical rules. From 1985 until the mid-1990s, fiscal policy in South Africa was guided by a 3 per cent deficit guideline. This guideline had no theoretical basis and proved to be ineffective when the budget deficit rose sharply during the early 1990s. In 1995, the post-apartheid government embarked on the very successful fiscal adjustment effort that was discussed in Section 15.6.3. This effort was guided by the goals of the GEAR strategy. The GEAR goals were pursued in a flexible manner, as became apparent when the time frame for reaching the 3 per cent deficit goal was extended by one year when the Asian crisis of 1997/98 precipitated an economic downswing. With the exception of a central-bank borrowing rule[20] and constitutional restrictions in the intergovernmental fiscal system, there were no permanent restrictions on fiscal policymaking during the adjustment.

From 1998 onwards the South African government adopted various measures to make fiscal policymaking in South Africa more transparent. The overarching framework for this endeavour is the Public Finance Management Act (PFMA) of 1999. The Act does not put limits on the absolute or relative values of fiscal aggregates, that is, it does not prescribe numerical fiscal rules. Instead, it aims to address the accountability dimension of fiscal transparency by emphasising regular financial reporting, sound internal expenditure controls, independent audit and supervision of control systems, improved accounting standards and training of financial managers, and greater emphasis on outputs and performance monitoring. The Act also compels the South African fiscal authorities to disclose their longer-term objectives and views about future trends in

fiscal policy annually. The Medium-Term Expenditure Framework referred to earlier (see Section 15.6.2) is in line with this approach. The broad fiscal framework currently in force in South Africa is therefore reminiscent of those used in Australia, New Zealand and the United Kingdom. In contrast to these countries, however, South Africa has not adopted separate legislation specifying binding annual or medium-term fiscal targets.

Both regimes that have been used since 1994 (target-guided discretion from 1994 to 1998 and transparency-based discretion since then) have worked well. The successful completion of the fiscal adjustment effort in 2001 and the maintenance of fiscal discipline thereafter were made possible primarily by the fiscal authorities' strong commitment to fiscal prudence. However, the flexibility of these regimes proved useful in a turbulent milieu marked by, inter alia, political democratisation, strong popular pressure for more expansionary policies, and three currency crises (1996, 1997/98, and 2001). Their discretionary nature was not a drawback from a credibility point of view. The authorities have earned considerable credibility for themselves and the regime, having established an enviable reputation for maintaining fiscal discipline. In fact, Frankel, Smit and Sturzenegger (2006: 71) suggested that the degree of credibility enjoyed by the South African fiscal authorities obviates the need for fiscal rules:

South African authorities have worked hard to earn credibility which has the benefit of allowing some margin of discretion. What would then be the logic of constraining themselves with fiscal rules which are just bound to be violated when shocks require the use of discretion?

The excellent reputation of the fiscal authorities is also evident from South Africa's

[20] Section 13(f) of the South African Reserve Bank Act of 1989 (as amended) prohibits lending to the South African government.

relatively good international credit ratings, which have improved consistently since the first official ratings were conducted in 1994.

These considerations suggest that there is no compelling reason why South Africa should adopt numerical fiscal rules. Rules are unlikely to add credibility benefits over and above those already enjoyed by policymakers and the transparency-based regime, especially if it is taken into account that rules as such cannot constrain future generations of policymakers. Moreover, the adoption of numerical rules will deny policymakers the valuable flexibility that they have used wisely until now. The present transparency-based regime seems to offer the best of both worlds: the commitment benefits that rules are supposed to reflect and the flexibility advantages of discretionary regimes. However, the high fiscal cost of social security benefits such as the proposed national health system will, if implemented, be a far greater challenge to **fiscal discretion** and might well strengthen the case for fiscal rules in future.

15.7 Fiscal reforms in sub-Saharan Africa[21]

Many of the fiscal issues with which South Africa has been grappling also feature on the fiscal agendas of other countries in sub-Saharan Africa. The public finances of most sub-Saharan African countries are inherently fragile as they have narrow revenue bases and government spending is under great pressure. During the 1970s and 1980s policy mistakes and global economic developments rapidly destabilised the vulnerable fiscal systems of many sub-Saharan African countries. Since then, efforts to correct these imbalances and to prevent them from re-emerging have dominated fiscal policymaking in the region.

When assessing fiscal trends in sub-Saharan Africa, one should keep in mind that the region consists of 54 countries whose fiscal situations and structures differ in many respects. Generalisation is always risky. Several broad shifts are nonetheless taking place. We highlight a few positive developments.

- Budget balances have improved in many countries, especially from the mid-1990s onwards. It appears as if the trend toward lower budget deficits in sub-Saharan Africa mainly reflects expenditure cutbacks, rather than revenue increases. Even in 2009, during the Great Recession, central government budget balances in 27 (about half of the) African countries were better than -3% of GDP.

- A considerable number of sub-Saharan African countries have reduced their dependence on taxes on international trade, partly because such taxes distort prices and partly to comply with World Trade Organisation agreements. A number of countries recouped the lost revenue by introducing value added tax. Countries in all parts of sub-Saharan Africa now use this high-yielding and relatively non-distorting tax.

- Reductions in income tax rates have been common, and many countries successfully broadened their tax bases and (or) improved tax collection. Of the 13 countries for which data was available for the period 1987 to 2002, 11 countries reduced their highest marginal income tax rates on individuals and 12 countries had their highest rate on corporations reduced. More recently (in 2006) Egypt and Ghana reduced their highest marginal income tax rates – from 34% to 20% and from 30% to 25% respectively (Global Finance, 2011). Reductions in corporate tax rates continued to occur: in 2008/09 rates were reduced in Benin (from 38% to 30%),

---

[21] This section draws on Calitz and Siebrits (2007).

Cape Verde (from 30% to 25%), Sudan (from 30% to 15%) and Togo (from 37% to 30%) (World Bank and PriceWaterhouseCoopers, 2010).

▶ Factors such as faster economic growth, accelerated debt relief, and smaller fiscal deficits have reduced the debt burdens of a number of sub-Saharan African countries. The resulting reduction in the interest burdens of these countries has released budgetary resources for more productive ends. In contrast to the 1980s, the norm during the 1990s was no longer to sharply reduce public investment when fiscal problems occur. This, together with indications that government spending on education and healthcare generally did not fall nearly as much during reform periods as is often claimed by critics of structural adjustment, suggest that government-spending priorities have improved in many sub-Saharan African countries. Before the global financial crisis public finances in a number of countries (e.g. Mozambique, South Africa, Tanzania and Uganda), were on a much sounder footing than a decade earlier, and they were in a better position to promote growth, efficient resource allocation and the reduction of poverty and inequality.

The average fiscal balance for African countries during 1986–1990 amounted to -7,5%, which improved to 2,6% during 2004–2008. The subsequent weakening of the economies together with stimulus packages caused fiscal balances in Africa to deteriorate on average by around 6,5 percentage points of GDP, that is, from a surplus of 2,2% of GDP in 2008 to a deficit of 4,4% of GDP in 2009, thus mitigating the downturn of aggregate demand.[22]

The fiscal challenges nonetheless remain formidable. Narrow tax bases and underdeveloped financial markets still make many African countries highly dependent on grants and foreign borrowing as sources of financing for government spending. Spending pressures and susceptibility to external shocks remain high and the gains of the recent past are therefore fragile. Moreover, governance and service delivery challenges remain acute, as was affirmed by the findings of a survey commissioned by the United Nations Economic Commission for Africa (2004).

---

[22] For this and other information on the past trends and economic outlook of African economies, see African Economic Outlook (2010).

IMPORTANT CONCEPTS

active or passive fiscal policies (page 291)
automatic or built-in stabiliser (page 289)
budgetary vote (page 287)
Budget Review (page 310)
Budget Speech (page 310)
contingency reserve (page 310)

contractionary fiscal policy (page 296)
conventional balance (page 291)
crowding-out (page 295)
current balance (page 292)
current-balance (fiscal) rules (page 305)
cyclically adjusted budget balances (page 292, 300)

decision lag (page 294)
discretionary policy (page 306)
dissaving (page 292)
expansionary fiscal policy (page 296)
expenditure-limiting (fiscal) rules (page 305)

IMPORTANT CONCEPTS

fiscal activism or anti-cyclical fiscal policy (page 288)

fiscal council (page 309)

fiscal discretion (page 319)

fiscal policy (page 285)

fiscal rule (page 305)

fiscal transparency (page 308)

full-employment income budget balance (page 300)

impact lag (page 294)

implementation lag (page 294)

Keynesian approach (page 289)

macroeconomic, sectoral, and microeconomic goals of fiscal policy (page 285)

Medium Term Budget Policy Statement (page 312)

medium-term expenditure framework (MTEF) (page 313)

multiplier (page 295)

multi-year budget (page 312)

multi-year fiscal or expenditure planning (page 312)

multi-year plan (of fiscal authorities) (page 312)

National Treasury (page 288)

net borrowing requirement (page 292)

net indebtedness (page 293)

ordinary revenue (page 293)

overall-balance (fiscal) rules (page 305)

potential-income budget balance (page 300)

primary balance (page 293)

primary deficit (page 293)

primary surplus (page 293)

public debt (fiscal) rules (page 305)

public sector borrowing requirement (page 292)

rational expectations hypothesis (page 306)

recognition lag (page 293)

stagflation (page 296)

structural approach to fiscal policy (page 297)

structural budget balance (page 300)

supply-side economists (page 296)

total revenue (of government) (page 291)

transparency-enhancing reforms (page 308)

trend-line budget balance (page 300)

SELF-ASSESSMENT EXERCISES

15.1 Distinguish between macroeconomic, sectoral and microeconomic fiscal policy goals and instruments. Provide an example of each.

15.2 Discuss the principles of Keynesian anti-cyclical fiscal policy and the reasons for its fall from favour since the mid-1970s.

15.3 Use a diagram to explain the distinction between automatic fiscal stabilisers and active fiscal policies.

15.4 'The conventional budget deficit is superior to other definitions of budget deficit as a measure of the stance of fiscal policy.' Do you agree? Explain your answer.

15.5 A general rule of thumb is that a negative primary balance can be maintained for some time without an increase in the government's debt-GDP ratio, provided that the real rate of economic growth is higher than the real rate of interest in the economy. Explain why this rule makes sense.

15.6 'Due to lags, fiscal policy is irrelevant.' Do you agree with this statement? Substantiate your answer.

15.7 Discuss the structural approach to fiscal policymaking.

15.8 Use a diagram to explain the distinction between the structural and the cyclical components of budget balances, and discuss the practical significance of this distinction.

15.9 Explain, with the aid of a graph, the significance of distinguishing between active and passive fiscal policy.

15.10 Explain, with the aid of a graph, the fiscal consequences of the 2007–2009 international financial crisis and the ensuing Great Recession.

15.11 Discuss the advantages and disadvantages of fiscal rules. Is fiscal policy in South Africa driven by rules or discretion? Substantiate your answer.

15.12 'Fiscal policy in South Africa has been driven by practical reality rather than sound theoretical principles.' Discuss critically.

Chapter
SIXTEEN

Estian Calitz[1]

Public debt and debt management

The aim of this chapter is to study the essence of, and rationale for, public debt as well as its impact on the economy. Public debt arises from the borrowings of government – as reflected primarily in the annual budget. A systematic study of public debt and its management provides important insights into both the relationship between the various components of public economics and the interaction between fiscal and monetary policy in their impact on the economy.

Our study begins with a discussion of the concept of public debt, followed by an overview of the size and composition of public debt in South Africa. Next we discuss various theories on the rationale for public debt, followed by an investigation of the question: should government tax or borrow? Our final section deals with public debt management.

Once you have studied this chapter, you should be able to:
▶ define public debt
▶ describe salient characteristics of the size, composition, and nature of public debt in South Africa
▶ explain and compare different theories of public debt and evaluate them critically
▶ argue the relative merits of debt and tax financing of government expenditure
▶ define public debt management
▶ identify and describe the different types of public debt cost
▶ identify the goals of public debt management and discuss their pursuance, with special reference to South Africa.

[1] The author would like to thank Louis Fourie and Zichy Botha for their critical comments and suggestions on sections of this chapter. The usual disclaimer applies.

16.1 **The concept of public debt**

Public debt may be defined as the sum of all the outstanding financial liabilities of the public sector in respect of which there is a primary legal responsibility to repay the original amount borrowed (sometimes called the **principal of debt**) and to pay interest (sometimes called **debt servicing**). Most of the time, especially when considering the macroeconomic implications, the term public debt is used to refer to the debt of the national government only (see Figure 1.1, Chapter 1). We use this narrower definition in this chapter.

Public debt arises primarily from the government's annual budget deficits, one of the consequences of fiscal policies as discussed in Chapter 15. The government borrows mainly by issuing treasury bills or bonds, collectively known as government securities, but also makes use of bank loans (using overdraft facilities), mostly for bridging finance. The **treasury bill** is a short-term debt obligation of the national government, representing a charge on the revenues and assets of the Republic of South Africa (Van Zyl, Botha, Goodspeed and Skerritt, 2009: Section 9.6.1). A treasury bill is normally issued for a 91-day period. Treasury bills form part of the liquid asset base of the private banking sector.

The majority of public debt is incurred through the sale of **government bonds** (also called stock) that have a maturity of more than three years. Most of the time these are fixed-interest bearing securities issued by the national government and they also represent a charge on the revenues and assets of the Republic. Other varieties of government bonds are variable-interest bonds (of which inflation indexed bonds are an example) and zero-coupon bonds. **Zero-coupon bonds** are bonds that do not pay interest during the lifetime of the bonds. Instead, investors buy zero-coupon bonds at a deep discount from their face value, which is the amount a bond will be worth when it 'matures' or becomes due. When a zero-coupon bond matures, the investor will receive one lump sum equal to the initial investment plus interest that has accrued. As financial markets develop and investor sophistication increases, the variety of bonds increases. All government bonds, irrespective of their maturities, are regarded as liquid assets in the hands of banks.

Occasionally debt is incurred outside the budget (off-budget debt) and is not reflected in the budget deficit. For example, in the early 1990s the government transferred bonds directly to the public employees' pension funds to improve their funding levels, instead of budgeting for the expense in the normal fashion.

Details of the national government debt are published in the Quarterly Bulletin of the South African Reserve Bank. This excludes the debt of extra-budgetary institutions (such as universities), provincial and local governments, and the non-financial public enterprises (such as Eskom and Transnet). Of course, if the national government were to take over the debt of any of these institutions, the legal responsibility to service and repay the debt is transferred to the national government. From that moment the debt will be counted as part of the public (i.e. national government) debt.

Our definition of public debt also excludes contingent liabilities (see Section 16.5.5), that is, the outstanding financial liabilities of public entities (such as public enterprises) and private entities whose debt carries an explicit guarantee by the national government. Only when such a guarantee is called up, will the payment obligation be transferred to the national government (as guarantor) and the amount involved will be added to the national debt.

16.2 Size and composition of the public debt

On 31 December 2010 the total debt of the South African government (public debt for short) amounted to R891 billion – this was 33,5 per cent of the GDP, or roughly R17 800 per head of the population. This tells us that, if all the public debt were to be repaid immediately, the government would on average have to impose a once-off tax of R17 800 on each citizen, which amounts to a rather high 34% of the average income per head of the population. Those citizens that are government bond holders as well, will of course also be on the receiving side when such debt is repaid. The impact of the international financial crisis of 2007–2009 and the subsequent recessionary conditions show how quickly the state of public finance can change in a country. At the end of 2007 public debt was 27 per cent of GDP.

The average size of public debt as a percentage of GDP declined during the 1970s and 1980s and then rose substantially during the 1990s (Table 16.1), both before and after the political change of 1994. The surge led various economists to warn against the dangers of a **debt trap**, a term used to signify an inability of a government to repay and service its debt. Part of this increased share was because the government borrowed money to fund the government employees' pension funds and took over the debt of the independent homelands under the apartheid system. From the beginning of the next decade government debt as a percentage of GDP fell quite dramatically: first averaging 40,9 per cent in 2000–2004, then reaching an even lower average of 29,0 per cent in 2004–2009. The lower debt-GDP ratio was mainly the result of the systematic reduction of the annual budget deficit as a percentage of GDP, the use of privatisation income to reduce

government debt and sustained economic growth. In 2008 the debt-to-GDP percentage reached its·lowest level (of 23,9 per cent) during the 51 years covered by Table 16.1, just when the global financial crisis erupted. South Africa incurred a substantial Keynesian-type debt increase in 2010, yet the debt ratio of 33,5 per cent[2] was still far below the average of 40 per cent during the previous 20 years. Macroeconomically South Africa had substantially more fiscal manoeuvrability than many developed countries. At the end of 2010, for example, the gross public debt as a percentage of GDP was about 77 per cent in Britain, 91 per cent in the United States, 119 per cent in Italy and 228 per cent in Japan.

Table 16.1 Public debt-GDP ratio in South Africa by sub-period, 1960–2010

Period	Public debt (year-end) as % of GDP, period average
1960–69	44,7
1970–79	39,7
1980–89	32,4
1990–94	41,1
1994–1999	49,0
2000–2004	40,9
2005–2009	29,0
2010[a]	33,5

Notes: [a] Preliminary figure.

Source: South African Reserve Bank, *Quarterly Bulletin* (various issues).

The South African government has traditionally made relatively little use of foreign financing, so that most of the public debt is domestic debt. During the period 1960 to 2000 foreign public debt as a percentage of total public debt fluctuated between 10,9 per cent (1976) and 1,6 per cent (1992).

---

[2] According to South African data. The IMF figure comparable to those of the countries listed in the rest of the paragraph was 35,9 per cent (IMF, 2011: 2).

During this period foreign debt never exceeded 4,3 per cent of GDP. In 1985, 1986, and 1987 foreign loans were used to counter private capital outflows, but access to the international financial markets subsequently became increasingly difficult due to international financial sanctions. Access to international financial markets was normalised in 1994. Although this has, together with the gradual phasing out of exchange control, provided the fiscal authorities with an increased array of foreign financing options, the rise in the share of foreign debt in recent years has remained modest. A substantial jump occurred in and was maintained after 2001, resulting in an average of 14,2 per cent of total debt for 2001 to 2010.

An analysis of the **ownership distribution** of public debt shows that the majority of public debt is in the form of long-term bonds held by pension funds (including the Public Investment Corporation (PIC)) and long-term insurers. At the end of 2010 the PIC alone owned about 26 per cent of the long-term domestic marketable bonds of the national government. The biggest investor remains the Government Employees' Pension Fund. This Fund's investment in government bonds is channelled, along with investable funds of other government pension funds and other public bodies, via the PIC. At the end of 2010 government bonds constituted 21,2 per cent of the PIC's assets.

Until 1989 insurance companies and private pension funds were compelled by law to hold 53 per cent of their untaxed liabilities and 33 per cent of their tax liabilities in fixed-interest bearing public sector securities (Abedian and Biggs, 1998: 261). This provided the government with a captive loans market. To the extent that the interest on such bonds was lower than would have applied if government had to compete for these funds in a competitive market, these prescribed investments constituted a hidden tax on the relevant institutions. For the government, the cost of debt was therefore below the market rate. This implicit tax, which impacted negatively on savings, was criticised for its unfairness and adverse influence on investment performance and was abolished in 1989.

For some time the PIC continued to be subject to strict investment requirements; however, this has also changed and during the 1990s the PIC was increasingly allowed to make market-related investment decisions. This was due to the fact that the PIC, as the investment arm of the government's pension funds, was responsible for the investment yield of these funds. Public employees contribute to a defined benefit fund. It means that the weaker the investment performance of the PIC is, the higher the government's future obligation to improve the solvability of these funds will be. For this reason the government transferred bonds to the pension funds at various occasions in the early 1990s – to ensure future solvability it reduced its contingent liability by increasing its actual debt. When the PIC was transformed into a public corporation in 2004, its investment freedom was formalised further, although this remains subject to political influences because it is wholly owned by the government.

An intriguing question, which we will address in Section 16.3, is whether, and on what basis, public debt is justified. When attempting to understand the nature and causes of public debt, an important issue that has to be considered revolves around the purpose for which debt is incurred. For example, are the borrowed funds to be used to finance current or capital expenditure? Spending on goods and services that are used up within a specified, usually short, period is called **current expenditure** or consumption expenditure (Bannock, Baxter and Rees, 1971: 82). In fiscal terms these goods and services are normally associated with tax rather than debt financing. **Capital**

expenditure refers to expenditure on durable items that yield services or revenue over a long period, such as roads, irrigation dams and electricity networks. This kind of expenditure is normally financed through loans (public debt).

The inverse of the question about the justification for debt is whether public debt is something that should be repaid. Most people would argue that a government is not like a business, the health of which is determined by factors such as the value of its shares, its profit, its debt-equity ratio, and measures of liquidity and solvency. These criteria are important determinants of whether a business is bankrupt or thriving. If the business is to be sold, one needs to know its value or net worth to determine the price. **Net worth** may be defined as the difference between the value of all assets and liabilities, that is, the 'shareholders' (or, in the case of government, the taxpayers') 'interest'. In the case of government, the mirror image is the **net indebtedness**, which is the difference between the value of all liabilities and assets.[3] Many would argue that this kind of information is irrelevant when analysing the financial state of a government, because a government allegedly cannot become bankrupt or is unlikely to be put up for sale. In fact, one type of government bond, known as a **consul**, is a perpetual bond, that is, a bond with an indefinite maturity – never to be repaid. This is well-known in the UK, but no such bond has thus far been issued in South Africa.

In recent times these ideas have been challenged. The government is not only the supplier of public goods and services. It is also the custodian of public assets owned collectively by the citizens (taxpayers) of the country. Informed and enquiring citizens have tended to become interested in the way

in which the government is managing their (public) assets and liabilities. The net worth of government has become important, not as an indication of the potential selling price of the government, but as a measure of the quality of fiscal management and of the impact on the next generation (i.e. the inter-temporal burden and its implications for inter-generational equity). Attention to the balance sheet of government has become a feature of public economics. Privatisation, for example, has raised questions like: is society becoming poorer if public assets are sold, and should the revenue from privatisation be used to repay public debt or to acquire new assets?

Incidentally, the balance-sheet accounting implied above, is also required to answer many of the questions raised by public auditors who have over the past two to three decades advocated the importance of value for money in a number of countries such as Canada and New Zealand. In South Africa we increasingly focus on commercially oriented questions such as the value of public assets, the (opportunity) cost of non-earning or badly managed assets, and the cost of excessive stockpiling – such as occurred in the defence force in the past.

16.3 Theory of public debt

16.3.1 Introduction

In Section 16.2 it was stated that loan finance (debt) is an acceptable method to finance capital expenditure, while current expenditure may be a better candidate for tax finance. Is this necessarily true, especially as the distinction between current and capital expenditure can be ambiguous? What is the rationale for debt finance and what are the criteria for choosing between tax and debt financing of government

---

[3] Sometimes 'net indebtedness' is only used in respect of the difference between the financial assets and liabilities of government.

expenditure? These are some of the oldest questions in economics and there are a number of divergent views on the issue. The answer depends in part on who actually pays the public debt, which is a question about the nature of the distribution or incidence of the public debt burden.

We begin our analysis of the rationale for debt finance by introducing the concept of the **inter-temporal burden**. This refers to the shifting of the burden of the public debt over time from one generation to the next. The burden of the debt refers to the responsibility for the actual payment of the principal and interest.

The American President Herbert Hoover once remarked: 'Blessed are our children, for they shall inherit the public debt'. Is this necessarily true? There are different views on this topic,[4] and before investigating them, a few preliminary observations are necessary. When debt is incurred, benefits accrue to the present generation since the proceeds of the loan are used to supply public goods and services. If capital goods such as infrastructure are provided, the future generation also stands to benefit. The debt furthermore establishes a responsibility to pay interest and to repay the loan or to refinance it. In repaying or refinancing the loan, a statutory burden will be conferred on the next generation. The next generation will pay interest to bond holders until the bonds expire. In the case of bonds that expire and are not replaced by the issuance of new bonds (refinancing), the next generation will transfer income to bond holders. In the case of the refinancing of maturing bonds – a common practice in public finance – the next generation will pay interest to the new bond holders.

In our study of tax incidence (Section 10.5 of Chapter 10) we saw that there may be a

marked difference between statutory and effective (or economic) tax incidence. The same applies to public debt. The chain of events set in motion by government borrowing may lead to an economic incidence that may differ substantially from the statutory or legal incidence. The actual incidence depends on the assumptions about economic behaviour and the concomitant relationships between economic agents. The answer obviously also depends on the balance of the fiscal benefit and burden, that is, the net fiscal burden.

Two kinds of public debt have to be distinguished. **Domestic** or **internal debt** is the debt incurred by government when borrowing from domestic residents or institutions. The value of the debt is expressed in terms of the home currency. The sale of the bond does not involve an inflow of foreign capital and the payment of principal and interest does not cause an outflow of funds from the country. The balance of payments is therefore unaffected by transactions in such bonds. **Foreign** or **external debt** is the debt incurred by government when borrowing from foreign governments, residents or institutions. The value of the debt is normally expressed in a foreign currency but can also be denominated in the home currency. The sale, repayment and servicing of the bond all affect the balance of payments. There is an impact on the balance of payments when:
- bonds are sold to foreigners, thus causing an inflow of foreign capital (affecting the financial account) – in Figure 1.3 (Chapter 1) this will reflect as an increase in S_f
- foreigners sell the bonds to South Africans before the expiry date (i.e. before maturity), resulting in an outflow of capital (financial account) – in Figure 1.3 this will reflect as a decrease in S_f
- bonds are repaid in the hands of foreign investors, also amounting to a capital outflow (financial account) – in

[4] The discussion of these views relies substantially on Rosen and Gayer (2008: 467–472).

Figure 1.3 this will again reflect as a decrease in S_f
▶ interest is paid to foreign bond holders, a payment for a foreign service affecting the current account – in Figure 1.3 this will reflect as an increase in M (a factor service).

Since South Africa started to liberalise its financial markets, foreign investors increasingly started buying government bonds in the secondary capital market (i.e. the Bond Exchange of South Africa on which government bonds are traded after the date of issue). This means that the bond may often change hands so that the debt associated with a bond may, during the 'lifetime' of the bond, at different times be counted as foreign or domestic debt, depending on the nationality of the registered bond holder at the time.

In financially integrated markets the distinction between domestic and foreign debt becomes blurred, since a foreigner can also purchase bonds issued domestically, just as a South African may buy foreign issued bonds of the South African government. It is thus more appropriate to distinguish between bonds issued in the domestic money and capital markets (domestically issued bonds) and bonds issued in foreign money and capital markets. The distinction between domestic and foreign thus becomes one of source rather than residence.

16.3.2. Internal versus external debt and the burden on future generations

A view that characterised economic thinking in the 1940s and 1950s was that internal debt does not create a burden for the future generation. This view is attributed, inter alia, to the American economist, Abba Lerner (1903–1982). The argument is that certain members of the future generation will inherit a debt repayment or debt-servicing obligation, but other members of the same generation will be the recipients of these payments. In other words, members of the future generation owe the debt to themselves. On repayment of the debt, income is transferred from one group of citizens (those who do not hold bonds) to another group of citizens (the bond holders). As a whole, the future generation is therefore not in a worse position since it is capable of the same aggregate level of consumption that would otherwise have been the case. The repayment of the debt results in an intragenerational transfer or redistribution of resources (i.e. a transfer within the same generation) rather than an inter-generational transfer (i.e. a transfer between two generations). In terms of this line of thinking, therefore, internal debt is neutral with regard to inter-generational equity.

The situation is different when external debt is used. In this case the distribution of the burden depends on the way in which the funds are used, the fact that interest payments constitute a net transfer of funds to the rest of the world, and the fact that bond holders are now external to the economy. If the borrowed money is used to finance current consumption expenditure, the future generation has to repay the loan without enjoying the benefits. In fact, their income will be reduced by the amount of the loan and (or) the accrued interest that needs to be paid to the foreign lender. Aggregate consumption will be lower than in the case of domestic debt repayment. Should the money be used to finance capital accumulation, for example a railway line, the project's productivity is crucial. If it is a long-term asset with a real investment return in excess of the marginal cost of funds obtained abroad (which, in a perfect market, will be the real interest rate on the loan), the combination of the debt and the performing asset actually makes the next generation better off. The opposite applies when the investment return is less than the marginal cost of funds.

Today it is realised that the incidence of the burden of public debt is a more complicated matter. Generations overlap and the inter-generational incidence of the debt burden may differ according to the income distribution, tax burdens, and inflation rates experienced by future generations, information which is unknown at the time of the decision to borrow.

It should be noted that, apart from the equity considerations, external debt could alleviate pressures on the domestic financial markets (i.e. on the domestic supply of saving) during an economic upswing. Should the government decide to borrow abroad during such times, external debt may therefore also fulfil a macroeconomic stabilisation role.

16.3.3 Inter-temporal burden

Lerner regarded a generation as consisting of everyone who is alive at a given time. However, if we define a generation as everyone who was born at the same time, several generations exist at any particular point in time and the burden of the debt may in fact be transferred across generations. An inter-temporal burden is said to exist.

Suppose the government introduces a new programme that benefits everyone alive at a specific point in time and debt financing is used. Suppose further that a special tax has to be instituted once the debt repayment commences. It may well be that older citizens who benefited from the programme are no longer alive. This implies that they escape the burden of the tax, which has to be carried by members of younger generations.

The burden of the debt can thus be transferred to future generations. The distinction between external and internal debt is of no relevance in this case. Even if the debt is completely internal, a burden is created for the future generation. It is, of course, possible for the next generation to shift the burden forward once again.

From the point of view of inter-generational income distribution, it is very difficult to anticipate whether the next generation will be richer than the present generation. It is not inconceivable, of course, that if this is to be known or suspected, the present generation may deliberately vote for an inter-generational redistributive fiscal policy such as using debt finance, much the same as they may vote for intra-generational redistribution from the wealthy to the poor. Of course, the wealth of the next generation cannot be known, but it could be that the present generation's actions add to the wealth of the future generation. If, for example, there is a legacy of high quality public infrastructure for the next generation, the present generation may judge that the next generation will have a much better prospect of generating wealth than they had. In the eyes of the present generation, debt financing would then be an appropriate policy instrument of inter-generational redistribution.

The inter-generational debt burden is more complicated in a country experiencing a major change (discontinuity) in its political dispensation, such as that experienced during the last quarter of the twentieth century by countries converting to democracy in Eastern Europe, Asia, South America and Africa (including South Africa during the 1990s). Often there are strong populist pressures on the new government to renege on repayment of inherited debt or on foreign countries (or institutions) for debt exoneration. The argument is that the present generation cannot be held ransom by creditors of the rejected previous regime. However, the discontinuity in the political system does not imply a discontinuity in debt commitments, which are legal obligations and represent investments in the hands of bond holders. Moreover, the new generation cannot claim debt forgiveness while enjoying the benefits of the assets that were accumulated in the process.

The inter-temporal fiscal burden reminds us that the distribution of fiscal benefits and burdens between generations cannot be measured in terms of what happens in a particular fiscal year – a lifetime perspective is required. In generational accounting, the present value of lifetime taxes to be paid by a representative person of each generation is compared to the present value of lifetime benefits to be enjoyed from government services. The difference is the **'net tax'** (at present value), or the **net fiscal burden**. A comparison of the 'net tax' of different generations provides a sense of how fiscal policy distributes income or purchasing power across generations (Rosen and Gayer 2008: 468–470).

16.3.4 **Fiscal neutrality and Ricardian equivalence**

We now consider the question whether the burden of debt financing is any different from that of tax financing. This introduces an old view on debt financing, associated with the British classical economist of the early nineteenth century, David Ricardo (1771–1823). This view, of which Robert Barro is probably the most important modern exponent, states that whether government uses tax or debt finance is immaterial or irrelevant. The behaviour of individuals will be the same in both cases.

The argument is as follows: when government borrows (sells bonds) instead of levying taxes to finance public expenditure, the current generation is 'under-taxed'. They are rational, however, and realise that the loan will have to be repaid from tax income at some future date. Debt finance is therefore a postponement of the tax burden that will fall on the next generation. The current

generation will not want their heirs to be in a worse position (i.e. enjoy a lower level of consumption) on account of the 'underfunded' benefit which they are enjoying and will therefore increase their bequests by an amount equal to the increase in the tax burden of the next generation. This constitutes a voluntary reduction in private spending, cancelling the impact on domestic aggregate demand of the debt-financed government expenditure. The result is that the government's choice of debt financing is neutralised in terms of its effect on aggregate demand, and the effect on the well-being of successive generations is nullified by the rational behaviour of taxpayers and bond holders (i.e. investors in government bonds). Tax finance is therefore equivalent to debt finance (the so-called **Ricardian equivalence**) and activist fiscal policy, e.g. increasing the budget deficit to stimulate the economy, becomes ineffective (see Section 16.3.5 and Section 15.4 of Chapter 15).

This argument has been the subject of much debate and empirical testing. A number of qualifications needs to be noted. Firstly, the type of public expenditure is important. It may be equally rational to argue that capital expenditure benefits future generations as well and that they should in fact co-finance the expenditure. Tax finance will place the full burden on the current generation, while debt finance will spread the burden over present and future generations, provided the maturity of the debt is long enough. In this case debt finance will be justified in that it will avoid an excessive burden on the present generation. Debt finance will, therefore, promote inter-generational equity.

Secondly, the neat theoretical separation of two generations has been criticised. Heirs are not universal to all families and generations overlap as well, as we saw in Section 16.3.3. Thirdly, information about the implications of debt finance for future generations will not be easy to determine. Finally, empirical results are an important test of the existence of Ricardian equivalence. If it were to apply, one would expect the current generation to increase private savings in the event of an increase in government debt. However, the opposite tends to occur. In South Africa, for instance, a decrease in private savings as a percentage of GDP accompanied an increase in public debt as a percentage of GDP during the 1980s and 1990s.

Our exploration of Ricardian equivalence has not exhausted all the arguments in our search for the rationale for debt finance. We now come to a very powerful argument for debt finance that strongly influenced economic policy thinking from the Great Depression to the first half of the 1970s and regained currency during and after the international financial crisis of 2007–2009.

16.3.5 Fiscal activism and Keynesian demand management

According to the famous British economist John Maynard Keynes (1883–1946), aggregate demand determines total production and income in the economy. Due to the working of the income multiplier (Section 15.3.2 of Chapter 15) the government is able to increase or decrease the national income by changing aggregate demand. During recessionary economic conditions the appropriate fiscal policy may either involve a reduction in taxes or an increase in government expenditure, both of which would increase the budget deficit (or reduce the surplus). The converse applies during an economic boom.

Keynesian demand management dominated fiscal and monetary policy thinking for more than 40 years. The government was not expected to present balanced budgets as advocated by classical economists (a view to

which we will return in the next section), but to stimulate domestic demand as long as there was unemployment. Budget deficits (or deficit spending) were regarded as an effective way of reducing unemployment in a non-inflationary manner. In Keynesian thinking, deficit spending can be the result of either an increase in government expenditure or a decrease in taxes. Rising public debt in periods of recession and falling public debt in boom periods were associated, conceptually at least, with macroeconomic stabilisation. The Keynesian approach entailed efforts to fine-tune the economy and ensure the correct level of domestic demand commensurate with full employment and price stability.

Economists and politicians gradually began to lose faith in attempts to manage domestic demand in this manner. Two reasons for this scepticism may be highlighted. The first is that it became much easier to increase budget deficits and the public debt in periods of economic downswing than to reverse the trend during upswings. In fact, increasingly higher deficit-GDP and public debt-GDP ratios were observed. It was problematic to justify further increases in budget deficits to increase employment in a non-inflationary manner if the existing high deficits were already fuelling inflationary expectations. It took a major external shock like the international financial crisis of 2007–2009 for governments in many countries to openly revert to fiscal activism. Yet, the concern about the ability to reduce public debts and deficits to sustainable levels remained.

Secondly, during the 1970s and 1980s a growing body of economists and economic policymakers in various countries came to realise that the economic problems of both industrial and developing countries were structural rather than cyclical in nature. Core or structural unemployment and inflation persisted to such an extent that short-term demand management was increasingly regarded as an ineffective way of trying to deal with unemployment and inflation. This resulted in a switch to the so-called supply-side approach in which debt financing had much less, if any, justification from a macroeconomic stabilisation point of view. The emphasis shifted to small(er) budget deficits, balanced budgets, and even budget surpluses. Neoclassical thinking and public choice theorists are the driving forces behind these views, which, incidentally, date back to the eighteenth and the nineteenth centuries. It would therefore be more correct to refer to the revival of old ideas rather than new insights, although some modern variations have been added.

16.3.6 **The crowding-out phenomenon**

Suppose an initial equilibrium in the goods and money markets is disturbed by a budget deficit incurred through an increase in government spending. What effect will it have on the economy? The increase in government expenditure means that aggregate demand increases, which sets the multiplier process in motion. The resultant increase in income leads to an increase in the demand for money. If the supply of money remains constant in real terms, the excess demand for money causes interest rates to increase. Higher interest rates dampen private investment and thus aggregate expenditure.

This secondary reduction in aggregate demand dampens the initial multiplier effect, resulting in a lower new equilibrium level of income than would have applied if interest rates had remained unchanged. Given the negative relationship between interest rates and investment, such a fiscal policy therefore dampens the rate of private capital formation (i.e. private investment) in the economy. This phenomenon is called **crowding-out** and may formally be defined as the dampening of private investment on account of increases in interest rates associated with an increase in public expenditure, especially if the latter is debt-financed.[5] Crowding-out can occur when government, through its borrowing, competes with the private sector for funds. This line of argument is associated with the neoclassical school of thought.

16.3.7 **The public choice view**

In Chapter 6 we studied the properties of the various social choice rules as well as the extent to which and the conditions under which an optimal allocation of resources would be possible. We also encountered the public choice argument that democratic institutions, through the behaviour of politicians, bureaucrats, voters and special interest groups, exhibit inherent biases towards an 'over-expansion' of the public sector, that is, the democratic process tends to lead to higher than optimal levels of government expenditure.

Public choice economists argue that there are two causes of this bias. Firstly, it is attributed to the alleged co-existence of concentrated benefits and a diffused or widely spread distribution of costs in respect of the government's expenditure programmes. Put differently, small groups tend to benefit from certain public expenditure programmes although the cost is spread over all (or a larger group) of taxpayers. A programme or set of programmes with clearly defined benefits will have a better chance of being approved if the advocating groups are well organised and the cost of financing is obscure or hidden.

Salary increases for highly unionised public officials are an example of this type of expenditure programme. Debt finance,

---

[5] More generally, crowding-out may occur whenever there is fiscal expansion that increases interest rates, implying its occurrence under tax financing as well. See Dornbusch et al. (1994: 171).

especially inflationary financing through money creation, is an example of a very diffuse financing mechanism. In the case of loan finance, only a part of the burden of the cost is incurred in the year in which the expenditure has to be voted. It may actually be a deliberate political strategy to sell debt-financed programmes to voters because it enables politicians to be vague about the cost. This form of strategic behaviour may be particularly prevalent prior to an election which the incumbent political party is in danger of losing or at the sub-national level in cases where the particular tier of government is highly dependent on transfer income from a higher tier of government (see Chapter 17, Sections 17.5 and 17.6). It is so much more tempting (and even easier) to sell expenditure programmes to voters if another politician is accountable to a different constituency for the financing. Provincial politicians, for example, may use these tactics to force larger transfer payments from the national government to the provinces with the result that the tax or debt burden at the national level is increased.[6] These practices rest on the assumed existence of **fiscal illusion** among the electorate, which may be defined as the belief that taxes are lower than they actually are or are going to be.[7]

The second cause of the bias towards high levels of government expenditure is the separation of benefits and costs in the budgetary process. This actually reinforces the first cause. Expenditure and revenue budgets are designed and voted on separately by parliaments. The one-year nature of budgeting is a further cause, because annual budgeting allows for the approval of expenditure programmes without information on the concomitant long-term expenditure commitments and the long-term tax or debt implications of the total of all expenditure programmes. The future gap between expenditure and revenue, which by definition amounts to future debt financing, may increase without anyone being aware of it. This separation of revenue and expenditure decisions is linked to the ability-to-pay approach to taxation, in other words, financing on the basis of equity rather than efficiency considerations. Public choice economists therefore tend to argue strongly for the increased application of the benefit principle of taxation (instead of the ability-to-pay principle). An additional method of correcting for these problems is to apply medium-term fiscal planning (see Chapter 15, Section 15.7). Nowadays many countries have adopted a medium-term fiscal framework in which the multi-year implications of budgetary choices are revealed, thus allaying some of the concerns of public choice economists.

Public choice economists also argue that the alleged bias towards 'over-expansion' of the public sector has been fed by the Keynesian legacy of budget deficits explained in Section 16.3.5. In many countries the size of the public debt and the budget reached such proportions that their concomitant fine-tuning properties were lost.

The public choice view on how to improve efficiency in the allocation of public resources has important implications for debt financing. Public choice economists argue that constitutional fiscal limits are required to correct for the overexpansion bias, that is, they favour more rules and less discretion in fiscal policy. A balanced budget – in other words, one without debt financing – is an extreme version of this prognosis. In the United States, the idea of a balanced government budget enjoyed substantial popularity well into the first decade of the

[6] Incidentally, taxation through inflation as a result of bracket creep, which was discussed in Chapter 12 (Section 12.4.4), falls in the same category.

[7] In 1903 the Italian fiscal economist, Amilcare Puviani, recognised that the existence of a fiscal illusion or the potential for its establishment would enable or ensure the continued tax financing of growing demands for public goods.

twentieth century. This can be attributed to the fact that there was a strong correspondence in this regard between public choice and neoclassical thinking which gained the upper hand in macroeconomic policy thinking in the United States at the turn of the century. The debate on fiscal rules was discussed in Chapter 15 (Section 15.4). Notwithstanding strong support for balanced budgets, the USA has recorded federal budget deficits in every year from 2002 to 2011. Clearly, the influence of this view waned much at the time of the international financial crisis of 2007–2009.

16.3.8 Summary of views on the impact of debt

We now summarise our findings. Table 16.2 consists of a matrix of the possibilities associated with the various viewpoints discussed (the rows) and the basic economic considerations of efficiency, equity, and macroeconomic stability (the columns). Where possible, the name of the major exponent or school of thought is also indicated.

16.4 Should the government tax or borrow?

On the basis of the foregoing discussion of the rationale for public debt and our analysis of taxation, we consider the question: which is the best financing instrument for public expenditure: taxation or loans (debt)? Remember that debt is nothing but postponed taxation; in a sense our question is therefore one of when to tax, rather than whether or not to tax. We explore the question by referring to the allocation (efficiency) and distribution (equity) of resources, and by considering the implications for macroeconomic stability.

16.4.1 Allocation (efficiency)

Is taxation more efficient than debt? The answer lies in its impact on allocative efficiency, that is, the amount of excess burden created. Earlier we noted that the difference between tax and debt is one of timing. In order to compare efficiency, therefore, we must inquire as to the impact of the time difference on efficiency. Consider a particular project that is completed in one year and which may be financed either through tax or debt. If tax finance is used, the full cost of the project is financed by levying a once-off tax. If loan finance is chosen, the loan will have to be repaid over a number of years, for purposes of which an amount of tax will have to be levied every year. If lump sum taxes are used in each case, there is no excess burden, efficiency is ensured, and there is thus no difference between tax and debt on efficiency grounds.

Not all taxes are efficient, however. In Chapter 11 (Section 11.2.3) we saw that, in the case of an *ad valorem* tax on a commodity, the amount of excess burden increases exponentially with increases in the tax rate. This means that the excess burden of a single, relatively high tax is bigger than the sum total of the excess burdens of a series of small taxes that generate the same revenue as the single tax. When a specific tax is collected by levying a once-off, relatively high tax rate, it will therefore be less efficient than if the same amount of tax is obtained by levying a succession of low tax rates. A succession of low tax rates occurs in the case of debt financing. The debt servicing cost is spread over a number of years and requires a corresponding series of tax revenues. In this case debt financing will be more efficient than a once-off tax to finance the entire project up front. The choice between tax and debt on efficiency grounds, therefore, depends on the type of tax used.

The efficiency issue has further implications, though. It extends also to the source of the funds. Generally speaking, taxation reduces private consumption and savings. Debt finance – that is, if the debt is not monetised – represents a direct use of savings, reducing the amount of savings available to finance private investment. To the extent that debt finance represents a larger reduction in the country's savings than tax, it will be less efficient than tax from the point of view of investment decisions. This is the crowding-out argument discussed in Section 16.3.6.

Table 16.2 Summary of views on the impact of public debt

Viewpoint	Efficiency	Equity	Macroeconomic stability
Internal-external debt argument (Lerner)		External debt creates a burden for the future generation; internal debt is an intra-generational transfer	External debt can relieve pressures on domestic saving during economic upswings
Inter-temporal burden		All (external and internal) debt can impose a burden on the future generation	
Ricardian equivalence (Ricardo)		Individuals behave in such a way that the impact of tax and loan finance on the future generation is equated	Individuals increase saving (reduce consumption), thus rendering activist fiscal policy ineffective
Fiscal activism (Keynes)			Debt-financed fiscal expansion increases aggregate demand to equate aggregate supply at full employment and price stability
Crowding-out of private investment (neoclassical)		Debt may accompany transfer of earning assets (e.g. infrastructure) to future generations	Debt-financed fiscal expansion reduces private investment rate and economic growth, or increases inflation
Public choice	Bias towards overexpansion of public sector (non-efficient expenditure levels) to be neutralised by balanced budget rule (no debt financing) (some correspondence with neoclassical thinking)		Excessive government spending is fed by deficit budgeting without achieving macroeconomic stability

Combined, it is impossible to know a priori which of the above efficiency effects will dominate, that is, whether tax or debt finance is more efficient. The net effect can only be established empirically.

16.4.2 **Distribution (equity)**

Intuitively debt finance constitutes the one method whereby more than one generation could contribute to the financing cost of activities that confer an inter-generational benefit, something that tax finance cannot effect. All debt imposes a burden on the future generation. The difficulty lies in knowing in advance what the concomitant benefit to the future generation will be. If we were to know, for example, that the future generation would be poorer than the present one, it would make sense to transfer income from the present to the future generation, for example by tax-financing an infrastructural project with long-term benefits. The opposite would, of course, apply in the case of a more wealthy future generation.

Ricardian equivalence theory suggests that the government need not concern itself with inter-generational equity, since society will voluntarily effect such equity as is preferred. By increasing their bequests in the face of debt finance, individuals will ensure that the impact of tax and loan finance on the next generation is equated. From an inter-generational equity point of view it is thus immaterial whether tax or debt finance is used.

The final equity consideration is linked to the benefit approach to taxation (see Chapter 10, Section 10.4.1). According to this approach, it is fair (and efficient) for a particular group to pay for a particular programme if they benefit from it. There is no reason why the future generation should not pay for programmes that benefit them. To the extent that a programme benefits a future generation, they should carry part of the financing burden, that is, pay for the benefit that will accrue to them. This could be achieved by means of debt finance.

16.4.3 **Macroeconomic stability**

From a macroeconomic perspective, the choice between tax and debt arises at the margin, that is, should additional expenditure be financed by taxes or by loans, thus incurring a deficit or increasing the size of an existing deficit? No one has suggested that the full budget be loan-financed. Keynesian economists argue that when unemployment is high, for example, debt-financed fiscal expansion is warranted in order to stimulate aggregate demand until it equals aggregate supply at the full employment level of income. Such a fiscal expansion may occur with or without a reduction in tax. Deficit finance is a choice in favour of new debt rather than tax and may also entail substituting new debt for existing tax. On the other hand, when unemployment is low in the Keynesian world, deficit financing may be inflationary and tax increases (a lower budget deficit or a higher budget surplus) will be necessary to constrain private spending.

In Section 16.3.5 we saw that the Keynesian consensus started to break down in the early 1970s when periods of high unemployment and high inflation were experienced and when it was no longer possible to increase employment in a non-inflationary manner. Lower budget deficits, preferably by keeping government expenditure in check, became the consensus view of Keynesians and monetarists (Dornbusch et al., 1994: 397), albeit for quite different reasons. The monetarist argument revolves around crowding-out, already encountered in Section 16.3.6: debt finance has to be reduced to 'crowd in' private investment. The positive impact of reduced budget deficits on investor confidence may outstrip the depressing effect on income in the short term and may on balance be 'good for growth'. In addition, lower budget deficits reduce the risk of inflationary financing. The Keynesian argument is that a reduction in the budget deficit should be effected by curtailing government expenditure in order to avoid the cost-push effects of higher taxation – that is, to avoid the cost of using tax rather than debt. The international financial crisis of 2007–2009 of course threw the debate about appropriate stabilisation policies wide open.

In the era of globalisation the freedom of choice that countries have to independently change budget deficits by large margins in order to pursue macroeconomic stability has been reduced substantially. The strong drive for macroeconomic policy coordination subsequent to the financial crisis of 2007–2009 was a case in point. In a world of competitive tax rates and increasing convergence of countries' budget deficit-GDP ratios at low levels, the choice in developing countries especially has become one of how much and how fast to reduce budget deficits, rather than of how high the budget deficit should be (i.e. how much debt instead of tax).

16.5 Public debt management

16.5.1 Introduction

Thus far our discussion has dealt with the economic justification (or not) to borrow or incur public debt. Once a government has decided to use debt finance, another important set of questions arises: when to borrow, for how long and at what cost, from whom to borrow, where to borrow, which debt instrument to use, and so on. These questions relate to debt management, and, due to their economic impact, are important in their own right.

Given the existing debt and debt structure at any point in time, we define **public debt management**[8] as decisions regarding the timing of borrowing, the term-structure of the existing debt, the desired future maturity structure, the financial instruments, the cost of borrowing and the markets in which new debt is to be issued. A somewhat more general definition is used by the International Monetary Fund and World Bank (IMF and World Bank, 2001): sovereign debt management is the process of establishing and executing a strategy for managing the government's debt in order to raise the required amount of funding, achieve its risk and cost objectives, and meet any other sovereign debt management goals the government may have set, such as developing and maintaining an efficient market for government securities. The approach by the South African government closely resembles this definition.[9]

We discuss the questions raised above with reference to the following objectives of public debt management (which may at times be in conflict):

- minimisation of state debt cost
- macroeconomic stability
- development of domestic financial markets
- financial credibility – ensuring access to financial markets (domestic and foreign).

Before exploring debt management in terms of these objectives, we explain a few basic concepts and operational issues.

Bonds and the cost of borrowing

Recall that the price of a government security (P) is inversely related to its yield (i). If

---

[8] We follow, with slight amendments, the definition used by Abedian and Biggs (1998: 280–281). Substantial parts of the discussion in this section rely on Abedian and Biggs (1998: 276–302).

[9] The interested reader will notice this from National Treasury (2004a: Chapter 5).

the coupon (the fixed amount of earnings) on a consul (a perpetual bond) is denoted as *E*, we can write:

$$P = \frac{E}{i}$$

Assuming efficient markets so that the long-term interest rate is equal to the yield rate on all bonds, higher interest rates imply lower bond prices (value) and vice versa. In the case of a security with a finite maturity, the price is given as the following:

$$P = \left[\frac{E}{(1+\frac{i}{100})}\right] + \left[\frac{E}{(1+\frac{i}{100})^2}\right] + \left[\frac{E}{(1+\frac{i}{100})^3}\right]$$
$$+ \ldots + \left[\frac{E}{(1+\frac{i}{100})^n}\right]$$

where *i* denotes the annual yield and *k* the number of years (periods) to maturity.[10]

Although the government cannot change the interest payments applicable to previously issued debt when changing inflation rates affect the real value of the debt, the owner of such bonds can be protected against capital losses and realise capital gains if the bonds are sufficiently marketable. The government, on the other hand, may for example be able to realise the benefits by buying back unexpired bonds during periods of rising inflation or when such buy-backs would reduce debt service cost.[11] Either the government itself (Treasury) or (more often) the central bank assumes the responsibility of marketing government bonds. To the central bank, government securities are an important instrument of monetary policy, as interest rates (and hence the money supply

control) are influenced by transactions in these bonds – these are so-called open market transactions.[12] As financial markets develop (and in order for these markets to develop), the liquidity of bonds in the secondary capital market becomes more important. At some stage private financial agencies are appointed as so-called **primary dealers** or **market makers**; their functions are to quote (on behalf of the government) two-way prices (selling and buying prices) for government bonds and to assume the responsibility of always buying and selling securities in the secondary market.

When interest rates are volatile, the market value of bonds (and the **government's net worth** or net indebtedness) changes accordingly. By valuing the government's outstanding liabilities at market prices (so-called **mark to market**), a more accurate picture of the state of the fiscus is obtained. If the financial assets and liabilities of government were to be managed by a profit-driven treasury, such valuation will be done continuously in order to maximise profits and minimise losses as a going concern. However, we will see later that when public debt management has macroeconomic stability as one of its objectives, it is not solely driven by the profit-and-loss bottom line.

How much does it cost the government to borrow? The immediate response would be that the answer depends on the interest rate. If the interest rate rises, so will the interest bill, and vice versa. Note that, due to the fact (or to the extent) that government stock is issued at a fixed rate of interest or coupon, a rising interest rate affects only the interest cost pertaining to new debt or debt incurred to replace maturing debt.

The interest cost is not the only cost. In modern capital markets bonds are often

---

[10] This equation can be used to calculate the yield to maturity, which is the interest rate that makes the present value of the future cash flow of a bond equal to the bond's market price, if the bond is held to maturity (Van Zyl, Botha, Goodspeed and Skerritt, 2009: Section 10.2.1). For a more detailed explanation of prices and yields on bonds, and of the market for government bonds, see Van Zyl, Botha, Goodspeed and Skerritt (2009: Section 10.2.1).

[11] Buying back bonds is the same as repaying a loan before the due date.

[12] For insight into these relationships, refer to the liquidity preference theory and the loanable funds theory; both are normally studied in a monetary economics course.

issued at a discount, which means that the government receives a smaller amount than that which will have to be repaid. The reason for the discount on bonds is that the market rate of interest may be higher than the specified yield (or coupon rate) on the bond when the bond is issued due to a number of market factors (such as changes in economic conditions, monetary policy, demand, risk, etc.). Instead of having to raise the coupon every time a bond is issued, the amount of cash received is adjusted. The discount, together with the coupon rate, therefore provides a better indication of the effective interest cost to the issuer (or yield to the buyer). In fact, because it is assumed that all future coupon payments can be invested at the current market rate during the remainder of the bond's lifespan, this market interest rate is actually known as the bond's yield to maturity (YTM). The YTM changes on a daily basis as market conditions change and, as a result, is beyond the control of the issuer.

Suppose that a bond of R100 (the nominal value) is issued at a discount of 5 per cent. This means that the bond will sell at a price of R100 – R(0,05 × 100) = R100 – R5 = R95. The investor thus pays R95 for an asset with a nominal (book) value of R100. The amount received when a bond is issued at a discount (i.e. the **discount price**) differs from the nominal value. In this example the government incurs an extra cost of R5 (in addition, that is, to the coupon or interest payment applicable to the bond). Suppose this bond has to be repaid after five years. In addition to the coupon payments paid over the five-year period, the government will have to repay R5 more in capital than the amount originally received, that is, the discount price of R95 plus the R5 discount cost. The **discount on a bond** is thus defined as the difference between the nominal value and the discount price of the bond.

The figures in our example may appear insignificant, but the amounts involved can be quite large. In 1998/99 for instance, the discount on public debt in South Africa amounted to R6,4 billion, which represented 12,8 per cent of the total debt cost in that year.

The budget deficit, which is announced by the Minister of Finance in the annual Budget Speech, does not account for discount on public debt on an accrual basis. Had this been done, it would have resulted in a higher budget deficit and state debt cost, and lower amounts of government debt in any particular financial year.

A bond may, of course, also be issued at a premium. If the market interest rate were to be below the coupon rate on the day of issue, the bond would be sold at a premium as the effective interest rate would be lower than the coupon rate. The premium will close this gap. For example, during March 2005, the R153[13] (with 2010 as year of maturity) traded at a price constituting a significant premium of about 24 per cent. This was due to the fact that the 13 per cent per annum (fixed) coupon rate on that bond exceeded its market yield (YTM) of about 7,5 per cent by a large margin. This means that for every R1 million in nominal value of the R153 that the government issued in March 2005, it received R1,24 million from the buyer. However, during fiscal year (2005/06) the government had to pay a coupon interest of R130 000 (13% × R1 000 000) to the holder of every bond with a nominal value of R1 million. When an R153, bought in March 2005, matured in 2010, the government had to repay the holder only R1 million.

There are various other costs associated with debt, such as conversion costs, which are incurred when bonds are redeemed before maturity and converted into other bonds, and the cost of raising loans. These costs are however relatively small.

---

[13] The practice is to allocate a number such as this to a particular bond.

Foreign borrowing

When foreign borrowing is undertaken, a **foreign exchange cost** may be incurred in the event of subsequent exchange rate depreciation. Suppose that South Africa issues a one-year bond of €100 on 1 January. To simplify the explanation, we assume an initial exchange rate of €1 = R10 on 1 January, a zero interest rate, no discount on bonds, and a 10 per cent depreciation of the rand against the euro during the year. On 1 January the government receives R1 000 as the proceeds of the loan. On 31 December the government has to repay €100. In order to do this, rands have to be converted into euros. After the depreciation of the rand the new exchange rate is €1 = R11. The government will therefore require R1 100 to repay the loan. The depreciation of the rand has caused an extra cost of R100. An exchange rate depreciation can therefore substantially increase the cost of foreign borrowing. The opposite happens in the case of an appreciation of the rand against the issue currency.

One must be careful, though, not to conclude that the cost associated with an exchange rate depreciation rules out foreign loans altogether. Nominal interest rates are usually higher in a country with a depreciating currency than in countries with stable or appreciating exchange rates. The countries with stable or appreciating exchange rates are normally also the sources of foreign financing. If, in this example, the bond rate was 2 per cent in Euroland and 10 per cent in South Africa, the total cost of the foreign loan after one year (assuming interest is paid at the end of the year) would be the exchange rate depreciation cost of R100 plus the interest cost, which, when converted to rand, amounts to R22 (calculated as $0,02 \times €100 \times 11$). The total cost equals R100 + 22 = R122. The cost of a local bond of equal value (ignoring discount cost) would be $0,10 \times$ R1 000 = R100. Had the South African bond

rate been 12,2 per cent (i.e. had the margin between the domestic and foreign interest rates been 10,2 percentage points), there would have been no difference between the cost of domestic borrowing (which would be $0,122 \times$ R1 000 = R122) and foreign borrowing. Due to the changing value of the South African rand against the currencies of countries in which foreign borrowing is undertaken, the fiscal authorities revalue (in rand terms) the value of maturing foreign loans in the year of repayment.

We now return to the objectives of public debt management, beginning with the minimisation of state debt cost and macroeconomic stabilisation.

16.5.2 Public debt management objectives I and II: minimisation of state debt cost versus macroeconomic stabilisation

At the end of fiscal year 2010/11 the total state debt in South Africa amounted to R988,7 billion. In fiscal year 2010/11 the debt service burden (i.e. interest paid and other costs) was R71,4 billion, which was 2,6 per cent of the GDP or 10 per cent of the government budget. From the perspective of cost effectiveness, no one will argue about the importance of debt cost minimisation. How is this effected?

To answer this question one must keep in mind that a bond is an investment to a bond holder. The return on this investment has two components: the regular coupon yield E (interest earnings) and the capital gain (the difference between the price at which it is sold and bought), both of which the investor would want to be as high as possible. From a cost minimisation perspective, the government as borrower would want the opposite: the lowest interest possible and the smallest capital loss. Note that in a liquid market the government can buy back bonds issued previously – even at a capital gain (which would amount to a capital loss for the bond holder).

Debt cost minimisation is the result of three factors.

- Firstly, the size of the budget deficit and, consequently, the total amount of debt. The lower the annual budget deficit, the smaller the total debt and the lower the debt service cost, all other things being equal.
- Secondly, the interest rate level, which is determined in the money market (short-term rates) and capital market (long-term rates). In South Africa the monetary authorities, through the repo-rate mechanism, play a key role in determining short-term interest rates. As we will see when we discuss macroeconomic stabilisation, the monetary and fiscal authorities may not always desire the same interest level.
- Thirdly, for any debt level, there exists a maturity structure, which minimises debt cost, that is, an optimal maturity structure. The national government dominates the primary bond market. At

the end of 2010, for example, the government was responsible for 78 per cent of new marketable public sector bonds issued. The government cannot, therefore, passively take the market interest rate as a given (as a small market participant would). Government policies (of which fiscal policy is an important component) and the open-market transactions in government bonds have a major impact on interest rates and thus on the borrowing cost. An optimal debt strategy therefore has to calculate the cost of debt, taking account of the impact on interest rates of the very same debt strategy.

The key factor in debt cost minimisation is the difference between short- and long-term interest rates. The **yield curve** (Figure 16.1) shows time-to-maturity of all bonds on the horizontal axis and bond yields to maturity on the vertical axis. A yield curve can be constructed for any of a number of bonds – we focus on government bonds, for which the curve is drawn relatively easily due to the homogeneous features of such bonds.

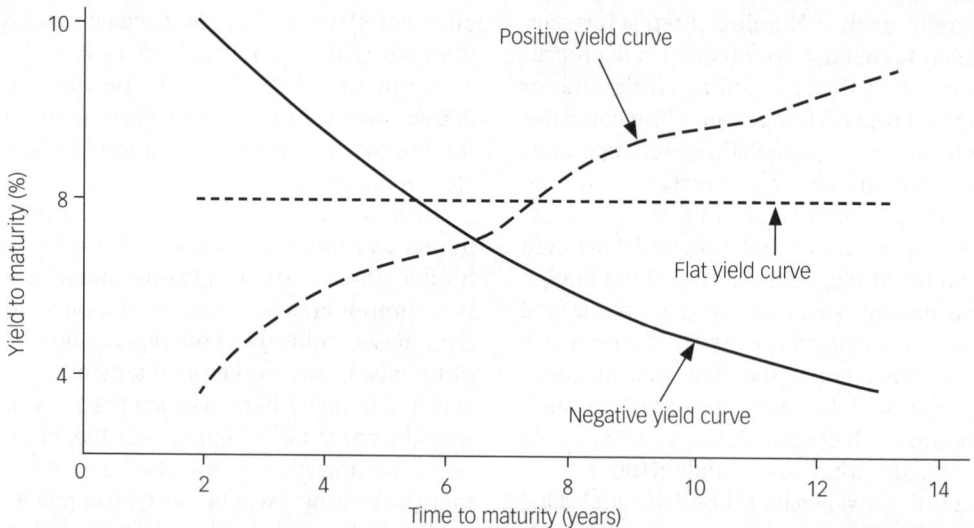

Figure 16.1 Yield curves of government securities

Points on the curve represent the relationship between yield and time-to-maturity of government securities, of which there would typically be a substantial number. Due to market volatility, the yield-to-maturity varies often, so that the yield curve may change frequently – sometimes even daily.

Generally, there are three types of yield curves:

- A **horizontal** or **flat curve** signifies no difference between short and long rates, so that there would be no cost advantage in changing the maturity structure of public debt.
- A **negatively** sloped or **inverse yield curve** is normally observed during periods of vigorous economic expansion and close to the peak of the business cycle. Short-term yields (rates) are higher than long-term yields (rates).
- When long-term yields (interest rates) are higher than short-term yields (rates), the yield curve has an **upward** or a **positive** slope. Typically this pattern is displayed during periods of economic recession and moderate economic growth. In this case, higher long-term rates may reflect longer-term inflationary expectations.

We will now discuss debt management with reference to the upward-sloping yield curve. (The reasoning in respect of the inverse yield curve can easily be derived by inverting the arguments.)

In the case of a positive yield curve[14] the forward-looking cost-minimising treasurer will sell (issue) short-term securities (which are relatively expensive)[15] and buy back long-term securities (which are relatively cheap).

A relatively bigger portfolio of securities with short-term expiry dates, provides the treasurer with much greater manoeuvrability to buy (lock into) long bonds once long rates begin to decline relative to short rates. The **maturity** or **term structure** of public debt will therefore shorten and the debt service cost will be reduced.

The increased supply of shorter-term bonds, on the other hand, will decrease their prices and put upward pressure on short-term interest rates. This may well be in conflict with macroeconomic stabilisation goals. The monetary authorities may at that point in time find no need for higher interest rates; on the contrary, low(er) interest rates may be viewed as compatible with the pursuance of higher economic growth. It is at this point that the cost-minimising objective of the fiscal authorities and the macroeconomic stabilisation objective of the monetary authorities may well be in conflict.

The question is whether debt management should actively be pursued as a macroeconomic stabilisation instrument. There appears to be stronger support for debt management as an instrument of cost minimisation than for pursuing macroeconomic stability. The argument is that the main contribution by the fiscal authorities to macroeconomic stability concerns the size of the budget deficit, rather than the financing thereof. The potential conflict between cost minimisation and macroeconomic stabilisation can give such confusing signals to the financial markets, that it would be more efficient if the fiscal authorities focused only on cost minimisation. The IMF and World Bank (2001) take this line. They recommend that, where the level of financial development allows, there should be a separation of debt management and monetary policy objectives and accountabilities. In countries with well-developed financial markets, borrowing programmes are based on the economic and fiscal projections contained

---

[14] The slope of a normal yield curve is indeed upwards as the yield on longer-dated bonds must be higher than short-dated ones due to the so-called risk premium on the longer one.

[15] This is due to the inverse relationship between the rate of interest and bond prices.

in the government budget, and monetary policy is carried out independently from debt management. This helps to ensure that debt management decisions are not perceived to be influenced by inside information on interest rate decisions, and avoids perceptions of conflicts of interest in market operations. In some countries a separate debt office was established with the sole brief of minimising public debt cost, given the size of the budget deficit and public debt. The South African government appears to have moved in the direction of greater distance between public debt management and macroeconomic policymaking, although a separate debt office has not (yet) been established.

The counter argument is that the fiscal and monetary authorities share the responsibility for macroeonomic stability and that proper policy coordination, rather than separate or independent policy entities, is the answer. The Keynesian world of integrated policymaking is more in line with this view.

One aspect of public debt that has been acknowledged as an important factor in stabilisation policy, is foreign debt management. In Section 16.3 we explored the theoretical views regarding the case for foreign debt. Suffice to say that during an economic boom, when $I>S$, foreign loans by government add to the supply of savings, relieving domestic demand pressures. Note, though, that cost minimisation may be in conflict with the goals of exchange rate policy. A situation may arise where foreign borrowing may be in the interest of the accumulation of reserves, at the same time that (or precisely because) the domestic currency is under pressure. Although the fiscal authorities may find it too expensive to borrow abroad, the monetary authorities may actually favour it. On the other hand, fiscal and exchange rate policy can also complement each other. During 2010/11, for example, when there was concern about the strengthening of the South African rand against major currencies, National Treasury contributed to a somewhat weaker currency by borrowing in foreign rather than domestic capital markets.

16.5.3 Public debt management objective III: development of domestic financial markets

In South Africa government bond issues have been a major factor in the development of the market for loanable funds and the development of financial markets in general. From the point of view of enhanced efficiency, in which greater liquidity and better information play an important role, various capital market developments may be traced to aspects of debt management in South Africa. Marketing of government debt through primary dealers, which was introduced in 1998, not only improved liquidity but also reduced the refinancing risk of government. To improve liquidity, a debt consolidation programme consisting of switches and buy-backs was introduced in 2002. Illiquid bonds were switched into benchmark bonds and (or) repurchased. As the majority of the illiquid bonds had high coupons, the debt consolidation through which they were replaced resulted in savings on debt service cost.

The National Treasury has also diversified the funding instruments available from fixed income bonds and treasury bills to inflation-linked bonds, variable rate bonds and zero-coupon bonds. An innovation that generated much interest is the fixed-interest retail bond that the government launched on 24 May 2004 and which was designed to offer an inexpensive and attractive saving opportunity to small savers.

16.5.4 **Public debt management objective IV: financial credibility**

Debt management is not only concerned with minimising cost: it is also concerned with the ability to borrow. Do prospective investors regard the security as a good investment? Does the issuer of the bond (the government) have financial credibility? South Africa's re-entry into international financial markets, the acquirement of international sovereign credit ratings in 1994, and the subsequent systematic improvement in the country's ratings tell the story of the long road to, and hard work in, successfully building financial credibility. Incidentally, a number of African countries have now acquired international credit ratings, albeit at substantially different levels. Besides South Africa, countries as different as Botswana, Burkino Faso, Cameroon, Egypt, Ghana, Madagascar, Mali, Morocco, and Mozambique have subjected themselves to the thorough investigation and scrutiny of international credit rating agencies. Credit rating agencies suffered reputational damage when they did not detect the default risk underlying high-rated mortgage-backed securities in the US, a major cause of the international financial crisis of 2007–2009. Despite this, ratings remain an important yardstick of financial creditworthiness.

These agencies basically ask two questions when assessing creditworthiness:
- Firstly, *can* the country service its debt? This question revolves around a country's economic ability and its prospects to pay the interest and repay the principal (debt).
- Secondly, *will* the country service its debt? This is a question about the political will to repay the debt.

These questions are relevant irrespective of whether the government borrows domestically or internationally. One of the asymmetries of economic life is that it is much easier for a government to impair or destroy its financial credibility than to build it up. The greater the credibility, the lower the debt cost, and the better the chances of raising loans per se. We highlight a number of factors that are decisive in determining financial credibility.

Market participants need to be convinced of fiscal sustainability. For example, during the first half of the 1990s fiscal sustainability in South Africa became a matter of concern (Calitz and Siebrits, 2003: 58–59). From a macroeconomic perspective the fiscal situation deteriorated from 1990 until 1994, when the long cyclical downswing depressed tax revenues and government expenditures were raised by several extraordinary transfer payments as well as the expansion of social services. Recall from Chapter 15 (Section 15.5.3) our outline of the consequences of government revenue and expenditure trends in the first half of the 1990s for the budget deficit (peaking at 7,3 per cent of GDP in 1992/93) and public debt (rising to 49,5% at the end of fiscal year 1995/96), which gave rise to a debate about whether or not a debt trap was looming.[16] A debt trap is said to be looming when the government has to borrow to pay interest on debt, in other words when a primary deficit arises. Recall from Chapter 15 (Box 15.1) that a primary deficit occurs when non-interest expenditure exceeds recurrent revenue. It means that the government is not able to pay any interest on public debt from current revenue. Consequently

[16] See, for example, Van der Merwe (1993). This debate clearly indicated the extent to which the private sector also had lost faith in the potential of anti-cyclical fiscal policy. Retrospectively, if not by design, the rising deficit portrayed a strong anti-cyclical policy stance. In financial circles, however, instead of being welcomed as an attempt to soften the impact of the cyclical downturn, this caused alarm.

the debt-GDP ratio increases. The rule of thumb is that a primary deficit can only be maintained without a rising debt-GDP ratio if the real rate of economic growth exceeds the real interest rate. It is now well-known that the South African fiscal authorities, to their credit, not only averted the debt trap, but also succeeded in systematically improving the government's (and the country's) financial credibility in the domestic and international capital markets. This was achieved by a combination of measures: greatly improved tax administration and compliance, expenditure restraint, and the use of privatisation income to repay debt. Given the share of government expenditure in the economy, the resultant reduction in the interest bill as a percentage of GDP released resources for reallocation to higher priority expenditure areas, notably in the field of social expenditure. Recent analysis (Calitz, du Plessis and Siebrits, 2011) has shown that the sharp increase in the ratio of public debt to GDP during the middle of the 1990s was less steep if the funding of the government employees' pensions fund and the takeover of the debt of the homelands of the apartheid state were counted as public debt when the obligations arose many years earlier (instead of when the national government took over the debt during the first half of the 1990s). Retrospectively, the accusation of 'weak aggregate fiscal discipline' in the early 1990s (see Ajam and Aron, 2007: 746) was excessive, more so because the improved funding of the pension funds reduced, if not removed, a major liability that otherwise would have required financing in the future.

Market participants also need to be convinced that the market rules of the game are upheld and reinforced by government. It is quite conceivable that, due to distortional interventions in the financial markets, governments may encounter difficulties in raising loans in the domestic market or may only be able to raise loans at high cost, even with relatively low budget deficits. We highlight three South African examples that contributed to the financial credibility of government. The first is the abolishment in 1989 of the prescribed asset requirements in respect of insurance companies and private pension funds, referred to in Section 16.2. In 2003, 14 years later, the less intimidating and less distortional, albeit quite forceful, technique of moral suasion was active in directing investment resources into targeted sectors of the economy. The financial sector charter (Financial Sector Charter Council, 2008) was developed voluntarily by the financial sector, naturally to avoid legislation of the kind aborted in 1989. Designed to underpin black economic empowerment (BEE), the charter embodies targets (in total and for institutions) in respect of BEE ownership, targeted investment in areas where gaps or backlogs in economic development and job creation have not been adequately addressed by financial institutions, investment in education, and so on.

The second example is the pre-1994 decision by the ANC to dispose of nationalisation as an economic policy position. In February 1990 Nelson Mandela stated that 'the nationalisation of the mines, banks and monopoly industry is the policy of the ANC and a change or modification of our views in this regard is inconceivable' (Nattrass, 1992: 624). Two years later, having been confronted by the universal disapproval of nationalisation by world economic leaders at the World Economic Forum in Davos, Switzerland, he told business people in Cape Town that he would try to persuade the ANC to dispose of the policy, as it had become clear to him that South Africa would not be able to attract foreign investment if investors felt that they had the 'sword of Damocles' of nationalisation hanging over their heads. During 2010 a hefty debate about nationalisation of the mines was instigated by the ANC Youth League.

Despite government statements that nationalisation was not policy, at the time of writing it was still a point of discussion within the ruling party.

The last example of a government that understands and upholds the rules of the (financial markets) game is the decision by the ANC government not to renege on public debt that accrued in the apartheid era.

These examples illustrate actions that strengthened the development of a nonpartisan style of governance that values and pursues international best practices of good governance in a market-based economy.

16.5.5 Contingent liabilities[17]

Finally, a word on **contingent liabilities**, which represent potential financial claims against the government. When triggered, a definite financial obligation or liability will arise. Contingent liabilities may be *explicit*, such as government guarantees on foreign exchange borrowings by certain domestic borrowers, government insurance schemes with respect to crop failures or natural disasters, and instruments such as put options on government securities.

Contingent liabilities may also be *implicit*, where the government does not have a contractual obligation to provide assistance, but (*ex post*) decides to do so because it believes the cost of not intervening is unacceptable. Examples include possible interventions in respect of the financial sector, state-owned enterprises or sub-national governments.

According to the National Treasury, total contingent liabilities in South Africa amounted to R298,2 billion (or 11,2 per cent of GDP) at the end of the fiscal year 2010/11

(National Treasury, 2011: 96). Government guarantees have the effect of reducing the debt cost to the borrowing institution and are therefore not free. In 2010/11 Government received fees of R43,9 million on various guarantees provided.

Unlike real government financial obligations, however, contingent liabilities have a degree of uncertainty: they may be exercised only if certain events occur, and the size of the fiscal payout depends on the structure of the undertaking. Experience indicates that these contingent liabilities can be very large, particularly when they involve recapitalisation of the banking system by the government (as was the case with huge bailouts of financial institutions in various industrial countries during the international financial crisis of 2007–2009), or government obligations that arise from poorly designed programmes for privatisation of government assets. If structured without appropriate incentives or controls, contingent liabilities are often associated with moral hazard for the government, since making allowances ahead of time can increase the probability of these liabilities being realised. As a result, governments need to balance the benefits of disclosure with the moral hazard consequences that may arise with respect to contingent liabilities. In Chapter 17 we discuss the issue of the borrowing powers of sub-national governments in South Africa with reference, inter alia, to moral hazard.

---

[17] This section draws strongly on IMF and World Bank (2001: Section IV.5.2: 31–32).

IMPORTANT CONCEPTS

capital expenditure
(page 326)
consul (page 327)
contingent liabilities
(explicit, implicit)
(page 347)
crowding-out (page 333)
current expenditure
(page 326)
debt servicing (page 324)
debt trap (page 325)
discount on a bond
(page 340)
discount price (page 340)
domestic or internal debt
(page 328)
fiscal illusion (page 334)

foreign exchange cost
(page 341)
foreign or external debt
(page 328)
government bonds
(page 324)
inter-temporal burden
(page 328)
mark to market (page 339)
maturity or term structure
(page 343)
net indebtedness (page 327)
net tax or net fiscal burden
(page 331)
net worth (page 327)
net worth of government
(page 339)

ownership distribution (of
public debt) (page 326)
primary dealers (market
makers) in government
bonds (page 339)
principal of debt (page 324)
public debt (page 324)
public debt management
(page 338)
Ricardian equivalence
(page 331)
treasury bill (page 324)
yield curve (horizontal or
flat, inverse or negative,
upward or positive)
(page 342, 343)
zero-coupon bonds
(page 324)

SELF-ASSESSMENT EXERCISES

16.1 Distinguish between:
  ◗ nominal and real debt
  ◗ interest and discount on public debt
  ◗ internal and external debt
  ◗ a positive, a negative, and a horizontal yield curve
  ◗ explicit and implicit contingent liabilities.

16.2 Explain the nature of the different public debt costs.

16.3 Suppose the South African government borrows $100 in the USA on 1 January. The exchange rate is R8 to $1. How much will have to be repaid in rand after two years if the rand appreciates by 10 per cent per annum against the US dollar over the period? What will be the net result of the loan transaction for the South African government at the end of the period if the US interest rate is 5 per cent per year? (Assume that interest is calculated and paid in arrears on the last day of each year.)

16.4 If the government issues a bond with a nominal value of R100 and a coupon rate of 5 per cent at a discount of 10 per cent, what will be the effective return on investment for the bond holder?

16.5 Compare the different theories of public debt in terms of efficiency, equity and macroeconomic stabilisation considerations.

16.6 Explain the contradictions (if any) between Ricardian equivalence, fiscal activism, and crowding-out as theories of public debt.

16.7 'Tax finance is always superior to debt finance on both efficiency and equity grounds.' Discuss this statement.

16.8 'If the home currency is depreciating, the home government should under no circumstances issue foreign bonds.' Discuss this statement.

16.9 Are the following statements true (T) or false (F)? Explain your answer.

(a) Contingent liabilities form part of the public debt.

(b) The net worth of government is the difference between the value of all assets and the liabilities of government.

(c) If the government borrows in another country and the relative value of the respective currencies does not change over the period of the loan, there will be no foreign exchange rate cost.

(d) Ricardian equivalence means that it makes no difference to the level of aggregate demand whether the government uses tax or debt finance.

(e) There is no need to be concerned about a rising public debt-GDP ratio because public debt is something that a country owes to itself.

(f) In the case of an inverse yield curve, the forward-looking cost-minimising government debt office will sell short-term securities and buy back long-term securities.

(g) The different debt management objectives are never in conflict.

(h) Debt management should not be used as an instrument of macroeconomic stabilisation.

PART

5

Intergovernmental fiscal relations

Tania Ajam

Fiscal federalism

The aim of this chapter is to study the rationale for fiscal federalism and the nature of intergovernmental fiscal relations from an efficiency and equity point of view, with particular reference to the South African situation.

We start by examining the economic rationale for fiscal decentralisation as opposed to the reasons for fiscal centralisation. This is followed by an explanation of the considerations on which the assignment of tax powers and expenditure functions to sub-national governments are based. Next we discuss tax competition and tax harmonisation as well as the borrowing powers and debt management at sub-national level, before proceeding with an analysis of different kinds of intergovernmental grants. The chapter concludes with an overview of intergovernmental fiscal issues in South Africa.

Once you have studied this chapter, you should be familiar with the key principles of fiscal federalism. In particular you should be able to:

- explain why sub-national governments exist at all and compare the merits of fiscal decentralisation and centralisation
- describe the Tiebout model
- describe the assignment of expenditure functions and revenue sources (tax powers) to the national, provincial, and local spheres of government in South Africa
- distinguish between tax competition and tax harmonisation
- explain the reasons for, and the nature of, intergovernmental grants
- list the types of intergovernmental grants
- explain the issues that surround borrowing powers and debt management at sub-national level
- review the role of the South African Financial and Fiscal Commission (FFC) in sharing revenue across the three spheres of government
- discuss trends and issues in provincial and local government financing in South Africa.

17.1 The economic rationale for fiscal decentralisation

In Chapter 1 we introduced the concept of general government (Figure 1.1). This concept signifies that governments typically consist of more than one level. That is, there may be provincial or local tiers of government in addition to central or national government. Budgetary decisions are generally made at different levels of government. The term **sub-national government** (i.e. provincial and local government) refers to those levels of government that have smaller jurisdictions compared to the national government. National government's jurisdiction would, of course, extend to the whole country, whereas the jurisdiction of a local government, for instance, would only be within a particular municipality.

The greater the discretion that sub-national governments have to make (e.g. policy decisions about spending, taxation, and borrowing) the more decentralised the fiscal system is. In a state with more than one level of government **intergovernmental fiscal relations**, also called 'fiscal federalism', is concerned with the structure of public finances: how taxing, spending, and regulatory functions are allocated between the different tiers of government, as well as the nature of transfers between national, provincial, and local governments. In contrast to approaches followed in political science and constitutional law, the generic meaning of the term 'federalism' in economics implies decentralisation, and fiscal federalism deals with the fiscal implications of a decentralised system of multi-level government.

The justification for a decentralised system embodying sub-national decision-making powers stems partly from our earlier analyses presented in Part 1 of the book. Firstly (and as discussed in Chapter 2), it may improve allocative efficiency or the ability of the public sector to produce the level and mix of public services that citizens demand and which correspond with their preferences. But this depends on the nature of public (and merit) goods produced and delivered by government. Some public goods are national in scope (like defence), or indeed global (as discussed in Chapter 3, Section 3.9). Local public goods, however, confer benefits that are confined to a limited geographical area. For instance, the transmission of a radio programme would benefit only those people within the broadcasting range of the transmitter, or parks would serve the recreational needs of people living close to them. Local public goods are therefore specific to a particular location. Consumers, by electing to locate in a particular geographic jurisdiction, can therefore choose the quantity and type of local public goods they receive. This theme is explored in greater detail in Section 17.1.1 where we discuss the Tiebout model and the allocative role of government.

Local and provincial governments therefore exist due to the fact that the spatial incidence of public goods differs. In practice, however, the boundaries of sub-national governments are often historically or politically determined. Therefore these may not coincide exactly with the benefit areas of the public goods that sub-national governments produce. As a result, **spatial externalities** may exist, that is, spillovers of costs and benefits at the boundaries between sub-national government jurisdictions.

A second rationale for decentralisation is provided by public choice theory generally and the limitations of a centralised majority-based democratic system in particular – as discussed in Chapter 6 and briefly elaborated on in Section 17.1.2 below.

17.1.1 The Tiebout model

Tiebout (1956) asserted that if there were a large enough number of local government jurisdictions and each of these local governments offered a different mix of local public goods and taxes, individuals would reveal their true preferences for local public goods by choosing a particular local government jurisdiction in which to live. In this model, citizens (who have different tastes) are mobile and choose to settle in the local government jurisdictions that produce a mix of tax and public good outputs, which correspond most closely to their preferences. Their choice of location thus reveals their preferences for public goods in the same way that their choice of private goods purchased in the market reveals their preferences for private goods.

> *Just as the consumer may be visualised as walking to a private market place to buy his goods, we place him in the position of walking to a community where the prices (taxes) of community services are set. Both trips take the consumer to market. There is no way in which the consumer can avoid revealing his preferences in a spatial economy.*
>
> Tiebout, 1956: 422

The greater the number of communities and the greater the variation in taxes and public services offered, the closer consumers will be to satisfying their preferences. Under these conditions, local public goods can be decentralised in a way that is immune to the free-rider problem. Tiebout's notion of 'voting with one's feet' permits the revelation of preferences by allowing people to sort themselves into groups with similar tastes. Furthermore, the equilibrium that will be achieved by voting with one's feet will be Pareto efficient. The Tiebout model thus describes a theoretical solution for the problem of preference revelation, a phenomenon that inhibits the achievement of allocative efficiency (see Chapters 2, 3, and 6).

It must be noted that the Tiebout model is based on a number of restrictive assumptions, namely:

- all citizens are fully mobile
- individuals have full information about the local public goods offered by each jurisdiction
- there is a large number of jurisdictions to choose from, spanning the full range of public good combinations desired by citizens
- there are no geographic employment restrictions: people receive income from capital only and are not tied to a particular location through job or family ties
- there are no spillovers across jurisdictions
- there are no economies of scale in the production of public goods.

If there are economies of scale in the production of public goods and hence declining average cost (for example the cost of an additional listener to a local radio programme or of an additional road user may be zero), then a local public goods equilibrium may not exist at all. Preference revelation once again becomes a problem.

If there is only a limited number of communities, these may compete with each other to attract outsiders. While this behaviour (analogous to a monopolistically competitive firm) may provide an incentive towards an efficient production of public services, the mix and level of public services provided may not be Pareto efficient. If there are fewer communities than types of individuals, a person might not be able to find a jurisdiction where people's tastes match his or her own.

Finally, there are issues concerning redistribution. As there is an element of redistribution involved in the provision of local public goods (e.g. health and education), the wealthy may attempt to avoid this redistribution by segregating themselves from the poor (Atkinson and Stiglitz, 1980).

Although the Tiebout model is based on a number of stringent assumptions, it does clearly demonstrate that a decentralised fiscal system – which can accommodate a diversity of preferences for public goods – can be welfare-increasing in relation to a centralised system which imposes a standardised public good-tax mix on people, no matter what their tastes. Fiscal decentralisation can in principle contribute to a more efficient provision of local public goods by aligning expenditures more closely with local priorities.

17.1.2 Public choice perspective on fiscal federalism

From a public good perspective we have already discussed (in Chapter 6) Arrow's impossibility theory and the maximising behaviour of politicians, bureaucrats and special interest groups within a centralised democratic system. Both explicit and implicit logrolling on the part of political parties and individual politicians, and the 'empire-building' motives of bureaucrats, coupled with rational ignorance among the broad electorate, can give rise to an over-supply of public goods in the economy. To the extent that they do, the net effect is clearly sub-optimal, with goods and services not being allocated in accordance with the relative preferences of the community as a whole.

This Leviathan hypothesis, first proposed by Brennan and Buchanan (1980), views government as a revenue-maximising monopolist which seeks systematically to exploit its citizens by maximising the tax revenue that it extracts from the economy. According to this perspective, fiscal decentralisation would place a powerful restraint on the government's Leviathan tendencies. Devolution of taxing and spending powers to sub-national governments would act as a disciplinary force on the size of government by forging a closer link between raising funds

and spending funds. For instance, any additional expenditure by a sub-national jurisdiction may have to be funded by increased sub-national taxation. Centralised fiscal systems break this link, encouraging the growth of government. In centralised fiscal systems, local residents have more opportunities to lobby for spending programmes that are financed out of nationally collected revenues or national loans.

17.1.3 Other reasons for fiscal decentralisation

Competition between sub-national jurisdictions may enhance innovation. Successful local government experiments may be replicated elsewhere and the failures discarded. This argument will be examined in greater detail later.

Furthermore, there may be a high cost associated with decision-making if it is completely centralised. Due to the smaller groups involved, the devolution of spending and taxing powers may reduce the cost of decision-making. Fiscal decentralisation could also encourage public participation in decision-making since local and provincial governments may be closer to the communities they serve and may foster fiscal accountability.

17.2 Reasons for fiscal centralisation

Although there are advantages associated with fiscal federalism, there are also factors that favour centralisation.

Firstly, spatial externalities may arise when the benefit or costs of a public service 'spill over' to non-residents of a particular jurisdiction. Goods with external benefits are likely to be under-produced, since each sub-national government is concerned primarily with the welfare of its own residents.

Similarly, public goods with significant external costs may be over-produced since the residents of a jurisdiction do not bear the full social cost. Under these circumstances it may be preferable to have a centralised provision to 'internalise' these costs and benefits.

Secondly, centralised provision of public services may be justified by economies of scale, that is, certain services (such as transport systems and water) may require areas larger than a single sub-national jurisdiction for cost-effective provision.

Thirdly, centralised provision may lead to lower administration and compliance costs in the financing of public services. For example, using one computer system for the whole country or one revenue collection system serving national and provincial governments may prevent the cost of duplication.

In practice, no country has a completely decentralised or completely centralised system. While the provision of certain goods is preferable at national level, others are best provided at sub-national level. The crucial question is therefore the following: what is the optimal degree of fiscal decentralisation? This brings us to the assignment problem.

17.3 Taxing and spending at sub-national level: the assignment issue

The **assignment problem** is concerned with how spending and taxation responsibilities should be distributed among national and sub-national governments. Fiscal federalism literature provides broad guidelines on this fundamental issue.

17.3.1 Stabilisation function

There is general consensus that macroeconomic policy should be assigned to central government. Sub-national governments cannot and should not conduct monetary policy. If the power to create money were decentralised to regional entities, there would be strong incentives for sub-national governments to print money to finance public service provision, rather than raising sub-national taxes or imposing user charges. Such behaviour would clearly lead to inflationary pressures, thus adversely affecting the national economy and compromising national government policies for which the particular sub-national government bears no responsibility.

The conventional wisdom in the fiscal federalism literature is that fiscal stabilisation policy would be ineffective at sub-national level. Provincial and local economies tend to be 'open' (i.e. they 'import' and 'export' large shares of what they produce or consume from other provinces or local jurisdictions). If a single sub-national government were to pursue an expansionary fiscal policy, for example, much of the increase in demand would be lost to outside jurisdictions due to the openness of such economies. If, for example, a provincial government were to cut taxes substantially in order to stimulate the provincial economy, most of the newly generated spending would flow out of the provincial economy in payment for goods and services produced elsewhere. The ultimate impact on employment levels in the province would be very small. Fiscal policy by sub-national governments is thus likely to prove impotent since the extent of import leakages would substantially reduce any multiplier effects. Taxes suitable for macroeconomic stabilisation, such as personal and corporate income tax, should therefore be centralised (Musgrave, 1983).

17.3.2 Distribution function

In the fiscal federalism literature it is generally argued that only a centralised redistribution policy by central government is likely to be effective. The argument is that any effort to redistribute income by a single sub-national government (e.g. by increasing taxes on high-income earners and firms and spending the proceeds on the poor) would ultimately be self-defeating. There would be an influx of poor migrants into the jurisdiction, attracted by the fiscal benefits (transfer payments or increased public services). This would be accompanied by an exodus of high-income earners and businesses from that jurisdiction. It then becomes more difficult for the jurisdiction to attain its distributional goals, given the dwindling tax base. Sub-national governments may therefore end up in a worse distributional position, which may in fact clash with the redistributive objectives of the national government.

17.3.3 Allocation function

Probably the most compelling economic case for fiscal decentralisation is its potential to secure efficiency gains. The static arguments linking fiscal decentralisation with improved efficiency include the following:

▶ Uniform centralised policy forces every region to consume the same mix of taxes and public spending, even though tastes and attitudes may vary widely across regions in a large country with many cultural and ethnic groups. Each decentralised jurisdiction could more closely tailor its service and tax package to the preferences of its citizenry. For instance, the residents of a particular province might want education in a particular language. Politically, decentralisation, which accommodates diversity, may be necessary to induce various regions to remain part of the federation (e.g. Quebec in Canada).

▶ Different public goods have different spatial characteristics. Some benefit the entire country (e.g. defence) whereas others benefit only a province (e.g. forestry services) or a locality (street lighting). Public services are provided most efficiently by a jurisdiction that has control over the minimum geographic area that would internalise the benefits and costs of such provision.

▶ Lower-tier governments may have more information about the needs and priorities of their citizens as well as region-specific conditions and prices than national governments, which could improve programme design and service delivery.

▶ Diseconomies of scale and increasing bureaucratic inefficiency arise when spending programmes become too large, that is, when they serve too large a geographical area.

The dynamic efficiency arguments point out that fiscal decentralisation can stimulate innovation. Contestability in the public sector arena may have similar beneficial effects to competition in private markets. Centralisation of functions may mean that national governments may be prone to inertia. With little experimentation, practices within government may become rigid and perpetuate themselves even when the underlying logic for their introduction no longer holds true. Variety in policy design and application at sub-national level is seen as desirable as it diversifies the country's exposure to disastrous policy experiments. Successful policy experiments at sub-national level can be replicated by other tiers of government as best practice and the failures can be discarded.

Improved allocative efficiency in a decentralised system depends heavily on the political and institutional mechanisms through which sub-national governments can be made aware of their electorates' preferences and are held accountable for their actions. However, in many developing countries these democratic structures are not in place, or if they are nominally in place, de facto do not function. Furthermore, sub-national governments may lack capacity and may be prone to corruption. Thus, while efficiency gains due to fiscal decentralisation are attainable in principle, the way in which fiscal decentralisation is implemented determines whether these are in fact realised. In a sense, while fiscal decentralisation can attenuate one form of government failure, it may introduce other forms. The above discussion also shows clearly that while a decentralised system may promote efficiency, it may prove detrimental to the equity goal (i.e. redistributive goals) and may even compromise stabilisation objectives.

17.3.4 Tax assignment

Tax assignment refers to the assignment of tax sources to different tiers of government. In the same vein, **expenditure assignment** refers to the assignment of expenditure functions to different tiers of government.

Intuitively, tax assignment should complement expenditure assignment. In principle, the more the spending responsibilities assigned to a particular level of government, the more the tax revenue sources should be assigned to it. As the difference between expenditure and tax assignments increases, sub-national governments will become more dependent on grants from national government in order to meet their spending obligations. As a result, the ability of the electorate to enforce fiscal accountability will decrease.

In determining the most appropriate tax assignment, two important factors for consideration are equity (ensuring vertical and horizontal equity among individual tax payers as well as across regions) and efficiency (minimising the cost of collection and compliance, as well as minimising any market distortions). In the light of equity and efficiency, Musgrave (1983) proposes the following assignment guidelines:

- Progressive redistributive taxes should be assigned to the national government (e.g. personal and corporate income taxes).
- Taxes appropriate for macroeconomic stabilisation should likewise be centralised (e.g. value added tax and personal income tax). As its corollary, taxes assigned to the sub-national governments should be less sensitive to economic and business fluctuations, that is, it should be cyclically stable (e.g. motor vehicle taxes).
- Unequal tax bases among jurisdictions should be assigned to the national government (e.g. mining tax).
- Taxes on mobile factors of production should be centralised (e.g. corporate income tax or value added tax where companies are able to shift the accounting base of the tax to lower-tax jurisdictions).
- Residence-based taxes such as excise taxes should be assigned to the provinces.
- The local authorities should levy taxes on immobile factors of production, such as property taxes.
- All levels of government may charge user charges and benefit taxes.

17.4 Tax competition versus tax harmonisation

When different sub-national governments impose different tax rates, citizens and businesses may react by moving to jurisdictions with lower tax rates. **Tax competition** occurs when sub-national governments adjust (lower) their tax rates to attract mobile factors of production (notably capital) from other jurisdictions. **Tax harmonisation** occurs when sub-national governments coordinate their tax policies (for instance, by limiting the degree of variation in tax rates levied, or by defining the tax bases in a uniform way).

Initially tax competition was regarded as distortionary, non-neutral, and leading to sub-optimal outcomes, and it was thought that it could be rectified by means of tax harmonisation. The rationale was that if one province decides to pursue a competitive tax strategy, the other provinces would respond likewise. This 'beggar-thy-neighbour' downward spiral caused by provinces attempting to undercut each other could eventually lead to identical but sub-optimally low tax rates on mobile production factors. In addition, the distribution of mobile factors (particularly capital) would be distorted. Uncoordinated tax policies could therefore lead to market distortions with regards to mobile factors of production as well as tradable goods and services.

More recent thinking sees tax competition as a positive influence and efficiency enhancing. Decentralised tax powers could promote innovation, as sub-national governments would be able to experiment with various fiscal packages. In the public sector analogue of private market competition and discipline, policy successes could be emulated elsewhere and failures abandoned. It could also permit sub-national governments to tailor tax mixes to their citizens' preferences and furthermore encourage accountability. If governments are providing services that individuals and firms want and are willing to pay for, the adverse effects of tax competition may be limited. If government overspends and tries to place the tax burden on those who do not benefit, tax competition may be construed as a positive spur to increased government responsiveness. One reason for the about-face is the intensifying global competition. Due to international mobility of

capital, investment that is merely displaced to another region at least remains within the country instead of migrating across national borders.

17.5 Borrowing powers and debt management at sub-national level

Sub-national governments generally have more limited capacity than central government in issuing debt obligations. In the interest of coordinated macroeconomic policy and the achievement of overall macroeconomic objectives, there must be a central government supervision of the debt operations of sub-national governments. Because the national economy is larger and more diverse, central government can absorb those shocks that a single region would find too great to deal with.

Another related aspect of sub-national debt is fiscal exposure, which refers to the total amount of both the direct liabilities of government (e.g. bonds) and the contingent liabilities (e.g. government guarantees). Sub-national borrowing requires an active market in government securities assisted by bond-rating agencies. Fiscally irresponsible behaviour of sub-national governments is then penalised by increased interest rates. The discipline of the market may, however, be undermined by contagion effects and negative pecuniary externalities. **Financial contagion** refers to a situation where a financial crisis in one government, or in respect of one particular type of financial instrument, triggers a loss of confidence in investors, which precipitates similar crises in other similar governments or similar classes of financial instruments. In this context, one province's inability to service debt could cause a loss of investor confidence in other provinces. Provincial tax bases are narrower and more elastic than national tax bases due to factor mobility. An adverse shock may render a province unable to service its debt, precipitating a financial panic. The perception that the financial panic is contagious might impose a negative externality on the other provinces. Alternatively, the higher interest rates in response to increased perceived risk will affect all the provinces.

Effective market discipline on the borrowing activities of provinces assumes, however, that private agents have sufficient information to assess provincial risk profiles accurately. For instance, if sub-national governments do not have their own substantial tax revenue sources, potential lenders and bond-rating agencies will set their interest rates based on their perceptions of the terms under which revenue sharing or intergovernmental grants are likely to be made. In some developing countries payments to sub-national governments are often suspended when central governments run into financial problems. In practice, information asymmetries are rife, creating the conditions for 'moral hazard' behaviour.

Moral hazard occurs in a situation where the actions of one party to a contract cannot be monitored by the other party or parties to the contract. This permits opportunistic behaviour on the part of the party whose actions are 'hidden', to the detriment of the other less informed parties. A classic example of moral hazard can be found in the insurance industry where drivers (whose driving style and ability cannot be observed by the insurance company) start to drive more recklessly once fully insured. Moral hazard behaviour and sub-national debt are described below.

In the instance of sub-national debt, moral hazard entails that one party (the lending institution) may behave in fiscally imprudent or risky ways, such as by extending risky loans to provincial governments of dubious creditworthiness, knowing that the debt will either be explicitly or implicitly guaranteed by the other party (the national government). To complicate the problem, provincial governments know that the national government is explicitly or implicitly underwriting their debt, and therefore also have an incentive to act fiscally imprudently. There is thus moral hazard between the lender and the provincial government as well as between the provincial and national governments.

Even if a government explicitly refuses to bail out a sub-national government, this may have very little credibility with markets. Although it would be best for a government to say in advance that it will not bail out sub-national governments in such an eventuality, it has every incentive to renege on its undertaking. In other words, no matter how emphatically national government refuses to aid bankrupt provinces, there will always be a strong incentive for the government to assist sub-national governments should they find themselves in financial trouble. The long-term costs of impassively standing by while a sub-national government fails may be so great that national governments invariably act as the government of last resort.

Anticipating this behaviour, markets would react as if the national government had implicitly underwritten sub-national government lending. The implicit guarantee by central government (which generally has a better credit rating than sub-national governments) will mean that sub-national governments will be able to borrow on more favourable terms than would have applied otherwise, thereby encouraging increased debt.

In addition, under these circumstances moral hazard behaviour by creditors could exacerbate the situation. The closer a sub-national government is to financial crisis and the more liabilities it accumulates, the more likely it is that the national government will have to step in and bail it out. Banks and financial institutions, anticipating this, may lend more rather than less to the sub-national government. This may result in even more unsustainable sub-national debt, which could have a destabilising effect on the macro economy.

As political circumstances render it untenable in most cases for a central government to allow a sub-national government to go bankrupt, national government may ultimately find itself liable for any default on public debt no matter which tier of government does the borrowing. This would apply even if the actual letter of the debt contract exempts the national government from any liability. There is thus a need for national government regulation in order to allow sub-national borrowing but under conditions that will minimise national government risk. In an international setting, irresponsible behaviour by, or on behalf of, a sub-national government could harm the country's credibility and credit rating, and thus impose a negative externality on other spheres of government.

17.6 Intergovernmental grants

Intergovernmental grants are transfer payments from one sphere of government (e.g. national) to another sphere of government (e.g. a provincial or local government). Intergovernmental grants may be unconditional or conditional. **Unconditional grants** may be spent by recipient governments as they see fit. **Conditional grants** must be spent on the specific service stipulated by the grantor (i.e. the sphere of government which is making the grant).

Grants may also be matching or non-matching. In a **matching grant**, the grantor government will match a certain percentage of each rand of spending by the sub-national government on the same activity. A **non-matching grant** is just a lump-sum allocation

that does not depend on the level of sub-national expenditure.

17.6.1 Unconditional non-matching grants

An unconditional non-matching grant is a lump-sum transfer to sub-national government on which no constraints are placed as to how it is to be spent. The national government could recommend that the grant be spent on certain public goods – referred to below as 'grant-aided public goods' – but the choice ultimately lies with the recipient government. The recipient government may spend it on any public good or service, or provide tax relief to its citizens. This grant acts to increase the income of the recipient government, but does not alter the relative price of any particular public good. A non-matching grant is in effect an income supplement. A **block grant** in the South African context refers to a type of unconditional non-matching grant where a global lump sum is transferred to a sub-national government to be spent at its discretion. This is also referred to as **revenue sharing**.

The effect of introducing such a grant is illustrated in Figure 17.1. We measure spending on the grant-aided public good in rand, on the horizontal axis. Spending on all other public goods is measured on the vertical axis. The line AB shows the government's budget constraint before receiving a grant. The line CD shows the government's new budget constraint after receiving the grant. I_0 and I_1 are the indifference curves of the median voter, indicating society's relative preferences.

Point E_0 shows the initial equilibrium, which could be thought of as reflecting the median voter's preferences (i.e. preferred combination of grant-aided and other public goods). An unconditional grant (of BD rand) shifts the recipient government's budget constraint from AB to CD. The new equilibrium is at E_1, signifying a higher level of social

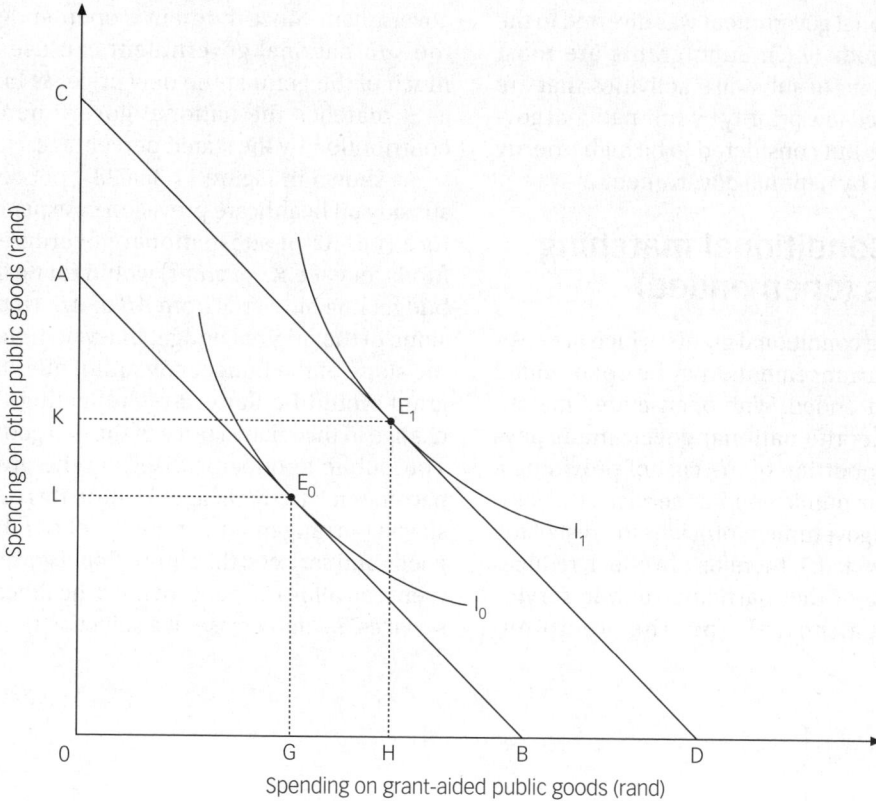

Figure 17.1 Unconditional non-matching grant

welfare. There is an increase in grant-aided public good expenditure by the sub-national government (*GH*). This increase is, however, less than the amount of the grant (*BD*). Unconditional grants, because they may be spent on any public good or to finance tax breaks, have the least stimulatory effect on the recipient government's consumption of the grant-aided public good.

17.6.2 **Conditional non-matching grants**

Conditional non-matching grants provide recipient governments with a given amount of funds (without sub-national matching) with the condition that these funds are used for a particular purpose. For example, a

conditional grant might be for spending on healthcare only. As shown in Figure 17.2, the sub-national government's budget line will therefore shift outwards by the amount of the grant (*AF*) from the original budget line *AB* to the post-grant budget line *AFD*.

From the sub-national government's perspective, *OJ* (equal to *AF*) of the grant-aided good is 'free'. Therefore at the new equilibrium E_1, at least *OJ* of the grant-aided public good will be produced and consumed. Note that this particular community can still reduce its own spending on the grant-aided good as long as the full grant (i.e. *AF=OJ*) is spent as prescribed. At E_1, therefore, the extra spending on the subsidised good (*GM*) is less than the grant (*OJ*), as part of the initial spending on the subsidised good by the sub-national government was diverted to the other goods (*LK*). Such grants are most appropriate to subsidise activities that are considered low priority by sub-national governments but considered to be high priority activities by national government.

17.6.3 Conditional matching grants (open-ended)

Matching conditional grants, which are cost-sharing arrangements, may be open-ended or closed-ended. With open-ended matching grants the national government pays some proportion of the cost of providing a particular public good or service. The sub-national government provides the rest of the funds needed. It therefore, in effect, reduces the price of that particular public service (say healthcare) for the recipient

government. Since the grant is open-ended, the sub-national government can use as much of the grant at the new price, as long as it matches the national government's contribution by the stated percentage.

As shown in Figure 17.3, a $33\frac{1}{3}$ per cent subsidy on healthcare provision or expenditure (i.e. R2 of sub-national government funds for each R1 of grant) would rotate the budget line outwards from *AB* to *AD*. (If the slope of the original budget line was 1, then the slope of the budget constraint after the grant would be flatter at $\frac{2}{3}$, reflecting the change in the relative price of the two goods. The public good subsidised by the grant becomes relatively cheaper.) Due to this cost-sharing arrangement, at any level of other goods and services, the sub-national government can afford 50 per cent more healthcare services. As in the case of a selective tax on

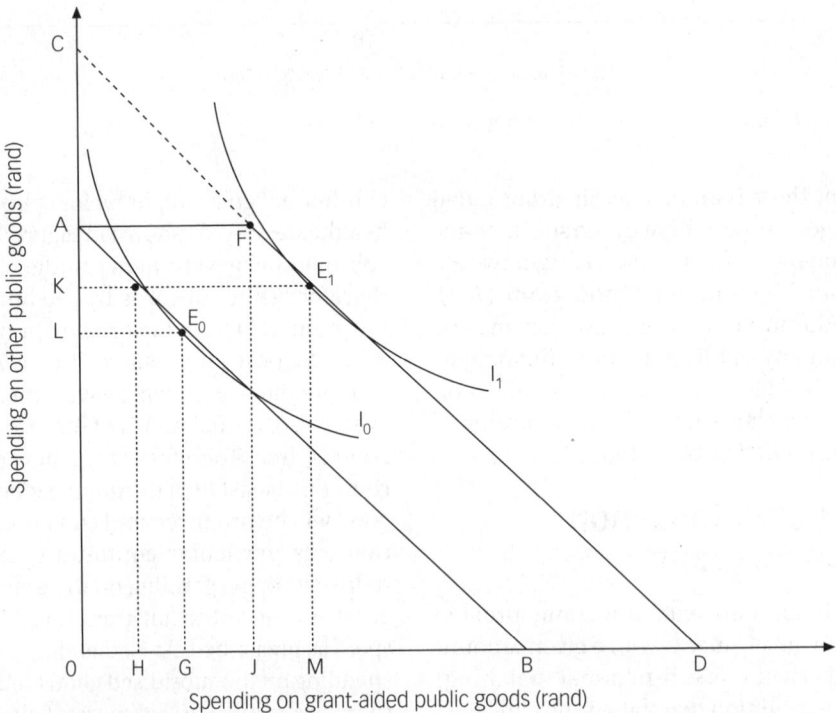

Figure 17.2 Conditional non-matching grant

income (see Chapter 12, Section 12.4.1), a grant that changes the relative price of public goods has an income and a substitution effect. The income effect in this case entails that the public (as represented by the sub-national government) is better off and can thus consume more of both the grant-aided and the other public goods. The substitution effect involves the substitution of the grant-aided good for other public goods. The *net effect* determines the position of E_1, the new equilibrium. As long as E_1 lies to the right of E_0, more of the subsidised public good is purchased. Both the income and substitution effects would prompt the sub-national government to increase expenditure on the public good.

If relative preferences were such that E_1 lay to the left of E_0, the income effect would dominate the substitution effect to such an extent that less of the subsidised good will be purchased than before the grant (i.e. the subsidised good or service is an inferior or Giffen good or service).

In general, open-ended matching grants are regarded as most appropriate for correcting inefficiencies in public good production that result from positive externalities (Shah, 1995). Positive externalities, or benefit spillovers, occur when the provision of goods and services by one sub-national government benefits other sub-national governments, which do not however bear the cost of provision. In this case there would be an incentive for the sub-national government to under-provide that public good or service unless it was subsidised. Note that open-ended matching grants may benefit richer

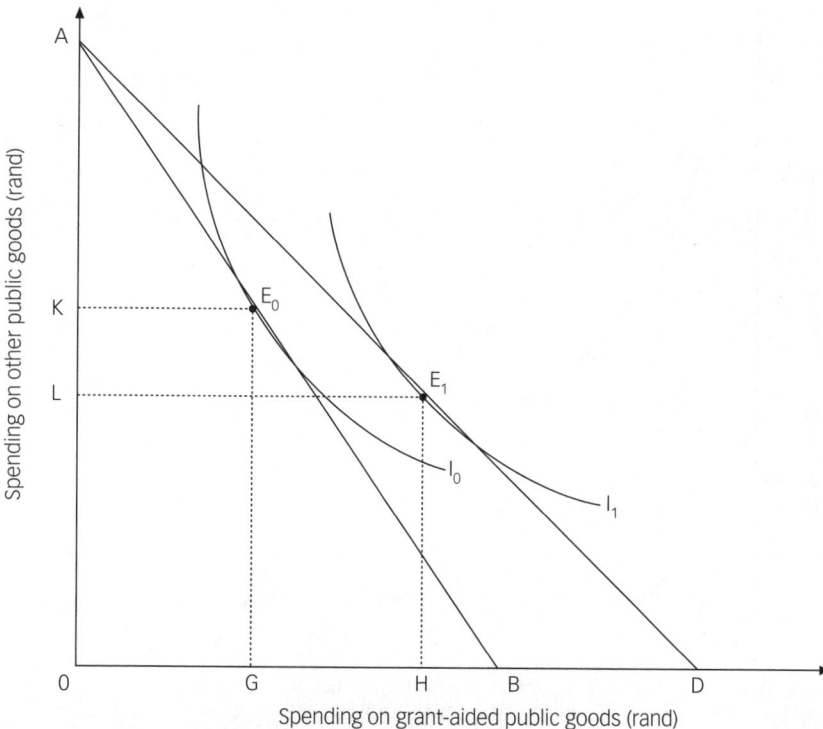

Figure 17.3 Conditional matching grant (open ended)

sub-national governments more than poorer ones who might not be able to match national government expenditure. Geometrically it can be shown that if E_1 were to lie directly above E_0, the cost to the sub-national government of the new bundle of public goods would be the same as the pre-grant combination. The response of a poor community to a conditional grant may well be to seek a combination of goods that does not increase or even decrease the total cost in respect of all public goods, that is, E_1 will be directly above or even to the left of E_0.

17.6.4 Conditional matching grants (closed-ended)

There are also closed-ended matching grants where the national government pays some proportion of the cost of providing a particular public good or service, up to a certain limit. The effect of a closed-ended matching grant is illustrated in Figure 17.4.

When there is a $33\frac{1}{3}$ per cent subsidy on, for instance, healthcare up to a limit, the budget line will move from AB to ACD. Costs of healthcare provision will be shared along AC until the subsidy limit (at spending level OJ) is reached. Beyond the subsidy limit, healthcare is unsubsidised and the sub-national government faces the full price of provision; hence the steeper slope of the section CD of the new budget line (the slope of CD is the same as that of AB). At the new equilibrium, E_1, more healthcare will be provided than would have been the case without the grant.

Grantor governments generally prefer closed-ended matching transfers as these allow them to retain control over their budgets.

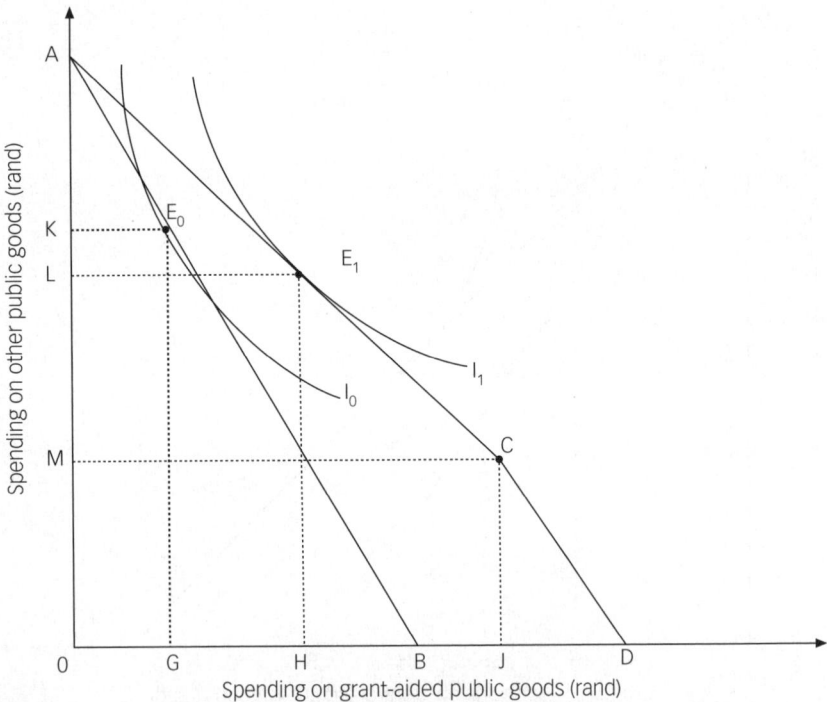

Figure 17.4 Conditional matching grant (closed-ended)

17.6.5 The rationale for intergovernmental grants

The main arguments for intergovernmental transfers are summarised below. The design of the grant should be appropriate to the objective it seeks to attain.

▶ Fiscal imbalances between expenditure needs and revenue generation capacities of sub-national government can be addressed. Under circumstances where it is not feasible to devolve increased tax powers to sub-national government, unconditional non-matching grants (i.e. block grants) should be considered. Sometimes revenue is collected at national level and then transferred to sub-national governments as block grants to address fiscal imbalances. This is known as revenue sharing.

▶ To ensure minimum standards in the provision of public goods and services across the nation, conditional non-matching grants are appropriate.

▶ To compensate for benefit spillovers, conditional matching transfers (open-ended) are suitable. The rate of subsidisation should reflect the degree of benefit spillover.

A conditional matching grant (closed-ended) may be considered to assist sub-national governments financially while promoting expenditures on an activity considered by the national government to be of a high priority, but at the same time affording the national government better control over its own budget. See Box 17.1.

BOX 17.1 Conditional grants in 2011/12

Conditional grants are made from national government departments to (a) provincial governments and (b) to municipalities. These grants are appropriated (i.e. budgeted for) in the annual Division of Revenue Act (DoRA) passed by Parliament at the same time as the Budget. To a much lesser extent, provincial governments may also occasionally give conditional grants to municipalities.

The amount budgeted for each conditional grant as well as indicative allocations for the next two fiscal years are listed in the DoRA. Each conditional grant has its own grant framework which spells out in detail the conditions attached to that particular grant, the service delivery outputs or outcomes expected from that grant, the criteria used to divide each grant among provinces or municipalities, a summary of the audited actual spending on that grant in the previous year, a grant payment schedule, and how and by whom the grant's performance will be monitored. Grant recipients report quarterly on their spending of the grant and on their delivery performance. Should provincial departments or municipalities receiving a grant not adhere to its conditions, the DoRA empowers the National Treasury to stop or withhold payments and to relocate grant payments to other recipients.

In 2011/12, there were 30 provincial conditional grants, collectively amounting to R57,9 billion. Examples of provincial conditional grants include:

▶ a Comprehensive Agricultural Support Grant for emerging farmers from the National Department of Agriculture, Forestry and Fishing to the nine Provincial Departments of Agriculture;

▶ the National School Nutrition Programme Grant from the National Department of Basic Education to Provincial Departments of Education;

▶ a Comprehensive HIV/AIDs Grant, a hospital revitalisation grant and a National Tertiary Services grant for specialised health services from the National Department of Health to Provincial counterparts; and

▶ the Human Settlements Development Grant for housing and related infrastructure from the National Department of Human Settlements to the Provincial Departments of Housing.

Ten types of conditional infrastructure grants were made available to local government in 2011/12, totalling R29,5 billion. In addition six conditional grants were also made in 2011/12 for municipal capacity-building amounting to a further R1,0 billion. Examples of local conditional grants include:

▶ the Municipality Infrastructure Grant paid by the Department of Cooperative

Government and Traditional Affairs to individual municipalities for the provision of basic services such as water and sanitation, roads and social infrastructure to poor households in non-metropolitan municipalities;

▶ the Public Transport Infrastructure and Systems Grant, administered by the National Department of Transport funds rural district municipalities to improve the condition of rural roads;

▶ the National Electrification Programme funds municipalities and Eskom to sustain progress in connecting poor households to electricity; and

▶ the Municipal Systems Improvement Grant assists municipalities in building capacity for management, planning and technical skills.

17.7 Intergovernmental issues in South Africa

17.7.1 Constitutional issues

Expenditure assignment

The South African constitution establishes a state with three spheres of government: national, provincial, and local. It assigns to each of these three spheres of government certain powers or functions. These competencies may be concurrent (shared responsibility of national and provincial governments) or exclusive (sole responsibility and discretion of the province, or sole responsibility of national government). Functional areas of concurrent legislative competencies are listed in Schedule 4 of the

constitution, and exclusive provincial responsibilities are detailed in Schedule 5.

Schedule 5 of the constitution specifies that certain expenditure responsibilities be devolved completely to the provincial sphere (e.g. provincial roads and abattoirs). Others (as described in Schedule 4) are administered jointly as concurrent competencies (e.g. primary and secondary education and health). Some functions remain at national level (e.g. foreign affairs and defence).

Provincial legislation in respect of these Schedule 5 functions takes precedence over national legislation, except when national legislation is necessary to establish national norms and standards, to maintain economic unity, to protect the common market in respect of the mobility of goods, services, capital and labour, or to promote economic activities across provincial borders. Provinces therefore do have a limited degree of fiscal (and political) autonomy although this is weighed against national interest.

Local government competencies are detailed in Part B of Schedule 4 and Schedule 5. Examples of concurrent functions of local government include air pollution, electricity and gas reticulation, municipal health services, etc. Exclusive local government competencies include beaches and amusement facilities, cleansing, dog licensing, local amenities, sport facilities, and municipal roads.

Revenue assignment and borrowing powers

The constitution permits a province to impose taxes, levies, and duties other than income tax, value added tax, general sales tax, and rates on property or customs duties. Most productive taxes are reserved for national government.

A province may also levy flat-rate surcharges on the tax bases of any tax (including individual income tax), levy or duty imposed by national legislation except corporate income tax, value added tax, rates on property, and customs duties.

Provinces may levy these taxes provided they do not prejudice national economic policies, economic activities across provincial boundaries, and national goods and services or factor mobility. Additional own revenue[1] raised by provinces or municipalities may not be deducted from their share of revenue raised nationally, or from other allocations made out of national government revenue. This is to provide an incentive for provinces to increase their tax effort.

To supplement own revenues and fiscal transfers from national government through the revenue sharing formula (see Section 17.7.2), provinces are also empowered to raise loans. The Borrowing Powers of

---

[1] Own revenue is taken to refer to revenue raised within the province or on behalf of the province. These include provincial taxes, user charges, licence fees, and so on.

Provincial Governments Act of 1996 and the Public Finance Management Act of 1999 set out the conditions under which provinces may borrow. Loans may be raised only to finance capital expenditure (e.g. bridges and other infrastructure) and not for current expenditure (e.g. wages). The only exception to the ban on borrowing in order to finance current expenditure, is for bridging finance, in which case such loans must be redeemed within the same fiscal year. No national government guarantee is available in respect of provincial borrowing.

Local governments are entitled by the constitution to impose rates on property and surcharges on fees for services provided by or on behalf of the municipality (e.g. for electricity or sewerage). In the past, municipalities were able to raise Regional Services Council (RSC) levies as a source of revenue. These were however abolished since they were unconstitutional. Until a new alternative revenue source is made available to municipalities, they will receive a temporary grant to replace lost RSC levy income. With the proposed restructuring of the electricity distribution industry, municipalities could also lose electricity user charge income that could further compromise local fiscal capacity. Municipalities are also allowed to borrow, subject to the same restrictions as for the provinces described above. The Municipal Finance Management Act (2003) describes the framework for municipal borrowing.

17.7.2 Intergovernmental transfers and the Financial and Fiscal Commission (FFC)

In South Africa most taxes are raised at national level because collection is easier to administer and it avoids the duplication associated with a more decentralised system. However, the constitution assigns provinces with certain responsibilities regarding the delivery of goods and services, either individually or jointly with national government. There is an imbalance between the expenditure mandate of sub-national levels of government and the financial resources that they can raise on their own account. This mismatch is referred to as **vertical fiscal imbalance** and arises due to the limited capacity of the provinces to raise revenue for themselves independently of national government. For most provinces, income raised within the province as 'own revenue' (mainly from car licences and hospital fees) amounts to less than 5 per cent of the provincial budget (see FFC, 1996). In terms of tax assignment criteria and the constitutional mandate of provinces, the scope to expand the provincial revenue base is thus limited.

The constitution states that provinces are entitled to an equitable share of the revenue collected nationally, in line with their new expenditure responsibilities and functions. The process by which government incomes are pooled and subsequently divided among national and sub-national governments is referred to as **revenue sharing**.

The Financial and Fiscal Commission (FFC) is an independent body established in terms of the constitution, to make impartial recommendations to the national parliament and the nine provincial legislatures on financial and fiscal matters such as the following: equitable allocations to the three tiers of government from the national revenue pool; intentions of provincial governments to levy taxes and surcharges; raising of loans by lower tier governments; and the criteria to be used for these purposes.

We now focus on the process of making equitable allocations to national, provincial, and local government from nationally collected revenues.

The vertical division of revenue

The allocation of funds from nationally collected revenue entails a vertical division of such revenue between the national, provincial, and local spheres of government. The vertical division of revenue for 2007/08 – 2013/14 is shown in Table 17.1. First a 'top slice', which consists mainly of funds to service the debt and a contingency reserve, is subtracted from the nationally collected revenue pool. The remainder is then split among the national, provincial, and local spheres. Note that the national share includes the budgets for national departments but excludes conditional grants to provinces and local government.

From Table 17.1 it is evident that in 2011/12, after the 'top slice' for state debt service costs and contingency reserves, R808,3 billion remained for division among the three spheres. National government's share of this amount was 47,0 per cent in 2011/12, and was expected to increase marginally to 47,4 per cent in two years' time. Provincial governments received 44,3 per cent of total revenue after the top slice was subtracted (consisting of their 'equitable share' which is an unconditional grant, as well as various conditional grants from national government). It was envisaged that the provincial share would decrease marginally between 2011/12 and 2013/14. Local government received only 8,7 per cent after the top slice was subtracted in 2011/12. While the FFC formulae were regarded as important inputs in the calculation of these vertical divisions, the Commission's recommendations apparently were not decisive. The government regards the vertical division of funds between the different spheres of government as a policy judgement that reflects the relative priority of functions assigned to each sphere of government and not something that can be captured in a formula (Ministry of Finance, 1999: 59).

The horizontal division of revenue

The vertical split is then followed by a horizontal division of the provincial and local pools of resources available among the nine provinces and the 283 municipalities respectively. To ensure that each provincial government receives an equitable allocation in order to meet its constitutional expenditure obligations, the FFC (1996) proposed a revenue sharing formula for the horizontal division of resources among the nine

provinces over a three- to five-year period. The FFC asserted that formula funding is more objective and less prone to manipulation by politicians and civil servants. In addition, it would enable provinces to predict with greater certainty the revenues that would accrue to them over the period in which the formula was in force. The formula is mainly population-driven with the population in a province being an indicator of the fiscal need of the province. It is also weighted in favour of rural people as a proxy

Table 17.1 Vertical division of revenue in billions of rands in South Africa, 2007–2014

	2007/08	2008/09	2009/10	2010/11	2011/12	2012/13	2013/14
R billions	Outcome			Revised estimate	Medium-term estimates		
Total revenue+ borrowing	541,443	635,953	747,197	809,923	888,923	968,132	1053,029
Less top slice of which:							
Debt-service cost	52,877	54,394	57,129	66,57	76,579	90,808	104,036
Contingency reserve	0,00	0,00	0,00	0,00	4,13	11,735	23,905
Resources to be divided	**488,566**	**581,56**	**690,068**	**743,353**	**808,254**	**865,919**	**925,617**
National departments	242,58	289,236	345,366	359,12	380,154	408,439	439,049
% of total to be divided	**49,7**	**49,7**	**50,0**	**48,3**	**47,0**	**47,2**	**47,4**
Provinces	207,504	246,836	293,164	323,08	357,929	380,45	404,251
% of total to be divided	**42,5**	**42,4**	**42,5**	**43,5**	**44,3**	**43,9**	**43,7**
Local government	38,482	45,487	51,537	61,152	70,171	77,029	82,317
% of total to be divided	**7,9**	**7,8**	**7,5**	**8,2**	**8,7**	**8,9**	**8,9**

for backlogs and for poverty. The formula aims to equalise rural weighted spending per capita across the provinces. As such, it addresses the **horizontal fiscal imbalances** between provinces that arise from differences in revenue (tax) capacity in relation to their expenditure responsibilities.

However, the FFC is only an advisory body and its recommendations are not binding on the Budget Council which actually makes the division of revenues. The Budget Council (see Chapter 15, Box 15.1) consists of the Minister of Finance and the nine provincial MECs for Finance, with the FFC as observers. The actual formula used by the Budget Council to determine each province's equitable share is based on the provinces' demographic and economic profiles. The formula used in the 2011/12 division of revenue consisted of the following:

▶ an education share (48 per cent), based on the size of the school-age population (ages 5–17) and the number of learners (Grade R–12) enrolled in public ordinary schools
▶ a health share (27 per cent), based on a combination of a risk-adjusted capitation index for the population, which takes into account the health risks associated with the demographic profile of the population and the relative share of case loads in hospitals. The risk-adjusted capitation is given a 25 per cent weighting and the caseload (i.e. patient-day-output component) is given a 75 per cent weighting. The risk-adjusted capitation index is estimated using General Household Survey (2009) demographic data of the non-insured population in each district and province drawn, adjusted for gender and age, and captures health needs. The caseload component captures health service supplying a basic share (16 per cent), based on each province's share of the total population of the country

▶ a poverty component (3 per cent) reinforcing redistribution in the formula
▶ an economic output share (1 per cent), based on the Gross Domestic Product by Region (GDP-R) data
▶ an institutional grant (5 per cent), equally divided among the provinces.

The formula determines the equitable share that is given to the provinces as an unconditional block grant. In order to determine the total allocation for each province, the conditional grants, which each province receives from national government, must be added to the equitable share. Table 17.2 shows the budgeted allocations to the provinces for 2011/12.

As will be illustrated later, local governments are (in aggregate) not as reliant as provinces on transfers from other spheres of government. There is, however, substantial variation among municipalities. Some poorer municipalities rely on grants for up to 92 per cent of their income (e.g. the Bohlabela municipality), while some urban municipalities raise up to 97 per cent of their own income (National Treasury, 2005a: 30). Transfers to the local sphere include unconditional equitable share grants, conditional grants, and grants in kind (e.g. the Water Services Operating Subsidy). Conditional grants are generally for municipal infrastructure and other capital expenditure, capacity building or in support of restructuring.

The individual municipality's claim to nationally collected revenue depends not only on the total size of the vertical division, but also on the nature of the horizontal division among municipalities. The FFC formula for the division of the local government resource pool, which is the basis of the method used by the Department of Provincial and Local Government and the National Treasury to distribute the equitable share, bases the claim for a share on the relative needs of jurisdictions, after taking the tax capacity into

Table 17.2 Budgeted provincial allocations in billions of rands for 2011/12

R Billions	Equitable share	% of total	Conditional grants	% of total	Total transfers	% of total
Eastern Cape	44,1	15,3	8,9	12,8	53,0	14,8
Free State	17,5	6,1	5,0	7,2	22,5	6,3
Gauteng	50,4	17,5	14,7	21,1	65,1	18,2
KwaZulu-Natal	62,9	21,8	13,3	19,2	76,4	21,4
Limpopo	36,3	12,6	6,9	10,0	43,3	12,1
Mpumalanga	23,4	8,1	5,2	7,5	28,6	8,0
Northern Cape	7,7	2,7	2,5	3,6	10,2	2,9
North West	19,3	6,7	4,5	6,5	23,8	6,7
Western Cape	26,8	9,3	8,2	11,7	34,9	9,8
Unallocated			0,3	0,4	0,3	0,1
Total	**288,5**		**69,4**		**357,9**	

account. The purpose of the formula is to provide financial assistance to those municipalities that cannot provide basic services to the poor from their own tax base.

Essentially, the latest version of the local government equitable share formula consists of five components:

▶ A basic services component for water, refuse removal, sanitation, environmental healthcare services and electricity reticulation to poor households earning less than R800 per month; for each of the subsidised services there are two levels of support: a full subsidy for those households that actually receive services and a partial subsidy for unserviced households set at one-third of the subsidy to serviced households.

▶ An institutional support component to support the basic administrative and governance capacity in local governments; it consists of a base allocation which will go to every municipality regardless of size, and a variable allocation depending on the population in the municipality and number of councillors.

▶ A development component to give effect to the developmental objectives of local government beyond the provision of basic municipal services, as envisaged in Section 214 of the constitution. This component has been set at zero until a suitable variable can be found to capture the development needs of local government.

▶ A revenue-raising capacity correction component to take into account the estimated revenue capacity of each municipality.

▶ A stabilising constraint to ensure municipalities are given in the current formula what they had been promised in the previous MTEF round of allocations, and to ensure that allocations would not be negative due to the revenue raising correction (National Treasury, 2008a).

The introduction of free basic services at municipal level in 2003/04 has created increasing pressure on the local government's equitable share. These pressures have only been partially addressed in the 2011/12 equitable share allocations, undermining municipal financial sustainability as the number of indigent consumers qualifying for free basic services has increased in the aftermath of the global recession.

17.7.3 Provincial financing issues

Until 1996 provinces were only spending agencies for the national government, disbursing funds according to the policies and priorities determined at national level. In the past, provinces were treated in much the same way as national departments with regard to the budget. They were concerned mainly with the implementation of national policy. They could not set their own priorities, nor did they have much accountability – problems could always be blamed on national government. Estimating and evaluating expenditures across functions and provinces were done by government officials in Pretoria, with little regard for provincial priorities. Under the provisions of the constitution the provincial governments have much more latitude to determine their own spending patterns.

Provincial budgets should therefore increasingly embody the provincial governments' responses to regional challenges and opportunities for development within the nine provinces. Under these circumstances, coordination between the spheres of government in setting expenditure priorities becomes crucial, so that differing needs can be provided for without jeopardising national goals.

However, the nine provinces have vastly differing capacities for financial management and expenditure control. Accountability and efficiency thus depend on the strengthening of managerial and administrative capacity in all provinces – especially the weaker ones. Given South Africa's history of government overspending, sound financial management is particularly important so that provinces can perform the spending functions devolved to them without the risk of provincial overspending. Provincial overspending would, of course, jeopardise national deficit targets and other stabilisation objectives.

It is also important that the share of national revenue received by the province be adequate to fulfil provincial spending obligations. If financing is not commensurate with the new distribution of responsibilities across spheres of government, this could also lead to persistent pressures for provincial overspending.

Probably one of the most pressing challenges facing provincial government is the need to diversify their tax bases and reduce dependence on national government. Provinces in South Africa have very little own revenue capacity compared to sub-national governments in other countries and thus are fiscally highly dependent on central government. Currently, provincial own revenues are generally less than five per cent of provincial expenditure. These are derived mainly from motor vehicle licenses, hospital fees, and gambling proceeds.

There are concerns that the over-reliance on funding from central government could undermine provincial fiscal autonomy. Furthermore, there is a weak link between the revenue-raising responsibility, which is mainly at the national level, and the responsibility for the spending decisions, which is provincial. This could dilute fiscal accountability in the sense that provincial executives are not called upon to justify expenditure patterns to provincial electorates as taxpayers. This could also induce perverse incentives such as inefficient increases in expenditure, since costs are de facto being shifted onto national government, as well as deviation from provincial electorate preferences. Fiscal federalism's supposed benefit of allocative efficiency is thus weaker. Tax legislation has recently been passed which should allow provinces limited leeway to extend their tax bases.

The FFC has proposed that provinces be allowed to 'piggy-back' a provincial surcharge on the national personal income tax. For a number of technical reasons, it is unlikely that provincial governments will be able to implement a surcharge on the personal income tax in the near future, although they may elect to levy smaller taxes in terms of the Provincial Taxation Regulation Process Act of 2001. If provinces were empowered to tax, this would probably only benefit the better-off provinces, which have viable tax bases (e.g. Gauteng, Western Cape, and possibly KwaZulu-Natal).

17.7.4 Local government financing issues

Cities around the world, with their high concentrations of economic activities and dense populations, provide significant opportunities for stimulating economic growth and development. However they also introduce considerable challenges in relation to pollution, traffic congestion, public transport, crime and the efficient and equitable provision and financing of services such as water, sanitation and electricity. South African cities also have to contend with the racially skewed spatial distribution of economic activity and land use as a result of apartheid segregation, where high concentrations of poverty and backlogs in housing and infrastructure co-exist with wealth and first world living standards.

Urban economics is a field of study that uses the analytical tools of economics to explain the spatial and economic organisation of cities and metropolitan areas, to analyse

their special economic problems and explore solutions. Urban economics considers land use and human settlement patterns and densities, transport costs and geographic location factors in production and consumption decisions. Unlike other economic disciplines, which virtually ignore geography, urban economics focuses on these spatial relationships to explain the economic motivations underlying why and how cities are formed, function and develop over time. Policies designed to change the distribution of populations and economic activity within cities, between cities, and between urban and rural areas would also fall within the domain of urban economics (Heilburn and McGuire, 1988; Henderson, 1987). Local government/municipal finance (or urban public finance as it is sometimes called) is an important component of urban economics that considers how cities raise revenues (through user charges, property rates and intergovernmental grants) in order to deliver services and promote economic growth and development.

Unlike the provinces, local government in South Africa in aggregate has a more substantial tax base and the 283 municipalities which make up the local government sphere generate more than 90 per cent of their aggregate budget as own revenues. Government transfers are therefore a much smaller percentage of local government revenue than at the provincial level. See also Box 17.2.

There are three main categories of municipalities: metropolitan councils, district councils, and local councils. There is considerable variation in terms of revenue and expenditure patterns both within and across these categories.

The key issue confronting local governments is sustainability. Municipalities are under extreme pressure (as evidenced by service delivery protests) to improve access to, and the quality of, the services they deliver, e.g. eradication of the bucket system and provision of effective sanitation and safe

BOX 17.2 Local government finances in 2010/11

In the 2010/11 local government financial year, municipal operating expenditure budgets amounted to R191,4 billion in total. In addition, municipalities collectively budgeted R41,2 billion on their capital budgets in 2010/11. The combined operating and capital budgets of all municipalities in 2011/12 amounted to R232,6 billion. This is expected to rise to R244,4 billion in 2011/12 and R269,7 billion in 2012/13. The six metropolitan municipalities[1] alone make up 57,8 per cent of the combined operating and capital budget of all municipalities in 2010/11. The local and district municipalities constitute 34,4 per cent and 7,8 per cent of combined municipal budgeted expenditure in 2010/11 respectively.

Local government capital expenditures are financed through historical operating surpluses, own revenues, loans, contributions from district municipalities and conditional grants, and other transfers from national and provincial governments. The key operating expenditures in 2010/11 included personnel expenditure, bulk purchases such as electricity bought from Eskom and retailed to residents, and bulk purchases in connection with water and sewage service provision. Other operating expenditures include general expenses and administration of the council, and interest and redemption on loans.

The main sources of operating revenue for municipalities in aggregate in 2010/11 were as follows (National Treasury, 2010):
▶ Property rates of R31,3 billion (15 per cent)
▶ Service charges for water, electricity and sanitation of R88,7 billion (43 per cent)
▶ Intergovernmental grants of R52,9 billion (26 per cent)

▶ Other own revenues of R31,6 billion (15 per cent).

In municipalities in the Western Cape, Gauteng and KwaZulu-Natal own revenues as a percentage of operating revenue were 92%, 84% and 84% respectively. This indicates that the municipalities in provinces with greater levels of economic activity and residents with higher income levels tend to be more self-financing, more sustainable and less dependent on intergovernmental grants. This is in contrast to municipalities in the Eastern Cape, Mpumalanga and Limpopo where own revenues as a percentage of operating revenues were only 69%, 65% and 56% respectively. Municipalities in these poorer provinces tend to be more dependent on grants from national and provincial governments, and less self-financing.

The main sources of capital revenue for municipalities in 2010/11 were the following (National Treasury, 2010):
▶ Grants and subsidies of R210 billion (54 per cent)
▶ External loans of R80,5 billion (21 per cent)
▶ Donations of R5 billion (1 per cent)
▶ Other income of R93,3 billion (24 per cent).

Outstanding consumer accounts in local government amounted to R22,6 billion in 2002/03, increasing to R37,1 billion in 2004/05, R52,0 billion in 2007/08 and R56,1 billion in 2009/10. These increases in debts owed by consumers to municipalities indicate their weak ability to recover the income that is due to them. Revenue management remains one of the weaknesses of municipal government.

---

[1] Johannesburg, Cape Town, eThekwini, Ekurhuleni, Tshwane and Nelson Mandela.

drinking water and electricity. Rural municipalities, in particular, are also faced with infrastructure backlogs that must be eliminated as well as existing infrastructure that must be maintained. Urban municipalities are under pressure to invest in economic infrastructure such as public transport, which is required to underpin economic growth. All of these create spending pressures on municipal budgets, but their revenue sources are also severely constrained. A culture of non-payment for municipal services has led to the accumulation of arrears and pressured the revenue side of municipal budgets. Many municipalities have experienced great difficulties in recovering the user charges owed to them for services rendered by households. One of the challenges of local government is to improve financial management to ensure that budgets are adhered to. This would include the introduction of uniform accounting standards and compliance with GAMAP (Generally Accepted Municipal Accounting Practices). Financial reporting systems also tended to be weak at municipal level, precluding early warning systems and effective monitoring and evaluation of financial and service-delivery performance. While improved credit control, debt collection and other forms of financial management can certainly contribute to the sustainability of

poor municipalities, their financial condition will remain vulnerable unless the underlying structural conditions of unemployment, poverty and the skewed spatial distribution of economic activity are also addressed.

Since 1994, local governments have been undergoing a fundamental transformation that culminated in the redemarcation of municipalities in December 2000. The number of municipalities has been reduced from 843 to 283. Other important changes include the reassignment of functions between district and local municipalities, the impact of the restructuring of the electricity industry, devolution of health and certain public transport functions, the funding of free basic services, and the introduction of a new property rates system. It would be important to assess the impact of all these factors cumulatively on local government finance. At present, however, there are too many transformation processes that are still either under way or newly completed for the true financial position of individual municipalities to be determined. The Municipal Finance Management Act of 2003 and the Property Rates Act of 2004 introduced a uniform valuation system that should go some way in providing a legal framework for enhancing the financial viability of municipalities. The challenge over the next decade will be to implement these acts.

IMPORTANT CONCEPTS

assignment problem
 (page 357)
block grant (page 362)
conditional grants
 (page 362)
expenditure assignment
 (page 359)
financial contagion
 (page 360)
fiscal federalism (page 354)
horizontal fiscal imbalances
 (page 372)

intergovernmental fiscal
 relations (page 354)
intergovernmental grants
 (page 362)
matching grant (page 362)
moral hazard (page 361)
non-matching grant
 (page 362)
revenue or tax sharing
 (page 362, 370)
spatial externalities
 (page 354)

sub-national government
 (page 354)
tax assignment (page 359)
tax competition (page 359)
tax harmonisation
 (page 360)
unconditional grants
 (page 362)
urban economics (page 375)
vertical fiscal imbalance
 (page 370)

SELF-ASSESSMENT EXERCISES

17.1 The fiscal federalism literature contends that stabilisation and distribution functions are best performed at national level, whereas allocative functions are best performed at sub-national level. Can you explain why?

17.2 Explain the assumptions and main arguments of the Tiebout model.

17.3 'A fiscally decentralised system is always more efficient and more equitable than a fiscally centralised system.' Discuss.

17.4 Which type of intergovernmental grant would be most suitable to ensure minimum educational standards across all provinces? Why? Illustrate your answer by means of a diagram.

17.5 'Tax competition by sub-national governments always has negative effects.' Do you agree?

17.6 Should provincial debt be formally guaranteed by the national government? Why (not)?

17.7 How does South African expenditure and revenue assignment compare with the guidelines of fiscal federalism theory?

17.8 What are the key issues and trends in provincial and local government finances in South Africa?

References

Abedian, I. & Biggs, M. (eds). 1998. *Economic globalization and fiscal policy*. Cape Town: Oxford University Press.

African Development Bank. 2001. *African Development Report*. Oxford: Oxford University Press.

African Development Bank. 2004. *African Development Report*. Oxford: Oxford University Press.

African Economic Outlook. 2010. *Past fiscal prudence and disinflation have created space for expansionary macro policies*. [Online]. Available: http://www.africaneconomicoutlook.org/en/outlook/macroeconomic-situation-and-prospects/facing-the-crisis-with-new-policy-responses/ [14 February 2011]

Agiobenebo, T.J. 2006. On the optimal quantity of public goods and related issues. *South African Journal of Economics*, 74(2): 274–300.

Ajam, T. & Aron, J. 2007. Fiscal renaissance in a democratic South Africa. *Journal of African Economies*, 16(5): 745–781.

Alence, R. 1998. *The economic policy-making process in South Africa: Report on a survey of an informed panel, late 1997*. Pretoria: Human Science Research Council.

Anderson, P., Baumberg, B., 2006. *Alcohol in Europe: A public health perspective*. A report for the European Commission. Institute of Alcohol Studies, UK, June 2006.

Anderson, J.E. (2003). *Public Finance: Principles and Policy*. Boston: Houghton Mifflin.

Ardington, E. & Lund, F. 1995. *Pensions and development: How the social security system can complement programmes of reconstruction and development*. Development Paper 61. Midrand: Development Bank of Southern Africa.

Arrow, K.J. 1951. *Social choice and individual values*. New York: John Wiley.

Arrow, K.J. 1962. The economic implications of learning by doing. *Review of Economic Studies*, 29.

Aschauer, D.A. 1989. Is public expenditure productive? *Journal of Monetary Economics*, 23(2).

Atkinson, A.B. & Stiglitz, J.E. 1980. *Lectures on Public Economics*. Maidenhead UK: McGraw-Hill.

Auerbach, A.J. 2009. Implementing the new fiscal policy activism. *American Economic Review: Papers & Proceedings*, 99(2): 543–549.

Bahl, R. 1998. Land versus property taxes in developing and transition countries. *Lincoln Institute of Land Policy conference on land value taxation in contemporary societies*. Phoenix. 11–13 January 1998.

Bank of Namibia. 2006. *Integrated Paper on recent economic developments in SADC*. 1 December 2006. [Online]. Available: http://www.sadcbankers.org/SADC/SADC.nsf/LADV/3CD719E2A8CEBD7442257257002EEFBC/$File/RED+Oct2006+(Final).pdf [27 March 2008]

Bannock, G., Baxter, R.E. & Rees, R. 1971. *The Penguin Dictionary of Economics*. London/New York: Allen Lane/The Viking Press.

Barreix, A. & Roca, J. 2007. Strengthening a fiscal pillar: The Uruguayan dual income tax. *Cepal Review*, 92: 121–140.

Baumol, W.J. 1982. *Contestable markets and the theory of industry structure*. San Diego: Harcourt.

Baumol, W.J. 1967. Macro-economics of unbalanced growth: The anatomy of urban crisis. *American Economic Review*, 57: 415–426.

Becker, G.S. 1985. Public policies, pressure groups, and dead weight costs. *Journal of Public Economics*, 28(3): 329–347.

Bernardi, L. Barreix, A. Marenzi, A. & Profeta, P. 2008. *Tax systems and tax reforms in Latin America*. London: Routledge.

Bhorat, H. 2004. Labour market challenges in post-apartheid South Africa. *South African Journal of Economics*, 72(5): 940–977.

Bird, R.M. 1971. Wagner's 'law' of expanding state activity. *Public Finance*, 26(1): 1–26.

Bird, R.M. 1992. *Tax policy and economic development*. Baltimore: Johns Hopkins.

Bird, R.M. 2008. The BBLR approach to tax reform in emerging countries. *International Studies Program Working Paper 08-04*. Andrew Young School of Policy Studies. Georgia State University. December 2008: 1–30.

Bird, R.M. & Zolt, E.M. 2010. Dual income taxation and developing countries. *Columbia Journal of Tax Law*, 1: 174–217.

Black, P.A. 1993. Affirmative action: Rational response to a changing environment. *South African Journal of Economics*, 61(4): 317–323.

Black, P.A. 1996. Affirmative action in South Africa: Rational discrimination according to Akerlof? *South African Journal of Economics*, 64(1): 74–82.

Black, P.A. 2004. Economic impact analysis: A methodological note. *South African Journal of Economics*, 72(5): 1068–1074.

Black, P.A. 2008. Alcohol taxes versus preventative measures: A theoretical note. *South African Journal of Economics*, 76(4): 607–611.

Black, P.A. & Dollery, B.E. 1992. *Leading issues in South African microeconomics: Selected readings.* Halfway House: Southern.

Black, P.A. & Mohamed, A.I. 2006. 'Sin' taxes and poor households: Unanticipated effects. *South African Journal of Economics,* 74(1): 131–136.

Black, P.A. & Saxby, G. 1996. Differential investment multipliers: An application of Weiss and Gooding. *South African Journal of Economic and Management Sciences*, 9(4).

Blinder, A.S. 1987. The rules-versus-discretion debate in the light of recent experience. *Welwirtschafliches Archiv*, 123: 399–413.

Blinder, A.S. 2006. The case against the case against discretionary fiscal policy. In: Kopcke, R.W., Tootell, G.M.B. & Triest, R.K. (eds). *The macroeconomics of fiscal policy.* Cambridge, Mass: MIT Press.

Blinder, A.S. & Zandi, M. 2010. *How the Great Recession was brought to an end.* 27 July. [Online]. Available: http://scholar.google.co.za/scholar?cluster=16640258663503337300&hl=en&as_sdt=0,5. [[PDF] from dismal.com]. [17 February 2011].

Boadway, R. 2005. Income tax reform for a globalized world: The case for a dual income tax. *Journal of Asian Economics*, 16: 910–927.

Boadway, R.W. & Wildasin, D.E. 1984. *Public sector economics.* 2nd edition. Boston: Little, Brown and Co.

Boadway, R. & Shah, A. 1995. Perspectives on the role of investment incentives in developing countries. In: Shah, A. (ed). *Fiscal incentives for investment and innovation.* Washington: World Bank.

Boadway, R., Chamberlain, E. & Emmerson, C. 2010. *Taxation of wealth and wealth transfers.* In: *Dimensions of tax design: The Mirrlees review chaired by Sir James Mirrlees.* Oxford: Oxford University Press: 737–814.

Bohm, P. 1978. *Social efficiency.* London: Macmillan.

Borcherding, T.E. (ed). 1977. *Budgets and bureaucrats.* Durham: Duke University Press.

Boshoff, W.H. 2008. Cigarette demand in South Africa over 1996-2006: The role of price, income and health awareness. *South African Journal of Economics*, (76)1: 118–131.

Boskin, M.J. (ed). 1996. *Frontiers of tax reform.* Stanford: Hoover Institution Press.

Bowles, S. 2004. *Microeconomics,* Princeton: Princeton University Press.

Brennan, G. & Buchanan, J.M. 1980. *The power to tax: Analytical foundations of a fiscal federalism constitution.* Cambridge, New York: Cambridge University Press.

Bromberger, N. 1982. Government policies affecting the distribution of income, 1940-1980. In: Schrire, R. (ed). 1982. *South Africa: Public policy perspectives.* Cape Town: Juta: 165–203.

Brown, C.V. & Jackson, P.M. 1990. *Public sector economics.* Oxford: Basil Blackwell.

Browne, G.W.G. 1983. Fifty years of public finance. *South African Journal of Economics*, 51(1): 134–173.

Browning, E.K. & Browning, J.M. 1994. *Public finance and the price system.* 4th edition. New York: Macmillan.

Buchanan, J.M., Tollison, R.D. & Tullock, G. (eds). 1980. *Towards a theory of the rentseeking society.* College Station: Texas A & M University Press.

Buchanan, J.M. & Tullock, G. 1962. *The calculus of consent.* Ann Arbor Mich.: University of Michigan Press.

Bundy, C. 1988. *The rise and fall of the South African peasantry.* 2nd edition. Cape Town: David Philip.

Burger, R. 2007. *Policy Brief: How pro-poor is the South African health system?* Stellenbosch Economic Working Paper 6/07. Department of Economics, University of Stellenbosch.

Burger, R. & Swanepoel, C. 2006. *Have pro-poor health policies improved the targeting of spending and the effective delivery of health care in South Africa?* Stellenbosch Economic Working Paper 11/06. Department of Economics, University of Stellenbosch.

Calitz, E. 1986. *Aspekte van die vraagstuk van staatsbestedingsprioriteite met spesiale verwysing na die Republiek van Suid-Afrika: 'n funksioneelekonomiese ondersoek.* Stellenbosch: University of Stellenbosch. (DCom. thesis.)

Calitz, E. 1992. The limits to public expenditure. In: Howe, G. & Le Roux, P. (eds). 1992. *Transforming the economy: Policy options for South Africa.* Indicator Project SA, University of Natal and Institute for Social Development, University of the Western Cape.

Calitz, E. 2000a. An assessment of fiscal policy in South Africa. *International Atlantic Economic Society Session of the Allied Social Science Associations Annual Meeting,* Boston, USA, 8 January 2000. (Unpublished.)

Calitz, E. 2000b. Fiscal implications of the economic globalisation of South Africa. *South African Journal of Economics*, 68(4): 564–606.

Calitz, E. 2002. Comparative international perspectives on structural economic reform in South Africa. *BMR Research Report 2002/01*, Pretoria: University of South Africa, Bureau for Market Research, Pretoria.

Calitz, E., Du Plessis. S.A. & Siebrits, F.K. 2011. An alternative perspective on South Africa's public debt, 1962-1994. *South African Journal of Economics*, 79(2): 161-172.

Calitz, E. & Siebrits, F.K. 2002. Changes in the role of government in the SA economy. *Absa Economic Perspective*, Second Quarter: 15-23.

Calitz, E. & Siebrits, F.K. 2003. Fiscal policy in the 1990s. *South African Journal of Economic History*, 18(1&2): 50-75.

Case, A. & Deaton, A. 1998. Large cash transfers to the elderly in South Africa. *Economic Journal*, 108(450): 1330-61.

Central Statistical Service. 1996. *Living in South Africa: Selected findings of the 1995 October household survey*. Pretoria: Government Printer.

Chalk, N. & Hemming, R. 2000. Assessing fiscal sustainability in theory and practice. *IMF Working Paper WP/00/81*. Washington, DC: International Monetary Fund.

Chia, N.C. & Whalley, J. 1995. Patterns in investment: Tax incentives among developing countries. In: Shah, A. (ed). *Fiscal incentives for investment and innovation*. Washington: World Bank.

Cnossen, S. 1990. The case for selective taxes on goods and services in developing countries. In: Bird, R. & Oldman, O. (eds). *Taxation in developing countries*. 4th edition. Baltimore: Johns Hopkins.

Cnossen, S. 2003. How much tax coordination in the European Union? *International Tax and Public Finance*, 10: 625-649.

Cohen, J.M. & Cohen, M.J. 1960. *The Penguin Dictionary of Quotations*. New York: Penguin.

Committee of Urban Transport Officials (CUTA). 2002. *Guidelines for conducting the economic evaluation of urban transport projects*. 3rd edition. Cape Town: Government Printer.

Cook, P. & Kirkpatrick, C. 1997. Globalisation, regionalisation and Third World development. *Regional Studies*, 31(1): 55-66.

Corlett, W.J. & Hague, D.C. 1953. Complementarity and the excess burden of taxation. *Review of Economic Studies*, 21: 21-30.

Cowen, T. & Crampton, E. 2011. *Market failure or success: the new debate*. Fairfax: George Mason University Press.

Crouch, L. & Mabogoane, T. 1998. When the residuals matter more than the coefficients: An educational perspective. *Studies in Economics and Econometrics*, 22(2): 1-14.

Dahlman, C.J. 1979. The problem of externality. *Journal of Law & Economics*, 22: 141-162.

Dasgupta, A.K. & Pearce, D.W. 1974. *Cost benefit analysis: Theory and practice*. London: Macmillan Press.

Debrun, X. & Kapoor, R. 2010. Fiscal Policy and Macroeconomic Stability: Automatic Stabilizers Work, Always and Everywhere. *IMF Working Paper WP/10/111*. Washington, D.C.: International Monetary Fund.

Demsetz, H. 1982. Barriers to entry. *American Economic Review*, 72: 47-57.

Department of Finance. 1996. *Macroeconomic strategy on growth, employment and redistribution*. Pretoria: Government Printer.

Department of Finance. 1997. *Medium term budget policy statements*. Pretoria: Government Printer.

Department of Finance. 1998. *Budget review 1998*. Pretoria: Government Printer.

Department of Finance. 1999. *National expenditure survey 1999*. Pretoria: Government Printer.

Department of Housing. 1995. *Annual Report*. Pretoria: Government Printer.

Department of Housing. 1996. *Annual Report*. Pretoria: Government Printer.

Department of Welfare. 1997. *White Paper for Social Welfare*. Pretoria: Government Printer.

De Wulf, L. 1975. Fiscal incidence studies in developing countries: Survey and critique. *IMF Staff Working Papers*. 22(1) March: 61-131.

Dornbusch, R., Fischer, S., Mohr, P. & Rogers, C. 1994. *Macroeconomics*. 3rd edition. Johannesburg: Lexicon.

Downs, A. 1957. *An economic theory of democracy*. New York: Harper & Row.

Du Plessis, S.A. & Boshoff, W. 2007. A fiscal rule to produce counter-cyclical fiscal policy in South Africa. *Stellenbosch Economic Working Papers 13/07*. Stellenbosch: University of Stellenbosch (Department of Economics) and Bureau for Economic Research.

Du Plessis, S.A., Smit, B.W. & Sturzenegger, F. 2007. The cyclicality of monetary and fiscal policy in South Africa since 1994. *South African Journal of Economics*, 75(3): 391-411.

Easson, A.J. 1992. Tax incentives for foreign direct investment in developing countries. *Australian Tax Forum*, 9: 387-439.

Econex. 2010. *The appropriateness of using excise taxes to address the question of external costs related to alcohol consumption in the South African context and alternative interventions*. Report prepared by Econex Pty (Ltd) for the South African Breweries Limited. Team leader: Professor Philip Black. Econex: Trade, Competition & Applied Economics: Cape Town.

Eichenbaum, M. 1997. Some thoughts on practical stabilization policy. *American Economic Review Papers and Proceedings*, 87(2): 236-239.

El-Khouri, S. 2002. Fiscal policy and macroeconomic management. In: Khan, M.S., Nsouli, S.M. & Wong, C-H. (eds). *Macroeconomic management: Programs and policies.* Washington DC: International Monetary Fund.

F.F.C. 1996. *The Financial and Fiscal Commission's recommendations for the allocation of financial resources to the national Government and the provincial Governments for the 1997/98 financial year.* Midrand: Financial and Fiscal Commission.

Fan, S. & Rao, S. 2003. Public spending in developing countries: Trends, determination, and impact. *EPTD Discussion Paper No. 99.* Washington, D.C.: International Food Policy Research Institute.

Faria, A.G.A. 1995. Source versus residence principle; Relief from double taxation; Aspects of tax treaties; International capital flows. In: Shome, P. (ed). 1995. *Tax policy handbook.* IMF: Washington.

Feldstein, M. 1997. How big should government be? *National Tax Journal,* 50(2): 197–213.

Fisman, R. & Wei, S. 2004. Tax rates and tax evasion: Evidence from 'missing imports' in China. *Journal of Political Economy,* 112(2): 471–500.

Fjeldstad, O. 2004. What's trust got to do with it? Non-payment of service charges in local authorities in South Africa. *Journal of Modern African Studies,* 42(4): 539–562.

Fourie, F.C.v.N. 1997. *How to think and reason in macroeconomics.* Kenwyn: Juta.

Frankel, J., Smit, B.W. & Sturzenegger, F. 2006. South Africa: Macroeconomic challenges after a decade of success. *CID Working Paper 133.* Cambridge, Mass: Harvard University (Center for International Development).

Franzsen Commission. 1968. *First Report of the Commission of Inquiry into fiscal and monetary policy in South Africa (Chairman: D.G. Franzsen).* RP 24/1969. November 1968. Pretoria: Government Printer.

Freeman, A.M. 1983. *Intermediate microeconomic analysis.* New York: Harper.

Frey, B.S. 1978. *Modern political economy.* Oxford: Martin Robertson.

Gale, W.G., & Scholz, J.K. 1994. IRAs and household savings. *American Economic Review,* 84: 1233–1260.

Gcabo, R. & Robinson, Z. 2007. Tax compliance and behavioural response in South Africa: An alternative investigation. *South African Journal of Economic and Management Sciences,* 10(3): 357–370.

Gillis, M., Shoup, C.S. & Sicat, G.P. (eds). 1990. *Value added taxation in developing countries.* Washington: World Bank.

Global Finance. 2011. *Income Tax Rates.* [Online]. Available: http://www.gfmag.com/tools/global-database/economic-data/10442-personal-income-tax-rates.html#ixzz1DxhKL2eS [14 February 2011]

Go, D.S., Kearney, M., Robinson, S. & Thierfelder, K. 2005. An analysis of South Africa's value added tax. *World Bank Policy Research Working Paper 3671*: 1–21.

Grabowski, R. 1994. The successful developmental state: Where does it come from? *World Development,* 22(3): 413–433.

Grobler, C. & Stuart, I. 2007. Health care provider choice. *South African Journal of Economics,* 75(2): 327–350.

Gupta, S., Schiller, C. & Ma, H. 1999. Privatisation, social impact and social safety nets. *IMF Working Paper WP/99/68.* Washington, DC: IMF.

Gustafsson, M. & Patel, F. 2006. Undoing the apartheid legacy: Pro-poor spending shifts in the South African public school system. *Perspectives in Education,* 24(2): 65–77.

Hall, R.E. & Rabushka, A. 1983. *Low tax, simple tax, flat tax.* New York: McGraw-Hill.

Hall, R.E. & Rabushka, A. 1995. *The flat tax.* Stanford: Hoover Institution Press.

Harberger, A.C. 1962. The incidence of the corporation income tax. *Journal of Political Economy,* 70(3): 215–240.

Harrod, R. 1952. *Economic essays.* New York: Harcourt, Brace & Co.

Haufler, A. 2001. *Taxation in a global economy.* Cambridge: Cambridge University Press.

Hayek, F.A. 1960. *The constitution of liberty.* London: Routledge & Kegan Paul.

Heilburn, J & McGuire, P.A. 1987. *Urban Economics and Public Policy.* New York: St. Martin's Press.

Hemming, R. & Kell, M. 2001. Promoting fiscal responsibility: Transparency, rules and independent fiscal authorities. *Bank of Italy Workshop on Fiscal Rules.* Peruglia, Italy: 1–3 February 2001.

Henderson, J. V. 1988. *Urban Development: Theory, Fact and Illusion.* New York: Oxford University Press.

Heracleous, L. 1999. Privatisation: Global trends and the Singapore experience. *International Journal of Public Economics,* 12(5).

Hochman, H.M. & Rodgers, J.D. 1969. Pareto optimal redistribution. *American Economic Review,* 59(4): 531–541.

Hofmeyr, A., Burns, J. & Visser, M. 2007. Income inequality, reciprocity and public good provision: An experimental analysis, *South African Journal of Economics,* 75(3): 508–520.

International Monetary Fund. 2000. *Republic of Poland: Article IV Consultation – Staff Report.* Washington, DC: IMF. [Online]. Available: http://www.imf.org/external/pubs/ft/scr/2001/cr0156.pdf [12 June 2008]

International Monetary Fund. 2000 & 2001. *Government finance statistics yearbook.* Washington: IMF. [Online]. Available: http://www.imf.org/external/np/mae/pdebt/2000/eng/guide.pdf [12 June 2008]

International Monetary Fund. 2001. *Government finance statistics manual.* Washington: International Monetary Fund.

International Monetary Fund (IMF). 2006. *Government finance statistics yearbook, 2006: Database and Browser,* March 2006. IMF: Washington.

International Monetary Fund (IMF). 2008. *Government finance statistics yearbook 2008.* Washington: IMF.

International Monetary Fund. 2010. *World Economic Outlook.* October. [Online]. Available: http://www.imf.org./ [13 February 2011]

International Monetary Fund, 2011. *Fiscal Monitor Update.* January. Washington, D.C.: International Monetary Fund. [Online]. Available: http://www.imf.org/external/pubs/ft/fm/2011/01/update/fmindex.htm [30 March 2011]

International Monetary Fund and World Bank. 2001. *Guidelines for public debt management.* Prepared by the Staff of the International Monetary Fund and the World Bank.

Janisch, C.A. 1996. *An analysis of the burdens and benefits of taxes and government expenditure in the South African economy for the year 1993/94.* Pietermaritzburg: University of Natal. (MCom-thesis.)

Jappelli, T, and Pistaferri, L. 2002. *Tax incentives for household saving and borrowing.* Working Paper no. 83, Centre for Studies in Economics and Finance. [Online]. Available: http://ideas.repec.org/p/sef/csefwp/83.html [12 June 2008]

Jorgenson, D.W. and Yun, K. 2001. *Investment, Volume 3, Lifting the burden: Tax reform, the cost of capital, and US economic growth.* Cambridge, MA: MIT Press.

Kagel, J.H. & Roth, A.E. 1995. *The handbook of experimental economics.* Princeton, NJ: Princeton University Press.

Kahn, A.E.1988. *The economics of regulation: principles and institutions.* Cambridge, MA: MIT Press.

Kahn, M.H. 2006. Determinants of corruption in developing countries: The limits of conventional economics. In: Rose-Ackerman, S. (ed). *International handbook on the economics of corruption.* Cheltenham: Edward Elgar Publishing.

Katz Commission. 1994. *Interim Report of the Commission of Inquiry into certain aspects of the tax structure of South Africa (Chairman: M.M. Katz).* Pretoria: Government Printer.

Katz Commission. 1995. *Third Interim Report of the Commission of Inquiry into certain aspects of the tax structure of South Africa (Chairman: M.M. Katz).* Pretoria: Government Printer.

Katz Commission. 1997a. *Fourth Interim Report of the Commission of Inquiry into certain aspects of the tax structure of South Africa (Chairman: M.M. Katz).* Pretoria: Government Printer.

Katz Commission. 1997b. *Fifth Interim Report of the Commission of Inquiry into certain aspects of the tax structure of South Africa (Chairman: M.M. Katz).* Pretoria: Government Printer.

Katz Commission. 1998. *Eighth Interim Report of the Commission of Inquiry into certain aspects of the tax structure of South Africa (Chairman: M.M. Katz): The Implications of Introducing a Land Tax in South Africa.* Pretoria: Government Printer.

Kaul, I., Grunberg, I. & Stern, M.A. 1999. Defining global public goods. In: Kaul, I., Grunberg, I. & Stern, M.A. (eds). 1999. *Global public goods.* New York: Oxford University Press.

Keen, M., Kim, Y & Varsano, R. 2008. The 'flat tax(es)': Principles and experience. *International Tax Public Finance,* 15: 712–751.

Keen, M. & Mansour. M. 2009. Revenue mobilization in Sub-Saharan Africa: Challenges from globalization. *IMF Working Paper,* WP/09/157. Washington: IMF: 1–47.

Kennedy, R. 2003. The day the traffic disappeared. *The New York Times Magazine,* April 20.

Khalilzadeh-Shirazi, J. & Shah, A. 1991. *Tax policy in developing countries.* Washington: World Bank.

Klasen, S. 1996. *Poverty and inequality in South Africa.* Mimeograph. (Accepted for publication in Social Indicator Research.) Cambridge: Centre for History and Economics: Kings College.

Klemm, A. & Van Parys, S. 2010. Empirical evidence on the effects of tax incentives. *Working Paper,* 2010/673. Universiteit Gent, Faculteit Economie en Bedrijfskunde, September 2010: 1–31.

Kopits, G. 2001. Fiscal rules: Useful policy framework or unnecessary ornament? *IMF Working Paper,* WP/01/145. Washington DC: International Monetary Fund.

Kopits, G. & Craig, J. 1998. Transparency in government operations. *IMF Occasional Paper 158.* Washington, DC: International Monetary Fund.

Kopits, G. & Symansky, S. 1998. Fiscal policy rules. *IMF Occasional Paper 162*. Washington, DC: International Monetary Fund.

Kruger, J.J. 1992. State provision of social security: *Some theoretical, comparative and historical perspectives with reference to South Africa*. Stellenbosch: University of Stellenbosch. (MCom-thesis.)

Lachman, D. & Bercuson, K. 1992. Economic policies for a new South Africa. *IMF Occasional Paper 91*. Washington DC: International Monetary Fund.

Lancaster, K. & Lipsey, R.G. 1957. The general theory of the second best. *Review of Economics and Statistics*, 24: 11–32.

Lane, T. 1993. Market discipline. *IMF Staff Papers*, 40(1): 53–88.

Leach, D.F. 1997. Concentration–profits monopoly versus efficiency debate: South African evidence. *Contemporary Economic Policy*, 15(2): 12–23.

Leftwich, A. 1995. Bringing politics back in: Towards a model of the developmental state. *The Journal of Development Studies*, 31(3): 400–427.

Leibbrandt, M., Poswell, L., Naidoo, P., Welch, M. & Woolard, I. 2004. *South African poverty and inequality: Measuring the changes*. Paper for Transformation Audit of Institute of Justice and Reconciliation. Cape Town. [Online]. Available: http://www.transformationaudit.co.za/articles/Poverty.pdf [November 2004]

Leibenstein, H. 1966. Allocative efficiency versus X-efficiency. *American Economic Review*, 56(3): 392–415.

Leibenstein, H. 1978. *General X-efficiency theory and economic development*. New York: Oxford University Press.

Lemboe, C.J. 2010. *Cigarette taxes and smuggling in South Africa: Causes and consequences*. Stellenbosch: University of Stellenbosch. (MCom-thesis.)

Leistner, G.M.E. 1968. Table insert. *Africa Institute Bulletin*, VI(6): 175–7.

Lim, D. 1993. Recent trends in the size and growth of government in developing countries. In: Gemmell, N. (ed). 1993. *The growth of the public sector: Theories and international evidence*. Aldershot: Edward Elgar.

Lindahl, E. 1958. Just taxation – a positive solution. In: Musgrave, R.A. & Peacock, A.T. (eds). *Classics in the theory of public finance*. New York: St Martin's Press.

Lindauer, D.L. & Velenchik, A.D. 1992. Government spending in developing countries: Trends, causes, and consequences. *World Bank Research Observer*, 7(1): 59–78.

Lipsey, R.G. & Chrystal, K.A. 1995. *An introduction to positive economics*. 8th edition. New York: Oxford University Press.

Lund Committee. 1996. *Report of the Lund Committee on child and family support*. Pretoria: Government Printer.

Lusinyan, L. & Thornton, I. 2007. The revenue-expenditure nexus: Historical evidence for South Africa. *South African Journal of Economics*, 75(3): 496–507.

Lutzeyer, S. (2008). *Climate trading: The Clean Development Mechanism (CDM) and Africa*. Mimeograph. Stellenbosch; University of Stellenbosch, Department of Economics.

Manuel, T.A. 2003. Finding the right path. *Finance and Development*, 40(3): 18–20.

Margo Commission. 1987. *Report of the Commission of Inquiry into the tax structure of the Republic of South Africa (Chairman: C.S. Margo)*. RP34/1987. Pretoria: Government Printer.

McConnell, C.R. & Brue, S.L. 2005. *Economics, principles, problems, and policies*. 16th edition. McGrawHill: Boston.

McGrath, M.D. 1983. *The distribution of personal income in South Africa in selected years over the period from 1945 to 1980*. Durban: University of Natal. (PhD-thesis.)

McGrath, M.D., Janish, C. & Horner, C. 1997. Redistribution through the fiscal system in the South African economy. *Conference of the Economic Society of South Africa*, Potchefstroom, 8 September 1997.

McManus, J. & Warren, N. 2006. The case for measuring tax gap. *eJournal of Tax Research*, 4(1): 61–79. [Online]. Available: http://www.atax.unsw.edu.au/ejtr/ [13 December 2010]

Meghir, C. & Phillips, D. 2010. Labour supply and taxes. In: *Dimensions of tax design: The Mirrlees review chaired by Sir James Mirrlees*, Oxford: Oxford University Press.

Meier, N.G., Breitenbach, M. & Kekana, R.D. 2008. An economic appraisal of the impact of traffic diversion – the N1 toll road and its alternative. *South African Journal of Economics*, 76: 4.

Meintjes, C.J. 1992. Impediments on the labour absorption capacity of the South African economy. *EBM Research Conference*, Port Elizabeth, 30 November 1992.

Meltzer, A.H. & Richard, S.F. 1981. A rational theory of the size of government. *Journal of Political Economy*, 89(5): 914–927.

Merriman, D. 2003. Understanding, measuring and combating tobacco smuggling. In: *World Bank economics of tobacco toolkit*. Washington, DC: World Bank, Chapter 7.

Meth, C., Naidoo, R. & Shipman, B. 1996. *Report of the Task Team on unemployment insurance and related coverage issues.* Pretoria: Department of Labour.

Ministry of Finance. 1999. *Medium Term Budget Policy Statement 1998.* Pretoria.

Mintz, J.M. & Seade, J. 1991. Cashflow or income: The choice of base for company taxation. *The World Bank Observer*, 6(2): 177–190.

Mohapatra S., Patra J., Popova S., Duhig A., Rehm J., 2010. Social cost of heavy drinking and alcohol dependence in high-income countries. *International Journal of Public Health*, 55(3): 149–57.

Mohr, P.J. 1994. Can South Africa avoid macroeconomic populism? *Development Southern Africa*, 11(1): 1–32.

Mohr, P.J., Fourie, L.J. & associates. 2008. *Economics for South African students.* 4th edition. Pretoria: Van Schaik.

Mosley, L. 2000. Room to move: International financial markets and national welfare states. *International Organization*, 54(4): 737–773.

Motala, S. 2006. Education resourcing in post-apartheid South Africa: The impact of finance equity reforms in public schooling. *Perspectives in Education*, 24(2): 79–93.

Mouton Committee. 1992. *Report of the Committee of Investigation into a retirement provision system for South Africa.* Vols. 1 & 2. Pretoria: Department of Finance.

Muchapondwa, E., Carlsson, F. & Kohlin, G. (2008). Wildlife management in Zimbabwe: Evidence from a contingent valuation study. *South African Journal of Economics*, 76(2).

Mukand, S. 1999. *Globalization and the 'confidence game'.* Discussion Paper 99-24. Medford, MA: Tufts University, Department of Economics.

Musgrave, R.A. 1959. *The theory of public finance: A study in public economy.* Tokyo: McGraw-Hill.

Musgrave, R.A. 1969. *Fiscal systems.* New Haven: Yale University Press.

Musgrave, R.A. 1983. Who should tax, where and what? In: McClure, C.E. (ed.) *Tax assignment in federal countries.* Canberra: Australian National University Press.

Musgrave, R.A. 1987. Public finance. In: Eatwell, J., Milgate, M. & Newman, P. (eds). 1987. *The new Palgrave.* New York: McMillan Press: 1055–1061.

Musgrave, R.A. & Musgrave, P.B. 1989. *Public finance in theory and practice.* 5th edition. New York: McGraw-Hill.

Nahman, A. & Antrobus, G. 2005. Trade and the environmental Kuznets curve: A literature review. *South Africa Journal of Economics*, 73(1): 105–120.

National Treasury. 2002. *Budget review 2002.* Pretoria: Government Printer.

National Treasury. 2004a. *Budget review 2004.* Pretoria: Government Printer. [Online]. Available: http://www.treasury.gov.za [31 March 2008]

National Treasury. 2004b. *Trends in intergovernmental finances: 2000/01–2006/7.* Pretoria: Government Printer.

National Treasury. 2005a. *Budget Review 2005.* Pretoria: Government Printer. [Online]. Available: http://www.treasury.gov.za [17 June 2008]

National Treasury. 2005b. *Estimates of national expenditure 2005.* Pretoria: Government Printer.

National Treasury. 2007a. *Budget review 2007.* Pretoria: Government Printer. [Online]. Available: http://www.treasury.gov.za [17 June 2008]

National Treasury. 2007b. *Local government budgets and expenditure review 2001/02 – 2007/08.* Pretoria: Government Printer. [Online]. Available: http://www.treasury.gov.za [17 June 2008]

National Treasury. 2007c. *Medium-term budget policy statement 2007.* Pretoria: Government Printer.

National Treasury. 2008a. *Budget review 2008.* Pretoria: Government Printer. [Online]. Available: http://www.treasury.gov.za [17 June 2008]

National Treasury. 2008b. *Estimates of national expenditure 2008.* Pretoria: Government Printer. [Online]. Available: http://www.treasury.gov.za [17 June 2008]

National Treasury. 2009. *Budget review 2009.* Pretoria: Government Printer.

National Treasury. 2010a. *Local government adopted capital and operating expenditure budgets for the 2010/11 Medium Term Revenue and Expenditure Framework (MTREF).* 2 December 2010. [Online]. Available: http://www.treasury.gov.za [1 March 2011]

National Treasury. 2010b. *Budget review 2010.* Cape Town: FormeSet Printers.

National Treasury. 2011. *Budget review 2011.* Cape Town: FormeSet Printers.

National Treasury. 2011. *Budget review 2011.* Pretoria: Government Printer. [Online]. Available: http://www.treasury.gov.za [1 March 2011]

Native Economics Commission. 1932. *Report of the Native Economic Commission 1930-32.* Pretoria: Government Printer.

Nattrass, J. 1988. *The South African economy: Its growth and change.* 2nd edition. Cape Town: Oxford University Press.

Nattrass, N. 1992. The ANC's economic policy: A critical perspective. In: Schirre, R. 1992. *Wealth or poverty: Critical choices for South Africa.* Cape Town: Oxford University Press.

Nelslon, R.R. & Winter, S.E. *An evolutionary theory of economic change*. Cambridge, MA: Harvard University Press.

Newbery, D. & Stern, N. (eds). 1987. *The theory of taxation for developing countries*. Washington: World Bank.

Nicholson, W. & Snyder, C. 2010. *Theory and application of intermediate microeconomics*. 11th edition. South-Western, Cengage Learning.

Niskanen, W.A. 1971. *Bureaucracy and representative government*. Chicago: Aldine-Atherton.

Norregaard, J. & Khan, T.S. 2007. Tax policy: Recent trends and coming challenges. *IMF Working Paper*, WP/07/274. Washington: IMF: 1–59.

North, C.C. 1991. Institutions. *Journal of Economic Perspectives*, 5: 97–112.

Nozick, R. 1974. *Anarchy, state and utopia*. New York: Basic Books.

Oates, W.E. 1972. *Fiscal federalism*. New York: Harcourt Brace Jonvanovich.

Oberholzer, R. 2008. Attitudes of South African taxpayers towards taxation: A pilot study. *Accountancy Business and the Public Interest*, 7(1): 44–69. [Online]. Available: http://www.adobe. com/supportservice/custsupport/LIBRARY/ acwin.htm [9 December 2010]

Organisation for Economic Co-operation and Development (OECD). 1988. *Taxation of net wealth, capital transfers and capital gains on individuals*. Paris: OECD.

Ouattara, A.D. 1997. Globalization's challenges for Africa. *IMF Survey*, 26(11): 177.

Parker, D. 2002. Economic regulation: A review of issues. *Annals of Public and Cooperative Economics*, 73: 2.

Parry, C. 2009. Supply versus demand reduction: Best practices for addressing alcohol abuse in the South African Context. *1st Biennial Regional Liquor Regulation Conference*, Johannesburg. 25–26 March, 2009.

Peacock, A.T. & Wiseman, J. 1967. *The growth of public expenditure in the United Kingdom*. London: George Allen & Unwin.

Pearce D.W. (ed). 1986. *The MIT Dictionary of Modern Economics*. Cambridge, Mass.: MIT Press.

Pienaar, W.J. 2008. Economic valuation of the proposed road between Gobabis and Grootfontein, Namibia. *South African Journal of Economics*, 76: 4.

Prest, A.R. & Turvey, R. 1978. Cost-benefit analysis: A survey. In: AEA and RES. *Surveys of economic theory*. London: MacMillan.

Ramsey, F.P. 1927. A contribution to the theory of taxation. *Economic Journal*, 37: 47–61.

Rawls, J. 1971. *A theory of justice*. Cambridge, Mass.: Harvard University Press.

Registrar of Pension Funds. 2005. *Forty seventh annual report*. Pretoria: Financial Services Board. [Online]. Available: ftp://ftp.fsb.co.za/public/ pension/Reports/PFAR2005.pdf [8 April 2008]

Republic of South Africa. 1969. *Bantu Taxation Act, No 92*. Pretoria: Government Printer. [Laws.]

Republic of South Africa. 2003. *Local Government: Municipal Finance Management Act, No 56 of 2003, Government Gazette*, 464, 13 February 2004. [Laws.]

Republic of South Africa. 2004. *Local Government: Municipal Property Rates Act, No 6*. Pretoria: Government Printer. [Laws.]

Republic of South Africa. 2009. *Money Bills Amendment Procedure and Related Matters Act, No 9 of 2010*. Pretoria: Government Printer. [Laws.]

Richardson, J. 1986. *The local historian's encyclopedia*. 2nd edition. London: Historical Publications.

Romer, P.M. 1986. Increasing returns and long-run growth. *Journal of Political Economy*, 94.

Rosen, H.S. 2002. *Public finance*. 6th edition. New York: McGraw-Hill.

Rosen, H.S. & Gayer, T. 2008. *Public Finance*. 8th edition. McGraw-Hill Irwin: Boston.

Rosenthal, L. 1983. Subsidies to the personal sector. In: Millward, R., Parker, D., Rosenthal, L., Sumner, M.T. & Topham, N. (eds). 1983. *Public sector economics*. London and New York: Longman.

Rostow, W.W. 1971. *Politics and the stages of growth*. Cambridge: Cambridge University Press.

Sadka, E. & Tanzi, V. 1993. A tax on gross assets of enterprises as a form of presumptive taxation. *IBFD Bulletin*, 66–73 (February).

Sahn, D.E., Dorosh, P.A. & Younger, S.D. 1997. *Structural adjustment reconsidered: Economic policy and poverty in Africa*. Cambridge: Cambridge University Press.

Samuelson, P.A. 1954. The pure theory of public expenditure. *Review of Economics and Statistics*, 36(4): 387–389.

Samuelson, P.A. 1955. A diagrammatic exposition of a theory of public expenditure. *Review of Economics and Statistics*, 37(4): 350–356.

Sandford, C. & Hasseldine, J. 1992. *The compliance costs of business taxes in New Zealand*. Wellington: Institute of Policy Studies, Victoria University.

Saunders, P. & Klau, F. 1985. The role of the public sector: Causes and consequences of the growth of government. *OECD Economic Studies*, 4 (Special Edition): 11–239.

Schumpeter, J. 1954. *Capitalism, socialism and democracy*. 4th edition. London: Allen & Unwin.

Schumpeter, J.A. 1987. *Capitalism, socialism and democracy* (first UK edition 1943). London: Unwin Paperbacks.

Shah, A. 1995. Introduction to fiscal incentives for investment and innovation. In: Shah, A. (ed). *Fiscal incentives for investment and innovation.* Washington DC: World Bank.

Shome, P. & Schutte, C. 1993. Cashflow tax. *IMF Working Paper,* WP/93/2, Fiscal Affairs Department. Washington: International Monetary Fund.

Shoven, J.B. 1976. The incidence and efficiency effect of taxes on income from capital. *Journal of Political Economy,* 84: 1261–1283.

Siebrits, F.K. 1998. Government spending in an international perspective. In: Abedian, I. & Biggs, M. (eds). *Economic globalisation and fiscal policy.* Cape Town: Oxford University Press.

Siebrits, F.K. & Calitz, E. 2004a. Observations about fiscal policy in sub-Saharan Africa. *Absa Economic Perspective,* Fourth Quarter: 2–9. [Online]. Available: http://www.absa.co.za/ABSA/PDFfiles/EP_2004_Q1_English_Focus_Web_4.pdf

Siebrits, F.K. & Calitz, E. 2004b. Should South Africa adopt numerical fiscal rules? *South African Journal of Economics,* 72(4): 759–783.

Simons, H. 1936. Rules versus authorities in monetary policy. *Journal of Political Economy,* 44(1): 1–30.

Skinner, J. 1991. If agricultural land taxation is so efficient, why is it so rarely used? *The World Bank Economic Review,* 5(1): 113–133.

Slemrod, J. & Sorum, N. 1984. The compliance cost of the U.S. individual income tax system. *National Tax Journal,* 38(4).

Sørensen, P.B. 2005. Neutral taxation of shareholder income. *International Tax and Public Finance,* 12: 777–801.

Sørensen, P.B. 2007. The Nordic dual income tax: Principles, practices, and relevance for Canada. *Canadian Tax Journal,* 55(3): 557–602.

Sørensen, P.B. & Johnson, S.M. 2010. Taxing capital income: Options for reform in Australia. In: *Melbourne Institute – Australia's future tax and transfer policy conference.* Melbourne: Melbourne Institute of Applied Economic and Social Research: 179–235.

Smith Committee. 1995. *Report of the Committee on strategy and policy review of retirement provision in South Africa.* Pretoria: Department of Finance.

South Africa. 1998. Developing a culture of good governance. *Report of the Presidential Commission on the reform and transformation of the Public Service in South Africa.* Pretoria: Government Printer.

South Africa Foundation. 1998. Big and small business in South Africa: Where the twine meets. *SAF Viewpoint,* December.

South African Financial Sector. 2003. *Financial Sector Charter.* [Online]. Available: http://fsc.cmcnetworks.net

South African Reserve Bank. *Quarterly Bulletin.* Various issues. Pretoria: South African Reserve Bank.

South African Revenue Service (SARS). 2008. *Budget Tax Guide 2008/09.* Pretoria: South African Revenue Service. [Online]. Available: http://www.finance.gov.za/documents/national%20budget/2008/guides/Budget%20Pocketguide%202008.pdf [12 June 2008]

South African Revenue Service (SARS). 2010. *Annual Report 2009–2010.* Pretoria: Government Printer. [Online]. Available: http://www.sars.gov.za [13 December 2010]

South African Revenue Service (SARS). 2010. Reference guide – *Environmental levy on carbon dioxide emissions of new motor vehicles manufactured in the Republic,* SE-EL-GU-03. Pretoria: SARS. [Online]. Available: http://www.sars.gov.za. [16 March 2011]

South African Revenue Service (SARS). 2011. *Pocket Tax Guide, Budget 2011.* Pretoria: South African Revenue Service. [Online]. Available: http://www.sars.gov.za [28 February 2011]

Spilimbergo, A., Symansky, S., Blanchard, O. & Cottarelli, C. 2008. Fiscal Policy for the Crisis. *IMF Staff Position Note* SPN/08/01, 29 December. Washington, D.C.: International Monetary Fund.

Statistics South Africa. 2002a. *Earning and spending in South Africa: Selected findings and comparisons from the income and expenditure surveys of October 1995 and October 2000.* Pretoria: Statistics South Africa.

Statistics South Africa. 2002b. *Income and expenditure of households, 2000 South Africa.* Statistical release P0111. Pretoria: Statistics South Africa.

Statistics South Africa. 2005. *Labour Force Survey,* September 2004. Pretoria: Statistics South Africa.

Statistics South Africa. 2008. *Income and expenditure of households, 2005/06.* Statistical release P0100. Pretoria: Statistics South Africa.

Steenekamp, T.J. & Döckel, J.A. 1993. Taxation and tax reform in LDCs: Lessons for South Africa. *Development Southern Africa,* 10(3): 319–333.

Steenekamp, T.J. 1994. Moet armes belasting betaal? *South African Journal of Economics,* 62(4): 371–392.

Steenekamp, T.J. 1996. Some aspects of corporate taxation in South Africa: the Katz Commission. *South African Journal of Economics,* 64(1): 1–19.

Steenekamp, T.J. 2007. Tax performance in South Africa: a comparative study. *Southern African Business Review*, 11(3): 1–16.

Stiglitz, J.E. 1984. *Theories of wage rigidity*. NBER Working Paper 1442. Washington DC.

Stotsky, J. & WoldeMariam, A. 2002. Central American tax reform: Trends and possibilities. *IMF Working Paper*, WP/02/227: 1–41.

Strydom, P.D.F. 1987. Structural imbalances in the South African economy. *The Economic Society of South Africa Conference*. Pretoria, South Africa.

Stowell, D. 2005. *Climate trading: Development of greenhouse gas markets*. New York: Palgrave MacMillan.

Sunley, E.M. 1989. The treatment of companies under cashflow taxes: Some administrative, transitional, and international issues. *Working paper 189 of Country Economics Department*. Washington: World Bank.

Swanepoel, J.A. & Schoeman, N.J. 2003. Countercyclical fiscal policy in South Africa: Role and impact of automatic fiscal stabilisers. *South African Journal of Economic and Management Sciences*, 6(4): 802–822.

Tanzi, V. 1995. *Taxation in an integrating world*. Washington DC: Brookings.

Tanzi, V. 1996. Globalization, tax competition and the future of tax systems. *IMF Working Paper*, WP/96/141. Washington DC: International Monetary Fund.

Tanzi, V. 2004. Globalization and the need for fiscal reform in developing countries. *Journal of Policy Modeling*, 26: 525–542.

Tanzi, V. 2005. The economic role of the state in the 21st century. *Cato Journal*, 25(3): 617–638.

Tanzi, V. & Schuknecht, L. 1995. The growth of government and the reform of the state in industrial countries. *IMF Working Paper* 95/130. Washington DC: International Monetary Fund.

Tanzi, V. & Zee, H.H. 2000. Tax policy for emerging markets: Developing countries. *National Tax Journal*, LIII(2): 299–322.

Thornton, J. 2008. Explaining Procyclical Fiscal Policy in African Countries. *Journal of African Economies*, 17(3): 451–464.

Tiebout, C.M. 1956. A pure theory of local expenditures. *Journal of Political Economy*, 64: 416–424.

Todaro, M.P. 1997. *Economic Development*. 6th edition. New York: Longman.

Toumanoff, P.G. 1984. A positive analysis of the theory of market failure. *Kyklos*, 37(4): 529–541.

Toye, J. 2000. Fiscal crisis and fiscal reform in developing countries. *Cambridge Journal of Economics*, 24: 21–44.

United Nations Development Programme. 2004. *Human development report 2004*. New York: Oxford University Press.

United Nations Economic Commission for Africa. 2004. *Striving for good governance in Africa*. Addis Ababa.

Van der Berg, S. 1991. Redirecting government expenditure. In: Moll, P., Nattrass, N. & Loots, L. (eds). 1991. *Redistribution: How can it work in South Africa?* Cape Town: David Philip: 74–85.

Van der Berg, S. 1992. Social reform and the reallocation of social expenditures. In: Schrire, R. (ed). 1992. *Wealth or poverty? Critical choices for South Africa*. Cape Town: Oxford University Press: 121–142.

Van der Berg, S. 2001. Trends in racial fiscal incidence in South Africa. *South African Journal of Economics*, 69(2): 243–268.

Van der Berg, S. 2005. Fiscal expenditure incidence in South Africa, 1995 and 2000. *Final report to National Treasury on aspects of expenditure incidence*. February.

Van der Berg, S. 2006. The targeting of public spending school education, 1995 and 2000. *Perspectives in Education*, 24(2): 49–64.

Van der Berg, S. & Burger, R. 2002. The stories behind the numbers: An investigation of efforts to deliver services to the South African poor. Study for World Bank as background paper to *World Development Report 2004*. Stellenbosch. November. [Online]. Available: http://econ.worldbandk.org/files/28003_van_der_berg.pdf

Van der Berg, S. & Burger, R. 2003. Education and socio-economic differentials: A study of school performance in the Western Cape. *South African Journal of Economics*, 71(3): 496–522.

Van der Berg, S. & Louw, M. 2004. Changing patterns of South African income distribution: Towards time series estimates of distribution and poverty. *South African Journal of Economics*, 72(3): 546–572.

Van der Berg, S., Louw. M. & Yu, D. 2008. Post-transition poverty trends based on an alternative data source. *South African Journal of Economics*, 76(1): 58–76.

Van der Merwe, E.J. 1993. Is South Africa in a debt trap? *South African Reserve Bank Occasional Paper* 6, Pretoria: Government Printer.

Van Heerden, J.H. 1996. The distribution of personal wealth in South Africa. *South African Journal of Economics*, 64(4): 278–292.

Van Zyl, C., Botha, Z., Goodspeed, I. & Skerritt, P. 2009. *Understanding South African financial markets*. Pretoria: Van Schaik.

Wagner, A. 1883. Three extracts on public finance. In: Musgrave, R.A. & Peacock, A.T. (eds). 1958. *Classics in the theory of public finance.* London: Macmillan.

Whiteford, A. & McGrath, M. 1994. Inequality in the size distribution of income in South Africa. *Occasional Papers 10.* Stellenbosch: Stellenbosch Economic Project.

Wilson, J.D. 1999. Theories of tax competition. *National Tax Journal,* 52(2): 269–304.

Woolard, I. & Leibbrandt, M. 2001. Measuring poverty in South Africa. In: Bhorat, H., Leibbrandt, M., Maziya, M., Van der Berg, S. & Woolard, I. (eds). 2001. *Fighting poverty: Labour markets and inequality in South Africa.* Cape Town: UCT Press.

World Bank. 1991. *Lessons of tax reform.* Washington: World Bank.

World Bank. 1994. *World development report 1994.* Washington: World Bank.

World Bank. 1997. *Congo – Poverty Assessment.* Report No. 16043-COB. Washington: World Bank.

World Bank. 2000. *Swaziland – Reducing poverty through shared growth.* Report No 19658-SW. Washington: World Bank.

World Bank. 2004a. *African Development Indicators 2004.* Washington: World Bank.

World Bank. 2004b. *World Development Indicators 2004.* Washington: World Bank.

World Bank. 2010. *World Development Indicators 2010. CD Rom.* Washington, D.C.: World Bank.

World Bank & PriceWaterhouseCoopers. 2010. *Paying Taxes.* [Online]. Available: http://www.scribd.com/doc/29675385/Paying-Taxes-2010-Global-Report-via-World-Bank [14 February 2011]

Yu, D. 2010. *Poverty and inequality trends in South Africa using different survey data.* Working Paper 04/2010. Stellenbosch: Stellenbosch University, Department of Economics.

Zee, H.H., Stotsky, J.G. & Ley, E. 2002. Tax incentives for business investment: A primer for policy makers in developing countries. *World Development,* 30(9): 1497–1516.

Zodrow, G.R. 2003. Tax competition and tax coordination in the European Union. *International Tax and Public Finance,* 10: 651–671.

Index